INDIAN PHILOSOPHY

INDIAN PHILOSOPHY

JADUNATH SINHA

Volume III:

The Philosophies of Bhāskara, Śaivism and different Śaiva schools and the problem of Post Śaṅkara Advaitavāda

MOTILAL BANARSIDASS PUBLISHERS
PRIVATE LIMITED • DELHI

3rd Reprint: Delhi, 2017
First Edition: Calcutta, 1971

ISBN: 978-81-208-1602-1 (Vol. III)
ISBN: 978-81-208-1603-9 (Set)

MOTILAL BANARSIDASS
41 U.A. Bungalow Road, Jawahar Nagar, Delhi 110 007
8 Mahalaxmi Chamber, 22 Bhulabhai Desai Road, Mumbai 400 026
203 Royapettah High Road, Mylapore, Chennai 600 004
236, 9th Main III Block, Jayanagar, Bengaluru 560 011
8 Camac Street, Kolkata 700 017
Ashok Rajpath, Patna 800 004
Chowk, Varanasi 221 001

MLBD Cataloging-in-Publication Data
Indian Philosophy (Vol. III)
The Philosophies of Bhāskara, Śaivism and different
Śaiva schools and the problem of
Post Śaṅkara Advaitavāda
by JADUNATH SINHA
ISBN: 978-81-208-1602-1 (Vol. III)
ISBN: 978-81-208-1603-9 (Set)
Includes, Abbreviations, Index of Authors and Subjects Appendix
I.Bhaskara, II. Saivism, III. Pasupata, IV. Saiva Siddhanta,
V. Advaita Vedanta, VI. Liberation VII Sinha, Jadunath.

Printed in India
by RP Jain at NAB Printing Unit,
A-44, Naraina Industrial Area, Phase I, New Delhi-110 028
and published by JP Jain for Motilal Banarsidass Publishers (P) Ltd,
41 U.A. Bungalow Road, Jawahar Nagar, Delhi-110 007

PREFACE

"A History of Indian Philosophy," Vol. I written by the present author elaborately deals with the philosophies of the Upaniṣads, the Epics, the Purāṇas, and the Gītās, the common ideas in Indian philosophy, and the philosophies of the Cārvākas, the Vaiśeṣika, the Nyāya, the Navya Nyāya, the Mīmāṁsā, and the Śābdika—Bhartṛhari. The second volume elaborately deals with the philosophies of the Sāṁkhya, the Yoga, the Jaina, early Buddhism, the schools of Buddhism, the foundation of the Advaita Vedānta of Śaṁkara, and the foundation of theistic Vedānta. It contains also brief treatment of the philosophies of Bhāskara, Yādavaprakāśa, Rāmānuja, Nimbārka, Vallabha, Caitanya, Jīva Gosvāmī and Baladeva Vidyābhūṣaṇa.

The present third volume elaborately deals with the philosophies of Bhāskara (900 A D.), the Pratyabhijñā school of Śaivism (Kashmir Śaivism) (800—1000), the Pāśupata (100 A.D.—1000 A. D.), the Śaiva Sidhhānta (Southern Śaivism) (1100—1300 A.D.), the Śaiva Viśiṣṭādvaitāvāda of Śrīkaṇṭha (1300 A.D.) Vīra Śaivism, Śrīpati Paṇḍita's (1400 A.D.) Śaivism, and the problems of the post-Śaṁkara Advaitavāda (900—1700 A.D).

A general account of the fundamental problems of epistemology, metaphysics, morality and religion based on the original Sanskrit works is given here. Criticisms of the rival schools by each system are given for clear comprehension of it. Detailed references are given, and Sanskrit texts are profusely quoted at the end to stimulate the readers to study them and form their own opinions of the different systems. Śaivism in the Upaniṣads and the Purāṇas is considered in "History of Indian Philosophy" Vol. I.

Śākta monism has great resemblance to Pratyabhijñā and Spanda schools of Śaivism in their theoretical teachings and practical spiritual disciplines. They are allied systems as Utpaladeva distinctly mentions in his "Sivadṛṣṭivṛtti." My brochure "Śākta Monism" will help the readers understand this interesting subject. My English translation of "Rāma Prasāda's Devotional Songs" explains Kuṇḍalinīyoga adopted by Pratyabhijñā Śaivism, Vīra Śaivism of Śrīpati Paṇḍita and Advaitavādins. The songs show how normal human life is transformed into divine life in Śākta religion by harmonizing works and devotion with knowledge, and enjoyment with renunciation.

Though the different schools of Śaivism discuss the thirty six principles, their fundamental philosophical standpoints are different. Pratyabhijñā Śaivism is monistic while the Pāśupata and Śaiva Siddhānta are dualistic. Both Śrīkaṇṭha and Śrīpati Paṇḍita are successors of Rāmānuja, and are profoundly influenced by his qualified monism (viśiṣṭādaitavāda), though their systems differ from Rāmānuja's view on some points.

The schools of Śaivism are more interested in religion than in metaphysics, and deal incidentally with metaphysical problems. But the post Śaṁkara-Advaita Vedānta is equally interested in epistemology, metaphysics, dialectic refutation of categories and concepts of rival schools, and rigorous spiritual discipline for the mystic intuition and realization of Brahman, though the modern exponents of Advaita Vedānta do not lay equal stress on its practical teachings.

This book elaborately deals with the problems of Brahman, Īśvara, jīva, Īśvarasākṣin, jīvasākṣin, pratyagātman, sākṣin, ahaṁkāra, avidyā and māyā, the locus and the object of avidyā, the nature and the cessation of avidyā, the nature of the world, its material cause and efficient cause, falsity of the world appearance, falsity of this falsity, Brahman as the truth and substratum of the world appearance, various theories of causation, three degrees of reality, the empirical reality of the world, the status of the object, its externality, presentability and capacity for evoking responsive actions, and the relation of the empirical self to a mental mode and an external object. It deals with intrinsic validity of knowledge, extrinsic invalidity of knowledge, tests of truth, pramāṇas—perception, inference, comparison, testimony, presumption, and nonapprehension, the problem of induction, kinds of inference, and hypothetical reasoning (tarka). The Advaita Vedānta criticisms of Vaiśeṣika categories,—space, time, cause and effect, being, difference, negation, some important qualities and relations are given. This book discusses some important metaphysical problems like ekajīvavāda, bahujīvavāda, dṛṣṭisṛṣṭivāda, sṛṣṭidṛṣṭivāda, eka-avidyāvāda, aneka-avidyāvāda, pratibimbavāda, avacchedavāda, ābhāsavāda, śabdādvaitavāda, bhāvādvaitavāda, and the like. The Advaita Vedānta sceptics' criticisms of valid knowledge (pramā), means of valid knowledge (pramāṇa)—perception, inference, vyāpti, comparison, testimony, presumption, nonapprehension, and of illusion, doubt, recollection, recognition, and hypothetical reasoning are given. This book discusses some important relations such as those of the knower, knowledge and the known object, the agent, action and the object of action, the enjoyer, enjoyment and the object of enjoyment, and the signifier and the signified. It treats of the psychological problems of the difference between recollection and meditation, contemplation and meditation, knowledge and action, and verbal knowledge and immediate knowledge, of the epistemological problems of conflict among the pramāṇas, the superiority of scriptural testmony to perception in supersensible matters, the ontological validity of the Veda or Vedānta, and the empirical validity of the other pramāṇas, of the ethical problem of moral imperative (niyoga), and of the religious problem of the relation of prudential duties, the occasional duties, the daily obligatory duties, and the specific duties pertaining to one's station in society and order of life to the knowledge of Brahman. It elaborately deals with hearing, reflection and meditation, the nature of liberation and its kinds, the external and the internal means to liberation, the state of release, the mystic intuition of Brahman and becoming Brahman, the destruction of the mental mode assuming the form of Brahman or infinite bliss, and the like. It especially treats of the Advaitists' views, which have been severely criticized by the Rāmānujists, the Nimbārkists, the Mādhvas, the Vallabhites, and Jīva Gosvāmī, which will be discussed in the fourth, fifth and sixth volumes.

The spiritual disciplines of the different systems prescribed by them are expounded carefully, for the continuous and ardent practice of them is an indispensable prerequisite for the realization of the deep spiritual truths propounded by them. They should not be lightly treated by the modern generation of intellectuals. There are different kinds and degrees of experience. Spiritual truths are not empirically verifiable. But they are based on empirical facts, and grow out of them by transcending or transforming them gradually in the light of the higher experience. The higher life grows out of the gradual transcendence and transformation of our bodily consciousness, intellectual consciousness, moral consciousness, æsthetic consciousness, and religious consciousness. The highest experience is a spiritual experience—an integral vision of all without negating anything. An all-embracing philosophy affirming and transforming our normal life including social life, national life, and international life can be built up on the basis of this experience. A new world order will be based on this experience. A new philosophy will be based on the mystic experience of the integral reality, which will be enlightened by the rational light of knowledge.

A brief critique of all the systems is given at the end. An elaborate criticism of the different topics in the different systems requires a decent volume. Criticisms of the divergent views of the contemporary scholars have been strictly avoided to keep the book within a modest compass.

The perusal of this book will bring to the mind of the readers of Western philosophy similar views of some Western philosophers. The views of some have simply been referred to. But quotations from their works have not been given, and similarities and dissimilarities have not been pointed out.

In chapters VII, VIII, IX and X the different views of the post-Śaṁkara Advaitavādins, Maṇḍana Miśra, Sureśvara, Padmapāda, Prakāśātman and his followers (Vivaraṇa school), and Vācaspati Miśra and his followers (Bhāmati school) under important topics are given. The Advaitists' criticisms of the Cārvākas, the Mādhyamika, the Yogācāra Vijñānavāda, the Buddhist realists' doctrine of of momentariness, the Vaiśeṣika doctrine of atomism, the Nyāya theory of self, Kumarila and Prabhākara's theories of self, and their theories of liberation are given. An attempt has been made to make the treatment of the problems of Post-Śaṁkara Advaitavāda comprehensive and critical from the Advaita standpoint.

My "Indian Epistemology of Perception" elaborately discusses some interesting problems of epistemology, which are mentioned in this book.

39, S. R. Das Road,
Calccutta-26
May 20, 1971·

JADUNATH SINHA

CONTENTS

PAGE

CHAPTER VI

CHAPTER VII

CHAPTER VIII

PAGE

CHAPTER IX

CHAPTER X

CHAPTER XI

ABBREVIATIONS

ŚD. Śivadṛṣṭi (Somānanda), K. S. T. S., Poona, 1934.
ŚDV. Śivadṛṣṭivṛtti (Utpaladeva), a commentary on ŚD., „ „ .
APS. Ajaḍapramātṛsiddhi („ „), 1921.
APSV. Vṛtti on APS. (Harabhaṭṭa Śāstrī) „ .
ĪPK. Īśvarapratyabhijñākārikā (Utpaladeva), „ „ .
ĪPKV. Vṛtti on ĪPK („) „ „ .
ĪS. Īśvarasiddhi („) „ „ .
ĪSV. Vṛtti on ĪS. („) „ „ .
SS. Sambandhasiddhi („) „ „ .
SSV. Vṛtti on SS. („) „ „ .
ŚS. Śivasūtra (Vasugupta), „ Allahabad, 1916.
SpPD. Spandapradīpikā (Utpala Vaiṣṇava), V. S. S., 1898.
BŚSV. Śivasūtravārtika (Bhaṭṭa Bhāskara), K. S. T. S., 1916.
VŚSV. „ (Varadarāja) „ Srinagar, 1925.
KŚSV. Śivasūtravṛtti (Kallaṭa), „ „ Allahabad, 1916.
SpK. Spandakārikā (Vasugupta) „ „ .
SpKV. Vṛtti on SpK. (Kallaṭa) „ „ .
SpS. Spandasaṃdoha (Kṣemarāja) „ Bombay, 1917.
ŚV. Śāktavijñāna (Somānanda) „ „ Srinagar, 1947.
ŚSVM. Śivasūtravimarśinī (Kṣemarāja) „ „ .
ṢTTS. Ṣaṭtriṃśattattvasaṃdoha „ „ Bombay, 1918.
ṢTTSV. Vivaraṇa on ṢTTS. (Rājānaka Ānandācārya), „ „ .
PPR. Parāprāveśikā (Kṣemarāja) „ „ Bombay 1918.
PH. Pratyabhijñāhṛdaya („) (edited by Jaideva Singh), Matilal Banarsidass, Delhi, 1963.
PHV. Vṛtti on PH. („) „ .
PS. Paramārthasāra (Abhinava Gupta), „ „ Srinagar, 1916.
PSV. Vivṛti on PS. (Yogarāja) „ „.
PTTV. Parātriṃśikātattvavivaraṇa (Abhinava Gupta), „ Bombay, 1918.
BPD. Bodhapañcadaśikā („) „ „ „ .
BO. Bhāvopahāra (Cakrapāṇinātha) „ .
APP. Anuttaraprakāśapañcāśikā (Ādyanātha) „ „.
RKBG. Sarvatobhadra (Rāmakaṇṭha) on 'Bhagavad Gītā', „ „. Srinagar, 1943.
ŚM. 'Śākta Monism' (Jadunath Sinha), SPH., 1966.
HIP. 'A History of Indian Philosophy', „ Vol I, 1956, Vol II, 1952.
LY. 'Lights on Yoga' (Aurobinda), Pondichery, 1953.
MLY. 'More Lights on Yoga' („), „ „ .
JRDL Jīva Gosvāmī's Religion of Devotion and Love, (Jadunath Sinha) Ch.S.S.
CAA. Chaitanyacharitāmṛta (Krishnadas Kaviraj) (Bengali).
TA. Tantrāloka (Abhinava Gupta), K. S. T. S. 1918 seq.
TAV. Viveka on TA. (Jayaratha) „ .
K.S.T.S. Kashmir Series of Sanskrit Texts, Srinagar.
AG. 'Abhinavagupta : an Historical and Philosophical Study' (K. C. Pandey), Ch. S.S , 1963
PO. Pañcopāsanā (Bengali) (J. N. Banerjee), Firma, Calcutta—12, Bengali year 1367.

T.S.S. Trivundrum Sanskrit Series.
PSS. Pāśupatasūtra (edited by Ananta Kṛṣṇa Śāstrī), T.S.S., 1940.
PAB. Pañcārthabhāṣya on PPS. (Kauṇḍinya), „ „.
G.O.S. Gaekwad Oriental Series, Baroda.
GK. Gaṇakārikā (Haradatta) (edited by C. D. Dalal), G.O.S., 1920.
RT. Ratnaṭīkā (Bhāsarvajña) on GK. „ „.
GKV., gloss on GK.
YS. Yogasūtra (Patañjali).
YBH. Yogabhāṣya (Vyāsa) on YS.
Bhāg. Bhāgavata.
SDS. Sarvadarśanasaṃgraha (Mādhava), Kalyan—Bombay, Śaka 1847.
TP. Tattvaprakāśa (Bhojadeva) (edited by T. Gaṇapati Śāstrī), T.S.S., 1920.
TD. Ṭātparyadīpikā (Śrīkumāra) on TP. „ „.
MT. Mṛgendra Tantra, K. S. T. S., Bombay, 1930.
MTV. Vṛtti on MT. (Nārāyaṇakaṇṭha) (edited by M. K. Śāstrī) „ „.
VSMRS. Vaiṣṇavism, Śaivism and Minor Religious Systems (R. G. Bhandarkar), Varanasi, 1965.
BS. Brahmasūtra.
ŚKBS. Śrīkaṇṭha's commentary on BS. (edited by Śrīnivāsācārya), Mysore, 1903.
ŚRBS. Śrīkarabhāṣya (Śrīpati Paṇḍita) on BS.
DHIP. 'History of Indian Philosophy' (S. N. Das Gupta), Cambridge University Press.
Up. Upaniṣad.
Kaṭh. Kaṭha.
Muṇḍ. Muṇḍaka.
Śvet. Śvetāśvatara.
ŚT. Śāradātilaka, Benares, 1934.
YH. Yoginīhṛdaya, S.B.T., 1963.
YHD. Yoginihṛdayadīpikā, „ „.
S.B.T. Sarasvatī Bhavana Texts, Benares.
CHI. Cultural Heritage of India, Calcutta
BG. Bhagavadgītā.
RBS. Śrībhāṣya (Rāmānuja) on BS.
NS. Nyāyasūtra (Akṣapāda.).
BBS. Bhāskarabhāṣya on BS., Ch. S.S., 1915.
ACK. Advaitacintākaustubha (Mahādevānanda Sarasvatī), a commentary on TA., BI., 1922.
ACM. Advaitacintāmaṇi (Raṅgojī Dīkṣita), S.B.T., 1920.
AS. Advaitasiddhi (Madhusūdana Sarasvatī), N.S.P., 1915.
ĀNM. Nyāyamakaranda (Ānandabodha), Ch. S. S., 1907.
NMV. Nyāyamakarandavyākhyā (Citsukha) „.
NKS. Nyāyakusumāñjali (Udayana), Benares, 1912.
ŚBS. Śārīrakabhāṣya (Śaṁkara) on BS, „ N.S.P., 1917.
Bhām. Bhāmatī (Vācaspati Miśra), a commentary on ŚBS., „.
VKT. Vedāntakalpataru (Amalānanda), a commentary on Bhām, „.
KTP. Kalpataruparimala (Appyayadīkṣita), a commentary on VKT., „.
RP. Ratnaprabhā (Govindācārya), a commentary on ŚBS., BI., 1863.
SNS. Naiṣkarmyasiddhi (Sureśvara), Adhyātma Prakāśa Kāryālaya, Holenarsipur, Mysore, 1968.
NSKA. Kleśāpahāriṇī (Satcidānandendra Sarasvatī), a commentary on SNS., „.
BBV. Bṛhadāraṇyakabhāṣyavārtika (Sureśvara).
PK. Pañcīkaraṇa (Śaṁkara), Ch. S. S., 1923.
PKV. Pañcīkaraṇavārtika (Sureśvara), a commentary on PK., „.
PKVV. Pañcīkaraṇavivaraṇa (Ānandagiri), a commentary on PK., „.

PĀV. Prakaṭārthavivaraṇa, a commentary on BS. (edited by P. R. Chintamani, University of Madras), 1935, Vol. I.
PPD. Pancapādikā (Padmapāda), a commentary on ŚBS., V.S.S., 1891.
PPV. Pañcapādikāvivaraṇa (Prakāśātman), a commentary on PPD., V.S.S., 1892.
VPS. Vivaraṇaprameyasaṁgraha (Vidyāraṇya), a commentary on PPV., V.S.S., 1893.
KKK. Khaṇḍanakhaṇḍakhādya (Śrīharṣa), Medical Hall Press, Benares, 1917.
ŚMV. Śaṁkara Miśra vyākhyā on KKK., ,, .
ĀVS. Vidyāsāgarī (Ānandapūrṇa), a commentary on KKK., Ch., S. S., 1908.
TPD. Tattvapradīpikā, (Citsukha) N.S.P., 1915.
NPD. Nayanaprasādinī (Pratyagrūpa), a commentary on TPD., 1915.
SB. Siddhāntabindu (Madhusūdana Sarasvatī), G.O.S., No. 64, 1933.
SBBS. Bindusandīpana (Puruṣottama Sarasvatī), a commentary on SB., ,, .
TA. Tattvānusandhāna (Mahādeva Sarasvatī) BI., 1922.
SLS. Siddhāntaleśasaṁgraha (Appyayadikṣita), Jīvānanda, Calcutta, 1897.
Or SL. Siddhāntaleśa (,,), V.S.S., 1890.
SLSV. Siddhāntaleśasaṁgrahavyākhyā (Jīvānanda), Calcutta, 1897.
VP. Vedāntaparibhāṣā (Dharmarājādhvarīndra) Venkatesvar Press, Bombay, Samvat 1968.
ŚMN. Śikhāmaṇi (Rāmakṛṣṇādhvari), a commentary on VP. ,, .
MP. Maṇiprabhā (Amaradāsa) ,, .
BRS. Brahmasiddhi (Maṇḍana Miśra), (edited by Kappusvami Sastri), Madras, 1937.
BRSV. Brahmasiddhivyākhyā (Śaṅkhapāṇi), ,, .
NDA. Nyāyadīpāvalī (Ānandabodha), Ch. S. S., 1907.
PM. Pramāṇamālā (,,), ,, .
IS. Iṣṭasiddhi (Vimuktātman), (edited by M. Hirianna), G O.S., 1933.
ISV. Iṣṭasiddhivivaraṇa (Jñānottama), a commentary on IS., ,, .
PD. Pañcadaśī (Vidyāraṇya), N.S.P., 1912.
PDV. Pañcadaśīvyākhyā (Rāmakṛṣṇa), ,, .
AUT. Aitareyopaniṣadṭīkā (Ānandagiri), Anandasram Press, Poona, 1931.
AUD. Aitaryopaniṣaddīpikā (Vidyāraṇya), ,, .
SŚR. Saṁkṣepaśārīraka (Sarvajnātman).
MVV. Mahāvidyāviḍambaṇa (Vādīndra), G.O.S., 1920.
TS. Tarkasaṅgraha (Ānandajñāna or Ānandagiri), G.O.S., 1917.
PP. Prakaraṇapañcikā (Śālikanātha Miśra), Ch. S. S., 1903-04.
ŚDP. Śāstradīpikā (Pārthasārathi Miśra), Ch. S. S., No. 188.
VSM. Vedāntasiddhāntamuktāvalī, (Prakāśānanda), Jīvānanda, Calcutta, 1897.
VS. Vedāntasāra (Sadānanda Vyāsa),. N.S.P., 1925.
VM. Vidvanmanorañjanī (Rāmatīrtha) a commentary on VS., ,, .
SBD. Subodhinī (Nṛsiṁhāśrama Sarsvatī), a commentary on VS., ,, .
US. Upadeśasāhaśrī (Śaṁkara), edited by Dinker Vishnu Gokhale, Bombay, 1917.

CHAPTER I

THE PHILOSOPHY OF BHĀSKARA

INTRODUCTION.—Bhāskara flourished in 900 A.D. after Śaṁkara. He criticises Śaṁkara's views of knowledge only as the means of liberation, of the world as a false appearance due to nescience, of an individual self as an unreal reflection of the Brahman in nescience or in an internal organ, its product, of an effect as an unreal appearance of a real cause, of an individual self as identical with the Brahman, and of the Brahman as indeterminate and unqualified. He does not criticise Somānada and Utpaladeva's (1000 A. D.) Śaiva monism. Nor does he criticise Rāmānuja's view (1200 A. D.). His view is criticised by Udayana (1000 A. D.) in his 'Nyāyakusumāñjali' as pointed out by the editor of Bhāskara's 'Brahmasūtrabhāṣya'. Vardhamāna explains 'Bhāskara' as an expounder of the Tridaṇḍin's view, who wrote a commentary on the 'Brahmasūtra' in his 'Nyāyakusumāñjaliprakāśa.' Udayana wrote 'Lakṣaṇāvalī' in (984 A. D.). Hence it is certain that Bhāskara flourished in 900 A. D. He refers to Śaṁkara as a crypto-Buddhist. Many other Vedāntists follow him in branding Śaṁkara as a disguised Mahāyāna Buddhist. Bhāskara's commentary is in conformity with Tridaṇḍī Vedānta.[1]

Bhāskara regards the Brahman as nondifferent as the cause of the world, and as different as the effect or the manifest world. He thinks of the world as a modification of the Brahman or as unfoldment of His powers (brahmpariṇāmavāda). He considers an individual self to be a real part of the Brahman, different and nondifferent from Him, its difference being conditional and nondifference being essential (bhedābhedavādā). He regards the Brahman as the qualified, omniscient, omnipotent Lord of the world. He thinks works combined with knowledge as the means of liberation (jñānakarmasamuccayavāda). After Śaṁkara he strikes out a new way of interpreting the 'Brahmasūtra' and propounding the doctrine of difference and nondifference or identity (bhedābhedavāda) which is adopted and modified by Nimbārka, Vallabha, and Jīva Gosvāmī as will be shown later. This doctrine is old and mentioned and criticised by Śaṁkara in his commentary. But Bhāskara is the first pre-eminent expounder of this doctrine and intetprets the 'Brahmasūtra' in the light of it.

BRAHMAN IS PROVED BY THE VEDAS ALONE.—Bhāskara holds that Brahman can be proved by the scripture or Vedas. The Mīmāṁsakas urge that the Vedas prescribe our duties (kārya) which ought to be done by us. Dharma is characterised by an imperative (codanā) or command. Brahman is an eternally accomplished reality. There can be no injunction or imperative about Him since it is relative to Ought which is to be accomplished.[2] Bhāskara rejects this view and holds that the Vedas lay down imperatives also relating to the knowledge of Brahman. Such an imperative is as follows : 'The Brahman is to be heard, reflected on, sought for, and enquired into.' All sentences in the Vedas are directly or indirectly related to the determination of the nature of Brahman. The Vedas convey the knowledge of Brahman and do not merely enuneiate our duties. For example, the scriptural sentences about creation explain the nature of Brahman as the cause of the world. If they are explained as injunctions about our duties, it will be a misinterpretation. The scripture is authoritative not only in regard to our duties, but also in regard to the nature of Brahman. It is authoritative for it is not a human creation but a revelation of Brahman. The Mīmāṁsakas may argue that scriptural sentences relating to sacrifices are authoritative because they determine the nature of our duties. This argument is wrong for they are authoritative in that they are not utterances of human beings but of Brahman. They are impersonal and independent of other means of valid knowledge (pramāṇa), and, therefore, authoritative. Brahman can be proved by the scripture only. An attempt to prove His existence by inference as the cause of the world is fruitless. He cannot be proved by inference.[3]

THE NATURE OF BRAHMAN : QUALIFIED GOD : CAUSE AND EFFECT : NON-DIFFERENT AND DIFFERENT.—The Brahman is the omniscient, omnipotent, omnipresent Lord. He is the creator, maintainer, and destroyer of the universe. He is the Providence and Moral Governor. He is transcendent and immanent. He is the Supreme Self, the Inner Controller (antaryāmin), dwelling in all creatures. He is the nondifferent cause and different effects. He is nondifferent as cause, and different as effects. He is the material cause of the universe. He is the creator of names and forms and their destroyer. He is the source of all individual souls. He is immanent in them as their Inner Controller, and transcendent of them as their Knower and Controller. He is the impeller of all souls in their free actions in conformity with their merits and demerits. He is the cause of their bondage and release. He afflicts them with nescience and destroys their nescience. He is the giver of boons. He is the object of their worship and meditation. He sustains all life, sense-organs and internal organs. He is cosmic life, intelligence, bliss, undecaying, and immortal. 'He is truth, knowledge, infinite.' 'He is bliss, immortality, and self-luminous consciousness.' He illumines the universe (bhāmanī). He is of the nature of being, knowledge, bliss, and infinitude. He is the all-comprehending unifying spiritual principle. He is the governor of all physical phenomena and guide of the laws of nature and moral laws. He is the Highest Good and attainable by all individual souls. He is the consumer of all sins. He is the giver of fruits of actions to all souls. He is the imperishable akṣara, the unseen seer, the unheard hearer, the unthinkable thinker, the unknown knower. He is not the experiencer of the fruits of the souls' actions. He is blissful and gives bliss to them. As blissful He transcends them all.[4]

Śaṁkara distinguishes between the unqualified Brahman or the Supreme Brahman and the lower or qualified Brahman or God, and regards the former as an ontological reality and the latter as a phenomenal appearance due to nescience (avidyā). He opines that God is imagined for the purpose of an individual soul's worship of Him. The Brahman is unqualified, but said to be qualified for the sake of worship or meditation.[5] Bhāskara refutes Śaṁkara's view by observing that the difference between the higher Brahman (parabrahma) and the lower Brahman (aparabrahma) is not due to the difference between the unqualified Brahman and the qualified Brahman, respectively.[6] The Brahman is always qualified. He is never unqualified. He is always the ommipresent, omniscient, ommipotent, infinite, eternal, blissful, adorable, pure, holy Lord. He is called Para Brahman because He is the Supreme Self worthy of worship. He is called Apara Brahman when His particular aspect is worshipped. Both unqualified and qualified, formless and formed Brahman should not be worshipped. Only the formless Brahman as pure cause should be worshipped.[7] He as the formed mutable world should not be worshipped. Only His luminous, spiritual, immortal form should be worshipped. Bhāskara identifies the Brahman with the Lord (īśvara).

THE BRAHMAN IS THE MATERIAL CAUSE OF THE WORLD.—The world is produced by the omniscient, omnipotent Lord, the First Cause ; He modifies Himself into names and forms, physical objects, for the experience and knowledge of the individual souls, with an inconceivable arrangement of parts, maintains and dissolves them. The Vaiśeṣikas prove that God is the efficient cause (nimitta-kāraṇa) of the world thus : the world is composed of parts because of its being an effect, like a jar ; therefore, it has an intelligent cause. Bhāskara refutes this argument on the following grounds. 1. This argument is false because the relation between the Lord and the world is not perceived. God is supersensible ; His relation to the world has never been perceived before. So He cannot be inferred to be the efficient cause of the world. 2. That an effect is produced by an intelligent agent is already known. Proving it is proving the already proven. Embodied life is due to merits and demerits (karman). They are due to voluntary actions of individual souls that are intelligent agents. 3. A potter, a weaver, etc., are not omniscient, and are endowed with bodies and sense-organs and tainted with love and hatred. If God is inferred to be the efficient cause of the world, then He is not omniscient, is emobdied and tainted with love and hatred, and ceases to be the Lord. His omniscience, omnipotence, bodilessness and perfection cannot be proved if He be the efficient cause of the world. 4. God is inferred to be the efficient cause of the the world because it is composed of parts, like a jar. The reason (hetu) is irregular since a sprout grows out of a seed without any intelligent efficient cause. The subtle elements of earth, water, etc., are not composed of parts. Only the gross elements are composed of parts. So being composed of parts is a fallacious reason (hetvābhāsa). Hence God cannot be inferred to be the efficient cause of the world. The aphorism 'from Whom the creation, maintenace, and dissolution of the world take place' is not intended to show that God is the efficient cause of the world. It shows that He is the material cause of the world. The Śruti says : 'From the Brahman these creatures are born, by Him they are maintained, and in Him they are dissolved.'[8]

THE DOCTRINE OF THE BRAHMAN'S MODIFICATION INTO THE WORLD (brahmapariṇāmavāda).—According to Bhāskara the Brahman of Himself is modified into the world by His nature, as milk is modified into curd, or as water is modified into ice. Milk has the natural power of being modified into curd, but water cannot be modified into it. A potter can make pots with pre-existing material (e.g., clay). A carpenter can make furniture with pre-existing material (e.g., wood). They are not ommipotent, and so require pre-existing material. But the Brahman is omniscient and omnipotent, and so can modify Himself into the world. The Śruti says : 'The Brahman is all-knower and all-experiencer. He has various powers'. Great sages and gods are said to produce various kinds of effects without any external means and material through their supernatural powers. God modifies Himself or His powers into the world as a spider spins a cobweb out of its body. It is objected that if the entire Brahman is modified into the world, no Brahman remains to be meditated on, and He ceases to be partless. Either the entire Brahman is modified into the world or parts of Him endowed with parts are modified into it. He cannot be partly modified into the world because He is partless as the Śruti says, 'The Supreme Person is supramundane, incorporeal, partless, inactive, immutable, and flawless.' 'He is neither large nor minute, nor short'. He has no magnitude. The words 'part' and 'whole' are inapplicable to Him, but applicable to entities composed of parts.[9] Some object that the aphorism applies to the prakṛti, that the application of the words 'whole' and 'parts' is not considered here, that the Brahman is devoid of any dimension, and that He is neither composed of parts nor partless. To this objection Bhāskara replies that the Brahman modifies Himself into the world without losing His nature, that modification is transformation of His powers, that His power of experiencing is modified into the conscious individual souls which experience insentient objects, and that His power of being experienced is modified into the insentient elements and gross objects. He creates the conscious souls and the unconscious objects by expanding His powers and then withdraws them into Himself. His creation is the expansion of His powers, and dissolution is the withdrawal of them. In the world we do not find a partless and bodiless being create an effect by indefinable māyā. Hence Śaṁkara's veiw of the Brahman's creating the false world-appearance by indefinable māyā is wrong. Bhāskara refutes Śaṁkara's doctrine without mentionning his name. God's powers must be admitted which can be modified into the multiform world. It is not inconceivable. Various dreams are experienced by individual souls. They are created in the souls by God through His powers. The Śāṁkhya view also suffers from the aforesaid difficulty, because, in his view, the entire partless prakṛti constituted by sattva, rajas and tamas, which are not its parts, is modified into the world. The Vaiśeṣika view also suffers from the same difficulty because, in his view, partless atoms are wholly modified into the world. So Bhāskara's view of the Brahman's modification into the world is more reasonable and in harmony with the Vedic testimony than the Sāṁkhya, the Vaiśeṣika, and the Advaita Vedānta views.[10]

The Śruti says, 'The Brahman modified Himself into the world'. God is the efficient cause and the material cause of the world. He modifies Himself into the world—the effect. The modification of Him is the unfoldment of His powers. His powers are infinite and inconceivable. He manifests His powers at the time of creation, sustains their expression during maintenance, and withdraws them at the time of dissolution, as the sun expands its rays in the day and withdraws them in the evening. The Śruti says, 'God has neither a cause nor an effect, neither an equal nor a superior; His powers are supreme and various and natural or spontaneous. His powers of knowledge, strength and action are essentinal to him, and not adventitious to His nature'. The Śruti distinctly declares that names and forms (nāmārūpa) or physical entities are modifications (vikāra) of the Brahman. But Śaṁkara following non-Vedic Mahāyāna Buddhists interprets modifications as false appearances (vivarta) of the Brahman and confuses the people. He and his followers propound the doctrine of the Mahāyāna Buddhists and regard the physical effects as false appearances due to māyā or avidyā. They are crypto-Buddhists and preach the false doctrine of māyā. They take the word 'modification' apart from the context and misinterpret it. The Śruti says : 'The Lord, the efficient cause of the world, is its root or material cause also'. Hence neither prakṛti nor atoms nor māyā can be the material cause of the world.

THE FORMLESS BRAHMAN SHOULD BE WORSHIPPED.—The Brahman is of the nature of difference and nondifference. Is the Brahman of the nature of difference to be worshipped ? Or, is the Brahman of the nature of nondifference to be worshipped ? The opponent argues that the Brahman both as formless and formed should be worshipped, because the Brahman as formless is the cause of the world, and because the Brahman as invested with forms is the world of physical events, and because the formless and formed Brahman is the real Brahman. Bhāskara urges that both formless and formed Brahman should not be worshipped—formless as the cause and formed as the effect or the world, but only the formless Brahman as the cause of the world should be worshipped, because the Śruti declares Him to be nonphysical. 'He is neither large nor minute, nor short'. All physical forms and qualities are denied of Him. The Brahman in Himself as a cause is immutable, eternal, one and secondless, and then becomes an occasional effect. The opponent may argue that the Brahman as cause is mutable, that He will lose His nature as a cause if He abandons His mutable nature, and that therefore the Brahman invested with the forms of earth and other elements should be worshipped. Bhāskara refutes this argument by observing that the Brahman in Himself is nondifferent, that the world is His adventitious form, that the world of physical things is of the nature of Him, but that He is not of the nature of the world of names and forms. All Upaniṣads declare that the Brahman devoid of the physical world should be worshipped. 'He is devoid of sound, touch, and colour ; He is infinite'. 'He is not this, not this'. He is devoid of physical elements and their modifications. There are no diverse effects in the cause. Names and forms are transitory but not nonexistent.[11]

THE NATURE OF BRAHMAN TO BE WORSHIPPED.—Bhāṣkara avers that the Brahman of the nature of being and knowledge, free of the forms of physical things and souls should be meditated on. God free of corporeal, incorporeal, and physical forms is the object of worship. Earth, water and fire are corporeal. Air and ether are incorporeal. Potencies of desire are psysical. So God transcendent of physical objects and individual souls, and unlimited by limited forms should be worshipped. The Brahman as truth, knowledge, and infinite is not limited by the forms of physical objects and of individual souls. His existence is the substratum, and consciousness or knowledge is the attribute. A nonbeing cannot have an attribute. His existence and consciousness are inseparable. His consciousness is His distinctive character. He is infinite and unlimited by nature, and not limited by space and time. There is no difference between a substratum and an attribute within His nature. There is no substance without attributes, and there are no attributes without a substance. He is extremely subtle and knowable with great difficulty. He can neither be grasped by the sense-organs nor described by speech. But He can be intuited by devotion, meditation and worship. He can be known through the Śruti and the Smṛtis. The mind is purified by clarity of knowledge ; He can be intuited through meditation by the purified mind. It is objected that if the Brahman is supersensible and knowable through meditation, then an individual soul is different from Him. To this objection Bhāskara replies that an individual soul is nondifferent from the Brahman, and that it knows its nondifference from Him in trance through repeated meditation on Him. Its identity with Him is manifested by repeated meditation. Those who think themselves to be identical with Him without trance through meditation are puffed up with false conceit. Bhāskara refers here to Śaṁkara and his followers.[12] The opponent argues that the Brahman in His real nature both as formless and formed, as cause and effect, should be worshipped. But Bhāskara avers that the Brahman as formless, pure, and cause, should be worshipped. His nature as an effect is His adventitious form. The Supreme Self is the inmost Spirit residing within all physical elements and conscious souls. So the opponent argues that the Brahman in the form of experients or souls and experienced objects should be worshipped because there is no difference between Him and the souls and the world. This argument is wrong since He is stated in the Śruti not to be identical with each soul and physical element. He is stated to be the luminous, immortal Person dwelling in each soul and element, and worthy of worship. He is the transcendent Spirit dwelling in each of them. Hence the Brahman in the form of individual souls and physical elements should not be worshipped. The individual souls are experients ; the physical objects are experienced ; the Inner Controller (antaryāmin) is their regulator ; they constitute the outer manifestation of Brahman. They are of the nature of Brahman in their essentional nature of His conscious and unconscious manifestations. His formlessness is His principal nature. 'He is the creator of names and forms.' 'He is incorporeal, eternal, without outside and inside, before and after'. 'He is the experiencer of all'. So the Brahman with the world should not be worshipped. Some opine that the Brahman as being(sat) should be worshipped. But the Śruti declares Him to be of the nature of knowledge or consciousness. He is not only being but knowledge or consciousness also. He is consciousness only, and devoid of any other form. 'This Ātman, Supreme self, is a mass of knowledge (vijñānaghana), a mass of intuitive consciousness (prajñānghana)' 'All shine by His light'. All are manifested by His consciousness. Yājñavalkya says, 'He should be meditated on as a light in the heart-ether, withdrawing the sense-organs, the manas, and the buddhi from all other objects'.[13]

THE INDIVIDUAL SELF(JĪVA).—An individual self is neither born nor does it die. Its so-called birth or death is that of its body. The Śruti says,'This self is said to be born when its body is born, and it is said to die when it departs from its body'. It also says, 'All souls emanate from God as sparks emanate from a fire'. It shows that souls are not generated. They are eternal and so cannot be produced. We have such experience as 'I perceived this in the past'. Such recognition proves that an individual self is permanent ; it perceived an object in the past, retained its residual impression, and remembers it at present. The Śruti declares it to be eternal. The 'Bhagavad Gītā' says, 'The individual self is unborn, eternal, immutable, ancient, and indestructible'. The individual souls are said to emanate from God. Emanation implies the absence of origination, and does not imply modification. It implies difference of a soul from God due to a limiting adjunct.

The Vaiśeṣikas hold that consciousness is not the essence of a soul but its adventitious attribute which it acquires in connection with its body and manas. But Bhāskara holds that an individual self is a knower by nature, and that consciousness is its essentional nature. The Śruti says, 'This self is self-luminous'. 'The knowledge of the self never lapses'. 'The self is a mass of consciousness'. 'The Brahman is knowledge and bliss'. 'The Brahman is truth, knowledge, and infinite'. These texts show that the essential nature of an individual self is the nature of the Brahman, and that its conditional nature is its inessential nature. Its consciousness is perceived by its self since its nature as a knower is always perceptible. It perceives external objects and internal cognitions, and itself as a knower. So it is no mere knowledge.[14]

The self (jīva) is atomic in dimension because the Śruti speaks of its departure from a body, movement, and return. After death of its body it moves to higher spheres of existence, and returns and enters into another body. If the self were not atomic or monadic, it would not be capable of departure, movement, and return. It is objected that the self is not atomic because the Śruti says, 'This self is great and eternal'. To this objection Bhāskara replies that the text applies to the Supreme Self, and that it implies the essential nature of an individual self as distinguished from its inessential nature. The magnitude of an individual self is asserted by the following scriptural texts : 'This self is atomic and to be known by the (illumined) manas'. 'The individual self is to be known as the hundredth part of the hundredth part of a hair'. It is situated in the heart, but feels sensations in all parts of its body, as a drop of sandal paste on one part of the skin soothes the entire body. The consciousness of the self pervades its body as the light of a lamp pervades a whole room. The opponent objects that knowledge cannot leave the self and spread out to the whole body for an attribute cannot leave its substrate. To this objection Bhāskara replies, that the self is atomic in the state of bondage, but that minuteness is not its essential nature because the Śruti says, 'That thou art'. The manas being atomic, the atomic dimension of the self is not permanent. So long as the self is in bondage it is united with its subtle body which is liable to contraction and expansion. It is freed of its subtle body when it is liberated. So long as it is embodied due to the knowledge of duality or difference, it is connected with its limiting adjuncts,--buddhi and the like. Knowledge exists in the self so long as it exists. It can never be divested of its essence of knowledge. Sometimes knowledge is manifested and sometimes it is not manifested. In the waking state it is manifested while in deep sleep and swoon it is not manifested. The internal organ should be admitted to be the limiting adjunct of an individual self because otherwise when the self is in proximity to a sense-organ and an object, it should not always perceive an object, or it should either perceive it always or it should not perceive it always.[15]

The self is a doer, because the scriptural injunctions and prohibitions are meaningful, and because an individual self is under moral obligation to perform the enjoined duties and not to commit the prohibited actions. The Sāṁkhya wrongly holds that the self is the experiencer of joys and miseries while the buddhi is the doer. The self is the experiencer of the fruits of its right and wrong actions in the form of joys and miseries. The buddhi is its organ of action. It has no power, but the self has power. The self is the doer, and the buddhi is its instrument of action. If the self were not a doer, it would not be capable of meditation on God and absorption in Him and abiding in its essential nature of identity with Him. Trance is not possible without stopping the instinctive tendencies of manas towards enjoyment of external objects. This depends upon an intense activity of the self. But its activity is not its essential nature because if it were so, it would never be liberated. If activity were its essential nature, it would always do actions, and experience pleasure and pain. But it does not act in deep sleep. Further, the nature of the self which is of the nature of consciousness cannot change. Nor is its conditional agency unreal. When a piece of iron is heated in fire, its heat is perceived and real, although it is adventitious and conditional. Likewise, when the self becomes active through the buddhi—its limiting adjunct and organ of action, its agency is real, although it is adventitious and conditional. Just as a carpenter is an agent when he uses his implements, and as he is not an agent when he does not use them, so the self is an agent when it uses its internal organ, and it is not an agent when it does not use the organ or when its organ is destroyed in release. The conditional agency of the self is not absolutely free but conrolled by the will of God who impels it to act in accordance with its merits and demerits, as the clouds are the general causes of the germination of the various kinds of seeds.[16] The self is endowed with limited freedom, and is, consequently, under moral obligation to do right or wrong actions. But its freedom is limited by its own merits and demerits acquired by it in the past births by its free actions. God limits its freedom by impelling it to do those actions which make it experience the fruits of its merits and demerits. If it has no freedom, scriptural injunctions and prohibitions are meaningless. If it is absolutely free and not under the necessity of experiencing the consequences of its actions, the demands of the Moral Law of Karma are not fulfilled. So its freedom is limited by the will of God who makes it suffer the consequences of its actions in accordance with the Law of Karma.

BHĀSKARA'S CRITICISM OF THE BUDDHIST'S VIEW OF THE WORLD.—The Buddhists hold that the self is a series of momentary cognitions. Bhāskara offers the same criticisms as the other orthodox schools of Indian philosophy against the Buddhist view. He urges that this view makes recollection and all practical actions which depend upon it impossible. All have such an experience as 'I perceived the object yesterday and remember and recognise it to-day.' Such recollection implies the permanence of the self. The Buddhist should be ashamed of himself in an assembly of learned persons when he denies the existence of the permanent self. He who denies the existence of the permanent self does not deny the existence of his own permanent self. The cognition of the existence or the nonexistence of entities other than the self are possible. But a self cannot have a cognition of its own nonexistence. An object perceived by one self cannot be remembered by another self. Hence the same permanent self is the subject of the perception and recollection of the same object. The Buddhist may argue that the cognition which perceived an object and the cognition which remembers it belong to the same series,that their belonging to the same series accounts for recollection. Bhāskara refutes this argument by pointing out that a series of cognitions is not different from the cognitions which are its members. In a series the momentary cognitions are different from one another. So an object perceived in the morning cannot be remembered at noon. Further, if the self is a series of momentary cognitions, it cannot have transmigration and future life.

There is no proof for the existence of an intermediate body through which the same series of cognitions may transmigrate to another body in future life. The last momentary cognition cannot jump over to the first momentary cognition in future life because it is incorporeal. There is no other entity that urges the last momentary cognition in this life to jump over to the first momentary cognition in future life. Merits and demerits (karman) cannot do so for there is no proof for their doing so. If the omniscient Buddha's preaching so be said to be its proof, his omniscience is not proven. Hence the self's transmigration or future life is not possible. Therefore the Buddhist view of the self as a series of cognitions (vijñānasantāna) is wrong.[17]

THE INDIVIDUAL SELF AND BRAHMAN.—One self-luminous Supreme Self becomes many individual souls through different limiting adjuncts (e. g., internal organs), as one luminous sun becomes many reflections of it in different vessels of water. It is objected that the sun is in the sky, and is reflected in water situated in a different place, but that the incorporeal, ubiquitous Brahman cannot have limiting adjuncts in different places in which He may be reflected. To this objection Bhāskara replies that the Brahman is not affected by increase or decrease of the limiting adjuncts as the sun is not affected by increase or decrease of the reflecting media, vessels of water, but that the different souls are affected by changing states of the limiting adjuncts as the reflections of the sun are affected by the changing states of the reflecting media. The Brahman dwells in His greatness as the common Self in the different souls without being affected by the attributes of the limiting adjuncts. The souls are parts of the Brahman. An individual soul's nondifference from the Brahman is natural or essential, and so it realises its identity with Him by destroying its nescience. The Śruti states both difference and nondifference or identity between an individual soul and the Brahman. 'A Yogin sees Him through meditation'. 'That thou art'. The former Śruti states difference while the latter states identity between them. The Brahman and an individual soul are like a serpent and its coiled state. The Brahman is the essential state of an individual soul while the state of an individual soul is its conditional state. A ray of light is both different and nondifferent from the sun. So an individual soul is both different and nondifferent from the Brahman. They have the common nature of consciousness and knowledge as a ray of light and the sun have the common nature of light[18]. It is objected that an individual soul is different from the Brahman because the Śruti speaks of the Brahman as a bridge, of His limited dimension, of His being related to, and of His being different from, other entities 'The Brahman is a bridge'. 'He has sixteen parts'. 'An individual soul becomes accomplished by uniting with Him'. 'He is seen as the golden Person within the sun'. So Brahman is not unlimited. This objection is groundless because although He is one and unlimited, He is said to be like limited entities to show His resemblance to them to a certain extent. He is like a bridge because He unites all worlds with one another. He is stated to be like a limited entity for the convenience of meditating on Him. There is no other entity than the Brahman. The existence of any other entity is denied. He is omnipresent, unlimited, and all-pervasive. The individual souls receive the fruits of their actions from God. He gives them fruits in proper time and place when their merits and demerits mature. The Śurti says, 'The Supreme Self is the giver of the fruits of actions'. Jaimini says, 'Dharma is the cause of the fruits of actions.' Bādarāyaṇa says, 'God is the cause of the fruits of actions.' The Śruti says, 'God makes a soul do prescribed actions whom He desires to elevate'. He is the regulator (niyantṛ) of the souls' actions in accordance with their deserts. So there is no inconsistency between Jaimini's view and Bādarāyaṇas view. Some think that the action of the Inner Controller (antaryāmin) in the form of a moral imperative (niyoga) is the cause of the fruits of actions. This view is wrong, because His action is eternal and common to all souls, and because an eternal entity cannot be accomplished. God alone can impel individual souls to act according to their deserts and receive the fruits of their actions.[19]

BHĀSKARA'S CRITICISM OF ŚAṀKARA'S VIEWS OF AN INDIVIDUAL SELF AND NESCIENCE.—Some Māyāvādins (e.g., Śaṁkara) hold that God Himself becomes bound, that His part called an individual self does not exist as an ontological reality, and that it is an empirical reality imagined by nescience, which is its limiting adjunct, and said to be different from Him. Bhāskara refutes this view by pointing out that the Brahman being of the nature of eternal knowledge and supreme bliss cannot have nescience, and so cannot be bound. He is omniscient and omnipotent and free of nescience, and cannot, therefore, make Himself bound to embodied life. He who is dependent can be fettered to bondage. An individual self, a part of God, is bound due to its nescience, and has desire for sentient pleasure and action. In the state of bondage its real divine nature is veiled by nescience, but when it is released its divine nature is manifested. It is not fulfilled in its adventitious nature as an individual self. God is the cause of its bondage and release.

Śaṁkara holds that the Brahman directly enters into a body and becomes a bound soul, that there is no individual soul different from Him, and that He becomes limited by names and forms—mind-body-complex—due to nescience (avidyā). Bhāskara offers the following criticism of Śaṁkara's view of nescience. To whom does nescience belong? It cannot belong to an individual self (jīva) because Śaṁkara does not admit it to be an ontological reality. Nor does it belong to God because He is of the nature of eternal knowledge and manifestation contradictory to nescience. He is devoid of pleasure, pain and delusion, and so cannot be bound for being bound consists in being subject to them. Being bound and being eternally free from bondage, being infected with nescience and being omniscient, and being subject to pleasure, pain and delusion and being supremely blissful, cannot exist in God since they are contradictory to each other. God is stainless, and so free of nescience which exists in individual souls in the physical world. Hence He must be admitted to be different from them, which are His parts, and which are bound to embodied life. Further, is there one nescience in all individual souls? Or, are there many cases of nescience in them? If there are many, they become like objects, and are neither real nor unreal but indefinable, and, consequently, inadmissible. If there is one nescience in them, one individual soul being liberated by the destruction of its nescience, all individual souls are liberated—which is not admitted by Śaṁkara. Hence Śaṁkara's doctrine of nescience is groundless.[20]

THE INDIVIDUAL SELF'S CONDITIONAL DIFFERENCE AND ESSENTIAL NONDIFFERENCE FROM BRAHMAN.—An individual self is a part of Brahman, although He is partless. The Śruti speaks of the individual souls as like sparks of fire. As ubiquitous ether is limited by the ear-hole, so an individual self is a limitation of the Brahman by an internal organ (antaḥkaraṇa), which is the limiting adjunct (upādhi). As five kinds of vital air are parts of air, and different and nondifferent from it, as desire, aversion, volition, etc., are modes of the manas, and different and nondifferent from it, so an individual self is a part of the Brahman or God, and different and nondifferent from Him. Its nondifference from Him is natural or essential, and its difference is conditional. An individual self is bound and transmigrates because of the strength of its limiting adjunct, viz., an internal organ, and because of the eclipse of its identy with the Brahman. When it realises its identity with Him, it is liberated. When a jar is destroyed, the ether enclosed in it becomes ubiquitous ether ; so when the limiting adjucnt, the mind-body-complex, is destroyed, an individual soul becomes one all-pervading self or God. There is natural nondifference between an individual self and the Supreme Self or God as well as conditional difference between them due to a limiting condition. When the limiting condition is destroyed, the conditional difference between them is destroyed.

Although an individual self is essentially identical with the Brahman, He is not affected by its joys and griefs. An individual self experiences joys and griefs because of its merits and demerits, but the Brahman does not experience them because He is devoid of merits and demerits. He is eternal, devoid of sattva, rajas and tamas, and is not affected by happiness and misery—the fruits of merits and demerits. But an individual self (karmātman) is bound by merits and demerits and subject to bondage and release. If individual souls were completely identical with the Supreme Self, who would be enjoined to perform the prescribed actions and refrain from committing the prohibited actions ? The individual souls alone, the parts of the Brahman, are the agents of the enjoined and the forbidden actions, as connected with their bodies. The Brahman is eternally pure and liberated, and cannot be under moral obligation to perform the enjoined actions and not to commit the prohibited actions. It is objected that if the individual souls were identical with the Brahman, then their actions would be intermixed with one another. To this objection Bhāskara replies that, in his view, there would be no intermixture of their actions because they are atomic and separated from one another. An individual self is not ubiquitous and does not pervade all bodies, but does actions with its own body. So its actions cannot be shared by the other souls. In the state of bondage its bodies in different births undergo change, growth, and decay. But in the state of liberation it is divested of its internal organ and physical body. So the actions of the individual souls cannot be intermixed. In fact, the liberated souls have no bodily actions. Those who admit the individual souls to be ubiquitous may encounter the difficulty of intermixture of their actions. Some hold that individual souls are reflections of the Supreme Self in nescience (avidyā), or in the internal organs produced by it, limited in dimension, bound to embodied existence, and discontinuous with one another, and that therefore their actions are not intermixed. Bhāskara urges that this view is wrong for a reflection is admitted to be unreal, like a hare's horn, and unconscious, and that, consequently, it cannot be bound or released, nor be under moral obligation. Nor is the Supreme Self bound or released.

An individual soul's bondage and release are due to the will of God. Bondage is transmigration from one body to another and experiencing joys and miseries of embodied life due to nescience (ajñāna). Liberation is the absolute extinction of embodied existence, and of its attendant happiness and misery due to right knowledge of one's identity with God. The Śruti says, 'On knowing the Lord there is the absolute destruction of all fetters of bondage; when they are destroyed, birth and death are destroyed.' The individual souls' essential identity with God is eclipsed by His volition, and its inessential difference from Him is destroyed by His volition, or its essential identity with Him is manifested by His volition. Let there be absolute difference between it and Him if its essential identity with Him is eclipsed by its relation to a body due to His will. What is the use of admitting its identity with Him? Bhāskara replies that the Śruti 'That thou art' declares an inividual soul's natural and eternal identity with Him and its conditional difference from Him due to a limiting adjunct which endures during bondage.[21]

SATKĀRYAVĀDA : REALITY OF THE WORLD.—The Vaiśeṣikas hold that a cause and an effect are absolutely different from each other, and that a cause produces a new effect which was nonexistent in its cause. A lump of earth is the cause; a jar is its effect. An effect is perceived as different from its cause. A jar can contain water, but a lump of earth cannot do so. In order to refute this view Bādarāyaṇa says, "They are nondifferent from each other". The Sruti says: 'O gentle one! as one lump of earth being known, all earthen products are known, so one Brahman being known, all beings are known. A modification is a name; earth alone is real'. Bhāskara explains the text as follows: the cause alone is modified into its effect; earth alone is modified into a jar; a jar is not distinct from earth; it is perceived as a modification of earth. An effect is dependent on its cause in the past, the present, and the future. An effect is a state of its cause, and is not perceived as different from its cause in space and time. It is real like its cause, and becomes unmanifest in its cause when it is destroyed. The world is real, and its cause, the Supreme Self, is real. An effect is both different and nondifferent from its cause. It is nondifferent from its cause in its essential nature, but different from the latter in its form and function. The world is nondifferent from its cause—the Brahman—in its essence, but different from Him in its physical form and in being experienced by individual souls.

Some Advaita Vedāntists called by Bhāskara Māyāvādins hold that a cause is real, that an effect is an unreal appearance of its cause due to beginningless nescience, and that an effect has no ontological reality, because the Śruti says, 'Earth alone is real'. The partless Brahman cannot be modified; so the manifest world is mere māyā. Bhāskara offers the following criticisms of Śaṁkara's view. 1. If the manifest world is false, then earth, etc., also are false because they are parts of the experienced world. How are earth, etc., known to be false? They are known by perception and inference, and not contradicted by the knowledge of defects in the causes (kāraṇadoṣa) of their knowledge or by a sublating knowledge (bādhakapratyaya). They are perceived by all persons. So they are real, and their difference is real. All worldly transactions follow from the perception of these real things. 2. If the knowledge of difference belonging to persons infected with nescience (avidyā) is false, then their knowledge of the nondual Brahman by inference also is certainly false in the absence of a sublating knowledge. If a sublating knowledge contradicts the false knowledge of the reality of empirical things, then the person having the knowledge is not infected with nescience. The Māyāvādin does not state the cause of the truth of the inference of the Brahman. So all knowledge is false, and nothing can be stated as the truth. 3. The knowledge of the Brahman is false, because it is knowledge, like the knowledge of empirical things, as the dreams of a person overcome by sleep are false because they are produced by defects in their causes and because they are not contradicted by a sublating knowledge during dream. There is no example to show that an unreal entity is perceived as a real entity. A hair's horn is not perceived by any body as a real entity. The argument that the empirical world is unreal like dreams is false, because dreams are recollections of real things perceived in the past. 4. The argument that the falsity of the empirical world is proved by testimony is wrong, because verbal knowledge or knowledge produced by the auditory organ is false. The sentence 'That thou art' consists of letters which do not exist at the same time. So a scriptural sentence cannot be perceived by the auditory organ. The Māyāvādin avers that the falsity of the empirical world is known from the Śruti 'There is no plurality in the Brahman'. Bhāskara interprets it thus : there is no plurality in the causal state of the Brahman ; but there is plurality of effects in His effected state ; hence there is no contradiction in this. He interprets the Śruti 'Ātman is not this, not this' as follows : the self is different from the mind-body-complex which is not-self. 'The Brahman devoid of difference appears to be different'. This text means that in the causal state of the Brahman there is no difference or plurality, but that it does not deny the existence of plurality altogether, because appearance is an appearance of what is known to be real. 5. Śaṁkara attributes the false knowledge of plurality to beginningless nescience (avidyā). Bhāskara asks whether nescience is real or unreal or neither real nor unreal but indescribable. Śaṁkara asserts its nature to be neither real nor unreal but indescribable (anirivacanīya). If it is so, then it gives rise to many undersirable contingencies. It is absurd to speak of nescience as indescribable whose effects are all empirical things which are objects of our practical actions. If nescience is indescribable, a teacher cannot explain its nature to a pupil, and a pupil cannot learn its nature from a teacher. Further, is nescience with origin or without origin ? If it is without origin, it is eternal, and cannot be annulled, and, consequently, there can be no release. If the Brahman be said to be its cause, that is not possible because He is of the nature of eternal knowledge and because eternal knowledge and nescience are contradictory to each other and cannot coexist in the same subject. If the nature of the self is the cause of nescience, then it being eternal, nescience, its effect, is eternal, and so there can be no release. Further, is nescience real or unreal ? It cannot be real and unreal at the same time as it is self-contradictory ; nor can it be known to be real and unreal at the same time for the same reason. If the unmanifest (avyākṛta) or ether (ākāśa) be said to be nescience, then it is a real entity since it is produced like a sprout. Nor is nescience nonapprehension for nonapprehension being the absence of apprehension is a nonentity, and cannot be the cause of bondage. If nonapprehension is a nonentity and yet the cause of bondage, then it is not a nonentity since a nonentity cannot cause bondage. So nescience is describable. Nescience (avidyā) is different from right knowledge (vidyā). It is the false knowledge of the mind-body-complex as the self ; it is the cause of the nonapprehension of the nature of the Brahman. If nescience be said to be names and forms (nāmarūpa), then it is describable. The different physical objects are names and forms. The perception of difference is not false knowledge. The world of different physical objects is a state of the Brahman ; it is a real entity because it exists. So nescience is not the perception of difference. The Māyāvādin asks how the partless Brahman can be modified into the world. He can be modified because of His nature as modifiable, like milk ; He is omniscient and omnipotent and modifies Himself of His will. It may be argued that milk composed of parts is modified into curd. The argument is wrong because being composed of parts is not the cause of modification. If it were so, water would be modified into curd. So being composed of parts is not the cause of modification of milk into curd. If milk is modified into curd because of its nature of modifiability, is a power of milk composed of parts the cause of its modification ? Or is the power of its parts the cause of its modification ? The Māyāvādin does not admit a liquid to be a composite whole distinct from its parts. So power of the parts is the cause of modification of a thing composed of parts. The parts are devoid of parts. If they had parts, they could be modified due to their being composed of parts. Are the parts of parts modified or not ? If they were not modified, milk would be found in curd. So all parts should be thought to be modified. If the parts of parts are assumed, it will lead to infinite regress because parts are infinite. Hence a thing devoid of parts is modified. Therefore the Brahman devoid of parts is modified into the world. Modification is the unfoldment of powers of a being that does not lose its nature thereby, as threads are modified into a cloth without losing their nature. Creation is expansion of causal power. Destruction is withdrawal of causal power. The conscious, omniscient, omnipotent, absolutely free Lord modifies Himself into the world of His will for the good of all according to His powers. He knows the manifest world consisting of the individual souls and physical things as different from one another at the time of creation, and does not know them to be different from one another at the time of dissolution because they are merged in Him. The Śruti says : 'He is the cause, the Lord of causes, but He has no cause or Lord'. It is wrong to argue that a being devoid of parts cannot be modified for the manas devoid of parts is modified into lust, anger, greed, delusion and the like, which are different from one another, without losing its nature. Śaṁkara argues that the scriptural sentences about creation do not prove its ontological reality, since there is no purpose of creation and since difference is disproved by other scriptural sentences, but that the scriptural sentences about the existence of the nondual Brahman have ontological validity. It is wrong to hold that the scriptural sentences about creation have empirical validity, and that those about the nondual Brahman have ontological validity. Creation is for the purpose of enjoyment and suffering as well as knowledge of the individual souls. Their enjoyment and knowledge depend upon the reality of their bodies and sense-organs. Enjoined works depend upon agents, actions, and fruits which are differnt from one another. Hence the individual souls, their bodies and sense-organs and the physical things are real. Śaṁkara infers the oneness of Brahman from the nondifference of an effect from its cause. The reason (hetu) of the inference is unproven. If creation is not admitted, then the physical elements and the world are eternal as the Mīmāṁsakas hold. Śaṁkara argues that the scriptural injunctions about works are unreal appearances, and that those about the reality of the nondual Brahman are ontologically valid. This argument is irrational because difference is proved by an equally strong pramāṇa and because it is proved by perception. Śaṁkara argues that works are enjoined by the Vedas assuming the reality of difference admitted by common people, but that the Vedas do not admit the ontological reality of difference. Bhāskara refutes the argument by pointing out that nondifference or identity also is perceived by common people through the notion of community (sāmānya) among all objects. Community is higher and lower. The genus of cows is a lower community. Beinghood (sattā) is the highest community. Thus nondifference or identity also is perceived and empirical, and not dependent on scriptural testimony only. Further, beinghood is not perceived by anybody, abstracting it from existing particular objects. So it is wrong to hold that beinghood alone is real, and that particular existents are unreal. The objects are different from one another in their nature. Their plurality called difference is well-known. The form of a jar does not exist in a piece of cloth; the form of a piece of cloth does not exist in a jar. The nonexistence of each in the other in another part of space is called mutual nonexistence. Further, the beinghood of particular objects is perceived by all sense-organs. So there will be intermixture of perceptions through the different sense-organs; a blind person would see colours, and a deaf person would hear sounds. It may be argued that there is no intermixture of different kinds of perception through the different sense-organs because they perceive their appropriate objects—sound, touch, colour, taste, and smell. Bhāskara urges that, in that case, beinghood is not perceived by the different sense-organs, that as beinghood—the highest community—is proved by the perception of community, so inferior communities (e.g., genus of cow, etc.) also are proved by the perception of them, and that the substrata of these generalities are proved by the perception of difference among them. Hence an object of the nature of community and individuality is real. Further, is beinghood known as distinct or nondistinct from these substances? If it is known as distinct from them, then duality or difference is real, and it will lead to infinite regress. If beinghood is known as distinct from a particular substance, then the beinghood of the knowledge of distinctness is known as distinct from beinghood, and so on to infinity. If beinghood is known as nondistinct from a particular substance, then beinghood is not known through any sense-organ. So knowable beinghood is not proved. If beinghood is said to be perceived by God, then Śaṁkara's thesis that beinghood is perceived by common people is disproved. Further, for the Advaitavādin, neither manas, nor a sense-organ, nor knowledge, nor a knowable object exists; all become nonexistent or void. How, then, can he know beinghood? And how can he make others comprehend it? Furthermore, the scriptures prescribe meditation on the mystic symbol '*Om*', and on cosmic life, etc., which are symbols of the Brahman. These acts of meditation can be performed by the individual souls if difference is real. They cannot realise the Brahman through these means if difference is not real. The Śruti says: 'I shall divide the elements into three parts and combine them in particular ways.' How, then, can plurality or difference be said to be a mere unreal appearance? If plurality be a false appearance, the scriptural texts regarding the creation of the elements are false. In fact, they are true. The elements created by the Brahman are real. Only the Śruti forbids the worship of the Brahman in the form of His manifestations as the physical elements and gross objects, and inculcates the worship of the formless, transcendent Brahman. The Śruti says, 'Prakṛti is to be known as māyā'. Śaṁkara interprets māyā as unreal appearance. This interpretation is wrong. Prakṛti is real and composed of sattva, rajas and tamas. It is called 'prakṛti' because it produces modifications. The 'Bhagavad Gītā' speaks of prakṛti as a real entity. It is called māyā because through it all are known. Māyā is not an unreal appearance as Śaṁkara wrongly thinks. Thus Bhāskara refutes Śaṁkara's doctrine of an effect being an unreal appearance (vivarta) of a real cause.

He regards both a cause and an affect as real entities, and an effect as a modification of its cause. He believes in the pre-exisiance of an effect in its cause (satkāryavāda). When a cause exists, an effect is produced. A cloth is produced out of threads wherein it pre-exists. A jar is produced out of earth wherein it pre-exists. A cloth is not perceived where and when threads are not perceived. A jar is not perceived where and when earth is not perceived. So an effect pre-exists in its cause. The Śruti says, 'O gentle one ! this was being alone in the beginning'. It means that the world (this) pre-existed in the Brahman (being) as its cause before creation. The Śruti says, 'This was nonbeing in the beginning.' It means that the world was unmanifest in the Brahman—its cause—before creation. The common people think an extremely subtle entity incapable of being used to be nonexistent, although it is not really nonexistent. A jar is produced out of earth, but curd or a hair's horn is not produced out of it. If a nonexistent jar were produced out of earth, then curd or a hare's horn would be produced out of it because they are equally nonexistent. So an effect pre-exists in its cause. If a nonexistent effect be said to be produced by the power of its cause, then what regulates the power of a cause to produce a particular effect ? The effects being nonexistent in their causes, particular causes cannot produce particular effects. If effects pre-exist in their causes, then only a power of a particular cause can produce a particular effect. Hence the pre-existence of an effect in its cause must be admitted. It may be objected that if an effect is pre-existent in its cause, the causal operation of a cause becomes useless to produce it. It may be argued that causal activity of a cause simply manifests an effect pre-existing in its cause. Then is manifestation of the effect existent or nonexistent in the cause ? If it is existent, then the activity of a potter or any other efficient cause is needless. If it is nonexistent, then a cause produces an effect which is nonexistent in its cause. Bhāskara replies to this objection by stating his view. A cause and an effect are two states of the same entity. A state and an entity are not absolutely different from each other. An attribute and a substance are not absolutely different from each other. They are the same entity. There is no substance devoid of an attribute ; and there is no attribute apart from a substance. The one being perceived, the other is perceived. They are different and nondifferent from each other. A cause and its effect also are different and nondifferent from each other. Their difference and nondifference are perceived. An effeet is unmanifest in its cause as a cloth is enfolded in a roll. An effect is the manifest condition of its cause. The world is the manifest condition of the Brahman.[22]

Bhāskara criticises the Buddhist realist's view that an entity is produced out of a nonentity (asatkāryavāda). A sprout is not found to be produced out of a nonentity (e. g., a hair's horn). If a nonentity were a cause of an entity, any effect would be produced out of any cause. There can be nothing to regulate the production of a particular effect out of a particular cause. All nonentities being alike, any effect can be produced out of any cause. But a sprout is not found to be produced out of anything other than a seed. A seed alone is modified into the state of a sprout. An entity is perceived to be produced out of an entity. This fact of perception cannot be controverted. Further, if an entity were produced out of a nonentity, then a person could produce a desired object without any effort or activity. But this is not found. Hence the Buddhist doctrine is irrational[23].

According to the Buddhist Vijñānavādin many momentary cognitions are real; external objects are unreal; all are soulless or essenceless; all are cognitions. The cognitions are invested with the forms of yellow, blue, and the like. Cognitions invested with forms alone are manifested and perceived. They are self-manifest and perceived. They are subjects, objects, and manifestation of objects. One and the same cognition appears to be the knowing subject, the known object, and knowledge. Its apprehended form is the object of knowledge; the apprehending form is the means of knowledge; self-apprehension is knowledge; they exist in the same momentary cognition. So an external object does not exist. Nor does a permanent self exist apart from a series of cognitions. Blue and cognition of blue are perceived together, and, therefore, identical with each other. A cognition is produced without an external object, like a dream-cognition. Bhāskara offers the following criticisms of the doctrine. 1. Extermal objects are not nonexistent for they are perceived. They are perceived as existing in outer space like a fire, a hill, earth, water, etc. Cognitions are produced by them in the self. Cognitions and objects are perceived as inward and outward, and so cannot be identical with each other. The cognition of a jar, the cognition of a cloth, etc., are apprehended with the forms of cognised objects. So the objects are real. 2. The Vijñānavādin argues that a cognition and an object are perceived together, and that therefore they are identical. What is the meaning of being perceived together? It means either being perceived in the same space or being perceived at the same time. In either case a cognition and an object are different from each other. So they cannot be proved to be identical with each other. 3. Further, there is no example to show that an apprehender is identical with the apprehended. A double moon is not an example since in the perception of it there is a difference between the knower and the known. 4. External objects are not nonexistent because they are like dreams, since the waking perceptions of objects are not similar to dream-cognitions. Dreams are vitiated by the defect of sleep and contradicted by perceptions on waking. 5. The argument that the cognitions of external objects are false because they are cognitions, like dream-cognitions, is false for 'being cognitions' is not the reason for their falsity. The falsity of dream-cognitions is unproven, for the sublating waking perceptions also are false according to the Vijñānavādin. Therefore dream-cognitions cannot serve as an example for the inference. The falsity of the waking perceptions cannot be proved by inference because perception is stronger than inference. 6. The Vijñānavādin argues that the variety of cognitions is due to the variety of residual impressions (vāsanā). The impressions do not exist because they are not perceived. There is no proof for their existence. The Vijñānavādin argues that the ālayavijñāna called ego-cognitions (ahaṁpratyaya) is the substratum of the residual impressions of the cognitions of the so-called external objects, and that these impressions and object-cognitions are related to each other as causes and effects. This argument is wrong because the ego-cognitions are momentary and cannot be the substratum of residual impressions, and because the impressions distinct from cognitions are not possible according to Vijñānavāda. Further, impressions are produced by perceptions, and are causes of recollections; they cannot produce variety of perceptions. Hence Vijñānavāda is unjustifiable. The world of external objects is real.

Bādarāyaṇa refutes the doctrine of the Māyāvādins also by refuting the doctrine of the Buddhist Vijñānavādins. If Bādarāyaṇa does not admit the reality of external objects, why does he try to disprove the nonexistenee of external objects? Waking perceptions cannot be proved to be false by inference since perception is stronger than inference as already shown.[24]

REFUTATION OF ŚAMKARA'S DOCTRINE OF FALSITY OF THE WORLD-APPEARANCE.—Śaṁkara holds that the world that is perceived is a false appearance due to nescience (avidyā) which is without an origin. Bhāskara condemns it as irrational on the following grounds. 1. The world is an effect or modification of the Brahman. An effect is always perceived to be permeated by its cause. An earthen jar is perceived to be permeated by earth. A gold ear-ring is perceived to be permeated by gold. An effect being produced by its cause subsists in it. An effect is as real as its cause, and is not perceived as separate from its cause in space and time and as destroying or overcoming the nature of its cause. So an effect is not a false appearance. 2. Truth or falsity of the world does not depend upon persons. Śaṁkara holds that the world is true for those who are not desirous of release, and that it is false for those who are desirous of release. This view is not reasonable for it cannot be said that colour is false for the blind, and that it is true for others. The existents are not dependent on persons so that they may be true for some and false for others. The existence and nonexistence of the objects do not depend upon persons. The world is true and false at the same time—which is self-contradictory—if it be true for the undesirous of release and if it be false for the desirous of release. The existence of the world is true for both the undesirous of release and the desirous of release, the ignorant and the wise. It cannot be false or unreal for the ignorant. It is wrong to say that the double moon existed at first and then became nonexistent. 3. If knowledge derived from perception and the other pramaṇas is proved to be false by scriptural testimony, then it is always false like the illussion of the double moon. The perception of the world is not vitiated by defects in its cause, as the perception of the double moon is so vitiated. So it is not false. The Brahman is both different and nondifferent from the world. He is nondifferent as the cause, and different as the effect, as gold is nondifferent as a cause and different as an effect. 4. Śaṁkara holds that the false world-appearance is due to nescience (avidyā). Bhāskara refutes his view of nescience and establishes his own view of it. If the knowledge of a person infected with nescience be false, then his knowledge of the Brahman also is false, because there is no distinction between the two kinds of knowledge, both being infected with nescience. A person infected with nescience is eligible for hearing the scriptural text 'That thou art'. If he has no nescience, then the scriptural injunction about his hearing of, and reflection and meditation on, the text would be needless. But the injunction is necessary. So the person is infected with nescience, and his knowledge of the Brahman is false. 5. Bhāskara asks what Śaṁkara means by nescience. It is either the perception of difference or the perception of nondifference. If it is the perception of difference, why is it so? Is it so, because it is different from knowledge (vidyā)? Or, is it so, because it is the absence of knowledge? It is not the absence of knowledge because the perception of difference is experienced. But there is a difference between higher knowledge (parā vidyā) and lower knowledge (aparā vidyā). But nescience cannot be the absence of knowledge. The knowledge of difference is neither a substance, nor a quality, nor an action. So it is not different from knowledge. Vidyā is knowledge. The knowledge of difference also is knowledge. If nescience is the opposite of knowledge, or false knowledge, then is it eternal or noneternal? If it is eternal, it cannot be destroyed, and there cannot be release. If it is noneternal or produced, then it is an effect and so a real entity, and Śaṁkara's thesis that nescience is unreal is abandoned. A nonentity, like a hare's horn, is not produeed. Where does nescience abide? It cannot abide in the Brahman because He is of the nature of pure knowledge and supreme bliss. Nor can it abide in an individual self (jīva) since Śaṁkara does not admit its ontological reality as distinct from the Brahman. A jīva is a reflection of the Brahman in nescience or an internal organ produced by nescience and so a nonenttity. Nescience without a substratum is a real entity. So the knowledge of difference is not nescience. Nescience does not belong to God. Hence it is a real individual soul's false kuowledge of body and the like, which are not-self, as self, and ignorance of the nature of the Brahman. It is both false apprehension and non-apprehension. It is destroyed by the knowledge produced by the hearing of the text 'That thou art.' The knowledge of the world of difference is not nescience because it is an effect of the Brahman. It is real as its cause is. He is real as cause and effect. He is nondifferent as cause and different as effect. The knowledge of the Brahman cannot be false. The opponent may ask how there can be release if the known world is real. Bhāskara asks Śaṁkara how he can account for release, who thinks the world to be a false appearence. As dreams contradicted by waking perception are produced again and again, so the false appearance of the world will be produced again and again in a released person. As in the states of deep sleep and dissolution nescience persists in the form of darkness and produces the false world appearance, so nescience is partially destroyed by the unsteady flame of the knowledge (vidyā) of the Brahman, and again reappears and produces the false world-appearance. It may be objected that nescience being completely destroyed by the knowledge of the Brahman cannot reappear. To this objection Bhāskara replies that the knowledge of the Brahman also being a false appearance (prapañca), cannot completely destroy nescience, which is a false appearance, since they are endowed with equal powers. It may be objected that the Brahman or Ātman always exists, that therefore the knowledge of Him destroys nescience completely as light destroys darkness, and that the false world-appearance cannot emerge again. To this objection Bhāskara replies that if the false world-appearance cannot emerge again, then all persons will be released. But this is an undesirable contingency. Hence bondage and release should be ascertained by scriptural testimony, and not by reasoning which is endless, and which can never get at the truth in regard to supersensible entities. Therefore the world is not a false appearance.[25]

WORKS AND KNOWLEDGE COMBINED ARE THE MEANS TO LIBERATION (JÑĀNAKARMA-SAMUCCAYAVĀDA).—Bhāskura thinks works (karma) and knowledge (jñāna) combined as the means to liberation. He is opposed to Śaṁkara's view that knowledge alone is the means to release, and that knowledge and works, like light and darkness, cannot be combined with each other. Śaṁkara traces actions to nescience or ignorance. Nescience (avidyā) of the nature of the Self is the cause of desire (kāma). Desire is the cause of action (karma). Hence works are products of nescience, and so cannot be combined with knowledge. Nescience is ignorance of the nature of the Self (ātman) or Brahman. Knowledge is the knowledge of the Self or Brahman. Bhāskara refutes Śaṁkara's view. Works are of four kinds: (1) some produce effects; (2) some get at something; (3) some modify an entity; (4) others purify an entity. Śaṁkara argues that release of the nature of the Brahman cannot be produced, since if He were produced He would be noneternal. So works (eg., Agnihotra) cannot produce release. Nor can they get at the Brahman since He is omnipresent. Nor can they modify Him since in that case He would be noneternal. Nor can they purify Him since no refinement can be produced in Him in that He is eternal. So works cannot produce release. Bhāskara refutes this argument of Śaṁkara. He agrees with Śaṁkara that works cannot produce, modify, or purify the Brahman. But Bhāskara admits that works combined with knowledge can lead to the attainment of the nature of the Brahman, as Śaṁkara admits that it can be attained by knowledge through the annulment of nescience. If release were an accomplished fact and always attained, as Śaṁkara holds, all would be released without any effort. Śaṁkara defends his position by arguing that release can be attained by knowledge through the annulment of nescience, and that nescience can be annulled by knowledge since they are contradictory to each other. This defence is unavailing since nescience or the knowledge of difference cannot cease so long as embodied life continues in asmuch as the body, the sense-organs, and the objects are its causes. Further, the wheel of nescience, desire and action always revolves in embodied life, which are the causes of each other. So the intuitive knowledge of the non-different Brahman is obstructed by the empirical knowledge of difference because the latter is stronger. Hence there can be no release so long as embodied life continues. So long as the body, the sense-organs, and the objects are present, the knowledge of difference is bound to reappear and obstruct the knowledge of nondifference. That the knowledge of difference is completely destroyed by the knowledge of nondifference in embodied life is contradicted by experience. Nescience cannot be said to have a trace since it is unreal according to Śaṁkara. A hare's horn cannot be said to have a trace left behind or not to have a trace left behind because it is unreal. If the knowledge of difference were completely destroyed by the knowledge of nondifference, there would be no difference between Śaṁkara (advaitavādin) and his opponent. But Manu, Vyāsa, Yājñavalkya and others who realised their nondifference from the Brahman instructed others. So their knowledge of difference persisted, although they were released. Further, if release is a state of mere knowlege without bliss, it is not a covetable end. Hence Śaṁkara's view of knowledge of nondifferece alone being the means of release is not tenable. Bhāskara does not deny the existence of nescience in a bound individual soul. He regards nescience as false knowledge of not-self—mind-body-complex—as self, and destruction of nescience as the destruction of this false knowledge. When a person's false knowledge is destroyed, he becomes omniscient, omnipotent, supremely blissful, and released. Besides, potencies of actions—merits and demerits—acquired in numerous births, which have not yet begun to bear fruits, and which have begun to do so, cannot be destroyed by the knowledge of the Brahman, since they are not contradictory to knowledge. If they are said to be destroyed by the knowledge of the Brahman, because they are the cause of bondage, how are they known to be the cause of bondage? If they are said to be known to be so from scriptural testimony, then Śaṁkara comes over to Bhāskara's view. Śaṁkara does not admit the ontological reality of external objects which he regards as mere nescience. Actions are different from nescience. They depend upon the knowledge of difference, which cannot be destroyed in embodied life. So Bhāskara holds that bondage in the form of nescience, desire and action is destroyed by the knowledge of the self combined with the performance of the daily obligatory duties prescribed by the scriptures. According to him, Bādarāyaṇa upholds the doctrine of knowledge combined with works as the means to the attainment of liberation.

Śaṁkara argues that works attain perishable ends, and that knowledge attains the eternal Brahman or release. The Śruti says: 'Heaven attained by merits due to right actions is perishable, but the knower of the Brahman attains the supreme Brahman'. So enquiry about the Brahman should be made after Dharma is known. Hence knowledge cannot be combined with works. Prudential duties for the attainment of empirical ends (kāmyakarma) and prohibited actions (niṣiddha karma) should not be done and combined with knowledge. But daily obligatory duties (nitya karma) should be done and combined with knowledge. Desire to know the Brahman arises after performance of sacrifices, charity, and austerities. Sense-control, mind-control, withdrawal of the sense-organs from their objects, endurance of pleasure and pain, and faith in the Brahman should be cultivated. Then the Self should be known in the self. The Self is extremely difficult to be known by the manas tainted with love and hatred. The self is identical with the Brahman in its essence. The Brahman should be heard, reflected on, meditated on, and sought to be known. Works should be combined with meditation or worship. The knowledge of nondifference being repeatedly practised uproots the potencies of nescience and the potencies of love and hatred. Nescience is the cause of love and hate; they are the causes of desires; desires are the causes of actions. So when potencies of nescience are destroyed, potencies of actions are destroyed. So after Dharma is known, enquiry about the Brahman is appropriate. Works uncombined with knowledge lead to the knowledge of Dharma, which ends in exaltation or the attainment of heaven. But Śaṁkara's argument that works lead to the attainment of perishable ends, but that knowledge leads to the attaiment of the Brahman is wrong, because works unaccompanied with knowledge are perishable, but because works accompanied with knowledge lead to the realisation of one's identity with the Brahman. The Śruti says, 'The works of a person who meditates on the Brahman do not perish.' Works are perishable in themselves, but they are not so when they are combined with knowledge. Works combined with knowledge are the cause of the attainment of the highest good. Works combined with the knowledge of the Brahman lead to liberation which is imperishable. If they cannot yield liberation, an ascetic's knowledge of the Brahman also cannot do so because he performs the unavoidable bodily, vocal and mental acts for the preservation of his life. Works uncombined with knowledge lead to the attainment of heaven. But works combined with knowledge lead to the attainment of liberation. The renunciation of all works is a vain pursuit. Offering all works to God is true renunciation of works, and brings about the realisation of Him. Works should not be renounced because they have conflict with knowledge. Śaṁkara holds that knowledge leads to liberation by destroying nescince which is the knowledge of difference. Bhāskara urges that nescience is not the knowledge of difference, and that the latter cannot be destroyed in embodied life as shown elsewhere. The knowledge of duality or difference cannot be entirely destroyed by the knowledge derived from the scriptural text 'That thou art'. The body continues to experience the fruits of one's merits and demerits which have begun to bear fruits. Further, if the knowledge of difference is false, God's omniscience is not possible, and all secular and spiritual actions of released persons become impossible. During embodied existence both works and knowledge, which are the means of liberation, should be practised, since there is no embodied release.

Some hold that house-holders should perform prudential duties and offer them to God. Bhāskara holds that they should not perform these duties if they desire to attain liberation. If they perform these duties for the acquisition of worldly happiness and heavenly happiness, they cannot acquire the saving knowledge thereby. The works which produce the desire to know the Brahman assist knowledge, and such works should be performed for they are a means to liberation. Those who are outside the sphere of duties relating to the four stages of life acquire knowledge by performing noninjury, truthfulness, uttering God's name, fasting, meditation on Him, and the like. The performance of the specific duties pertaining to one's stage of life is an aid to the acquisition of knowledge. After firm knowledge is acquired, yoga should be practised in order to strengthen it. Silence should be observed to assimilate the knowledge. Meditation is the common duty of persons in all statges of life. Works cannot be abandoned completely in any stage of life. Works and knowledge both lead to liberation which is uniform. There are defects and excellence of the means, but the end is one and identical.

LIBERATION.—Bhāskara regards liberation as abiding in the state of the Brahman or Supreme Self. The Vaiśeṣika holds that release is a state of unconsciousness when an individual soul's specific qualities of knowledge, pleasure, pain, desire, aversion, volition, impression (saṁskāra), merit and demerit are destroyed. He argues that if it has bliss in release, it has attachment (rāga) to pleasure, that attachment is a cause of bondage, that when the body, the sense-organs, and the manas are destroyed, knowledge cannot be produced, and that in the absence of knowledge, it becomes unconscious like a stone. Bhāskara urges that attachment to the objects of pleasure alone is a cause of bondage, but that attachment to God is a cause of liberation. A released soul attains the nature of the causal Brahman, and becomes the omniscient, omnipotent Self of all creatures, like Him. This is the view of Jaimini and Bādarāyaṇa according to Bhāskara. A released soul experiences its own bliss. The Brahman is of the nature of supreme bliss. Release is a state of nondifference from Him, and so replete with bliss. Bliss is not mere absence of pain as the Vaiśeṣika wrongly thinks. His view of release as a state of unconsciousness is repugnant to the teaching of the Upaniṣads and so heterodox and unacceptable. The atheistic Sāṁkhya holds that liberation is a state of pure consciousness devoid of bliss or a soul's abiding in its essential nature attainable by superconscious trance. Release without bliss is not a covetable end of a conscious soul. Bliss is not painlessness. If consciousness itself is bliss, then there is bliss even in the state of pain. Hence a released soul's experience of its innate bliss should be admitted. The theistic Sāṁkhya holds that a liberated soul remains separately from God. The Śruti says, 'A released soul attains to God.' There is a relation of a substratum and a content, realised and what is to be realised, an object and an agent, between God and a soul. Bhāskara holds that a soul remains nondifferent from God in release. There is natural or essential nondifference or identity between a soul and God, but there is a conditional difference between them due to a limiting adjunct. When the limiting adjunct is destroyed, a soul becomes nondifferent from God.

Is an individual soul fulfilled in an adventitious form of consciousness or its own nature as soul ? Some hold that it is fulfilled in an adventitious form since liberation also has a fruit. This view is wrong because liberation is experienced by a soul in its own form as heavenly happiness is enjoyed by a bound soul in a supramundane form. In dream and deep sleep a soul is tainted with nescience, but in release it is fulfilled as the pure Supreme Self. The Śruti says, 'A released soul becomes supreme light.' Here 'supreme light' means the Supreme Self or Brahman of the nature of self-manifest, infinite consciousness. According to Jaimini, liberation is a state of consciousness, sinlessness, true resolve, omniseience, omnipotence and the like. According to Auḍulomi liberation is a state of being and consciousness alone devoid of the knowledge of objects like deep sleep. Bādarāyaṇa holds that liberation is a state of consciousness and lordship, there being no conflict between them. A liberated soul's sinfulness and other adventitious qualities are destroyed, and it enjoys the lordship of God. Bhāskara interprets the views of Jaimini, Auḍulomi and Bādarāyaṇa in the aforesaid manner.[26]

A raleased person sees his departed father and the like at his mere will without any effort. He can see all objects of the empirical world at his mere will. He becomes free and autonomous, and has no other Lord. He can go to any world of supramundane beings at his will. According to Bādari a released soul has no body and sense-organs since it does every action through mere will. According to Jaimini a released soul has a body and sense-organs since it takes various forms. According to Bādarāyaṇa a released soul has both a body and the sense-organs since it is omnipotent and can create a body at its will with or without any material. In the absence of a body and the sense-organs a released soul can enjoy various objects with its manas only as a bound soul does so in dream. In the presence of a body and the sense-organs a released soul enjoys various objects with them.

No thoughtful person makes an endeavour to attain release of the nature of unconsciousness or the absence of the knowledge of objects. There are degrees of joy in the worlds of gods enjoyed by a bound soul. But a released soul has not dim consciousness as in deep sleep since it is equivalent to unconsciousness. A released soul cannot have consciouness without the knowledge of other objects. But the Advaita Vedāntin does not admit the existence of any other experience. If he admits it, then his nondualism or monism is contradicted. Hence the Māyāvādin's view of release as dim conseiousness devoid of the knowledge of objects is not right. But if release be admitted to be a state of consciousness, a released soul can be both different and nondifferent from the Brahman, become omniscient and omnipotent like Him, and of the nature of being and consciousness, and enjoy various kinds of objects. A released soul is ubiquitous, but a bound soul is atomic owing to its limiting adjunct—an internal organ—and capable of departure and movement. Its ubiquity is natural while its minuteness is conditional.

In deep sleep and death a soul is unconscious. But in release it has special knowledge of all objects. It has also general knowledge of them due to its capacity for knowledge and action. Those released souls which are united with the Brahman can enjoy His lordship without any limit including creation, maintenance, and dissolution of the world. But those who are not united with Him enjoy His lordship except control over the world. Their lordship is always in conformity with God's lordship, and never surpasses it. They enjoy freedom or autonomy subject to God's freedom, and supernatural powers such as minuteness and the like, but can never create, maintain, or dissolve the world. God's lordship is eternally accomplished in His supramundane greatness and also manifested in the mundane modifications of the physical world. The released souls enjoy those objects which are enjoyed by God. They never return again to embodied life.

Bhāskara rejects Śaṁkara's doctrine of embodied release. So long as the body and the sense-organs are present, the knowledge of difference which is called nescience by Śaṁkara continues, hunger and thirst afflict the body, and actions for the maintenance of the body persist. The body is conducive to the experience of joys and griefs due to merits and demerits which have begun to bear fruits. They and their potencies cannot be destroyed by the knowledge of the nondifferent Brahman. They are bound to reapprear during embodied existence. Hence Bhāskara denies the possibility of embodied release.[27]

[1] BBS., pp. 85, 124.
[2] Ibid, i, 1, 3.
[3] Ibid, i, 1, 4 & 2.
[4] BBS., i, 1, 2, 11-12, 14, 22-24, 28-31 ; 1, 2, 1, 4-15, 24 ; i, 3, 10-12 & 16.
[5] SBS., i 2, 14. HIP., Vol. II, p. 504-08.
[6] BBS., i, 3, 13.
[7] Ibid, iii, 2, 11-12.
[8] BS., BBS., i, 1, 2,.
[9] Ibid, ii, 1, 24 ; ii, 2, 26.
[10] Ibid, ii, 1, 26-29 ; i, 4. 25.
[11] Ibib, iii, 2, 11,.
[12] Ibid, iii ; 2, 23-25.
[13] Ibid, iii, 2, 11-17.
[14] Ibid, ii, 3, 17-18.
[15] Ibid, ii, 3, 21, 29-32.
[16] Ibid, ii, 3, 33, 36-37, 40-42.
[17] Ibid, ii, 2, 25.
[18] Ibid, iii, 2, 19-22 & 28.
[19] Ibid, iii, 2, 28-41.
[20] Ibid, i, 2, 6 ; i, 3, 19 ; iv, 4, 7 ; i, 4, 21 & 25.
[21] Ibid, ii, 3, 43, 46-50 ; iii, 2, 5-6.
[22] Ibid, ii, 1, 14-19.
[23] Ibid, ii, 2, 16-17. HIP ; Vol. II, p. 542-44.
[24] Ibid ii, 2, 28-30.
[25] Ibid, i, 1, 4.
[26] Ibid, iii, 4 20, 26, 38-39, 45, 50 ; iv, 4, 1-2, 4-5.
[27] Ibid, iii, 4, 26 ; i, 1, 4 ; iv, 4, 1-2 & 5, 7-22.

CHAPTER II

THE PRATYABHIJÑĀ SCHOOL OF ŚAIVISM

INTRODUCTION.—Vasugputa (800 A. D). wrote 'Śivasūtra' and 'Spandakārikā.' Kallaṭa (900 A.D.) wrote a commentary on the latter. Somānanda (900 A. D.) wrote 'Śivadṛṣṭi'. Utpaladeva (1000 A. D.) wrote a commentary on it. He wrote also 'Ajaḍapramātṛsiddhi,' 'Iśvarasiddhi', 'Sambandhasiddhi,' 'Iśvarapratyabhijñākārikā' and a commentary on it. He was a disciple of Somānanda. Abhinavagupta (1000 A. D.) wrote 'Iśvarapratyabhijñā-' vimarśinī', 'Śivadṛṣṭyālocana' not available at present, 'Tantrāloka', 'Tantrasāra', 'Paramārtha-asāra' 'Parātriṁśikāvivaraṇa', a commentary on the 'Bhagavad Gītā', Mālinīvijayavārttika' and other works. Yogirāja wrote a commentary on 'Paramārthasāra'. Kṣemarāja (1000 A. D.), a pupil of Abhinavagupta, wrote 'Pratyabhijñāhṛdaya', a digest of the Pratyabhijñā school of Śaivism, 'Spandasandoha', Śivaśūtravimarśini', 'Tattvasandoha', and other works. Utpala Vaiṣṇava wrote 'Spandapradīpikā'. Bhāskara wrote 'Śivasūtravārttika,' and Varadarāja also wrote another 'Śivasūtravārttika.' Śaṁkara refutes the Pāśupata doctrine but not the Pratyabhijñā school of Śaivism. Vasugupta might be a contemporary of Śaṁkara. There is great similarity between Pratyabhijñā Śaivism and Śākta monism, the former laying stress on Śiva and the latter laying stress on Śakti, though they are inseparable from each other according to both.

ARGUMENTS FOR THE EXISTENCE OF THE LORD.—Utpaladeva gives the following arguments for the existence of the Absolute Knower. The insentient objects cannot exist without being known or manifested by a knower. Their manifestations through cognitions rest in a conscious knower. All objects of the universe cannot be known by limited knowers, who wrongly identify themselves with their subtle bodies, who have limited knowledge and limited agency, and who are devoid of perfect 'I'-consciousness. Hence all objects of the universe are known by the Absolute Knower, Who is omniscient, omnipotent, absolutely free, unlimited by adjuncts, and endowed with manifestation and perfect 'I'-consciousness. He is the Lord. His lordship consists in creating or manifesting the world of different objects full of the nonapprehension of nondifference due to His power of māyā, which is nondifferent from Him, and yet which conceals His nature. His power of māyā is the cause of the nonapprehension of nondifference. He is the creator of the world or the manifester of different objects. He is the unlimited Knower of different objects, because He distinguishes them from one another, and because He synthesises them with one another by His consciousness. The manifestations of all objects in the form of His cognitions rest in Him, Who is their eternal unlimited Knower. They rest in His universal self-aware consciousness and perfect 'I'-consciousness. He can create, manifest and know all objects. He is all-pervasive, and can unite them with one another, and make them a 'universe'. 'I'-consciousness, all-knowerhood, all-pervasiveness, and unity of apperception are not possible in an insentient entity. All differences are manifested by the one unlimited Knower (amita-pramātṛ).[1]

Utpaladeva gives the following argument for the existence of the Lord (īśvara). Bodies and worlds have a particular arrangement of parts adapted to particular ends. Therefore they are created by the intelligent Lord Who creates them without any material to realise His purpose. He has knowledge of the variety of existents, and power of creating them by His mere volition. He cannot be a knower of limited knowledge and agency. He is the omniscient and omnipotent Lord. There is no evidence to prove that many agents have the power of creating the universe. Hence one omniscient and ominipotent Agent creates it. It can be created by the intelligent Lord alone. The entire universe with an arrangement of parts adapted to one another and to particular ends can be created by the Lord. He is the creator of the variety of objects in the universe. Many individual souls with limited knowledge and agency cannot know and create it. One Lord different from many individual souls can know and create it. The inference of one intelligent Lord as the creator of the universe because of its arrangement of parts adapted to one another is flawless and unvitiated by false reasons. The Lord is not a fiction of the imagination, but is recognisable by the individual souls as their Supreme Self, internal Knower and Agent. The last is the psychological argument for the existence of the Lord. He can be intuited by a long course of spiritual discipline prescribed by the Śaiva monists. The cosmological argument involves the teleological argument also because it considers the adaptation of the different objects to particular ends and their harmony, order and unity.

The Nyāyā-Vaiśeṣika infers the existence of the intelligent Lord as the creator of the universe with an arrangement of parts as external to it out of the pre-existent eternal atoms. But the Śaiva monists prove the existence of the intelligent Lord as the creator of the universe by His mere volition without any pre-existing material. The former regards the Lord as the efficient cause (nimitta kāraṇa) of the universe, while the latter regards Him as the efficient cause, the inherent cause, and the noninherent cause of the universe. He creates it by His mere volition, and is, consequently, its efficient cause. His power of māyā is modified into unmanifest prakṛti and the manifest universe, and so He is its material cause. He creates the conjunction of the parts of the universe by His mere volition, and is therefore its noninherent cause. The Nyāya-Vaiśeṣika is a Deist while the Śaiva monists are Theists. The former regards God as transcendent of the universe while the latter regard God as both transcendent of, and immanent in, the universe[2].

CRITICISM OF THE SĀṀKHYA ATHEISM.—The Sāṁkhya holds that the insentient prakṛti composed of sattva, rajas and tamas is modified into the universe in order to realise the ends of the individual souls (puruṣa), viz., their experience of joys and sorrows (bhoga) and liberation (mokṣa). It does not require the guidance of the intelligent Lord to realise the ends of the individual souls. He does not create the universe. The guṇas—sattva, rajas and tamas—are its material cause. The ends of the individual souls are its efficient cause. Prakṛti is unconscious, but individual souls are conscious and intelligent. Their proximity and transcendental influence throw the guṇas into disequilibrium, and start the evolution of prakṛti. Particular individual souls' complete isolation (kaivalya) from prakṛti, or complete detachment from it, stops its evolution for them, but it goes on for the experience of the other individual souls. Hence one intelligent Lord is not necessary for the creation of the universe and its adaptation to the individual souls' ends. He is neither its material cause nor efficient cause.

Utpaladeva offers the following criticisms of the Sāṁkhya atheism. If prakṛti is the material cause of the world with an arrangement of parts and diverse effects, if the effects are objects of the individual soul' joys and sorrows, if their ends are their efficient causes, and if the world does not require God as its material cause and efficient cause, then a potter is not necessary for the production of a jar. A lump of earth modifies itself into a jar for the use of an individual person by its nature. Earth is its material cause, and the end of a person is its efficient cause. It should not require a potter to shape earth into a jar as its efficient cause, and a wheel and a staff as its auxiliary causes. If the Sāṁkhya argues that earth, a modification of prakṛti, has a particular nature so that it requires an intelligent agent (e. g., a potter), and a wheel and a staff as auxiliary causes to be modified into a jar of a particular shape for the use of an individual person, then it may be equally argued that prakṛti is of such a nature that it requires the intelligent Lord to produce bodies and the like for the ends of the individual souls. If invariable concomitance between smoke and fire is known in some places at some times, then it must exist elsewhere between another instance of visible smoke and an invisible fire. Hence an intelligent agent, the omniscient and omnipotent Lord, can be inferred from the arrangement of parts in the world, because invariable concomitance between an arrangement of parts is an effect and an intelligent agent is known in all other instances. The Lord is necessary for the creation of the world, as a potter is necessary for the production of a jar. A particular arrangement of parts cannot be produced without an intelligent agent's activity entering into the parts with the aid of the auxiliary causes. Various arrangements of the parts in different effects cannot be produced without prior knowledge of them and volition to produce them. Variety of construction is intelligently designed and executed in a methodical manner, and cannot be produced accidentally, because it is intelligently adapted to definite ends of individual souls. If jars are produced by prakṛti with the assistance of a potter, bodies and the like also are produced by prakṛti with the assistance of the Lord. Their particular arrangements are adapted to particular ends, and the infinite variety of arrangements can be produced by the omniscient and omnipotent Lord. Prakṛti is insentient, and cannot have knowledge and volition, and cannot realise the ends of the individual souls. They do not know prakṛti, and cannot adapt prakṛti to their ends. Further, they are inactive, and so cannot act upon it. The buddhis of the individual souls have knowledge and volition according to the Sāṁkhya ; but they are ignorant of prakṛti, and, consequently, cannot adapt it to the ends of the individual souls. If all individual souls together are omniscient, then each of them is omniscient. If each of them is omniscient, then the cognitions and volitions of the souls will come into conflict with one another, and cannot adapt prakṛti to their particular ends. Hence prakṛti is known by one Lord from whom all individual souls are nondifferent, and who is omniscient and omnipotent. He is the intelligent agent of the world. The insentient prakṛti cannot be the efficient cause of the world ; nor can the individual souls be its efficient cause.

Utpaladeva avers that the Lord does not require any proof to prove His existence, since He is self-existent and self-proved, and since He cannot be proved or disproved by any individual soul. He is the foundation of all proofs of the objects of valid knowledge. He is self-manifest and of the nature of the only Supreme Knower. His knowledge and agency are proved by self-awareness. No individual soul can prove or disprove His existence. But He can only be recognised by an individual soul as its essential nature when it ceases to be overcome by His power of māyā. It can have immediate experience or intuition of the Lord, Ātman, or universal consciousness as its inmost essence. This is called the psychological proof for His existence.[3]

ŚIVA AND ŚAKTI.—Somānanda says: "Śiva is never devoid of Śakti or divine power, and Śakti or divine power can never exist apart from Śiva. Śiva is endowed with divine power, and desires to create entities by His volition. Śaivism does not recognise difference between the Lord and His divine power." Śaivism never recognises difference between Śiva, the Supreme Lord, and His divine power. Śāktaism also recognises this truth. Both believe in Śiva-Śakti as the supreme reality. So Utpaladeva designates the Śāktas as belonging to the cult of Śaivism or allied to it (svayūthya) because they regard Śiva as the unconditioned form of Śakti whom they worship, and does not criticise Śāktaism.[4] If Śakti be assumed to be an independent entity with various capacities to manifest various kinds of objects, then an infinite number of such capacities have to be assumed. If Śakti independently produces various kinds of existents, She does so either as endowed with power or as devoid of power. If She did so as devoid of power, then even void would produce all kinds of existents. If She does so as endowed with power, then Śiva endowed with power creates different kinds of existents. This is the doctrine of monistic Śaivism. If divine power be assumed to be endowed with some other power to create various kinds of existents, it will lead to infinite regress. Does divine power create various kinds of existents? Or, does Śiva endowed with divine power create them? Somānanda replies that Śiva endowed with divine power creates them because He is the agent and because His power is the instrument of action. If divine power were independently the agent of the various kinds of existents, then they would not be of the nature of Śiva, and this would contradict the Śaiva doctrine. But the Śāktas do not contradict this Śaiva doctrine. Power is an attribute of a powerful entity. Heat is not different from fire. So all kinds of existents being of the nature of Śiva endowed with divine power should be known. They are not of the nature of divine power independent of Śiva. Independent divine power is not their agent. Śiva endowed with the power of will, the power of knowledge, and the power of action creates all kinds of existents and exists in them. The powers of all entities are the power of the Supreme Lord. There is nondifference between power and a powerful entity.

Somānanda descrites five powers of Śiva—power of consciousness (cit), power of bliss (ānanda), power of volition (icchā), power of knowledge (jñāna), and power of action (kriyā). The last three powers exist in a very subtle state in Him as nondifferent from Him. He is the Supreme Lord endowed with infinite consciousness and bliss, Who is one, nondifferent and indivisible. Śiva is of this nature before creation. His consciousness (cit) is infinite, self-complete, and independent of objects of knowledge. His bliss is infinite, perfect and independent of objects knowledge. He experiences His infinite consciousness and bliss, and does not experience any external objects. He is the Self, Ātman, or absolutely free 'I' in all existents. He is of the nature of manifestation (prakāśa) and 'I'-consciousness (vimarśa). There being no objects before creation, His manifestation is confined to Him, and is of the nature of innate meditation in the form of 'I am'. His powers of volition, knowledge and action exist in a very subtle state in Him before creation. They are distinctly manifested in relation to other objects when they are created. In the highest state His nature is manifested as 'I am perfect'; this manifestation is of the nature of knowledge. His act of shining is of the nature of action. It depends upon His volition to shine. But His powers of volition, knowledge and action are very subtle because they cannot be imagined separately from one another, and because there are no other existents at the time. They exist in Śiva or Ātman as nondifferent from Him of the nature of infinite consciousness and bliss, and are manifested by His infinite consciousness. Utpaladeva avers that this is the indivisible state of Śiva in the highest state (parāvasthā). Even after creation of the mixed and impure existents Śiva exists as the Supreme Knower untainted by the distinction of knowledge and objects of knowledge. Before the production of all cognitions and after their cessation He exists as the self-manifest Self (ātman). He knows the cognitions before their production and after their cessation; so they rest in Him. He creates the objects, knows them, and makes them rest in Him. Without resting in Him they cannot be known at all. In all states He is endowed with power of consciousness and power of bliss. His powers of volition, knowledge and action are said to be distinct from one another in relation to objects of votition, knowledge and action. But He, the Absolute Knower, is never devoid of these powers.[5]

Kṣemarāja avers that Śiva is of the nature of manifestation (prakāśa) and 'I'-consciousness (vimarśa). 'I'-consciousness is the transcendental delight in the experience of supreme 'I' (pūrṇahantā-camatkāra) in creating, maintaining and dissolving the universe. If He were without 'I'-consciousness, He would cease to be the Lord and become insentient. The Supreme Lord is of the nature of self-manifest supreme 'I' with the created principles manifeted in all existents. He manifests Himself in the variety of the universe through His power of 'I'-consciousness. Ādyanātha avers that Śiva is of the nature of manifestation (prakāśa) and supreme 'I'-consciousness nondifferent from Himself. Abhinavagupta mentions the five powers of consciousness, bliss, volition, knowledge and action which exist in Parama Śiva as nondifferent from Him. He manifests Himself as Śivatattva, Śaktitattva, Sadāśivatattva, Iśvaratattva and Śuddhavidyātattva according as these powers are predominant respectively. He manifests Himself as appearances of external objects. He is absolutely free, manifests and merges the empirical world in Himself as the basis, and makes it appear as different from Him, although it is really nondifferent from Him. Somānnda avers that the Ātman, the Supreme Self, manifesting Himself in all existents is Śiva of the nature of universal consciousness and bliss and endowed with irresistible will and all-pervasive knowledge and action. He is the Supreme Self in all existents. His consciousness, bliss, volition, knowledge and action are manifested in the creation of all objects.

The universe is the expression of Śiva's æsthetic experience of His delight and creative 'I'-consciousness. His being intent on creating the manifold universe is the first stage of His volition. His consciousness is due to introversion because of its being independent of other objects. His creation of the manifold universe is the construction of various objects due to nonapprehension of nondifference consequent on māyā by the empirical knowers. There is no distinction of time before the creation of māyātattva. All His powers are in a mixed state before creation. It is objected that Śiva's intentness on creating the universe of a variety of of ugly effects full of nonapprehension of His nature due to māyāśakti by the bound souls is unreasonable because He rests in His bliss and because He experiences His delight in unfolding His nature in the universe. How can the beautiful Lord be intent on creating an ugly universe? Śomānanda replies that Śiva performs the fivefold acts of creation, maintenance, dissolution, veiling the individual souls' knowledge, and granting them grace. There are no other causes of these acts. Utpaladeva explains it thus. When Śiva assumes the state of Sadāśiva and Īśvara, He knows the universe as 'I am the universe'. At the stage of impure creation also He knows in the form 'I know this jar' or the like. The knowledge of duality is manifested by Śiva of the nature of consciousness. It would not be known if it were not manifested by Him. But there is nonapprension of nondifference due to the power of māyā. Hence the unfolding of His nature in the creation of the pure, mixed and impure existents is not ugly. The nonapprehension of nondifference is of the nature of error and ugliness. But this ugliness is insignificant because it consists in mere nonapprehension. There is no unfolding of what was nonexistent. Śiva of the nature of consciousness assumes the nature of the universe, even as a mirror assumes a variety of reflections of objects. All existents with the principles (tattva) exist in transparent universal consciousness or Śiva as reflections. So He does not become impure or ugly by his intentness on creating them. The motive of His creation is not compassion for human souls as the Nyāya holds. His fivefold acts of creation, etc., are the expression of His nature with five powers. Creation means the unfolding of the principles.

Śiva's intentness on creation (aunmukhya), Somānanda avers, is His knowledge of the construction of the universe and unfoldment of His effort for its accomplishment. His knowledge abides in Himself. The first manifestation of His knowledge in regard to the creation of the universe in the form of initiation of volition is called intentness. It is a little swollen or manifest state of His volition to create the universe. His volition is directed towards an effect to be produced on account of which He is said to be endowed with a volition. The outward extension of intentness is called volition, although it is not yet expressed in an effect. But Śiva never becomes gross (sthūla) because of His intentness.[6] Volition is the later part of intentness, which is capable of producing an effect. Śiva does not become gross when He exerts His volition to create the universe.

When Śiva wills to know or act, His volition is an action. The prior and posterior parts of a volition are assumed because it consists of subtle parts which are distinguishable. A volition to act also is an action. A volition, a cognition, and an action are involved in one another. Hence, in reality one power exists in Śiva endowed with power. His mere delight undetermined by any condition is His power of bliss. His delight determined by an object of action is intentness. Intentness attains its completion when the intended act is accomplished. It is an expression of an effort of cousciousness.

Śiva's power of knowledge consists in His power of manifesting the knowledge of the universe to be created by Him because of which unknown objects are manifested to the minds of the empirical knowers. His power of action consists in the effort to create gross effects which are known by all empirical knowers. The effort is the object of His volition in His power of action which produces gross effects of empirical use. Thus the entire universe comes into existence. In the act of creating the universe His power of consciousness, power of bliss, power of volition, power of knowledge, and power of action are involved. These five powers, especially the last three, are involved in the act of creating each object of the universe. Neither the three powers nor intentness to create nor delight cease. Delight here means Śiva's assumption of the five powers, Who is of the nature of infinite consciousness. In the absence of any of these powers no effect can be produced. If one of the complement of causal conditions is absent, an effect cannot be produced. So Śiva's five powers must co-operate with one another in the creation of all effects. Śivatattva consising of all principles must be present in the production of all effects. One indivisible Śiva with His powers must be present in each of them.

Śiva endowed with all these powers is present in the apprehension of all effects. When a jar is known, the act of knowing is an action. The act of knowing yields knowledge. Knowledge involves volition since a knower devoid of volition cannot know an object. When an object is known, there is a prior volition to know it. One does not know an object if one does not will to know it. One knows an object with one's power of consciousness. When a desired object is known the self feels delight. Hence the power of volition, the power of knowledge, the power of action, the power of consciousness, and the power of delight are involved in the act of knowing an object.

It is objected by the Sāṁkhya that there can be no knowledge in Śiva because it is a modification of prakṛti which is regarded by Śaivaism to be an impure creation produced later. To this objection Somānanda replies that Śiva's knowledge is essential to His nature and unlimited by time and space. Utpaladeva avers that Śiva's knowledge is natural to His essence and not due to buddhi which is an insentient effect of prakṛti, that it is not limited by space and time, and that it is not an object of any other knower's knowledge. Only the knowledge of the empirical knowers who identify their selves with their subtle bodies is due to buddhi due to their nonapprehension of nondifference. But Śiva's knowledge is mere universal consciousness. When the empirical knowers have knowledge due to their buddhis, it cannot be manifested without Śiva's light of consciousness which is self-manifest and natural to Him. Hence the Sāṁkhya objection is baseless.[7]

The Nyāya and the Vaiśeṣika object that the Śaiva view is identical with their view since they hold knowledge to be a quality of the self (ātman) and since Śiva (ātman) has knowledge according to the Śaiva. They hold that knowledge inheres in the self. The Śaivas hold that Śiva is the Self or Ātman endowed with knowledge. Somānanda and Utpaladeva refute this objection thus. The Nyāya and the Vaiśeṣika really take knowledge in the sense of knowledge produced by buddhi, a modification of insentient prakṛti, which they consider to be a quality of an individual self because they hold that it acquires knowledge in conjunction with manas or buddhi. But the Śaivas hold that knowledge is Śiva's essential nature, Who does not acquire it in conjunction with manas or buddhi which is a modification of prakṛti at the stage of māyāśakti. There is no trace of māyāśakti in Śiva's knowledge. Similarly, the Nyāya and the Vaiśeṣika hold that volition is a quality of the self, which it acquires in connection with manas or buddhi, and argue that Śiva conceived by the Śaivas is the Self, that volition inheres in Him, that therefore the Śaiva view is identical with their view, and that volition cannot be the essence of Śiva. Somānanda and Utpaladeva rejoin that volition constitutes Śiva's essence, and that it is not His adventitious quality acquired in conjunction with manas or buddhi. An individual self has the quality of volition at the stage of empirical difference. So the Nyāya and the Vaiśeṣika contention is not valid.

Śiva assumes some forms through His power of volition. He assumes some forms through His power of knowledge. He assumes some forms through His power of action. He assumes some forms by veiling Himself in the form of appearances. In this manner He assumes the forms of thirty six principles (tattva). Gross matter appears to be insentient. Śiva with His power of consciousness and power of bliss, which constitute His essence, is endowed with the powers of volition, knowledge and action. He becomes intent on creation through His powers of consciousness and bliss not related to any objects. He is unfolded in the pure, mixed and impure creations. He is always perfect and of the nature of consciousness and bliss. His intentness on creation is turned into volition to create the world under the influence of His māyāśakti due the nonapprehension of the Ātman. It becomes volition, knowledge and action. All existents are of the nature of Śiva or Ātman, since He is present in them all, and since He assumes those forms. Hence they are of the nature of Śiva or Ātman. He creates the manifold universe without any pre-existent material through His mere volition, even as yogins create things without any material through their mere volitions. So all pure, mixed and impure existents are of the nature of Śiva, since they are manifestations of His powers of consciousness, bliss, volition, knowledge, and action. The infinite Śivatattva always shines in the manifold universe of diverse objects. They are the diverse true manifestations of the Supreme Lord.[8]

CATEGORIES : (1) ŚIVATATTVA.—Kṣemarāja defines Śivatattva as Parama Śiva of the nature of volition, knowledge and action and full of perfect delight. Śivatattva is the first vibration of Parama Śiva in His volition to create the universe. He manifests the principles in Himself as the foundation. Śivatattva is His first desire to manifest the principles as reflections of towns and the like in a mirror because of His being possessed of five powers and absolute freedom, which exist in Him as nondifferent from His nature as of the nature of manifestation, and in which His powers of consciousness and the like predominate. Abhinavagupta defines Śivatattva as the highest principle of the nature of universal consciousness, perfection, and infinite delight because of His resting in Himself, endowed with infinite powers, full of the rays of consciousness and volition, devoid of all differences, pure, calm, beginningless and endless. The universe to be created rests in Him. He transcends all other principles. Yogirāja elaborates this definition. The universe to be created exists and shines in Him as nondifferent from Him. He is of the nature of infinite manifestation. He is perfect because of His desirelessness. He is infinite bliss because He is self-complete, self-fulfilled, and delights in His nature consisting in the artistic experience of infinite 'I' (akhaṇḍāhantācamatkāra-rasa). Thus He is different from insentient matter manifested by Him because He is of the essence of manifestation (sphurattā) and infinite delight. He is of the nature of the power of volition, the power of knowledge, the power of action, etc. He is different from the unqualified and powerless Brahman of Śaṁkara and his followers, who is almost insentient. He is endowed with infinite powers. He is unlimited in nature and so devoid of limiting determinations and differences. He is pure since He is devoid of the impurity of differences. He is calm since He is free of agitation due the distinction of subjects and objects. He abides in His nature united with His powers. He is not like a piece of stone. He is without origin and end since He is eternal. There is no time—past, present and future—in Him since time is produced by Him. Śivatattva is universal consciousness, which is of the nature of great manifestation, which transcends all principles, and which is manifested in the hearts of all empirical knowers as perfect 'I'-consciousness and æsthetic experience of delight. He is the first cause of all existents, and the origin of all differences, although devoid of all differences; He is originless and absolutely free. He assumes the state of Bhairava full of the artistic experience of delight due to the power of manifestation consequent on the unfolding of infinite diverse absolute freedom. Bhaṭṭa Bhāskara defines Śivatattva as the self-luminous principle.[9]

ŚAKTITATTVA.—Kṣemarāja defines Śaktitattva as the first vibration of the Supreme Lord desirous of creating the universe because of His power of volition being unrestrained. He calls this principle icchāśaktitattva. Bhaṭṭa Bhāskara defines Śaktitattva as Parama Śiva's powers of knowledge and action. Yogirāja defines Śaktitattva as Parama Śiva's experience full of creative delight desirous of creating the universe, the seed of all existents, assuming a slightly manifest state. His blissful experience of 'I' desires to create the universe. Śaktitattva is the experience of 'I' because of the desire to create the external universe owing to absolute freedom and predominance of the artistic experience of supreme delight. Ādyanātha defines Śaktitattva as Parama Śiva's volition desirous of creating the universe and veiling it with 'I'-consciousness. Śaktitattva is Parama Śiva's transparent volition, which exists always in Him, which is the seed of the universe that is merged in Her. His absolutely free power of volition becomes Śaktitattva--the seed of the universe to be created. The Supreme Lord Himself assumes the state of Śaktitattva because of the degrees of His artistic experience of perfect 'I' due to the upsurging of His power of lordship. Hence His power of delight predominates in Śaktitattva. His logical experience is not the cause of the universe. But His volition to create it with the predominance of creative delight and the æsthetic experience of delight is the cause of the universe. His power of 'I'-consciousness veils the universe to be created; it remains merged in His power as nondifferent from Him. The Supreme Divine Power, dynamic consciousness, absolutely free and full of perfect 'I'-consciousness, and nondifferent from Parama Śiva, is the cause of the universe.[10]

(3) SADĀŚIVATATTVA.—Somānanda regards Sadāśivatattva as the state assumed by Parama Śiva when His power of knowledge predominates, and Īśvaratattva as the state assumed by Him when His power of volition predominates. Kṣemarāja defines Sadāśivatattva as the principle wherein the universe exists as potential and dominated by His 'I'-consciousness. The universe exists in Him as indistinct consciousness of 'this' which is dominated by His 'I'-consciousness. Utpaladeva averse that Parama Śiva's power of knowledge and power of action are inseparable from each other, that they are directed inward and outward, that when His introversion predominates He assumes the state of Sadāśivatattva or

Sādākhyatattva, and that when His extraversion predominates He assumes the state of Īśvaratattva. His enfolding within is Sadāśivatattva while His unfolding without is Īśvaratattva. Somānanda avers that Parama Śiva's power of knowledge called the state of Sadāśivatattva is the supreme state of Logos or experiencing subtle speech (paśyantī) of the Śābdikas. His power of knowledge predominates in Sadāśivatattva, but his power of action is not absent since it is said: 'His power of knowledge and power of action are Sādākhya'. Utpaladeva observes that both Sadāśivatattva and Īśvaratattva have power of knowledge and power of action since power and powerfull Being are nondifferent from each other, that power of knowledge is predominant in the former while power of action is predominant in the latter. According to Yogirāja there is nondiscrimination of 'this'-consciousness and 'I'-consciousness in Sadāśivatattva, and He has consciousness 'I am this'. His power of knowledge predominates in this principle—the seed of the origin of the universe in the state of the void, since His power of action rests in His 'I'-consciousness attended with an æsthetic experience of delight. Sadāśivatattva is also defined as Parama Śiva engaged in the act of bestowing His grace on all, ready to manifest the universe by ejecting it out of His power of volition, and veiling Himself by it. Rājanakānanda opines that His power of volition predominates in this principle because of indistinctness of 'this'-consciousness, and that He assumes the role of bestowing His grace on all because of His desire to manifest the principles out of Himself, which are not yet manifested.[11]

(4) ĪŚVARATATTVA.—Kṣemarājā defines Īśvaratattva as the germinating universe existing in Parama Śiva dominated by His 'I'-consciousness, although it is not yet created. In this principle both 'this'-consciousness and 'I'-consciouness are distinct and coexist in the same substratum. In Sadāśivatattva 'this'-consciousness is indistinct and dominated by distinct 'I'-consciousness. The universe to be created is known as 'this'-consciousness. Utpaladeva defines Īśvaratattva as Parama Siva's unfolding outward, and avers that His extraversion predominates herein. His power of action is predominant in this principle. Bhaṭṭa Bhāskara defines Īśvaratattva as the principle that urges the universe to be created. Īśvaratattva is also defined as Parama Śiva experiencing all principles as 'this', although they are not yet created. He has distinct consciousness of all principles as 'this' and imbues them with 'I'-consciousness. Rājānakānanda holds that His power of knowledge predominates in Īśvaratattva because of His distinct knowledge of the objects of knowledge. Yogirāja avers that Parama Śiva assumes the state of Īśvaratattva when He knows the principles as 'I am this' because of His equally distinct consciousness of 'I' and 'this' which He does not discriminate from each other and when He experiences a flash of delight in 'I'-consciounsness.[12]

(5) ŚUDDHAVIDYĀTATTA.—Kṣemarāja defines Śuddhavidyātattva as the knowledge of identity of 'this'-consciousnessness and 'I'-consciousness. The universe is known as an object of knowledge whose essence is difference. Utpaladeva defines Śuddhavidyātattva as coexistence of 'I'-consciousness and 'this'-consciousness in the same substratum. Parama Śiva at this stage identifies Himself with the universe and knows it as 'I am this universe.' Existents are of the nature of consciousness. Parama Śiva assumes the state of objects of knowledge, and

knows them as His own states and of the nature of pure consciousness so that His knowledge is pure. Rājānakānanda opines that His power of action predominates in this state since the principles are more distinctly known in it. Yogirāja avers that the Lord's Śuddhavidyātattva is a flash of delight in the experience 'I am I'. 'This is this' wherein 'this'-consciousness predominates and 'I'-consciousness is subordinate. Abhinavagupta opines that Śuddhavidyā does not make any distinction among knowers, knowledge, and objects of knowledge, that it apprehends all differences as reflected in māyā, that it is really the cause of the universe, that it is a triangular great cave (mahāguhā) because it is not known in its real nature since the distinction of knowers, knowledge, and objects of knowledge is dominated by the knowledge of nondifference, and that it is triangular mahāvidyā the object of worship and the source of all religious sentiments. This great cave full of śuddhavidyā is the basis of the creation of the universe. It is absolute freedom of Parama Śiva, of the nature of 'I'-consciousness (vimarśa) manifested by His supreme consciousness or manifestation (prakāśa) apprehending the universe as 'this'. It is the resting place of His 'I'-consciousness. His manifestation is full of æsthetic experience of delight apprehending His natural, innate power of Logos and power of mantra. His manifestation is realised in His 'I'-consciousness. These are the stages of creation. Bhaṭṭa Bhāskara opines that Śuddhavidyā enlightens a bound soul on the nature of Parama Śiva taught by the Śaiva scriptures. Varadarāja avers that when a yogin acquires śuddhavidyā at the will of the Lord, when he experiences his innate bliss, and when he does not care for trifling supernatural powers, he attains the state of manifestation of Parama Śiva dwelling within him, which is devoid of difference, and which is full of perfect bliss, and attains transcendence of the universe.

The knowers known as Mantramaheśvaras are governed by Sadāśivatattva. The knowers known as Mantreśvaras are governed by Īśvaratattva. The knowers known as Mantras are governed by Śuddhavidyātattva. The first have realised Sadāśivatattva; the second have realised Īśaratattva; and the third have realised Śuddhavidyātattva.[13]

(6). MĀYĀTATTVA.—Kṣemarāja defines māyā as the appearance or manifestation of difference among the existents with their specific natures. Utpaladeva defines māyaśakti as the Lord's knowledge of difference among the existents, although He is of the nature of consciousness and the sole agent of them. Some hold that He knows the universe as different from Him, although He knows Himself to be its agent full of consciousness. Vidyā makes the bound souls recognise their identity with the Absolute. Māyā veils their knowledge of identity with one universal consciousness. It creates two kinds of illusion in them: it produces the illusion of their difference from Parama Śiva, although they are nondifferent from Him; it generates the illusion of their identity with not-self, e.g., the void, buddhi, or gross body. It produces three kinds of taint (mala) in them. Somānanda defines māyātattva as the Lord's sportive power of concealing His nature as one universal consciousness, and of assuming the state of the impure principles. Māyātattva is also defined as the knowledge of difference among its modifications and among all individual souls, which veils the Lord's absolutely free spiritual wealth. In creating impure states He conceals Himself and generates the knowledge of difference of the principles from Himself and from one another for the experience of bound souls by His māyāśakti because of His power of doing the impossible. Abhinavagupta deseribes māyā as the cause of the world. It is the cause of distinction of the knowers, knowledge, and objects of knowledge. Paramo Śiva full of supreme powers is present in the empirical distiction of these factors. He assumes the distinction through māyā. He is of the nature of self-manifest consciousness and devoid of the taint of all differences and yet He assumes the empirical distinction through māyā. Abhinavagupta defines māyāśakti as Śiva's supreme freedom, which veils the nature of His Self and which makes the impossible possible. It is called the principle of māyā (māyātattva). Yogirāja explains it in the following manner. Māyāśakti is Śiva's power which does not depend upon any other Being. It is free in the sense that it is the power of creating the world. It is Śiva's power and divine (devī). It is called māyā, because the empirical world of knowers and known objects is definitely known because of māyā, and also because it deludes the individual souls and binds them to the world. It is not foreign to the nature of the Brahman as the Advaita Vedāntins hold. It is the power of the Lord for His sport. Is is His power of freedom through which He creates the world of subjects (pramātṛ) and objects (prameya), which cannot be created by any other Being. His power of māyā creates the three taints (mala) which veil the real nature of the embodied bound souls (paśu). They are nothing but Śiva Who of His own will assumes the state of bondage by contraction.

Māyā is nondiscrimination of the coverings (kañcūka) and the other principles from kalā to earth. Varadarāja explains its nature thus. Māyā consists in a soul's not knowing the principles as the Ātman because of its being covered by its coverings and because of its identifying itself with its subtle body and gross body. Māyā deludes an individual soul which knows itself to be a limited agent, and which does not know itself to be the ommipotent agent on account of its coverings. The world of diversity is due to nonapprehension of the principles. Delusion (moha) consists in a soul's nonapprehension of its real nature as the Ātman—Absolute consciousness. It is nescience. A soul that is overcome by nescience and identified with it becomes a victim of sufferings, is tainted with merits and demerits, and called Karmātman. Ādyanātha defines māyātattva as the Lord's knowledge of difference among the existents which are like His own parts or states[14].

(7—11) KAÑCŪKA : KALĀ, VIDYĀ RĀGA, KĀLA, AND NIYATI.—Kṣemarāja deseribes the nature of the coverings (kañcūka) of the bound souls in the following manner. Parama Śiva's omnipotence, perfection, eternity, and all-pervasiveness are contracted, and become kāla, vidyā, rāga, kāla, and niyati, respectively, although they are unlimited in their real nature. The Lord Himself assumes limits and contracts His powers. His powers are not limited by any external entities. The contractors (kañcūka) of His powers are due to His volition. Kalā is the cause of an individual soul's limited agency. Vidyā is the cause of its limited knowledge. Rāga is the cause of its love for particular objects. Kāla is the cause of sequence among the existents, which are known and cease to be known. It is the cause of temporal order—the past, the present, and the future. Niyati is the cause of regulation in regard to righteous and unrighteous actions. It is the cause of limitation in regard to space and cause. It connects specific causes to specific effects. Thus

Śiva becomes an individual bound soul, being limited in His powers. When its powers are expanded fully, it becomes the Absolute. Utpaladeva avers that a bound soul has limited knowledge and agency due to the agency of vidyā and kalā, although it is insentient and dependent because of its false identification with its mind-body-complex. Its limited knowledge and limited agency are due to Parama Śiva's knowledge and action, which are contracted by vidyā and kalā respectively. Rājānakānanda avers that existents reflected in a bound soul's buddhi cannot be rightly known because of their being composed of sattva, rajas and tamas, and that they are rightly known through the agency of vidyā. He avers that Parama Śiva's power of eternal, perfect delight being limited becomes a bound soul's affection for particular objects of pleasure. Particular affections for particular objects are branches of common love for objects of enjoyment. He also avers that Parama Śiva's absolute freedom being limited regulates the relation between virtues and vices and their effects, and specific causes and specific effects.

Abhinavagupta calls māyāśakti and its five prodcuts—kalā, vidyā, rāga, kāla, and nityati—six coverings (kañcūka-saṭka). Parama Śiva is omnipotent, omniscient, universal consciousness unlimited by time, space and conditions. Although He is absolutely free, He assumes the nature of an atomic (aṇu) individual soul through His power of Māyā. His power of knowledge and power of action are contracted, and thus an individual soul acquires vidyā and kalā. It is deprived of its omniscience, omnipotence, etc., by its āṇava mala which veils them up. Yogirāja explains Abhinavagupta's view in the aforesaid maner. The five principles produced by māyā are called coverings (kañcūka) since they veil the real nature of a bound soul as the Absolute. They are called bondage since they bind individual souls to embodied existence by deluding them, since they generate their sufferings, and since they make them empirical knowers.[15]

(12) PURUṢATATTVA.—Kśemarāja avers that when the Supreme Lord assumes the state of a limited knower owing to His power of māyā which conceals His nature, He is called an individual soul (puruṣa). It is deluded by māyā, bound by merits and demerits, and becomes subject to transmigration. Its delusion does not affect the Lord, although it is nondifferent from Him. When it recognises its identity with Him owing to vidyā, it attains liberation and becomes one universal consciousness or Parama Śiva. It is conscious, but its consciousness is contracted, and it has the universe in a contracted form as its body. The Lord's power of māyā conceals its nature, and, consequently, its consciousness appears to be contracted. It appears to be a limited knower, although it is really identical with Parama Śiva whose body is the universe. In reality, all knowers are the venerable Lord Whose body is the universe, and identical with the light of one universal consiousness. Even contraction of Parama Śiva's consciousness, which is self-imposed, is full of His consciousness since it is revealed to be identical with Him on close consideration. He is the only supreme reality. Either contraction is He or nothing. All His powers of lordship are contracted in an individual soul. The Lord limited by His power of māyā and with all His powers of lordship contracted assumes the state of an individual soul, even as the red sun with its rays withdrawn into itself is unable to manifest itself. An individual soul is atomic (aṇu) because it is denuded of its powers of lordship owing to contraction. It is rot able to recognise its identity with Parama Śiva, and

transmigrates. When it recognises its powers of lordship through vidyā owing to the descent of the power of the Lord (śaktipāta) or His grace, it becomes Parama Śiva. He is the Supreme Knower and knows the universe as His own parts or states since He is possessed of the powers of Lordship. But an individual soul tainted with afflictions, potencies of actions and dispositions becomes bound, and knows the existents as different from itself and from one another owing to His power of māyā. Utpaladeva draws a distinction between the Lord and a bound soul in this manner. He describes a bound soul as universal consciousness limited by a subtle body. It has nonapprehension of nondifference from the Absolute due to māyāśakti, distinguishes between subject and object, and becomes subject to embodied existence. It is atomic, ignorant, dependent, impotent, imperfect, and subject to the power of māyā. It is tainted with impurities (mala). Somānanda defines an individual bound soul as ignorant of its real nature as the Absolute, and a released soul as recognising its nature as the Absolute and devoid of agitation due to the distinction of subject and object. Utpaladeva avers that a bound soul is atomic owing to its limitation, although it is eternal and incorporeal in its real nature, that it is ignorant owing to its renouncing the knowledge of its pervading the universe, that it is of limited powers due to its dependence or loss of absolute freedom and due to its loss of infinite power of knowledge and infinite power of action, that it has affection for particular objects due to its being limited by rāga, and that it is subject to māyā in that its mind-body-complex is created by māyā. Abhinavagupta avers that an individual soul experiences objects owing to powers arising from a mass of sounds or words because of its being deprived of its powers by kalā. It is an empirical knower of objects, and its knowledge is subject to the distinction of subjects and objects, words and objects. It does not know that subjects and objects as well as words and objects are creations of, and identical with, the Abosolute. Parama Śiva Himself becomes a bound soul when He assumes limitation through His power of māyā and becomes tainted with impurities, and when He is related to the five coverings of kalā, vidyā, rāga, kāla, and niyati. Abhinavagupta mentions avidyā instead of vidyā in contradistinction from śuddhavidyā. Avidyā is not the absence of knoweldge. Vidyā enables an empirical knower to know present objects and prevents it from knowing the past, future and remote objects.[16]

(13) PRAKṚTITATTVA.—Kṣemarāja defines prakṛti as the root cause of the principles from mahat to earth and other gross elements. Utpaladeva defines prakṛti as the one root cause of twenty three principles which are not separated from one another in it. Abhinavagupta regards prakṛti as a manifestation of Parama Śiva's wealth of powers. Yogirāja regards it as full of sattva, rājā and tamas,—which is modified into causes and effects, which binds the individual souls by generating their pleasure, pain, and delusion, and which is experienced by them. Prakṛti is also defined as Parama Śiva's powers of volition, knowledge and action together devoid of agitation and contracted, or as equilibrium of sttava, rājas and tamas, which are of the nature of His aforesaid powers, and which are not yet separated from one another. When they are thrown into disequilibrium they produce the different kinds of existents.[17]

(14-16) Buddhi, ahaṁkāra and manas exist in citta as nondifferent from it. Parama Śiva's power of knowledge and power of action are the principal ingredients in the creation of empirical knowers. They contract and become Iśvaratattva and Śuddhavidyātattva. They further contract and become vidyātattva and kalātattva. Further contracting they become the sense-organs of knowledge and the sense-organs of action. His power of action contracting to the extreme limit becomes the subtle elements. His power of volition becomes rajas of a bound soul and turns into its egoism (ahaṁkāra). His power of knowledge becomes sattva and turns into buddhi, which is characterised by determinate knowledge of an object. His power of action becomes tamas and turns into manas, which is characterised by doubt.[18]

(17—26).—Parama Śiva limits Himself and becomes the cognitive sense-organs and their objects owing to the predominance of His power of knowledge. He limits Himself and becomes the motor sense-organs and their functions owing to the predominance of His power of action. The auditory organ, the visual organ, the tactual organ, the gustatory organ, and the olfactory organ are the five organs of knowledge. They apprehend sound, colour, touch, taste, and smell, respectively. The vocal organ is the organ of speaking. The prehensive organ is the organ of grasping. The locomotive organ is the organ of walking. The generative organ is the organ of procreation. The excretory organ is the organ of evacuation. These are the organs of action[19].

(27—36).—Sound-essence, touch-essence, taste-essence, and smell-essence are the subtle elements (sūkṣma bhūta, tanmātra). Ether, fire, air, water, and earth are the gross elements. Earth has smell. Water has natural liquidity. Fire has hot touch and colour. Air has touch and absence of colour. Ether has sound. The gross elements are the lowest limits of Parama Śiva's manifestation of His apparent insentience due to His extreme contraction. A lower principle is pervaded by a higher principle. Parama Śiva endowed with powers permeates all principles, is immanent in them, and transcendent of them. His power is the source of thirty six principles. He assumes the forms of Mantras, Mantramaheśvaras, Mantreśvaras, etc , by differentiating knowers and known objects. The universe of different objects of knowledge is gross because it is full of difference. The knowers also are gross due to Parama Śiva's volition, although they are of the nature of knowledge. Hence their knowledge also is gross since it depends upon the means of knowledge and the objects of knowledge. It is called vidyā. Some regard vidyā as mahāmāyā due to the appearance of difference. Parama Śiva veils the nature of His Self and creates the empirical world of difference full of nonapprehension of nondifference. He assumes māyāśakti and creates the world of difference of empirical knowers and objects of knowledge. He assumes the forms of thirty six principles.

INDIVIDUAL SELF.—Utpaladeva gives the following arguments for the existence of a conscious limited knower. Manifestation and 'I'-consciousness are the characteristics of the Absolute Knower. Objects depend for their manifestation on a conscious knower. Their existence and nonexistence are known by a conscious knower. Otherwise, there would be no distinction between them. So their existence is attended with their being known by a conscious knower. Their being is attended with their being manifested; their existence is attended with their manifestations in a conscious knower in the form of cognitions. Existent objects can induce a knower to perform practical actions (arthakriyā), but nonexistent objects cannot induce him to do so. Hence practical actions depend upon a knower who knows objects. They cannot produce any distinction in a knower unless they are manifested by his cognitions. An existent object can be distinguished from a nonexistent object through the conditions (upādhi) of their manifestations in the knower ; an existent object induces a knower to react upon it ; a nonexistent object does not induce him to react upon it. Otherwise, an existent object cannot be distinguished from a nonexistent object in its nature. Both an existent object and a nonexistent object depend upon the consciousness of a knower. An object which is known to be existent can evoke a practical action in a knower. But an object which is known to be nonexistent cannot evoke a practical action in a knower. Thus the being of an object depends upon the consciousness of a knower. Śaiva monism advocates the doctrine of idealism. If consciousness is of the nature of manifestation only and devoid of 'I'-consciousness, it is insentient. Here Utpaladeva refutes Śaṁkara's doctrine of Brahman as universal consciousness devoid of 'I'-consciousness. Consciousness devoid of 'I'-consciousness does not know itself to be the self's consciousness, and, consequently, cannot be the abode of another existent, or cannot know it. 'I'-consciousness is the foundation of 'this'-consciousness. Different objects cannot be manifested by mere 'this'-consciousness, but can be manifested by 'this'-consciousness attended with 'I'-consciousness. A knower is self-manifest or self-aware ; but an insentient object is manifested by a conscious knower ; it is proved by a conscious knower to exist when he knows it through its manifestation. Insentient objects unmanifested by a conscious knower are as good as nonexistent ; their manifestation depends upon a conscious knower, either 'I' or any other knower. The relation between an insentient object and a conscious knower as a known object and a knowing subject depends upon consciousness (saṁvid). A conscious self devoid of 'I'-consciousness cannot have apprehension of difference and nondifference. 'This'-consciousness of insentient objects is fulfilled in 'I'-consciousness in the form 'I am' or 'This I am'. The knower or Ātman, is either limited by vital forces or unlimited by them. The former is a bound individual soul which is atomic while the latter is the Supreme Self unlimited and all-pervading. Both are of the nature of consciousness or manifestation, and the abodes of the manifestations of objects. Both know the discrete objects and combine them into a unity. Multiplicity exists in the objects. Their unity is due to their knower's synthetic act of apperception. One conscious Knower manifests all insentient objects and withdraws them and makes them unmanifest, which are really nondifferent from Him in their essential nature. He is of the nature of manifestation and 'I'-consciousness. Hence He is more than insentient objects. He is the Lord. But a limited knower in whom consciousness and knowledge inhere is devoid of perfect 'I'-consciousness, and, consequently, insentient. He is partly insentient because his vital forces with which he wrongly identifies himself are insentient objects of knowledge. He cannot, therefore, be the Absolute Knower. The Lord contracts His consciousness and manifestation at His will, and assumes the nature of a limited knower through the limiting adjunct of vital forces and the like. A limited knower is limited by his subtle body and so called a puryaṣṭaka-pramātṛ. He has a limited knowledge of objects. But the Supreme Self (paramātman) is unlimited and unconditioned, and the Absolute Knower. When a limited knower recognises his identity with the Lord, he attains to His status. All objects cannot be manifested by a limited knower identified with vital forces, etc., which are insentient, because he is devoid of perfect 'I'-consciousness. But the manifestations of all objects rest in the Absolute Knower or Ātman in the form 'I am the universe'. Perfect 'I'-consciousness is the resting place of the manifestations of all objects because of its absolute freedom and omnipotence and the absence of dependence on all other entities. These are characteristics of lordship. When a limited knower recognises his identity with the Absolute Knower, he knows the world to be full of nonduality and non-difference from Him.

Abhinavagupta asserts that Śiva of the nature of the light of consciousness assumes the power of māyā, and becomes a tainted individual soul called paśu. A bound soul is called a paśu. An individual soul is bound to embodied life owing to its being limited by kāla, kalā, niyati, rāga, and vidyā, which are called the five coverings or contractors (kañcūka) of the universal consciousness of Śiva, the Absolute. The omniscient and omnipotent Śiva is limited by āṇavamala owing to His assumption of the power of māyā, and to His concealment of His omniscience and omnipotence, assumes the taint of āṇavamala of the nature of nonapprehension of nondifference, and becomes limited even as the ubiquitous ether is limited when enclosed in a jar, and is called an individual soul (puruṣa, jivātman). It is called paśu because it is fettered and maintained by māyā and its products called āṇava-mala, māyīya-mala, and kārma- mala, which taint it.

An individual soul is identified with its internal organs. Manas, buddhi, ahaṁkāra, and citta are the internal organs. They are composed of sattva, rajas and tamas—sattva being predominant in them. A soul bound by them tinged with the impressions (saṁskāra) of external objects and intent on operating on them transmigrates from one species to another in accordance with its merits and demerits because of its inability to know its essential nature as the Ātman. It is a spiritual atom or monad (aṇu) because it is tainted with āṇava-mala which contracts its essential universal consciousness very much. But the Ātman or Śiva does not transmigrate from one species to another because He is of the nature of one pure universal consciousness only and endowed with the power of creative volition, knowledge and action. He is the essential nature of the universe. A bound soul becomes monadic (aṇu) owing to contraction manifested by His freedom, and identifies itself with the internal organs.[20]

Somānanda describes five kinds of individual souls (jīvātman) or bound souls (paśu). (1) Some do not know their nature[1] as Śiva or universal consciousness, and are so called paśu or bound souls. Their nonapprehension of nondifference is due to Śiva's māyāśakti. They live an empirical life characterised by the difference between empirical knowers and empirical objects of knowledge. The empirical knowers are bound souls or universal consciousness limited by their subtle bodies. So they are called knowers limited by their subtle bodies (puryaṣṭaka-pramātṛ). They are atomic (aṇu) because their consciousness is limited. They are eternal and incorporeal because they are of the nature of consciousness (caitanya). They are possessed of finite knowledge because they have lost the consciousness of their immanence in the universe. They are possessed of finite agency because they have lost their freedom and lordship. They are tainted with attachment (rāga) because they identify themselves with their subtle bodies and because they think of the means of enjoyment. They are influenced by māyāśakti, and are in the womb of māyā. They are members of the empirical world due to māyāsakti. The venerable Śiva cannot be ignorant of His nature as Śiva, because He is eternally pure, because impurities cannot be produced without His volition, and because they subsist in Him being full of His volition. Hence the individual souls are atomic (aṇu) because of their ignorance of their nature as Śiva or universal consciousness and because of their being overcome by Śiva's māyāśakti. Their āṇava-mala, māyīya-mala, and kārma-mala are produced by His power of māyā. Really there is no difference between knowers (grāhaka) and known objects (grāhya). The difference between them is due to nescience (ajñāna). (2) Some individual souls know themselves of the nature of Śiva under the influence of mahāmāyā or power of vidyā, to be immanent in the universe, and to be calm (śānta), as it were. They are always of the nature of Śiva whether they know this fact or whether they do not know it. So it is said that they are calm, as it were. (3) Some individual souls acquire the firm conceit that they are identical with God (Īśvara) as conceived by the Vaiśeṣikas owing to a certain degree of the power of vidyā. Some individual souls acquire the conceit that they are Śiva owing to a certain degree of the power of vidyā. (4) Some individual souls are devoid of any knowledge of objects as different from them, which is due to the taint called māyīya-mala, although their being bound remains intact. Their knowledge is due to a different state. They are called pralayakevalins. (5) Some individual souls know their nature as Ātman, do not identify their selves with their subtle bodies, and do not know objects as different from themselves as the pralayākalas do. They are not tainted by kārma-mala and are called vijñāna-kevalins.[21]

Kṣemarāja defines an individual soul as the Absolute, Ātman, or universal consciousness contracted, which has the universe in a contracted form as its body. It is a knower or subject of the universe as a known object. It is nothing but Parama Śiva, Absolute, or universal consciousness pervading the universe in a contracted state. It is a knower of the universe as a contracted state of universal consciousness, which manifests the universe in its own basis. There is identity between an individual soul and Parama Śiva. An individual soul is identical with Him Whose body is the universe, because universal consciousness is His real nature, but it appears to be contracted because its real nature is not manifested owing to His power of māyā. Contraction also is full of universal consciousness because of its being manifested by consciousness. If it is not manifested, it is a mere nonentity. Thus every individual knower is identical with Parama Śiva Whose body is the universe. Kṣemarāja says elsewhere : "If nonapprehension is never apprehended, then knowledge alone remains. If it is apprehended, then it is of the nature of apprehension. Thus knowledge alone remains." Spandaśāstra also says : 'The individual soul is identical with Parama Śiva. There is no state in a word, object, or apprehension, which is not Śiva. The knowledge of identity of an individual soul with the Absolute constitutes its liberation, and the ignorance of it constitues bondage.

It may be objected that an individual subject is of the nature of differentiation which is a function of the mind, that as such it cannot be identical with Parama Śiva, the light of universal consciousness. To this objection Kṣemarāja replies that universal consciousness descends to the state of mental consciousness to apprehend particular objects, and becomes individual consciousness, because it contracts itself in order to apprehend particular objects of knowledge. The individual consciousness is nothing but the universal consciousness. When the universal consciousness conceals its real nature, and is contracted, it has two aspects. Sometimes its contraction becomes subordinate, and the universal consciousness becomes predominant. Sometimes contraction becomes predominant, and universal consciousness becomes subordinate. An individual soul is vijñānākala when the natural state of universal consciousness is predominant with its manifestation without 'I'-consciousness. An individual soul is vidyāpramātā when both manifestation and 'I'-consciousness of Parama Śiva are predominant. As contraction gradually decreases, the stages of Īśa, Sadāśiva, and Anāśrita Śiva are reached. The highest stage of being a knower of the pure path is gradually reached when universal consciousnes becomes predominant owing to the effort of meditation and trance. The stage of being a knower of the void is reached when contraction becomes predominant. Thus the universal consciousness assuming the form of a contracted subject descends from the stage of universal consciousnes being intent on apprehending objects, is limited by its external objects of knowledge and by its internal objects of knowledge like pleasure, pain, etc.,is limited by both limitations, and becomes the individual consciousness. It is said in the 'Pratyabhijñā', 'The Lord's powers of knowledge, action, and māyā become sattva, rajas and tamas in an individual soul.' Thus the universal consciousness of the nature of absolute freedom with the powers of knowledge, action, and māyā becomes the individual consciousness with sattva, rajas and tamas owing to the excess of contraction. Individual consciousness is the nature of a knower of māyā, that is full of limited consciousness. Vasugupta says, 'The knower of māyā is individual consciousness.'

Śiva is one Ātman of the nature of universal consciousness, since consciouness is not divided by space, time and other limiting conditions, and since an insentient entity cannot know it. He is twofold as universal consciousness of the nature of manifestation, and as individual consciousness or a limited knower of limited objects due to His freely assuming vital forces and the like and limiting Himself by them. He becomes threefold as being covered by the taints called āṇava-mala, māyīya-mala and kārma-mala. He becomes fourfold as He assumes the nature of void, vital forces, a subtle body, and a gross body. Void is the object of a pralayakevalin's experience. He becomes thirty five principles from Śivatattva to earth. He becomes seven kinds of knowers, viz., Śiva-pramātṛ, Mantramaheśvara, Mantreśvara, Mantra, Vijñānākala, Pralayākala, and Sakala. He becomes fivefold according as His powers of consciousness, bliss, volition, knowledge, and action are limited owing to nonapprehension, and become kalā, vidyā, rāga, kāla, and niyati, which are the five modifications of māyā and called coverings in that they veil the universal consciousness and are its contractors. Mantreśvara is a subject who has experienced Īśvaratattva. Mantra is a subject who has experienced Śuddhavidyātattva. Vijñānākala is a subject who is above māyā, but who has not experienced Śuddhavidyātattva. Pralayākala is a subject who abides in māyātattva. Sakala is an individual soul that abides in māyātattva and has knowledge of difference alone.[22]

KINDS OF SOULS.—Utpaladeva describes Vijñānakevalas as those individual souls, which are different from one another despite their nondifference in being of the nature of knowledge, eternity and the like,—their difference being due to God's volition,—and which are like puruṣas conceived by the Sāṁkhya. He describes Pralayākalas as those individual souls, which do not identify themselves with void, their vital forces, or their bodies, which know themselves as of the nature of 'I' and agents, which are tainted with subtle impressions of merits and demerits, and whose māyīyā-mala is imagined because of their relation to objects of knowledge at times. He describes Vidyeśvaras as those individual souls, which are endowed with agency, whose knowledge is not limited by merits and demerits, and which are tainted with māyīya-mala because of their knowledge of different objects of knowledge. All individual souls comprising gods are tainted with three kinds of taints. Nevertheless, merits and demerits (kārma-mala) are the main cause of transmigration and embodied life. The principle of consciousness endowed with agency is limited by kalā in an individual soul, and the principle of apparent insentience, like the void, vital forces, and bodies, is of the nature of sattva, rajas, and tamas. They derive from Parama Śiva's powers of knowledge, volition, and action, respectively. Knowledge and agency are the principal characteristics of Him of the nature of consciousness. But an individual soul's knowledge and agency are due to its being related to Him.

Śaivaism evaluates the doctrines of the Ātman in different systems. The Cārvākas regard the Ātman as the body endowed with consciousness. But the body is a product of Śiva's māyāśakti, and so cannot be the Ātman of the nature of universal consciousness. The self is of the nature of manifestation, but the body is insentient and manifested. The body. is endowed with mental consciousness, and the mind also is a product of Śiva's māyāśakti. The body and the mind are characterised by difference, but Śiva or Ātman is universal, undifferentiated consciousness. The Naiyāyikas regard the Ātman in empirical life as a substance endued with the qualities of cognition, pleasure, pain, desire, aversion, volition, impression, merit and demerit, and the Ātman in release as a substance devoid of these qualities. Kṣemarāja opines that the Naiyāyikas identify the Self with buddhi in bondage, and identify it with void in release. The Mīmāṁsakas regard the Ātman as a substance endued with these qualities, which is an object of 'I'-consciousness. Kṣemarāja opines that they also identify the Self with buddhitattva, since cognition and other qualities are the modifications of buddhi. The Buddhist realists and idealists regard the Ātman as a stream of cognitions. Kṣemarāja opines that they also identify the self with buddhitattva, since cognitions are the modes of buddhi. The Buddhist Mādhyamikas regard the Ātman as void or nonexistent. Kṣemarāja opines that void is an object of knowledge, and that for that reason it cannot be the knowing self. The Sāṁkhyas regard the Ātman as an eternal, enlightened, individual knower of the nature of consciousness. Kṣemarāja opines that they identy the Ātman with vijñānākala individual souls. The Śābdikas regard the Ātman as Śabdabrahma in the form of paśyantī. Kṣemarāja opines that they identify the Self with Sadāśivatattva. Somānanda's criticism of this doctrine is given elsewhere. Some Aupaniṣadas regard the Ātman as Being (sat). Kṣemarāja opines that they identify the Self with Īśvaratattva. Other Aupaniṣadas regard the Ātman as vital force. Kṣemarāja asserts that vital force is a product of māyāsakti. The Tāntrikas regard the Ātman as transcendent of the universe. Other sacred texts describe the Ātman as immanent in the universe, which is only a form of the Self. The Trika philosophy of monistic idealism regards the Ātman as both transcendent and immanent. The non-Śaiva systems do not know the real nature of the Ātman or Śiva, and identify Him with the various stages of His manifestations or concealments by His absolutely free will beyond which their limited knowledge cannot extend. None can have a complete knowledge of Him without His grace or descent of His supreme power. All the stages are the manifestations of one universal consciousness or the Lord through His free will, and differ from one another owing to the various degrees of free revelation or concealment of His nature. The Vaiṣṇavas and others' minds are tinged with vidyā and rāga, and so cannot know the omniscieut supreme Lord. Vidyā contracts their knowledge of the all-pervasive Śiva. Rāga limits their desires to particular desires. So their minds cannot experience the Absolute consciousness which is universal and all-pervasive. 'They are overcome by māyāśakti, and pursue liberation in bondage'. 'They cannot attain to the highest status of Śiva because they pursue the limited (e.g., the gross body, the subtle body, buddhi, etc.) as Ātman'. The Śaivas take the word 'Ātman' in the sense of the universal Self, Absolute, Parama Śiva, and they call an individual self a 'jīvātman' or 'paśu'. Śaṁkara also calls the Absolute 'Brahman' or 'Ātman', and an individual self as 'jīvātman' or 'jīva'. Parama Śiva is universal consciousness with absolute freedom of will. Why is He tainted with the three taints, and why does He become an atomic individual soul bound to empirical life? Kṣemarāja gives the following reply. Parama Śiva contracts His consciousness by His absolutely free will, and assumes the nature of an atomic individual soul. Parama Śiva of the nature of universal all-pervasive consciousness conceals, by His free volition, pervasion of nondifference, and assumes pervasion of difference. Then His power of will and other powers, though unlimited by other objects, appear to be limited. Then only He is tainted with taints, and becomes an individual bound soul.

Does an individual self perform the fivefold acts of creation, maintenance, dissolution, concealment, and granting grace in the empirical condition? Kṣemarāja replies that even in the empirical condition an individual self performs the fivefold acts. The Lord, entering into a body, vital forces, etc., turns outward, and makes 'blue' and other objects appear in definite portions of space and time. Thus it is His act of creation in regard to them. When He withdraws them and makes them appear in other parts of space and time, it is His act of dissolution. When He continues to make 'blue' and other objects appear, it is His act of maintenance. When He makes 'blue' and other objects appear to be different from one another, it is His act of concealment, since they are really nondifferent from one another and universal consciousness manifesting them. When He makes them appear as nondifferent from the Absolute, it is His act of granting grace. Those individual souls which meditate always on these fivefold acts of the Lord in their empirical life, and which know the universe to be an unfoldment of His essential nature of consciousness, attain to embodied release. But those souls, which know the objects of experience as entirely different from one another and the Lord, remain bound to embodied existence.

From the standpoint of the highest end whatever appears through the successive unfolding of the powers of the presiding Deities of the external sense-organs is created. While the self delights in the created object for some time without shutting its eyes, it is maintained by the Deity of maintenance. When it is withdrawn at the time of artistic experience, it is dissolved. When the objects of experience are withdrawn, sometimes they generate various subconscious impressions of doubt in the mind. Then they may reappear in experience, and continue empirical life and generate concealment of the real nature of the Self. But when the different objects of experience are known to be identical with the Self, then a soul enters the state of grace. Until it acquires the knowledge of identity, it remains deluded and bound. An individual soul is deluded by its own powers. To be bound to embodied existence is to be deluded by its own powers because of the ignorance of the agency of the fivefold act of creation, maintenance, dissolution, concealment, and act of grace. Its ignorance is due to the absence of the unfoldment of its own power which can be effected by the descent of the Divine Power or grace of Śiva. Being bound to empirical life is due to delusion consequent on various doubts generated by the conflicting scriptural texts and views of common people. It is said: 'The cycle of birth and death is due to fear, and fear is due to ignorance.'

Abhinavagupta avers that Parama Śiva Himself assumes the state of a bound soul, and becomes an embodied experiencer of external sensible objects through a body, which is a vehicle of its experience, and the sense-organs, which are the organs of its experience. This is his reply to the objection why the individual souls, which are not really different from the Supreme Knower, become embodied and possessed of finite knowledge and agency. Yogirāja explains his statement thus. Śiva, the Supreme Lord, of the nature of infinite consciousness, bliss and freedom, conceals His nature at His will, and assumes the rôle of the embodied knowers, and becomes the experiencers of the objects of knowledge through bodies full of pleasure and pain constructed by Him, who are bound and maintained by Him. But they are not entities which are different from Him. The difference between the embodied individual souls and the Absolute is empirical and serves practical purposes. The Lord, Śiva, freely becomes the individual experiencers and the objects of experience—subjects and objects—as His objects of sport. His freedom is so unsurpassable that He continues to be the experiencer of all empirical knowers, and experiences Himself as infinite consciousness and bliss, although He assumes the nature of empirical knowers and empirical objects by renouncing His infinitude and perfection. But how can one become many, which differ from each other as darkness and light, and acquire different attributes? Abhinavagupta replies that the Lord becomes many bound souls and empirical objects, even as a crystal is tinged with many colours of objects, and becomes many. But though they are many, or though one Lord becomes many bound souls and objects, yet He remains as one Being of the form of consciousness. The Lord, absolutely free, experiencing all bound souls, and being manifested as their experiencer, remains intact in His essential nature, while the bound souls are born and perish. Hence one Ātman becoming manifold subjects and objects, is manifested as one as the experiencer of all bound souls and thus monism is not compromised.

Śaiva monism differs from Patañjali's view that God is a particular self devoid of potencies of actions, their maturation, and dispositions different from the individual selves, which are are subject to them. It differs from the Nyāya-Vaiśeṣika view that God is different from individual souls as father is different from children. Śaiva monism holds that individual souls are different from Śiva, because they are under the influence of His māyāśakti, and because they wrongly identify themselves with their subtle bodies, but that they are in their real nature Śiva, and that they apprehend themselves as many and different from Him and one another owing to their nonapprehension of nondifference[23].

STATES OF AN INDIVIDUAL SOUL.—An individual soul has five states : waking state, dream, deep sleep, ecstasy and superecstasy. Kṣemarāja describes the waking state as the perception of external objects through the sense-organs, common to all empirical knowers. He describes dream as the internal perception of different objects produced by the manas only, which are peculiar to a particular empirical self. He describes deep sleep as nondiscrimination, nonapprehension, and full of māyā. He describes ecstasy as a flash of supreme delight due to the experience of the manifestation of the Ātman even when empirical objects are perceived as different from one another. A yogin who is always in the state of meditation can have ecstasy. Kallaṭa avers that a yogin knows himself as of the nature of Ātman even in the waking state as the result of constant endeavour and exertion to unfold the nature of spanda. Kṣemarāja recognises superecstasy as the result of the perfection of the practice of ecstasy, in which a yogin becomes like Śiva of the nature of translucent, free, pure consciousness and bliss because his body is not yet destroyed. He becomes Śiva Himself when his body perishes. In ecstasy a yogin experiences the sentiment of delight of ecstasy due to the manifestation of śuddha-vidyā even at the stage of the waking state, dream and deep sleep. He does not swerve from the state of being the experiencer of the supreme delight of ecstasy when he perceives the different empirical objects created. Ecstasy is replete with pure delight. Though it is veiled by māyāśakti, it flashes forth at intervals of enjoyment of objects because of meditation on Ātman and introversion of the manas. It is sustained by the introverted mind, although the body and the sense-organs are extraverted. When a yogin's desire for empirical objects is destroyed, he acquires the state of ecstasy and valid knowledge of Ātman, and ceases to be an empirical knower identified with his subtle body.

Utpaladeva defines waking state as the perception of external objects common to all individual souls through the sense-organs. He defines dream as the knowledge of distinct cognitions of objects through manas alone like the percepts of external objects through the sense-organs due to illusion. Dream-cognitions are false, acquired through manas only, and resemble the percepts of external objects. He defines deep sleep as the knowledge of void resembling dissolution when an individual soul knows itself to be 'I' and an agent in the absence of buddhi and the like which become inoperative, and when it has indistinct, formless subconscious impressions only, and when it has no knowledge of objects. In deep sleep an individual soul is a knower of the subtle body when it identifies itself with the vital forces which sustain the internal function of the sense-organs, and is tainted with māyīyamala whether it has objects of knowledge or whether it has none. Waking state, dream, and deep sleep are reprehensible because of the predominance of the vital forces in the agency of an individual soul and because of its relation to pleasure and pain subject to increase and decrease. In waking state and dream inhalation (prāṇa) and exhalation (apāna) are prominent. In deep sleep they become subordinate to samāna. In ecstasy udāna ascends through suṣumnā—the middle nāḍī—with Īḍā on the left and with Piṅgalā on the right, which is full of fire. Vyāna becomes dominant in Vijñānakevala and Mantreśvara, and makes them pervade the universe with their consciousness. Śaiva yaga is referred to here.

Bhaṭṭa Bhāskara defines waking state as the internal perception of mental modes and the external perception of sounds, temperatures, colours, tastes, and odours, in which Ātman's power of knowledge is manifested, and assumes the forms of an empirical knower, empirical knowledge and empirical objects, and which is due to a bound soul's loss of its essential nature. It perceives mental modes and external objects as different from one another because of its loss of the knowledge of its nature as Ātman. He defines dream-cognitions as recollections of different objects in the absence of external objects, which conceal the real nature of a bound soul. He defines deep sllep as nonemergence of the Lord's powers of knowledge and known objects, nonapprehension of Ātman of the nature of pure consciousness, in which the objects and their recollections exist in the empirical self that rests in the Lord, and which conceals its real nature. He defines ecstasy as the experience of Ātman as the real nature of the empirical self, as the consciousness of Him as the only experiencer, in which all false knowledge is destroyed, and which flashes in all the states. Ecstasy is manifested by trance. Varadarāja defines ecstasy as apprehesion of nondifference, which destroys nonapprehension of nondifference, full of supreme delight, which is experienced in all states. A yogin immersed in trance attains to superecstasy in which Ātman alone shines constantly. Utpaladeva states the first three states thus. Waking state consists in the knowledge of objects common to all knowers and known as external to them through all sense-organs. Dreams are distinct cognitions produced by manas alone but wrongly known to be objects perceived through the external sense-organs. Deep sleep is like dissolution in which there are indistinct, formless, subconscious impressions in the self in the status of 'I'-consciousness due to the absence or inactivity of buddhi, in which there is 'I'-consciouness in the nature of the subtle body, and in which there is an internal mode which urges the vital forces. Deep sleep is tainted with the impurity of māyā and yet untainted with it, with objects of knowledge and yet without them.[24]

DESCENT OF DIVINE POWER.—Abhinavagupta says: "The luminous Lord is reflected in buddhi purified by the descent of Śiva's divine power (śaktipāta), even as a face is reflected in a transparent mirror". Yogirāja explains descent of Śiva's divine power of granting grace as expansion of the rays of His light of pure consciousness, which destroy the threefold taints of a bound soul. Some individual souls' buddhis are covered with āṇava-mala, kārma-mala and māyīya-mala due to Śiva's power of veiling. Hence, though their Ātman is luminous light of pure consciousness, it is almost unmanifested. They are called bound souls. Others are on the path to liberation owing to the descent of the divine power to them. Others are liberated because of the greater descent of the divine power, or to the grace of the Lord. God's grace is the only real cause of purification of the enlightend buddhi of a bound soul. Thus there are different degrees of the descent of the divine power to bound souls, great, mediocre, and slight. When a bound soul's heart becomes pure owing to the descent of Lord's power of granting grace, it acquires the knowledge 'I alone am the Supreme Lord'. So its coverings which make for its bondage are automatically dissolved owing to the emergence of its knowledge of Ātman, and consequently, its potencies of actions—merits and demerits—due to the power of niyati consequent on māyā cannot generate birth and death. A bound soul's covering of the body and the like is due to its nonapprehension of nondifference from Śiva. It is destroyed by its knowledge of its nature as Śiva. Its flaw of nescience is due to its own imagination of difference. When the Lord's qualities of omniscience and the like are manifested to a bound soul, and when its real nature as Ātman is somehow manifested to it, it becomes like a liberated soul even in an embodies state. Kṣemarāja avers that bound souls' great pervasion to universal consciousness manifested in the universe is not possible without the supreme descent of the divine power.[25]

TAINTS.—Utpaladeva says : "There are three kinds of taints (mala). Āṇava-mala consists in the loss of freedom of universal consciousness and in the loss of consciousness of freedom. Māyīya-mala consists in the apprehension of the different objects of knowledge, which gives rise to the experience of pleasure, pain and rebirth. Kārma-mala consists in not knowing Śiva as the only real agent or doer." These three kinds of taints are involved in one another. Āṇava mala contracts one universal and absolutely free consciousness to an atomic, dependent, ignorant individual soul. It involves māyīya-mala since it makes the nondifferent universal consciousness appear as different. Merits and demerits are the qualities of the subtle body, which an individual soul wrongly thinks to be its qualities. Thus kārma-mala also involves māyīya-mala since it involves false knowledge. Parama Śiva's volition, power of māyā, is the cause of the formation of the three kinds of taints.

Kṣemarāja describes how an individaul soul is covered by three kinds of taints. Śiva's power of will, which is absolutely free and unrestricted, becomes contracted and assumes the form of āṇava-mala, which consists in the sense of being imperfect. His power of knowledge is gradually contracted in the world of difference, and His omniscience becomes fragmentary knowledge of a limited number of objects. It becomes extremely contracted when it assumes the internal organs and the external organs of knowledge, and becomes māyīya-mala, which consists in apprehending all objects infected with difference. His power of action is gradually contracted in the world of difference, and His omnipotence becomes limited power of doing a limited number of acts. His power of action is extremely contracted when it assumes the external organs of action and becomes kārma-mala, which consists in doing right and wrong actions.

Yogirāja gives the following account of the taints. Āṇavamala is an internal impurity of the nature of nonapprehension which conceals the real nature of an individual soul even as a stain veils the nature of gold. Māyā, kalā, vidyā, kāla, niyati, and rāga are subtle coverings, which conceal the nature of an individual soul. Māyīya-mala is full of difference, or of knowledge of difference, which manifests its little knowledge and little agency. It is an internal impurity while skin, blood and the like are external impurities. Kārma-mala makes an individual soul an impure, empirical knower, who performs righteous and unrighteous actions, and acquires merits and demerits. Āṇava-mala, māyīya-mala and kārma-mala are the subtle taints of an individual soul while skin, blood, etc., are its gross taints. Owing to these taints an individual soul gets contracted, like ether enclosed in a jar, although it is all-pervasive. Thus an individual soul is enclosed in three sheaths—the bodily sheath, the vital sheath, and the mental sheath, and becomes atomic, although it is all-pervasive in its real nature.

Varadarāja defines āṇava-mala as knowing the mind-body-complex or not-self as the Self wrongly. An impurity is imagined in the self itself by itself at its will, and constitutes bondage. It is of the nature of nescience. Bondage is created by an individual soul's will. Varadarāja describes māyā as the cause of the appearance of difference. Kalā and other principles down to earth are of the nature of māyā. He defines māyīya-mala as full of the appearance of different objects of knowledge, and as cause of the limited knowledge of different objects. He defines kārma-mala as merits and demerits or potencies of actions which produce birth and death and joys and sorrows. These taints produce bondage.[26]

AN INDIVIDUAL SOUL BECOMES THE ABSOLUTE.—Kṣemarāja describes how an individual soul or consciousness becomes the Absolute, universal consciousness, by introversion and rising to the status of the consciousness of Ātman or Parama Śiva after acquiring the perfect knowledge of its authorship of the fivefold act of creation, maintenance, dissolution, concealment, and act of grace. When it knows its authorship of the fivefold act, the causes of its ignorance are removed, and its delusion generated by its own powers is destroyed. Then it acquires free agency, gives up the contracting powers of extraversion, becomes introverted, rises to the status of the Supreme Knower, and becomes universal consciousness owing to the destruction of the limiting kalā. Thus it enters into the highest stage of universal consciousness which is its real nature. It is objected that the power of universal consciousness, by its very nature, cancels all difference, and should do so even at the stage of māyā, even as the sun manifests all objects even when it is covered by clouds. To this objection Kṣemrāja replies that the power of universal consciousness, which is like fire, and which by its real nature, consumes the universe of different objects, partly consumes the fuel of the objects of knowledge, although it is covered by māyā. When it descends to the sphere of māyā, it does not burn them completely but only partially. It leaves behind their subtle impressions and rouses them to consciousness. Its power of devouring or assimilating the objects of knowledge to itself is proved by one's experience. When an individual soul practises creation by unfolding the powers of the presiding Deities of the sense-organs, and when it practises dissolution by withdrawing the powers of these Deities, it acquires the power of universal consciousness, and assimilates the universe to itsself. When it acquires the power of universal consciousness, its coverings of the body and the vital forces are eclipsed, its essential nature is manifested, it assimilates the principles from Sadāśiva to earth to itself, and makes them appear as identical with its real nature. It is said : 'Just as a kindled fire consumes fuel, even so an individual soul consumes the fetters of the objects of knowledge.' An individual attains to perfection when it experiences its body and other entities constituting the thirty six principles as forms of Parama Śiva.

Kṣemarāja gives the following account of the means of attaining identity-consciousness called śāmbhavopāya. Mantras are composed of letters ; all letters are of the nature of universal consciosness of Śiva. Logos, supreme speech (parā vāk), is nondifferent from the light of universal consciousness, of the form of the eternally sounding great mantra, full of perfect 'I'-consciousness containing all the powers represesented by the letters. It is expressed through the stages of paśyantī, madhyamā, and vaikharī. Parā vāk is more subtle than paśyntī vāk. Paśyantī vāk is more subtle than madhyamā vāk. Madhyamā vāk is more subtle than vaikharī vāk which is an articulate sound. It assumes the rôle of a limited subject. It does not reveal its form as Logos to an empirical knower, but reveals particular objects as different from one another. It reveals also the pure stage of nondifference but as veiled by difference. An ignorant person wrongly regards himself as limited to his body, vital forces, etc., being deluded by the various powers of the letters presided over by their Deities. In the stage of a bound soul the aforesaid Deities manifest creation and maintenance in regard to difference, and withdrawal or dissolution in regard to nondifference, and generate only fitness for limited difference. But, in the stage of the Lord, they manifest creation and maintenance in regard to nondifference, gradually reduce difference, and finally manifest the stage of nondifference. Utpaladeva says : "He who knows that all this glory is mine, and that all this universe is 'I' possesses lordship even when differences have their play." An individual soul is bound to empirical life because of its being deluded by its own powers. It can realise its identity with the Absolute by immersion in supreme consciousness and bliss with the aid of Logos embodied in all mantras and enshrined in the divine power of perfect 'I'-consciousness.

Kṣemarāja describes the Śākta means of attaining identity-consciousness (śaktopāya) as follows. The supreme power of consciousness called Vāmeśvarī, because she ejects the universe out of herself, and because she displays the empirical world of different objects for the experience of individual souls, manifests herself as a bound soul, as an empirical knower endowed with limited knowerhood, limited agency, etc, because of the coverings of katā, vidyā, rāga, kāla and niyati, in the form of khecarī, as internal organs in the form of gocarī, as external sense-organs in the form of dikcarī, and as external existents in the form of bhūcarī. She conceals the real nature of self as ether of pure consciousness through the group of khecarī powers, which consist in the powers of kalā, vidyā, etc. She shines through the group of gocarī powers, which preside over the internal organs whose main functions are ascertainment of difference, false identification of Self with different things, and apprehension of things as different, by concealing her real nature, which consists in ascertainment of nondifference. She shines through the group of dikcarī powers presiding over external sense-organs whose main function is the perception of difference, by concealing her real nature which consists in the ascertainment of nondifference. She shines through the group of bhūcarī powers in the form of external objects of knowledge, which appear to be different from one another, by concealing her real nature as the Supreme Self of all and deluding bound souls. But, in the stage of the Lord, the Supreme Power (śakti) of pure consciousness manifests herself as the ether of pure consciousness whose nature is omnipotence and other powers of lordship, as gocarī whose nature is ascertainment of nondifference, as dikcarī whose nature is perception of nondifference, and as bhūcari whose nature is manifestation of objects as nondifferent from one another, as parts of one's Self—all these revealing the inner nature of the Lord. 'Śakti' (power) is feminine in Sanskrit.

Kṣemarāja describes the means of attaining identity-consciousness called āṇavopāya as follows. When the supreme power of pure consciousness unfolds the power of udāna which ascends through Suṣumnā through the centres of mystic consciousness (cakra) and induces ecstasy, when she unfolds the power of vyāna which makes a soul pervade the universe with its consciousness, and when she unfolds superecstasy which is a mass of pure consciousness and delight, a bound soul attains the state of the Lord and embodied release even when it is endowed with a body. When it ceases to identify itself with the void, the subtle body, vital forces, and the gross body, and when it recognises its identity with one universal consciousness, it attains identity-consciousness and embodied release. Śaiva monism believes in embodied release. (Cp. Śaṁkara).

Kṣemarāja describes how the internal consciousness of perfect 'I'-consciousness, which is supreme trance, and which shines in all states, can be attained by controlling the vital forces. The vital forces of inhalation (prāṇa) and exhalation (apāna) which run through Iḍā and Piṅgalā do not flow in a straight path. Only when they are equilibrated by breath-control, and when Kuṇḍalinī rises upward through Suṣumṅā, vital force flows in a straight path. Breath-control is not necessary in an advanced stage of spiritual discipline. Concentration on the internal supreme consciousness results in trance which persists even in the waking state, dream, and deep sleep. It is not broken by the waking experience. Bhaṭṭa Bhāskara opines that the intuition of Self emerges as a result of, concentration on the internal supreme consciousness, of the cessation of the mental modes, and of the complete control of the vital forces. Then a bound soul becomes pure Ātman or or Śiva. Varadarāja observes that concentration on the internal supreme consciousness or the centre (madhya) results in the perfect intuition of it, and in the transcendence of the empirical world. In this state an advanced yogin is immersed in pure 'I'-consciousnes transcending the universe. The internal supreme consciousness is called the centre, because it is the foundation of the universe, because it dwells within all created beings as their essence, and because it is full of experience. Vasugupta calls the process control of the centre. In this state a yogin is not deflected by determinations and differences due to the power of māyā, and his Śivahood is manifested. Vaśugupta's use of the word' madhya-saṁyama' has covert reference to arousal of Kuṇḍalinī, Serpent Power, dormant Divine Power, at the basic centre and making Her ascend through the middle path, Suṣumnā, and pierce the higher centres.[27] Sir John Woodroffe translates Kuṇḍalinī as Serpent Power. But really it is Divine Power.

WORLD AND ŚIVA-ŚAKTI.—The world is the unfoldment of the Lord's power of action. Its creation is the expansion of divine power. Its maintenance is the continuance of it as external. Its dissolution is its resting in the Supreme Knower. These three acts are the expression of the Lord's power. 'His powers are the entire universe ; the Lord is endowed with these powers'. All known entities are of the nature of consciousness, which unfolds and contracts ; otherwise they would never be known. This is the Śaiva doctrine of Idealism. It is Absolute Voluntarism as distinguished from Śaṁkara's Absolute Idealism. The Lord persists in the acts of creation, maintenance and dissolution of the world. There is a difference between an agent and an effect. An effect is perishable, but an agent is imperishable. When an effort to produce an effect is suppressed, the effect is destroyed. But the agent's agency is not destroyed. The divine agent is omniscient and omnipotent, and never divested of His power of 'I'-consciousness. When His power of 'I'-concsousness is enfolded, the created world ceases to be manifested. An advanced yogin who has realised his identity with the Lord, has the experience that the world is created, maintained and dissolved by his powers. Parama Śiva, Who is absolutely free, is the cause of the creation, maintenance, and dissolution of the world. The supreme divine power full of perfect 'I'-consciousness, nondifferent from Him, is the cause of the universe. When this divine power is unfolded, the universe is created. When it sustains the universe, the latter is maintained. When it is enfolded, the universe is dissolved. Māyā, prakṛti, atoms and the like, are different from the manifestation of universal consciousness,and, consequently, nonexistent. Hence they are not the causes of the universe. If they are of the nature of manifestation, they are universal consciousness of the nature of manifestation. For the same reason, space, time and form which are created by universal consciousness cannot manifest its real nature because it is all-preveding, eternal and self-complete. It may be objected that the universe is nonexistent if it is different from universal consciousness, that it is not the effect of universal consciousness if it is nondifferent from the latter, and that causal relation is not possible between two nondifferent entities. To this objection Kṣemarāja replies that the supreme divine power of universal consciousness, pure and absolutely free, is unfolded in the form of the universe, and that, in this sense, the causal relation between them is ontologically true. Hence the power of universal consciousness is the cause of the manifestation of the universe consisting of knowers, means of valid knowledge, and objects of knowledge. The means of valid knowledge are not capable of proving the power of universal consciousness, that is absolutely free, unlimited and self-manifest; they have the function of manifesting new objects. The Absolute is self-existent and salf-manifest.

The power of absolute consciousness does not require any material to create the universe. It unfolds the universe in itself as the basis of its free will. Although the universe is nondifferent from the power of absolute consciousness in its real nature, yet the fromer is unfolded by the latter as if the former were nondifferent from the latter, even as the reflection of a town in a mirror is manifested as different from it, although the fromer is really nondifferent from the latter. Unfoldment consists in manifesting what is unmanifest but existent. The existence of the universe means its identity with the power of absolute consciousness that is self-manifest. The universe is manifold owing to the empirical difference between knowers and known objects. Parama Śiva assumes the forms of empirical knowers and objects of knowledge by contracting His universal consciousness, and becomes all principles, pure, mixed and impure, from Śivatattva down to earth and other gross elements. Bound souls are universal consciousness limited by kalā, vidyā, rāga, kāla and niyati produced by the Lord's māyāśakti. Empirical objects are modifications of prakṛti, a power of the Lord. They are not insentient but dormant consciouness. Neither individual souls nor objects are unconsous ; they are contractions of universal consciousness, and limited by time and space. When individual souls realise their identity with one universal consciousness, they pervade the universe with their consciousness and transcend it,and experience that it is created, maintained and dissolved by them. (Cp. Śākta Monism.) Parama Śiva is omniscient, omnipotent, and absolutely free. The body, vital forces, buddhi, and the void are not Ātmaṇ. Universal consciousness is the ontological nature of the universe consisting of existents and nonexistents. A known entity, being nondifferent from consciousness, is full of consciousness. So consciousness alone is the ontological reality of the world. The supreme, subtle, all-pervading, taintless, divine power of Parama Śiva, of the nature of supreme bliss and immortality, the mother of all powers, is the creator, maintainer and destroyer of the universe. The internal vibration of the unfolding power of 'I'-consciousness, identified with all powers, that is capable of destroying the universe of differences and determinations, is appropriately called Bhairava. He is the internal vibration of the nature of perfect 'I'-consciousness. It permeates the universe of different entities.[28]

The manifold world of different entities is reflected in the Absolute, transparent, nondifferent, universal consciousness, even as a town of diverse objects is reflected in a mirror. The universal consciousness of the supreme Lord is dovoid of differences ; yet the world of different entities is reflected in it. Entities appear to be different from one another and from the Lord's consciousness, even as different parts of a town reflected in a mirror appear to be different from one another and from the mirror. The difference of entities from universal consciousness and from one another is valid from the empirical standpoint. Their nondifference from one another and from universal consciousness is valid from the ontological standpoint. The empirical knowers know their difference at the stage of common experience. But when they reach the stage of ecstasy, they know their nondifference. The former identify their selves with their gross bodies, vital forces, subtle bodies, or void, while the latter identify their selves with Ātman. Ātman is capable of receiving reflections of different entities, even as a mirror is capable of recciving reflections of different objects. Ātman is not made different by different reflections, even as the mirror is not made different by different reflections. Although universal consciousness is one, transparent, and nontemporal, yet it is manifested because of the excess of creative delight, as the manifold, temporal world of different subjects and objects despite its being nondifferent from the latter, even as a mirror is not affected by the difference of the objects due to space and time, which are reflected in it. Universal consciousness in different entities transcends them, although it is manifested in their forms, even as a mirror transcends the reflections of different objects in it. Universal consciousness transcends different entities as their experiencer, as capable of receiving their reflections, and is manifeted to itself in its essential nature. Although it appears to be manifold,yet it is one as consciousness, like a variegated cognition. But there is a difference between a mirror and universal consciousness. Different objects are reflected in a mirror, but are not created by it. But different entities reflected in universal consciousness are created by the latter out of the stuff of its consciousness at its will in itself as the foundation, and known to be nondifferent from itself with artistic experience of delight. A mirror is insentient. But universal consciousness is of the nature of manifestation. An empirical knower's knowledge of difference is illusory, but the Lord's knowledge of nondifference is valid. An empirical knower has nonapprehension of nondifference. Nonapprehension is the absence of apprehension of the perfect nondual Ātman. The perfect universal consciousness is not manifested to an empirical knower, but the imperfect dual nature of subjects is manifested to him Hence the doctrine of reflection is irreproachable.

Māyā, prakṛti and earth are objects of knowledge. They are manifested as mere being as the final result of meditation on nonduality. The objects do not exist without being known ; so they are of the nature of consciousness. The entities cannot be known without knowledge ; so knowledge assumes the forms of objects. Thus Śaiva monism upholds the doctrine of idealism and regards the universe as of the nature of knowledge. Bhaṭṭa Kallaṭa says, "When differences are transcended, they are manifested as mere being" or universal consciousness. It is the supreme Brahman, of the nature of nondifference, omnipresent, eternal, and true, that abides in divine power of the nature of consciousness. Hence differences are ultimately unreal. When the knowledge 'I am all' is repeatedly practised, the appearance of all differences is dissolved, delusion of māyā in the form of false conceit of the mind-body-complex as self is destroyed, contraction of an atomic soul is removed, and it merges in Brahman of the nature of perfect consciousness and bliss. It ceases to identify itself with the gross body, vital forces, the subtle body, or void, and becomes Brahman. Thus Bhaṭṭa Kallaṭa, Abhinavagupta and Yogirāja regard differences as reflections in the Absolute and as ultimately unreal. Somānanda holds that all are of the nature of Śiva. Utpaladeva avers that all are Śiva since they are of the nature of consciourness. In a sense, Śiva is not different entities, but they are of the nature of Him. In another sense, Śiva assumes the forms of different subjects and objects with his power of māyā.[29]

Vasugupta calls Parama Śiva or Ātman, a dancer, an individual soul a stage, and its sense-organs spectators. He displays the world-drama in Himself as the foundation by His sportive internal vibration, and manifests the mental stages of waking, dream, deep sleep, and ecstasy by veiling His real nature as universal consciousness in an individual self or knower. He is the universal consciousness contracted by the five coverings, wrongly identifies himself with his vital forces, subtle body, or void, has the states of waking, etc, and called the stage because it delights in the world-play and fun. Śiva, the Supreme Yogin, manifests the world-drama from Sadāśivatattva to earth and other elements. The sense-organs are spectators. Śiva manifests the world-play to an individual soul's sense-organs, which execute their functions with the powers of the Lord, and which cannot veil His nature as omniscience and absolute freedom. They are enchanted with the world-drama manifested to them. Śiva veils Himself in an individual soul, called the inner self, and unfolds His world-drama outside.[30]

ENJOYER, ENJOYMENT AND ENJOYED.—Enjoyment (bhoga) means enjoyment of pleasure. It includes suffering pain. Pleasure and pain are objects of enjoyment and suffering, respectably (bhogya). Enjoyment implies an enjoyer (bhoktṛ) or experient. Kallaṭa argues that an object of pleasant or painful experience is produced and destroyed, but that an experient being of the nature of pure consciousness is neither produced nor destroyed, and is therefore eternal. There is difference in the objects of enjoyment or suffering, which originate and perish. But the enjoyer, being of the nature of pure consciousness (cit), has neither origin nor end. The experiencer is omnipresent, and persists in waking state, dream, and deep sleep, and is always awake. Ecstasy and superecstasy are knowable through Āgama. There is no state in which Śiva, Absolute Experient, does not exist in thoughts, words and objects. He always exists as objects of pleasant and painful experiences in all states. So the Absolute Experient (bhoktṛ) alone exists in the forms of objects of experience. There are no other self-existent objects of enjoyment and suffering. Śiva is the experient, pleasant and painful experiences, and objects of enjoyment and suffering. Somānanda avers that Śiva is both nondifferent and different, nondifferent as the experient, and different as objects of enjoyment and suffering. Being an experient is the constant state of Śiva in all objects of pleasant and painful experiences.[31]

KNOWER, KNOWLEDGE AND KNOWN.—Kallaṭa argues that the omnipresent Lord endowed with supreme power shines in knowledge and knowable objects in the waking state and dream, and that He shines as of the nature of pure consciousness in deep sleep and ecstasy. The Supreme Knower, Śiva, shines in individual souls or limited knowers of empirical objects through His power of māyā in waking state and dream. But Śiva in harmony with His power shines in deep sleep and ecstasy as pure consciousness. Empirical objects of knowledge are made of sattva, rajas and tamas, and abide in Śiva's power of māyā ; yet they cannot exist without being known by the Supreme Knower, Who is omniscient. He ejects them out of Himself for the knowledge of limited knowers. The distinction between empirical knowers and objects of knowledge is made by Him through His power of māyā, and is transcended by Him. They cannot veil His self-luminious nature[32]. Utpaladeva argues that Śiva is the one inner Ātman of all individual souls, is immanent in the universe, assumes its form, and is endowed with undivided 'I'-consoiousness in the form 'I am this'. He creates the universe by His volition, which is of the nature of 'this' or object of knowledge. He creates buddhi which knows objects. He knows both subjects and objects through His 'I'-consciousness as of the nature of 'this'. He creates them by His power of action and His power of delight, so that the former may know the latter, and experience joys and sorrows. Individual souls experience joys and sorrows because of sattva, rajas and tamas due to his power of māyā. They are overcome by māyā, and do not know their essential nature as Śiva. The guṇas are modified into sense-organs, internal organs and objects of knowledge. Their differences are due to his power of māyā, He has powers of being, delight and action, when He assumes these forms through His power of māyā. Individual souls do not possess these powers, but they are endowed with sattva, rajas and tamas produced by His power of māyā, and experience pleasure, pain and delusion. The objects of knowledge are 'this'-consciousness of Śiva, mixed modes of the guṇas, different from one another, and produce different feelings in different souls. They appear different from one another owing to the souls' acts of discrimination due to their vital forces. They appear to be common objects of their perceptions because of their distinct manifestations through the cognitions produced by them in the souls. When the souls destroy their distinct cognitions by concentration and meditation on Śiva—One universal consciousness, they gradually attain to the status of the Lord. When a limited knower knows himself to be the Supreme Ātman of the universe, while knowing different objects, as 'I am this' or 'this is my creation', he is released. His consciousness expands and permeates the universe, identifies itself with universal consciousness immanent in it, and transcends the limits of his knowledge created by Śiva's power of māyā. A bound knower knows the objects of knowledge as different from one another and from himself. But a released ciousness, he is called the Lord. Śiva knows the universe as His body, but a bound knower knows it as diverse because of his being tainted with attachment, aversion, nescience, egoism, merits, demerits, their maturation, and dispositions of actions. His nescience of his essential nature as universal consciousness is the cause of his knowledge of difference. When he is purified of taints due to his nescience. he becomes an unlimited knower, and knows himself to be so. The Lord is the Supreme Knower of all valid knowledge because of His absolute freedom. He alone is the independent Knower, and does not depend upon any means of valid knowledge. The Supreme Knower creates external objects, internal cognitions in limited knowers and their temporal order. He creates objects, means and different kinds of valid knowledge. He creates the difference between knowers and known objects by His volition, knows them to be different from each other, and yet knows them to be nondifferent from Him as universal consciousness.

Diverse objects of the universe are proved by means of valid knowledge, founded in Him, the Supreme Knower. They have dependent existence due to His volition with the aid of His power of māyā in the inferior empirical order ; they are created or manifested by Him and dissolved or made unmanifest by Him. He is their real essence. They are universal consciousness in their real nature. He is the foundation of the world of diverse objects. Thus Śiva, the Supreme Knower, is the foundation of knower, knowledge and known object[33].

Abhinavagupta adduces the following arguments elucidated by Jayaratha to prove that Śiva, of the nature of manifestation, is the ontological reality of a knowable object. What is of the nature of nonmanifestation cannot be manifested, nor can it be real. Manifestness of blueness of a blue object is not its ontological nature. Were it so, it would always be manifested to all, and it would not be manifested to some at some time, and all would be omniscient. Śiva of the nature of manifestation, the Supreme Knower, is the ontological nature of an object of knowledge. Any other limited knower is not its ontological nature, since it does not know the object as nondifferent from itself. No object can exist, which cannot be manifested. A blue object being manifested in relation to manifestation is itself of the nature of manifestation, and as such is manifested. (Cp. Berkeley). What is not of the nature of manifestation is not manifested. Even the absence of an object (eg., a jar) on the ground is of the nature of Śiva because of its being perceived as different from the ground. So it is said, "Nonapprehension also being cognised is of the nature of Śiva of the nature of knowledge." What is manifestation is always manifested. This fact being undeniable, it does not require any proof. Śiva is the ontological reality and manifester of the proofs of entities. A proof depends on Śiva of the nature of 'I'-consciousness in order to prove its manifestness, or that of another entity. The Lord of the nature of manifestation of other entities is the foundation of all proofs. The Mādhyamikas deny a knower, knowledge, and a knowable object. The Yogācāras deny a knower and a knowable object. The Vaibhāṣikas deny a knower. But a proof in order to prove the non-existence of an entity presupposes the existence of a prover. Provability of an object depends on the existence of the self-existent and self-proved Lord, Who makes one prove it. So the Buddhists' proofs are invalid, since they presuppose the existence of the Supreme Knower of the nature of manifestation. He is the foundation of a knower, knowledge and a knowable object. A proof is so called, since it proves a knowable object as characterised by 'thisness', and since it depends upon different kinds of manifestation. They rest upon the Supreme Knower of the nature of consciousness. He is not provable by any proof. If He were so, the act of proving Him would dedent upon another Knower and so on to infinity. So He is self-existent and self-proved. He is independent and free, controls all entities, is unlimited by space, time and form, ubiquitous, eternal, and of the form of the universe. He manifests the variety of empirical knowers and empirical objects.[34]

AGENT AND OBJECT OF ACTION.—An action implies an agent or doer and an object of action or effect. Kallaṭa argues that an effect is destroyed, but that an agent is not destroyed, since ultimately Śiva is the only agent. An agent is of the nature of pure consciousness, and is neither produced nor destroyed. An effort which produces an effect is destroyed, but an agent who makes an effort is not destroyed. Power to produce an effect, of the nature of activity of external organs of action, is destroyed. When the activity of the motor organs ceases, the power to act ceases. But the conscious agent or Self does not cease. Śiva, the Supreme Agent, is imperishable, although an effect is perishable. He Who is inward-looking, omniscient, omnipotent, cannot be destroyed, and experiences the universe as His manifestation. Somānanda avers that from the standpoint of the highest knowledge Śiva is an agent or doer, an object of action, an instrument of action, activity and fruit of activity. Utpaladeva adduces the following arguments to show that Śiva is the Supreme Agent. His act of manifesting diverse objects is His creative act, which is an act of volition. Unconscious entities —prakṛti, atoms, etc —cannot create nonexistent entities. A conscious agent is a cause, and an object of action is an effect. A nonexistent entity cannot come into existence. An existent entity also has no use of coming into existence, for it is already existent. Śiva alone can create a nonexistent entity by His volition, and make it knowable by limited knowers through external sense-organs and internal organs. He alone is capable of acting within and without and creating or manifesting external objects and internal cognitions in a temporal order. External entities and internal cognitions can equally abide in Him for their manifestation, existence, extermality, and actions, Who creates, maintains and knows them. Seeds are unconscious and so cannot create sprouts. The Lord is conscious, and can create them by His volition. His power of niyati connects specific causes with specific effects. Some yogins also can create jars and sprouts by a mere fiat of will. Insentient entities which are not related to each other cannot be related as cause and effect. So prakṛti and atoms cannot produce diverse objects of the world as the Sāṁkhya and the Vaiśeṣika, respectively, suppose. So the relation of the causal act and the agent of action can exist in Śiva alone—the Supreme Knower. If cause and effect are of the nature of each other, they are identical ; if they are different in nature, they are not of the nature of each other. The Lord's act is temporal. He is an agent, and so can be a cause, for He can create an effect by His free volition. He can create a difference of cause and effect within Him, which is empirical only. Difference and nondifference cannot exist in an insentient entity, as it is nondifferent in nature. Each insentient entity has its own nature ; so different insentient entities have different natures, and so cannot be related to each other as cause and effect. But they can exist in one Lord of the nature of universal consciousness, since He is capable of receiving reflections of many insentient entities in the mirror of His consciousness. An insentient entity has no will to become, and so cannot become an agent owing to the absence of freedom. The one Absolute Knower causes the diversity of manifestation of different objects by His creative will, and assumes their forms. So the free Lord's volition to manifest Himself as the diverse objects of the world is their cause. All causation is will-causation. (Cp. James Ward & Martineau).

The Lord's eternal act of 'I'-consciousoess is His nature and devoid of origin, end, and sequence. But His act of manifestation of different entities out of His power of māyā has sequence due to His power of time. Time produces sequence. Sequence depends upon difference. Difference depends upon the manifestation and nonmanifestation of entities. He manifests spatial order by creating diversity of co-existent objects external to one another. He manifests temporal order by creating diversity of successive events which cannot coexist with each other. A limited knower alone knows different events in succession. But the Absolute Knower does not know them in succession. A limited knower alone knows the spatial order of external entities. But the Absolute Knower knows all entities together, as nothing is unknown to Him. He creates the difference between subjects and objects by His will, and knows them as different from one another and yet as nondifferent from Him in their essence. Different entities are related to one another, and are known to be so by the one Absolute Knower in Whom they abide. Agent, action, effect, temporal order, spatial order, etc., can be created, related to each other, and known to be so by the Absolute Knower alone. They are real to the limited knowers, because they serve their practical purposes. External entities have no innate power of producing their effects; causes can produce their effects because of the Lord's volition. Even they do not independently produce their effects, and they do not by themselves cease to exist. They exist so long as they are manifested by Him. Thus the Lord is the Supreme Agent of all effects or objects of action[35].

SIGNIFIER AND SIGNIFIED.—Kallaṭa argues that empirical knowers distinguish between words and objects signified by them. Their cognitions of objects are interpenetrated with words. But when they cease to identify their souls with their gross bodies, subtle bodies and void, they transcend the distinction of words and objects, and become universal consciousness. Śiva assumes the forms of cognitions, words and objects with His power of māyā, and deludes bound souls. He destroys their delusion with His power of granting grace, and enables them to transcend the distinction of cognitions, words and objects due to His power of māyā, and makes them realise their identity with Him. Śiva's power of action existing in bound souls is the cause of their bondage, and is not known by them. They are deluded by His power of māyā, and identify themselves with their mind-body-complexes. Their essential nature is veiled by the divine powers presiding over letters constituting words, and by those presiding over the objects of cognition. They experience joys and sorrows, because they identify their souls with manas, buddhi, and ahaṁkāra owing to the absence of freedom. But when they know Śiva's power of action existing in them, it generates superior and inferior supernatural powers. When they cease to identify their souls with their subtle bodies, they create objects of knowledge and objects of enjoyment and suffering, and become the transempirical Knower and Experient. When they attain to this stage, they become the Lord of the circle of powers (cakreśvara)[36].

MĀTṚKĀ—Vasugupta says, 'The powers presiding over the letters (अ to क्ष) are the basis of empirical cognitions'. Bhartṛhari says, 'There are no cognitions which are unattended with words ; knowledge is always of the nature of words. It is not manifested without a word.' Varadarāja observes, that empirical cognitions of external objects and internal cognitions of empirical egos are attended with the knowledge of words and differences, and that they do not rest in the knowledge of one's Ātman. The presiding Deities of the letters delude bound souls by veiling their real nature as pure consciousness and bliss and by producing false conceit of self in their bodies and the like, and overcome them with empirical cognitions of objects attended with their names. These souls do not know that they are identical with divine power in their essence, and that objects and names are their own creations in that they are creations of divine power. When their pure knowledge is eclipsed, the powers of mātṛkā delude them.[37]

MANTRA—A mantra is so called for the real nature of one's self is known through reflection on it as nondifferent from the Supreme Self. Reflection on the Deity represented by a mantra results in the knowledge of identity of a soul with the Deity. The mind of a worshipper reflecting on the Deity embodied in a mantra becomes identical with Him. So Vasugupta calls a yogin's mind a mantra. It experiences Ātman, and becomes the Supreme Knower unlimited by time, space, and endowed with omniscience and the like. A mantra is so called for it releases a soul from bondage through reflection on it. Reflection is meditation on the manifestation of Ātman of the nature of perfect 'I'-consciousness. It unites a soul with divine power. A mantra is a mystic syllable (e. g., 'Om'), a word, or a group of words charged with mystic, divine, spiritual power. The secret of a mantra lies in its power of manifesting pure knowledge because of a soul's immersion in pure, undifferentiated, supramental, transcendental consciousness. A mantra consists of sounds, and embodies pure knowledge. It is composed of letters, and all letters are of the nature of Śiva. Vowels are like seeds, and consonants are like the womb ; they are of the nature of Śiva and Śakti. So mantras are of the nature of the Lord and His divine power, though empirical sounds are full of empirical knowledge of differences. They are, in their real nature, one universal consciousness and power. Āgama says, 'Mantras ought not to be discussed or disputed by persons of small intelligence. Wise persons ought to put faith in them on the authority of Āgama'. 'All gods are of nature of mantras ; all mantras are of the nature of Śiva. Know a mantra to be of the nature of Śiva, and meditate on Him, and mutter a mantra repeatedly'. 'The Lord, the dispenser of mantras, consumed all nescience of a sage by the virility of a flame rising from the fire of His mystic sound'. The Śāktas regard mantras as rays of divine consciousness. The Vaiṣṇavas regard them as composed of infinite consciousness and bliss, and identical with the Lord. The nature and power of mantras are incomprehensible by the intellect. But they are facts of spiritual experience, and should not be brushed aside by the sceptics.

A mantra is the real nature of the power of universal consciousness. A yogin's inner effort to reflect on the meaning of mantra generates the experience of its identity with divine power embodied in it. He can experience its real nature by continuous meditation on the Deity enshrined in it, and by constant repetition of it for certain periods. Its power is revealed by the Lord at His will through meditation on the Great Lake (mahāhrada). But it is not revealed to a yogin of limited power of meditation, who strives for trifling supernatural powers produced by nāda, bindu and the like. Vasugupta says, "The experience of the power of a mantra is acquired through meditation on the Great Lake. The Supreme Divine Power permeating the universe unlimited by time and space, the essence of mantras, transparent and profound, and replete with perfect 'I'-consciousness, is called the Great Lake. Meditation on it generates the experience of a yogin's identity with it—revelation of Ātman. Mahāmantra is the essence and power of all mantras, which is replete with perfect 'I'-consciousness. The experience of it takes the form of the revelation of one's Ātman. It is acquired through constant meditation on one's identity with the Great Lake after completely withdrawing the mind from external objects[38].

MASTER.—Vasugupta says, "A master is the means." He is the means of liberation of a disciple from bondge, since he initiates him in a mantra, since he teaches him the potency of a mantra, a mudrā and the like, and since he instructs him in the ways of spiritual culture. Śiva is the supreme end. A master is the means of realising the end, for he reveals the pervasion of a mantra and the like. Or, he is the supreme divine power in the nature of God's grace, which becomes a means of liberation through a human teacher. A master is equal to Śiva for he reveals the potency of a mantra. Mantras are eternal and devoid of origin and end. A master has awakened his divine power through a mantra, and can impart it to a disciple. Vasugupta says, "A master who is avipastha is competent to impart the saving knowledge to an eligible disciple." One who has acquired mastery over the divine powers presiding over letters can awaken divine power in a disciple by one's power of knowledge. A prince of yogins, who has identified himself with Ātman pervading the universe, who has recognised mantras as rays of the Lord of the nature of pure consciousness, and who has mastered the powers presiding over letters, is called avipastha, and is competent to be a master. The universe is known by him to be the unfoldment of His power, and to be created maintained, and dissolved by His power. He abides in his being as one universal, pure consciousness in the states of creation, maintenance, and dissolution. He has realised his identity with the Lord[39]. The Śāktas and the Vaiṣṇavas also regard a master as equal to the Lord. Regarding him as a human being is a sin, like regarding a mantra as a mere collection of letters or sounds.

INITIATION.—A master initiates a disciple in a mystic syllable or word or a group of words (mantra) and instructs him on spiritual practice. Initiation (dīkṣā) is so called because it gives the knowledge of Ātman and because it destroys the fetters of bondage. A person enlightened with saving knowledge and identified with Śiva alone can initiate another eligible person because of the descent of divine power (śaktipāta). An unenlightened person cannot enlighten another. One who has realised one's identity with Śiva is able to rouse in a disciple recognition of himself as Śiva or universal consciousness, freedom and bliss. Initiation in supreme liberation brings about realisation of one's Ātman, identity with Śiva, and attainment of supreme bliss. It brings on transcendence of the empirical universe, complete control over the powers of internal organs, and entrance into the inner supreme consciousness.

When there is very strong descent of divine power on a soul through a competent master who initiates a disciple, he realises himself as Śiva or the Absolute. He does not require repeated practice of any spiritual discipline. This way is called no-means (anupāya). Initiation is necessary for release. Śiva is eternally manifested as ubiquitous consciousness, which is His nature. He does not forsake His ubiquity when He assumes various forms. Those souls, which are interpenetrated by the most intense divine power descending on them, and which are purged of all determinations enter into the consciousness of Ātman without any means or spiritual discipline. Their means is gradual entrance into perfect consciousness. Abhinavagupta calls it no-means or the fourth means.

A person, who experiences that the whole world is full of him, and his play, is identified with Śiva, and released in embodied life. Śiva, the object of meditation, is manifested in his mind. Whenever he desires to realise his identity with Śiva, he utters his mantra which embodies Him. Because he is devoid of false knowledge, he experiences immortality in the form of consciousness of his essential nature unveiled by nescience. He abides in the essence of a mantra, supreme, transcendental consciousness and bliss, and thus experiences Ātman or Śiva. This is initiation in beatitude, which gives identity with Śiva or manifestation of his nature[40].

ALL RELATIONS PRESUPPOSE THE SUPREME KNOWER.—Entities are of two kinds : sentient and insentient. Insentient entities are known and acted upon by sentient souls. Knowledge and action are the essence of sentient souls. Knowledge is self-proved or self-aware in one's self. Its action is expressed in a bodily action which is perceived by oneself and others. Ātman, Supreme Self, the Lord of one's soul and other souls, is known by 'I'-consciousness. Their essence, Ātman, is veiled by His power of māyā. Some hold that there is one indeterminate consciousness. Others hold that there are many determinate cognitions such as recollection, doubt, inference and the like attended with words. Both these views are wrong. The permanent Ātman is different from indeterminate and determinate cognitions, and is not manifested in them. Common persons do not apprehend Ātman transcending the mind-body-complex by 'I'-consciousness atteneded with a word. Ātman is the knower of apprehension. When apprehension is destroyed, its recollection persists. Hence Ātman is the permanent knower[41].

The Buddhist raises the following objection to the Śaiva view. When the apprehension of an object is destroyed, the object no longer exists since all entities are momentary. So even if self's recollection persists, it is without an object, and, consequently, cannot lead to an action on the object. Apprehension produces a residual trace, which produces a recollection ; recollection imitates the previous apprehension, and manifests it with its object. Hence there is no use of the so-called permanent self to account for recollection. If a residual trace be regarded as self, it can account for recollection. The remembering self is as unnecessary as the apprehending self. The so-called permanent self is not made different by its different states—pleasure, pain, cognition, volition, etc., and so cannot recollect the object of the previous apprehension. Hence the remembering self is as imaginary as the apprehending self. If a cognition were of the nature of consciousness, it would be permanent like self. If it were not conscious, it could not manifest an insentient object. It may be argued that a cognition is buddhi, which is insentient, that as it receives a reflection of self, so it receives a reflection of the object, and that thus an object is manifested. An action also exists in an object and is produced in its place, because it has no permanent self which can combine its successive parts into a unity. Nor has it any substratum persisting for a long time and being of the same nature. An action is a mode of motion, and has a unique existence in a body and the like enduring at many times and in many places, because no other action than this is perceived. The relation of an action and an agent cannot be known without the relation of cause and effect. An antecedent event occurring, a subsequent event occurs. A cause occurring, an effect occurs. An effect is known through causal relation. A relation exists between two relata. One self cannot exist in two relata. Two self-existent entities also cannot depend upon each other. Hence a permanent actor is as imaginary as a permanent knower, and so Ātman cannot be the Lord of all beings. The Śaiva gives the following reply to the aforesaid objection. It is true that a past apprehension produces a residual trace, and that a residual trace produces a recollection, but that recollection exists in the self which is permanent. The self remembers the object of the past apprehension, but recollection does not manifest the object of the past apprehension. All knowledge, which manifests the nature of an object, is self-aware, and is not apprehended by another cognition. The cognition of a colour is self-aware and manifests a colour. The cognition of a taste is self-aware and manifests a taste. The cognition of a colour does not manifest a taste, and the cognition of a taste does not manifest a colour. A recollection produced by a residual trace of a past apprehension merely resembles the latter, but does not manifest it, and because it cannot do so its similarity with the latter cannot be definitely known. It may be argued that a recollection wrongly cognises the object of the past apprehension as the cognition produced by a shell wrongly cognises silver[42]. The Śaiva replies that the past apprehension being not manifested and its object being destroyed, the cognition of the object at present should not be called a recollection of it. An illusory cognition also cannot cognise the object of a past cognition without being related to it. So it is better to hold that a recollection is produced by a residual trace of a past apprehension, and that the former cognises the object of the latter. A recollection is a determinate cognition. A determinate cognition is insentient, and so cannot cognise the object of the past apprehension. But the conscious self can manifest or cognise a past object. Cognitions being different from one another, and being self-aware, they cannot cognise other cognitions and their objects. But practical actions of common people are produced by cognitions cognising the objects of one another. Thus there will be collapse of practical life. Hence the Śaiva holds that the Lord of the nature of consciousness assumes the form of the universe of diverse objects. Cognitions, recollections, negations, etc., are His powers. He relates different cognitions to one another, and apprehends their objects. He apprehends the object of a past apprehension because its object is not unmanifest to Him. So recollection is the recognition of an object cognised by a past apprehension by Him. He manifests the specific individual apprehended in the past because He is eternal and because He apprehended it in the past. He can remember the object of a past apprehension even when it is destroyed. Otherwise, the recollection of the object of a past apprehension cannot be accounted for. If a recollection were different from the past apprehension of the object, the remembered object would not be manifested. Hence the present recollection and the past apprehension have identity in nature, and He is their Knower. The objects perceived in the past and remembered at present are manifested separately, but the past apprehension of it is not manifested separately, because one's Self is manifested as 'I perceived it in the past'—Self being the object of 'I'-consciousness and enduring in the past and the present. The cognitions of the omniscient yogins also are not manifested by other cognitions, but are self-manifest ; they are manifested by the Self in which they subsist. When they are objects of knowledge, they are manifested by themselves. Sometimes the past apprehension and the present recollection are cognised separately by the Self in such a form as 'I perceived the object in the past and I remember it now'. When the Self perceives an object in such a form as 'I perceive this jar' or 'this is a jar', it perceives the object as related to or known by the Self ; it does not perceive the object as unrelated to the Self. Sometimes the self knows an object in such a from as 'This is perceived by me' or 'This was perceived by me'. Thus the subject and the object are manifested separately in the self. But the distinctness of the manifestations is due to the power of māyā. Even when an object is manifested separately from the percepient Self, really it is manifested as perceived by the self as existing outside it. An object would not be manifested if it had not the nature of being manifested ; it would not be manifested by a cognition if it were not manifested before its cognition. An object's being manifested is its manifestation ; they are not different from each other. An object which is of the nature of being manifested can be manifested by a cognition. The existence of an object can be proved only when it is manifested. If it is of the nature of being manifested, then only can it be manifested by a cognition. If external objects were proved by the occasional manifestations of object-cognitions, then mere consciousness, which is nondifferent, could not be the cause of a variety of manifestations or object-cognitions. The manifestations of insentient objects prove their existence ; their being manifested only proves their existence. Hence mere consciousness is the ontological reality in them. Although it is nondistinct, yet distinct cognitions or manifestations of objects prove the existence of the latter as external, like the objects of perception. The revival of diverse residual traces is not the cause of the variety of manifestations or cognitions of objects, since there is no cause of the revival of the variety of residual traces. The revival of various residual traces is not different from consciousness. The revival of them is uncaused. Hence external objects are the causes of the different manifestations or cognitions of them. But practical actions of people follow upon the manifestations of objects ; the latter are of the nature of manifestations. Hence the assumption of external objects is needless. Further, they cannot be proved by any means of valid knowledge, since they appear to be both composed of parts in that they are possessed of contradictory qualities, and since they appear to be devoid of parts ih that they are related to six directions in many ways. The Lord of the nature of infinite consciousness manifests all objects existing within Him as external to Him through His volition without any external material, even as a yogin manifests objects external to him without any material.[43]

There was never any manifestation of a self-existent external object. So the existence of the latter cannot be inferred from the former, as a seed is inferred from a sprout. The external objects cannot be inferred from their manifestations, since they were never perceived as external to consciousness. All objects are manifested as existing in the Lord, and cannot be manifested without His volition. They cannot be the objects of His volition if they do not exist within Him as nondifferent from His cognitions. His volitions and creation of objects refer to the same manifestations of the same objects. 'I'-consciousness is the essence of the manifestation of an object. Otherwise, the manifestation tinged with an object would be insentient like a crystal. But it is transparent and receives the reflection of a seemingly insentient object; it is consciousness attended with 'I'-consciousness. The manifestation of an object exists in Ātman which alone has consciousness; the act of consciousness is the agency of the conscious Self. So Self is different from an insentient entity or matter. Self is of the nature of consciousness attended with 'I' consciousness ; freedom is its essential nature ; this is lordship of the Supreme Self or Lord. His agency of manifestation and all-pervading being unaffected by time and space are of the nature of 'I'-consciousness. It is the essence of His nature. He knows Himself, and yet His freedom is not affected by His knowing Himself. He does not know an unknowable entity under the influence of something over which He has no control. If He knew such an entity, His freedom would be compromised. The Lord freely creates the diverse objects of His knowledge, and manifests them as external to Him to fulfil the practical purposes of common people. He is identical with His 'I'-consciousness. He knows Himself, but does not make Himself different by knowing Himself. The Lord of the nature of manifestation manifests the universe of diverse objects, which is really His Self, as if it were different from Him through His power of māyā. The Absolute Consciousness is knowledge, perception, recollection, doubt, determination,—modes of manas and buddhi—in their essence. They refer to the manifestations of objects which appear to be different from Ātman. But really they are nothing but universal consciousness. There is 'I'-consciousness even at the time of immediate apprehension. It is Ātman's consciousness of an object. Ātman's action on an object depends upon its desire to appropriate it or reject it. So it depends upon Self's consciousness of the object. The determinate knowledge 'this is a jar' is manifested as different from Ātman. But it is really nothing but the power of Absolute Consciousness different from names and forms—diverse objects—and is manifested to Ātman as nondifferent from Him, and not as 'this'-consciousness. Absolute Consciousness appears to be different objects because of the Lord's power of māyā, in space and time and as successive through perception, recollection and other kinds of determinate knowledge. 'I'-consciousness, which is of the nature of manifestation embodies Logos in the form of 'I' ; yet it is not a false cognition, but a true determinate cognition devoid of duality, difference, or a counterentity.[44] A jar and a non-jar different from each other are manifested as negating each other. But there is no manifestation of a nonmanifest entity as there is manifeetation of a manifest entity. So there is no nonmanifest entity which a manifest entity may negate. Hence the manifestation of the manifest Ātman is not a false cognition. The cognition of a jar is ontologically false because it appears to be different from the free and independent Knower in Whom it is manifested as a cognition. But an empirical self, which wrongly identifies itself with its body, vital forces, buddhi, or void appears to be different from Ātman or Lord because of His power of māyā. The cognition of it is false because its 'I'-consciousness negates other objects and because it is not perfect 'I'-consciousness in the form 'I am the universe'. In Ātman's perfect 'I'-consciousness there are no other objects different from it. His 'I'-consciousness does not negate other objects different from it. An empirical self's cognitions of objects are ontologically false,because they appear to be different from Ātman because of His power of māyā. Its cognitions of objects modified by the residual traces of its past cognitions with the help of its egoism are ontologically false because it wrongly identifies itself with its body, vital forces, egoism, or the like. The Lord Himself enters into a body and the like, and manifests diverse objects at His will outside Him, which really exist within Him. He manifests them through His power of agency successively. He enters into a body and the like, and manifests Himself as an empirical self or knower. He manifests Himself as 'I' and 'this' simultaneously. He abides in all cognitions of objects,—determinate cognition, recollection, negation, etc.,—in empirical knowers, and manifests Himself within them. He directly manifests Himself in the internal cognitions in the form of the manifestations of external objects. But in recollections He manifests Himself in the form of the past perceptions. Therefore recollections are said to be produced by their residual traces. The Lord's omniscience and omipotence are manifested in the cognitions of all objects, which He desires to create or manifest. He is the Supreme Knower and creator of all objects which are manifested in succession. But He transcends the temporal order, and is of the nature of infinite and eternal consciousness. (Cp. Green). He is the Supreme Knower of different objects related to each other as cause and effect and known through different cognitions. Their causal relation is due to His act of combining them with each other. He is the Supreme Knower of different objects existing at different times and in different places, relates them to one another by His act of uniting them with one another. Their spatial and temporal relations are due to His synthetic act of apperception. Sometimes causes are perceived and effects are inferred or remembered; sometimes effects are perceived and causes are inferred or remembered. Causes precede effects, and effects succeed causes. There is sequence between them. They do not relate themselves to each other, but they are related to each other by the Supreme Knower by His synthetic act of unifying them. Different objects existing in different places and at different times are unrelated to one another, and can be related to one another by the Supreme Knower alone Who knows them simultaneously by a flash of intuition. (Cp.Green). The causal relation between a perceived effect and an unperceived cause can be established by the Supreme Knower Who can perceive and remember them respectively. Recollection is its own proof since it is self-aware and present; it proves its validity. Past apprehension being absent, its self-awareness is absent, and so cannot prove the validity of recollection. Recollection cannot establish the relation between cause and effect, because when it occurs the prior apprehension is absent, which cognised a cause. Present recollection recalls it. Present apprehension cognises an effect. So recollection cannot establish causal relation between two events. A sublated cognition (e.g., the cognition of silver) and a sublating cognition (e.g., the cognition of a shell) cannot coexist in the same subject at the same time, since they are contradictory to each other. They can be related to each other as sublated knowledge and sublating knowledge by the

Supreme Knower alone Who knows them both together. 'There is the absence of a jar on the ground.' Here the cognition of the absence of a jar is nothing but the cognition of the bare ground. The cognition of the bare ground does not prove its being the absence of a jar, although on that ground a different jar capable of being perceived does not exist. The ground is always exclusive of the nonground; so the cognition of the bare ground cannot prove the absence of a jar, which is different from it. Exclusiveness of a jar different from the ground would be its accidental character, if being together with a jar were its accidental character. Similarly, the cognition of a shell proves the absence of the cognition of silver, and invalidity of the cognition of silver at the moment. But it does not prove the invalidity of the prior cognition of silver. Sublation is not known by inference, because at the time of the cognition of a shell the prior cognition of silver does not exist, and because the subject of inference is not proved to exist. The prior cognition of silver is the subject of inference, and its invalidity is the predicate of inference. The sublating cognition and the sublated cognition both are known together by the Supreme Knower in Whom they coexist, and they are known to be related as such by Him alone Who is the eternal self-aware consciousness. He knows the harmony of the sublating cognition of a shell with its object (eg., a shell). All pure and impure practical actions based on the knowledge of different objects due to the Lord's power of māyā are possible in the Supreme Knower Who knows them in their real nature. The pure knowers know them as nondifferent from Him, while the impure knowers know them as different from Him. Sometimes practical actions follow upon perceptions of objects present to the sense-organs. Sometimes they follow upon recollections of objects perceived in the past. Recollections, expectations, etc., which succeed perceptions and other determinate cognitions which cognise different objects, are cognitions of objets existing in the past, the present, and the future, but they do not differ in their real nature because they are manifestatlons of objects.[45] In pleasure, pain, etc., their causes are absent, although the manifestations of pleasure, pain, etc., are present. The causes cannot produce pleasure, pain, etc., unless they exist in consciousness. They qualified by the past time can produce these feelings. So the causes of these feelings exist at present in consciousness. Pleasure, pain, etc., are manifested at present because their causes are cognised by consciousness at present. So both the causes of the feelings and the feelings are known by one Supreme Knower. Externality is an adjunct (upādhi) of the manifestations of entities and nonentities, but not their essential nature. Recollections cognise external objects, but the externality manifested by them is not their essence. The absence of an object is manifested by a cognition as existing outside it, but its externality is not the essence of the cognition. Externality is a limiting condition of the aforesaid cognitions. It exists in consciousness, but does not exist in the essence of the internal cognitions. It is their adventitious condition. Practical actions are due to the different manifestations, which exist within consciousness, and which are known by one knower; and they are not due to the externality of their objects. The manifestations are of the nature of consciousness, and always exist within consciousness, but they also exist without because they are made to appear to be outside consciousness by the Lord's power of māyā. The external appearances of the manifestations or cognitions are popularly called objects. They exist whithin the Lord's consciousness when He desires to create or manifest them. The so-called external objects are cognised as 'this'-

consciousess. They are cognised by internal cognitions which are known by 'I'-consciousness. Thus the manifestations of jars, etc., exist both within and without. They are known as internal cognitions and external objects knowable through the internal organ and the external sense-organs. Pleasure, pain, etc., are internal cognitions knowable through the internal organ alone. The Lord has immediate experience of the determinate cognitions of objects, and of pleasure, pain, etc. The cognitions of the empirical knowers cannot exist and produce practical actions without being combined into a unity by the one Supreme Knower. The Lord of the nature of infinite consciousness and perfect 'I'-consciousness is the Self of the universe. He has pure knowledge and action. His impure knowledge and action in the empirical knowers are contracted by His power of māyā, and related to different objects composed of sattva, rajas and tamas. Hence the Supreme Knower is necessary for the combination of plurality into a unity in the empirical knowers' knowledge of the universe of diverse objects in time and space and bound by causality.[46] These arguments of Utpaladeva unmistakably show how adept he was in epistemological thinking.

CRITIQUE OF OTHER SYSTEMS.—Monistic Śaivaism holds that there is no difference between Śiva endowed with powers and His powers, even as an action does not exist separately from a substance which acts, and that powerful Śiva creates the world of manifold objects through His various powers. This is not possible according to any other system of philosophy.

Some Vedāntins hold that Brahman is variegated. Somānanda criticizes this doctrine of multiform Brahman. There is no cause of Brahman's manifoldness. Various entities in Brahman are different from one another by their very nature. Jars are different from the lump of earth from which they are made. They have no dual nature in the forms of earth and jars, for in that case jars would always exist. Various entities in Brahman may be said to be due to avidyā. If they be produced by avidyā, they are unreal like it. But the Śaivas admit the reality of all entities. If various entities in the world be not related to avidyā, then they are different from it and consequently real.[47] Some Vedāntins hold that Brahman Himself becomes the world because He is its material cause. Others hold that Brahman becomes the false world-appearance. Others hold that the world is not real. Others hold that Brahman is the Supreme Self of all individual selves. Others hold that individual selves are like sparks of Brahman. Others hold that they are the reflections of Brahman in avidyā or in internal organs produced by it. Others hold that Brahman Himself assumes the forms of diverse objects of the world for His sport. Others hold that individual souls differ from Brahman owing to their mind-body-complexes, even as the reflections of the sun in different earthen vessels of water differ from the sun owing to the earthen vessels of water. Individual souls are not aware of their real nature as Brahman in the state of heir bondage, and become aware of it in the state of their liberation. Many Vedāntins regard the world as a false appearanee, and existents as unreal.[48] The Śaiva monists regard individual selves as identical with Śiva endowed with infinite consciousness and powers contraetcd by five coverings produced by His power of māyā, and the manifold world as created by His various powers.

The Pāñcarātrikas regard Vāsudeva, the Supreme Lord, as Brahman Who possesses vidyā and avidyā as His powers. He creates the world through His power of avidyā, and liberates individual selves through His power of vidyā. He is not tinged by avidyā and vidyā because He is the omniscient Lord. Others hold that the Lord creates the world through His semen or virility. The 'Bhagavad Gītā' states that the Lord revealed His cosmic form to Arjuna through His power of revelation. Both these views of the Pāñcarātrikas are not reasonable. If avidyā be a positive entity,it is identical with vidyā. If it be a negative entity, it cannot be the means of creating the real world. A negative entity cannot be related to the real world since it involves self-contradiction. Therefore some other entity than avidyā should be assumed to be the material cause of the world. If avidyā be the material cause of the world, the Pāñcarātrika view becomes identical with the Vedāntin's view. If the Lord create the world through His power of vidyā, then another God should be assumed to relate His vidyā to the insentient world.[49]

The Jainas hold that individual souls differ from one another, that they are not pervasive, that they become bound owing to avidyā which generates infraatomic particles of karma-matter, which encrust their souls, and that they are liberated by the destruction of the particles of karman. Somānanda criticizes the Jaina doctrine. The Jainas cannot account for the souls' acquiring avidyā and being bound by it to embodied life. Further, when a soul completely destroys particles of karman due to avidyā, it becomes a conqueror (jina) or Lord. Somānanda urges that the Jaina's concept of the Lord is tantamount to a formless void. The Jainas are atheists, and do not admit the reality of God. They believe in liberated souls which are conscious of their innate infinite knowledge, infinite perception, infinitite happiness, and infinite power. So Somānanda's criticism of the Jaina view is not fair. But he is right in observing that a liberated soul is not equivalent to God, because God can create the world while a liberated soul cannot create it.[50]

The Buddhist realists, the Vaibhāṣikas and the Sautrāntikas, admit the reality of momentary external objects,which are different from one another. Somānanda urges that they cannot account for the difference among them. They cannot trace their difference to the volitions of God because they are atheists The Buddhist Vijñānavādins,the Yogācāras,hold that momentary cognitions are real, but that external objects are unreal.Somānanda offers the following criticism of it. He asks how a real cognition can produce an unreal external object. The Vijñānavādin may reply that just as a lustful person creates the false hallucination of an unreal woman, so a real internal cognition produces an unreal external object. Somānanda urges that a lustful person experiences the hallucination of an unreal woman, whom he perceived as real on a former occasion. Further, a cognition is a means of knowledge,and depends upon an agent of knowledge or a knower. But the Vijñānavādin denies the existence of a permanent knowing self If he regards a mere act of knowing as a knower, then it must have a means of knowledge. If he regards a cognition as being both a knower and a means of knowledge, then it involves self-contradiction, and becomes successive. If a cognition is nontemporal and devoid of sequence and a knower, then he accepts the Śaiva view that Śiva is the Supreme Knower, regards a cognition as permanent, and thus abandons the doctrine of momentariness. The Vijñānavādin holds that a momentary cognition knows in such forms as 'I know' and 'he knows me' as a knower and a means of knowledge. But if a cognition exists for two moments, it ceases to be momentary. If a cognition cognises an object as a knower and as a means of knoWledge at diferent moments, then it exists at different moments. If it is momentary, it cannot have a sequence, and consequently cannot have a result of the act of cognition. The Vijñānavādin argues that a single cognition appears to be subject and object different from each other, and that a pure cognition appears to be an unreal external object through avidyā of the nature of a subconscious impression (vāsanā). Somānanda urges that a pure cognition cannot be tainted with the subconscious impression of avidyā, that a volition arises prior to a cognition, and that, consequently, there must be a knowing self before a cognition can arise. There is no indeterminate jar which may be apprehended by a pure knower. When the cognition of a jar comes into existence, it cannot apprehend a determinate jar with its many qualities simultaneously. If it apprehend a qualified jar with its qualities simultaneously, then it exists at least for two moments, and thus ceases to be momentary. A cognition cannot apprehend an external object at the moment when it is produced. External objects are not unreal, because unreal objects cannot be cognised. A cognition of an object is manifested, whether the object is manifested or whether it is not manifested. A cognition is of the nature of valid knowledge (vidyā), and is not therefore momentary. A cognition is real, and, consequently, nonmomentary, since what is real is nonmomentary. The Vijñānavādin may argue that a light manifesting an object is neither permanent nor an agent. Somānanda replies that a light is an agent of manifestation or a manifester, and that the visual organ is the means of manifestation. Similarly, the manifesting self, which knows an object, is permanent. If a cognition is a means of knowledge, then it leads to infinite regress. It is a means of manifesting an object. Another cognition is a means of manifesting the cognition, and so on to infinity. Therefore a cognition is not momentary if it cognises an object. The Mādhyamikas hold that the reality is Void (śūnya), and that both internal cognitions and external objects are false appearances (saṁvṛti). Somānanda offers the following criticism of it. Void is devoid of consciousness, and so cannot enlighten a void on the nature of void. Nor can it be contradicted by a void. It can neither be proved nor disproved. Further, one phenomenal appearance (saṁvṛti) cannot be contradicted by another phenomenal appearance, because Void is the absolute reality which is veiled alike by all phenomenal appearances.[51]

Some Sāṁkhya thinkers are atheists and believe in the reality of many individual souls, which are independent and free. They hold that their bondage is due to nondiscrimination, and that their release is due to discrimination. Somānanda urges that they cannot account for the origin of nondiscrimination. Some Sāṁkhya thinkers are theists, believe in the existence of God, an omniscient Soul, and also believe in many individual souls. Somānanda urges that they cannot account for the difference between God and individual souls. Some Sāṁkhya thinkers identify God with prakṛti, and think of Him as devoid of consciousness. They think of God as an emergent of prakṛti. Somānanda urges that God devoid of consciousness is nothing but insentient matter. Some Vedāntins also regard Brahman as devoid of consciousness. Somānanda urges that such Brahman is like insentient matter.[52]

The Śābdikas hold that one eternal sound (śabdabrahma) is the supreme reality. Bhartṛhari describes it as one eternal sound of the nature of supreme word or speech (parā vāk) which is manifested as paśyantī or seeing or experiencing. It is devoid of the functions of the sense-organs, unlimited by space, time, causality, forms, and sequence. It is free of the distinctions of subject and object. It is the self which pervades all bodies. It is the formless consciousness which experiences internal cognitions. It experiences all objects. It is the supreme reality. It is a principle of sound which is imperishable and without origin and end. It assumes the state of madhyamā and becomes cognitions. It becomes articulate and assumes the state of vaikharī. It is manifested as manifest sounds or words and external objects. It assumes the forms of internal cognitions and external objects. All cognitions are attended with words and cognise objects. No objects can be cognised by cognitions unattended with words. Paśyantī is indivisible and nontemporal or devoid of sequence. One who knows Śabdabrahman well can know Supreme Brahman. Somānanda opines that Śiva's power of knowledge in the form of Sadāśiva conceived by the Śaivas is the Śābdika's supreme reality called paśyantī or experiencing ultimate sound (Logos). Utpaladeva expounds the Śābdika view thus. What is of the nature of infinite consciousness or Supreme Brahman is of the nature of eternal sound or supreme word. It experiences and is so colled paśyantī. Even Supreme Brahman, although of the nature of consciousness or manifestation, cannot be manifested without a word. The word or sound experiencing within is an experient. It is of the nature of mere consciousness and devoid of objects of knowledge and called the self because it pervades the entire body, which is its vehicle of experience. It is also the omniscient Supreme Self. The eternal sound that experiences the endless world is the Supreme Self. It is devoid of subjects and objects, and the supreme experiencing sound (paśyantī). When it is tainted with avidyā and experiences different objects owing to avidyā, it becomes a bound individual self. Its empirical existence is subject to space, time, genus, and form. Its experience of sensible objects is due to the operation of the sense-organs. But the Supreme Self is not limited by space, time, genus, and form. Its experience is independent of the operation of the sense-organs. Thus the experiencing, supreme, eternal sound called paśyantī is the supreme reality. It becemes a cognition (madhyamā vāk) when it desires to experience an object. It becomes an articulate sound (vaikharī vāk) when it desires to express itself in the external world. It assumes the forms of external objects owing to avidyā, which are known through external sense-organs, and become objects of knowledge. It is tinged with the subconscious impressions of external objects owing to avidyā, and assumes the unreal forms of external objects. Thus the experiencing eternal subtle sound becomes the Supreme Self, individual selves, and external objects—the two latter being unreal appearances due to avidyā and the first being the only ontological reality. The Śābdika believes in monism of an eternal sound[53].

Śomānanda offers the following criticism of the Śābdika view. Common people admit articulate words only which are perceived. Therefore parā vāk and paśyantī are rejected. Words are uttered by the vocal organ which is a motor organ. It is an organ of a bound individual self, and consequently cannot be the Supreme Self. Words and the vocal organ are due to avidyā, a product of God's māyāśakti, and consequently cannot be the Supreme Self. If they be of the nature of Brahman, then hands and feet also are of the nature of Him. If paśyantī were said to be of the nature of Brahman because of its being subtle apprehension involved in all kinds of experience, then the vital forces entering into the heart, the seat of manas and self, would be real since they involve inner experience. When there are voluntary actions in regard to external objects, there is always an inner experience. But external objects signified by words do not constitute the nature of Ātman. So the words including the subtle experiencing speech do not constitute the nature of Ātman. It is objected that those yogins who meditate on inner speech attain supernatural powers, and that therefore the inner speech is Ātman. Somānanda replies that the Deities presiding over the sense-organs and the gross elements grant supernatural powers to them. So the objection is not sound.Their hands and feet, which are motor organs, are not of the nature of Brahman. So their vocal organ also is not Brahman. The Sāṁkhya regards it as a contsruction of prakṛti related to an individual soul for whose experience it is constructed. It is not related to the experience of the Supreme Self. All objects are real when they are experienced. The entities which are not experienced are unreal. Experience devoid of 'I'-consciousness is not experience. 'I'-consciousness, which is the essence of all reality when it is experienced, is attended with a name. But hands and feet are not attended with names. So the subtle experiencing sound is not like hands and feet. Somānanda considers paśyantī by its nature and name. Paśyantī refers to an act at the present time. 'To see' is a transitive verb. What does paśyantī see or know ? What is the objective case of the verb 'to see ?' The transitive verb 'to see' abides in an agent who sees. What is the object that is seen or known ? If paśyantī saw external objects as 'this,' then it would be unreal since they are unreal. They are unreal appearances, and so paśyantī does not really see them, and thus ceases to be paśyantī. The Śābdikas do not regard external objects as real entities. If paśyantī were said to see unreal objects due to avidyā, then paśyantī would be unreal, and would be related to avidyā. Avidyā is unreal by its nature. So paśyantī cannot be related to unreal avidyā. If paśyantī be unreal, then its being of the nature of Brahman is not conceivable. The Śābdikas may urge that paśyantī first creates external objects, and then sees them. But it is strange that real paśyantī creates unreal objects, and that it attains the nature of paśyantī after creating them. If paśyantī is unreal at first because it does not see any objects before creation, then it cannot create any objects. If any unreal entity were the cause of any effect, then any effect would be produced by any cause. If a cause were unreal without producing an effect, then a real cause also cannot produce an unreal effect. Then does paśyantī create unknown objects or known objects ? If paśyantī first creates objects and then sees them, then it creates unknown objects. But the Śābdikas do not admit that paśyantī creates unknown objects. If it be said to create unknown objects, it is not possible since it cannot create them without knowing their nature and the means of their construction. Paśyantī cannot create them without any motive or end. The Śābdikas do not admit that paśyantī creates objects without any end or motive in sport. Hence paśyantī cannot create objects either with or without prior knowledge of them. But paśyantī is real. If objects known by it are real, then it is not real and cannot know them, because it involves dualism. The Śābdikas are monists and admit the reality of paśyantī only. If objects are unreal, then paśyantī becomes tainted by creating them, and by creating them it makes its knowledge of them illusory. Further, whether paśyantī knows real or unreal objects, it cannot create them because it has no motive or end to realise in doing so.[54] Further, is avidyā paśyantī's own attribute or another's attribute ? If avidyā is its own attribute, then it is tainted. If avidyā is an attribute of another entity, what is that other entity? The Śābdikas are monists and do not admit the reality of any other entity than paśyantī or Śabdabrahman. They do not admit the reality of avidyā as another entity. If it is another independent entity, it cannot be destroyed. If it were produced and destroyed by another entity, then it would cease to be independent. Further, if avidyā is indescribable, either as real or unreal, or as eternal or noneternal, then it is a nonentity since it is devoid of any nature. A nonentity devoid of any nature cannot be known by paśyantī. If avidyā is not known by paśyantī, then the latter becomes insentient since it does not know anything. If avidyā is known by paśyantī definitely as distinguished from other entities, it becomes describable. Hence avidyā is not indescribable. Further, if avidyā is not known by paśyantī, by what means of valid knowledge do the Śābdikas know that avidyā is indescribable? How do they prove that avidyā is indescribable? If avidyā is said to be proved by inference from the knowledge of difference, then it is not undescribable. If it is inferred from the knowledge of difference in order to account for it, then it is known by inference to be of a definite nature. Hence it is not of an indefinable nature or indescribable. Further, the Śābdikas' inference of avidyā from the knowledge of difference is not valid for the same reason. If it is inferred to be of a definite nature, then it is not indefinable. Bhartṛhari says, "The existent entities are known by inference to be different because of the difference in condition, space, time, and different powers." Hence different entities are definite in nature and describable. Indefinite and indescribable avidyā cannot be inferred from different entities, which are of a definite nature, and which are describable. If different entities are perceivable, they are not indefinite and indescribable. If they are not perceptible, they cannot be proved.[55]

Avidyā is either existent or nonexistent. But it connot be both, since existence is the negation of nonexistence, and since nonexistence is the negation of existence. Avidyā is not vidyā, but is not mere negation of vidyā or knowledge, but like vidyā in that it appears as the world. Hence avidyā is certainly existent, and is consequently neither indescribable nor consistent with monism. If both avidyā and paśyantī are real, the Śābdika doctrine involves dualism. If avidyā be mere negation of valid knowledge, then it is mere void or a nonentity since negation is its chief characteristic. Void cannot contradict paśyantī that is of the nature of valid knowledge, since it is devoid of any form or character. If void contradicts paśyantī of the nature of valid knowledge, then it is real, and leads to dualism. But a nonentity cannot contradict paśyantī that is real. Further, paśyantī is not of the nature of sound, but is a power of God. But the Śābdikas do not admit the reality of God. They hold that paśyantī is a subtle sound which exists as nondifferent from an object which is signified by it. A sound is composed of air or its modification, and not the supreme reality, even as hands being composed of earth or its modifications are not the supreme reality. A mere sound cannot exist in the states of parā, paśyantī, madhyamā and vaikharī, like the roar of an ocean. The Śābdikas may urge that real paśyantī is not contradicted by avidyā, but that madhyamā is contradicted by it, that a word in the state of madhyamā apprehends an external object which appears to be different from it, that madhyamā is related to buddhi, an internal organ, which assumes the form of a cognition of an object, but that paśyantī is not related to buddhi. What is the cause of madhyamā? Paśyantī cannot be its cause, since the former is pure whereas the latter is impure, and since the latter apprehends an external object as diffrent from it whereas the former does not apprehend it. Paśyantī is pure and devoid of the distinction of subject and object. But madhyamā is impure and tainted with the distinction of subject and object. Hence paśyantī cannot produce madhyamā. If paśyantī be the efficient cause of madhyamā, the former is different from the latter, even as a potter is different from a pot. If paśyantī be the material cause of madhyamā, the former is identical with the latter in nature, like threads and cloth. If paśyantī be different from madhyamā, then the Śābdika doctrine is not monism. If madhymā be of the nature of paśyantī, then it cannot be impure and apprehend an object as different from it or apprearing as nondifferent from it. If paśyantī be of the same nature as madhyamā, then it ceases to be pure, and becomes tainted with avidyā. If paśyantī know external objects as nondifferent from itself, then madhyamā also should apprehend them as nondifferent from itself, and should not apprehend them as different from it and one another. But different objects are perceived through different sense-organs. This fact would not be possible if madhyamā did not apprehend them as different from itself and one another. Further, paśyantī either exists inside the body at the stage of 'I'-consciousness or extends outward to an external object. If it exist inside the body only, it becomes limited. If it extend also to an external object, and if it know the latter as 'this', then the distinction of paśyantī, madhyamā and vaikharī is useless. If paśyantī extend through nāda and bindu in the form of vital forces, and create and destroy the world, then also it is not pervasive but limited, and not one, but many. Hence paśyantī cannot perform the function of God, and the Śābdika doctrine of paśyantī is atheistic. Moreover, paśyantī is different in different bodies or identical in them. If it be different, then there are different paśyantīs, and the Śābhika abandons monism. It it be one and the same, then one person uttering a word, all would utter a word without making an effort. If one paśyantī appear to be different in different bodies as limiting adjuncts, even as one crystal appears to be different according as it is tinged by different coloured media, then the bodies are real, like the media. But the Śābdikas do not regard the bodies as real. Unreal entities are incapable of performing any function. Further, paśyantī is a transitive verb and must have a real objective case. Hence the object of paśyantī is real. Paśyantī is real if its object of knowledge be real. But paśyantī is one, indivisible, nondifferent and nontemporal while its objects are composite, divisible, different and temporal. Its objects being limited by time and space, it cannot be nonspatial and nontemporal. If paśyantī know its objects as limited by time, space and forms, then its knowledge is valid. If it know them as not limited by their forms, space and time, then its knowledge is false, and paśyantī becomes of the nature of nescience. If it know them as limited by their forms, space and time, then it cannot be one, indivisible and nondifferent. Furthermore, paśyantī existing at present cannot know a nonexistent future object as present, but it can rightly know a present object only. If it know a past object or a future object, then it knows a nonexistent object. But paśyantī knows all objects, past, present and future according to the Śābdikas. They regard space and time as mere distinctive marks. The Śābdikas may argue that paśyantī knows different objects limited by different portions of space and time as different cognitions, and that then it knows a common entity in them as a common cognition, and that it thus knows all entities. Somānanda refutes this contention thus. Let the cognition be common to all objects. Its nature as paśyantī experiencing them should be determined. Its nature as paśyantī or experiencing depends upon particular objects limited by particular portions of space. Its objects being particular and different, the so-called common cognition also is different in cognising different objects. It is not common to them because of its nondifference from them. If it were nondifferent from them, it would never cognise a past object or a future object. Paśyantī nondifferent from a past object or a future object cognises it in the past or in the future. Or, it is different in cognising different objects such as 'blue', 'yellow', etc.; so the cognitions of them are different from one another. The Śābdikas may argue that paśyantī as mere consciousness is nondifferent. Somānanda refutes this contention by observing that mere consciousness cannot cognise particular objects, e.g., 'blue', 'yellow', etc., and that if paśyantī cannot cognise them, it ceases to be paśyantī because it does not experience any object.[56] The Śābdikas hold that paśyantī is devoid of sequence or temporal order, and argue that because it is devoid of sequence, it is one, indivisible and partless, and that it does not differ in cognising different objects. Somānanda asks what destroys the sequence of parts or events in it and collects them together. If another entity destroys the sequence of parts or events, it destroys their sequence in paśyantī or in some other entity. If it do so in paśyantī, then the latter has sequence, which is denied by the Śābdikas. If it do so in another entity, then they admit dualism. If they admit that paśyantī had at first sequence and then became devoid of sequence when its sequence of parts was destroyed by some other entity, then there are two natures in paśyantī. But it cannot possess two natures since it is indivisible. The Śābdikas may argue that paśyantī experiences itself by itself by its own powers of object and instrument of experiencing without having parts. Somānanda refutes it by observing that paśyantī becomes insentient and ceases to be paśyantī, if it assume the nature of an object and an intsument of experiencing and become dependent. Paśyantī, being of the nature of mere consciousness, is incorporeal, unextended and devoid of parts, and consequently it becomes insentient, if it has parts in that it is an object of experience and if it is an instrument of experience. Further, either paśyantī experiences itself as not experienced before or as experienced before. Both these alternatives are not reasonable. If paśyantī experienced itself before, it cannot have desire to experience it. If it did not experience itself before, it is not paśyantī. Paśyantī is of the nature of manifestation and so cannot but manifest itself. If it do not manifest itself, it ceases to be an experiencing principle. The nature of paśyantī does not change every moment so that it may experience itself as existing at present. Further, paśyantī experiences itself either as of the nature of manifestation or as of the nature of nonmanifestation. If it experience itself as of the nature of nonmanifestation, then it becomes insentient. If it experience itself as of the nature of manifestation, then it already knows it and so cannot have any desire to know it. If it experience itself although it know itself already, there will be no end to its knowing itself. If the Śābdikas hold that paśyantī experiences itself as subtle and pure and untained with determinations such as 'blue', 'yellow', etc., then they come to accept the Śaiva view that Ātman, infinite self-luminous consciousness, knows itself as devoid of the distinction of the act of knowing, the agent of knowing, and the object of knowing, and devoid of the determinations of time. In fact, if paśyantī be assumed to be an object of the act of knowing, then its being an agent of knowing will be dependent. Further, it involves self-contradiction because paśyantī, the agent of knowing, cannot be the object of the act of knowing.[57]

The Śābdikas admit the reality of a sphoṭa over and above paśyantī. Somānanda asks whether a sphoṭa is identical with paśyantī or whether it is something different from it. They admit both to be real and eternal, and so advocate dualism. Whether a sphoṭa be identical with paśyantī or whether it be different from the latter, paśyantī experiences a real object or comprehends the meaning of a sentence through the experience of a sentence-form (vākyasphoṭa), which is different from the constituent words. All sphoṭas are perceived to be different from the sentences which are admitted to be real. If a sphoṭa be different from paśyantī, and if a real sphoṭa convey the meaning of an unreal object, then there is no harm. But if paśyantī of the nature of pure consciousness apprehend an unreal object, there is a flaw because a sphoṭa identical with paśyantī conveys the meaning of a real sentence. Further, a verbal sentence is valid if it is uttered by a reliable person ; and a sphoṭa is uttered by a reliable person because it is eternal. So the sounds represented by the letters are noneternal. They are not the cause of the comprehension of the meaning of a sentenee ; nor are they valid. A sound in the form of a sphoṭa is the cause of the comprehension of the meaning of a sentence. It is not noneternal ; nor is it produced or uttered by a reliable person. Thus the admission of a sphoṭa would destroy the rule about the validity of a sentence uttered by a reliable person and about the invalidity of a sentence uttered by an unreliable person, because all sentences would be equally valid. Further, if all sphoṭas be real and eternal, then monism advocated by the Śābdikas will be overthrown. Further, how can a sphoṭa of a sentence be manifested by words and letters which are false and unreal ? If the former can be manifested by the latter, then the latter are true or real. A sphoṭa is immutable, eternal and real, and so cannot be manifested by false, unreal words, letters and sounds representing them, which are entirely different from it. If the former can be manifested by the latter, then the latter are real. If a sphoṭa be of the nature of paśyantī, then it cannot, for that very reason, be manifested by unreal, false words, letters and sounds represented by them. If a sphoṭa identical with paśyantī be manifested by them, then they cease to be avidyā, because they manifest the meaning of a sentence. But the Śābdikas regard them as unreal due to avidyā.

Further, Somānanda asks what means of valid kowledge establishes the reality of paśyantī. The Śābdikas regard paśyantī as imperceptible. Inference is based on the perception of invariable concomitance between a probans and a probandum. If paśyantī be imperceptible, it cannot also be inferred. Nor can it be proved by testimony, because it is a sentence uttered by a reliable person who has perceived an object. But the Śābdikas hold that paśyantī is not experienced by a person. So testimony cannot prove the existence of paśyantī. The Śābdikas may argue that paśyantī is perceived by self-experience due to meditative trance. Then paśyantī becomes an object of the act of self-experience in the form of meditative trance. But they regard paśyantī as the supreme reality which cannot be an object of the act of trance. He who experiences paśyantī is the supreme Lord Who experiences the omniscient paśyantī. But this admission undermines the doctrine of the Śābdikas who consider paśyantī to be the supreme reality. The Śābdikas may regard a flash of intuition as the means of valid knowledge which proves the reality of paśyantī. A sister has sometimes an intuition 'My brother will come tomorrow'. It is produced by an object, undoubted and uncontradicted; nor is it produced by a cause vitiated by defects. If it is contradicted by a contradictory cognition, then it becomes invalid. Otherwise it is valid. Somānanda refutes the validity of pratibhā. It resembles perceptual apprehension, but it is not perception since the object of perception (e.g., brother) does not exist at the time. The Śābdikas may argue that intuition apprehends a future object as future. But futurity is prior nonexistence. Nonexistence is not related to existence. The Śābdikas may argue that pratibhā is like the intuition 'there is water in the well'. There is no apprehension of its being produced by a nonexistent object or by a future object; and therefore it is valid knowledge. Somānanda refutes this argument by observing that pratibhā is without any cause, and, consequently, of the nature of doubt, and that its doubtful nature is not experienced at the time. 'Is it silver or non-silver?' This is doubt. A person in doubt is not engaged in an action. But a person who has undoubted knowledge is engaged in an action. Hence pratibhā, which is of the nature of doubt, is not valid knowledge, and cannot establish the reality of paśyantī. Pratibhā is not inference because it is not based on the ascertainment of the invariable concomitance of a probans with a probandum according to the Sābdkas. If the invariable concomitance be not determined, it cannot infer the existence of a probandum. If pratibhā be trance due to meditation, it is not always manifested, but is acquired by an expert yogin at some time. Paśyantī is proved by pratibhā at a particular time when it is intuited. But paśyanti is not eternal, if it be apprehended and proved by a discontinuous intuition. But the Śābdhikas regard paśyantī as eternal[58].

The Śābdikas may argue that paśyanti experiences itself through itself always. Somānanda refutes this argument. If paśyantī experience itself through itself, then it cannot be proved in order to convince another person. If paśyanti be self-manifest, another person is not convinced by one's self-experience. Instruction is of the nature of an injunction which enlightens another person on an unknown object. If paśyantī be self-manifest, it cannot communicate its nature to another person who does not know it. If paśyanti do not know itself through apprehension but through itself, then it becomes an object of itself that is said to be proved. If it be proved, it becomes limited; and if it be limited, it ceases to be paśyantī because it is known by its apprehension of its limited nature. If it be an object of its apprehension, it ceases to be self-manifest because manifestation of it by its apprehension becomes predominant. Further, if paśyantī be the object of its apprehension, it becomes impure because all objects of apprehension are impure. But the Śābdikas assume paśyantī to be pure and self-manifest, and all other entities to be false and unreal. Hence paśyantī cannot be established by any person by any means of valid knowledge. If paśyantī be established by some pramāṇa, then that pramāṇa is true, and consequently paśyantī and the pramāṇa which establishes it are true. This position overthrows monism. If the pramāṇa be false, then paśyantī is not established by it.

Some Grammarians hold that there is an unproduced and eternal sound over and above sphoṭas. Somānanda refutes it. The unproduced and eternal sound also cannot be established by any pramāṇa like a sphoṭa. A sound uttered by an unreliable person is equally eternal like a sound uttered by a reliable person, and is equally valid like the latter. Nor can an eternal sound be manifested by a produced sound, because an eternal sound is always of the same nature and cannot be unmanifest or manifest. The Śābdikas may argue that the eternal sound is manifested by a produced sound, even as the eternal ether (ākāśa) is manifested by the ether enclosed by a jar or the like. This argument is not valid because ether is always inferred from its quality (viz., sound) and because it is neither manifested nor perceived.

The Śābdikas may argue that what is created by Śiva according to Śaivaism is equally false and unreal like the objects produced by paśyantī according to the former. Somānanda contends that this argument is not valid because what is created by Śiva according to the Śaivas is of the nature of Him and real. But, according to the Śābdikas, what is produced by paśyantī is unreal due to avidyā. The Śābdikas may argue that paśyantī corresponds to Śiva's power of knowledge. Somānanda refutes it thus. This argument is wrong, because paśyantī is insentient in that it is of the nature of sound, and because sound cannot be Śiva's power of knowledge which is sentient. Further, the Śābdikas regard paśyantī as vocal organ (vāk) and sound which is an object of knowledge. But no system of philosophy identifies a sense-organ with its object. The unproduced and eternal sound cannot be experienced by paśyantī, even as a hand cannot be grasped by it. The supreme subtle sound (parā vāk) is the vocal organ and the supreme reality experienced by paśyantī which is its form. If it were true, then a hand would be grasped by itself. But an organ cannot be its object. So parā vāk cannot be experienced by paśyantī. Further, paśyantī is an action ; it is an act of seeing or experiencing, and so has prior and posterior parts. First there is a volition to create an object (e.g., a jar), which is prior to the act of seeing or experiencing. The volition cannot act to create an object without prior intentness (aunmukhya) of the Self on creation of such an object and the knowledge of it. Thus there is a sequence of volition, knowledge and action, which depends upon and is known by Śiva or the Self. Hence paśyantī is Śiva's power of knowledge, but not a vocal organ or an eternal sound. Paśyantī of the nature of a word or a sound cannot take the place of Śiva. If paśyantī of such a nature be the supreme reality, then a jar or the like may be the supreme reality. Paśyantī is a word or the vocal organ, and is a product of Śiva's māyāśakti, which is of the nature of nonapprehension of nondifference. It is a motor organ full of difference and belongs to the lowest order or māyā. Hence the supreme subtle sound (parā vāk) or the experiencing sound (paśyantī) cannot be the supreme reality. But subtle and gross sounds are creations of Śiva and of the nature of Him like other created objects through His māyāśakti. Power of māyā arises from Śiva, and is of the nature of nonapprehension of nondifference from Him.[59]

OBJECTIONS REFUTED.—It is objected that if all existents be of the nature of Śiva, He becomes mutable, insentient, composed of parts, dependent on other entities, pure and impure, higher and lower, perishable, and leads to collapse of practical life, but that He is said to be immutable, conscious, partless, independent, pure, supreme, imperishable, and not to cancel practical life. Śiva is of the nature of pure consciousness and devoid of increase and decrease. If earth, water and the like were of the nature of Śiva, He would be modified into them, and if He assumed their forms, He would become insentient and composed of parts like them, and depend upon other entities for being produced and experienced by other experients. If He were modified into the elements, as milk is modified into curd, He would become pure and impure, higher and lower. If an effect were nonexistent in its cause, the cause would be destroyed in order to produce an effect, and Śiva, the cause, would be destroyed when He produced the elements. If all objects were of the nature of Śiva, we would walk upon Him, spit upon Him, and do such acts as would entail atonement for our sins, and in this way our practical life would cease. Further, if all existents were of the nature of Śiva, bondage and liberation would become nonexistent, the scriptures teaching the means of attaining liberation from bondage would become meaningless, all would be liberated and dispense with instructions, and the Deities and the spiritual teachers would become unnecessary. Further, Śiva being devoid of kārma mala, He would not produce dharma and adharma. He would not be the cause of individual souls' voluntary actions, since false knowledge, attachment, etc., are their causes. Thus dharma prescribed by the Śaivas would become useless. Besides, there would be no distinction among the efficient cause, the inherent cause, and the noninherent cause of an effect, since they are all of the nature of Śiva. All persons would become omnipotent, omniscient, and eternally liberated. There being no distincion between good and evil, there would be no distinction between worshippers and the worshipped, disciples and teachers, means and ends, and there would be an excess of materialism. All being liberated, none would require instructions about the scriptures. Moreover, if Śiva imagined Himself to be the elements, He would be possessed of imagination. But He is devoid of imagination, for Śaivism, since vikalpas are of the nature of avidyā in that different objects are nonexistent. If Śivatattva be devoid of imagination, He is possessed of apprehension, and apprehension is not false or does not know a nonexistent object. He apprehends either His Self or another self, an unapprehended entity or an apprehened entity. There is a distinction between an apprehender and an apprehened object. This difference will give rise to many difficulties. Further, if Śiva's volition be the cause of an effect, then another volition of Him is the cause of another effect. Different effects are produced by different causes. This means that different effects are produced by different volitions of Śiva according to Śaivaism. What are the causes of His different volitions ? Furthermore, if all existents be of the nature of Śiva, then they are equally true or real. But the Śaiva scriptures sometimes declare them to be false and unreal like magic shows. Thus the Śaiva doctrine of all existents being in the nature of Śiva contradicts the Śaiva scriptures, and comes into conflict with the other systems.

Somānanda and Utpaladeva refute the above objections in the following manner. If Śiva were gross, He would be modified into the elements, as milk is modified into curd. If He were subtle, He would be modified into them, as māyā and prakṛti are modified into them. But He is of the nature of pure consciousness, and neither gross nor subtle, since material things alone are either gross or subtle, and since they are modified into gross and extended objects. He cannot be modified into them, since He is of the nature of pure consciousness. He creates the elements by his sheer fiat of will, even as yogins can create them by their mere volitions. He does not create them by modifying Himself into them. They are His creations at His will, and not modifications of Himself; they come into existence just after His volitions. There is difference of superior, mediocre and inferior entities among His creations, as there is such distinction in the creations of the yogins. Or, there is a distinction between Śiva and the universe, as there is a distinction between an ocean and its waves despite their identity. The divinity of the universe is not destroyed, even as water does not lose its nature as water when it becomes a wave. Unmoving water is unqualified, and moving water is qualified. Similarly, Śiva in His acosmic form is unqualified, and He in His cosmic form is qualified. Thus even in the state of an existent its divinity persists.[60] Hence Śiva does not become insentient and composed of parts, as a yogin does not become insentient and composed of parts by creating different objects by mere volitions. The elements created by Śiva by His mere volition are neither insentient nor produced out of māyā and prakṛti which are insentient because they are His particular volitions, like the objects created by a yogin by his mere volitions. (Martineau : atoms are standing volitions of God.) The defence that they are insentient because they are apprehended as of the nature of 'this' is useless, since what are apprehended as 'this' are not necessarily insentient. Śivatattva is the Self of all existents, and, consequently, not composed of parts. He is the knower of all existents, and so cannot be reduced to them which are known, and which consist of parts. He exists as transcendent of the universe and immanent in it independently through His absolute will. So He is independent of other experients or individual souls. Because He creates existents by His will, He does not depend upon other entities for doing so. If He were modified into them, even as milk is modified into curd, He would become insentient and subject to increase and decrease, purity and impurity. But He does not cease to be conscious at any time, and His consciousness is not modified into insentient existents. So He does not become insentient, impure, less and the like. His nature is not divided into different existents, but He creates them by His mere volition. They are all alike of the nature of Śiva. But there is a distinction among them for the purpose of empirical life only. It is an imaginary distinction of mere names for practical purposes. Practical actions are not nescience as Śaṁkara and others hold. Śiva exists as practical actions through His volition. They are not another entity called avidyā. He exists as practical actions for the purpose of common people's empirical life. He creates them and persists in them. There is no difference of His nature in them. The scriptures do not make any distinction in Śivatattva existing in them. They simply give instructions about purification relating to our practical actions. They being only particular volitions of Śiva, they do not make any real difference in Śivatattva nor make Him impure. He does not lose His real nature when He assumes forms filled with His powers. What is the cause of Śiva's passing from an acosmic state to a cosmic state ? The question does not arise because in the acosmic state He is Śiva and because in the cosmic state He is Śiva. His acosmic state is real ; what is real is existent ; existence is being ; being is agency of being ; agency is freedom of Śiva of the nature of consciousness and possessed of the powers of volition, knowledge and action. Action is of the nature of agency ; an agent is free and conscious because freedom is voluntary action according to one's free will. Hence, wherever there is being there is will to be ; will to be depends upon knowledge. Created entities depend upon, and are of the nature of, Śiva possessed of the powers of volition, knowledge and action. How can difference among existents exist in uniform and nondifferent Śiva of the nature of pure consciousness ? Somānanda replies that the mutual difference among the existents also is of the nature of Śiva. All are of the nature of Śiva, and differences among them also are of the nature of Śiva. The power of an existent is nothing but the power of Śiva ; power and a potent being are nondifferent from each other. Hence all existents and their differences are nothing but Śiva since they are of the nature of pure consciousness.[61] It is objected that all entities being of the nature of Śiva, Śaivism cannot account for the usefulness of spiritual teachers and the scriptures. To this objection Somānanda replies that Śiva Himself becomes a spiritual teacher as omniscient and enlightened by His volition, and that He Himself becomes a bound soul by His volition by assuming contraction, and receives instructions and is enlightened by His volition. He gives instuctions through the scriptures by His volition, and He receives instructions by His volition. He becomes the means by His volition, and He becomes the end by His volition. It is objected that all entities being of the nature of Śiva, virtue and vice cannot differ from each other. To this objection Somānanda replies that virtue which realises the good is created by Śiva by His volition and is of His nature, and that vice which realises evil is created by Śiva by His volition and is of His nature. Both are His creations and their difference also is His creation. All entities which are apprenhended by our consciousness are of the nature of Śiva or universal consciousness. This absolute voluntarism is tantamount to pantheism and negation of human freedom. It is objected that all entities being of the nature of Śiva, an efficient cause, an inherent cause, and a noninherent cause do not differ from one another. To this objection Somānanda replies that an efficient cause (e. g., a weaver), an inherent cause (e. g., threads), and a noninherent cause (e. g., conjunction of threads) are created by Śiva's volitions, and that they differ from one another, although they are alike His volitions, even as a king's commands differ from one another, although they are alike his commands. Utpaladeva accounts for their difference in two other ways. Śiva Himself is the efficient cause ; His volition is the inherent cause ; His volition in the form of conjunction of the parts of an entity is the noninherent cause. Or, although Śiva is one, He becomes threefold, an efficient cause, an inherent cause, and a noninherent cause for the purpose of empirical use which is of the nature of nonapprehension of nondifference.[62] It is objected that gross elements being imagined by Śiva, He is endowed with imagination. To this objection Somānanda replies that Śivatattva does exist in gross elements, and that they are imagined in the sense that their real nature as Śivatattva is not apprehended by bound souls. He creates gross elements by His volition. Hence they are real and should not be said to be imaginary. They do not differ from one another in being of the nature of Śiva. It is objected that all entities being of the nature of Śiva according to Śaivism, there is no difference between its proponent and opponent. Somānanda refutes this objection by asserting that the difference between them is intended for empirical use, which is not based on ontological reality, but which is based on nonapprehension of nondifference. Empirical life is based on appearances of Śiva, empirical differences, subjects and objects. Although they are unreal, they appear to be real and are illusory. Even nonentities are of the nature of Śiva as appearances. Śivatattva of the nature of pure consciousness and experience of the universe is not like paśyantī vāk—experiencing Logos. He experiences existents of the nature of names and objects named, devoid of space, time, and temporal order, and is devoid of the cognition of difference because He manifests them as perfect 'I'. Although He has the experience of 'I', He is devoid of the cognition of difference, even as a perfumer experiences a large number of scents without experiencing their specific scents. The experience of 'I' being of the nature of Logos or supreme speech is not the cognition of difference. What is of the nature of the light of consciousness or manifestation has no counterentity different from it. No entity different from it is manifested by it. It is objected that the state of Śiva before the commencement of any particular knowledge and action and after their cessation is devoid of experience and insentient because it is devoid of the power of volition and the like. Somānanda replies that this objection is baseless, since Śiva is never devoid of all powers and insentient. He is always endowed with the powers of volition, knowledge and action in a subtle state. So there is no difference in Him. He is not powerless after the completion of one action and the commencement of another action. After the completion of one action He has another volition with a distinct cognition of another object of action. He has never any state of powerlessness. His experience never ceases. It presupposes a prior volition to experience. His experience is in the form of 'I am', and is always manifested since unmanifested experience is not possible. Hence it is not insentient. It is objected that stones and the like being of the nature of Śiva, He becomes insentient. Somānanda observes that Śiva is not insentient, although stones are of the nature of Śiva and appear to be different from Him because of nonapprehension of nondifference. One volition of Śiva being accomplished, He initiates and accomplishes another volition. His powers always exist in Him, and He moves on from one volition to another because of their natures, since they are endless. He is absolutely free, and His volition is not determined by any other cause. The endlessness of His new volitions follows from His absolute freedom. The delight of His ever new volitions to experience His inexhaustible wealth of spiritual perfection is the cause of the endlessness of His volitions. It is objected that if all existents are of the nature of Śiva, then this view contradicts the assertion of the Āgama that the univease is unreal like a bubble. Somānanda replies that it is aimed at inculcating dispassion for the transient world and its really being of the nature of one universal consciousness. The statement that all existents are Śiva does not prove that they are many Śivas. Śiva is not of the nature of a jar and the like, but they are of the nature of Śiva. He is of the nature of one pure consciousness, and does not differ owing to the absence of the difference of space, time and nature.[63]

SPIRITUAL CULTURE : 1. WORKS.—The monistic Śaivas describe a few acts of spiritual discipline for advanced aspirants. Initiation is necessary for entering upon the way of realisation of the highest reality. It consists in imparting knowledge of Ātman to another person, and breaking his fetters. Both a master and a disciple should be eligible. Kṣemarāja avers that a person, who has acquired command over the powers of the Lord, can enlighten a disciple by his power of knowledge. Bhaṭṭa Bhāskara also avers that a person, who has acquired the knowledge of Ātman due to the descent of divine powers, is competent to initiate a disciple. Rāmakaṇṭha avers that the Lord is the supreme Master, Who initiates a disciple, through a human master (guru), by granting His grace, and making His divine power descend upon him. A disciple should have earnest desire to be free of his fetters. Abhinavagupta regards a vow as relishing the experience of identity in the perception of difference in the world. Yogirāja explains a vow as firmness in the experience of identity acquired by repeatedly listening to scriptural testimony, reasoning on monistic texts, and intuiting identity in the midst of difference in such a form as 'I am manifested in all this'. It is the experience of one divine consciousness as perfect 'I'-consciousness, the essence of differences, with a flash of delight. Kṣemarāja regards a vow as maintenance of the body with the experience 'I am Śiva'. Bhaṭṭa Bhāskara regards a vow as abiding in one's Ātman without any hindrance and as feeling a vibration of the Lord in one's bodily actions. Varadarāja regards a vow as maintaining the body for service of one's self, which is identical with the Supreme Self, Śiva, with devotion to Him. An aspirant constantly prays for the maintenance of his body as a vehicle for the experience of Śiva, and of pure devotion to Him surging from the heart. Charity consists in discarding the nature of a limited self and assuming the nature of Śiva-Śakti of the nature of infinite consciousness. The highest gift is the gift of one's self to Ātman—Śiva (ātmadāna). The self should be completely dedicated to Śiva (ātmanivedana). The experience of His nature is the result of the offering of all works performed without any desire for fruits to Him. Somānanda regards ablution as purification by knowing one's bondge and release both to be taints, and as delight due to the experience 'I am the universe full of infinite consciousness' in happiness or misery. He regards worship as that of Śiva as nondifferent from one's self, for worship, a worshipper, and the worshipped are He. Abhinavagupta regards worship as the experience of Śiva as the only ontotogical reality. Chanting hymns, offering oblations to a sacrificial fire, making obeisance to a Deity, and the other acts of devotion are not necessary for an aspirant, who has acquired integral knowledge of identity, since they depend upon the knowledge of difference. He is replete with perennial bliss, and does not take delight in artificial joy derived from chanting, sacrifice, or obeisance. There being none besides Śiva, there is none to make obeisance to. A sacrifice, for Somānanda, is the experience of delight in all forms,—the experience 'I am Śiva', the sacrificer and the Lord to Whom a sacrifice is made—the experience that the place of sacrifice and the instruments and material of sacrifice are 'I' or Śiva. Offering oblations to a sacrificial fire, for him, is the experience 'I am desireless and perfectly contented Śiva', and the knowledge of all existents as the forms of Śiva. Abhinavagupta regards offering oblations to a sacrificial fire as consuming the subconscious impressions of all desires (vāsanā) in the fire of Śiva-Śakti with the molten butter of supreme love for all, and offering the knowledge of external and internal differences to the blazing fire of one universal consciousness. It is consuming the seeds of external and internal differences in the blazing fire of the integral experience of Śiva. Yogirāja explains it as consuming the difference of subjects and objects in the fire of the experience of perfect 'I'-consciousness replete with a flash of delight without any effort. An aspirant enters into one universal consciousness because of the destruction of his false conceit of identity with his body, vital forces, buddhi and the like. Abhinavagupta regards meditation as contemplating that Śiva Himself always creates diverse forms in the mirror of buddhi, and that there are no entities other than manifestation of divine power. Yogirāja explains all forms as pictures painted in the scene of divine consciousness, and all mental modes as unfoldment of supreme divine power. Somānanda regards meditation as the experience 'I am Śiva' in all forms and all thoughts. He regards repeated muttering of the Lord's name or mantra (japa) as the continuous experience 'I am all and create all by volition' while uttering it. Abhinavagupta regards japa as transforming all principles, worlds, and sense-organs into the internal experience of perfect

'I'-consciousness, and as recognising their identity with it every moment. Yogirāja observes that such transformation can be effected by controlling the vital force in Suṣumnā, by awakening divine power (Kuṇḍalinī), making Her ascend through it, and unite with Parama Śiva in Sahasrāra. Japa is the recognition of the universe as nondifferent from perfect 'I'-consciousness every moment. The uttering of a mantra, a signifier, awakens the Deity signified by it, and makes the vital force in the form of a thread vibrate and sound in Suṣumnā, pervade the universe, and transform it into perfect 'I'-consciousness. The process refers to the esoteric practice of yoga according to monistic Śaiva Tantras. Kṣemarāja regards it as continuous repetition of the experience of perfect 'I'-consciousness, which is the essence of a mantra. Vasugupta defines japa as muttering a mantra. Kallaṭa explains it as continuous transformation of the universe into the spontaneous 'I'-consciousness for a mantra of Śiva is full of contemplation of perfect 'I'-consciousness. Bhaṭṭa Bhāskara recognises four kinds of japa : sākta, haṁsa, paudgala, and niṣkala. Breathing goes on 26000 times in 24 hours in a person. This is called paudgala or ajapā. Haṁsa is of the nature of nāda—a subtle sound—heard in the heart-centre not due to the impact of two sounding bodies. Niṣkala is the utterance of 'Aum' or 'Om'. Śākta is the experience of one's self as perfect 'I' or Supreme Lord. Varadarāa regards japa as meditating on the Supreme Lord resulting in the manifestation of nāda expressing divine power—the essence of a mantra. Constant japa or meditation on Him inverts the outgoing vital current, and turns it into the experience—'I am He' (so'ham). Japa is so called because it creates and sustains the universe.[54]

2. DEVOTION.—Rāmakaṇṭha, a disciple of Utpaladeva, gives a monistic account of the nature of devotion. It is the worship of Ātman, or the Lord, or a Deity by meditating on Him as of the nature of Brahman or nondual transcendental consciousness. When it reaches the highest stage of immediate experience of the nature of the Lord, it is called integral knowledge (vijñāna). Supreme devotion is the result of the knowledge of all entities as nondifferent from the nature of the Lord. The highest knowledge of the nature of immediate experience of absolute nondualism itself is the highest devotion. So Rāmakaṇṭha identifies the highest knowledge with the highest devotion. Abhinavagupta avers that Parama Śiva's divine power (Śakti) should be worshipped with supreme devotion, and the worshipper's self should be dedicated to Her. Worship requires supreme devotion, self-dedication, self-surrender, and self-consecration. Devotion is humility of a devotee's mind fit for entering into identity with the divine power, that creates the difference between a worshipper, worship and the worshipped Deity, Śakti is the supreme end, absolutely free, entirely different from insentient entities because of Her absolute freedom, and full of transcendental consciousness. Self-dedication is complete dedication to Ātman, for there is no other reality. Worship is the apprehension of the pure, ontological nature of Śiva. Self-offering is offering of a limited self and all belonging to it to Śiva-Śakti of the nature of absolute consciousness. A sacrifice is consuming all seeds of subconscious dispositions in the fire of Śiva-Śakti ready to consume the fuel of all entities. Devotion consists in transcending bodily, vital, and mental consciousness, and merging the limited soul in the Absolute Consciousness. Supreme devotion consists in acquiring the certain knowledge of identity of

one's soul with all--the Absolute. (Cp. Vallabha's concept of becoming all). Worship with supreme devotion and self-dedication should be continued until the limited soul is purified of all taints and identified with Śiva-Śakti—integral reality.[65]

3. YOGA.—Somānanda regards yoga as offering all acts—walking, sitting, running, eating, etc., to Śiva, and as thinking 'I am all beings', and 'all entities are created by my volition by unfolding my powers'. The Śaiva monists describe some acts of yoga for advanced yogins. Posture, according to Varadarāja, consists in discarding the fixation of mind on certain parts of the body, meditation and other acts of yoga, in abiding in identity with Śiva-Śakti of the nature of universal consciousness and power, in being immersed in the Great Lake already explained, and in drowning 'this'-consciousness in the infinite 'I'-consciousness. In this state a soul identifies itself with the Divine, destroys delusion, acquires pure knowledge (śuddhavidyā) owing to excess of immersion in Śiva-Śakti, and assimilates divine bliss. Varadarāja regards breath-control as equilibrating prāṇa flowing upward through Iḍā and apāṇa flowing downward through Piṅgalā, pushing udāna upward through Suṣumnā, rousing coiled divine power (Kuṇḍālinī) at Mūlādhāra, carrying Her upward through Svādhiṣṭhāna, Maṇipūra, Anāhata, Viśuddha, and Ājñācakra, uniting Her with Parama Śiva in Sahasrāra, and identifying one's limited consciousness with universal consciousness. It consists in first equilibrating prāṇa with apāṇa, then discarding the control of gross vital forces, then controlling the subtle vital force in Suṣumnā, and then acquiring extremely subtle supreme vibration of divine power. A yogin, who practises the last kind of breath-control, does not fall from his union with the supreme power of universal consciousness. Varadarāja regards withdrawal as drawing the mind away from external objects, and entering into the supreme abode of the Lord. It is entrance of a soul's limited consciousness into universal consciousness, which breaks the fetters of bondage. Varadarāja regards fixation as fixing the mind on the Supreme Ātman, which releases a soul from bondage. He regards trance as the sense of equality in all beings, and as the experience 'I am Śiva without a second'. Meditation has already been explained. All acts of yoga from breath-control to trance lead to complete inmersion in the Supreme Reality.[66]

4. KNOWLEDGE.—Vasugupta says, "Knowledge is food." Kallaṭa explains knowledge (jñāna) as a soul's recognition of one's nature as 'I'-consciousness, which is its food because it generates complete fulfilledness, and because it is the cause of resting in one's Ātman. Bhaṭṭa Bhāskara explains knowledge as supreme knowledge of Śiva, which is the means of supreme contentment and perfection. Varadarāja observes that when a yogin is firmly established in the experience of Śiva of the nature of perfect manifestation, his causal body, subtle body, and gross body due to potencies of actions are consumed in the fire of this knowledge, and he acquires a divine body, which is pervasive and composed of pure consciousness. So long as he lives, his three bodies are permeated by the knowleege that he is Śiva—the Supreme Knower. When his pure knowledge (śuddhavidyā) is eclipsed, he perceives empirical differences, which are like dreams. Just as dreams are destroyed by waking perceptions, so the perception of differences is destroyed by the knowledge of nondifferent, universal consciousness.[67]

A bound soul is released from bondage by meditating on Parama Śiva, and becomes the Lord of the world, like Sadāśiva. A soul in bondage has knowledge implying the distinction of subjects and objects. But a yogin is attentive to their relation to Ātman, knows them to be 'I', and experiences the bliss of trance. A bound soul delights in external insentient objects and physical pleasures. But a yogin delights in his Ātman within and the bliss of trance. Ātman is Parama Śiva, Supreme 'I', universal consciousness, dynamic 'I'-consciousness—Integral 'Self-consciousness distinguished from vital ego, mental ego, empirical, limited ego, or egoism.

A yogin who delights in Ātman freely in the waking state, dream, and deep sleep is called a prince of yogins (vīreśa) or heroes. He rests in Ātman or Parama Śiva, experiences his identity with Him, and delights in the bliss of ecstasy (turīya). He experiences identity-consciousness devoid of difference in the three states, bliss of identity-consciousness as the result of concentration at the centres of mystic consciousness (cakra), and of meditation on the ether of transcendental consciousness at the heart-centre, and a flash of transcendental wonder and delight. He experiences all knowers and objects, and is yet not attached to them. He becomes autonomous and unrivalled in spiritual powers and wealth. His sense-organs become almost inoperative owing to his experience of unique supreme bliss even when he experiences their objects. He is not contented with the experience of Ātman—Supreme Self—common to all stages of the experience of ecstasy. He gradually rises to the higher stages of ecstasy, and reaches the highest stage of superecstasy (turīyātīta) resting in Ātman. The bliss of ecstasy is delight in abiding in the state of the Supreme Knower in the midst of the knowledge of empirical subjects and objects[68]. When a yogin practises ecstasy for a long period, and when he acquires excellence in it, he transcends ecstasy, and acquires superecstasy. He become *like* Śiva of the nature of translucent, infinite consciousness and absolute freedom and bliss because his body continues. When his body is dissolved, he *becomes* Śiva. He achieves embodied liberation in life, and disembodied liberation after death[69] (Cp. Śaṁkara).

Parama Śiva's power of creative will is called Virgin Umā, the divine power of His absolute freedom engaged in the sportive acts of creating, maintaining, and dissolving the universe. A prince of yogins experiences his internal states and external objects as parts of himself, and not as different from him. When he is completely absorbed in and identified with Umā, he acquires a body according to Her or the Lord's creative will, and acquires supernormal powers. He can perceive objects remote in time and space, separate physical elements from one another, appease all afflictions of the body like diseases, foster animate and inanimate beings, and acquire the experience of being identical with the world if he desires to do so. Supreme fulfilment is within his power. He can acquire the status of the Lord of the circle of divine powers, if he applies his powers with a view to experiencing his identity with the Supreme Self of the universe. When he acquires the pure knowledge (śuddhavidyā) of his identity with the universe, he attains to the status of supreme lordship (cacreśa). In the plane of śuddhavidyā—pure knowledge 'I am the universe'—'I'-consciousness and 'this'-conciousness abide in the same substratum. When the pure knowledge of the supreme nondual consciousness emerges, the pure ether of consciousness called khecarī mudrā is manifested. It is the state of the Absolute[70].

Impure knowledge is the empirical knowledge of difference, finite knowledge, false knowledge of various determinations (vikalpa) called dream from the standpoint of the Absolute. It is incomplete, imperfect, inferior knowledge. When a yogin disregards the supernatural powers which accrue to him unsought, and when he resorts to śuddhavidyā, he achieves supreme fulfilment. An advanced yogin should discard the gross means of breath-control and the like implying the knowledge of difference, enter into his essential consciousness with his mind purged of the taint of difference, and immerse his nature as a limited knower identified with his mind-body-complex in ecstasy—inner consciousness permeated with a flash of delight. Gradually when his buddhi enters into the supreme status, his vital forces are purified by immersion in the unfolding divine Śakti, and he experiences nondifference because of his becoming of the nature of transcendental consciousness and bliss. Until he becomes independent of his mind-body-complex, he cannot acquire the pure knowledge of nondifference. When he transcends bodily, vital, and mental consciousness, he acquires the saving knowledge of nondifference.

A bound soul overcome by delusion is tainted with merits and demerits, and has knowledge of difference because of its false egoism. When Śiva's divine power of grace descends on a bound soul, its false conceit of ego-sense is destroyed, its consequent knowledge of difference is removed, its innate freedom is manifested, and it acts in a higher order of creation. Its knowledge of difference due to kāla, vidyā, rāga, kalā, and niyati, the five coverings (kañcūka)—products of the power of māyā—is eclipsed, and it rises to a higher plane. The power of freedom is the essence of a knower, which is veiled by māyā. When māyā is destroyed by Śiva's power of grace, its innate power of freedom is manifested, it attains to the state of ecstasy replete with delight, and abides in it constantly. Ecstasy permeates its waking state, dream, and deep sleep, which assume the forms of creation, maintenance, and dissolution. It is the state of delight in Ātman and detachment from all external objects. A yogin's power of freedom of the nature of Self-delight can create objects at his will. When his āṇava mala and kārma mala—atomicity and merits and demerits—are destroyed by the Lord's grace, his desires for external objects are destroyed, his subtle body with which he identifies himself is attenuated, and he attains to the state of self-completeness and self-delight.[71]

A yogin, who rules over the powers, and who is like Śiva, experiences that the universe is the unfoldment of his powers, that its creation is the manifestation of his power of action, that its maintenance is the continuance of its manifestation outward, that its dissolution is the involution of his power of manifestating the universe and its resting in the Supreme Knower of the nature of transcendental consciousness. He does not lapse from his experience of ecstasy full of perfect 'I'-consciousness of the nature of transcendent wonder and delight in the midst of its creation, maintenance and dissolution full of difference. He is not affected by pleasure and pain, for he ceases to identify himself with his subtle body. He does not consider them to be 'mine', but considers them to be 'this'-consciousness or external objects. A yogin, who is completely freed of the experience of pleasure and pain, and of their subconscious impressions, becomes a free knower of the nature of pure consciousness. Pure consciousness is supramental, transcendental consciousness.[72]

A yogin whose volition is identical with Śiva's power of absolute freedom, experiences his body as a known object, like a jar, a lifeless thing, wherewith he does not identify his self. A known object appears to him like a body, and his body appears to him like a known object. His internal cognitions and external objects, which are known, appear to him like parts of his self, and not as different from him. As his mind is concentrated at the heart-centre on Ātman, the universe is experienced by him like dream-cognitions. The binding power of delusion due to nescience is destroyed in him. So he experiences the universe including his body as full of the Lord, and becomes the ruler of the universe, like Sadāśiva.[73]

NESCIENCE AND TRUE KNOWLEDGE.—Utpaladeva regards nescience (ajñāna) as the knowledge of difference, and true knowledge (jñāna) as the knowledge of nondifference or identity. Nescience is due to nonapprehension of nondifference. It is the knowledge of a limited knower wrongly identified with his mind-body-complex, relating to different objects, and producing practical actions. His congnitions of different objects have empirical validity since they lead to successful actions, but they have no ontological validity since they do not cognise the ontological reality—one universal consciousness or the Absolute. When an empirical knower recognises his identity with Śiva, his false egoism is destroyed, and he is liberated. Varadarāja defines nescience as false knowledge of self as not-self and not-self as self, and true knowledge as recognition of one's identity with Śiva. Nescience is knowledge of difference due to māyā. True knowledge is knowledge of supreme nondifference (Cp. Śaṁkara). Bhaṭṭa Bhāskara regards nescience as false knowledge of 'I' and 'mine' in the mind-body-complex, as knowledge of difference interpenetrated with words or verbal images due to māyīa mala, and as bondage characterised by the veiling of reality. He regards true knowledge as supreme knowledge of nondifference, which destroys the knowledge of difference.

Abhinavagupta avers that nescience (ajñāna) is the cause of bondage and that true knowledge (jñāna) is the only cause of liberation. A taint (mala) is nescience and the seed of birth and death. Jayaratha avers that nescience is of the nature of incomplete knowledge, āṇava mala, false conceit of self in not-self, and of not-self in self, and not a substance. Nescience is of two kinds : self-nescience (pauruṣa) and buddhi-nescience (bauddha). Self-nescience is nescience in an individual self (puruṣa). Buddhi-nescience is nescience in buddhi. Self-nescience is the cause of bondage. Buddhi is an internal organ produced after self's embodied life. So nescience in buddhi is not the cause of bondage. When nescience in self is removed by initiation, it is independently the cause of liberation. It is said, "Bonds in a self are purified by initiation, and not those in buddhi. Even if bonds in buddhi persist, initiation is not infructuous." A self is really of the nature of mere knowledge. Complete knowledge is the absolute negation of nonapprehension itself, that is the real nature of Ātman,—a mass of manifestation and bliss. Liberation is the apprehension of this real nature of a self, or its Śivahood.[74]

It is asked why nescience is not mere absence of knowledge, but incomplete knowledge. Abhinavagupta replies that if nescience were mere absence of knowledge, even a stone and the like would have nescience and be bound. So nescience is defined as incomplete knowledge (apūrṇa jñāna). Vasugupta says, "Knowledge is bondage". Here knowledge means positive incomplete knowledge or knowledge of an object in its partial aspect. 'This is blue'. 'This is pleasure'. These cognitions are of the nature of apprehension of duality or difference and so incomplete. 'The real nature of known objects is Śiva of the nature of manifestation. So the aforesaid cognitions are nescience or incomplete knowledge. Vasugupta says, "Consciousness is Ātman." Abhinavagupta avers that the positive word 'consciousness' (caitanya) means mere freedom (svātantrya) devoid of any distinctive characters. In Vasugupta's aphorism 'knowledge is bondage' knowledge means an act of knowledge or an organ of knowledge. It means knowledge of duality of mere consciousness. Apprehension of duality is nescience because it is false, and so it ought to be destroyed. Jayaratha avers that the act of consciousness is common to all cognitions. Ātman has complete act of knowledge. The quality of possessing the complete act of knowledge is consciousness. That is called the nature of supreme lordship or freedom, So it is mere freedom, Eternity, ubiquity, etc., are its distinctive features (viśeṣa). 'Knowledge' in Vasugupta's second aphorism means the act of knowledge by which an object is known. It makes a distinction between a knowing self, act of knowledge, and an object of knowledge. It refers to different factors involved in knowledge, and does not describe its complete form (pūrṇarūpa). Here 'knowledge' is apprehension of duality—incomplete knowledge. It is incomplete because of its incompleteness. It is not complete for it does not apprehend Ātman of the nature of nondual consciousness, which is its real nature. This incomplete knowledge is stained by three taints, and contracted by good and evil dispostions, and forms of body and objects. So it is called bondage. Because it is of the nature of bondage it should be eradicated.[75]

Abhinavagupta divides nescience into two kinds : nescience in buddhi and nescience in a soul, and true knowledge into two kinds : true knowledge in buddhi and true knowledge in a soul. Soul-nescience (pauruṣa ajñāna) produces a taint, which veils the soul's Śivahood of the nature of omniscience and omnipotence. It is indeterminate knowledge of the bound soul, of the nature of contracting knowledge and action. But buddhi-nescience (bauddha ajñāna) is determinate, since determination is the function of buddhi. Buddhi-nescience is of the form 'I know this'. This kind of knowledge produced by the relation of a knowing self and a knowable object is called nescience ; it arises in buddhi owing to reflection of nescience in a soul limited by atomicity (āṇava mala) and contracted by its five coverings. When the atomic, bound soul's impurities are destroyed, and when it attains to the state of Śiva, its soul-knowledge expands, becomes ubiquitous and indeterminate. When soul-nescience is destroyed by initiation, ubiquitous, indeterminate knowledge of Ātman is distinctly manifested after death. When buddhi-knowledge destroys buddhi-nescience, embodied release is achieved. Buddhi-knowledge arises from listening to scripture teaching nonduality of the Lord. Initiation too prior to buddhi-knowledge contributes to release. So buddhi-knowledge produced by listening to monistic scripture has a prime importance. It is not mere intellectual comprehension of scripture but a spiritual discipline. When buddhi-knowledge is produced, buddhi-nescience is destroyed, and the knowledge of being liberated arises in buddhi. This state is embodied liberation. Soul-nescience is destroyed by initiation, but the soul's inner state of freedom from its atomicity is not known until buddhi is purified and until buddhi-knowledge arises. So long as the body continues, false conceit of identity of a soul with body and buddhi persists. If soul-nescience were already not removed by initiation, liberation would not be achieved even after death. When buddhi-nescience is removed, all determinations (vikalpa) of buddhi are eradicated, and liberation is achieved.[76]

BONDAGE AND LIBERATION.—Somānanda opines that difference being due to Śiva's volition and as such being of His nature, there is no difference between bondage and release. There being no real bondage, there is no real release, which depends upon prior bondage. Bondage and release are only phenomenal appearances, and not ontologically real. (Cp. Śaṁkara). Utpaladeva opines that embodied life is called bondage characterised by nescience. Somānanda thinks of bondage and release as mere experiences (pratīti). Utpaladeva thinks of liberation as mere experience of nondifference from Śiva, and of bondage as nonexperience of this nondifference. Śiva at His will assumes the state of bondage and release of the nature of mere experiences of difference and nondifference. Difference is of the nature of Śiva. So there is no real bondage, and in its absence there is no release. It may be objected that, all being of the nature of Śiva, bondage and liberation are not different from each other, and that therefore every person should know 'I am Śiva.' Somānanda replies that bondage is of the nature of nescience, and that liberation is of the nature of true knowledge. In bondage there is no firm knowledge that all existents are of the nature of Śiva endowed with the powers of volition, knowledge and action. In liberation there is firm knowledge that they are of such a nature. Firm knowledge or immediate experience of the nondifference of all existents from Śiva is liberation. The absence of such knowledge is bondage. Nonapprehension of nondifference is bondage. Apprehension of nondifference is liberation. It may be objected that even if bondage and liberation be of the nature of Śiva, Śaivism ought to prove that they are of the nature of experience, and that if they are of the nature of Śiva, they should not be spoken of as different from each other. Somānanda refutes the objection by observing that Śaivaism proves that all existents are of the nature of one Śiva, but that it does not disprove that they are one or many. All being of the nature of Śiva, whether they be one or many does not involve any conflict. Śaivism advocates monism, and holds that all existents are of the nature of one Śiva, that no existent is better than any other, and that no existent is worse than any other. To assert the existents to be one or many is to admit their independence. But Śaivism denies this, and admits the existence of one Śiva alone. There is no difference between bondage and liberation in reality, since both are of the nature of Śiva. There being no bondage, there is no release from it.[77]

Abhinavagupta avers that there is no abode of release nor movement of a soul to another region, but that release is manifestation of a soul's own power of breaking the knot of nescience. He believes in embodied release. When the knot of nescience is broken asunder, all doubts are dispelled, all false knowledge is destroyed, merits and demerits are worn out, and a soul is released even in embodied life. Merits and demerits burnt by the fire of knowledge do not produce birth again, even as seeds burnt by a fire do not sprout. Yogirāja expounds Abhinavagupta's view. Liberation is destruction of false conceit of 'I' in its mind-body-complex, and manifestation of a soul's own powers characterised by freedom of its Ātman. Its consciousness contracted by false conceit is called bound', as it were. When bondage by the mind-body-complex is destroyed by manifestation of a soul's real nature as Ātman, its innate powers expand, and it is called 'released', as it were. So bondage and release are mere false conceits. In Reality—integral consciousness—nothing new is accomplished; Its own nature is manifested. So a soul, that has acquired the saving knowledge, and whose limitation by nescience has been destroyed, is released, though it continues to exist in an embodied state for bestowing grace on others. Nescience is false conceit of self in not-self due to nonapprehension. It is a knot since it contracts a soul's perfect nature. Its complete freedom, ubiquity, eternity, etc., are contracted by its false conceit due to nescience. The knot of false conceit is broken asunder by firm practice of complete freedom of its Ātman. When the knot is torn, its innate powers expand and it realises its eternity, ubiquity, omniscience and omnipotence. This state is called liberation. It is complete isolation of a soul from its body and experience of its essence, which is æthetic delight of the experience of perfect 'I'. It has no distinct abode for it is not limited by space, time, and form. So there is no movement of a released soul to any abode. It is identical with ubiquitous Absolute consciousness in its real nature. So when it recognises its identity with universal consciouness, it need not go anywhere to realise its essence as supreme 'I'. It may be contended that an embodied soul is bound, and that therefore it cannot be released. Yogirāja observes that this contention is false, since bondage consists in false conceit of the self in the mind-body-complex, and since a soul that has destroyed its nescience, false conceit, merits and demerits, and subconścious potencies of bodily, vital and mental desires, has achieved embodied release despite its connection with a body. It achieves disembodied release after death. Mere connection with a body is not bondage. Its nescience has been burnt by the fire of its knowledge of identity with Śiva, and by the knowledge of identity of the world with Him, and by the experience of its perfect 'I'-consciousness. Its actions do not produce merits and demerits, for it has no desire for their fruits. It has recognised its real nature as free, omnipotent, omniscient Supreme Self immanent in all empirical knowers and of the nature of infinite pure consciousness. It has known that it is not a real doer as an empirical self or ego, or that the supreme divine power of absolute freedom does all actions. So as pure universal consciousness it is not affected by its desireless actions. An action produces a fruit, if an agent has a desire for it, and if he strongly identifies himself with it. But it does not produce a fruit, if an agent has no desire for it, and if he has no false conceit that he is the agent of the action. A released soul is egoless, and has destroyed desires for appropriation of some pleasant objects and rejection of painful objects, and is devoid of the knowledge of difference. It is awakened to the consciousness of its identity with the Absolute, and shines as Ātman. It has transcended the knowledge, of empirical knowers and objects, of the difference of pleasure and pain, become tranquil, and realised its nature as Supreme Self in all creatures, and is released wherever it lives. It is purged of all taints, merits and demerits, and has realised the supreme end. The potencies of actions acquired in this birth are burnt by initiation. Those acquired in past births which have not yet ripened and begun to bear fruits are burnt by the experience of identity with Śiva, and cannot bear fruits. Those which will be acquired in future births are prevented by restraints, moral observances and other acts of yoga. The prārabdha karmans, which have begun to bear fruits, will be worn out by the experience of their fruits in this birth. So after achieving embodied release a soul continues to live an embodied life until the aforesaid potencies are exhausted.[78] Yogirāja opines that Śiva's power of veiling the nature of a bound soul is the cause of its bondage owing to which its nature as Śiva is not manifested, and that it performs moral and immoral actions, experiences pleasures and pains, and transmigrates. His power of granting grace is the cause of its liberation.

Abhinavagupta describes liberation as no other than free Ātman. It has no distinct name from that of Ātman. (Cp. Śaṁkara). What is false is bondage. What is true is Ātman. Jayaratha defines liberation as the knowledge or intuition of Ātman. What is the characteristic of Ātman is the characteristic of liberation. A bound soul is gradually released by removing limitations by lower principles. When these are destroyed, limitations of a self by higher principles persist, and it is reborn in a plane of higher principles after death. When it acquires the highest knowledge of Ātman, free of all limitations by principles (tattva), with absolute freedom and consciousness devoid of distinction, it achieves liberation.[79] Abhinavagupta regards release as nothing over and above the manifestation of the essential nature of a self, and its essence is consciousness of Ātman. Consciousness is the essence of Ātman. True knowledge of it is Its manifestation. The distinction between knowledge and emancipation—means and end—is imaginary, and not real. Powers of actions and the like are nothing distinct from consciousness. If they are conceived to be attributes of an unconscious entity (e. g., self), the reason is unproven, since the existence of the attributes has not been proved. Pratyabhijñā Śaivism does not accept any substrate of the attributes like power of action and the like as Kaṇāda does, and it does not conceive of powers as attributes of a powerful being—a substrate. Kaṇāda thinks of a self as the unconscious substrate of cognition, pleasure, pain, desire, volition, aversion, merits and demerits. Just as there is no difference between a fire and its power of burning, so there is no difference between powerful Ātman and Its powers. So supreme free consciousness is designated as endowed with powers which are mere adjuncts (upādhi). If there were a difference between powers of knowledge and action and Ātman or Śiva, Śaiva monism that Śiva alone is the Reality would be contradicted. The different powers are of the nature of consciousness and freedom. Śiva is endowed with manifold powers nondifferent from Him. So knowledge of Ātman itself is liberation. In fact, there is no cause-effect relation between knowledge and liberation. But one who has acquired intuition of Ātman is certainly released. It is said, 'Knowledge is a means to liberation'. So there is a cause-effect relation between knowledge and liberation. Abhinavagupta opines that the text asserting the aforesaid relation between them is not primary but secondary. An action is of the nature of knowledge, because it cannot exist apart from knowledge. An action is not devoid of knowledge. Different actions and their external objects are not different from knowledge. So liberation is of the nature of knowledge. It is one. The doubt that different means would produce different kinds of liberation is dispelled by the aforesaid reasoning. There is no difference between means and ends. Knowledge of the essence of Ātman is the only means. There being no difference in means, there is no difference in liberation. It is objected that many means have been enjoined in monistic Śaivism. Abhinavagupta replies that though many means have been inculcated, they have the same end, viz., destruction of all taints and their powers. Though there are many causes of the destruction of a jar, the effect is one. So the argument that different means must realise different ends is false. Here the difference between means and end is unreal. So the objection that ends must differ is groundless. The power of volition, the power of action, and the power of knowledge being threefold, liberation—the end—is only one. Śāmbhavopāya, śāktopāya and āṇavopāya already explained result in one liberation.[80]

Abhinavagupta avers that Ātman exists in the state of manifestation of consciousness, that undifferentiated consciousness endowed with manifold powers constitutes Its nature, and that It assumes the form of a bound soul by veiling Its lustre. Its release is brought about by a prescribed method of manifesting Its nature as self-luminous. Manifestation of Ātman is that of consciousness distinct from that of an external object. Consciousness is undivided, of the nature of one, integral manifestation. Infinite powers are innate in Its nature. Though It is one and nondual, and possessed of inconceivable, infinite powers and freedom, It conceals Its omniscience and omnipotence, assumes duality of subjects and objects, and becomes an individual soul. This is called bondage. Liberation is nothing more than manifestation of Ātman's nature as consciousness. It is manifestation of Its lustre characterised by omniscience and omnipotence. Atomicity (āṇava mala) itself is false knowledge—incomplete knowledge in the form of manifestation of difference. It produces flaws in Ātman in the form of false conceit of 'I' in not-self. So pure, complete knowledge becomes impure owing to false knowledge. It is manifested as incomplete knowledge because of Ātman's freedom. When a self knows itself as the Absolute Knower, its knowledge becomes complete. Ātman veils Its nature by false conceit of 'I' in not-self. In reality, there is neither bondage nor liberation. So there is no variety in liberation[81].

Kṣemarāja opines that when Śiva conceals His omniscience and omnipotence, and generates delusion in a soul by investing it with a subtle body and gross body, its being deluded by them is bondage. But when He generates the state of ecstasy (turīya) in it, it pervades the universe and transcends ecstasy, and becomes a mass of pure consciousness and bliss, and achieves identity with Śiva and embodied release[82].

CRITICISM OF OTHER VIEWS OF LIBERATION.—The Yogācāras regard liberation as the cognition : 'I am devoid of love, hate and the like.' The mind is naturally luminous but veiled by love, hate, etc., adventitious impurities due to beginningless nescience. These constitute bondage, and when they are destroyed by meditation on four noble truths, luminous consciousness is manifested, which is called liberation. Jayaratha refutes this view. The Yogācāras regard the mind as a series of momentary mental modes. Meditation is the cause of the destruction of its impurities. But it cannot produce an excellence in the momentary psychoses ; it can do so in a permanent substance alone. Fragrant flowers can perfume sesame seeds, because they are permanent. Momentary impure mental modes cannot produce a pure luminous cognition, but they can produce only impure cognitions. Meditation cannot produce an illuminating cognition. The advocates of the doctrine of momentariness cannot account for bondage and liberation. Those philosophers alone who believe in permanent souls can account for them. A permanent soul is bound and released. A series of momentary cognitions is neither bound nor released, since a single cognition is not so. The Yogācāras regard the same cognition as of the forms of joy, grief, etc., and so consider the knowledge of buddhitattva to be liberation, and call it omniscience. There is the cessation of the lower principles when buddhitattva is attained. A soul that has attained this principle is born in higher planes of existents. Jayaratha interprets the Yogācāras' view of emancipation in this way.

The Mādhyamikas regard the cognition 'I am void within' as liberation. They think all external entities to be essenceless (niḥsvabhāva) and false and all internal cognitions also to be so, and therefore think liberation to be void (śūnya). Jayaratha refutes their view. For them, 'blue' and other external objects are false, and cognitions also are false like them. Consciousness also being merely of the nature of manifestation is false and nonexistent, since nothing is manifested. The Mādhyamikas' argument in defence of their position that consciousness of manifestation is undeniable is invalid. They contend that what is devoid of all substrates, all attributes, all afflictions, and all dispositions, is not really a void, and that what is devoid of imaginary distinction of subject and object, etc., is not devoid of consciousness. This contention amounts to the Yogācāras doctrine of Vijñānavāda: momentary cognitions alone are real, and the world is manifested as varied cognitions of the mind. This doctrine has already been refuted.[83]

The Sāṁkhyas regard liberation as discriminative knowledge of the self : 'I am not a doer, but a conscious neutral knower different from prakṛti and its modifications.' Mind (buddhi) is active, but the self is an inactive neutral spectator. If it were active, it would never be conscious. Prakṛti and its modifications alone are unconscious and active. Jayaratha refutes this view. If the self were inactive, it would never be released. Even if a self acquired discriminative knowledge of itself, it would not abide in its essential nature, since prakṛti being by nature active it would not be neutral to the self, and would bind it again. Prakṛti being unconscious cannot know : 'I am seen by this self', 'I shall no more act for its experience', and so it would act for the self's enjoyment and suffering, although it has acquired discriminative knowledge of its self. So the self cannot be released. The Sāṁkhyas regard the self's abiding in its essential nature after completely discriminating itself from prakṛti or not-self of the nature of pleasure, pain, etc., as liberation. So liberation, for them, is the attainment of puruṣatattva devoid of pleasure, pain and the like. The Sāṁkhya concept of liberation is higher than that of the Buddhists, since the doctrine of self is higher than that of not-self, mind, or cognition. This is Jayaratha's interpretation of the Sāṁkhya view of release.[84]

Patañjali regards liberation as complete aloofness (kaivalya) of the self from prakṛti and its effects through meditation on God. Jayaratha interprets Patanjali's concept of liberation as the attainment of niyatitattva, which regulates causes and effects, actions and fruits. Niyatitattva is higber than puruṣatattva. Jayaratha interprets liberation conceived by Mausula as the attainment of māyātattva, Pāsupatas' concept of liberation as the attainment of Īśvaratattva, that is higher than māyātattva. The Buddhists' concept of liberation means the destruction of māyīya mala. Mausula's concept of release means the destruction of kārma mala. Pāsupatas' concept of liberation means the destruction of āṇava mala, which is the false conceit of self in not-self. Abhinavagupta regards release as the destruction of limitations, and complete release as the destruction of all limitations. A principle (tattva) is a limitation which generates bondage in a self. A self that has destroyed a lower principle is reborn in a plane of a higher principle. God binds it again in a higher plane, which has achieved release from a lower principle. The Śaiva attains the highest emancipation by destroying all principles and limitations and by realising his Śivahood. Knowledge of all principles, destruction of all limitations by them, and extermination of all nescience are liberation. It is manifested as knowledge of supreme 'I'-consciousness devoid of all kinds of 'this'-consciousness and their subconscious impressions.[85]

SOMĀNANDA : ALL IS ŚIVA.—Śiva produces the world of diverse objects by His volitions. Different objects are products of His volitions without any external material. They are His externalised volitions. All are Śiva in this sense. They are created out of His creative delight for His play. There is the nature of Śiva in all entities, which exists equally in them all. Differece is real, because it is the creation of Śivatattva, which is multiform. The manifoldness of the world is real, and not a false appearance. All categories are of the nature of the Lord, Śiva. All cognitions also are of the nature of Śiva, because He infuses His power into them. So all are of the nature of Śiva. He assumes the forms of all existents by His volitions, not by modifications of His nature. The world in its subtle state and gross state both is full of existence, or being ; being is the agency of becoming ; agency is the quality of acting, of the nature of freedom and consciousness of Śiva. So all entities are Śiva. His action is voluntary. His act is an act of will. Being full of the powers of volition and action is being of the nature of Śiva, since powers and powerful Being are nondifferent from each other. Though there are many things of the nature of Śiva, He is not many consciousnesses. He is one transcendental consciousness (cit). Thus all are Śiva.[86]

UTPALADEVA : ĀBHĀSAVĀDA.—Śiva is the light of universal consciousness. Śakti is the mirror of dynamic consciousness wherein He is reflected, and He sees Himself. He turns back upon Himself through Śakti, and becomes self-conscious or 'I'-conscious. Śiva is consciousness and self-consciousness or 'I'-consciousness while Śaṁkara's Brahman is mere consciousness. Consciousness is manifestation (prakāśa), and self-consciousness is self-manifestation (vimarśa). Śiva is self-manifest through Śakti. She makes Him self-manifest through His reflection in Her. She is the power of self-manifestation. She is sovereignty (aiśvarya), freedom (svātantrya), power of differentiating into subjects and objects, psychic or spiritual vibration (spanda), power of action (kriyāśakti), power of manifesting diverse objects of the world, and of reflecting them on the screem of Śiva's transparent consciousness, and power of synthesising different elements into a unity. So Śiva is the archetype (bimba) whereof the world is a manifestation (ābhāsa) or reflection (pratibimba). Or, Śiva is the reflection of Himself in Śakti or dynamic consciousness, and the world is a secondary reflection (ābhāsa) of Śiva. The world is real, though it is a reflection, and is projected by His volition outward for the experience of limited knowers or souls. Diverse objects are the materials of His world play which is real. They are not false appearances. The world play is real, souls are real, and different objects are real. They are products of His māyāśakti. They are known because they are of the nature of illumination, but they are insentient, since they are devoid of self-illumination or 'I'-consciousness. Śiva is their material cause, since He enters into their constitution. He is their efficient cause, since His māyāśakti and other powers are their efficient cause. His powers are inseparable from Him. Niyati due to His māyāśakti connects specific causes with specific effects. Space, time, causality, recollection, differentiation, sublation and the like are due to His act of synthetic apperception. He apprehends diverse objects as nondifferent from Him, though bound souls know them to be different from themselves, and from one another. Released souls apprehend them as nondifferent from themselves. So diverse objects, though reflections of Śiva in His dynamic consciousness, are not unreal. They are not subjective ideas of bound souls. Utpaladeva does not advocate subjective idealism. He advocates Ideal-Realism, like Somānanda, his teacher. Somānanda mentions pratibimbavāda in 'Śivadṛṣṭi'

Utpaladeva says, "An object is not manifested, if it is not of the nature of manifestation; manifestation to a self is its manifestation. A manifestable or knowable object of the nature of manifestation cannot be proved to be of the nature of nonmanifestation. So an object is proved to be of the nature of manifestation. The Lord of the nature of consciousness manifests all objects outside Him by His internal volition like a yogin without any external material. The Lord manifests the objects which exist in Him; if they did not exist in Him, He would not have volition to manifest them outside Him. He projects the objects which exist as nondifferent from Him outward to be known by limited knowers. "The essence of manifestation is the urge of the Lord (vimarśa) to creat an object. A manifestation (prakāśa) tinged with an object is like an insentient crystal tinged with the reflection of an object. Ātman or Śiva is different from an insentient crystal, since He is the agent of dynamic consciousness which manifests an object. The Lord knows 'this is a jar' as His power, and not as 'this'. The Lord enters into a body, and manifests internal objects by His volition outside Him. Manifestations full of consciousness exist always inside the Lord or Ātman; they exist outside Him also when they are projected outward by Him through His māyāśakti. They exist inside Him when He wills to create them and make them perceptible to limited knowers. Manifold manifestations or reflections constituting the world can exist in the permanent self-luminous Lord's consciousness, though He is devoid of variety. This Lord alone can manifest manifold objects of the world because of His ommipotence by His volition. This divine will constitutes His creativeness of the world. "Different manifestations (ābhāsa) cannot be created by the one Lord of the nature of consciousness without His 'I'-consciousness characterized by the volition to create them". "His will to exist as the world of the nature of manifestations is the cause of its continued existence. The one Lord assumes the form of the manifold world, which is the unfoldment of His 'I'-consciousness in the form of 'this'. The Lord is the creator of diversity. Śiva is the creator of all objects (artha) with their relation to Him, and of difference and nondifference. The objects (vastu) are the forms of consciousness alone (cinmātra). Differences are constructed by māyāsakti. They are nondifferent from Śiva. Externality of objects is inessential." These statements clearly show that Utpaladeva was realistic in his approach to the world, and advocated Ideal-Realism. The objects are reflections on Śiva's consciousness, and yet they are real.[87]

Abhinavagupta also advocates the doctrine of manifestation (ābhāsa) or reflection (pratibimba). He says, "Śakti, māyā, prakṛti, and the earth are manifested by the Lord because of His omnipotence. The world consists of various bodies, sense-organs, spheres of existence ; it is the unfoldment of His powers ; He assumes the forms of embodied souls that enjoy the world. Śiva of the nature of consciousness is reflected in His transparent consciousness of the nature of Śakti, as a face is reflected in a transparent mirror. Śiva, the pure, tranquil, indeterminate, supreme Reality is reflected in the world consisting of thirty six principles. As a town with its various objects is reflected in a mirror without annulling their difference, so diverse objects are reflected in the indeterminate consciousness of the Lord. They are reflected in His differenceless consciousness as different from one another. They are due to His māyāśakti. When a soul conquers māyā producing difference, it merges in Brahman."[88] "The Lord manifests the play of creation and dissolution of the limited world in His ether of consciousness by His absolute freedom. The events of the world are reflected in the Lord's consciousness as different from one another, as earth, water, etc., are reflected in water. What is repulsing in the world is made of māyātattva, and what is not repulsing in it is made of sadvidyātattva. The Lord unfolds the world in two forms of manifestations and shines as archetype (bimba) and reflections (pratibimba)"[89]. These statements show that Abhinavagupta advocates the doctrine of reflection. But they do not show that reflections of different objects of the world are unreal phenomenal appearances. Abhinavagupta says, "What is repulsing and what is unrepulsing in the world are mere reflections (ābhāsamātra) in their essence, and not ontologically real (tāttvika)". This statement shows that the world is a phenomenal appearance. It may be interpreted in the sense that from the absolute standpoint of Śiva the world is a phenomenal appearance, but from the empirical standpoint of a bound soul, it is real. But when it acquires recognitive intuition of its identity with Śiva, it knows the world to be nondifferent from its Ātman or Śiva. Vasugupta describes determinate cognitions as dreams. Utpaladeva says, "The manifestations of objects always exist in Śiva, but they exist outside Him also projected outward by His māyāśakti". So they are empirically real to a bound soul fettered by bonds, tainted by impurities, and contracted by coverings, created by māyāsakti. But they are unreal to Śiva because He knows them to be nondifferent from Him. Abhinavagupta says, "As invisible Rāhu reflected in the moon is manifested, so the ubiquitous Ātman is reflected in buddhi in the form of objects. Ātman or Śiva is reflected in buddhi rendered transparent by the descent of Śiva-Śakti, as a face is reflected in a transparent mirror. The world is reflected in Śiva Himself as jars, etc., are reflected in water ; all issue out of Śiva like dreams issuing out of a sleeping person's mind"[90]. So the world is reflected in Śiva's consciousness and reflected back in a jiva's buddhi.

PRATYABHIJÑĀ SCHOOL OF ŚAIVISM AND ŚAṀKARA'S ADVAITAVĀDA.—The former differs from the latter in the following points. 1. Śaṁkara regards Brahman as the ontological reality while Somānanda regards Śiva endowed with divine power (Śakti) as the ontological reality. Śiva and Śakti are inseparable from each other. Śiva is endowed with the power of consciousness or illumination, self-illumination, bliss, volition, knowledge and action. Brahman is infinite existence-consciousness-bliss. They are Its essential characteristics.

2. Śaṁkara regards God (Īśvara) as a phenomenal appearance of Brahman limited by nescience (avidyā). God is the omniscient and omnipotent creator, sustainer and destroyer of the world, while Somānanda regards Śiva as the omniscient and omnipotent creator, sustainer and destroyer of the world. Śiva is not a phenomenal appearance. 3. For Śaṁkara, māyā is neither real, nor unreal, nor both, nor either, but indefinable, while, for Somānanda, māyā is a real power of Śiva, a principle of self-limitation whereby He produces the world. 4. For Śaṁkara, the world is a false appearance (vivarta) of Brahman due to māyā, while, for Somānanda, the world is created by Śiva by His power of volition and by His power of action without any extraneous material ; it is the product of His volition. Śaṁkara advocates absolute idealism while Somānanda advocates absolute ideal-realism or voluntarism (svātantryavāda). The former regards the world as an unreal appearance while the latter regards it as real : all are Śiva. Somānanda regards the diverse objects of the world as created or projected outward by Śiva, and sustained and dissolved by His volitions. Abhinavagupta regards them as created by Śiva and reflected in the foundation of His transparent consciousness as houses and trees are reflected in the water of a tank by His powers. 5. For Śaṁkara, the individual soul is an unreal appearance, a reflection of Brahman in nescience, while, for Somānanda, the jīva is real in that Śiva limits Himself by māyāśakti and becomes the jīva. 6. For Śaṁkara, the soul's bondage is due to its nescience or ignorance of its identity with Brahman, and its liberation is due to the destruction of nescience by the knowledge of its identity with Brahman. But, for Somānanda, bondage is due to the taints due to nescience, and liberation is due to the destruction of the impurities and nescience, the acquisition of omniscience and omnipotence, and the recognition of the soul's Śivahood. 7. For Śaṁkara, Brahman is mere infinite knowledge, while, for Somānanda, Śiva is the unlimited Knower. 8. For Śaṁkara, the jīva, in its real nature, is mere knowledge, while, for Somānanda, the jīva is a limited knower, doer and enjoyer ; it derives its consciousness or illumination (prakāśa) and 'I'-consciousness or self-illumination (vimarśa) from Śiva, and is a limited self-conscious knower of its cognitions, feelings and volitions. 9. For Śaṁkara, Brahman is transcendent of the false world-appearance and unreal empirical selves, while, for Somānanda and Utpaladeva, Śiva-Śakti is both transcendent and immanent. 10. For Śaṁkara, Brahman as pure identity is real, while, for Somānanda, Śiva is real as unity, plurality, and unity of plurality. 11. For Śaṁkara, time, space and causality are mere categories of the intellect infected with nescience and inapplicable to Brahman, the Reality, while, for Utpaladeva, they are real, applicable to the real world, and presuppose Śiva, the Supreme Knower, Who unifies plurality and synthesizes different elements into a unity. 12. Śaṁkara advocates vivartavāda while Utpaladeva advocates ābhāsavāda or pratibimbavāda. Certainly, the Pratyabhijñā school of Śaivism is more satisfactory from the monistic standpoint than Śaṁkara's absolute idealism as a philosophical doctrine[91].

PRATYABHIJÑĀ ŚAIVISM AND DUALISTIC ŚAIVISM.—Both accept Śiva as the supreme, independent reality, and the soul and the world also as real. Both accept thirty six categories (tattva), and three taints as real, though their accounts of them slightly vary. But the former is monistic while the latter is dualistic. The former regards Śiva as the ontological reality of the soul and the world while the latter regards them as eternally distinct from Him. The Pāśupata regards Śiva as the efficient cause and prakṛti as the material cause of the world while Pratyabhijñā Śaivism regards Śiva as the efficient, material, and auxiliary cause of the world. Śrīkaṇṭha's Śaivism and Śrīpati Paṇḍita's Vīra Śaivism are influenced by Rāmānuja's qualified monism (viśiṣṭādvaitavāda). Their views represent Śaiva Viśiṣṭādvaita. There are other differences also.

SPANDA ŚĀSTRA.—'Śiva Sūtra' of Vasugupta and his 'Spandakārikā' are the basic works. They do not expound any new philosophy, but Pratyabhijñā works and Spanda Śāstra expound the same doctrine of Śaiva monism or Trika philosophy. The accounts of knower, knowledge and knowable object, of enjoyer, enjoyment and enjoyable object, agent, action, and effect given already were based on 'Spanda Kārikā' also. 'Spanda Śāstra' lays greater stress on the spiritual discipline for the recognitive intuition of a soul's identity with Śiva. 'Śiva Sūtra' also lays greater stress on the method of realisation of the supreme goal. Somānanda's 'Śivadṛṣṭi' and Utpalavadeva's 'Īśvarapratyabhijñākārikā' and 'Siddhitrayī' expound the philosophy of the Pratyabhijñā school of Śaivism. Abhinavagupta's 'Paramārthasāra' expounds the Pratyabhijñā Śaiva philosophy. His 'Tantrāloka' and 'Parātriṁśikā-tattvavivaraṇa' expound the Pratyabhijñā theology and Śaiva Kuṇḍalinī-yoga.

Vasugupta describes spanda as psychic enery, throb or vibration in a body, which is agitated in intense anger, joy, deliberation and the like. It is expressed in self-appropriation of a particular object and determination to do a particular action. It is divine power in the form of serpent power (kuṇḍalinī) which is asleep or coiled at the basic centre, awakened by breath control and concentration on the Divine at it, and made to pierce six centres (cakra) in Suṣumnā, spinal cord, and ascend to the highest centre above the cerebrum and unite with Śiva. An ignorant soul is freed of nescience, and aquires the knowledge of its Śivahoot, which is no more veiled. Kallaṭa avers that when powers are calmed, psychic vibration distinctly emerges. Its nature is known from an adept Master. When inhaled air and exaled air are calmed, and when the mind is concentrated on the ether of Śiva's consciousness, a soul's real nature as universal consciousness, Ātman or Śiva is manifested. An earnest, aspiring, and persevering soul constantly making efforts to know spandatattva knows is essential nature in no distant time in a waking state. It knows its essential nature in a state of ecstasy (turīya).[92] Kṣemarāja speaks of throbbing consciousness of the Lord, which is the heart, and which transcends the world, and which is immanent in it. The Lord is of the nature of illumination and self-illumination (vimarśa) or 'I'-consciousness. If He were devoid of 'I'-consciousness, He would be insentient. Vimarśa is transcendental consciousness (cit), dynamic consciousness (caitanya), freedom (svātantrya), sovereignty (aiśvarya), agency, throbbing, heart, essence, vibration and the like. Kṣemarāja speaks of Śiva as possessed of spanda and self-existent. So spanda is vibration of divine power of freedom nondifferent from Him. Spanda is not vibration of physical energy, or vibration of vital force, or vibration of mental energy, but spiritual vibration of divine power. In the human body it remains coiled at the lowest centre of mystic consciousnes and completely awakened at the highest centre. It can be roused by Kuṇḍalinīyoga. It is common to

Śaivayoga and Śāktayoga. Spanda is the one power of Śiva's 'I'-consciousness. It is so called because it assumes the form of slight movement, throbbing, wave, strength, effort, heart, essence and the like. Though it is one, it simultaneously unfolds and enfolds, evolves and involves. (Cp. Vallabha and Aurobinda)[93].

PRATYABHIJÑĀ ŚAIVAYOGA : KUṆḌALINĪYOGA.—There are seven circles (cakra), lotuses, or centres of mystic consciousness in Suṣumnā in the spinal cord with the nerve Iḍā on the right and the nerve Piṅgalā on the left. There is the basal centre above the anus, mūlādhāra of four yellow petals with the letters 'vaṁ', 'śaṁ', 'ṣaṁ', and 'saṁ' inscribed on them. Divine power, serpent power, Kuṇḍalinī, lies asleep, coiled, dormant, in three coils and a half around Śivaliṅga. Divine power or Mother ascends from it to the higher centres. She is awakend by breath-control and concentration at the centre on the Divine Being. Aurobindo dispenses with breath-control in Kuṇḍalinīyoga. At the base of the sex-organ there is a lotus called Svādhiṣṭhāna of six white petals with the letters 'baṁ', 'bhaṁ', 'maṁ', yaṁ', 'raṁ' and 'laṁ' inscribed on them. Śivaliṅga resides in this lotus. At the base of the navel there is a lotus called Maṇipura of ten red petals with the letters 'ḍaṁ', 'ḍhaṁ', 'ṇaṁ', 'taṁ', 'thaṁ', 'daṁ' 'dhaṁ', 'naṁ', 'paṁ' and 'phaṁ' inscribed on them. Fire-god resides in this lotus. At the heart-lotus there is Anāhata lotus of twelve smoky petals with the letters 'Kaṁ', 'Khaṁ', 'gaṁ' 'ghaṁ' 'ṅaṁ', 'cham', 'chhaṁ', 'jaṁ', 'jham', 'ñaṁ', 'ṭaṁ' and 'thaṁ' inscribed on them. The Divine Being as the Inner Controller and the jīva reside here. The lotus is called Anāhata because an occult sound 'Auṁ'—nāda—is heard here when the mind becomes calm and tranquil after prolonged practice of Kuṇḍalinīyoga. At the base of the throat there is the Viśuddha lotus of sixteen blue petals with the letters 'aṁ', 'āṁ', 'iṁ', 'īṁ', 'uṁ', 'ūṁ', 'ṛṁ', 'ṝṁ', 'liṁ', 'lliṁ', 'eṁ', 'aiṁ', 'oṁ', 'auṁ', 'aṁ' and 'aḥa' inscribed on them. Śivaliṅga resides here. Between the eye brows there is the Ājñācakra of two yellow petals with the letters 'ha' and 'kṣa' inscribed on them. Śivaliṅga resides here like a luminous lamp. In the centre of the crown of the head above the cerebrum there is the Sahasrāra lotus of a thousand multicoloured petals with fifty letters inscribed on them. At the centre there is a circle of effulgent light inside which there is a triangle. Parama Śiva and Divine Power (Śakti) reside here. This lotus is called Akula. Kuṇḍalinī is aroused, ascends through Suṣumnā, pierces all the lotuses, and is united with Parama Śiva, in this highest lotus, in the state of fully awake, infinite consciousness and bliss. The Śāktas call it the abode of Divine Mother. The Śaivas call it the abode of Śiva. These centres of mystic consciousness are not found on dissection through a microscope. They are revealed to yogins through occult vision. The Pāśupatas enjoined meditation on 'Oṁ' at the heart-lotus but not at the other centres. They were not aware of Kuṇḍalinīyoga. Vīra Śaivism expounded by Śrīpati Paṇḍita enjoined Kuṇḍaliniyoga. But it is unique to Pratyabhijñā Śaivism and Spandasāstra, especially emphasized by Vasugupta, Kallaṭa, Abhinavagupta and Kṣemarāja, and Śāktaism. Somānanda briefly expounds it in his 'Śāktavijñāna'. I have explained it in my 'Śākta Monism'. Aurobindo regards the Mūlādhāra as governing the physical, the Svādhiṣṭhāna as governing the lower vital, the Maṇipūra as governing the larger vital, the Anāhata as governing the emotional, the Viśuddha as governing the expressive mind, the Ājñācakra as governing the dynamic mind, and the Sahasrāra as governing the higher thinking mind, and illumined mind. He describes the Mulādhāra with four red petals, the Svādhiṣṭhāna with six deep purple red petals, the Maṇipura with ten violet petals, the Anāhata with twelve golden pink petals, the Viśuddha with sixteen grey petals, the Ājñā with two white petals, and the Sahasrāra above the head with blue petals surrounded by gold light. He dispenses with the letters inscribed on them, and simplifies Kuṇḍalinīyoga. He emphasizes concentration at the centres and meditation on the Divine with perfect self-surrender, opening to higher consciousness, persevering, aspiring, and seeking for Divine grace. Breath-control should not be practised without the guidance of a yogin. Kuṇḍalinīyoga should be practised while sitting erect with folded legs.[94]

PRATYABHIJÑĀ ŚAIVISM AND ŚĀKTA MONISM.—Both are types of spiritual monism and allied systems. They resemble each other in many respects. They regard Śiva-Śakti as the supreme ontological reality, believe in māyāśakti, the world as unfoldment of the Divine, the individual soul as the Divine limited by five contractors (kañcuka), and as tainted with three taints (mala), the thirty six principles (tattva), bondage as due to nescience, and release as due to destruction of nescience and taints, and Kuṇḍalinīyoga. They differ in some respects. Śaiva monism regards Śiva as higher than Śakti, and transcendent of the world, creating the world with His power. Śākta monism regards Śakti as higher than Śiva, transceudent of, and immanent in, the world, evolving in it, and enfolding it. It regards Śakti as endowed with illumination (prakāśa) and self-illumination (vimarśa) whereas Śaiva monism regards Śiva as endowed with these qualities. The former regards Śiva as static, calm Absolute while the latter regards Him as dynamic and endowed with the powers of consciousness, bliss, knowledge, volition and action, creating, sustaining and dissolving the world. Somānanda regards the world as real and produced by Śiva's volition while Śāktaism regards the world as a phenomenal appearance. Utpaladeva and Abhinavagupta regard the world as a reflection of Śiva in His universal consciousness. Besides Kuṇḍalinīyoga Śaiva monism enjoins āṇavopāya, sāmbhavopāya, śāktopāya and anupāya, which are foreign to Śāktaism.

Somānanda criticises Sāktaism which enjoins the worship of Śakti's highest state devoid of Śiva. His criticism of Śaivism has already been dealt with. But later Śāktaism does not recognise Śakti as devoid of Śiva. Therefore Somānanda's criticism does not apply to it[95]. Lakṣamana Deśikendra quotes from authoritative Śākta works about the nature of Śiva. "Śiva with His Divine Power (Śakti) pervades the universe, and assumes the forms of diverse objects through His Śakti." "Sakti nondifferent from Śiva issued from Him, and created the universe." Śiva is the transcendent, self-manifest, infinite, undifferentiated consciousness. He is the static, impersonal Absolute. Śakti is the personal, dynamic, Divine Power invested with 'I'-consciousness. She creates the universe by Her free will. She is the cause of bondage and liberation of jīvas. She projects the world of phenomenal appearances with Her māyāśakti, and entangles jīvas in embodied life by veiling their spiritual nature by nescience. Śiva and Śakti are inseparable from each other. Thus many functions of Śiva of Śaiva monism are assigned to Śakti by Śākta monism. She is 'I'-consciousness (vimarśa), and differentiated into subjects and objects, and modified into thirty six principles[96].

[1] APS., 23-26.

[2] ĪS., 6-7, 14, 36, 41-42, 53-54, & 56 ; ĪPK., i, 38, 51-56,59 ; iii, 10-11 ; ŚD., ŚDV., i, 44-45 ; iii, 80-81.

[3] ĪS., ĪSV., 18-27, ĪPK., i, 2-3 ; ĪPKV., 1-2 ; ĪS., 26-42.

[4] ŚDV., iii, 1.

[5] ŚD., iii, 1-6, 20, 64-65 ; i, 3-6 ; ŚDV., i, 3-7 ; cp. ŚM., pp. 1-5.

[6] APP., i ; PS., PSV., 46 ; ŚD, i, 7-8, 11, 15, 17 & 27 ; ŚDV., i, 2, 8 & 12.

[7] ŚD., ŚDV., i, 19-20, 24-25 & 27.

[8] ŚD, i, 28, 39-41, 44 & 49 ; ŚDV., i, 28, 40, 44-48.

[9] PPR., p. 6 ; APP., p. 18 ; ṢṬTS., ṢṬTSV., i ; PS., 10-11, p. 32 ; PSV., 10-11, p. 32 ; 14, p. 41 ; ŚSV., iii, 3, p. 45. PTTV., p. 178.

[10] PPR., 6-7 & 11 ; PSV., 14 ; PHV., 1.

[11] ĪPK., ĪPKV., iii, 3-4 ; ŚD., ŚDV., ii, I ; ŚD., i, 30 ; BŚSV., ii, 3 ; ṢṬTS., ṢṬTSV., 4.

[12] PHV., 3 ; ṢṬTS., ṢṬTSV., 4 ; PPR., p. 7 ; ĪPK., ĪPKV., iii, 3-4 ; ŚD., i, 3 ; ŚDV., ii, 1 ; BŚSV., ii, 3 ; PSV., 14 ; VŚSV., ii, 3.

[13] PHV., 3 ; PSV., 15 ; ĪPK., ĪPKV., iii, 3-4 ; ṢṬTS., ṢṬTSV., 5; VŚSV., ii, 3.

[14] ĪPK., ĪPKV., iii, 6, 7 & 16 ; ŚD., ŚDV., i, 32 ; PPR., p. 7 ; PS., PSV., p. 15 ; SS., SSV., iii, 3, 14-16 & 35 ; BŚSV., iii, 3 ; APP., 21 ; ṢṬTS., ṢṬTSV., 5.

[15] PPR., pp. 8-9 ; ṢṬTSV., 7-12 ; VŚSV., ii, 7, 42-46 ; PHV., 9, PSV., 17 ; ĪPKV., iii, 9 ; APP., 23-25 ; BŚSV., ii, 25 ; pp. 43-44 ; cp. ŚM., pp. 20-21.

[16] PPR., pp. 7-8 ; APP., 22 ; PH., PHV., 4 ; ĪPK., iii, 10 & 14 ; PS., PSV., 4 ; ṢṬTSV., 6.

[17] APP., 26 ; PPR., p. 9 ; ṢṬTSV., 13 ; cp. AG., pp. 362—72.

[18] ṢṬTS., ṢṬTSV., 14-15 ; PPR., p. 10 ; APP., 26-27.

[19] ṢṬTS., ṢṬTSV., 16-20 ; PPR., p. 16.

[20] APS., 2-14, 17-23 ; PSV., 16 ; VŚSV., iii, 1, 1-7.

[21] ŚD., ŚDV., i, 41-43 ; ṢṬTS., 6 ; ĪPK., iii, 13-20 & 31.

[22] SpK., ii, 3-4 ; SS., i, 1 ; PH., PHV., 3-5 & 7.

[23] ŚD., ŚDV., iii, 98-99 ; ĪPK., IPKV., iii, 18-23 ; Svacchanda Tantra, X, 1141 ; Netra Tantra, viii 30 ; PHV., 8-12 ; PSV., 5-7 & 16.

[24] SpK., SpKV., 21 ; KŚSV., iii, 20, 25, 32, 38-39 & 41 ; VŚSV., i, 55-56, 38-45 ; SS., i, 7-10 ; ĪPK., iii, 24-31 ; cp. ŚM., pp. 5-7, 10-11, 29-35, 40-41.

[25] PSV., 18, 33, 8-9 ; PTTV., pp. 136-37.

[26] ĪPK., iii, 15-16 ; PHV., 9 ; PSV., 24 ; VŚSV., i, 2, śl., 15-20.

[27] PHV., PH., 12-13, 15-17 ; ŚS., KŚSV., BŚSV., iii, 44 ; VŚSV., iii, 44, śl., 198-205 ; cp. ŚM., pp. 5-7, 29-35 ; cp. AG., pp. 314-15.

[28] KŚSV., i, 1 ; iii, 30-31 ; VŚSV., i, 9, 12-13 ; i, 5, 33-35 ; iii, 43, śl., 191-92 ; iii, 30-32 ; PHV., 1-2, 10, 12-13 ; ŚD., i, 40 & 48 ; cp. AG., pp. 319-42.

[29] PS., PSV., 13, 41-43 & 51 ; ŚD., ŚDV., i, 2 & 32.

[30] ŚS., KŚSV., VŚSV., BŚSV., iii, 9-11.

[31] SpK., SpKV., 14, 17 & 29 ; ŚD., vii, 99

[32] SpK., SpKV., 18-19.

[33] ĪPK., ii, 2, 8, 30-31 ; iv, 1-15 ; iii, 14 ; ĪPKV., iii ; 14 ; PS., PSV., 41 ; ĪPK., ĪPKV., iii, 15-23 ; ii, 31, 33 & 39 ; i, 2.

[34] TA., TAV., i, 52-62.

[35] ĪPK., ii, 2, 9, 12, 14-15, 27, 33-42, 46, 48, 50-52 ; ĪPKV., ii, 2, 33-34, 36-38, 40-41 ; 46-47, 52-53 ; SpK., SpKV., 14-15 ; ŚD., vii, 100-01.

[36] SpK., SpKV., 47-51.

[37] ŚS., i, 4 ; iii, 19 ; KŚSV., VŚSV., i, 4 ; iii, 19 ; BŚSV., iii, 19.

[38] ŚS., ii, 3 ; i, 22 ; BŚSV., KŚSV., VŚSV., ii, 2-3, 4-9 ; i, 22, śl., 103-08, 110-11 ; PHV., 12 ; PTTV., 148 & 243 ; TTV., i, 46 ; cp. ŚM., pp. 17-18 ; CCA., ii, ch. 17 ; J R DL.

[39] ŚS., KŚSV., BŚSV., ii, 6 ; iii, 29-31 ; VŚSV., ii, 6, śl., 26-29 ; cp. ŚM., pp. 14-15, J R DL.)

[40] PTTV., pp. 260 & 299 ; VŚSV., iii, 29-30 ; śl., 123-36 ; BŚSV., iii, 28-29 ; TA., TAV., ii, 4 & 7 ; SpK., SpKV., 30-32.

[41] ĪPKV., i, 5 ; ĪPK., i, 4-5.

[42] ĪPKV., ĪPK., i, 9-18.

[43] ĪPK., i, 19-25, 27-36 ; ĪPKV., i, 26-34, 37-38.

[44] ĪPK., i, 40-44, 49, 51 & 53 ; ĪPKV., i, 51 & 53.

[45] ĪPK., i, 54, 56, 59, 64 & 66 ; ĪPKV., i, 70 & 79.

[46] ĪPK., i, 4-72, 84-85 & 87 ; ĪPKV., i, 4-72, 75 & 88.

[47] ŚD., vi, 1-7. [48] ŚD., vi, 8-15.

[49] ŚD., vi, 16-24. [50] ŚD., vi, 24-26.

[51] ŚD., vi, 32-49, 84-85.

[52] ŚD., vi, 27-29. [53] ŚD., ŚDV., ii, 2-11.

[54] ŚD., ŚDV., ii, 13-16, 20-28 ; ŚD., ii, 24-25.

[55] ŚD., ŚDV., ii, 28-33 ; VPD., i, 32.

[56] ŚD., ŚDV., ii, 34-49. [57] Ibid, ii, 50-57.

[58] Ibid, ii, 58-65. cp. HIP., Vol. I, pp. 870-71.

[59] ŚD., ŚDV., ii, 65-69, 76-90.

[60] ŚD., iii, 34 ; ŚD., ŚDV., iii, 21-39 ; ŚDV., i, 32.

[61] ŚD., iii, 42-44, 47, 52-57 ; ŚDV., iii, 40-44, 48-49, 56 & 59.

[62] ŚD., 77-79 ; ŚD., ŚDV., iii, 71, 73-76.

[63] Ibid, iii, 82-83, 85-97.

[64] ŚD., vii, 78-80, 85-86, 88-92, 96-67 ; ŚS., KŚSV., BŚSV., VŚSV., iii, 26-28, śl., 110-15 ; PS., PSV., 73-78 & 80 ; RKBG., iv, 24 ; xvi, 24 ; PTTV., 32, p. 267 ; cp. ŚM., pp. 27-29.

[65] PTTV., 32, pp. 266-67 ; RKBG., ix, 24 & 27 ; xiii, 11 ; xviii, 55 ; cp. ŚM., pp. 42-44.

[66] ŚD., vii, 81-84 ; ŚS., VŚSV., iii, 16, śl., 60-65 ; iii, 6, śl., 30-39 ; iii, 5, śl., 21-25 ; iii, 16, śl., 60-63.

[67] ŚS., KŚSV., BŚSV., VŚSV., ii, 9-10, śl., 56-61.

[68] ŚS., i, 16-18 ; KŚSV., i, 18 ; VŚSV., i, 16-18, śl., 82-90 ; i, 11-12, śl., 57-66 ; BŚSV., i, 17-18, śl., 76-81 ; cp. ŚM., pp. 39-42.

[69] ŚS., KŚSV., iii, 25.

[70] Ibid, i, 21 ; ii, 5 ; i, 13-14, 19-21 ; VŚSV., i, 19-21, śl., 91-101.

[71] ŚS., ii, 4 ; VŚSV., śl., 17-19 ; iii, 21-22, śl., 87-93, ŚS., KŚSV., iii, 35-41.

[72] ŚS., KŚSV., iii, 30-34.

[73] Ibid, i, 15-16 ; ŚS., VŚSV., i, 14, śl., 73-76 ; i, 15, śl., 77-81 ; cp. ŚM., pp., 29-32.

[74] TA., TAV., i, 22 & 24.

[75] TA., TAV., i, 25-30 ; ŚS., VŚSV., BŚSV., i, 1-2.

[76] TA., TAV., i, 36-45, 47-50.

[77] ŚD.. iii, 68-70 & 72.

[78] PS., 60-62, 67-70 ; PSV., 9, 60-61, 67-68 ; cp. Post-Śaṁkara Vedānta.

[79] TA., TAV., i, 31-32.

80 Ibid, i, 156-70.

[81] Ibid, i, 330-31.

[82] PH., PHV., 16.

[83] TA., TAV., i, 33, pp. 64-67.

[84] Ibid, pp. 68-70. HIP., Vol. II, pp. 737-42.

[85] TA., TAV., i, 34-35, pp. 70-73.

[86] ŚD., i, 41, 45, 47-49 ; ii, 88 ; iii, 17, 20, 29, 34-35, 55, 60-61, 64-65 ; V, 2.

[87] ŚD., V, 33-34 ; ĪPK., i, 38, 41-43, 51-53 & 59 ; ii, 30 ; IV, 1; ĪPK., ĪPKV., i, 30-31, 33-34 & 84 ; ii, 33, 52-53, ĪS., 35 ; ŚS., i, 8. See also 'Kashmir Śaivism' (J. C. Chatterjee), K. S. T. S., 1914, pp. 53-61 ; AG., pp. 319-21, 323-41.

[88] PS., 4-5, 9-10, 12-13 & 51.

[89] TA., iii, 3-4 & 10.

[90] ŚS., i, 9 ; ĪPK., i, 84 ; PS., 8-9 & 48.

[91] ŚD,, i, 3 ; iii, 2-3, 34-35 ; iv, 1 ; vi, 1 & 7 ; vii, 99 ; ĪPK., i, 42, 44, 49, 51, 57, 59, 66 & 88 ; ii, 2-12, 23, 26, 30, 34, 36, 39-40, 49-53 ; PS., PSV., 12-13. See also 'The Doctrine of Recognition' (R. K. Kaw), pp. 330-33.

[92] SpK., SpKV., 1, 21-25.

[93] SpS., pp. 1 & 5 ; PPR., pp. 1-2 ; ŚV., pp. 47-49. Cp. ŚM., pp. 29-32 ; LY., pp. 16-19, 66-68 ; MLY., pp. 34-36.

[94] ŚV., PTTV., SpK., SpKV., i, 24-25 ; cp. ŚM., pp. 29-35 ; LY., pp. 18-19 ; MLY., pp. 35-36.

[95] ŚD., iii, 1.

[96] ŚM., pp. 1-5, ŚT., i, 6 ; VS., YH., i, 9 ; YHD., i, 50-52. cp. HIP. Vol. II, pp. 744-46.

CHAPTER III

THE PHILOSOPHY OF THE PĀŚUPATA

INTRODUCTION.—The account of the Pāśupata Śaiva given here is based mainly on the 'Pāśupatasūtra' and the 'Pañcārthabhāṣya' of Kauṇḍinya. It is based on Haradatta's 'Gaṇakārikā' and Bhāsarvajña's 'Ratnatīka' on it and on Mādhava's 'Sarvadarśanasaṁgraha' (1400 A.D.) also which summarises the 'Pañcārthabhāṣya' and the 'Gaṇakārikā' and reproduces portions of the 'Ratnaṭīkā'. The Pāśupatasūtra' with the 'Pañcārthabhāṣya' edited by R. Anantakṛṣṇa Śāstrī was published in Trivandrum in 1940 A.D. A. Śāstri dates the former about 100-200 A.D. and the latter about 400-600 A.D. S. N. Das Gupta is inclined to place the latter one or two centuries earlier. Śāstrī dates Haradatta about 800-900 A.D. and Bhasarvajña 1000 A.D. Akṣapāda, the author of the 'Nyāyasūtra' (200 B. c.) and his followers (400-1000 A.D.) were Pāśupatas. Kaṇāda, the author of the 'Vaiśeṣikasutra' (300 B.C.) does not explicitly mention God in the aphorisms. His followers, Praśastapāda, Udayana and others, were theistic Pāśupatas. They regarded God as the efficient cause of the world,—and not as its material cause.[1]

The 'Pāśupatasūtra' is said to have been written by the Lord (paśupati) who incarnated in a village on the bank of the Narmadā in Gujrat and taught a Brāhmaṇa named Kuśika at Ujjayinī. His teachings took the form of the aphorisms. They contain very little metaphysical speculation and elaborately deal with the rituals practised by the Pāśupata ascetics. They do not refer to the theory of Karma, transmigration the worship of the phallic symbol, and the doctrines of māyā and attributeless Brahman. They reject the worship of the gods and sacrifices to them and srāddha—offering of food to the spirits of the departed ancestors. They regard the Brāhmaṇas alone as eligible for initiation into the Pāśupata spiritual discipline, look upon women and the Śūdras with disrespect, recommend a rigid code of conduct for the ascetics, and stress meditation on the mystic syllable 'Om' in the heart. They prescribe taking refuge in God, devotion to Him, offering one's self to Him, muttering His mantra or 'Om' or gāyatrī in honour of Śiva, the supreme Lord, and invoking His grace. Kauṇḍinya explains the nature of the effects, the cause, the union of the soul with God, the method of effecting it, and the extinction of pain, He refers to prakṛti and its modifications advocated by the Sāṁkhya in his account of cosmology, and affiliates it to his theistic cosmology. He often refers to the Sāṁkhya and the Yoga and criticises their views, but not to the Vedānta. He does not refer to the Advaita doctrines of the attributeless Brahman and māyā and falsity of the world, and falsity of individual souls. He flourished certainly before Śaṁkara and the articulate formulation of the atheistic Sāṁkhya philosophy and the Yoga system of Patañjali. His account of restraints and moral observances partly differs from that of Patañjali. He explains breath-control, withdrwal of the sense-organs from their objects, fixation of mind, meditation, and trance, mentions posture without elaborating it, but emphasises muttering of a mantra or 'Om', fixation of mind in the heart, meditation on 'Om', constant recollection of God, abiding of mind in Him, offering of all actions to Him, offering of the self to Him, taking refuge in Him, devotion to Him, and invoking His grace. Patañjali regards meditation of God as one of the methods of attaining liberation but does not regard it as the only method. Patañjali considers yoga to be the arrest of all mental modes and liberation to be complete isolation of the self from prakṛti and its modifications. Kauṇḍinya, on the other hand, regards yoga as union of the self with God, and liberation as the absolute cessation of pain and the acquisition of divine powers, close proximity to, or intimate union with, God. Thus Kauṇḍinya's yoga substantially differs from that of Patañjali and his followers. Kauṇḍinya, like Akṣapāda, refers to the grace of God, His being the efficient cause of the world, and individual souls' merits and demerits. But, unlike him, Kauṇḍinya admits perception, inference, and scriptural testimony as the means of valid knowledge, and rejects comparison as a distinct pramāṇa. He mentions knowledge, pleasure, pain, desire, and volition as the qualities of the self from which its existence can be inferred, like Akṣapāda. But unlike him, he regards consciousness as an essential quality of the self. Kaṇāda does not distinctly refer to God in the 'Vaiśeṣikasūtra', though his followers prove His existence as the efficient cause of the world. Kauṇḍinya does not mention Kaṇāda's doctrine of atoms, though he mentions the five subtle elements. His cosmology is similar to the Sāṁkhya cosmology, but he regards prakṛti and its modifications as the effects of God, who is the supreme Cause. Neither the 'Pāśupatasūtra' nor Kauṇḍinya refers to meditation on God at the six centres of mystic consciousness in the Suṣumnā within the spinal cord or Kuṇḍalinīyoga nor to the worship of Umā as the power or consort of Śiva emphasised by the Pratyabhijñā school of Śaivaism in Kashmir and Vīra Śaivism as expounded by Śrīpati Paṇḍita in the 'Śrīkarabhāṣya' on the 'Brahmasūtra'.

The Pāśupata system is called Lakulīśa philosophy because Lakulīśa was its founder. The word means one who bears a staff in his hand. He was an incarnation of Śiva born at Karavan, the account of which is given in the 'Kāravaṇamāhatmya'. 'Lakulīśa' is called also 'Nakulīśa'. Viśuddhamuni mentions twenty eight incarnations of Śiva including Lakulīśa, the last. Haribhadra (1400 A.D.) mentions eighteen incarnations of Śiva including Nakulīśa, the first, in his 'Ṣaḍdarśanasamuccaya.' Mādhava gives an account of 'Nakulīśa-Pāśupata-darśana'. Evidently, 'Nakulīśa' and 'Lakulīśa' are the names of the same person, the founder of the Pāśupata system. Haribhadra avers that the Naiyāyikas also called the Yaugas are Śaivas and that the Vaiśeṣikas are Pāśupatas, although their systems differ little from each other, because their categories are comprised in one another despite their difference in number, and although the means of valid knowledge recognised by them differ in number. Rājaśekhara (1400 A.D.) identifies the Yauga school with the Śaivas, and mentions eighteen teachers of whom Nakulīśa is the first. He mentions Akṣapāda, Jayanta, Udayana, and Bhāsarvajña, the Naiyāyikas, as Śaivas in his 'Ṣaḍdarśanasamuccaya'. Guṇaratna (1400 A.D.) avers that the system of Akṣapāda is called the Śaiva, and that the system of Kaṇāda is called the Pāśupata, since the former is devoted to Sadāśiva while the latter is devoted to Paśupati, in his commentary on Haribhadra's 'Ṣaḍdarśanasamuccaya'.

J. N. Banerjee opines that Lakulīśa flourished in Kathiavar in the second century A.D. He revived and strengthened the Pāśupata religion which originated even before Buddha and Mahāvīra.[2]

EPISTEMOLOGY.—Kauṇḍinya admits three means of valid knowledge : perception, inference, and testimony. Perception is of two kinds : sense-perception and self-perception. Perception of external objects and their qualities is called sense-perception because it is acquired through the sense-organs. Sound, touch, colour, taste, and odour are the qualities of physical substances. Jars and the like are external substances. Self-perception is acquired through the grace of God when a self whose essential nature is consciousness is purified of all stains due to attraction towards physical objects and sense-organs, and due to emotions such as love, hate, anger, greed, envy, delusion and the like. A self is perceived when the pure mind is completely concentrated on it dissociated from the body, sense-organs and the like. Inference is preceded by perception. The existence of God is inferred from the world as an effect as its efficient cause. The Nyāya and the Vaiśeṣika hold this view. They are Pāśupatas. Inference is of two kinds : dṛṣṭa and sāmānyatodṛṣṭa. Dṛṣṭa is of two kinds : pūrvavat and śeṣavat. 'This is that of the dimension of six fingers' is a pūrvavat inference. 'This is a cow'. This fact is inferred from the perception of horns and the like. The movement of the sum is inferred by sāmānyatodṛṣṭa from its passing from one place to another in the sky. Testimony is scriptural tesimony derived from God and seers. These are the three pramāṇas. Comparison, presumption, inclusion, nonapprehension, tradition, flash of intuition and the like are included in them. A pramāṇa is a means of valid knowledge. It is generated by the intercourse of the sense-organs with their objects which manifest knowledge, and by the assistance of virtue, vice, manifestation, place, time, a moral imperative, or a command of God, and the like. God is the inducing cause of a pramāṇa, and makes a pramāṇa produce valid knowledge. A self is the knower of valid knowledge. Effects, sense-organs, union of a soul with God, the method of accomplishing the union, and release, which includes the absolute extinction of pain, are the objects of knowledge. Consciousness is valid knowledge. Consciousness, thought or knowledge is the manifestation of vidyā.[3]

ONTOLOGY : CAUSE : GOD.—God is called Śiva because He is self-complete and self-fulfilled. He is absolutely devoid of pain. He is the Lord (pati) because He is the supreme cause of the bound souls, the world, fetters and the like. He is called Īśvara because He is the ruler of all bound souls. He is the supreme Lord of all rulers, Brahmā and the like. He is the fulfilment of all desires. He is eternal and exists in all times. According to the atheistic Sāṁkhya prakṛti is the cause of the world. But the Pāśupata regards God as the cause of the world, Who is different from prakṛti. God is the ruler of all kinds of vidyā and the like, which are the means of virtue, wealth, happiness, and absolute isolation from prakṛti and its effects. He is the ruler of prakṛti and its effects. He is the ruler of the souls that pursue wealth, happiness, virtue, and isolation from prakṛti. He is the ruler of all conscious entities and unconscious elements. He is called 'Īśvara' since He is possessed of supreme lordship intrinsic to His nature. Some souls acquire lordship which is their acquired quality. He is the Lord of Brahmā who rules over vidyā, kalā, and creatures. Brahmā is an individual soul. God is the Lord of Brahmā and other rulers, and so called the 'Supreme Lord'. He is called 'Pati' since He knows, maintains, and enjoys all effects—the bound souls and the physical elements. He is called 'Ṛṣi' since He rules over all effects, vidyā, kalā, and bound souls. He is called Vipra since He knows all objects and since He pervades them with His power of knowledge. He is called 'Mahat' since His power of knowledge and power of action are His essential poweıs and not aquired powers. He is called 'Eṣa' because He is eternally present with a constant nature. He is untainted by words, since He is indescribable by words through qualities and characteristics, since He is different from them and unspecified by them, and since He should be contemplated as different from physical qualities, vidyā, kalā, individual souls and the like through the manas, discarding words. He is said to be free of association with words because He is the supreme cause, because He is endowed with essential powers of sovereignty, and because He is indescribable by words. He is called 'Maheśvara' since His powers of lordship are the greatest and not acquired like those of Brahmā and other individual souls. He is called 'Vāma' because He is endowed with the most excellent qualities and virtues and because He is the supreme cause among the subordinate causes and because He is the cause of the virtues that generate liberation.[4] He is called 'Deva' since He is endowed with the power of producing all effects by His mere volition and since He veils the knowledge of individual souls and binds them to embodied life, produces vidyā, kalā, and bound souls (paśu) and removes their nescience playfully. He is called 'Jyeṣṭha', because He is superior to the released and the aspirant souls, whose nature is controlled by Him, and whose desires for happiness, renunciation of desires, and abiding in Him are controlled by Him, and because His power of knowledge, power of action, power of lordship are eternal and greater than those of individual souls. He is called 'Rudra' because He associates individual souls with various kinds of fear arising from names. He is called 'Kāla' because He produces all effects from Brahmā down to earth and other elements, associates individual souls with particular places, bodies, sense-organs, and their objects, and dissociates the former from the latter and destroys the former's internal organs through the function of time. He is called 'Kalavikaraṇa' since He associates individual souls with particular places, bodies, sense-organs and their objects, and with virtue, vice, knowledge, nescience, detachment, attachment, sovereignty, and its absence, although He is devoid of internal organs and external sense-organs, because of His unobstructed power of knowledge and power of action. He is the Lord of the different worlds, bodies, sense-organs, and their objects. He is called 'Balapramathana' because He has the power of the operation, suppression, and destruction of virtue, vice, knowledge, nescience, detachment, attachment, sovereignty, nonsovereignty, desire, aversion, and volition called vidyā. He is called 'Sarvabhūtadamana' since He destroys excessive attachment of gods, men, beasts and birds to particular places, bodies, sense-organs, and their objects by producing in them the insight that all are done by God, according to Kaundinya. But Bhāsarvajña avers that God is so called because He produces excessive attachment in all gods, men, beasts, and birds to the objects of pleasure. Both the statements are correct because God is the cause of both bondage and release by veiling individual souls' knowledge and manifesting it. God is both immanent and transcendent. He is immanent since He rules over all effects—physical things and their qualities—and sense-organs, and since He favours the operation of all cognitive and motor organs. He is transcendent, since He is devoid of all effects and sense-organs, since He is possessed of infinite powers, and since He knows all beings and objects but is not known by any other being. He is called 'Amana' since He is devoid of the internal organ. He is called 'Manas' since He favours the functioning of the internal organ. He is called 'Paśupati' for He is the Lord of bound souls (paśu). He protects them by His power of pervasion by His unlimited power of knowledge, and by His power of ruling over them. Their voluntary actions for the acquisition of wealth and happiness, and for the acquisition of virtue and release, their existence, their attainment of good and evil, and their association with places, bodies, sense-organs, and their objects depend upon His will. He has the power of obscuring their knowledge and binding them to embodied life. He has the power of revealing their knowledge and liberating them from bondage. He has the power of bestowing His grace on bound souls by destroying their miseries. He has the power of creating, maintaining, and destroying the world. His lordship consists in His infinite power of knowledge and power of action, and His being the First Cause consists in His being eternally related to His powers of lordship or in His being endowed with them which are not acquired by Him. He is called 'Śaṁkara' because He is the cause of mind-control or equanimity, happiness and liberation. He is called 'Aghora' because He rules over an infinite number of bodies which afford pleasures to individual souls. He is called 'Ghoratara' because He rules over an infinite number of bodies which cause pain to them. He is called 'Puruṣa' because He pervades and rules over all kinds of knowledge, which are effects, and because He has the power of producing an infinite number of bodies as desired by Him. He is called the 'Brahman' because He is the greatest. He is called 'Bhagavat' because He always exists with an unchanging nature everywhere. He is called 'Śiva' because He is completely fulfilled. These qualities of God should be contemplated at the time of muttering His name or mantra. Such contemplation quickly increases the purification of the soul.[5]

Kauṇḍinya asks whether God is dependent on individual souls' merits and demerits or whether He is independent of them. He replies that He is independent of souls' merits and demerits. Individual souls depend upon God in performing their actions, but He does not depend upod them or their voluntary actions and consequent merits and demerits. So God is independent of souls' merits and demerits. He is absolutely free and independent.

Mādhava discusses this question in his account of the Pāśupata system. It is objected that if God were the absolute cause of all effects irrespective of individual souls' merits and demerits, they and souls' voluntary actions which are their causes would become useless and they would produce their fruits simultaneously. This objection is not valid because there is no fault in this view. If God is the absolute cause of all effects, souls' merits and demerits become useless. There is no defect in this view. If it is objected that, in that case, there is no end or motive of an action, whose end of action is absent? If souls' merits and demerits become useless, who is the cause of their becoming useless? Are souls its cause? Or, is God its cause? The answer is: when souls' actions and consequent merits and demerits are favoured by God, they bear fruits. So souls are not the cause of their actions and their merits and demerits becoming useless, since their volition and actions are controlled by God's volition. Nor is God the cause of souls' actions, merits and demerits becoming useless, since He is completely self-fulfilled and devoid of an end in doing an action. The objection that all merits and demerits of individual souls will produce their fruits simultaneously is not sound, since God is endowed with inconceivable power and unrestricted power of action whereby He can make the subordinate causes or "second causes" produce their effects according to His volition. Kauṇḍinya avers that God can make souls' merits and demerits produce their fruits either simultaneously or gradually according to His absolute will. A Pāśupata scripture says. 'God is independent of souls' merits and demerits, and absolutely free in His volitions and actions. So He is the cause of all causes.'[6]

EFFECTS.—A bound soul is an effect. Effects are vidyā, kalā, and paśu. Bound souls are produced, favoured, veiled, influenced by time, and modified. Kalā is of two kinds: effects and organs of knowledge and action. Bound souls are of three classes: gods, men, and beasts, birds and insects. They are impure and pure. Vidyā, Kalā, and bound souls are different from one another. According to the Sāṁkhya, prakṛti and some of its modifications are causes, but they are effects according to the Pāśupata doctrine because they are known by souls and fetter them to bondage (pāśa). According to the Sāṁkhya, bound souls are causes, but according to the Pāśupata they are effects because they are bound by God. Physical elements are effects as they are modifiable. Bound souls are modifiable since they are effects. Their knowledge can be veiled and manifested by God. They can be bound and liberated. They are subject to the influence of time. According to others, souls are causes, but they are effects according to the Pāśupata because they are bound by God. An individual soul is called 'ātman' or 'kṣetrajña' since it pervades the unconscious effects—prakṛti, physical things, and sense-organs, and knows them. It is conscious while they are unconscious. It is the hearer, toucher, seer, taster, smeller, thinker, speaker, and comprehender. It is conscious, atomic, and immortal. It is a knower of objects, an experiencer of pleasure and pain, and a witness. It is known from its pleasure, pain, desire, aversion, volition, and consciousness. It is unborn and not generated by physical elements and qualities—sound, touch, colour, taste, and odour. It is eternal. It is not non-eternal. When it is dissociated from prakṛti, effects, and sense-organs, and united with God through meditation and trance, it is said to be eternal.[7] Consciousness is not its acquired quality but its essential quality. Though the Naiyāyikas and the later Vaiśeṣikas are Pāśupatas, they hold that consciousness is an acquired quality of an individual soul generated by its conjunction with manas and sense-organs. When it fixes its mind on God dwelling in all creatures as their Supreme Soul, when it renounces desire and aversion and voluntary actions for the attainment of happiness, it is filled with friendship and good will for all. Universal good will arises from equality towards all. When its mind is fixed on God steadily, an attached, nonmeditative, unsteady, noneternal, born, unfriendly soul becomes detached, meditative, eternal, unborn, and friendly to all beings. A soul's steady abiding in God is acquired by the complete control of all sense-organs. They are controlled by withdrawing them from evil objects and associated with good objects. Men, beasts, birds, reptiles, etc., all are embodied individual souls. The masters of yoga are included in gods because they abound in merits. The souls residing in hell are included in beasts, birds, etc., because they abound in demerits. The fourteen worlds with their denizens are called 'saṁsāra' because they are the fields of birth and death. They are produced by God—the efficient cause. Souls are the experiencers of the fruits of these worlds. God causes their enjoyments and sufferings, destroys them, and manifests their experience by associating them with the appropriate bodies, sense-organs, and objects. He is the cause of kalā in the forms of effects and sense-organs. Earth, water, light, air, and ether are effects. The ears, the skin, the eyes, the tongue, the nose, the hands, the legs, the vocal organ, the generative organ, the evacuative organ, manas, buddhi, and ahaṁkāra are the sense-organs. God associates individual souls with the different worlds, bodies, sense-organs, and objects, and with virtue, vice, knowledge, nescience, attachment, detachment, sovereignty, and nonsovereignty. All souls except those which are released in embodied life are endowed with consciousness. They are of two classes: those which are tainted with the five physical elements and the sense-organs, and those which are neither attracted towards nor detached from effects and sense-organs since being associated with bodies, sense-organs, and their objects depends upon merits, demerits, manifestation, place, time, sacred commands and the like. Bhāsarvajña divides individual souls into tainted souls and taintless souls. The former are related to the bodies and the sense-organs. The latter are of three kinds, viz., those which are not attached to sense-organs and their objects, those which are in the state of steadiness, and those which are completely isolated from prakṛti and its effects.[8]

GOD AND EFFECTS.—God is the supreme cause. Vidyā, kalā, and bound individual souls are effects. They are produced, maintained, and dissolved in Him as stars appear and disappear in the sky. They abide in Him, and He is their abode, seat, or substratum. Effects are modifications of His power, and exist in it. He exists in them by His volition and power as inexhaustible and immortal. All subordinate causes and their effects exist in Him. They are inseparable from Him—the supreme cause. But causes and effects are not intermixed with each other as the sun and the objects illumined by it are not intermixed with each other. The supreme cause and the antecedent subordinate causes are more pervasive than the succeeding effects which are permeated by them. So they are distinguished and separated from each other. God is all-pervasive and pervades twenty five entities beginning with individual souls. Souls are more pervasive than twenty four entities beginning with prakṛti, which are permeated by souls. Prakṛti is more pervasive than twenty three entities beginning with buddhi, which are permeated by it. Buddhi is more pervasive than twenty two entities beginning with ahaṁkāra, which are permeated by it. Ahaṁkāra is more pervasive than eleven sense-organs and ten subtle elements and gross elements, which are permeated by it. Eleven sense-organs are more pervasive than five subtle elements and five gross elements, which are permeated by them. Five subtle elements—sound-essence, touch-essence, colour-essence, taste-essence, and odour-essence—are more pervasive than five gross elements, which are permeated by them. Ether, air, light, water, and earth are five gross elements. Ether is more pervasive than air, light, water, and earth, which are permeated by it. Air is more pervasive than light, water, and earth, which are permeated by it. Light is more pervasive than water and earth, which are permeated by it. Water is more pervasive than earth, which is permeated by it. Earth is more pervasive than earthen products—gods, men, beasts and birds, trees, plants, creepers, grass, and the like, which are permeated by it. So causes and effects are not intermixed with each other. It may be objected that there is no example of nonintermixture of entities by their functions. The answer is: turmeric water is an example in which there are the qualities of water—coolness, wetness, etc.—and the qualities of turmeric—odour, colour, pungence, density, etc. In the mixture earth is permeated by water. God is all-pervasive, associates individual souls with places, bodies, sense-organs and their objects, and pleasures and pains produced by them. He knows prakṛti, souls' merits and demerits, and gives them pleasures and pains in accordance with them, and remains immutable in them. So He is not intermixed with them, although they abide in Him. Immutable God is not intermixed with His mutable effects. Causes and effects are not intermixed with each other owing to their different functions, although they are pervasive, the former being more pervasive than the latter. They abide in God—the substratum. So effects are eternal for God in them is eternal. They are maintained by God. Because God, the maintainer, is eternal, effects maitained by Him are eternal. They exist in Him in the past, the present, and the future, as a seed exists in earth.

God is the cause of vidyā, kalā, and bound individual souls. He produces, favours, and dissolves them. They are produced, favoured, and dissolved by Him. So He is their cause, and they are His effects. He produces gods, men, beasts, birds, and insects. He produces virtue, knowledge, detachment, and sovereignty, and vice, nescience, attachment, and the absense of lordship. He binds them, and He liberates them.[9] He binds them by eclipsing their knowledge and powers, and liberates them by extending His grace to them and manifesting their knowledge and powers playfully. Effects and the sense-organs are fetters of bound souls. Wealth, happiness, virtue, liberation, and the means of attaining them are vidyā. God is their Lord, and rules over them. Vidyā is the knowledge which reveals the nature of one's self, and of other selves, like a lamp. It is the result of austerities, and reveals the distinction between good and evil, and the actions which are conducive to recollection of, union with, and abidence in, God, and the way to the attainment of supreme perfection. Vidyā is the knowledge which manifests the nature of the real entities described in the Nyāya system which advocates the Pāśupata philosophy. One who has acquired the knowledge of acquisition, impurities, and the means of attaining to liberation, is called wise. God is the cause of knowledge.

Kalā includes effects and sense-organs. Earth, water, light, air, and ether are effects. Sound is the quality of ether. Sound and touch are the qualities of air. Sound, touch, and colour are the qualities of light. Sound, touch, colour, and taste are the qualities of water. Sound, touch, colour, taste, and odour are the qualities of earth. The ears, the skin, the eyes, the tongue, the nose, the legs, the hands, the vocal organ, the generative organ, the excretive organ, manas, buddhi, and ahaṁkāra are the sense-organs. There are five cognitive organs, five motor organs, and three internal organs. The sense-organs are so called because they receive, discard, and move towards, objects. The mind (citta) is so called because it makes the soul know objects, feel pleasure and pain, and acquire virtue and vice. The internal organ is called citta, or manas.[10]

Mādhava gives the following account of vidyā, kalā, and bound souls. The entities which are dependent on God are effects. They are of three kinds, viz., vidyā, kalā, and paśu. Bound souls are included in vidyā since they are endowed with vidyā. Vidyā is of two kinds, viz., conscious and unconscious. Conscious vidyā is of two kinds, viz., discrimination and nondiscrimination. Discrimination is the function of the internal organ. All animate beings endowed with it know objects generally and individually. Bound souls' merits and demerits are unconscious vidyā. The entities which depend upon God, a conscious Being, but which are themselves unconscious are called kalā. Mādhava following Kauṇḍinya divides kalā into effeects and sense-organs. Five elements and their five specific qualities are effects. Five organs of knowledge, five organs of action, and three internal organs, manas, buddhi, and ahaṁkāra,—are the thirteen sense-organs. Doubt, determinate knowledge, and ego-sense are the functions of manas, buddhi, and ahaṁkāra, respectively.

A bound soul is an individual soul fettered by bonds. Bound souls are of two kinds, viz., impure and pure. The souls related to bodies and sense-organs are impure. The souls devoid of them are pure. They are elaborated in the 'Pañcārthabhāṣya' and the 'Dīpikā'. The bondage of individual souls consists in their lack of supernatural divine powers, or in the concealment of God's causal power, or in dependence. It is beginningless. Effects and sense-organs called kalā are the fetters. Individual souls are fettered by them, and become subject to their influence. This constitutes their dependence, nonsovereignty, bondage. Individual souls are bound because they are fettered by effects and sense-organs. They perceive effects and are attached to them, and are thus fettered by them to embodied life. It is implied that divine powers of lordship are inherent in individual souls, but that they are suppressed in bondage, and liberated in release.[11]

YOGA.—Yoga is the union of an individual soul with God. Patañjali defines yoga as the suppression of mental modes by withdrawing the mind from all objects. But, according to the Pāśupata, yoga is the union of a soul with God through trance or complete absorption of the mind in Him. The mind can be fixed on God when it is withdrawn from all objects of pleasure and when it becomes pure and free of distracting emotions and passions. Mere suppression of mental functions is not yoga, but complete union of a soul with God is yoga. Kriyāyoga consists in the mind's abiding in God for a long time, meditation, recollection and the like. It leads to the union of a soul with God. Penance also generates it. The union is brought about by a soul's meditation, recollection, and abiding in God, and by the command and grace of God, and by both. It is a state of an individual soul, and it is produced in God. When a soul is united with God, He is united with the soul.[12]

SPIRITUAL DISCIPLINE.—The union of a soul with God is not acquired by mere knowledge of the scriptures, but by a method of spiritual discipline prescribed by the Pāśupata scriptures. Mādhava avers that the union of a soul with God is effected through the mind. It is of two kinds, viz., yoga characterised by actions, and yoga characterised by the cessation of actions. The former consists in the repeated uttering of a name or a mantra of God, meditation, and the like. The latter consists in the movement of the mind. Vidhi is the action which generates virtue or merit. It is of two kinds, viz., principal actions and subordinate actions.

The principal actions directly generate virtue or merit. Good conduct is of two kinds, viz., vows and actions preparatory to them. Besmearing the body with holy ashes, lying in them, offering actions to God, repeatedly uttering a name or a mantra of Śiva, and walking round a temple are the vows. The offering of actions is that of loud laughter, singing God's excellent qualities, dancing in the prescribed manner, crying in an appropriate manner, bowing to God, and uttering His name or mantra to Him. These actions should be offered mentally to Him if other people are present. The preparatory actions are pretending to sleep while one is awake, shaking the limbs as if one is struck by epilepsy, dragging one's feet as if one is lame, making gestures like a lewd person towards a young beautiful woman, performing reprehensible actions like a person devoid of the power of discrimination between right and wrong actions, and speaking incoherent and meaningless words.[13] These are certainly repulsive actions.

The body should be besmeared with holy ashes in the morning, at noon, and in the evening. An aspirant should lie in holy ashes, but should not sleep. He should study the scriptures, teach other aspirants, meditate on God, and remember Him. After satisfying the calls of nature, eating, spitting, etc., he should touch ashes to purify himself. He should bear flowers offered to Śiva at the time of worship. The body should be besmeared with ashes, and flowers should be borne as the signs of being a Śaiva as prescribed by the Pāśupata scriptures. He should live in a village, a forest, a holy place, or a temple of Śiva. If he lives in any other place than a temple, e.g., under the sky, at the root of a tree, or in an open space, he should walk round the place and treat it as a temple. He should offer these actions to God. He should offer all his bodily, vocal, and mental actions to Him, and wait on Him as a servant after withdrawing his mind from the functions of all the sense-organs. These actions should be performed for the increase of devotion to God. Devotion to other gods is prohibited. Wearing a single cloth or a loin-cloth to cover one's nudity, or wearing no cloth in order to practise nonpossession, not seeing human urine and stool, and not talking to women and Śūdras in order to avoid the loss of knowledge, penances, and learning acquired from the scriptures, are prescribed. If an aspirant is compelled to talk to them in a village, he should atone for it by touching ashes and not water,—practising breath-control, and muttering gāyatrī in honour of Śiva—not Vaidikī gāyatrī. Japa is a mental act of muttering. Seeing impure things and talking to women and Śūdras make the mind impure by exciting desire, aversion, and anger. Women and Śūdras were not justly treated at the time. The 'Bhagavad Gītā' also condemns both despite its lofty and liberal teachings. Mendicancy should be adopted for one's livelihood, penances should be undergone, journey from one place to another should be made, and one should not remain in one place for some days.[14]

Then an aspirant should practise restraints, moral observances, breath-control, withdrawal of the sense-organs from their objects, concentrate his mind on a vital part of the body, meditate on God, and be absorbed in and united with Him. Non-injury, celibacy, truthfulness, abstention from trade and commerce, and not-stealing are the five restraints. The absence of anger, service to the preceptor, purity, temperance in eating and drinking, and vigilance are the five moral observances. One who does not do any injury to any creature in mind, and by words or by deeds, becomes immortal. Non-injury is greater than sacrifices, penances, celibacy, truthfulness, vows, study of the scriptures, and charity. An aspirant should strictly observe celibacy. A woman is the root of all evils. So no wise man should embrace a woman. Abstention from sexual union generates equanimity and penance. Strict celibacy makes an aspirant immortal, or emancipates him from bondage. The mind is the chief of the sense-organs, which should be controlled by it. External sense-organs are controlled by the mind, and it is controlled by the self. So sense-restraint is the control of the self by itself. Celibacy, in a wider sense, means the control of all sense-organs. Speaking the truth is truthfulness. An aspirant should speak words which agree with facts. Speaking the truth for the harm of others is forbidden. Speaking an untruth for the good of all beings is enjoined. A wholesome truth should be spoken ; an unwholesome truth should not be spoken ; a wholesome falsehood should not be spoken. A falsehood conducive to the good of all beings becomes a truth, and is enjoined by the Pāśupata scriptures.[15]

Trade and commerce should be shunned. Commerce consists in buying and selling merchandise. It causes pain to oneself and to other persons. In the former case a person suffers in this life. In the latter case he acquires vice which generates pain either in this life or in future life. So an aspirant should not engage in commerce. One who commits sins, one who praises sins, one who assists sinners to commit sins, and one who enjoys sins, are all sinners. One who does not enter upon an enterprise, who is not boastful, who ungrudgingly performs right actions, who performs restraints and moral observances, becomes a sage, and conquers old age and death. Nonstealing should be practised. There are six kinds of stealing, viz., taking what is not given in charity, seizing wealth from children, insanes, intoxicated persons, old persons, and sick persons, taking undesirable articles, e.g., insects, bees, birds, flies, etc., taking unapproved articles, e.g., land, cattle, birds, beasts, etc., seizing gold, clothes, etc., from others through deceit, magic, and other dishonest means, and eating, drinking, licking, and chewing any food without offering a part of it to a preceptor. Nonstealing is abstention from these six kinds of stealing. A thief suffers in this world and in the next world. He is wicked, malevolent, and dreadful to all persons. The five kinds of restraints are described. The absence of anger should be cultivated. There are four kinds of anger, viz., anger relating to emotions, e.g., intolerance, aversion, pride, conceit, envy, and the like, anger relating to actions, e.g., quarrel, enmity, beating, etc., anger causing mutilation, chastisement of hands, legs, nose, fingers, etc., and anger causing suicide or killing others. The absence of anger is eschewing these four kinds of anger. It consists in enduring all bodily and mental conflicts due to bodily, mental, or supernatural causes. An aspirant should not be angry if his country, caste, family, or conduct is condemned by any person, because his self is conscious, pervasive, and pure. One's own self and others' selves are not perceived. An angry person commits sins, speaks sinful words, and becomes shameless. So anger should be discarded. His muttering God's name or mantra, sacrifice, penance, charity, study of the scriptures, and even equanimity become fruitless. Those who can pacify their anger are great. Knowledge is accompanied by penance ; penance is accompanied by fulfilment ; fulfilment is accompanied by forgiveness. Forgiveness is the greatest friend ; anger is the greatest enemy. Forgiving persons conquers this world and the next world. Service to a preceptor should be practised. He should be served day and night and respected by rising before him, bowing to him, doing him good, executing his commands, dedicating one's self to him, following him like a shadow and looking up to his favour. A disciple should impart his knowledge acquired from his preceptor to many pupils and thus serve him and praise his greatness. If sense-restraint is accidentally relaxed, respect for a preceptor always expiates the lapse. The past, the present, and the future are revealed to a disciple by his preceptor's instructions. He is the instructor of the way to liberation. He is the giver of immortality. God imparts knowledge through a preceptor, who enlightens a person by imparting the saving knowledge to him. One who disrespects one's preceptor goes to hell, since he is the giver of immortality. One who honours one's preceptor in all conditions worships God. A preceptor is a person, who initiates a disciple in the Pāśupata cult, and who knows the nature of the supreme cause, effects, union of the soul with God, the means of effecting the union, and liberation. A disciple is born in a noble Brāhmaṇa family, endowed with keen sense-organs, and possessed of a strong desire to know the truth and attain divine powers.

Purity should be practised. Purity is of three kinds, viz., bodily purity, mental purity, and purity of self. Holy ashes burn impurities due to association, inheritance from the parents, eating and drinking impure food and drink, and inherent in bones and marrow. They destroy the most heinous sins due to theft, sexual congress with a preceptor's wife, and killing a Brāhmaṇa. They are consumed by muttering Śiva's name or mantra or gāyatrī in His honour. One who besmears one's body with holy ashes every day with sense-restraint attains the highest good. Bodily purity should be observed with restraints and moral observances. Mental purity is acquired by truthfulness, penances, sense-control, compassion for all creatures, desirelessness in receiving gifts, in entering on an enterprise, and in experiencing the objects of the sense-organs. Even the gift of all one's wealth with an impure mind is not conducive to virtue. Good dispositions lead to the fulfilment of all noble desires. One who remains unperturbed even when one is despised, humiliated and calumniated, attains purity of self. There is no other greater spiritual discipline than being insulted as it produces endurance, humility, impurturbability, and egolessness.[16]

Begged food is the best and purest food. Mendicancy is the best penance, and generates the highest good. One should beg food of Brāhmaṇas, Kṣatriyas, Vaiśyas and Śūdras, but not of depraved sinners. One should not associate with them in all conditions. Even an ascetic falls owing to association with them. Evil company should be eschewed by all means. Begging food from door to door, begging food without any desire, begging food with an intention, accepting unsolicited food, and receiving food got by chance are the five kinds of begging. Temperance in eating and drinking should be cultivated. It consists in taking light diet. Overeating is forbidden as it is injurious to self-control. One should perform breath-control three times while taking a morsel of food. This act is not prescribed by any other religious sect. Vigilance should be practised. Negligence and inadvertence should be shunned. Restraints should be performed with vigilance and constant recollection of duties. A Brāhmaṇa should meditate on God with vigilance, mind-control, renunciation and good conduct. By doing so he destroys fears due to confinement in the womb, pangs of rebirth, old age, and death, and becomes like God. Accidental talking to women and Śūdras should be expiated by performing breath-control. A morsel of food should be taken with breath-control thrice. It should be performed with knowledge, desire, and volition. The time of retention of breath should be four times that of inhalation, and the time of exhalation should be double that of inhalation. It should be done under expert guidance according to one's capacity. An easy squatting posture is a precondition of breath-control. It destroys impurities and sins, gradually steadies the mind, and makes it fit for meditation. Japa is the repeated muttering of a name or a mantra of God. It is of three kinds : audible, inaudible and mental. Audible muttering is ten times better than sacrifices or oblations to a sacrificial fire. Inaudible muttering is a hundred times better than sacrifices. Mental muttering is a thousand times better than sacrifices. Mental japa should be performed ; it destroys vices, increases virtues, deflects the mind from wrong actions, and fixes it on God. 'Om', or a mantra of Śiva, or gāyatrī of Śiva, should be muttered mentally. Unconditioned and undivided devotion to Śiva, the supreme Lord, is required of an aspirant in the Pāśupata cult. Devotion to any other subordinate god is forbidden. Śiva is the grantor of bliss and liberation, and so called Śaṁkara. Devotion is meditation.[17] An aspirant should speak of God, think of God, and act for God. He should always meditate on God while walking, sitting, waking, or sleeping. (Cp. Caitanya). All emotions should be directed towards God, and not to any other being. (Cp. 'Bhāgavata') Śiva alone should be worshipped by a Pāśupata ascetic. Sacrifices to gods and offering food to the souls of the ancestors are prohibited. They are in God's power, and created, maintained, and destroyed by Him. They are bound souls. Devotion should be withdrawn from them, and directed towards God. God is the cause of vidyā, kalā, and bound souls. He associates individual souls with their bodies, sense-organs and their objects, and dissociates the former from the latter ; He is the cause of their bondage and release. Eight kinds of obeisance are the means of offering and dedicating oneself to God. Self-dedication implies complete self-surrender to Him. It eradicates a worshipper's egoism, and awakens divine powers in him.

The objects of the sense-organs and their qualities, sound, touch, colour, taste, and odour are blemishes, for they are causes of the fulfilment of desires. Desire, anger, greed, fear, dream, love, hate, delusion, and the like states, emotions, and passions are causes of voluntary actions. They are the motives of action. So acquisition, preservation, loss, of the objects of pleasure, association with them, and injury to others are blemishes. The acquisition of the objects of enjoyment causes pain to oneself and to others. Causing others pain generates a demerit which produces pain in the next world. The preservation of them with the aid of weapons causes pain to oneself and to others. The loss of them due to seizure by a king, arson, theft, etc., causes pain to oneself and to others. So renunciation of them is better than acquisition, preservation, and loss of them. Renunciation destroys all suffering. So it should be cultivated by an aspirant for the destruction or prevention of all his sufferings. Without discarding the objects of sentient pleasure he can never be truly happy. Food, women, and power and domination are the three sources of danger, which bring about the degradation of all persons. There is no greater enlightener than knowledge ; there is no greater enemy than anger ; there is no greater misery than greed ;

there is no greater happiness than renunciation. Desire is never pacified by gratification but intensified by it. Rich crops, cattle, gold, and women can never produce contentment. So a wise person should acquire detachment and equanimity. Attachment should be destroyed, and detachment should be cultivated. Attachment is due to nescience. The objects of enjoyment, attachment and other consequent emotions and passions, which are blemishes, can be dissociated from the soul by the mind favoured by virtue, recollection, knowledge of the sacred injunction, etc., and fixed on God. Vice is the cause of distraction of the mind, and virtue is the cause of concentration of it, and its steady abiding in God. Meditation, recollection, abiding in God, and the like are due to virtue. The abiding of the mind in God without anything intervening between them is called abiding (sthiti). The sense-organs should be gradually controlled by the mind with the help of self-control, mental concentration, recollection, meditation, and muttering a mantra of God. When the sense-organs are withdrawn from their objects, when the mind is disengaged from all objects of pleasure, when merits and demerits cease to function, and when the mind is fixed on God without flickering, the soul becomes one, inactive, fearless, and devoid of grief. Oneness consists in the soul's being unaffected by its body and sense-organs. Inactivity consists in the cessation of all bodily and mental actions. Fearlessness consists in the soul's conquering all fears. Grieflessness consists in freedom from all thoughts, good and evil. The study of the scriptures, recollection, meditation, etc., are good. Nonstudy, nonrecollection, nonmeditation, etc., are evil. In this state a seeker becomes entirely free of grief whether or not it engage in muttering a mantra, fixing the mind, meditating on God, and remembering Him.[18]

The withdrawal of the mind from the objects of the senses, and its fixation on God are absolutely necessary for union with God. It depends upon the control of the mind by the self. Then the mind should be concentrated in the heart. The self abides in it. Then the mystic syllable 'Om' should be meditated on. Mental concentration is a prerequisite for meditation. Kauṇḍinya calls abiding of the mind in God for a very long time 'adhyayana', which generally means the study of the scriptures. Transcendent and formless God unassociated with words and endowed with essential powers of lordship should be meditated on. 'Om' should be meditated on, as it is a symbol of God. Meditation leads to the merging of the self in His power of knowledge and power of action. He impels it to unite with these powers. Its union with Him is not possible without His volition. Meditation is uninterrupted thinking of God represented by 'Om', which results in the merging of the self in Him. Merging is absorption. Meditation with or without breath-control even for a short time destroys sins. Meditation, recollection and the like produce the withdrawal of the functions of the uncontrolled sense-organs, purification of the soul, acquisition, conquest of the senses, and constant proximity to God.[19] Regular meditation for six months unites the self with God constantly.

Recollection is constant thinking of God. The object of meditation should be constantly contemplated. Constant thought or recollection destroys merits and demerits. When these are destroyed, blemishes are destroyed, and the mind is not deflected from God but is constantly united with Him. Constant recollection of God or 'Om' brings about the continuous abiding of the mind in Him. It is firmly established in divine consciousness.

'Adhyayana' ordinarily means the study of the scriptures. Kauṇḍinya explains it also as mental muttering of gāyatrī in honour of Śiva. It steadies the mind like meditation, and facilitates the formation of a habit of uninterrupted meditation. Recollection brings about the mind's constant proximity to God or His constant presence. Kauṇḍinya also explains adhyayana as the abiding of the mind in God for along time. Kriyāyoga consists in the study of the scriptures, mental muttering of a mantra or gāyatrī of Śiva, meditation on Him, and the like. The practice of meditation for six months produces constant proximity to God. The self is gradually unaffected by its body and sense-organs, and acquires supernatural powers by the grace of God. These powers are called 'guṇa'.

Ascetics who have acquired supernatural powers are not associated with merits and demerits owing to these powers and soul-force, and not associated with bodies and sense-organs. They do not acquire vices, and commit sins. The union of the self with God can be attained by the performance of duties prescribed by the Pāśupata scriptures with a pure mind purged of immoral emotions and passions. It can be attained by the performance of penances without performing the prescribed duties mentioned above. Prescribed conduct and penances produce merits which bring about joy due to the revelation of supramundane entities. Then supernatural powers such as minuteness, lightness, largeness, extension of the powers of external sense-organs and internal organs, acquisition of distant objects, fulfilment of all desires, subduing others, and irresestible will are acquired. The first three are the qualities of the effect. The other five are the qualities of internal and external organs. These eight supernatural powers are called 'aiśvarya' in the other systems, but they are called 'joy' in the Pāśupata system. An ascetic becomes joyful and vigilant if he does not take pride in these supernatural powers due to virtue, knowledge, and soul-force. An ascetic acquires greatness by performing the prescribed duties, by undergoing penances, and by practising restraints, moral observances, withdrawal of the sense-organs from their objects, fixation of mind, muttering Śiva's mantra or gāyatrī, meditation, recollection, and steady abiding in God, with supreme devotion. Greatness is the power generated by austerities.

An advanced ascetice should perform supreme offering, supreme worship, and supreme penance for the attainment of supreme union with God. Supreme offering is the offering of one's self to God. The self is the giver of offerings to God. If the self is given to Him, there is no need for an ascetic's giving any other articles. The offering of the self results in the cessation of rebirth. It does not result in the further association of the self with any place, body, sense-organs, and their objects, but in the attainment of the soul's absolute proximity to God and of the cessation of rebirth. It is supreme offering, as its fruit is the highest good. The 'Bhāgavata' says, 'God gives Himself to a devotee who gives his self entirely to Him'. Aurobindo says, "The Divine gives itself to those who give themselves without reserve and in all their parts to the Divine." He requires an aspirant to offer all his actions to God. Jīva Gosvāmī also requires a devotee to offer all his actions, physical, vocal and mental, and considers this act to be a precondition of pure devotion. Oblations to a sacrificial fire are a bad mode of worship, for they produce temporary, relative, and limited goods. But the worship of God with all bodily, vocal and mental actions is supreme worship, because it does not entail the labour of collecting requisite articles, the trouble of accepting gifts, and the sin of killing animals. The common penances stated above produce merits and destroy demerits. Supreme penance produced by supreme offering and supreme worship generates joy and greatness explained above. Supreme penance makes an ascetic attain supreme union of the soul with God even without the study of the scriptures, meditation, and the like. It produces infinitude and constant union with God. The virtue produced by supreme offering, supreme worship, and supreme penance engenders absolute and perfect proximity to God, which stops rebirth. An ascetic should not be attached to the joy produced by the penances and should continue to perform them.[20]

An advanced ascetic does not exhibit the signs of a Śaiva, but performs actions which are contrary to the Pāśupata cult. He acts like an insane, an idiot, a dullard, or a person of reprehensible conduct. He conceals his knowledge, vows, purifying words, and actions preparatory to vows. He is despised by ignorant people for his reprehensible conduct, chastised and persecuted by them, and slandered and calumniated by them. Their actions are beneficial to him. He imparts his sins to them and receives their virtues, and his fortitude is enhanced by their actions. They increase his virtues and decrease his vices, bring him in close proximity to God, and make him acquire supernatural bodies, sense-organs, and objects. Despisement, persecution, and condemnation make him acquire the fruit of all austerities—the intuition of the self. Calumniation becomes praise, and makes him immaculate. Dishonour is his best honour. This is the best way ; it destroys his pride, eradicates his egoism, brings him in close proximity to God, stops his rebirth, and prescribed by the omniscient Lord. A Brāhmaṇa ascetic attains constant proximity to God, and is not born again.[21]

LIBERATION AND ITS MEANS.—For the Sāṁkhya and the Yoga, a soul's complete isolation or dissociation from prakṛiti and its products is liberation. It is a state of absolute extinction of bodily and mental pain, and of misery due to supernatural agencies. Bodily pain is due to diseases of the body. Mental pain is due to anger, greed, delusion, fear, dejection, envy, intolerance, hate, pride, conceit, malice, attachment, and other passions. Pain is due to fear of confinement in a womb, fear of birth, fear of nescience, fear of old age, fear of death, fear of this world, and fear of the next world, and due to the loss of good, the advent of evil, and obstruction to desire. Liberation is the extinction of rebirth. Released souls, according to the Sāṁkhya-Yoga, are devoid of the knowledge of their own souls and other souls, and almost unconscious. But, according to the Pāśupata, they are omniscient, and acquire the knowledge of their own souls and other souls ; they not only completely exterminate their sufferings, but also acquire divine powers of independence and lordship through the grace of God and vigilance. The classical Sāṁkhya holds that souls are eternally pure, enlightened, and free, and not unconscious. Kauṇḍinya describes an older Sāṁkhya-Yoga view. According to the Sāṁkhya-Yoga detached souls are released and attain peace and extinction of suffering. Their systems are impure. But, according to the Pāśupata, the attainment of supernatural divine powers,—omniscience, lordship, etc.,—is liberation. It is not mere isolation from prakṛti and its modifications. A soul's union with God is the supreme end. It is direct and perfect contact of a soul with Him, but it is not the extinction of a soul in Him. A liberated soul retains its integrity in the state of complete union with God. Liberation includes the absolute cessation of pain, but it is not only complete extinction of suffering, but it is also the acquisition of omniscience and omnipotence of God. It is attained through a soul's vigilance in spiritual discipline and God's grace. His grace consists in His volition to bestow liberation on a bound soul. The complete destruction of all kinds of suffering and the attainment of the divine qualities and powers of lordship depend upon the grace and will of God.

Mādhava discusses the means of attaining liberation in his account of the Pāśupata doctrine. Is liberation attained by the knowledge about God, or by the immediate intuition of God, or by the ascertainment of the real entities ? The first alternative is untenable, since then the repeated study of the scriptures will become unnecessary in that the common people will be liberated without studying the scriptures by simply knowing that God is the Lord of gods. The second alternative also is untenable, since bound souls tainted with an excess of impurities are incapable of acquiring the immediate intuition of God. The third alternative is in accord with the Pāśupata view. But the real entities cannot be ascertained without the help of the Pāśupata scriptures which describe the five kinds of real entities,—cause, effect, union of a soul with God, the means of such union, and liberation. Mādhava avers that absolute extinction of suffering is liberation according to the Sāṁkhya, but that the Pāśupata regards it as the attainment of the lordship of God also.[22] A soul's complete isolation from prakṛti and its modifications is the result of meditation according to the Sāṁkhya, but its attainment of divine powers, and of the total extinction of pain is the result of meditation according to the Pāśupata. Supernatural powers are acquired by penances, meditation, and the like. Seeing subtle, remote, hidden, and all visible objects is occult vision. Hearing all audible sounds is occult hearing. The knowledge of the objects of all thoughts is occult thinking. A liberated person acquires the knowledge of the thoughts of gods, men, beasts and birds, about wealth, happiness, virtue, and liberation. He acquires the occult knowledge of all real entities described in the scriptures. He becomes omniscient. Omniscience is the occult knowledge of all sensible objects, and of all bound souls and liberated souls. It is the knowledge of all real entities collectively and individually. The power of knowledge is one, but appears to be manifold according as its objects are manifold. Omniscience is acquired by a soul while it is essential to God. A liberated person acquires the power of acting most quickly like the mind. As soon as he has a volition to do an action, it is done for his power of knowledge and power of action are unobstructed. If he desires to destroy a thing, it is destroyed at once. His volitions in regard to other persons also are executed at once. A liberated person can assume all forms according to his volitions. This power consists in assuming infinite forms by mere volitions without any bodily actions. Earth, water, light, air, and ether are under his control. His sense-organs being pervasive can act upon these objects. He can rule over all forms at the same time. He becomes nondifferent from God in pervasiveness. He acquires the power of performing the functions of all sense-organs even though they are deficient and inoperative. His sense-organs become subtle, perfect, and grasp all objects. Hence liberation is the power of knowing and acting on objects without the help of the sense-organs. According to the Sāṁkhya and the Yoga a liberated soul is divested of all qualities except pure consciousness, but according to the Pāśupata it acquires the qualities and powers of God through His grace,—the power of assuming all forms, the power of knowing all objects without the help of the sense-organs, lordship, all-pervasiveness, omniscience, and the like.[22] A liberated person can subdue all bound souls, even gods, but he can never be subdued by them. He is endowed with divine powers, and so cannot be subdued by the powers of all bound souls. He can not only subdue all bound souls but can also enter into them, suppress their consciousness by his power, and fill them with his presence due to the pervasiveness of his power of knowledge and power of action. But others cannot enter into him, suppress his consciousness, and overpower him. He cannot be possessed by ghosts, demons, and other evil spirits. He can not only subdue and influence others powerfully, but can also compass their death by his supernatural power. But none can bring about his death. He becomes absolutely fearless, and has no fear of the past, the present, and the future. Unsubduability consists in complete independence of others. Unpossessibility consists in unsuppressibility of one's knowledge and consciousness by other beings. Indestructibility consists in not being deprived of one's life by others. Fearlessness consists in conquering all kinds of fear. A liberated person becomes imperishable owing to the possession of divine lordship which is eternal. Imperishability consists in acquiring eternal relation to divine lordship. A liberated person conquers old age, and does not suffer any loss of the power of knowledge and power of action due to the deficiency of his sense-organs. Unagingness consists in not suffering from the consequences of the infirmity of his body, and of his sense-organs. A liberated person becomes immortal. He does not experience pain due to the cessation of the function of the vital forces. His movement to all places becomes unrestricted. He can go anywhere he desires to go. He becomes endowed with eight supernatural powers, viz., unsubduability, unpossessability, indestructibility, undaumtability, imperishability, unagingness, and immortality called irresistibility. He becomes greater than all bound souls owing to the excess of his supernatural powers. He acquires the power of ruling over all effects including all bound souls. Minuteness, lightness, largeness, heaviness, obtaining objects out of sight, irresistible will, power of ruling over others, and power of fulfilling all desires are acquired by meditation and penances. Liberated souls are called 'siddha', because they have acquired all supernatural powers, and because they have destroyed all seeds of suffering and have acquired resemblance to God.[23]

FIVE KINDS.—Haradatta mentions acquisition, means, places, conditions, purifications, and requisites for initiation each to be of five kinds. Bhāsarvajña enumerates them as acquisition of knowledge, acquisition of penances, acquisition of constant proximity to God, acquisition of the state of abiding in God, and acquisition of supernatural powers, and avers that they consist in the manifestation of those powers which were dormant in an aspirant's soul. His account bears resemblance to that of Kauṇḍinya, who describes them as acquisition of knowledge, acquisition of penances, acquisition of constant proximity to God, acquisition of constant union of the soul with God, and acquisition of excellent qualities. Kauṇḍinya states nescience, vice, strong attachment to the objects of pleasure, nonacquisition of abiding in God, and lack of supernatural powers as the five kinds of taints of the soul. Haradatta mentions the taints to be of five kinds. Bhāsarvajña states them to be false knowledge, vice, attachment, lapse from one's essential nature, and bondage. Kanndinya states the five means of the purification of the soul, viz., residence in a holy place, meditation, restraint of all sense-organs, recollection of God, and God's grace. Bhāsarvajña states them as residence in a proper place, performance of the prescribed rituals, muttering a mantra, meditation, constant recollection of God, and God's grace. He states the total destruction of false knowledge, vice, attachment, lapse from the spiritual nature of the self, and bondage as the five kinds of purification. Kauṇḍinya mentions the five places, viz., a holy place, a human habitation, an empty house, a cremation ground, and a temple of Śiva. Bhāsarvajña mentions five places as the following—a preceptor's house, a village, a cave, a cremation ground, and a temple of Śiva. Haradatta mentions five conditions of an ascetic, viz., manifest, concealed, conquest of the sense-organs, snapping, and steadiness of mind. When an ascetic exhibits the signs of a Pāśupata, smears his body with ashes, lies in them, and bears the signs, he is in a manifest condition. When he does not express the conduct of a Pāśupata ascetic and conceals the signs characteristic of the sect, he is in a concealed condition. When he has conquered his sense-organs and passions, he is in a condition of conquest. When he has reached the state of dispensing with all external rituals, he is in the state of snapping. When he has absolutely stopped all acts of spiritual discipline, he is in a state of steadiness. The state of a ghost, an insane, a fool, etc., is the state of concealment. The states of conquest and snapping are not admitted to be the state of concealment. The state of steadiness is the state of self-realisedness, because then there are no taints to be destroyed, and because there is no end to be realised. Those who are not eligible cannot attain to these states. Uninitiated persons are ineligible. Eligible persons can attain right knowledge and sinlessness. In the first state an ascetic should live in a place (e.g.a village) approved by his spiritual teacher. In the second state he should live in a place where persons of different ages and castes live and perform actions, which generate their merits and demerits. In the third state he should live in an empty house or a cave where there are no objects of attachment. In the fourth state he should live in cremation grounds until he dies. In the last state he should live with the supreme Lord Who is bodiless. Bhāsarvajña takes the word 'vāsa' in a technical sense. It means reception, retention, association, rejection, comprehension, knowledge of the scriptures, service to the spiritual teacher, and constant effort. Reception is the power of adequately understanding the meaning of a sentence uttered once. Retention is the power of recollecting what was received once after an interval of a long period. Association is the power of understanding the meaning of another part of a system of knowledge on hearing one part of it. Rejection is the power of selecting the rational part and rejecting the irrational part of the assertions of those who are like the spiritual teacher. Comprehension is the power of reflecting on a subject heard from another in various ways and arriving at a rational conclusion. Right knowledge of the scriptures consists in finding out scriptural statements, which are free from contradiction and repetition, and in manifesting one's right knowledge, which destroys the taint of false knowledge, and which satisfies a teacher by uttering a flawless scriptural statement. Action consists in service to the spiritual teacher by rising before him and rising from one's seat when he rises. Constant effort consists in excessive endeavour in comprehending the meaning of the scriptural statements in due consideration of the antecedent and subsequent parts in their proper relation to one another. Haradatta states that five things are necessary for initiation, viz., articles, time, a ritual, an image, and a spiritual teacher. Bhāsarvajña enumerates the requisite articles as kuśa grass, ashes, sandal paste, a thread, flowers, incense, and a mantra. A Brāhmaṇa is eligible for initiation. Time is forenoon. Ceremonial act consists in purifying an image of Śiva and a disciple. There are two kinds of teachers, viz., superior and inferior. The supreme Lord is the superior teacher, and a human teacher is His instrument, who is an inferior teacher. He is expert in propounding the Pāśupata cult according to the scriptures, possessed of excellent wisdom, efficient, and capable of communicating knowledge. Haradatta states the five kinds of strength as devotion to a spiritual teacher, purity of mind, conquest of mental conflicts, virtue and vigilance. Baāsarvajña explains them as follows. Devotion to a spiritual teacher consists in faith in his ability to save one from the misery of bondage by instructing one in the five topics. Mental purity is freedom from impurities. It is of two kinds, viz., destruction of the existent impurities despite the presence of the seeds of future impurities and destruction of the seeds of all impurities and nonproduction of future impurities. The conquest of mental conflicts is the conquest of the causes of bodily, mental, and supernatural sufferings, or endurance of them. The performance of the prescribed actions produces virtue. Vigilance is supreme wisdom acquired by an ascetic in the state of steadiness. There are three means of livelihood, viz., mendicancy, taking food left by others, and taking food which is got without being asked for. Mendicancy is the means of livelihood in the first state. Taking food left by others is the means of livelihood in the second state. Living on food acquired without being solicited should be resorted to by an ascetic living in cremation grounds. In the last state there is no necessity for livelihood because the body is then absent. Livelihood consists in acquiring food by means which are not conducive to one's honour or dishonour for the attenuation of the five kinds of impurities of the soul. There are eight topics in the Pāśupata system, viz., acquisition, taints, means, places, states, purifications, requisites for initiation, and strength. Each of them is of five kinds as described above.[24]

Bhāsarvajña gives the following account of the taints of the soul. False knowledge is invalid knowledge such as doubt, error and the like. Lust, anger and aversion are sins and included in false knowledge since they spring from it. Demerit is a cause of sinful acts. Its various forms also are demerits, since modifications are nondifferent from what is modified. The objects of the sense-organs are the causes of attachment. Attachment is clinging to the objects of sentient pleasure which is false conceit of pleasure. Sensible objects, causes of attachment, absorb the mind in them, and make it impure. So they are a kind of impurity. Lapse or even the slightest deviation of the mind from God is a kind of impurity. False knowledge with its seeds or causes is a taint. Demerit with its modifications is a taint. The cause of attachment with its modifications is a taint. Lapse of the mind from God with demerit—its seed—is a taint. Boundness is a quality of the soul, distinct from merit and demerit, which is inferred from the restriction of its innate powers of knowledge and action which are infinite. Nonomniscience, dependence, etc., are the fourteen kinds of boundness. They are the beginningless causes of the wheel of birth and death. Those souls, which have achieved complete isolation from prakṛti and its modifications, and whose four kinds of taints have been destroyed, are not born again. Virtue, knowledge, and detachment are not taints.

Bhāsarvajña avers that muttering a mantra and meditation are the means of attaining close proximtty to God. Japa is of two kinds, viz., japa resulting in the withdrawal of the sense-organs from their objects and japa resulting in trance. It may be objected that japa with a mind attached to other objects, even if continued for a hundred years, cannot withdraw the sense-organs from their objects. To this objection Bhāsarvarjña replies that there are two kinds of withdrawal of the sense-organs from their objects, superior and inferior. Japa with a conscious effort of the mind is inferior. When it is practised repeatedly for a long period, it purifies the mind, and makes it rest in God without a conscious effort. Such withdrawal is superior, and said to be preceded by japa. It makes the mind fixed on God by consuming merits and demerits acquired in many births. Meditation consists in a continuous stream of similar thoughts of God. It is of two kinds, viz., meditation preceded by japa and meditation preceded by fixation of mind. The first has already been mentioned. The second is preceded by fixation of the mind without an object for the wise. In deep sleep and swoon the mind becomes objectless because of the cessation of all mental modes. But the wise make their minds objectless by acquiring the true knowledge, which favours their minds, and makes them objectless. Their minds purified by concentration on God do not lapse from Him for a long time. Such meditation preceded by concentration is superior to meditation preceded by japa. Meditation should be continued till death in all conditions with the best of one's ability. Constant recollection of God is close proximity to God (cp. Rāmānuja). Recollection is the principal means of achieving abiding in God. Some hold that close proximity to God and the conquest of passions are nondifferent from each other. Bhāsarvajña criticizes it by pointing out that they are different in their nature. The conquest of sense-organs and passions consists in mastering the enjoyment of sense-organs and rejection of objects by them. But close proximity to God consists in repeated practice of meditating on Him. God's grace consists in the desire to achieve the qualities of God. It does not depend upon any other cause than His grace.[25]

[1] PSS., Introduction, p. 11 ; DHIP., Vol. V, p. 145; PO., p. 150.
[2] PO., p. 153.
[3] PAB., i, I, p. 7 ; iii, 19 ; V, 8 & 40. Cp. HIP., Vol. II, pp. 731-33.
[4] PAB., ii, 2 & 21.
[5] Ibid, ii, 2-3, 23-27 ; V, 26-28, 40, 42-44, 46-47 ; RṬ., pp. 11-12 ; Karaṇapadārtha, 1-26 ; SDS., Ch. vi, 10.
[6] PAB., ii, 6 ; SDS., ch. vi, 15.
[7] PAB.. V, 3-4, 47 ; ii, 22 ; PSS., V, 3 ; RṬ., p. 10.
[8] PAB., V, 26 & 28, 5-7 ; i, 23-24 ; ii, 24-25 ; i, i; RṬ., pp. 10-11.
[9] PAB., i, 12 & 44. 24.

[10] Ibid, i, 9 ; V, 42 & 47 ; ii, 24-25 ; vi, I ; iii, 19 ; V, 7 & 37.

[11] SDS., ch. vi, 9 ; PAB., I. [12] PAB., i, 20.

[13] SDS., ch. vi, 11-12 ; RṬ., pp. 14 & 19.

[14] PAB., i, 2-19 ; BG., ix, 22.

[15] PAB., i, 9 ; Cp. YS., ii, 32.

[16] PAB., i, 9 ; V, 16 ; ii, 20 ; V, 21 ; i, 17 & 39. Cp. YS., i 27, 28 & 32 ; ii, 49-52 ; YBh., i, 28 ; ŚM., pp. 27-29, 42-44.

[17] PAB., ii, 10, 11 & 21 ; V, 37-39 ; GKV., p 16.

[18] PAB., V, 20, 25, 27-28 & 30 ; iv, 12, 23-24 & 30.

[19] Ibid, V, 34, 21 & 28 ; ii, 11, 13-14 ; V. 31 & 35 ; ii, 15-19. Cp. Bhāg., X, 86, 33 ; XI, 3, 22; LY., pp. 40 & 73.

[20] PSS., PAB., iii, 1-3, 5-11, 18-19 ; iv, 1-9, 13-20.

[21] Ibid, V, 33, 40-41 ; i, i, vi, 16 ; SDS., vi, 14 & 16.

[22] PAB., i, 21-26 ; RṬ, p. 10.

[23] PAB., i, 27, 29-38 ; RṬ., pp. 10 & 16 ; HIP,, vol. II, p. 167.

[24] GK., 1-8 ; RṬ, 2-8, pp. 4-5, 6-9, 17, 22-23 ; SDS., vi, 2-4 ; PAB., V, 30.

[29] RṬ., pp. 21-23.

CHAPTER IV

THE ŚAIVA SIDDHĀNTA

INTRODUCTION.—The South Indian School of Śaivism is called the Śaiva Siddhānta. Mādhava's account of the Śaiva Darśana is that of the South Indian School. It is based on twenty eight Śaiva Āgamas. Mādhava quotes from the 'Mṛgendra Āgama', the Jñānapāda of the 'Kāmikā', the 'Pauṣkara', 'Kirana', 'Karaṇa,' and the other Āgamas in 'Śarvadarśana-saṁgraha'. The Śaiva Siddhānta flourished from the eleventh to the thirteenth century. The account of the doctrine given here is based on king Bhojadeva's (1100 A.D.) 'Tattvaprakāśa,' 'Tātparyadīpikā', Śrīkumāra's commentary on it, 'Mṛgendratantra' and 'Mṛgendratantravṛtti', a commentary on it by Nārāyaṇakaṇṭha. The doctrine propounded in these books is dualisic Śaivism as distinguished from Pratyabhijñā monistic Śaivism of Kashmir. It recognises souls to be distinct from God and bonds. The Pāśupatas regard God as the independent efficient cause of the world, while the Śaiva Siddhānta regards Him as its efficient cause with the help of souls' merits and demerits (karma). Śakti, His conscious energy, is the instrumental cause, and māyā, His unconscious energy is the material cause of the world. Śakti is not independent of God. Individual souls are eternal, and become indentical with Śiva in release without losing their distinctness.[1]

The Śaiva Āgamas treat of the three chief entities : the Lord (pati), bound souls (paśu), and the bonds (pāsa). Bound souls are atomic. Mala, karma, māyā, the world produced out of māyā, and God's power of veiling are bonds of the souls. Some souls are bound to embodied life. If their existence be not admitted, there cannot be embodied life. If there be no bondage consisting in the experience of pleasures and pains and birth and death due to merits and demerits, there can be no cessation of embodied life, and the scriptures which propound the means of release from bondage become useless. If the bonds called mala, karma, māyā, and the objects produced by māyā do not exist, there can be no bodies, sense-organs, and their objects, there can be no heaven and hell, and birth and death, because the souls being inactive cannot bind or liberate themselves. If God do not exist, there can be no creation, maintenance, and destruction of the world, and bondage and liberation of the souls, because nonomniseient souls without bodies cannot be their causes. So the existence of God, souls, and bonds must be admitted. One God assumes the three states of the Lord, souls, and bonds without losing His nature. The 'Śivarahasya' says, "God Himself becomes atomic souls by veiling His qualities. He becomes a taint which is a trace of His power." The pure principles are comprised in God. The mixed principles and the impure principles are included in bound souls and bonds, respectively. These there realities are the chief ones. The 'Pārameśvara' says "God is the binder ; individual souls are bound, and bonds are their fetters." The 'Vāyavīya' discusses the nature of conscious souls, unconsciovs entities, and their controller—God. The Śaiva Āgamas also discuss the nature of the Lord, bound souls and bonds. They are created by God, Who is omniscient and so devoid of nescience, illusion, love, hate, etc., and cannot compose false works. So they are authoritative.[2]

ŚIVA : GOD (PATI).—The Śaiva Siddhānta discusses the nature of the Lord, bound souls, and bonds. Bhojadeva describes God as one, ubiquitous, eternal, self-existent, transcendent Lord, Who is of the nature of pure consciouness, the cause of the world, and the bestower of grace on all beings. His lustre of the nature of the power of knowlenge and of the power of action is neither created nor destroyed. He is not released, but bestows release on bound souls. He emancipates them by His power that is one, original, and of the nature of pure consciousness. His power is not different from Him. He is eternally free, one, and embodied in five mantras. He performs fivefold acts : creation, maintenance, dissolution, act of veiling, and act of bestowing grace. God is one, and without a second, because the Vedas declare Him to be so, which are eternal revelations to the seers, and the most authoritative. The authority of the Vedas cannot be overridden by perception and inference which are weaker than scriptural testimony. He is of the nature of pure consciousness. The Śruti says : "He is indeed a mass of knowledge, supreme bliss, without inside and outside, and infinite." So He is a mass of consciousness, of the nature of consciousness, and of the essence of conscionsness. He is ubiquitous and omnipresent. He pervades all formed entities without movement. He is ubiquitous because He is the essence of all entities. He is ubiquitous like ether, but not insentient like it. He is eternal. The Śruti says : "God is immutable and eternal, but prakṛti is mutable." He is eternal as pervading the past, the present, and the future, or as being nontemporal. He is eternally self-existent and self-manifest. His manifestation is never produced or destroyed. The Śruti says, "This Person (God) is self-luminous." The 'Īśvaragītā' says : "He is the supreme Person." He is Lord in the sense that His lordship is unrestricted, and that He is the creator, objects of creation, and instruments of creation. Or, He is the Lord in the sense that He creates all effects without any instruments. Or, He is the Lord in the sense that He creates the world without any physical action. A creator with physical action ceases to be the Lord because He undergoes physical strain. God's lordship is devoid of it. He is transcendent, and so devoid of all physical actions. Or, He is devoid of a physical body subject to merits and demerits, because His being possessed of such a body would make Him bound and subject to transmigration. But He is incapable of transmigration because He is devoid of all physical actions of another entity (body), neutral, omniscient, independent, and omnipotent. The Śruti says, 'He is partless, inactive, transcendent, immaterial, and pure'. The 'Īśvaragītā' says, 'Liberated souls vision the supreme Soul as really immutable, blissful, devoid of sorrow, and infinite'. The Smṛti says, 'God is one, free, indifferent, uncreated, infinite, inactive, transcendent, supreme Lord'. He is the mintuest and the greatest, the supreme Lord, unrivalled and unsurpassed. He is the one root cause of the world. All effects are subordinate to Him. God with māyā as His body is the material cause and the efficient cause of the world, and is yet immutable. He bestows His grace on all beings—conscious and unconscious. He grants all bound souls exaltation and liberation. It is objected that if He creates the world to realise an end, then He is not self-fulfilled and of the nature of supreme bliss, and that if He creates the world without an end, then He cannot have a volition to create it. Śrīkumāra urges that this objection is unsound, because God creates the world either out of compassion or out of His nature. It may be objected that if He creates the world out of compassion, then He should create all souls as liberated, and should not create the world for their bondage in the shape of enjoyments and sufferings, since that shows His cruelty. He should not create sufferings for them and then create the world out of compassion to remove their sufferings. So it is not reasonable that He should create the world full of sufferings. To this objection Śrīkumāra replies that He creates the world in order to give liberation to bound souls, which consists in the destruction of their nescience, which depends upon knowledge and its cause and the like. Immediate knowledge of the nature of the self and God is the cause of liberation. Immediate knowledge is due to meditation and the destruction of the impressions of nescience. Listening, reflection, and meditation generate the immediate knowledge of God and the self, which depends upon the purification of the mind. The purification of the mind is generated by the performance of the daily obligatory duties and the occasional duties and by the discarding of the prudential duties for the fulfilment of desires and the prohibited actions. Hence the creation of the world is ultimately for the liberation of bound souls. Or, God creates the world out of His nature as full of compassion. He does not liberate all souls because He considers their merits and demerits. He liberates only those bound souls whose merits and demerits have become ripe and borne their fruits. He is of the nature of bliss. It may be objected that if He is of the nature of bliss, He is made of sattva which produces pleasure, and thus possessed of a guṇa, and undergoes modification. To this objection Śrīkumāra replies that God's bliss is not pleasure produced by sattva, but always uniform, eternal, and supreme essence of the self, while pleasure is produced by the intercourse of the sense-organs with their objects, noneternal, various, and limited. So He is not endowed with sattva, and so unmodifiable. Pleasure is a reflection of God's bliss in sattva, and a false conceit of bliss. He is devoid of nescience, love, hate, merit, demerit, body, and sense-organs. He is devoid of nescience because He is omniscient. He undergoes neither increase nor decrease because He is eternal and uniform. His lustre is of the nature of omniscience and omnipotence. His mantra is His lustre, which is the means of attaining Him. His image is eternal and devoid of origin and destruction. The Vedas are His lustre and eternal. He is a knower and an agent. He grants liberation to His devotees.[3]

ŚAKTI (DIVINE POWER).—God cannot extend His grace and liberate bound souls without the help of His power. Śiva is omnipresent, transcendent, inactive, and neutral, and, consequently, cannot grant them exaltation and liberation. He can bestow His grace on them only with the aid of His power. Divine power is one and without a second. The objection, that God being one and without a second, His power cannot be one and without a second, is not valid, since every entity being of the nature of God and His power both, God and His power are one and without a second. Liberation is of the nature of consciousness and bliss, because it is the abiding of the self in its essential condition, and, consequently, of the nature of God and His power. If liberation be not of the nature of consciousness and bliss, it cannot be the highest good. The objection, that the absolute extinction of pain also may be the highest good because of its being devoid of pain although it be not of the nature of bliss, is unsound, since the absence of pain is not the principal end in that it is sought for as favourable to pleasure, and not as the supreme end. Bliss being pursued as a higher end than the absence of pain, liberation must be admitted to be of the nature of bliss. Even if it be not experienced in the state of bondage, then also its experience in the state of liberation must be admitted, since otherwise it cannot be pursued as the supreme end. Hence liberation is of the nature of consciousness and bliss which are experienced, and, consequently, of the nature of God and His power; the experience of supreme bliss is the divine power, and the bliss of the experience is God. Consciousness and bliss should not be considered to be the qualities of the self and different from it, because the Śruti says, 'Brahman is consciousness and bliss', and because if they were different from the self, they would not be its qualities. The objection, that if consciousness and bliss were nondifferent from each other, they being self-manifest and not experienced from any other source, bondage and liberation would be nondifferent from each other, is groundless, because in the state of bondage bliss cannot be experienced not because it is nonexistent but because it is experienced as reflected in the consciousness and pleasure of a bound soul. Bliss is of the nature of God, and is manifested in the state of release. The objection, that a pure principle is of the nature of God and His power, but that God, the supreme cause, endowed with māyā, cannot be of the nature of God and His power, is not valid, because He can be so as the efficient cause and the material cause of the world. As the efficient cause, He is God, and as the material cause He is divine power. Or, God is the efficient cause, and His power of māyā is the material cause. The effects being of the nature of consciousness and unconsciousness are of the nature of God and His power. The creatures as souls are of the nature of God, and as bodies are of the nature of His power. God and His power being nondifferent from each other, both are one and without a second. God is devoid of sex. He is neither male nor female nor neuter. Śiva is of the nature of consciousness. Śakti is of the nature of consciousness. There is no difference between them. Śiva and Śakti are one reality, like a gem and its ray, or like fire and heat. It may be objected that a powerful being or substance is endowed with the quality of power, that for that reason a substance cannot be nondifferent from its quality of power, that if they were nondifferent from each other, they would not be related to each other. To this objection Śrīkumāra replies that if a substance and its power be different from each other, then also power cannot be said to be a quality of the powerful substance, that if a relation be admitted between a substance and its quality, which are different from each other, it will require another relation to relate them to each other, and so on to infinity, that if a relation be not admitted between a substance and its quality, the quality cannot be said to belong to the substance, because it is common to all substances, and that therefore nondifference between a substance and its quality must be admitted. Hence God and His power are nondifferent from each other.[4]

GOD'S KNOWLEDGE AND ACTION.—God is omniscient, because He is omnipotent, and because He knows the means and the ends of His action. He who knows an act, its means and end, can act. He who does not know an act, its means and end, cannot act. God's omniscience does not depend upon any condition to manifest it, like human knowledge, because it is not veiled. Nor is it of the nature of doubt, illusion, and indefinite knowledge, like human knowledge. The knowledge of individual souls is veiled by taints and hindered in regard to its objects, because its manifesting agents, kalā and the like, have limited power of manifesting objects. But God's knowledge is not veiled by the powers of taints, and so He is omniscient. Divine knowledge is neither perception nor inference, nor testimony. It always apprehends all objects. God is devoid of the sense-organs, and, consequently, His knowledge is not perception. It is not inference, since inference depends upon perception. Nor is it testimony, since testimony is mediate knowledge in that it depends upon perception and inference. God does not know any object mediately. He knows all objects immediately. His knowledge and action are independent of the sense-organs, and depend upon His mere volition. He is omniscient and omnipotent by nature. He creates, maintains, and destroys the world by mere volition. Though His knowledge is one, it appears to be many because of the manifestation of many objects to it. Its multiplicity is due to the limiting conditions. His action is one, but appears to be many, since He creates many objects. His action is manifold, since it is nondifferent from His knowledge which appears to be manifold. The manifoldness of His knowledge and action is due to the limiting conditions.[5]

PROOF FOR GOD'S EXISTENCE.—Śrīkumāra states the following inference for God's existence. All effects from time to earth and the like are produced by an intelligent agent, because they are effects; whatever is an effect, is produced by an intelligent agent, like a jar and the like; all entities from time to earth are effects; so they are produced by an intelligent agent, viz., God. Their being effects is proved by inference and testimony. Earth and the like are effects, because they are insentient and distinct from māyā—the chief material cause; whatever is insentient and distinct from māyā—the chief material cause, is an effect, like a jar and the like; earth and the like are so; therefore they are effects. It may be objected that earth and the like being composed of atoms, which are their chief material cause, are not distinct from their material cause (cp. Nyāya). This objection is unsound, since the Śaivas do not admit the atoms to be the chief material cause of earth and the like. Further, earth and the like are effects, since they are dependent, since they are of the nature of sattva, rajas and tamas, and since they are different from souls, like a jar and the like. Further, the Śruti says: 'Ether was produced from Brahman; air was produced from ether; fire was produced from air; water was produced from fire; and earth was produced from water'. So earth and the like are effects. Thus all entities other than souls are produced out of māyā as the chief material cause. The 'Īśvaragītā' says: 'Māyā is the material cause of the twenty four principles'. Hence the nature of earth and the like being effects is not an unproven reason for inferring the existence of God. The Śaiva argues that earth and the like are produced by an intelligent agent, viz., God. The opponent contends, that earth and the like are produced by an intelligent agent like us, who produces effects with the aid of merits and demerits, and that therefore the agent of earth and the like is like a human agent. This contention is false, since earth and the like are produced by an intelligent agent who perceives their material cause, the auxiliaries, the ends, and the souls for whom He creates them. Finite beings like us are devoid of perceptual knowledge of all these, and, consequently, cannot be the agents of earth and the like. Being an effect consists in being produced. Production depends upon the action of a cause. The action of a cause depends upon the action of a soul. The action of a soul depends upon a volition of a soul. A volition depends upon a desire. A desire depends upon the knowledge of the means to the attainment of the desired end. Hence an effect is not produced without an intelligent agent. Being an effect is present in positive instances, like jars and the like, and absent from a negative instance, like God. Hence being an effect is not a contradictory reason. Earth and the like are produced by an agent who has perception of their material cause, the auxiliary causes, the ends, and the souls for whose enjoyments and sufferings they are produced. So their agent or efficient cause is omniscient, and cannot be like human agents. This argument reminds us of the Nyāya argument for the existence of God. The opponent contends that earth and the like are produced by an intelligent agent endowed with a body, as jars and the like are produced by intelligent human agents with bodies. Śrīkumāra urges, that when there is a doubt whether earth and the like are produced by an agent, the thesis to be proved is that earth and the like are produced by an agent; that when there is a doubt whether earth and the like are produced by an intelligent agent, the thesis to be proved is that earth and the like are produced by an intelligent agent; that when there is a doubt whether earth and the like are produced by an intelligent agent who has perception of their material cause, auxiliary causes, etc., the thesis to be proved is that earth and the like are produced by an intelligent agent who has perception of these. Both the probans viz., being an effect, and the probandum viz., being produced by an intelligent agent who has perception of the material cause, etc., are present in the positive instances, e.g., jars and the like. The thesis to be proved is not that earth and the like are produced by an omniscient, embodied agent, because there is no doubt about it. Being an effect is not an invariable concomitant of being produced by an intelligent agent endowed with a body. The invariable concomitance of grass, sprouts, etc., being effects with being produced by an intelligent bodiless agent is perceived. Their being produced by an intelligent agent endowed with a body is not present in them. They are effects, and yet are not produced by an intelligent agent endowed with a body. Just as fire in general is inferred from smoke in general, so being produced by an intelligent agent capable of perceiving the material cause, etc., is inferred from earth and the like being effects. Just as a special fire is not inferred from a special smoke, so an intelligent agent endowed with a body is not inferred from earth and the like being effects. There is no contradiction between bodilessness and being an intelligent agent of an effect. The invariable concomitance between being an effect in general and being produced by an intelligent agent in general is known, and not between their special forms, because the former is perceived in grass, sprouts, and the like. The contention that there can be no agency if there is no organ like a body is false, because there is agency in the self's action on the body through a desire or a volition. When a soul impels its body to act, the impelled body cannot be an organ of the soul. The body acted upon by a soul cannot be the organ of its action. A finger cannot touch itself. Another body cannot be the organ of a soul's action on its body, because it will lead to infinite regress. Similarly, God acts upon the material causes of earth and the like without a body, and produces them. He produces them through His volition. He has no body except māyā—the chief material cause of earth and the like. Hence He is bodiless. A body is insentient, and cannot be an agent, like an axe. The bodies of a potter, a weaver, etc., are not agents; they are the organs of their souls' actions. The action of the souls cannot be denied. The actions of the potter's soul, the weaver's soul, etc., cannot be said to be nonexistent because they are not perceived. They are not perceived because they are subtle. Our own souls' actions on our bodies are perceived. There are two kinds of effects, viz., effects produced by bodily actions and effects produced by mere volitions. Jars and the like are produced by bodily actions, and depend upon the presence of bodies. But attraction is produced by mere volition, and does not depend upon the presence of a body. A soul can attract an object at a great distance. Others hold that God with a body creates the world, but that it is not perceptible by us. It may be argued that, a body being noneternal, and God not creating His body, His body is created by another God, and so on to infinity, and that this assumption will involve infinite regress. Some reply that the argument is valid, since the series of God's bodies are beginningless like seeds and sprouts. God with a body creates a world in one cycle. After its dissolution He assumes another body, and creates another world in another cycle. Others hold that God's body is eternal because of its being without an origin. His body must be admitted to be without an origin, since He creates with it a beginningless series of worlds, and māyā constitutes His body. Others think His body to be made of Logos (śabdabrahma). It may be objected that the inference 'earth and like are produced by omniscient God, because they are effects' is thrown out by the counter-inference 'earth and the like are produced by nonomniscient God, because they are effects'. This objection is invalid, because the alternatives are not tenable. Does the counter-inference deny the omniscience of the agent of earth and the like, or their agent's being a limited knower and a limited doer, or their being produced by an agent? The Śaiva desires to establish that earth and the like are produced by an omniscient agent or God. This thesis can be denied by the denial of earth and the like being produced by an agent. But their being produced by an agent is not denied by the opponent. He denies the omniscience of their agent. His denial of their agent's omniscience does not throw out the Śaiva's thesis. Even jars and the like are produced by omniscient God, the creator of the world, who activates the merits and demerits of the souls for whose enjoyments and sufferings they are produced by some potters. God's volition is the general cause of all effects. The activation of the souls' merits and demerits is not done by any other agent, since there is no evidence for it. It cannot be argued that a large effect is produced by a plurality of agents. Earth and the like are produced by God by mere volition, and, consequently, they do not require a plurality of agents. When an effect is produced by a physical action, a large effect requires a plurality of agents, one of whom cannot produce it by one's physical action. Hence a large effect is produced by one infinite God, and the assumption of many Gods is needless, since it violates the law of parsimony. The Mīmāṁsakas and others deny that earth and the like are produced by an agent. They do not affirm that earth and the like are produced by an agent with limited knowledge and agency. They cannot be produced by such an agent. God endowed finite knowledge cannot produce all effects. Hence the inference 'earth and the like are produced by God Who knows their material causes, etc., because they are effects, like a jar', is valid. Śrīkumāra's refutation of antitheistic objections is similar to the Nyāya refutation of similar objections. He is certainly influenced by the Naiyāyika theists. Śrīkumāra proves God's existence by scriptural testimony also. Śruti says, 'God's eyes are everywhere in the world'. So Vedic testimony proves His existence. It is proved by yogic intuition too due to meditation.[6] God is the efficient cause, His conscious power, the instrumental cause, and His unconscious power of māyā, the material cause, of the world. His conscious power being nondifferent from and dependent on Him, and His unconscious power of māyā being dependent on Him, He may be said to be its efficient cause, instrumental cause and material cause. In His own nature, He is the efficient cause, through His power He is the material cause.[7]

THE PRINCIPLES (TATTVA).—There are five pure principles : Śivatattva, Śaktitattva, Sadāśivatattva, Īśvaratattva, and Vidyātattva. Individual souls, māyā, time (kāla), destiny (niyati), kalā, vidyā, and rāga are the mixed principles. Avyakta, guṇas—sattva, rajas and tamas, buddhi, ahaṁkāra, the five cognitive sense-organs, the five motor sense-organs, five subtle essences, and five gross elements produced from māyā are the impure principles. These are produced for the bound souls' enjoyments and sufferings as fruits of their merits and demerits. The souls are knowers and active agents. Avyakta, guṇas, etc., are produced from māyā for their knowledge, activity, and pleasures and pains. They are impure principles. Bodies are the vehicles of experience, the sense-organs are the instruments of experience, and sound, touch, etc., are the objects of experience. The souls are born and endowed with bodies and sense-organs for their enjoyments and sufferings. Bodies and the like are not entirely different from avyakta and sattva, rajas and tamas, which are their causes. Twenty four principles—avyakta, buddhi, ahaṁkāra, manas, sound, touch, colour, taste, odcur, the five cognitive sense-organs, the five motor sense-organs, and the five gross elements—are of the nature of sattva, rajas and tamas. They are not different in nature from the guṇas. Avyakta is a product of māyā. The guṇas are the effects of avyakta. Buddhi is a product of the guṇas. Ahaṁkāra is an effect of buddhi. Manas, buddhi, ahaṁkāra, the cognitive sense-organs, the motor sense-organs, and the subtle essences are the products of ahaṁkāra. And the gross elements are the effects of the subtle essences. These are the impure principles. Māyā is the cause of time, destiny, kalā, vidyā, and rāga, which are its products. They are the mixed principles which limit the souls.[8] The Sāṁkhya identifies avyakta with prakṛti. But Śrīkumāra thinks avyakta to be a product of māyā, and the cause of the guṇas.

1. ŚIVATATTVA.—Śivatattva is the one, ubiquitous, eternal cause of all principles, and endowed with the power of knowledge and the power of action. He is one, without a second, unrivalled, unexcelled, and the essence of all elements. He is all-pervasive and immanent in all elements. He is eternal and imperishable, and so different from ubiquitous ether since

it is noneternal. He is the cause of all principles, and so different from an individual soul, which is one, ubiquitous and eternal, but which is not the cause of all principles. He is of the nature of knowledge and action which constitute His essence. Māyā also is one, ubiquitous, eternal, and the material cause of all impure principles, but not conscious and active. So Śivatattva is different from māyā. The 'Śivadharmottara' says : 'Śiva is without origin, middle and end, pure in nature, omniscient, perfect'. The 'Siddhānta hṛdaya' says : 'Śivatattva is one, immutable, immortal, eternal, unrivalled, minutest, greatest, self-manifest, transcendent, immanent, unthinkable, supersensible, peerless, characterless, incomprehensible, inexpressible, of the nature of being, consciousness and bliss, devoid of pain, actor and enlightener, and creates the universe with the aid of māyā'.[9]

2. ŚAKTITATTVA.—The first wink or awaking of God desirous of creating the world in order to bestow His grace on the conscious souls and the unconscious entities is called Śaktitattva that is nondistinct from Śivatattva. God and His power are nondifferent from each other. It may be asked how the existence of Śakti is known. Śrīkumāra replies that the effects cannot be produced without power. Inactive God cannot create, maintain, and dissolve the world, veil the knowledge of the souls, and manifest it without His power. Effects cannot be produced without the existence of the power of God. Kumārila avers that the powers of all entities are known by presumption from their effects. Śrīkumāra avers that they are God's powers which are nondifferent from Him. His power of volition, power of knowledge, and power of action are not different from Him.[10]

3. SADĀŚIVATATTVA.—Śivatattva becomes Sadāśivatattva when His power of knowledge and power of action neither increase nor decrease but are in equilibrium, and when His power of volition predominates over them.[11] God's power of knowledge, power of volition, and power of action are modifications of His supreme power. When they are unfolded, and when His power of knowledge and power of action reach a state of equipoise, and when His power of volition predominates over them, He becomes Sadāśivatattva, that is absolutely pure and transparent.

4. ĪŚVARATATTVA.—Śivatattva becomes Īśvaratattva, the creator of all principles, when His power of action predominates over His power of knowledge and power of action, which are in a state of equilibrium. It may be objected that God's power of action cannot act when His power of knowledge and power of volition are in equipoise because action depends upon antecedent knowledge and volition. Śrīkumāra urges that God's power of knowledge and power of volition manifest their objects and exist in an inactive state.[12]

5. VIDYĀTATTVA.—When God's power of knowledge predominates over His power of volition and power of action which are in a state of equipoise, Śivatattva becomes Vidyātattva that manifests all, being of the nature of knowledge. This is the principle of pure knowledge.[13] Nāda and Bindu that are endowed with kalā, always depend upon Śivatattva, and are nondifferent from Him. Others hold that they depend upon Sadāśivatattva. Vidyeśvaras exist in Īśvaratattva. Mantras and Vidyās exist as depending upon Vidyātattva.

because they manifest things. These five principles are devoid of temporal order because they are free of time. But they are imagined to be in this order in the scriptures owing to their functions in creation. Śivatattva is one in reality endowed with various powers, but differences in Him are imagined owing to the difference in their functions. God is not many. He is one and nondifferent. The five pure principles are due to the adjuncts of the functions of His powers. No real differences are possible in Him.[14] The five pure principles are imagined in the nature of God as different moments in the act of creation, though His is nondual. They are pure and of the nature of consciousness.

The nature of difference cannot be conceived. What is the substratum of difference? Is it different or nondifferent? If difference exist in a nondifferent entity, then such an entity does not exist because there is difference in it. If difference exist in different substrata, difference in them becomes useless because the entity is already different. If difference exist in an entity that is different, then such difference is the substratum of another difference, and so on to infinity, and this involves infinite regress. It cannot be argued that a nondifferent entity by itself is the substratum of difference because it involves begging the question. Hence imaginary difference in a nondifferent entity should be admitted to exist, even as the appearance of two moons exists in the one moon. The appearance of the two moons is not real because they exist in the same moon. Similarly, the appearance of the five pure principles exists in one, nondifferent God. They appear to be different owing to the difference of the functions of His powers.[15]

God assumes the five forms in order to bestow His grace on the conscious souls stained by the beginningless taint which restricts their innate powers, and on unconscious bonds (pāśa). "The world is of the nature of God. Śiva is the substratum cause; Śakti is modified into the world; Sadāśiva is the controller; Īśvara is the creator; and Śuddhavidyā is the manifester; Śiva bestows His grace on all through these imagined different principles."[16] Creation is an act of grace on the conscious souls and the unconscious entities. He gives the bound souls enjoyments and sufferings and liberation in the form of eternal bliss, and enables the unconscious bonds to perform their functions. It may be objected that giving pleasures and pains to the bound souls is not a matter of favour but of punishment, even as giving rice mixed with honey and poison to a person is a matter of punishment. Śrīkumāra urges that the bound souls' experiences of pleasures and pains are means to the production of their dispassion for the objects of pleasure and attachment to liberation, and, consequently, are a matter of favour. But why does He not liberate the souls without making them experience pleasures and pains? The reply is: liberation in the form of equality with God, which depends upon His grace, cannot be attained without the destruction of merits and demerits, which cannot be worn out without enjoyments and sufferings owing to their beginninglessness.[17] A soul's liberation in the form of union is nondifference from God without losing its distinctness. Granting liberation is His principal favour while granting happiness and misery is His subordinate favour. He creates the world, bodies and sense-organs for the souls' enjoyments and sufferings, which are necessary for the exhaustion of their merits and demerits. He is ultimately their cause as shown already.

Māyā is one, eternal, pervasive, beginningless, endless, and pure. It is one since there is no evidence for its manifoldness. It is objected that it is many, since there is no evidence for its being one. This objection is groundless, since its existence proves its oneness, and since the existence of many depends upon a prior entity. It is eternal because it is not an effect, being without a material cause. It is the root cause and material of the world. It is pervasive since it permeates all its effects. It is without orgin and end, since it is neither produced nor destroyed. It is pure since it is devoid of sattva, rajas and tamas. It is subtle for it is imperceptible.[18] It is common to all bound souls, because its effects are the common objects of their enjoyments and sufferings. It is modified into their bodies and sense-organs, and stamped with their merits and demerits. The liberated souls do not require bodies because their merits and demerits have beed destroyed. In the state of dissolution the bound souls' merits and demerits remain in māyā. It produces delusion by nature by veiling their spiritual nature owing to its insentience by inducing them to regard it as their nature. The 'Kiraṇa' says : "Māyā deludes the souls, connecting them with its mala and karma, and makes them experience objects". It may be objected that avyakta is the material cause of all effects, and that therefore māyā, which is different from it, should not be assumed. Śrīkumāra urges that avyakta being of the nature of sattva, rajas and tamas, which are effects, its eternal material cause must be admitted. It cannot be argued that avyakta is not proven to be of the nature of sattva, rajas and tamas, because it is of the nature of their equipoise. The 'Īśvara-gītā' and the 'Viṣṇu-purāṇa' speak of māyā as the material cause of prakṛti and the world. God produces the bodies and the sense-organs of the bound souls with the aid of their merits and demerits by agitating māyā by His powers for their respective enjoyments and sufferings.[19]

Māyā urged by God's various powers creates the principle of time in the beginning. The principles produced by time cannot be produced if time is not created at first. Māyā, the material cause of all impure principles, first creates time. Time is produced by God, His power, merits and demerits of the souls, and māyā. It is not produced by time for that would involve infinite regress. The past, the present, and the future are its forms.[20]

Māyā produces destiny after producing time. Time also is a cause of it. Destiny is so called because it regulates causation or makes specific causes produce specific effects. Oil seeds are the cause of oil. Paddy is the cause of rice. Destiny determines causal relation. It also makes specific merits and demerits produce specific pleasures and pains.[21] Thus niyati is natural order and moral order. Māyā produces kalā after producing time and destiny. Kalā attaches āṇava mala to the bound souls, and manifests their limited agency. It is said : "Māyā produces kalā after time and destiny, and manifests a soul's limited agency." The "Mātaṅga" says : "A bound soul pierced by kalātattva can experience pleasures and pains,—which is not possible without it. So kalātattva must be admitted. Māyā produces the subtle essences, destiny and the gross elements with the aid of time and kalā.[22] Kalātattva manifests a bound soul's limited agency and produces vidyātattva in order to manifest objects to it. Vidyātattva is of the nature of manifestation, and can produce the apprehension of objects. The 'Śaivarahasya' says : "Vidyā produced by māyā is of the nature of manifestation, and manifests buddhi ; it is experienced by a bound soul affected by pleasure, pain and delusion." It pierces the veil of a bound soul's power of knowledge by its power of action and shows it objects, and is its excellent instrument in the state of bondage. It may be objected that buddhi gives the determinate knowledge of objects and that the assumption of buddhitattva is useless to manifest objects to a bound soul. Śrīkumāra urges that a bound soul experiences objects determined by buddhi through impure vidyātattva, that impure vidyātattva is capable of modification because it is different from a soul, and because it is an effect of māyā, that buddhi does not manifest itself, because it is an effect, and because it is made of sattva, rajas and tamas, like a jar and the like, but that it is manifested by an entity different from itself, that buddhi is manifested because it is insentient, that it is insentient because it is an effect, like a jar and the like, that buddhi is not manifested by another buddhi because of its nonexistence, that it is not manifested by its another mode because it cannot have two modes at the same time, that impure buddhi is not manifested by pure vidyātattva, and that therefore it is manifested by impure vidyātattva.[23] Rāgatattva is of the nature of love, the common cause of a bound soul's voluntary action without the apprehension of objects, and is different from the attributes of buddhi. Some hold that it is an attribute of buddhi. This view is wrong. It is different from an attribute of buddhi. Common love (rāga) is an attribute of buddhi, because it is the cause of a soul's voluntary actions after manifesting objects to it. But rāgatattva is the cause of a soul's voluntary actions when it does not manifest objects to it. A bound soul desirous of release and attached to objects has voluntary actions without the apprehension of objects in regard to the means to release. Hence rāgatattva must be admitted as the cause of such voluntary actions. The 'Kiraṇa' says: "A soul is bound by sattva, rajas and tamas through the relation to buddhi and the other organs, being affected with the attributes of buddhi and being tinged with rāgatattva". The 'Matanga Pārameśvara' says, "A bound soul, being pierced by kalātattva and tinged by desire and unfolded by vidyātattva, experiences the objects of pleasure and pain. A bound soul is urged by rāgatattva to do voluntary actions to adopt the means to liberation, which is different from common love and desire."[24] When God being related to time, niyati, kalā, vidyā, and rāga assumes the state of a bound soul, and becomes an experiencer of pleasure and pain, He is called puruṣatattva—a bound soul. It is called a puruṣa because it lies in an abode made of twenty four principles and because it is counted among the principles different from Śivatattva.[25]

Avyakta is produced from māyā to produce the bound soul's experiences of pleasures and pains. It is so called because it is possessed of sattva, rajas and tamas which are not manifested. The Sāṁkhya regards it as the equilibrium of sattva, rajas and tamas. So the guṇas are not manifested in it. Avyakta is of the nature of the three guṇas because it is the cause of the gross elements, the subtle essences, manas, buddhi, and ahaṁkara, which are its effects, and which are causes of pleasure, pain and delusion. The nature of avyakta is incomprehensible by reason.[26] From avyakta, the equilibrium of sattva, rajas and tamas, the guṇas in the state of disequilibrium are produced. Their functions are manifestation, activity, and arrest—pleasure, pain, and delusion, respectively. Sattva produces knowledge or manifestation because it is transparent. Rajas produces activity because it is restless. Tamas produces arrest of activity because it is heavy. Buddhi is produced from sattva, rajas and tamas. Its functions are determination of objects, virtue, knowledge, detachment, supernatural powers, vice, ignorance, attachment, and absence of supernatural powers. Virtue is the cause of exaltation and liberation. A virtue produced by the performance of a sacrifice without desire for fruits produces happiness in heaven. A virtue produced by the performance of a sacrifice without a desire for fruits or by the eight-fold yoga produces liberation. Knowledge is of two kinds, viz., valid knowledge and recollection. Recollection is the exact remembrance of what was apprehended in the past. It is produced by a residual impression produced by a past apprehension. Valid knowledge is right apprehension. It excludes doubt, illusion and the like. Apprehension excludes recollection. Valid knowledge manifests the self or the not-self. The Cārvākas admit perception as the only means of valid knowledge. The Jainas admit two kinds of valid knowledge, viz., vivid knowledge and nonvivid knowledge. Immediate knowledge is vivid knowledge. Mediate knowledge is nonvivid knowledge. The Buddhists and the old Vaiśeṣikas admit perception and inference as valid knowledge, and reject testimony as a pramāṇa. The Buddhists reject its validity. The earlier Vaiśeṣikas include testimony and other pramāṇas in inference. The Sāṁkhya, the later Vaiśeṣikas, and Bhūṣaṇakāra accept perception, inference, and testimony as the pramāṇas. The earlier Naiyāyikas regard perception, inference, comparison, and testimony as the pramāṇas. The Prābhākaras admit these four and presumption as the pramāṇas. The Bhāṭṭas admit nonapprehension also as a pramāṇa. The Paurāṇikas admit tradition, inclusion, gesture, and noncontradiction also as pramāṇas. The Śaivas admit perception, inference and testimony as pramāṇas. Perception is indeterminate and determinate. Indeterminate perception is devoid of any reference to a name, a genus and the other determinations, and manifests an object alone owing to the intercourse of a sense-organ with an object. Determinate perception apprehends an object with its name, genus, substance, quality, and action. Determinate perception is of five kinds, viz., perception of an object with its name, or substance, or genus or quality, or action. (Cp. Old Nyāya). Again, it is of two kinds, viz., yogic perception and nonyogic perception. The former is the immediate perception of past, future, remote, and supersensible objects. The latter is the immediate perception of sensible objects present 'here and now' to the sense-organs. Inference is the mediate knowledge of a probandum produced by a probans that is known. It is of three kinds, viz., pūrvavat, śeṣavat, and sāmānyatodṛṣṭa. (Cp. Pāśupata). The first kind of inference infers an effect from a cause, e.g., future rain from specific clouds. The second kind of inference infers a cause from an effect, e.g., rainfall in an upper hilly region from a flood in a river. The third kind of inference infers a quality (e.g. colour of a mango) from another quality (e.g., its taste) which invariably accompanies it. It is not based on uniformity of causation but on uniformity of coexistence. (Cp. Nyāya). Again, inference is of two kinds, viz., inference for oneself and inference for others. The Naiyāyikas recognize five parts of the latter, viz., thesis, reason, example, application, and conclusion. The Mīmāṁsakas recognize its three parts, viz., thesis, reason, and example. The Buddhists recognize its two parts, viz., example and application. Testimony is right knowledge produced by the statement of a reliable authority. It is of two kinds, viz., personal and impersonal. The statements made by Manu and found in history, Tantras, and Purāṇas are personal. The sentences found in the Vedas are impersonal because they are not uttered by persons. Hence they are eternal and revealed to the seers. They are only manifested by utterance and neither produced nor destroyed.

In the state of dissolution the Vedas exist in and are sustained by God. God is not the cause of the Vedas because there is no reason for the rejection of the antecedent Vedas before creation. In the former creation there was no absence of the Vedas. Their existence is proved by inference. The prior creation was accompanied by the Vedas, because all creations are accompanied by them, because they are creations, like the present creation. Hence the Vedas are impersonal and authoritative and valid. (Cp. Rāmānuja). Comparison (e.g. 'a wild cow is similar to a cow') is nothing but testimony, because it is produced by the statement of a reliable person. The knowledge of the relation of a name (e.g., 'a wild cow') and an object (e.g., an animal) is nothing but inference. The perception of resemblance to a cow in a wild cow is nothing but perception, since it is due to the intercourse of a sense-organ with an object. Presumption is nothing but inference. The existence of Devadatta outside his house is inferred from his nonexistence in his house because he his known to be alive. Nonapprehension is not a pramāṇa, because there is no negation which is said to be known by it. The negation of a jar on the ground is nothing but the bare ground or a particular modification of the ground. (Cp. Prabhākara). Even if negation exist as different from an entity, it is known by perception, inference, or testimony. So nonapprehension is not a distinct pramāṇa. Inclusion is inference. Tradition is testimony. Gesture also is testimony. Noncontradiction is inference. Hence perception, inference and testimony are the three pramāṇas. Detachment is the absence of attachment due to the control of the sense-organs and the internal organs. It is due to the discernment of faults in noneternal earthly and heavenly objects. Supernatural powers are due to the nonobstruction of the sense-organs. Knowledge, virtue, detachment, and supernatural powers are due to the predominance of sattva in buddhi. Ignorance, vice, attachment, and the absence of supernatural powers are due to the predominance of tamas in buddhi. Vice is the cause of the absence of exaltation and the absence of liberation. Ignorance is wrong knowledge. It is of three kinds, viz., illusion, vikalpa and sleep. Illusion is false knowledge of an object (e.g., silver in a nacre). Vikalpa is the knowledge of a nonexistent object (e.g., a ghost), which follows a word alone. (Cp. Patañjali). Sleep is a mode of buddhi, in which tamas predominates, and which is devoid of waking cognitions and dreams. Patañjali defines sleep as the cognition of nonexistence. Attachment is affection for sensible or supersensible objects. The attribute of buddhi, which opposes the emergence of supernatural powers, is their absence. Others hold that the knowledge which apprehends the nature of God is right knowledge, and that any other knowledge is ignorance. Buddhi is of three kinds according to the merits and demerits acquired in the past births. Sattva predominates in buddhi owing to merits; tamas predominates in it owing to demerits; rajas predominates in it owing to merits and demerits.[27] Ahaṁkāratattva is produced from buddhitattva. Egoism is the function of ahaṁkāra. It is threefold and is apprehended as 'I live', 'I do', and 'I am strong' according as it takes the forms of life, action, and pride. The self is devoid of sattva, rajas and tamas, inactive, neutral, and of the nature of pure consciousness. So the existence of ahaṁkāra must be admitted to account for ego-sense. "Conceit or egoism is the function of ahaṁkāra which manifests the relation of a knowing self to a known object limited by time and space" ('Śaivarahasya'). Ahaṁkāra is of three kinds—sāttvika, rājasa, and tāmasa according as sattva, rajas, or tamas predominates in it, respectively. With the predominance of sattva it is called 'vaikārika'; with the predominance of rajas it is called 'taijasa'; with the predominance of tamas it is called 'bhūtādi' or primal matter.

Manas is produced from rājasa ahaṁkara, and is restless because rajas is of the nature of activity. The ten sense-organs are produced from sāttvika ahaṁkāra, because sattva is of the nature of manifestation and lightness. The subtle essences are produced from primal matter, because they abound in tamas. The Sāṁkhya holds that the eleven sense-organs are produced from sāttvika ahaṁkāra, and that the subtle essences are produced from tāmasa ahaṁkāra. Manas is of the nature of desire. Its function is doubt. The ears, the skin, the eyes, the tongue, and the nose are the cognitive sense-organs. The existence of manas is inferred from the nonsimultaneous production of the auditory, tactual, visual, gustatory, and olfactory cognitions. (Cp. Nyāya). If manas were nonexistent, these cognitions would be simultaneously produced. The objects of the aforesaid cognitive sense-organs are sound, touch, colour, and odour, respectively. Their functions are the apprehension of them, respectively. The vocal organ, the hands, the legs, the anus, and generative organ are the motor organs. Speaking, receiving, walking, evacuation, and generation are their functions, respectively. Manas, buddhi, and ahaṁkāra are the internal organs. There are five subtle essences. The five gross elements are produced from the five subtle essences. The principles are dissolved in their causes in the opposite order. They are dissolved in māyā. The pure principles are dissolved in Śaktitattva. Śaktitattva exists in union with Śivatattva. In dissolution māyā, the bound souls, and God exist. From them again creation follows. God dissolves the world to give respite to the bound souls. He again creates the world in order to ripen their merits and demerits, and associates them with their fruits—joys and sorrows. He wears off their merits and demerits by giving them enjoyments and sufferings, initiates them into the cult of Śiva, and liberates them through His grace.[28]

The 'Mṛgendratantra' gives the following account of the mixed principles. Time is produced by māyā, agitates an individual soul tainted with impurities and determined by niyati, and makes it active, and is the cause of the cognitions of the different periods of duration. Destiny makes a bound soul experience pleasures and pains due to its merits and demerits till dissolution. A bound soul experiences pleasures and pains which follow the principle of time through the cognitive sense-organs, the motor sense-organs, and the internal organs, on which it depends for the manifestation of its powers of knowledge and action. An individual soul's power of action is eternal and pervasive like God's power. It is not manifested in regard to objects without the aid of God's grace because of its being veiled by the beginningless taint called 'darkness'. Kalātattva is its aid. God agitates māyā, makes it ready to produce kalā, and makes a bound soul ready to experience pleasure and pain. Kalā is full of lustre, and manifests a bound soul's power of action. It removes the veil of its innate taint in one part, and manifests its power of action; thus it is the cause of a soul's limited action. Without its aid a bound soul cannot have limited action. God manifests a part of a soul's power of a consciousness and manifests its power of action limited by its taint with the aid of kalātattva which is full of lustre. Kalātattva removes taint from one part of a bound soul. Niyatitattva removes taint from a soul in a particular degree. A bound soul, whose power of action is manifested, being desirous of knowing buddhi in which objects are reflected, and being unable to perceive them unaided, depends upon vidyātattva. God created it after agitating kalātattva and making it prone to produce its effects and manifest the principles, which is an excellent instrument, because it excites a soul's power of knowledge and because it connects a soul with its internal organs and external sense-organs. A soul knows buddhi in which external objects are reflected, and external objects which are reflected in it through its cognitive sense-organs and motor sense-organs with the aid of vidyātattva, which manifests its power of knowledge. A bound soul, whose power of knowledge has been manifested by vidyātattva, and which perceives an external object, does not exert itself to appropriate it until its desire for it is produced. So God created rāgatattva from kalātattva. A bound soul being tinged with desire or love desires an object produced by māyā, and exerts itself, appropriates it, experiences pleasure or pain, and does not give up attachment to it under the influence of rāgatattva.[29]

INDIVIDUAL SOULS (PAŚU).—The souls become atomic because they are related to the taints which cause their atomic nature, and which make them possessors of finite knowledge and agents of limited actions, although they are in their essence of the nature of God,—omniscient, omnipotent, and omnipresent. Celestial souls, human souls, and the like—all are bound and subject to birth and death. They are bound because they are bound by the bonds, and atomic because they have the power of acquiring limited knowledge and of doing limited actions, and not because they are like atoms. They are conscious but nonpervasive, and are not unconscious atoms. It may be objected that the souls are of the nature of God, that therefore they cannot be related to the bonds of mala, karma, and māyā, that their relation to these being beginningless, their relation to the bonds does not depend upon any cause. What has a beginning has a cause. But the relation of the souls to the bonds being biginningless, is not produced by a cause. Śrīkumāra rejoins that the souls are essentially of the nature of God because the Śrutis and the Āgamas assert their divine nature, and that therefore God binds them to embodied life with the bonds. They are mala, karma, māyā, the world produced by māyā, and God's power of veiling the souls' knowledge and action. The 'Śaivarahasya' mentions three bonds—mala, karma, and māyā—of which the innate, beginningless mala is the chief one. The 'Prayogamañjarī' also mentions three kinds of bonds. This view is wrong because God's power of veiling also which favours the bonds is a bond. Mala, karma, māyā, the world produced by it, and God's power of veiling are the five kinds of bonds. The liberated souls are of the nature of God, but they are liberated by His grace. They are not eternally free like Him. God is eternally free and one. They are liberated and many. They can be liberated by muttering His mantras and meditating on Him. They are not like God in the state of bondage because they are stained with taints. But God is never stained with taints. The 'Vāyavīya' says, "God is called Śiva because He is absolutely pure in nature because of the prior negation of relaton to beginningless mala". The 'Lingodbhova' says, "God is transcendent, subtle, unmanifest, and immanent in the world. He is Liṅgin, and assumes prakṛti as liṅga in order to create, maintain, and dissolve the world". The 'Pārameśvara' says, "God is independent Lord Who destroys the bonds of the bound souls".[30]

There are three classes of the individual souls : vijñānakala, pralayākala, and sakala. The first are tainted with mala ; the second are tainted with mala and karma ; and the third are tainted with mala, karma, and māyā.[31] The last are of two classes : those whose sins have been destroyed and those whose sins have not been destroyed. The bound souls are called paśu because they are fettered by the bonds. God bestows His grace on the vijñānakalas whose sins have been destroyed, initiates them into the proper spiritual discipline, induces them to hear of, reflect on, God, and gives them mediate knowledge of their spiritual nature and of God. He does not give them immediate knowledge of their selves and of God, because it is produced by meditation, which destroys merits and demerits, and which prevents all hindrances. He appoints such souls to the office of Vidyeśvaras who are almost like the liberated souls. He appoints the others to the office of Mantras and Mantreśvaras.[32] He appoints some pralayākalas whose mala and karma have been burnt by the fire of knowledge to the office of the lords of the worlds. He makes some of them the lords of the gaṇas, and others Mantreśvaras. He makes the sakalas transmigrate with their subtle bodies from one birth to another under the influence of their merits and demerits. The subtle body, some hold, is composed of manas, buddhi, ahaṁkāra, the five cognitive organs, the five motor organs, sound, touch, colour, taste, and odour. Others think it to be composed of manas, buddi, ahaṁkāra, sound, touch, colour, taste, and odour. Others consider it to be made of the five cognitive organs, the five motor organs, manas, buddhi, ahaṁkāra, citta, five vital forces, desire, karma, nescience, and the five subtle essences.[33]

The 'Mṛgendratantra' describes an individual soul as having consciousness, knowledge and action always in regard to all objects, which are said to exist in it in liberation alone. It is not nonpervasive, momentary, one, insentient, inactive, and not the substratum of knowledge as an adventitious quality, because it is declared by the Śruti to become equal to God when its bonds are destroyed. It is pervasive, permanent, essentially conscious, and active. It is not unconscious in its essential nature as the Naiyāyika and the Vaiśeṣika maintain. It is not inactive as the Sāṁkhya maintains. Consciousness is not its adventitious quality, which it acquires in conjunction with manas and the sense-organs as the Nyāya-Vaiśeṣika holds, because the Śaiva scriptures assert a soul to be identical with God after its bonds of nescience and the like are destroyed. It is said : "God grants knowledge to a bound soul in order to manifest its divine nature and destroy its mala, karma, and māyā". Its divine nature does not consist in its nonpervasiveness or in being devoid of knowerhood or agency. It consists in pervasiveness, knowerhood, and agency. Nor does it acquire pervasiveness, eternality, omniscience, and omnipotences in liberation because what were nonexistent cannot be produced.[34] There are many souls.

It may be objected that there is no proof for the existence of a bound soul transmigrating from this world to a future world as an entity different from the body, the sense-organs, and the like. Śrīkumāra urges that sometimes a person remembers wealth buried in the previous birth, and recovers it in the present birth. His soul is permanent, although his past body has been destroyed. Such recollection is not false because it is not contradicted. The Āgmas assert the transmigration of the permanent souls, and so they are distinct from their bodies. The soul is not identical with the vital force, because it is of the nature of air, like external air, and because we speak of 'my vital force' and thus distinguish between a soul and vital force. Some hold that a soul is identical with the sense-organs. This view is wrong, because there is recollection of the objects perceived in the past through a sense-organ even when it is destroyed, because an object perceived by a sense-organ cannot be remembered by another, because a soul perceives all kinds of objects while the sense-organs perceive their proper objects, and because a soul recognises itself in such a form as 'I that perceived a colour through the eyes, hear a sound through the ears'. Nor is a soul identical with manas, because it is an instrument of knowledge, like an axe, and because it is limited in that it is an effect, like a jar, and because the existence of manas is proved by the impossibility of simultaneous cognitions of the objects of the sense-organs, but because the existence of a soul cannot be proved by it. The Buddhists identify a soul with a stream of momentary cognitions. This view is wrong because it cannot account for recollection : cognitions being momentary cannot remember what was perceived by them. But a soul is permanent, and can remember what it perceived before. The Buddhists hold that momentary cognitions can remember because they belong to the same series, and because the residual impressions of the previous cognitions can perfume the subsequent cognitions. This argument is invalid, because the residual impressions and the series also are momentary, and because they are nondistinct from the cognitions. If they are held to be permanent, the Buddhists contradict the doctrine of momentariness. Thus a soul is different from the body, the sense-organs, vital force, manas, and cognitions.[35] (Cp. Nyāya).

The 'Mṛgendratantra' criticizes the Cārvāka's view of the self, and Nārāyaṇakaṇṭha explains his arguments and criticisms. The Cārvāka holds that the soul is a product of earth, water, light and air, and that therefore the world cannot exist for the experience of the individual souls. This view is wrong, because the body made of earth, water, light and air is a means for the experience of another conscious entity, until conciousness emerges from it. The Cārvāka argues that consciousness emerges in a fœtus from the vital forces which are modifications of earth, water, light and air, as intoxicating power is generated by the particles of rice when they are fermented in water, and that the body is perceived as the self such as 'I am lean', 'I am fat', etc., that the self distinct from the body is not perceived, and that therefore the self exists in the body. It may be argued that the sense-organs are aggregates of the elements and the organs of knowledge, and that therefore they must depend upon a self as an actor different from them. This argument is wrong because the Cārvāka denies the validity of inference, and because he recognises the validity of perception alone. Even if inference be supposed to be valid, it can prove that the self inferred is different from consciousness. Consciousness manifests itself, and what is manifested by it is different from consciousness. Hence the self different from the body cannot be inferred. The body endowed with consciousness alone is perceived, and it is the self. Further, consciousness increases and decreases on the increase and decrease of a body, and so it is of the nature of a body, even as heat increases and decreases on the increase and decrease of a fire, and so it is of the nature of a fire. The 'Mṛgendratantra' urges that a body is not conscious because it is an object of enjoyment and suffering and because it is modifiable, as cloth and the like are devoid of consciousness, because they are objects of enjoyment and suffering, and because they are modifiable. The Cārvāka argues that an entity is an effect of another entity, if the latter being present, the former is present, and if the latter being absent, the former is absent. When the conjuction of a sperm and an ovum, which causes a fœtus, is present, consciousness is present, and when the former is absent, the latter is absent. Hence consciousness is an effect of a body. This argument is invalid, because there is no consciousness in a dead body, and because sometimes consciousness does not appear in a fœtus. So it cannot be argued that whenever there is a body, there is consciousness. If consciousness is said to be an effect of a particular modification of the body, then there can be no recollection, because it presupposes a permanent self, which remembers an object, which it perceived in the past. The present modification of a body cannot remember its past modification. So the remembering self is different from its body. Recollection cannot be denied because it is experienced by all. Though the body always undergoes modification, yet the self remains identical in its nature. It is different from its body and its cognitions of the objects. So the remembering self is not identical with its body. The Cārvāka denies the validity of inference, and makes the most of the elements of earth, water, light and air. But he cannot know their qualities without inference. Further, the fact, that perception alone is a means of valid knowledge, and that inference is not so, is not known by perception. Hence the self is different from the body.[36] (Cp. Nyāyā).

BONDS (PĀŚĀ).—The bonds are nonspiritual stuff, which corrupts the soul. Nescience, āṇava mala, karma, māyā and God's power of veling are the bonds, on the removal of which the bound souls are liberated and become like God. So the souls are bound by the bonds. If their dependence is natural to them, and not due to the bonds, then they cannot be said to be liberated. They are said to be so, because they are realeased from the bonds. A bound soul is dependent on the independent Lord, but a released soul becomes the independent Lord. This is the difference between bondage and liberation. When the bonds are broken, a soul's independence is manifested. Dependence for the attainment of the coveted good is bondage. Independence of a released soul is not obstructed. If a bound soul's dependence be eternal, then it can never be destroyed, and its cultivation of the way of knowledge for the breaking of the bonds becomes fruitless, because its independence can never be manifested. So its dependence is due to the bonds. If a soul's power of knowledge is not veiled by beginningless nescience,—being possessed of eternal and ubiquitous power of consciousness, —then it cannot depend upon the strength of the bonds for the attainment of happiness, and upon the strength of God for the attainment of liberation. If its omniscience and omnipotence be not veiled by the bonds, it would always be pure and omniscient and omnipotent. Hence the existence of the bonds which veil a soul's powers of knowledge and action must be admitted.

The veil of a bound soul is called a taint in the Śaiva scriptures. It is called nescience. It is one in all souls, and not different in the different souls. Although it is one, it is endowed with various powers which veil their nature. It is one in all bound souls, without origin, impenetrable, and veils the ubiquitous souls.[37] It is beginningless, innate, and one. It is not adventitious like the products of māyā. If it were many, it would be insentient and be produced by other causes, and would thus not be without origin. God cannot be bound because He is devoid of nescience. But the powers of nescience are manifold, because they veil the nature of many souls. Nescience exists in a bound soul from the beginningless time, and is without an origin. If it existed in a soul with an origin, then its association with it would depend upon the origin. But there is no origin of its association with a soul. If it binds a liberated soul also, then all efforts for liberation will become needless. Hence nescience is not an adventitious quality of a bound soul, produced by a cause, but is uncaused. The 'Svāyambhuva' says, "The taint—nescience—is originless, and constitutes the bondage of a soul." It is one, because there is no evidence for its being many. What is modified into many is found to be produced by causes, like jars and the like. But nescience is not produced, because it is without an origin, and because it veils the nature of a soul. So it is one. But its powers are many, because all bound souls are not released simultaneously. Its many powers veil the different souls' powers of knowledge and action. If its powers were one, nescience being destroyed in one soul, all souls would be released simultaneously. But they are not released simultaneously. So the manifold powers of nescience must be admitted. But the powers of nescience do not veil a soul's powers of knowledge and action nor are they removed from it independently. They are favoured by God's power to do so, because it favours all. His power of veiling is called a bond in a secondary sense, because it follows the power of nescience which veils a soul's powers of knowledge and action. His power favours all by its nature, and so does good to them all. It may be objected that if God's power favours all conscious souls and all unconscious bonds—nescience, merits and demerits, and māyā and its effects, then it cannot favour them all simultaneously. When it favours the unconscious bonds to fetter the conscious souls, it chastises the latter because their powers of knowledge and action are veiled and because they lose their independence. So God's power cannot favour the conscious souls and the unconscious bonds simultaneously. This objection is not valid, since His power does not favour the unconscious bonds in order to give sufferings to the conscious souls but in order to favour them. The taints can be destroyed after they have produced their fruits in the form of enjoyments and sufferings of the bound souls; when they are destroyed, the souls are released. Hence God's favouring the unconscious bonds and His favouring the conscious souls are not contradictory to each other. The unconscious bonds cannot act without the guidance of God's conscious power. He gives the pains of birth, disease, old age and death to the bound souls in order to release them, even as a physician causes pain to a patient in order to cure him of a disease by operating on him or by giving him bitter drugs. God is ubiquitous and omnipotent, and consequently pervades unconscious bonds also and makes them act. He does not remain inactive in regard to them when He has to do some actions. This is the reason why He, though perfectly pure, activates the unconscious bonds to produce their effects. Thus His power favours all conscious souls and unconscious bonds simultaneously. His power favours all entities to perform their functions, as the sun favours all lotuses and makes them bloom. There is no entity which is not activated by God's favour. His favour to those bound souls whose powers of knowledge and action cease to be veiled by nescience, karma, and māyā is excessively enhanced. His favour acts on the unconscious bonds which undergo modifications in order to free the other souls from their fetters. To make the bonds undergo modifications for the release of the bound souls is to favour them. When nescience ceases to function, and when God's power of veiling is a little loosened, He favours a bound soul by awakening in it the knowledge of its essential divinity, and He favours the bonds by making them produce all their effects. Thus God's power favours both a conscious bound soul and its unconscious bonds simultaneously—which does not involve any contradiction. He favours unconscious māyā to produce its effects from the kalātattva to earth, and unconscious merits and demerits by activating them to produce their fruits in the form of pleasures and pains, respectively. The unconscious entities are always directed by a conscious being.

The conjunction of a bound soul with a future particular body, particular kinds of sense-organs, and particular objects of experience is not uncaused. It is caused by a soul's merits and demerits acquired by it by its right and wrong actions. The conjunction exists in a particular place, and is various, temporary, peculiar to a soul, continuous in its future birth, and is not transferred to another soul. Its cause is an unseen principle because it is subtle and imperceptible. It is called 'karma' because it is produced by voluntary actions. It is an auxiliary cause of the conjunction, because it depends upon God's power of veiling, nescience, and māyā, and because it does not produce the conjunction independently. It produces a soul's conjunction with a future body, sense-organs, and objects in order to afford it proper enjoyments and sufferings. It sustains the conjunction for a certain period of time necessary for the soul's joys and sorrows. It is an object of experience in the sense that its fruits are experienced. The body, the vocal organ, and manas are the means of the experience of pleasures and pains, which are physical, mental and supernatural. The unseen principle is of two kinds, viz., merit and demerit, which are of the nature of truth and falsehood. During dissolution it persists as an impression in māyā, and undergoes maturation. It is not destroyed without producing the appropriate pleasures and pains. Though it is produced by voluntary actions, it is said to be without origin, because it belongs to a continuous stream. Though karma manifests merits because of its auspicious nature, it veils a soul's powers of knowledge and action, and fetters it to embodied life. Though it is of the nature of merits, it does not conduce to a soul's liberation. On the contrary, it hinders a soul's release. The soul achieves liberation when its merits are destroyed along with its demerits by the descent of God's power of grace to it.[38]

Māyā is one, evil, possessed of various powers, the seed of the world, fetters souls until merits and demerits have produced their fruits, pervades its effects, and is not destroyed. It is one, because it is the chief material cause of the world, and because there is no evidence for its being many. It is evil since it deludes the souls. It is the material cause of the world. It is possessed of various powers because it binds the souls until their merits and demerits have borne their fruits. When they are worn out by producing their fruits, the bonds cease to fetter the souls. Māyā is pervasive, since it pervades all its effects. It is not destroyed, since it is eternal, and since it exists even during dissolution, like the souls and God. The 'Tattva-trayanirṇaya' says: "God, the souls, and māyā are eternal, pervasive, and endowed with activity. When the modifications of māyā are dissolved, the three realities persist." The world with an arrangement requires an agent or efficient cause—God, and a material cause—māyā, even as a cloth requires a weaver as its efficient cause and threads as its material cause. Māyā is insentient, for its effects are insentient. If it were thought to be conscious despite its effects being unconscious, there would be no universal causal relation, no inference, and no practical actions. All practical actions depend upon inferences. All inferences depend upon the universal causal relation. Thus, if māyā were the conscious material cause of its unconscious effects, there would be complete cessation of practical life. So it is unconscious. If māyā were destroyed on the destruction of the world—its effect, then the world would not be created again owing to the absence of its material cause. So it is not noneternal. To argue that God creates the material cause of the world before creating the world involves infinite regress, because even its material cause would require another material cause, and so on to infinity. When the world is dissolved, māyā exists as a power of God. This view is not vitiated by any defect. If māyā were limited, its effects in all times and places would not be produced. So it is pervasive. If it were many and unconscious, it would be produced like its effects—jars, cloths, and the like. But it is not produced since it is their root material cause, which cannot be many. What is the good of assuming one māyā as the material cause of the world? One cloth is produced out of many threads. So let the world be produced out of many causes (e.g., atoms). This view is wrong, since many material causes (e.g., atoms) are produced out of one material cause. The view, that all insentient effects in the world are produced out of one, insentient, material cause—the māyā, is flawless. Some hold that unconscious effects are produced out of one conscious God. This view is wrong, for water may be inferred from smoke, if unconscious effects are produced out of the conscious Lord. An effect can be produced out of a material cause of the same nature. An unconscious effect is never found to be produced out of a conscious material cause. If an effect were produced out of a material cause of a contrary nature, then all effects would be produced out of all material causes. Some hold that atoms are the material cause of the world. This view is wrong, because atoms are not made of atoms, because they have parts in that they produce things of extensive magnitude in conjunction with other atoms, and thus cease to be atoms, and because, being unconscious and many, they are produced by other causes, and, consequently, cannot be the root material cause of the world. Some hold that insentient effects are produced by their material causes, as a new body is produced by a sperm and an ovum conjoined togther. This view is wrong, since new bodies cannot be produced at the time of dissolution when all bodies will be destroyed. Hence all effects subsist in māyā as God's powers, which are unfolded again at the time of creation, and which act to realize their ends.[39] So māyā is the eternal, pervasive, material cause of the world. Some hold that, if the world existed in māyā—its material cause, then no person would collect threads, a loom, a shuttle, and the like, to produce a cloth, since a cloth already exists in threads. If a cloth pre-existed in threads, they would not be its cause. A material cause is a cause if it produces a nonexistent effect, and not otherwise. This view is wrong, since all effects would be produced out of all material causes, if a nonexistent effect were produced out of a material cause. But all effects cannot be produced out of all material causes. A specific effect is produced out of a specific cause. According to Asatkāryavāda there is nothing to regulate the production of a specific effect out of a specific cause. Hence a specific cause alone has the power of producing a specific effect, and no other cause has this power. If a specific cause has the power of producing a specific effect, then an effect exists in its cause as a power, and this view is in accord with the Śaiva view. Otherwise, if a nonexistent effect is produced out of its material cause, there is no use of assembling a collocation of causal conditions to produce an effect (e.g., a barren woman's son). A lump of earth, a wheel, and a stick are unnecessary to produce a nonexistent jar. It may be contended that an effect does not exist in its material cause, but that a cause has the power of producing an effect. This contention is foolish, since there is no difference between the two views except in language. The causal power of a cause produces a specific effect. When the causal power is present, the effect is produced, and when the former is absent, the latter cannot be produced. Thus the former being the cause of the latter is proved by the method of agreement in presence and agreement in absence. When a lump of earth is present, a jar is produced, and when the former is absent, the latter cannot be produced. So the former is the cause of the latter.[40] It may be objected that a jar does not exist in a lump of earth, but that it is produced by a potter out of a lump of earth, and that after it is produced by his physical action, it is perceived. This objection is groundless, since a jar is not perceived because the conditions of its perception are absent, and since a jar is not perceived, not because it does not exist in a lump of earth. When the form of a jar is manifested by a potter's physical action, it is perceived, as water existing under the earth is manifested by digging. It may be objected that there is evidence for the existence of water under the earth, but there is no evidence for the existence of a jar in a lump of earth, and that therefore a nonexistent jar is produced out of a lump of earth, and that a jar is not manifested. The reply to the objection is that production is manifestation out of a material cause, and that the form of threads obstructs the form of a cloth hidden in them. The form of threads is removed by a loom, a shuttle, and the like, and the form of a cloth is manifested by them. A nonexistent thing cannot be manifested. Hence the kalātattva and other principles exist in māyā—the material cause—as powers, and are manifested by the action of God, and māyā is the chief material cause of the world.[41]

Bhojadeva regards māyā as a real, eternal, positive principle, which is the material cause of the world. Śrīkumāra avers that the world is real, and that māyā—its material cause—is real, because it is the material cause of the world. Māyā and the world are not false appearances of God as the Advaitavādins hold. The world—the effect of māyā—is real. It is not a false appearance, since there is no proof for it.[42]

Others hold that māyā is a positive entity of the nature of God, and that the world—its effect—is of the nature of Him, because nothing different from God can exist.[43] God of the nature of knowledge is manifested as māyā and its effect—the world. So He is both māyā and the world. This view does not make God modifiable, because He appears to be the world. It adopts the doctrine of false appearance (vivarta), which is an entity's becoming a different entity without losing its nature, as a rope appears to be a serpent. A rope is not modified into a serpent. Similarly, God is not modified into the world, but appears to be māyā and its effect. The 'Īśvaragītā' says: "God Himself is the root prakṛti, mahat, and the other modifications of it, and individual souls." Śatakakāra says: "The supreme reality is devoid of all determinations, pure, transcendent, and without origin and end. The world consisting of thirty six principles is manifested in it, as towns and villages with their distinctions are manifested in a mirror. Though they are nondistinct from one another in God's knowledge, they appear to be distinct from one another. One nondistinct God appears to be the manifest world."

BONDAGE, LIBERATION, AND YOGA.—God is the cause of the souls' bondage and emancipation. He has two kinds of power in regard to the souls—binding power and liberating power. The first binds them with a network of bonds from the beginningless time. When His binding power has ceased to operate in course of time, and when the souls' merits and demerits have been destroyed, His liberating power in quest of a favourable time descends into them. Then He ripens their taints, assumes the form of a spiritual teacher, initiates them into the cult of Śiva, destroys their taints, and unites them with Śivatattva. He liberates them with the sword of knowledge after destroying their bonds. He engages the sakala souls endowed with subtle bodies in actions for their enjoyments and sufferings in contact with sensible objects in the different worlds after associating them with gross bodies. He infuses His power into those souls whose taints have become ripe in order to destroy them, and engages them in the pursuit of the supreme reality.[44]

There are four kinds of bonds : mala, karma, māyīya, and God's power of veiling the souls' knowledge. Mala is the first kind of taint, because it is the cause of their merits and demerits. Some consider it to be the prior negation of knowledge. Others consider it to be an insentient positive entity like darkness destroyed by knowledge. The Śaiva teachers think it to be a potency or impression of nescience. The 'Śivasūtravārtika' says : "The knowledge of 'I' and 'mine', which manifests difference, which is produced by association with words, and which is the cause of māyīya mala, is characterised by the function of nescience." The 'Kiraṇa' says : "Mala is nescience, darkness, swoon, which veils the knowledg of a soul. Karma is the second kind of taint. Merits and demerits are called karma. Māyīya is produced by māyā, and is of the nature of the subtle body and the gross body. It is the third kind of taint. God's power of veiling is the fourth kind of taint. The existence of the bonds is proved by the fact that bondage or the cycle of births and deaths is not possible without them which bind the souls. Bondage is proved by the Śruti and other pramāṇas. The objection, that there is a vicious circle in the argument that mala and karma are produced when māyā operates, and that māyā operates when mala and karma are produced, is groundless, because mala, karma, and māyā are beginningless like seeds and sprouts.[45] Mala is one but possessed of various powers, and veils a soul's power of knowledge and power of action. There are many karmas and māyīyas. But mala is one and so different from them. God's power of veiling is one but not possessed of various powers, and so is not mala. The 'Kiraṇa' says : "Though a soul is ubiquitous, mala restricts its power of knowledge and power of action, and so makes it ignorant of God, as a mantra obstructs the consuming power of fire." "A soul is essentially pure like God ; but its mala conceals its essential purity consisting of pure consciousness." Power of knowledge and power of action constitute its essence ; they are omniscience and omnipotence. But mala conceals them, manifests its finite knowledge and limited power of action, and makes it bound. The objection, that when innate mala is destroyed, the soul that is possessed of it is destroyed, is unsound, because the soul's essence is not destroyed when its innate mala is destroyed, even as the essence of gold is not destroyed when the stain of gold due to copper is destroyed. Karma is beginningless, of the nature of merits and demerits, and various. It is beginningless as a stream, and not in the form of constant existence of one karma. If karma were one positive entity and without any origin and end, it would be eternal like a soul, and therefore liberation would not be possible. Further, if karma were eternal, bondage would not be destroyed. Karma is of two kinds : merit and demerit. It is various because it is the cause of various kinds of fruits. The variety of karma or merits and demerits is the cause of a variety of objects, which produce a variety of experience. Māyā is the material cause of all manifest objects, time, kalā, niyati, vidyā, and rāga. It is said, "Māyā is nondiscrimination of the principles." The world is material and so produced by one material cause, as earth is the material cause of all earthen vessels. Māyā is a real, positive entity, because it is the material cause of the world, like God, Who is its efficient cause. It is eternal since it is the root of the world, like God. If it were noneternal, it would be produced by another cause. The argument, that God is the cause of the world, and that māyā is not its cause because the Śruti and Bādarāyaṇa assert it, is wrong because God and māyā related to each other are the causes of the world. Insentient māyā is not the material cause of the world as independent of God. The Lord, though conscious, is not the cause of the world without māyā because He is neutral and without physical action. They are the causes of the world as related to each other. The world produced by māyā is a real positive entity. Māyā is real, and, consequently, its product, the world, is real. The world is not a false appearance, because there is no proof for its falsity, and because the nature of its falsity cannot be ascertained. God's power of veiling the souls' knowledge favours the bonds which bind them, and is so called a bond. The effects of mala, karma, and māyā are incapable of binding them because of their insentience. God's power veiling their knowledge alone enters into them, and enables them to bind the souls, and is therefore called a bond. Thus there are four kinds of bonds.[46]

The Vaiśeṣika holds that the right knowledge of the nature of substance, quality, action or motion, generality, and particularity with their similarities and differences destroys ignorance, love, hate, cognition, pleasure, pain, desire, aversion, merit, demerit, and impression due to a soul's conjunction with its body. When all these qualities are destroyed, the soul becomes unconscious ; and if such a soul is liberated, even a dead body should be considered to be liberated.[47]

The Sāṁkhya holds that liberation is due to discrimination between the self and prakṛti and the mind-body-complex—its effect. This view is wrong because the Sāṁkhya regards prakṛti, an effect of kalā produced by māyā as the chief cause of the world. It does not know that kalā and other distinct principles, which have different ends and functions, are the effects of māyā. Prakṛti is the equilibrium of sattva, rajas and tamas, and not different from them according to it. The guṇas are many, and hence prakṛti is manifold and insentient, and, consequently, must be produced by another cause, like threads. So prakṛti is not the chief cause of the world. Again, the Sāṁkhya holds, that conjunction of a soul with prakṛti is the cause of its bondage, that conjunction is preceded by disjunction between them, and that this disjunction is the cause of liberation. The conjunction of a soul with prakṛti is the relation of a knowing self to known objects, and not of the nature of union because both are formless. Prakṛti is not perceived by its nature, because it is assumed to be imperceptible. Nor can the self, which knows mahat, ahaṁkāra, and its other modifications, perceive prakṛti. So there can be no conjunction of a self with prakṛti, and therefore there can be no disjunction prior to it. Thus conjunction and disjunction between a self and prakṛti being not possible, prakṛti cannot be the chief cause of the world. The Sāṁkhya does not believe in God. A self, according to it, is not an experiencer of pleasure and pain. What, then, is the use of its body, sense-organs, and their objects, and pleasures and pains? A self's being an experiencer of pleasure and pain cannot be denied, because it is endowed with its body as the locus of its pleasure and pain, and with its sense-organs, which are the organs of its experience. A self, which is an experiencer of pleasure and pain, cannot be inactive, because an inactive entity cannot be related as a cause to any other entity. Further, a self is of the nature of knowing and activity; and if it is inactive, it cannot be a knower because knowing is of the nature of activity. Further, insentient prakṛti without being guided by an intelligent agent cannot produce an effect independently. It is absurd to hold that insentient prakṛti can produce effects, and that a conscious self cannot act.[48]

According to the Advaita Vedānta there is one Self or undifferentiated consciousness in all unconscious and conscious entities, that appears to be many souls and the manifold world in connection with different limiting adjuncts. The nondifferent supreme Brahman appears to be different, and the appearance of difference is illusory, like the appearance of the double moon. But this statement is a mere thesis which is not proved, because there is no reason or example for the inference. If the supreme Self be considered to be the pramāṇa, then it is the object of the proof also. If it is the means of valid knowledge and the object of valid knowledge, then it is also the knower of valid knowledge and valid knowledge. If it is fourfold, it undermines monism. Otherwise, the one supreme Self is unproved. Further, the Advaitavādins do not admit an individual soul's equality of enjoyment with Brahman in release, and real liberation. They consider bondage and liberation as phenomenal appearances only. But the reality of the perceptible world of plurality and of individual souls must be admitted. The variety of objects is the cause of pleasures and pains of the individual souls. They must experience these feelings in order to endeavour to attain release from them, since the scriptures inculcate the practice of a spiritual discipline for achieving liberation. If the individual souls are real, then only some can be happy and others can be miserable. If the bound souls are mere appearances of Brahman, and if they merge in It and emerge from It, their liberation is not real. Further, if Brahman be the cause of conscious souls and unconscious objects, It becomes conscious and unconscious, because effects are of the nature of their causes. But the presence of consciousness and the absence of consciousness cannot exist in It, because they are contradictory to each other. It is partless, and, consequently, cannot be partly conscious and partly unconscious. If It has parts, It is an effect, and ceases to be the chief cause. Further, a material cause is always unconscious, like earth and the like. Thus, Brahman, the material cause of the world, is unconscious. If It be conscious, It cannot be the material cause of the world. If It is unconscious, It cannot be the cause of the conscious souls. It cannot produce the world until It becomes conscious, because an unconscious entity, like earth, unguided by an intelligent agent, cannot produce an effect, like a jar. If the souls knowing themselves and objects be produced by Brahman, they also become unconscious, like jars and the like. So the doctrine of monism is vitiaied by many defects.[49]

The 'Mṛgendra Tantra' describes the eightfold Yoga as the means to the attainment of liberation. Nārāyaṇakaṇṭha elaborates it. Breath-control, withdrawal of mind from the objects of the sense-organs, fixation of mind, meditation, discernment, muttering God's name or mantra, and trance are the parts of yoga. Yoga consists in the immediate experience of the Self or its divinity and absoluteness, and a yogin is one who has realised his Self or divinity. One who has mastered one's sense-organs and passions can become a yogin. Passions can be gradually conquered by breath-control. It consists in inhalation, retention and exhalation of breath in the proportion of 1, 4 and 2 in respect of duration with the muttering of God's name or without it under an expert's guidance. It removes the defects in the humours of the body, and the flaws in the objects of the sense-organs by pacifying the passions which motivate them to function towards them. Then the mind should be withdrawn from the objects of the sense-organs after tasting a trace of inner joy on achieving mental equanimity. Then the mind withdrawn from the objects of sentient pleasure becomes fit for being concentrated on a desired object. Then meditation or thinking of a form of God for a period of time should be practised. Then trance should be practised. It is the continuity of the thought of some form of God without interruption in which alone the object of thought is manifested. It is the complete absorption of the mind in the object of meditation. Concentration is fixation of the mind at the heart or some other vital part of the body in order to make it fit for meditation on God. When the mind is distracted, concentrate it at the heart, and it will become steady. Breath-control, concentration and meditation should be accompanied by the repeated muttering of God's name, either audible, or inaudible, or mental, in order to confront the mind with the object of meditation.[50] Discernment is insight into the highest good which is covetable and the evils which are to be eschewed. A yogin who practises these parts of yoga individually and collectively perceives the world as pervaded by divine powers. He cannot be harmed by any evil powers, human and superhuman, because he achieves excellent knowledge, power of action, strength, and invincibility. Breath-control attended with muttering God's name steadies the mind. Concentration and meditation lead to a vision of God as a luminous form. Trance generates eight kinds of supernatural powers. Concentration of the mind on God residing in earth, water, and the other elements generates the manifestation of His powers pervading them. Concentration on Śivatattva after complete withdrawal of the mind from all objects practised for a long time leads to the attainment of divinity after death. When the mind becomes completely detached, it is no longer attached to worldly objects, and all its functions are arrested. A detached yogin with a completely controlled mind can concentrate on God with the whole world as His body. He does not concentrate on a limited object or place as pervaded by God, but on the whole world as pervaded by Him. He always perceives God in all beings and does good to them. Meditation on Him makes the mind steady and tranquil. Meditation on formless God repeately practised reveals Him with omniscience, omnipotence, and infinite bliss. The body becomes surcharged with divine light and consciousness, the mind is destroyed, and egoism is eradicated. The body is discarded at the proper time, and one's own divinity is realized.[51] (Cp. Post-Śaṁkara Advaita Vedānta). The account of 'Śaiva Siddhānta' based on 'Sarvadarśanasaṁgraha' is given in Vol. II. Śaivism in the Upaniṣads and the Purāṇas is discussed in Vol. I.

[1] SDS., ch. vii ; HIP., Vol. II, 1952, pp. 733-37.
[2] TP., i, 5. [3] TD., i, 1-3, 6-7.
[4] Ibid, i, 3 ; pp. 14-18. [5] MT., MTV., i, 5, 13-17.
[6] TD., ii, 17 ; pp. 88-91, 96-97, 99-110. Cp. HIP., Vol. I, pp. 677-95.
[7] CHI., 1st edition, Vol. II, p. 43n ; DHIP., Vol. V, pp. 162, 163n. & 168.
[8] TP., TD., ii, 1-4 ; ŚR., pp. 75-76.
[9] TP., ii, 5 ; TD., ii, 5, pp. 75-77.
[10] Ibid, ii, 7 ; pp. 77-79. [11] Ibid, ii, 8.
[12] TP., TD., ii, 9. [13] Ibid, ii, 10.
[14] Ibid, ii, 13. [15] TD., ii, 14.
[16] Ibid, ii, 14. [17] TP., ii, 16.
[18] Ibid, iii, 1. [19] TP., TD., iii, 2-3.
[20] TP., iii, 4. [21] Ibid, iii, 4-5.
[22] Ibid, iii, 6-7. [23] Ibid, iii, 10.
[24] Ibid, iii, 11. [25] Ibid, iii, 12.
[26] Ibid, iv, 1. [27] Ibid, iv, 2-3.
[28] Ibid, iv, 4-10 ; V, 6-7 ; vi, 1-2. cp. Sāṁkhya.
[29] MT., MTV., i, 10, 4-6, 8-14.
[30] TP., TD., i, 5-6. [31] TP., i, 8.
[32] TP., TD., i, 10. Cp. Pratyabhijñā school of Śaivism.
[33] Ibid, i, 11-13. [34] MT., i, 2, 5-7.
[35] TD., i, 8.
[36] MT., MTV., i, 6, 3-6. [37] MT., i, 7, 4-5 & 8.
[38] MT., MTV., i, 7, 11-23. [39] MT., i, 9 & 13.
[40] MT., i, 9, 16 & 19 ; MTV., i, 9, 15.
[41] MT., i, 9, 20-21 ; MTV., i, 9, 13-16 & 21.
[42] TD., i, 18 ; p. 62. [43] Ibid, i, 19, pp. 71-72.
[44] TP., TD., i, 15-16. [45] Ibid, i, 15-17.
[46] Ibid, i, 19. [47] MT., MTV., i, 2, 22-23.
[48] MT., MTV., i, 2 & 15.
[49] MTV., i, 2, 12-14, pp. 64-70.
[50] MT., yogapāda, i, 2; i, 7-9.
[51] Ibid, i, 28-29, 49-50, 52-54, 56-60, HIP., Vol. II, 1952, pp. 733-37.

CHAPTER V

ŚAIVA VIŚIṢṬĀDVAITAVĀDA : ŚRĪKAṆṬHA

INTRODUCTION.—Nothing is known about the life of Śrīkaṇṭha. He mentions in the beginning and at the end of 'Śrīkaṇṭhabhāṣya' on the 'Brahmasūtra' that he was a disciple of Śvetācārya. This is the only work written by him, which is known. It was published in Mysore in 1903. He does not mention the names of Śaṁkara, Bhāskara, Rāmānuja, Nimbārka, or Madhva. But he says in the Introduction to his commentary, that 'Brahmasūtra' is the eyes with which the wise can have a vision of Brahman. It was misinterpreted by the earlier commentators. It is being rightly interpreted by Śrīkaṇṭha (6). Evidently he hints here at Śaṁkara who interpreted it in the light of monism (800 A.D.) He criticises Śaṁkar's doctrines of attributeless Brahman, of an individual soul as Brahman limited by a false adjunct, viz., nescience, of its being a knower as a reflection of Brahman in egoism, of an effect as an unreal appearance of its material cause, and of the world as a false appearance of Brahman.[1] So he was later than Śaṁkara. He criticises the doctrine of difference and identity between Brahman and an individual soul held by Bhāskara (900 A.D.).[2] Nimbārka (1300 A.D.) also held the doctrine of difference and identity in another way. So he was later than 900 A.D. He quotes a verse from Abhinavagupta's 'Bodhapañcadaśikā',[3] and a verse from Utpaladeva's 'Īśvarapratyabhijñākārikā' (1000 A D.).[4] Both Utpaladeva and Abhinavagupta belonged to the Pratyabhijñā school of Śaivism, and flourished in 1000 A.D. So Śrīkaṇṭha was later than 1000 A.D. He calls himself a Viśiṣṭādvaitavādin—a qualified monist. This doctrine resembles the doctrine of difference and identity between Brahman and the individual soul.[5] Śrīkaṇṭha conceives of Brahman as essentially qualified by the powers of conscious souls, and of unconscious matter, which are His attributes and accessories, and which constitute His body.[6] Brahman is the Supreme Soul with the conscious souls and unconscious matter as His body. He is the substance while they are His attributes. He is the Principal while they are His accessories.[7] He is the Whole while souls are His parts because they are His body.[8] Śrīkaṇṭha regards Brahman as qualified by the subtle conscious souls and unconscious matter as the material cause of the world, and Brahman as qualified by the gross embodied souls and unconscious matter as the effect. He regards an individual soul as a knower, enjoyer, and doer, and a released soul as similar to Brahman, and not identical with Him. He regards an effect as a real modification of its material cause, and the world as a real modification of Brahman endowed with power. These are the views of Rāmānuja. Especially, none other than Rāmānuja conceived of Brahman as qualified by the conscious souls and unconscious matter as His body, attributes, and accessories.[9]

So Śrīkantha adopted Rāmānuja's doctrine of Viśiṣṭādvaita, and was later than he was. Śrīpati Paṇḍita, the author of 'Śrīkarabhāṣya' on the 'Brahmasūtra' (1400 A.D.) calls

Śrīkaṇṭha a follower of Rāmānuja, a qualified monist. The later Vedāntists call the Śaivas plagiarists of Rāmānuja's doctrine. So Śrīkaṇṭha could not be earlier than Rāmānuja. He criticises the doctrine of difference between Brahman and an individual soul.[10] He could not be later than Śrīpati Paṇḍita (1400 A.D.) who explicitly refers to him. Śrīkaṇṭha criticises the Pāśupata doctrine that God is only the efficient cause of the world.[11] But he stresses, like the Pāśupata, meditation on 'Om' in the heart-ether, which he identifies with Śiva accompanied by Umā—the pure, infinite, universal consciousness attended with power, which is transcendent of, and immanent in, the universe. The Pratyabhijñā school of Śaivism emphasised meditation on Śiva-Śakti at the centres of mystic consciousness including the powerful heart-lotus.[12] Śrīkaṇṭha was a successor of Bhojarāja (1100 A.D.). R. G. Bhandarkar thinks Śrīkaṇṭha's philosophy to be qualified monism, like that of Rāmānuja. Anantakṛṣṇa Śāstrī assigns him 1350 A.D., and thinks that he belonged to the Southern school of Śaiva Siddhānta. Sūrya Nārāyaṇa Śastrī thinks him to be a contemporary of Rāmānuja (1100-1200 A.D.). S. N. Das Gupta and J. N. Banerjee assign him to the thirteenth century. Roma Choudhury places him after Śaṁkara and Rāmānuja. R. K. Kaw dates him 1270 A.D. It is undoubted that Śrīkaṇṭha was influenced by Rāmānuja's qualified monism, and that he was his junior contemporary.[13] His 'Śrīkaṇṭhabhāṣya' is a famous commentary on the 'Brahmasūtra', which is not brief and concise like Nimbārka's 'Vedāntapārijatasaurabha' nor elaborate and exhaustive like Rāmānuja's 'Śrībhāṣya'. He describes his commentary as the essence of all Upaniṣads, sweet and fragrant, and a great treasure to the revered devotees of Śiva. Appayadīkṣita (1600 A.D.) wrote a sub-commentary entitled 'Sivārkamaṇidīpikā' on 'Śrīkaṇṭhabhāṣya'. Śrīkaṇṭha based his doctrine on the Upaniṣads whereas the Saiva Siddhānta based its doctrine on the Śaiva Āgamas.

THE NATURE OF BRAHMAN.—Śrīkaṇṭha calls Brahman Śiva. He is of the nature of being, consciousness, and bliss, and of the nature of 'I', the Supreme Self. He is the creator of all worlds through His power, the source of all scriptures, the repository of all goods, the principal of all conscious souls and unconscious physical things, which are His accessories, and the grantor of emancipation. He is devoid of all blemishes and endowed with supreme knowledge, bliss and other qualities and powers, and greatness.[14] Creation, maintenance, and dissolution of the world, obscuration of the knowledge of the individual souls, and granting them grace are His acts.[15] Bondage is the obscuration of the souls' knowledge of their real nature. Emancipation is the manifestation of their knowledge of their real nature. He is the cause of their bondage and release. His being the creator, maintainer, destroyer of the world, and binder, and liberator of the souls is as essential as His being omniscient, omipotent, and the like. He is omniscient, eternally contented, independent, possessed of powers which are never destroyed, omnipotent, and endowed with beginningless knowledge. His omniscience consists in eternal immediate apprehension of all objects, independent of the external sense-organs. He is the efficient cause of the world and the bodies capable of producing joys and miseries appropriate to the various merits and demerits of the conscious souls. His being eternally contented consists in being full of supreme bliss and in being devoid of all blemishes. He enjoys His unsurpassable bliss through His manas, which is independent of the external sense-organs. His manas is of the nature of the power of pure knowledge. He enjoys His essential bliss through it. He has no trace of pleasure due to the external sense-organs. He is devoid of sentient pleasure due to the physical mind. His being endowed with beginningless knowledge consists in His being possessed of self-evident, innate, supreme knowledge. His knowledge of His essential bliss is due to His internal organ. It gives Him the apprehension of His bliss. It is of the nature of originless knowledge. "He is immortal, and abounds in peace and tranquillity." He is supramundane and untouched by all imperfections of the world. His independence consists in His being devoid of wretchedness due to dependence on another being, and in controlling and subduing all other entities. He controls and regulates all conscious souls and unconscious things. He is the creator of all, since He is independent of all other entities. His being endowed with indestructible powers consists in His being possessed of natural, innate, spontaneous powers. His being qualified by the powers of conscious souls and unconscious physical things is natural to Him. He is never unqualified. Śrīkaṇṭha rejects Śaṁkara's view of unqualified Brahman, like Rāmānuja, and regards conscious and unconscious powers as His qualities. Brahman is omnipotent in the sense that He is endowed with unlimited powers.[16] Because He has infinite powers, He is the material cause of the limitless world. The Supreme Lord Himself endowed with subtle and gross, conscious and unconscious powers, is the cause and the effect.[17]

He is called 'Bhava', since He always exists. He is the eternal Being, that persists in all beings. He is the material cause of all existents. He is called 'Śarva', since He destroys all entities. He is called 'Īśāna', since He is endowed with unconditional supreme lordship. "He rules over these worlds with His ruling powers". He is called 'Paśupati', since He is the ruler of the bound souls, which depend upon Him. The word 'paśu', or bound soul, implies bonds. Māyā or prakṛti and its effects are called bonds (pāśa) because they bind the souls to embodied existence. Brahman is the controller of the conscious souls and unconscious matter. He is called 'Rudra', because He cures the disease of embodied life. "The knower of Brahman transcends grief." He is called 'Ugra', because He cannot be overpowered by others' lustre or splendour. He is called 'Bhīma', because He is the cause of fear of all conscious souls. He is called 'Mahādeva', because He shines in His infinite greatness, or because He discards the imperfections of all existents, and because He is established in His self-knowledge and sovereignty. He is designated by other names. He is called 'Śivatattva', since He is devoid of all imperfections of empirical life, and since He is the abode of all kinds of goods. He is called 'Brahman', because He is the efficient cause and material cause of the world, and because He is endowed with infinite greatness. He is called 'Śiva', because He is possessed of supreme bliss and other qualities. Brahman as endowed with subtle consciousness and unconsciousness is the cause. He as endowed with gross consciousness and unconsciousness is the effect.[18] He is knowable through the Vedas alone. They were hidden in Him before creation and revealed at the time of creation. So they are impersonal and yet created by God.[19] He is the supremely trustworthy Person, because He has flawless perception of all entities, which is intrinsically valid. So His words which constitute the Vedas are valid. He is the promulgator of all kinds of learning. The Vedas manifest all kinds of entities, and are made or revealed by God. So His omniscience is known for certain by them. If He were not omniscient, He would not be able to speak about all entities through them. He is ubiquitous and in contact with all entities, and therefore omniscient, and knows them all. He also manifests them all through the Vedas made by Him, which manifest all objects. He communicates the knowledge of them to the bound souls through them. It may be objected that if God is omniscient, seers also are omniscient, because they know all the Vedas. This objection is not sound, because God's knowledge is greater than that of seers. Some Vedic sentences convey their meanings in a primary sense. Other Vedic sentences convey their meanings in a secondary sense. But God is the witness of all, and perceives them directly. So there is a difference between Him and the Vedas. He is greater than the conscious souls and the unconscious world. He communicated the knowledge of the Vedas to Brahmā at the time of creation, which are the means of acquiring all knowledge. So He is the maker of all the Vedas.[20]

The existence of God cannot be known by inference from the world as made of parts. Many agents are inferred from the world with a wonderful arrangement of parts, as many masons are inferred from a huge gateway to a temple. One God cannot be inferred as the creator of the world. Even if one God be inferred from the world as its creator, He is possessed of merits and demerits and a body, as a potter is possessed of them. Even if one God be inferred from the world as its agent, He cannot be inferred as its efficient cause and material cause. So He is known through the Vedas alone.

Brahman is the supreme reality, transcendent of the world and the souls, and possessed of the highest excellence.[21] He is of the nature of supreme 'I', and endowed with extraordinary, supreme qualities. Because He is the most excellent Being, He is the object of our reverence and worship.[22] He is the Supreme Person, the supreme light, attainable by the released souls. He is devoid of reprehensible qualities and endowed with auspicious qualities.[23] In the aforesaid senses He is both attributeless and endowed with attributes. He is devoid of imperfections and endowed with auspicious qualities. He is full of attributes—supreme purity, absolute holiness, auspicious qualities, supreme good, and devoid of all blemishes. He is called Śiva because of His twofold nature, because of His freedom from connection with beginningless impurities, and because of His being endowed with supreme purity, infinite bliss, and infinite auspicious qualities. He is devoid of attachment, aversion and other imperfections. He abounds in bliss and imparts bliss to others. He is pure consciousness and a conscious knower. Consciousness is His essence, and He is omniscient, and knows all entities at all times. As supremely merciful He resides in the heart of a person as full of light, although He is unlimited, for his meditation on Him. He is the favourer of all, destroys their bonds of embodied existence, and grants them emancipation. He is the sovereign remedy for the disease of bondage.[24] He is the Universal and Infinite, because He alone is of the nature of infinite bliss. He alone is the Universal, and none else. "When the Universal is experienced, nothing else is perceived". When infinite bliss is experienced, no desire for less pleasure disturbs the soul. Brahman is eternally self-fulfilled, abounds in tranquillity, and is full of infinite delight. "He is endowed with the body of ether ; His soul is truth ; His vital force is pleasure ; His manas is bliss ; He is rich in tranquillity, and immortal". 'Ether' is not physical ether, but of the nature of manifestation, the ether of pure consciousness.[25] He is transcendent of the unconscious world and the conscious souls. He is present in all, and the substratum of all, the Soul of the universe and the Inner Controller of the universe and the souls. He is immanent in the universe, and is manifested in it. He assumes the form of the universe, and is transformed into it. He is the ruler of all, the Supreme Lord, transcendent of all, greater than the universe, greater than all, and higher than all.[26] He is pure and immutable, though He is immanent in the universe and the bound souls. Though He is transformed into the universe, He is untouched by its mutability. Though He is immanent in the bound souls, He is not affected by their nescience, sins and imperfections. He is eternally pure and immutable. He is supremely holy, infinite, eternal, and omniscient. The universe is mutable, physical, finite and perishable. The bound souls are ignorant and afflicted with misery. Brahman is the Supreme Lord. The unconscious things and the conscious souls are govered by Him. He is the Soul of all, excels all, and is worshipped by all. His being of the form of the universe is not denied, but His being confined to it is denied.[27] Though He is of the nature of unconscious powers and conscious powers, though He is qualified by the unconscious world and the conscious souls, He is not tainted with their impurities, because He is the abode of all auspicious qualities. Their impurities are denied of Him.[28] Though He is the cause of the universe and the bound souls, and though He is qualified by them, He is not affected by mutability, ignorance and other imperfections, because He is omniscient, eternally fulfilled, independent, omnipotent, possessed of indestructibe powers and eternal knowledge, and the repository of the supreme goods realizable by the bound souls. Though He enters into all mutations, He is absolutely free from any taint of mutation, because He is imperishable and immortal. Though He enters into all conscious souls and unconscious matter, He ever remains the pure, holy, immutable, immortal Lord.[29] There is no other supreme reality than Brahman. His supreme power is manifested in all conscious souls and unconscious, physical things. He is free from the potencies of actions and possessed of omniscience and all other auspicious qualities.[30] He is the knower, enjoyer, and doer. He is the knower of all, experiencer of His infinite bliss, creator, maintainer, and destroyer of the universe, and binder and liberator of the souls. He is not mere knowledge, bliss and powers, which constitute His essence.[31] He is stern, just and merciful. He creates the embodied souls or associates the souls with their bodies in accordance with their merits and demerits. He gives them the fruits of their actions appropriate to their deserts. He is neither partial nor cruel. He is the chastiser and redeemer. He is severe and benign. He is terrible and loving and attractive. The souls and the world are real. God is real. They are His attributes, powers, parts, accessories. He is their substratum, substance, whole, principal. He is one in many, an organic whole, Supreme Individual. Many are internal differences within Him. He is devoid of homogeneous difference and heterogeneous difference. But there is internal difference within Him. There is none similar to Him. There is none dissimilar to Him. He is devoid of external difference. (Cp. Rāmānuja).[32]

Though God is the Inner Controller of all created entities, He is not tainted with their flaws, since the Śrutis assert Him to be devoid of all blemishes and endowed with the highest good. He is different from the bound souls and the physical causes and effects which bind them to embodied existence. He is the creator of all worlds and their Inner Controller, and not tainted with their imperfections.[33] It is objected that as the soul which is pure becomes impure in connection with a body, so God, Who is pure, is tainted with the blemishes of the embodied souls and physical things, of which He is the Inner Controller. This objection is not sound, since the Śruti unambiguously asserts that God is the Inner Controller of the earth, etc., which are His body, and is immortal. So He is flawless and pure. But the bound soul's real, spiritual, pure nature is concealed by God's volition. His pure, auspicious, holy nature is never obscured by the imperfections of the created beings. Although God and a soul reside in the same body, they exist as different from each other ; God exists as a neutral spectator while the soul exists as the experiencer of joys and sorrows—fruits of its actions. So God is not tainted with the blemishes of the body. He exists in celestial, human, and animal bodies as the formless Supreme Self, since He is the creator of names and forms. As formless, He is not tainted with the blemishes of the forms created by Him.[34] The Śruti says, 'Brahman is partless, inactive, and tranquil' ; 'He is sinless' ; 'He is omniscient and all-knowing' ; 'He is the ruler of prakṛti and the souls, the ruler of sattva, rajas and tamas' ; 'His powers are various and supreme'. He is called Mahādeva because He discards all forms, and glories in supreme self-knowledge, yoga, and sovereignty. So He is flawless and endowed with auspicious qualities.[35] Otherwise, numerous Śrutis would become meaningless. The Śruti 'Brahman is truth, knowledge, and infinite' simply asserts that He is of the nature of limitless knowledge, but that it does not deny other auspicious qualities of Him, because there is no specific statement about it, and because His being endowed with other auspicious qualities does not contradict the aforesaid Śruti. His being supremely self-manifest and of the nature of supreme knowledge does not contradict His being omniscient and all-knowing. So there is no contradiction. The Śruti asserts repeatedly that Brahman is devoid of inauspicious qualities and endowed with auspicious qualities. 'Ether is the body of Brahman ; His soul is truth, vital breath is joy, mind is delight ; He is rich in tranquillity, and immortal'. It means that He is of the nature of manifestation, that He is of the form of the ether of pure consciousness and existence, that His delight is in His self, and independent of external objects and external sense-organs, that He is flawless and omniscient, devoid of attachment, aversion, and other inauspicious qualities, possessed of supreme self-delight, favourable to virtues, hostile to sins, and endowed with supreme sovereignty. He is called 'Śiva' because He is absolutely free from beginningless impurities and endowed with absolute purity and holiness, infinite bliss and auspicious qualities. Śiva is Brahman invested with these twofold characteristics, absolutely immaculate, and the repository of the highest good. Brahman is present in all entities, but is not tainted with their changes and blemishes, as ether is present in all pots but is not affected by their limitations, and as the sun is reflected in water in different vessels but is not affected by their increase, decrease and other faults. The Śruti says, 'Brahman has two forms—corporeal and incorporeal' ; 'Brahman is not this, not this'. So both kinds of forms are denied of Him. This objection is not sound, since limitedness of forms alone is denied of Him, and since His power of assuming corporeal and incorporeal forms is not denied of Him. Physical qualities and limitedness alone are denied of Brahman, but His absolute flawlessness and infinite holiness and auspiciousness are not denied.[36]

GOD'S GRACE.—God is supremely merciful. He is free from all blemishes and endowed with all auspicious qualities. He creates the world of conscious embodied souls and unconscious subtle and gross matter for His sport. He is eternally self-fulfilled, and does not realise any end in creating the world. His creative delight is the cause of creation. He veils a soul's innate knowledge of its essential spiritual nature and community of nature with Him, and causes its bondage to embodied existence. He reveals the Vedas or eternal wisdom to the seers, and lays down injunctions and prohibitions. A bound soul freely performs prescribed actions and commits prohibited actions, and earns merits and demerits. God creates an appropriate body for it to experience the fruits of these merits and demerits. There is a beginningless series of creation and dissolution. God dissolves the world to give respite to embodied souls afflicted by the miseries of births and deaths out of His grace. He inclines them to listen to the Vedas, reflect on them, meditate on God with detachment and devotion, and acquire immediate knowledge of Him, and releases them through His supreme grace. He removes the veil of their knowledge of their innate divine nature, aud takes them to His spiritual abode, and makes them share in His supreme knowledge and power and bliss out of His grace. The Śāktas, the Śaivas, and the Vaiṣṇavas all believe in the grace of God. He is the repository of the souls' highest good. He is the destroyer of their sins and impurities. He destroys their merits and demerits, gives them absolute purity, and makes them similar to Him. His supreme grace is the principal cause of their release from bondage. Śrīkaṇṭha lays great tress on this aspect of Southern Śaivism.[37]

GOD'S BODY.—God has a spiritual body. He assumes a body at His will. His body is nonphysical and not due to merits and demerits, like a human body. So He does not experience pleasure and pain, although He has a body.[38] But human souls experience pleasures and pains with their bodies, because they are due to their merits and demerits, and because these produce their pleasures and pains. Human souls have physical bodies, but God has a nonphysical body. The Śruti says, "God is sinless, devoid of old age, death, grief, hunger, and thirst, and has true desires and true resolves". So He is free from the qualities of physical bodies. He can assume various bodies to reveal Himself to His worshippers at His will. His bodies are nonphysical, devoid of sins, old age, death, grief and the like, voluntarily assumed by Him for His sport, and for the good of His devotees, and eternal. They exist in His eternal, spiritual body, and are revealed to them for their good. Hence, although He has a body, He is not subject to bondage, like us. The Śruti asserts His being possessed of a body and devoid of sins, old age, death, grief, hunger and thirst which afflict a physical body.[39] Śrīkaṇṭha quotes the authority of scriptural testimony, because He does not depend upon reasoning unsupported by it in regard to supersensible realities. Even a fire cannot burn a powerful being. God assumes stable nonphysical bodies full of pure knowledge with the powers of mahāmāyā.[40]

THE ABODE OF ŚIVA.—Śiva abode is above Viṣṇu's abode, which is above Brahmā's abode. Brahmā's abode is above the mundane world. Brahmā is superior to all human souls. Viṣṇu is superior to Brahmā. Śiva is superior to Viṣṇu. Heaven is full of supreme empirical happiness. Celestial souls or gods reside there.[41] They are endowed with celestial bodies, with which they enjoy happiness for ages, and then are reborn on earth, or are released through the intuitive knowledge of Śiva. Their celestial bodies are perishable. Heavenly happiness is perishable. So the abode of Śiva should not be regarded as identical with heaven, since it is far above heaven. It is pure, eternal, imperishable, composed of pure consciousness, knowable through trance and super-trance, full of bliss, and devoid of pain.[42] It is full of pure, nonempirical, immutable objects of desire. It is free from attachment, aversion, greed and other passions, which are mental modes—effects of prakṛti. The abode of Śiva is supra-mundane and eternal. It is made of supramundane ether different from the physical element of ether, abounding in supreme bliss, and full of manifestation of Supreme Reality. It is devoid of increase and decrease, origin and destruction. Śiva is different from the bound souls and their bonds, which are prakṛti and its effects. So His abode is supramundane and imperishable. The bound souls are bound to the wheel of births and deaths. The bonds also undergo various modifications, and are created and dissolved. Śiva is the Lord of creation and dissolution, birth and death. So His abode is eternal and immutable. It is different from heaven which is attainable because of merits, and which is subject to increase and decrease. The abode of Śiva is attainable through the destruction of merits and demerits and realisation of the supreme bliss of Śiva and intuition of Him. It is attainable through supramoral, nonphenomenal, absolute purity. It is more luminous than millions of suns and inhabited by Śiva, Umā, and the freed souls. (Cp. Nimbārka's aprākṛta, Rāmānuja's śuddhasattva, and Jīva Gosvāmī's Vaikuṇṭha).

UMĀ—Śiva, the transcendent, omniscient Lord, accompanied by His supreme power—Umā—and qualified by Her is the material cause of the world. He is beyond the cosmic darkness.[43] The immutable Supreme Brahman—Śiva—variegated by His supreme power called Umā is the Highest Being. She is the supreme prakṛti of the nature of supreme consciousness and delight, supreme ether nonseparate from Him, manifested in the empirical world of effects created by Brahmā, which are Her different states.[44] The Pāśupatas do not worship Umā as a Consort of Śiva. She is His supreme power of pure consciousness. She is different from Him, as power is different from a powerful being, and yet She is nondifferent and nonseparate from Him, as power cannot exist separately from a powerful entity. There is duality in unity between Śiva and Umā. Without Her Śiva is static and ineffective. She is called supreme prakṛti, not physical, subordinate prakṛti, which is modified into the physical world. Yet the world is a manifestation of supreme prakṛti—God's supreme power of consciousness and delight, which is the ultimate material cause of the world. It is a state of His supreme power of consciousness and delight. Without delight there can be no activity of God, for He creates for His sport. Creative delight is the motive of creation. Brahman is neither differenceless nor powerless. Umā, His supreme power, constitutes His internal difference. Śakti is identical with Śiva, and yet different from Him. Śakti is dependent on Him as His power and attribute. Śiva is dependent on Śakti for His activites. Yet they are not two Deities. The ether of consciousness is supreme prakṛti, God's supreme power, that constitutes His body. It is the ultimate material cause of the world.[45] Natural supreme power is the nature of Śiva and His attribute, the being of His supreme existence, conciousness and bliss, His great glory manifested in all conscious souls and unconsious things, unlimited by space, time, causality and the like. His omniscience, omnipotence, being the cause of all, being the regulator of all, being worshipped by all, being the favourer of all, being the abode of all goods, and the like are not possible without His supreme power. He cannot be called the Supreme Lord, the Supreme Deity, and the Supreme Good without His supreme power. As a hair, nails, etc., are not produced from insentient body alone nor from a conscious soul alone, but from the body animated by a soul, so the world is not produced from māyā alone nor from God alone, but from God endowed with māyā. God alone is not the cause of the world, nor is māyā alone its cause, but God endowed with māyā is its material cause and efficient cause.[46] Umā is pure māyā posseded of the qualities of Śiva—supreme, pure consciousness, power and bliss. She is not impure māyā or prakṛti possessed of sattva, rajas and tamas, which is modified into the world. "Śiva united with Umā should be meditated on as transcending prakṛti. Umā is 'Om', supreme prakṛti, supreme power of Śiva."[47] Māyā is the unconscious power of God. At the time of dissolution it discards its gross forms, and persists in a subtle state as the body of God. At the time of creation it assumes gross forms, and is modified into physical things. It is impure māyā or prakṛti.[48]

HEART-ETHER.—Śrīkaṇṭha holds that God Himself is the heart-ether, since He is sinless and flawless. An individual soul tainted with sins and impurities is not the heart-ether. The greatness of the Supreme Lord is experienced in the heart-ether, as the support and unifier of the worlds. "The lotus of the heart-ether is free from grief." "God accompanied by Umā, the tranquil Master, should be meditated on in the heart-ether". "The Supreme Lord, Friend of Umā, abiding in the heart-ether should be meditated on".[49] Śrīkaṇṭha holds that God Himself is the heart-ether. Not only should God be meditated on in the heart-ether, but the heart-ether itself should be meditated on as the ether of consciousness. There is no conflict between the two modes of meditation. Supreme Brahman is intuited by an aspirant by the repeated and continuous practice of meditation on Śiva with Śakti, of the nature of Supreme Light, in the heart-ether of the nature of the ether of consciousness. He is attained by the released souls.[50] The 'Pāśupatasūtra' inculcates meditation on 'Om' in the heart-cavity, which represents Śiva. Śrīkaṇṭha emphasizes it, and identifies Śiva with the heart-ether, and regards it as of the nature of pure consciousness. He identifies it with Śiva-Śakti. 'Om' is a mantra of Śiva. Umā is 'Om' with a slight variation in its order. 'Om'= A+U+M=Śiva. U+Ma+A=Umā. So 'Om' or Śiva-Śakti should be meditated on in the heart-ether, and the heart-ether should be meditated on as the ether of pure consciousness according to Śrīkaṇṭha. He carries on the tradition of the teaching of the Upaniṣads regarding meditation on 'Om' in the heart-cavity. This kind of meditation is called daharavidyā. The heart-cavity is a vital centre of mystic consciousness according to Śaivism and Śāktaism. Śrīkaṇṭha quotes a verse, which has a cryptic reference to the union of Śiva and Śakti on the crown of the head above the twelve centres of mystic consciousness, where a soul experiences itself as spiritual 'I' as distinguished from empirical 'I' or ego, because of its being divested of sattva, rajas and tamas. So he is aware of Kuṇḍalinīyoga inculcated by Śaiva Monists and Śāktas.[51]

GOD IS THE MATERIAL CAUSE AND EFFICIENT CAUSE OF THE WORLD.—The Pāśupatas hold that God is only the efficient cause of the world, that māyā or prakṛti is its material cause, and that His powers are its instrumental cause. They argue that if He were its material cause,

He would be modified into this world, as clay is modified into a vessel. Śrīkaṇṭha refutes this doctrine on the following grounds. 1. This doctrine contradicts many Śrutis which assert God to be the material cause of the world. 2. It is not reasonable. God is bodiless, and so cannot act upon māyā, the material cause, and produce the world out of it. A potter with a body alone can act upon clay, and produce a vessel out of it. So the example of a potter is not appropriate. If God be not admitted as the efficient cause to act upon māyā, then the Pāśupatas adopt the Sāṁkhya view, since the concept of God becomes useless. Thus bodiless God cannot be the efficient cause of the world. 3. It may be objected that, though God is bodiless, He can act upon māyā, as a soul, though bodiless, rules over its body and sense-organs. This objection is not valid, since then God would experience pleasures and pains belonging to māyā, as a soul experiences pleasures and pains of its body and sense-organs. So God is not only the efficient cause of the world.[52] 4. It may be argued that God possessed of a body acts upon māyā, and produces the world out of it, as a potter possessed of a body acts upon clay and produces a vessel out of it. This argument is not valid, since in that case God would be noneternal and nonomniscient, like a potter. 5. If God rules over māyā, different from Him, the following Śrutis will be contradicted : 'I shall become many' ; 'He made Himself into the world' ; 'All are Rudra' ; 'He shines without experiencing joys and sorrows'. These texts show that God is also the material cause of the world. Though He is the efficient cause and material cause of the world, He remains unmodified and changeless, since the Śruti says, 'He is partless and inactive'. Śiva endowed with Śakti is the material cause of the world. Unconscious, impure māyā is not its material cause.[53] The Śruti says, "Brahman resolved : 'May I be many'." It shows that Brahman is the efficient cause and material cause of the world, because He resolves to be modified into it. So its material cause is nondifferent from its efficient cause. It may be objected that the transcendent Lord created the world out of māyā different from Him, which is its material cause, since the Śruti says, 'Māyā should be known to be the material cause (prakṛti)' of the world' ; 'Śiva, higher than the universe, the great sage, saw Hiraṇyagarbha being born'. Śrīkaṇṭha replies that Brahman is the efficient cause and material cause of the world, since the Śruti says : 'Śiva is higher than the universe' ; 'All are Śiva' ; 'That created Himself.' Although He is absolutely pure and flawless and full of infinite auspicious qualities, and transcendent of the world, and as such its efficient cause, He can transform Himself into the conscious embodied souls and the unconscious world. It may be objected that transformation is a change in the form of a cause, that it discards its causal form and assumes the form of an effect. Śrikaṇṭha replies that Brahman transforms Himself into the world without undergoing a change by His volition.[54] Śrīkaṇṭha believes in Avikṛtaparināmavāda like the other theistic Vedāntists, and holds that God remains unchanged and immutable while transforming Himself into the world. The Supreme Lord in His causal state, endowed with the subtle powers of conscious and unconscious entities, without concrete names and forms, was transformed into particular conscious states and concrete physical things. He separated the subtle, conscious, and unconscious powers, forming His body, from Himself, turned them into gross forms, being and objects, and entered into them.[55] So it is proper to hold that God endowed with conscious and unconscious powers is both cause and effect in His different states. (Cp. Rāmānuja).

BRAHMAN AND THE WORLD.—The world is pervaded by Brahman, and so nondifferent from Him, just as a jar is pervaded by earth and so nondifferent from it. Divine power down to earth is pervaded by God, and so nondifferent from Him. If the universe be not pervaded by God of the nature of being and consciousness, it cannot exist and be known, and becomes a false appearance. But it is real and manifested to knowledge. So it is pervaded by God, and so nondifferent from it.[56] Creation is the state of expansion of God endowed with powers, or of His powers. Dissolution is the state of His contraction or contraction of His powers.[57] (Cp. Vallabha). Creation is transition from the subtle state of God's unconscious and conscious powers to their gross state. Dissolution is transition from the gross state of God's unconscious and conscious powers to their subtle state. Before creation God exists as pure and endowed with subtle unconscious and conscious powers and supreme divine power nondifferent from Him, in which concrete names and forms are undistinguished from one another. God of the nature of pure consciousness manifests the world out of Himself through His mere volition without any external material, like a yogin. He Himself becomes the material of the world without depending on any other material. So the world, the effect, is nondifferent from Śiva—the Supreme Brahman—the chief cause.[58] Brahman with a contracted form is the cause, and He with an expanded form is the effect. He becomes Śadāśiva down to earth owing to the difference in the operation of His powers. So the world is nondifferent from Brahman—its cause. Though the world is nondifferent from its cause, Brahman, yet He is greater than, and different from, the conscious embodied souls and the unconscious world. The Śruti says, 'Śiva is greater than the world'; 'One God rules over the mutable world and the individual souls.' So Brahman called Śiva is greater than the world. Śrīkaṇṭha does not advocate absolute difference between Brahman and the world and the individual souls, because it contradicts the Śrutis which assert their nondifference from Him. Nor does he advocate their absolute nondifference from Him, because it contradicts the Śrutis which assert difference between their essential qualities. Nor does he advocate their difference and nondifference from Him, because it involves self-contradiction.[59] He advocates the doctrine of qualified monism, according to which the world and the individual souls are related to God as the body and the soul, as attributes and a substance.[60] (Cp. Rāmānuja). The world and the souls cannot exist apart from Brahman. There is a relation of inseparable existence between them. The powers of the unconscious world and the conscious souls cannot exist without Brahman; He cannot exist without His powers, as a fire cannot exist without the power of combustion. So Brahman is qualified by them, and nondifferent from them. Still He is greater than, different from, and transcendent of them. This doctrine does not contradict the texts asserting difference and the texts asserting nondifference. The aforesaid passages from the 'Śrīkaṇṭhabhāṣya' clearly show Śrīkaṇṭha being posterior to Rāmānuja and being influenced by his doctrine. Śrīpati Paṇḍita also was a qualified monist, like Rāmānuja. He admits it in his commentary on the 'Brahmasūtra', and avers that Śrīkaṇṭha also was an advocate of Viśiṣṭādvaitavāda, like Rāmānuja. Some followers of Vallabha assert that Śaivas were plagiarists of Rāmānuja's doctrine, meaning Śrīkaṇṭha and Śrīpati Paṇḍita. So Śrīkaṇṭha flourished in 1300 A.D. He refers to the doctrine of difference and identity as held by Bhāskara.[61]

It is objected that if Brahman be modified into the world, He is wholly modified into it, and no Brahman remains to be worshipped, and that therefore He cannot be modified into the world. Śrīkaṇṭha replies that the Śrutis, which alone prove the existence of supersensible realities, prove the modification of Brahman into the world by His inconceivable power. He alone, the complete reality, can be the cause and the effect.[62] He can be the cause and the effect because of His various infinite powers. As a conscious soul, though dissimilar to a physical body, comes into contact with it, as a fire, though dissimilar to water, can come into contact with it, so Brahman, though dissimilar to the world and the embodied souls, can be modified into them through His infinite power. Prakṛti is wholly transformed into the world, since it is partless and unconscious. But Brahman can be modified into the world through His various spontaneous powers, and yet not wholly modified into it because of His omnipotence. He remains changeless despite His being modified into the world. Māyā is His power ; He is endowed with the power of māyā. The world is His part, and pervaded by Him. All powers abide in Him. The Supreme Lord endowed with the supreme power of māyā variegated with various infinite powers assumes the form of the world with a part of His power, and remains transcendent of it.[63] The distinction between the possible and the impossible does not apply to Him. Brahman is eternally fulfilled, and has no purpose to fulfil in creating the world. He creates it in sport. Though He has no unfulfilled desires, He creates the world out of His delight. He is free from attachment, aversion and the like, equal to all, and neutral to all. How can He then create some souls with celestial bodies, some with human bodies, and some with animal bodies ? How can He create the embodied souls with unequal lots ? Because He does so, He is partial to the happy souls, and cruel to the unhappy souls. Śrīkaṇṭha replies that He is neither partial nor cruel, because He gives unequal lots to the different souls in accordance with their merits and demerits acquired in their past births by their free voluntary actions. The Śruti asserts that the souls of good conduct are born in high species, and that those of bad conduct are born in low species. The souls are beginningless, and their potencies of action are beginningless. Their embodied existence is due to the beginningless stream of their potencies of actions.[64] During creation their bondage is due to their contact with gross matter and bodies ; during dissolution their bondage is due to their contact with subtle matter. The omniscient Lord knows the diverse potencies of actions of the different souls, and creates the diverse bodies for them according to their diverse merits and demerits for their appropriate enjoyments and sufferings through His power. So the diversity of creation is due to the diversity of the different souls' merits and demerits. They are not independent of God. They are unconscious and guided by Him, and made to operate and produce their fruits, joys and miseries, by Him. They produce their fruits by their powers. God merely helps them produce their effects, and is not guilty of partiality or cruelty. He creates proper bodies for them in order to mature their merits and demerits, and make them bear their fruits. The souls cannot acquire the saving knowledge until their potencies of actions have fructified and been exhausted. Without the dawn of the saving knowledge, they cannot experience the highest bliss, which constitutes emancipation. God generates their knowledge of Him, reveals their highest bliss, and grants them release, when their minds are purified of all impurities. Just as the sun rises and blooms mature lotuses and not immature ones, so God releases those souls whose taints have matured and borne fruits, and not those whose taints have not yet matured and borne fruits and been worn out. Though He is the favourer of all, He releases them at different times for their good according to the law of karma. Prakṛti, atoms, merits and demerits, or time cannot create the world. God dissolves the world to give respite to the bound souls, which are fatigued by the miseries of embodied existence.[65]

INDIVIDUAL SOUL.—A soul is not produced out of Brahman, since the Śruti says, 'The soul is neither born nor does it die'; 'The Lord is eternal among the eternal souls'; 'The two unborn ones are omniscient and ignorant, the Lord and the nonlord.'[66] The soul is a knower by its nature. Knowledge is its essence. It becomes a knower of pleasures and pains in relation to manas, which is a products of prakṛti, and wrongly identifies itself with the mind-body-complex, and transmigrates from one body to another, because its innate knowledge is obscured by the power of māyā.[67] When its relation to three kinds of impurities is removed by the repeated practice of meditation on Brahman, its innate supreme knowledge is manifested, it becomes like Brahman, and is released. Thus the soul has omniscience as its essential nature, which is contracted by the power of māyā in the state of bondage, and which is manifested in the state of release, when its relation to māyā is destroyed. A bound soul is ignorant or endowed with finite knowledge, but a released soul is omniscient. So the soul is certainly a knower.[68] It experiences its innate bliss through its internal organ. It is atomic because it departs from its body, moves to higher and lower worlds, and returns to the earth again. If it were ubiquitous, it would not be capable of doing these actions. When its three kinds of impurities are destroyed, it is released, and can pervade the world with its rays of knowledge. The Śruti says, 'This soul is atomic and knowable through the illumined mind.' It experiences sensations in all parts of the body through its knowledge which can expand, though it resides in the heart, as a drop of sandal paste on one part of body cools the whole body, or as a gem illumines proximate objects by its ray of light. Its quality of knowledge is eternal. It is said to have knowledge as its attribute, because it is its essence. Knowledge is its attribute and essence. The soul is of the nature of knowledge and a knower, and not mere knowledge, as Śaṁkara holds. Knowledge exists so long as the soul exists. The soul is eternal, and so its knowledge is eternal. Its knowledge is manifested in the waking state, and not in deep sleep, as the power of procreation is dormant in childhood and manifested in youth.[69] If the soul were of the nature of mere knowledge and ubiquitous, as the Sāṁkhya holds, it would always have knowledge due to the absence of its contraction, or it would always have no knowledge if the soul by its nature were not-knowing, and it would not sometimes know and sometimes not know. If the soul were ubiquitous and if it had adventitious knowledge due to its contact with manas and the sense-organs, as the Nyāya-Vaiśeṣika holds, it would always perceive because of its contact with manas and the sense-organs at all times in that it is ubiquitous. The soul's merits and demerits also cannot regulate its perception at some time and nonperception at another time, since they are always present in the soul. Perception and nonperception being contradictory to each other, they must be either the causes of perception or the causes of nonperception. The soul is an agent because it freely performs actions prescribed by the scripture. If prakṛti were an agent, it would be the experiencer of their fruits. If prakṛti were active, the soul woul not be able to meditate on the truth 'I am different from prakṛti', and have a trance. Prakṛti, as unconscious, is incapable of meditation and trance. The soul acts when it desires to act, and it does not act when it desires not to act, like a carpenter. But prakṛti or buddhi, its effect, is insentient and devoid of desire, and, consequently, cannot act or refrain from acting at its will. But the soul's agency is subject to the will of God. The Śruti says, 'Brahman resides in a soul, and controls it from within.' The soul acts or abstains from an action at its will according as its merits and demerits mature and ripen for bearing fruits. God impels it to perform an action or abstain from it by giving it permission considering the cause of its volition to act or not to act. His impulsion is known from His favour or punishment shown to it as expressed in the fulfilment or nonfulfilment of its actions, or from the observance of scriptural injunctions or the commission of prohibited actions. Although the soul is impelled by God to do an action or not to do it, it becomes responsible for its actions because it freely performs its actions. Its volitions depend upon its merits and demerits partly, though the soul is free, but they are the result of its past free volitions. So it cannot escape from accountability for its free actions. Hence God is not partial. The soul is eternal, a knower, enjoyer, doer, and dependent on God for its free volitions and actions. It does not know its merits and demerits, and so cannot consciously act in accordance with them. God knows its merits and demerits, and makes it act in conformity with them, and experience the fruits of its actions.[70]

The soul is a part of God, a part of His form.[71] He does not become a soul by being limited by an adjunct, e.g., an internal organ, as ether limited by a jar becomes jar-ether. The Śruti 'This self is Brahman' means that the soul is nondifferent from Him because of its being pervaded by Him, even as a piece of wood is called a fire, since it is pervaded by a fire. Just as a piece of wood is not identical with a fire, so a soul is not identical with Brahman. Hence a soul is a part of Brahman, and acquires His nature.[72] It acqures some of His qualities by meditation, but can never become identical with Him even in the state of release. The Advaita doctrine of Brahman becoming a soul by being limited by an adjunct contradicts many Śrutis. A soul is a part of Brahman because the Śruti says : 'All creatures are a quarter of Brahman'. A soul is a part of Brahman endowed with souls as His body, as a ray of light of a luminous gem is its part.[73] It is different from Him, Who is qualified by it as an attribute. Attributes are parts of a qualified substance, and different from it. So the souls are the attributes of God qualified by them, and different from Him.[74] Though they are equally parts of God, some of them are pure, and others are impure, because of their connection with their bodies. They are different in different bodies and atomic, and so their cognitions and feelings do not intermix with one another in the state of bondage. But when their false conceit of 'I' and 'mine' in their bodies is destroyed by their special knowledge of Brahman in the state of release, they acquire their essential nature as the supreme 'I', pervade the world with their supreme, eternal, and essential knowledge. Thus their knowledge and delight in release are different from their cognitions and feelings in bondage.[75] The reasonings of the Advaita Vedāntists for Brahman being limited by true adjuncts, like the body and the like, or by false adjuncts, like nescience, and becoming jīvas, are fallacious. He never becomes individual souls. If Brahman be limited by real limiting adjuncts or by false nescience, they belong to Brahman Himself, and there is no restriction even by merits and demerits. If the souls are one and the same as Brahman, they cannot have different experiences. Their merits and demerits belong to Brahman, Who is limited by them, and cannot be restricted to the different souls, and produce their different experiences. If the limiting adjuncts are said to be connected with different regions of Brahman, then also there can be no differences among the souls' experiences, because all the regions are connected with the limiting adjuncts moving about. Hence Brahman being limited by real limiting adjuncts or false adjuncts cannot restrict particular experiences to the different souls. So it is reasonable to hold that a soul is a part of Brahman, and of the nature of His attribute. So Śrīkaṇṭha's doctrine is different from those of Śaṁkara and Bhāskara.[76]

BONDAGE AND LIBERATION.—God is the cause of a soul's bondage and emancipation. Its real attributes such as true desires, true resolves, etc., are concealed by the volition of God because of the beginningless flow of impurities in the form of merits and demerits.[77] At the time of creation its bondage is due to its connection with gross matter in the form of a body. During dissolution its bondage is due to its connection with subtle matter in which there is no distinction of names and forms. Its bondage and emancipation are due to God's will.[78] He reveals its essential nature and real attributes when its mind is purified of all taints in the form of merits and demerits which are worn out after maturing and bearing their fruits. He gives it the saving knowledge of Him and its essential nature, and makes it experience its supreme knowledge, delight and powers after maturing and exhausting its merits and demerits. It cannot achieve its release independently of Him.

A soul's bondage consists in suffering unlimited misery, being overcome by the wheel of births and deaths, and being associated with various bodies conducive to the experience of joys and sorrows appropriate to various merits and demerits due to the impressions of beginningless nescience.[79] Its supreme end is emancipation which consists in the experience of supreme knowledge and bliss resembling those of God on the destruction of its bonds due to His supreme grace, which is evoked by its particular knowledge and devotion consequent on its hearing, reflection and meditation. He is supremely merciful, and the favourer of all, and His grace is evoked by an aspirant's particular knowledge and devotion. So He is the grantor of emancipation.

KARMAYOGA.—Prohibited actions or sins and prudential actions for the fulfilment of desires for happiness here and hereafter should be discarded. The daily obligatory duties, the occasional duties, and the specific duties relating to one's caste and stage of life should be performed without desire for their fruits, because they purify the mind. Sense-restraint, mind-control, endurance of pleasure and pain, withdrawal of the sense-organs from their objects, dispassion for enjoyment here and hereafter, and desire for release should be practised. (Cp. Śaṁkara). Śiva's grace is evoked by these virtues of an aspirant, and He arouses devotion in him. He inspired with devotion should meditate on God, because meditation is the principal means to the supreme knowledge of Him. Śrīkantha inculcates, like a Theist, works, devotion and knowledge as the ways to emancipation, but regards knowledge as the principal means to release, and works and devotion as auxiliary to knowledge. The performance of one's specific duties without desire for fruits purifies the mind, and prepares it for the dawn of the saving knowledge. Sense-control and the like virtues are indispensable for purification of the mind. Craving for release from bondage is a prerequisite for the achievement of it. Desire for release should be attended with devotion to God. Devotion is granted by the merciful Lord through His supreme grace. His grace is evoked by an aspirant's moral purity and aspiration. Release ultimately depends upon His volition and grace, and cannot be achieved by the unaided and independent spiritual discipline of an aspirant. A Śaiva, a Śākta, and a Vaiṣṇava, who are Theists, equally believe in the grace of God and devotion to Him. But Śrīkaṇṭha gives superiority to knowledge and meditation over devotion and regards desireless works as subsidiary to knowledge because they purify the mind.

The Śruti says, 'An aspirant should be calm, self-controlled, virtuous, patient, collected, and intuit the self in the self'; 'Know Him through faith, devotion, and meditation'. Calmness consists in the conquest of attachment, aversion, and other passions. Withdrawal of the sense-organs from prohibited actions constitutes self-control. Abstention consists in nonperformance of prudential works and noncommission of prohibited works. Patience consists in endurance of opposites, e.g., heat and cold. Collectedness consists in turning the mind towards God, and in turning it away from all distractions. Faith consists in strong desire for learning the Upaniṣads teaching superior knowledge, and dealing with the Supreme Self, and in aversion to all other treatises which do not teach the means to salvation. Devotion consists in serving Śiva with the internal organ, the organs of knowledge, and the organs of action to the exclusion of the other Deities. Desire for salvation consists in yearning for the direct knowledge of God, or for the experience of the supreme bliss. It depends upon renunciation of all desires for happiness here and in heaven, or dispassion, discrimination between the eternal and the noneternal, calmness, self-control, patience, abstention, and collectedness. The persons belonging to all stages of life should cultivate these supreme virtues.[80]

The performance of the specific duties relating to one's caste and stage of life without desire for their fruits purifies the mind, and facilitates the dawn of superior knowledge. The Śruti says, 'The Supreme Self is sought after through penance, celibacy, faith, and knowledge.' Even those who do not belong to any stage of life acquire superior knowledge by muttering God's names or mantras or prayers. The persons in all stages of life can certainly acquire the knowledge of Brahman.[81] Renunciation is renunciation of the fruits of actions. Asceticism is the conquest of the sense-organs.

JÑĀNAYOGA.—The Śruti says, 'The knower of Brahman achieves the highest good'; 'On knowing Śiva one attains supreme peace'. So knowledge alone is the means to the attainment of the highest good. But it is objected that the Śruti says, 'Whatever action one does with knowledge'. So knowledge is said to be subsidiary to action. It purifies the agent who does an enjoined action. Knowledge and action coexist in the same person. Knowledge is subsidiary to action, because even one who has attained the knowledge of Brahman is enjoined to perform prescribed actions throughout life. The Śruti says, 'One should desire to live for a hundred years, doing works in this world certainly'. To this objection Śrīkaṇṭha replies that Bādarāyaṇa is right in holding that knowledge is not subsidiary to works, because knowledge alone directly leads to the attainment of the highest good. Works are subsidiary to knowledge, because desireless, prescribed works are aids to knowledge. Desires for their fruits should be renounced. So knowledge is superior to works. There is no conflict between desireless works and knowledge. 'One should perform works throughout life'. 'One should envelop the world with God.' These texts show that knowledge is not subsidiary to works. A knower of Brahman performing works always is not touched by them because of the superiority of knowledge. So knowledge alone is the principal means to the attainment of salvation. 'When Brahman is intuited, all works are destroyed'. This text shows that works are not superior to knowledge. Hence knowledge alone is the principal means to release, and prescribed works without desire for their fruits are subsidiary to knowledge, and should be continually performed.[82]

MEDITATION.—Meditation on God should be practised repeatedly, because it generates the direct knowledge of Brahman, as paddy is threshed repeatedly until it is husked. An individual soul acquires absolute purity by knowing Brahman directly. Though Śiva is greater than an individual soul, yet an aspirant should meditate on Him as 'I am Śiva'. The Supreme Brahman favours those worshippers who meditate on Him as identical with their souls, although He is greater than, and different from, Him. Salvation is the attainment of flawless Śiva full of unsurpassed supreme bliss. The attainment of divinity is not possible without the destruction of bondage, or of connection with the body. Bondage cannot be destroyed without meditation on Him. So a worshipper becomes Śiva Himself or like Him, when his bestiality is destroyed by continuous meditation on Brahman as 'I am Śiva'. Śivahood consists in being the abode of the highest good free from all blemishes. Supreme Brahman is of such a nature. A worshipper attains His nature by continuous meditation on Him as identical with his self. None but Śiva, Supreme Brahman, should be meditated on by a worshipper desirous of salvation. False conceit of 'I' in the body can be destroyed, and one's nature as 'Supreme 'I' can be achieved, by meditation on Śiva alone as identical with one's self, Who is of the nature of supreme intrinsic bliss, self-manifest, and omniscient. A worshipper should meditate on Brahman as identical with his self to attain his salvation. Otherwise, his wheel of births and deaths will never cease. Here Śrīkaṇṭha appears to betray his inclination towards monism, like a Śaiva of the Pratyabhijñā school. So some call his doctrine Śivādvaitavāda.[83] But his doctrine is Viśiṣṭādvaitavāda like that of Rāmānuja as shown elsewhere. 'A soul becomes Śiva Himself.' The text means that it becomes like Śiva, because a part can never become the whole, and because an attribute can never become a substance. Meditation on Brahman brings about assimilation of His qualities. As meditation advances, His qualities are more and more assimilated. Continuous meditation leads to assimilation of the divine nature. Brahman is greater than a symbol. So a symbol should not be meditated on as Brahman. But Brahman Himself should be meditated on in a symbol. A minister is respected as a king, but a king is not respected as a minister. So symbols should be worshipped as pervaded by Brahman, the most excellent Being.[84] They should not be worshipped as Brahman. Supreme Brahman alone as the most excellent of all beings is worthy of being revered and worshipped by all.[85] Brahman should be meditated on in the heart-lotus by a worshipper, while he is sitting, as this posture is favourable to meditation, in a pure and solitary place. Meditation is preceded by concentration. Concentration of mind requires the withdrawal of the sense-organs from their objects, and of the mind from distracting thoughts. Meditation is facilitated by concentration, because it is of the nature of contemplation or uninterrupted thought or remembrance of Brahman undisturbed by the intervention of dissimilar thoughts. Concentration is facilitated by the sitting posture. Continuous meditation depends upon a fixed posture with an unmoving body. One should meditate on God in a pure, solitary place while sitting on a seat, neither very high nor very low, restraining the sense-organs and manas, with a focused mind, and stopping all movements of the body. Meditation on Him purifies the mind of all impurities. There is no restriction as to the time, direction, and the like, in regard to meditation, since concentration is its chief means, and since it does not depend upon direction and the like. The mind is concentrated, when there are no causes of attachment, aversion, and other evil passions. Purity and tranquillity of mind are conducive to concentration. So there is no fixed rule as to the place, time, direction and the like in worshipping God in the form of meditation, whose chief means is concentration. Meditation should be practised every day until death. There should be no discontinuity in meditation on God, because continuous meditation brings on the realization of the divine nature. Brahman reveals Himself to those worshippers who meditate on Him as identical with their selves without discontinuity. Uninterrupted and continuous meditation on Brahman leads to the revealation of His nature.[86] The sins acquired in the past births are destroyed, and sins do not accrue to the soul of a worshipper in future, who has acquired the direct knowledge of God, since sins are opposed to it. The past merits also of the knowing soul are destroyed, and merits do not accrue to it, since they also are opposed to the knowledge of Brahman. Both merits and demerits are destroyed by the direct knowledge of Brahman, since He is devoid of merits and demerits, and absolutely pure and holy. Sivahood is absolute purity. Divinity is supramental, supramoral, supramundane, supreme purity. It cannot be attained without the complete destruction of merits and demerits, which are mental impurities. The merits and demerits, which have not yet begun to bear fruits, are destroyed by the direct knowledge of Brahman. But those which have begun to bear fruits produce all their fruits in this birth, or in a succeeding birth, but cannot destroy the knowledge of Brahman already acquired by a soul, just as acquired knowledge is not destroyed by intervening sleep. Hence the souls, that have acquired the direct knowledge of God, are certainly released from bondage, and do not undergo a succession of births, because there is no cause of it. The barrier of birth and death, like sleep, cannot destroy their knowledge of Brahman. The knowledge of Brahman is the immediate cause of salvation. Meditation is the chief means of the knowledge.[87]

The realisation of Brahman full of supreme bliss is the highest good. A person desirous of salvation should discard the worship of all other manifestations of Śiva than Himself alone, the cause of auspiciousness. Meditation on the Supreme Brahman as identical with one's self and full of supreme bliss is the principal form of worship.[88] Śiva united with Umā, His supreme power, is the Supreme Brahman. He is endowed with all excellent attributes, and the Supreme Self of all, immanent in, and manifested in, them. Meditation on Him is the cause of salvation. He is never divested of His essential attributes.[89] Brahman endowed with attributes is attained by the released soul. It becomes similar to Śiva. It attains similarity in nature to Him. Śiva devoid of all reprehensible qualities and invested with all auspicious qualities is attained by it. 'It enjoys all objects of desire with Him—the all-knower'. One's self freed from its bondage and empirical qualities and invested with sinlessness and the like should be meditated on. Repetition of the mystic syllable 'Om' while meditating on Śiva united with Umā or 'Om' in the heart-ether brings on union with Him. When He is meditated on in the heart-ether, He should be meditated on as the Universal Soul pervading all the worlds. A worshipper should adopt one kind of meditation on Brahman until he realises the Supreme Brahman, and not adopt various kinds of meditation, for their results are one and the same. Only he should meditate on Brahman as identical with his self. The adoption of various kinds of meditation entails unnecessary exertion, delay, and distraction. Śrīkaṇṭha himself prefers meditation on the Supreme Brahman or Śiva united with Umā in the heart-ether with repetition of the mystic syllable 'Om'.[90]

THE STATE OF THE FREED SOUL.—The Śruti says, 'The disembodied soul, rising from this body, attains the form of supreme light, is accomplished in its essential nature.' The form of supreme light is not the soul's adventitious nature, but its essential nature. It is always existent in the soul, but is manifested by the removal of its impurities. Brahman is of the nature of supreme light or pure universal consciousness. The soul also is of the nature of supreme light or pure omniscience. Its essential nature is like that of Brahman. When it attains Brahman, its impurities are removed, and it becomes like Him, and attains the qualities similar to His. Its divine qualities were existent already in it but were concealed by the impurities. If supreme light were its adventitious nature, the Śruti would not have stated it to be its 'own form' or essential nature.[91] When the soul's impurities are destroyed by the grace of God, its essential nature, like His attributes, is manifested, and not produced, like the fruits of its merits and demerits. Its bondage to embodied existence is due to its connection with beginningless impurities. So the released soul's essential nature—a mass of pure consciousness and bliss, full of omniscience and the like—is manifested. Unlimited knowledge, bliss, and power are manifested in release. They constitute its essential nature. The freed disembodied soul becomes sinless and free from old age, death, grief, hunger, and thirst, and acquires true desires and true resolves. So its attributes resemble those of God. The Śruti says, 'The freed soul becomes stainless and acquires supreme resemblance to Brahman'; 'The freed soul becomes similar to Śiva.' Because the freed soul acquires resemblance to God, it experiences its essential nature as nondistinct from God's nature.[92] The Śruti, 'The knower of Brahman becomes Brahman Himself' means that the soul that experiences Brahman becomes like Him. Because the freed soul becomes similar to Him, it feels its nature to be nondistinct from Him. It cannot create, maintain, and destroy the world, but it becomes equal to Him in respect of enjoyment alone. Brahman is not limited by time, space, etc., independent, eternally fulfilled, omniscient, omnipotent, possessed of unhidden powers, the cause of all, the Self of all, the supreme Lord, the favourer of all, and capable of releasing all bound souls. The freed soul united with Him enjoys all objects of desire with its natural internal organ through a particular kind of knowledge. Brahman and the freed soul can assume bodies and sense-organs at their will.[93] The nature of the freed soul is similar to that of God; it is endowed with auspicious qualities, e. g., sinlessness, self-manifestness, and the like. It is of the nature of pure knowledge.[94] It attains all objects of desire through mere volition. The fulfilment of its desires does not depend upon external objects. Because it has acquired the nature of God and become sinless and pure, it becomes independent of another ruler. It is no longer under the sway of merits and demerits, because they have been destroyed. God is no longer its controller, because it has transcended the scriptural injunctions and prohibitions—His commands—which are binding on the bound souls for their release, because it is divested of its bondage, and because it has attained divinity owing to the destruction of its impurities. God has omniscience and other qualities. So the freed soul, like God, becomes omniscient, self-fufilled, independent, omnipotent, possessed of unhidden powers, eternal knowledge, and infinite powers. Bondage is due to contraction of infinite knowledge due to the impurities. When they are removed, the soul becomes omniscient. When nescience, the cause of bondage, is exterminated, its false conceit of 'I' in the body is destroyed, it becomes free from grief due to old age and death, and independent because of the absence of the sway of merits and demerits, delights in the self because of its enjoyment of its supreme intrinsic bliss, becomes self-fulfilled, and free from hunger and thirst, and acquires true desires and true resolves because of its being possessed of unhidden powers. So it becomes independent and similar to God. Sometimes it assumes bodies at its will. Sometimes it does not do so, and enjoys objects with its manas created by God, as a bound soul enjoys the pleasures created by God during dream with its mind. The freed soul perceives and enjoys the world as a form and manifestation of God.[95]

Śrīkaṇṭha does not believe in embodied release. He holds that salvation is attained after the death of this body, when there are no other stronger merits and demerits that obstruct the direct knowledge of Brahman. When there are stronger merits and demerits, salvation is attained in another birth, when they are worn out after bearing their fruits.[96]

CREATION.—A potter makes an earthen vessel out of clay. He is the efficient cause, and clay is the material cause, of the vessel. But God creates the world out of His nature, and is both its efficient cause and material cause. Brahman withdraws the gross world of embodied souls and matter into Himself at the time of dissolution. It is transition from the gross state of matter to its subtle state. There is no distinction of day and night, the sun and the moon, names and forms, subtle and gross, gods, men, and beasts, and the like at the time. It is a state of utter darkness, when God alone remains, self-manifest, Witness of all. The embodied souls and their bonds, matter and material things, exist in their subtle state ; they are not completely destroyed. Only their gross states of names and forms no longer exist.[97] Then the bound souls remain with their subtle bodies but have no knowledge of particular objects or effects because of the destruction of their powers, bodies, and sense-organs, and because of the destruction of names and forms or concrete physical objects. Then Śiva also has no knowledge of His self-manifest form as before, because the organ of His self-knowledge is obscured by the taint of darkness. Dissolution is a great state of deep sleep called darkness wherein all distinctions of particular effects are destroyed.[98]

God, again, creates or manifests all conscious souls and unconscious matter endowed with concrete names and forms by manifesting His first creative power through His mere volition at the time of creation without depending upon any external material cause. The

Supreme Self of the nature of pure consciousness creates all objects by His mere volition without any material cause, like a yogin. (Cp. Somānanda and Utpaladeva). It is wrong to hold that God is the efficient cause, and that māyā is the material cause, of the world. The subtle form of God, called Māyāpuruṣa, incapable of existing apart from Him, is the material cause of the world. God resorts to His power called māyā to become the diverse world of names and forms, of the nature of creative will, and creates the world, considering the bound souls' merits and demerits, and creates the world through His power of action, and enters into it. He becomes the manifest world composed of sattva, rajas and tamas through His powers of knowledge, volition, and action. He is the creator and destroyer of the world.[99] Śrīkaṇṭha, like Rāmānuja, holds that the conscious embodied souls, the unconscious subtle nature, and the gross physical world cannot exist apart from God. There is inseparable relation (apṛthaksiddhi) between them.

SATKĀRYAVADA.—Śrīkaṇṭha, like other Theists, advocates the doctrine of Satkāryavāda that an effect pre-exists in its cause. An earthen vessel pre-exists in clay, its material cause, and is nondifferent from it. The effect is a real modification of its cause. It is designated by another name and has a different function. An earthen vessel is called a 'pot', and can carry water while a lump of clary is not called a pot, and does not carry water. It cannot exist apart from clay, and so clay is its essential nature. An earthen vessel is a diff-rent state of earth, and performs a different function, but it is not a different substance from earth. It is not an unreal appearance of clay, but another state of clay, although it is not different from clay. Because an effect pre-exists in its cause, the former is nondifferent from the latter.[100] An earthen vessel pre-existed in earth before its production. So it is perceived as of the nature of earth. It pre-existed in earth in a subtle form as nonseparte from earth, and becomes gross when it is produced. So an effect is a manifest state of its cause, which is its unmanifest state. It is not nonexistent in its cause. "The world existed as unmanifest before creation, and become manifest in names and forms after creation." A cause (e.g., a seed) is a contracted form of an effect (e.g., a sprout). An effect is an expanded form of a cause. An effect is the unfoldment of a cause while a cause is the involution of an effect.[101] Both cause and effect are real.

THE REALITY OF THE WORLD.—Brahman is the creator, maintainer, and dissolver of the world. So the world is real. He obscures the knowledge of the individual souls, and binds them to embodied existence. He removes the veil of their knowledge, makes them intuit Him, attain resemblance to Him, and achieve salvation. He is the binder and liberator of the individual souls. So they are real. He is different from the bound individual souls and the world which binds them at His will. So Brahman, individual souls and the world are real. His five acts are real and His essential characteristics.[102] The Śruti says, 'Brahman resolved : I shall become many' ; 'All this world belongs to the Supreme Self ; it is real' ; 'The world is created as diverse and multiform. All are Śiva.' So the world is real.[103]

[1] ŚKBS., i, 1, 2 ; ii, 1, 15-20 & 22 ; ii, 3, 19 & 33.
[2] Ibid, ii, 1, 22. [3] Ibid, i, 2, 1. BPD., 3.
[4] IPK., i, 38. [5] ŚKBS., ii, 1, 22.
[6] Ibid, i, 1, 2 ; i, 4, 2-7. [7] Ibid, ii, 1, 22.
[8] Ibid, i, 3, 45.
[9] Ibid, i, 1, 2 ; RBS., iii, 2, 29 ; ii, 3, 45 ; ii, 1, 15.
[10] ŚKBS., ii, 1, 22. [11] Ibid, ii, 2, 35-38.
[12] Ibid, i, 3, 13, 15-16 ; PSS., V, 2-25 ; PTLV., 2, 25 & 31. HIP., Vol. II, 1952, pp. 742-44.
[13] 'Śivādvaita of Śrīkaṇṭha', p. 27 ; DHIP., Vol. V, pp. 10-11 & 72 ; 'Doctrine of Recognition' ; VSMS., p. 127 ; PO., pp. 203-04 ; 'Doctrine of Śrikaṇṭha', Calcutta, 1962, pp. 5-7; PSS , Introduction, p. 5.
[14] ŚKBS., i, 1, 1. [15] Ibid, i, 1, 2. [16] Ibid, p. 12.
[17] Ibid, i, 1, 5. [18] Ibid, p. 14. [19] Ibid, i, 1, 3, p. 16.
[20] Ibid, p. 18. [21] Ibid, iii, 2, 31.
[22] Ibid, iv, 1, 5. [23] Ibid, iii, 2, 17 ; Ibid, iii, 2, 15.
[24] Ibid, i, 1, 13, 15, 17, 21 & 35 ; i, 3, 24 & 35; i, 4, 27.
[25] Ibid, i, 1, 2 ; p. 11.
[26] Ibid, i, 1, 2, 9-11 ; ii, 2 ; 4, 19 & 24 ; iii, 2, 31.
[27] Ibid, iii, 2, 21, [28] Ibid, iii, 2, 29.
[29] Ibid, i, 2, 19. [30] Ibid, iii, 2, 30.
[31] Ibid, i, 2, 22. [32] Ibid, iii, 2, 37 & 40.
[33] Ibid, iii, 2, 11. [34] Ibid, iii, 2, 14. Ibid, iii, 2, 12-13.
[35] Ibid, iii, 2, 15. [36] Ibid, iii, 2, 16-21.
[37] Ibid, iii, 2, 4-5, 11, 15 & 17 ; i, 1, 2&4 ; iv, 3, 1 ; i, 2, 1 ; ii, 1, 35 ; iv, 4, 22.
[38] Ibid, i, 2, 8. [39] Ibid, i, 1, 21.
[40] Ibid, iv, 4, 22. [41] Ibid. [42] Ibid.
[43] Ibid, i, 4, 28. [44] Ibid, iv, 3, 14 ; i,1, 16.
[45] Ibid, i, 2, 7. [46] Ibid, i, 4, 27.
[47] Ibid, iv, 4, 22.
[48] 'Doctrine of Śrīkaṇṭha', pp. 44-52.
[49] ŚKBS., i, 3, 13, 15-16 & 22. [50] Ibid, i, 3, 22.
[51] Ibid, iv, 4, 19. Cp. ŚM., pp. 29-33.
[52] ŚKBS., ii, 3, 35-36. [53] Ibid, ii, 2, 38.
[54] Ibid, i, 4, 27. Ibid, i, 4, 24-26. [55] Ibid, i, 4, 27.
[56] Ibid, ii, 1, 17. [57] Ibid, ii, 1, 18. [58] Ibid.
[59] Ibid, ii, 1, 20. Ibid, ii, 1, 19 & 22.
[60] Ibid, ii, 1, 22.
[61] Ibid, ii, 1, 19-20 & 22. [62] Ibid, ii, 1, 27.
[63] Ibid, ii, 1, 31. Ibid, ii, 1, 28-30.
[64] Ibid, ii, 1, 34-35. [65] Ibid, ii, 1, 35-36.
[66] Kath. Up., ii, 18 ; V, 13 ; Śvet. Up., i, 9; ŚKBS., ii, 3, 18.
[67] Ibid, ii, 3, 19. [68] Ibid.
[69] Ibid, ii, 3, 21-31. [70] Ibid, ii, 3, 41. Ibid, ii, 3, 32-40.
[71] Ibid, ii, 3, 42. [72] Ibid.
[73] Ibid, ii, 3, 45. [74] Ibid, ii, 3, 46.
[75] Ibid, ii, 3, 47. [76] Ibid, ii, 3, 52.
[77] Ibid, iii, 2, 4. [78] Ibid, iii, 2, 5 ; ii, 1, 35.
[79] Ibid, i, 1 ; 1, p. 7.
[80] Ibid, iii, 4, 23. Ibid, i, 1, 4, pp. 24-25.
[81] Ibid, iii, 4, 37-38 & 47. [82] Ibid, iii, 4, 1, 4-9, 13-17.
[83] Ibid, iv, 1, 1 & 3. Sūrya Nārāyaṇa Śāstrī, 'Śivādvaitavāda'.
[84] Ibid, iv, 1, 5. [85] Ibid, iv, 1, 4-5.
[86] Ibid, iv, 1, 12. [87] Ibid, iv, 1, 7-12, 15&19 ; iii, 1, 13.
[88] Ibid, ii, 3, 14-16. [89] Ibid, ii, 3, 39.
[90] Ibid, iii, 3, 40&43. [91] Ibid, iv, 4, 1.
[92] Ibid, iv, 4, 4 ; Muṇḍ. Up., iii, i, 3.
[93] ŚKBS., iv, 4, 18 & 21. [94] Ibid, iv, 4, 7.
[95] Ibid, iv, 4, 8-9, 12-14. [96] Ibid, iv, 4, 50.
[97] Ibid, 1, 2, 9. [98] Ibid. [99] Ibid.
[100] Ibid, ii, 1, 15-17. [101] Ibid, ii, 1, 15-20.
[102] Ibid, i, 1, 2 ; iii, 2, 4 ; iv, 4, 22.
[103] Ibid, ii, 1, 15. E.T., of ŚKBS., (Roma Choudhury, Calcutta, 1959.

CHAPTER VI

THE PHILOSOPHY OF VĪRA ŚAIVISM

VĪRA ŚAIVISM.—Vīra Śaivas are Liṅgāyatas or Liṅgāyets, because they carry the phallic symbols of Śiva, the cosmic creative principle, on their heads or in their bodies. This fact is mentioned in 'Sūtasaṁhitā' included in 'Skandapurāṇa' (600 A.D.). This practice influenced the Liṅgāyatas. Basava (1200 A.D.) was born in a Brāhmaṇa family in Kannada in South India. He strengthened and propagated Vīra Śaivism. He did not write any work. But many sayings in Kannada are ascribed to him. He refers to Śiva as 'ṣaṭsthala', a mysterious religious tenet, which he larned from his master. The tenets of Vīra Śaivism are found in 'Basavapurāṇa' (1300 A.D.), 'Channabasavapurāṇa' (1600 A.D.) in Kannada, 'Śrīkarabhāṣya' of Śrīpati Paṇḍita (1400 A.D.), 'Siddhāntaśikhāmaṇi' of Śivayogi Śivācārya, 'Śivādvaita-mañjarī' of Śivaprabhānanda and 'Anubhavasūtra' of Mogge Māyideva (1440 A.D.). Some believe that Basava was the founder of Vīra Śaivism. R. G. Bhandarkar thinks that it had its origin one or two centuries earlier.[1]

According to Vīra Śaivism Śiva is the Supreme Brahman called sthala, because the world is founded (stha) in Him, and dissolved (la) in Him. He is divided into liṅgasthala and aṅgasthala, or Rudra-Śiva, the worshipped, and the self, the worshipper, owing to His innate power. Śiva's power is divided into kalā and bhakti. Kalā abides in Śiva, and bhakti abides in the self. Bhakti means meditation, which generates union between the self and Śiva. Liṅgasthala is divided into bhāvaliṅga, prāṇaliṅga and iṣṭaliṅga. The first is the manifestation of Śiva's being ; the second, of His consciousness ; and the third, of His bliss. Each of these three principles is subdivided into two parts, and becomes mahāliṅga, prasādaliṅga, caraliṅga, śivaliṅga, guruliṅga, and ācāraliṅga. These six liṅgas are called ṣaṭsthala. The power of Śiva energised by these liṅgas becomes power of consciousness, transcendent power, original power, power of volition, power of knowledge, and power of action. Bhāvaliṅga is the infinite Divine which intuits its essence and becoming in its essence. Prāṇaliṅga is the universal Divine which comprehends the possibilities to be actualised in the finite. Iṣṭaliṅga is the individual Divine which actualises the possibilities. Mahāliṅga is, the great, prasāda-liṅga, the gracious, caraliṅga, the dynamic, śivaliṅga, the auspicious, guruliṅga, the preceptive, and ācāraliṅga, the practical.[2]

Vīra Śaivism accepts the doctrine of thirty six principles. The power of being predominates in Śivatattva. It is prasādaliṅga with parā śakti, the transcendent power. Śaktitattva is almost simultaneously manifested with Śivatattava because consciousness presupposes being. This principle is caraliṅga with originative power. The power of volition predominates in Sadāśivatattva. This principle is śivalinga with power of volition. The power of knowledge predominates in Īśvaratattva with its objective content. This principle is guruliṅga with the power of knowledge. The power of action predominates in Sadvidyātattva. This principle is ācāraliṅga with the power of action. These are the first group of five pure principles. Māyā, kāla, niyati, rāga, vidyā, kalā, and puruṣa are the second group of seven pure and impure principles. Māyā is voluntary self-limitation, and generates the five coverings. Śiva assumes them, and appears to be a finite soul. The last group of impure principles are twenty four principles—prakṛti, mahat, ahaṁkāra, five organs of knowledge, five organs of actions, five tanmātras, and five elements. The universe exists in an unmanifest state in Parama Śiva, and is manifested at the time of creation.[3]

ŚRĪPATI PAṆḌITA'S PHILOSOPHY OF VIŚIṢṬĀDVAITA.—He was a systematic exponent of Vīra Śaiva philosophy and religion. He flourished in the fourteenth century, and wrote a commentary on the 'Brahma Sūtra' entitled 'Śrīkarabhāṣya'. He avers that his commentary is based on the 'Agastyasūtravṛtti' which is not available. He adores Remuṇa, a self-realised Vīra Śaiva, and Rāma of the Dvāpara yuga, profusely quotes from the Upaniṣads, the Smṛtis, and the Śaiva Purāṇas, and claims to base his interpretation on the Vedas and the Śaiva Āgamas. He criticises the Pāśupata doctrine that God is only the efficient cause of the world. He mentions Śiva and Śakti and their nondifference from each other, like Somānanda of the Pratyabhijñā school of Śaivism, and refers to ṣaṭsthala. He criticises the Śaiva Siddhānta view of Śrīkaṇṭha, who follows Rāmānuja in his commentary on the 'Brahma Śūtra'. His main target of attack is Śaṁkara's monism. He criticises his doctrines of the indeterminate and attributeless Brahman, of Īśvara as the phenomenal appearance of Brahman limited by māyā, of an individual self as a false appearance of the Brahman limited by an internal organ produced by its avidyā, individual nescience, and of the world as a false appearance subsisting in Brahman due to māyā, cosmic nescience, and of its creation by Īśvara as apparent only. His criticisms closely follow those of Rāmānuja and Madhva. He criticises Rāmānuja's doctrine of God and the world related to each other as the soul and the body. He criticises Madhva's doctrine of difference between God and the soul. He advocates a type of dualistic monism which he calls Viśiṣṭādvaita, and recognises both difference and nondifference or identity between God and the soul. His doctrine is similar to Bhāskara's doctrine of difference and identity, though not identical with it. Śrīpati regards works, knowledge and devotion as the means to liberation. He accepts Bhāskara's doctrine of the combination of knowledge and works, though he does not mention his name. His dualistic monism is quite different from the Pratyabhijñā school of Śaivism which is a type of monism. His system is much influenced by Rāmānuja's qualified monism and Madhva's dualism. Though he flourished in the fourteenth century, Mādhava does not mention the Vīra Śaiva system in his 'Sarvadarśanasaṁgraha'. Mādhava also flourished in the same century.[4]

THE NATURE OF BRAHMAN.—Brahman, the substratum of all, the cause of all, is knowable from the testimony of the Vedas alone. He cannot be conclusively proved by the other means of valid knowledge. The Upaniṣads say, 'The existent alone existed before, one, secondless Brahman'. 'All Vedas speak of Brahman'. All scriptural sentences propound the doctrine of difference and nondifference and speak of Brahman as the material cause and efficient cause of the world, and reject the doctrine of prakṛti as the material cause of the world. The Mīmāṁsaka avers that the Vedas lay down injunctions about our duties, that there would be two classes of Vedic sentences if some of them prove the existence and nature of Brahman, that some texts speak of prakṛti as the material cause of the world, that Brahman being proved by inference to be the efficient cause of the world, He is not knowable from scriptural testimony alone, and that Brahman being an accomplished reality and foundation of all good, He cannot be proved by the Vedas. Śrīpati rejects the Mīmāṁsaka view. He avers that the Vedas speak of the nature of Brahman and lay down the method of meditation on Him, that they determine His nature by describing His essential characteristics, inessential characteristics, and other distinguishing characteristics.[5] Brahman is inferred by the Nyāya to be only the efficient cause of the world. But He is its material cause also and permeates it. The world is an expression of Brahman's energy. Energy exists in a substance. There is no energy without a substance as its possessor. They are nondifferent from each other. The world is of the nature of Brahman and created by Him. Brahman is its substratum and material cause and efficient cause. Hence insentient prakṛti cannot be its material or efficient cause. The world and individual souls are both different and nondifferent from Brahman. Individual souls are unborn and eternal. The Vedas speak of Brahman's fivefold acts of creation, maintenance, and dissolution, of the world, and binding and liberating individual souls. The texts speaking of them are praises of Brahman.[6] Scriptural testimony is the principal source of proving the existence and nature of Brahman. Perception and inference are subordinate proofs. Perception is intuition generated by meditation on Brahman. Intuition is a convincing proof, but it depends upon the practice of meditation based on scriptural testimony. So it is not an independent proof. Inference unsupported by scriptural testimony is a weak and unreliable proof. Śrīpati does not deny that some Vedic sentences speak of our duties, but insists that the performance of duties purifies the mind and prepares it for meditation on Brahman. Hence the principal end of the Vedas is enquiry into the nature of Brahman—our Highest Good. The Mīmāṁsaka objects that the Vedas enjoin the worship of many gods, and, consequently, reject the concept of one God. Śrīpati replies that there are superior, mediocre, and inferior worshippers, that the inferior ones worship many gods because they are incapable of worshipping the one supreme Brahman, and that the superior ones worship Him as full of all gods and their Lord. The worship of Him alone leads to liberation.[7] Śrīpati agrees with Somānanda, the exponent of the Pratyabhijñā shchool of Śaivism, that God is the material cause and efficient cause of the world, that the world is an expression of His energy, that His energy cannot exist without Him, and that He is the Highest Good. But he differs from Somānanda in that for him God's energy is both different and nondifferent from Him while the latter holds God's energy to be nondifferent from Him. Somānanda is an advocate of the doctrine of nondifference or monism whereas Śrīpati is an exponent of the doctrine of difference and nondifference, like Bhāskara. Thus Vīra Śaivism substantially differs from the Pratyabhijñā school of Śaivism. Śrīpati regards the individual souls to be eternal, like the Lord, and to be different and nondifferent from Him. He regards Brahman as determinate, qualified, and invested with difference while Somānanda regards Brahman as indeterminate, unqualified, and differenceless as known by a released soul. Both Somānanda and Śrīpati believe in God as invested with diverse powers which are real and essential. But Somānanda considers the experienced world to be false, although it is an expression of His power of māyā, whereas Śrīpati emphatically asserts its reality and being of the nature of Brahman, like Rāmānuja. Somānanda sometimes speaks of the reality of the world because it is created by the divine will. But a liberated soul, for him, has no knowledge of difference but knowledge of identity or perfect 'I'-consciousness. Śrīpati denies it unequivocally and insists, like Bhāskara, that a liberated soul's knowledge of difference persists, although it is eclipsed by the knowledge of different entities being full of Brahman. Śrīpati severely criticises Śaṁkara's doctrines of falsity of the world appearance due to māyā or avidyā or false attribution, and of Brahman as indeterminate, unqualified, and differenceless, like Rāmānuja and Madhva. But he agrees with Śaṁkara that Brahman is knowable through scriptural testimony alone.

CRITICISM OF ADVAITAVĀDA: ATTRIBUTELESS BRAHMAN.—Śaṁkarites hold that Brahman is unqualified, undifferentiated, and indeterminate. Śrīpati refutes this concept on the lines of Rāmānuja and Madhva on the following grounds. 1. Is the indeterminate or differenceless Brahman existent or nonexistent? If It is nonexistent, then Śaṁkarites accept the view of the Mādhyamika that void is the ontological reality. If It is existent, then existence is affirmed of It, and It ceases to be indeterminate, since affirmation is different from It. The affirmation that 'the indeterminate Brahman exists' makes It determinate. According to Śaṁkarites the existence affirmed of Brahman would be false. If the nature of Brahman be said to be imagined, then indeterminateness ceases to characterise It. The statement 'That is Brahman where Its nature is imagined' involves self-contradiction, since the indeterminateness of Brahman cannot be imagined, or since It cannot be related to imagination. The Upaniṣads do not speak of the indeterminate Brahman. They make verbal statements which consist of different parts, and therefore cannot make any statement about the indeterminate Brahmam. Hence the indeterminate Brahman cannot be proved by scriptural testimony. 2. The difference between false objects and Brahman is either ontologically real or ontologically unreal. If it is ontologically real, then it contradicts Śaṁkarites' principal thesis that Brahman is the only ontological reality. If it is not ontologically real, then Brahman also becomes ontologically real and unreal, since no difference exists between It and false objects. Śaṁkarites may urge that there is no flaw in this position for both difference and non-difference or identity are false. If it were so, then they should admit the falsity of both an individual self and Brahman. But they admit Brahman alone to be real and an individual soul to be false. If they urge that they do so because of the superiority of the scriptural texts regarding identity, then Śrīpati rejoins that the scriptural text 'All are indeed Brahman' emphatically asserts that Brahman is determinate and immanent in diverse objects. 3. Is the indeterminate Brahman of the nature of knowledge or nescience? It cannot be nescience for that contradicts Śaṁkarttes' thesis that Brahman is differenceless knowledge. If It is knowledge, it has an object or it is objectless. If it is objectless, it ceases to be knowledge. If it has an object, the object is eternal, since eternal knowledge must have an eternal object. Hence Brahman is not indeterminate and differenceless. Further, if Brahman is eternal knowledge with an eternal object, a released soul which has acquired the right knowledge of Brahman will have knowledge of diverse objects. But Śaṁkarites hold that it has no knowledge of difference. If it has no knowledge of objects, it ceases to have any knowledge, since knowledge can never be without any object. Knowledge without an object and a self is never experienced.[8] (Cp. Rāmānuja) Knowledge is always experienced in such a form as 'I know a jar'. Śaṁkarites' concept of selfless and objectless knowledge is as fictitious as a sky-flower. 4. Is the indeterminate Brahman a substance or a nonsubstance? If It is a substance, It is the substratum of qualities, and therefore not indeterminate or differenceless. If It is devoid of qualities, like a jar at the moment of its production as the Nyāya-Vaiśeṣika holds, then Brahman acquires qualities at some time, but an indeterminate entity cannot have qualities at any time. If the qualities of Brahman are said to be imagined, then also It is not indeterminate, since It is related to imagination and since buddhi cannot imagine qualities without the material of nescience. If Brahman is not a substance, then It subsists in a substance, like a quality or an action. Further, it will contradict the Śruti 'He is founded in His greatness.' If the indeterminate Brahman subsists in a substratum, It ceases to be inditerminate. Hence It is neither a substance nor a nonsubstance. Thus Brahman conceived as existent or nonexistent, as different or nondifferent from false objects, as knowledge or nonknowledge, and as a substance or a nonsubstance, is contradicted. Hence It is not an ontological reality. Further, the scriptural text 'That thou art' does not prove the identity of an individual soul with the differenceless Brahman. The word 'that' denotes the determinate Brahman, and the word 'thou' denotes a determinate individual self.[9] In the scriptural text 'That resolved: I shall become many' the word 'that' denotes the determinate Brahman, the Lord, the cause of the world. Śaṁkarites urge that the aforesaid sentence should be interpreted in a derivative sense. The word 'that' denotes Brahman limited by cosmic nescience or the Lord; and the word 'thou' denotes Brahman limited by individual nescience or an individual self. The limiting adjuncts should be discarded. Then the substratum of God and an individual self is identical, and this identity is not contradicted by any sublating knowledge. Śrīpati asserts that this interpretation of the text is wrong and farfetched for there are scriptural texts, which declare that Brahman is the impeller of all individual souls and giver of four kinds of release to them, and which prove that Brahman and individual souls are determinate. Further, if Brahman is determinate and qualified, then the knowledge of the one can lead to the knowledge of all beings. If Brahman is indeterminate and differenceless, the knowledge of the one will not lead to the knowledge of all beings. Śaṁkarites may argue that the intuition of Brahman acquired through meditation in an appropriate manner produces the knowledge of all beings. This argument is wrong for whatever is seen is destroyed according to them. Brahman is seen through meditation, and therefore destroyed. So meditation is useless and cannot produce the knowledge of all entities. Śrīpati further asks whether a pure soul which has intuited the supreme Brahman of the nature of infinite knowledge is different or nondifferent from It. A pure soul is not different from Brahman as a ray of the sun is not different from it. Nor is a pure soul nondifferent from Brahman for the Śruti says: 'Brahman is omniscient and omnipotent and an individual soul is endowed with limited knowledge and limited power'; 'Brahman is the Lord of prakṛti and individual souls'. It may be objected that, if an individual soul is like a ray of Brahman, it cannot have an immediate experience of the latter. The objection is groundless, because God can be intuited by an individual self purified by initiation by a competent teacher through His grace. So there is no conflict between an individual soul being a ray of God and its intuition of Him, as a ray of light, a part of the sun, in the eyes can see the sun. If an individual soul cannot have an immediate experience of God, the following scriptural texts will be false : 'The knower of Brahman becomes Brahman' ; 'This subtle Ātman is to be known through the illumined mind' ; 'On knowing Śiva an individual soul achieves peace'. Hence Brahman is not indeterminate and differenceless.[10]

CRITICISM OF ĪŚVARA AS AN APPEARANCE (ŚAṀKARA).—Some Śaṁkarites hold that God (Īśvara) is a reflection of Brahman in cosmic nescience (māyā), and that an individual self is a reflection of Brahman in individual nescience (avidyā). Śrīpati offers the following criticisms of this view. 1. Brahman is formless and colourless, and māyā is ontologically unreal. So Brahman cannot be reflected in māyā. If Brahman were reflected in māyā, then the incorporeal and formless air would be reflected in water. 2. Brahman is all-pervading and exists in māyā also. So the former cannot be reflected in the latter. Only the distant sun can be reflected in water in another place. The original and its reflection cannot coexist in the same locus. 3. When a reflecting medium (e.g., water) is destroyed, a reflection (e.g., a reflection of the sun) is destroyed. So when in the state of release cosmic nescience will be destroyed, God will be destroyed. To admit this is to accept the atheistic doctrine of the Buddhist. No one would make any effort to attain release, if God were a false destructible appearance.

Some Śaṁkarites hold that Īśvara is a limitation of Brahman by cosmic nescience, which is His limiting adjunct. Śrīpati refutes this view on the following grounds. 1. When the limiting adjunct of māyā will be destroyed by the knowledge of Brahman, God will be destroyed. But the destruction of God cannot be regarded as the Highest Good. The Śruti says : 'God is the giver of release'. 2. Māyā, according to Śaṁkarites, is ontologically unreal. So Brahman cannot be limited by it. If māyā is a false appearance, then God also is a false appearance. This view is unacceptable to Śrīpati who identifies God with the supreme Lord. 3. The Śruti 'Aum or Om is Brahmā, Viṣṇu and Rudra' implies that māyā is energy of the supreme Lord. It is not ontologically unreal.[11] God is the cause of the world. His being the cause of the world is not His essential characteristic but His inessential characteristic indicative of His nature. So creation, maintenance and dissolution belong to the world, and do not constitute the essential characteristic of God. He is identical with Brahman Who is determinate and qualified.

CRITICISM OF ŚAṀKARITE CONCEPTS OF JĪVA.—Some Śaṁkarites hold that an individual soul is a reflection of Brahman in individual nescience. Others hold that it is a reflection of Brahman in an internal organ, a product of individual nescience. Others hold that a jīva is Brahman limited by individual nescience or by an internal organ. Śrīpati refutes these views. 1. The limiting adjunct cannot be gross because in that case a jīva would not be able to go to the other world after death of its body. Brahman is declared by the Śruti to reside in the heart of a person. So Brahman cannot be reflected in the internal organ of a person. An original and its reflection cannot coexist in the same locus. 2. If a jīva is a reflection, it is false and incapable of doing a successful action. If it is false, the Śruti 'Brahman exists in a jīva as its Inner Controller' is contradicted. 3. In the state of release individual nescience is destroyed, and so a jīva reflected in it is destroyed. So release or destruction of an individual self cannot be the Highest Good of a person. 4. No person would make any effort to bring about the destruction of his individual self. All would endeavour to achieve earthly happiness, and none would seek for renunciation of desires for earthly enjoyments. None would act upon Vedic injunctions and prohibitions because they are false. 5. If a jīva is a limitation of Brahman by individual nescience or by an internal organ, it will be destroyed at the time of release when its limiting adjunct will be destroyed by the knowledge of Brahman. But the destruction of an individual self cannot be pursued as the Highest Good. 6. If a jīva is a limitation of Brahman by an internal organ, which is insentient, it may as well be regarded as a limitation of Brahman by any other insentient thing, like a jar or a cloth. 7. A spurious text says : 'Brahman creates an individual self and God being reflected in māyā'. So Śaṁkarites argue that they are imaginary appearances. This text is overridden by the superior text : 'Brahman is the omniscient and omnipotent Lord, and a jīva is endowed with ignorance and impotence'. This text emphatically asserts the ontological reality of God and an individual self.[12]

CRITICISM OF THE PĀŚUPATA VIEW.—An opponent argues that God is not the material cause of the world because He is devoid of qualities. Śrīpati asks whether He is not the material cause of the world as different from it or as its Inner Controller, or as invested with forms, or as formless. The first alternative is not tenable since He is all-pervading. If an efficient cause is without any condition or external material, then a potter cannot produce a jar, and a weaver cannot produce a cloth. The second alternative also is not tenable. If God were different from the world, He would be limited like a jar, and be a content in a substratum. The third alternative also is not tenable, since Brahman being invested with forms would consist of parts and would not be conceived of as partless and incorporeal like ether, and would be limited as mentioned already. Nor is the fourth alternative tenable, since the formless and partless Brahman cannot produce the world consisting of parts. An opponent futher argues that if Brahman of the nature of truth, knowledge and bliss were the material cause of the world, it also would be of the nature of existence, knowledge and bliss. If the world were not produced, it would not be of the nature of transcience, insentience and pain, and would not be modifiable like earth and the like. Further, is the Brahman or prakṛti the efficient cause, or the material cause, of the world, or both ? Brahman is not the efficient cause of the world for the Śruti says : 'All are indeed Brahman'. An efficient cause (e.g., a potter) requires external material (e.g., clay) to produce an effect (e.g., a jar). Nor is God the efficient cause of the world for the Śruti says : 'Brahman is one and without a second'. Nor is He both the efficient cause and material cause of the world, since they are of contradictory nature like light and darkness. Prakṛti cannot be the efficient cause of the world, since it is unconscious. Nor can it be both the material cause and efficient cause of the world, since they are of contradictory nature. If Brahman be the material cause of the world as milk is the material cause of curd, then He cannot be of the nature of bliss. If He is the material cause of the world as gold is the material cause of gold ornaments, then He becomes modifiable. If the world be assumed to be nonexistent before creation and then to emerge as a false appearance like an illusory appearance of a serpent in a rope, then a hare's horn also would emerge as an illusory appearance. Hence the empirical world cannot be produced by Brahman or Prakṛti.

Śrīpati holds that Brahman, the substratum of all, of the nature of being, knowledge and bliss, dwelling in six esoteric centres of the human body, called supreme Śiva, is the cause of the creation, maintenance and dissolution of the world. Though He is partless, He is the efficient cause of the world without any external material. He has the natural power of consciousness, which is the substratum of the world. He has the supreme power of bliss. He produces the world without any external material. Though He is partless, yet He can produce the world even as the partless air can shake a tree, or as a partless individual self can produce dream-cognitions. The corporeal sun can create incorporeal time. The omnipotent Brahman, Who can do what is inconceivable, can certainly produce the world. There is no flaw in the doctrine that Brahman assumes the supramundane auspicious form of Śiva, produces incorporeal and corporeal elements and their modifications for the benefit of His devotees out of His grace.[13] All things of the world are created, maintained and dissolved in Him, as the waves are created, maintained, and dissolved in the ocean, and are of the nature of Him. God's power is the material cause of the world which is a part of Him. He is the cause of all worlds which are His parts. The Śruti 'From Whom all creatures are born' shows that Brahman is the efficient cause of the world. The Śruti 'In Whom the creatures are dissolved' shows that Brahman is the material cause of the world. He is both the efficient cause and material cause of the world.[14] He is not only the efficient cause nor only the material cause. The material cause and the efficient cause are different from each other in their nature. Yet Brahman can be both the efficient cause and material cause of the world because it is a part of Him. The entire Brahman is not modified into the world. He was qualityless before creation. Then He resolved to create the world. He becames intent to create it by unfolding His power. Śrīpati rejects the view of the Pāśupata that God is only the efficient cause of the world.

THE WORLD IS REAL.—A Śaṁkarite holds that the world is false attribution and, consequently, a false appearance. Attribution is false ascription of a quality of an entity to another entity. It is either false ascription of not-self to self or false ascription of self to not-self. It is not the first for the illusion of a serpent in a rope is produced by the residual impression of a real serpent. A Śaṁkarite does not admit the reality of the world-appearance distinct from Brahman, and the reality of any place outside Him. Nor is attribution the second for in that case Brahman would be false. If attribution were false ascription of self to not-self, then the Self would be false and become insentient like the world. If attribution be due to a beginningless series of prior attributions, then it involves infinite regress. What is perceived in an entity cannot be attributed to it. Hence the perceived world cannot be attributed to the Self or Brahman. The character of a serpent cannot be attributed to a serpent, and so the illusion of a serpent cannot be accounted for. Further, Brahman and the world are without an origin. So Brahman cannot be attributed to the world. Besides, it would contradict the Śruti 'From Whom the creatures are born', which asserts that Brahman is the cause of the world and prior to it. If the world be false because it is seen or known, then Brahman also is false because He is known. If He is said to be unknown in order to avoid this difficulty, then persons cannot have any experience of Him. Moreover, it will contradict the Śaṁkarite view that an individual self is proved by 'I'-consciousness of which it is an object, and for which it is an object of immediate experience.[15] If Brahman is not known, He cannot be an object of immediate experience. But a Śaṁkarite admits Brahman to be directly experienced. A Śaṁkarite argues that Brahman is not an object of 'I'-consciousness, but that an individual self is an object of 'I'-consciousness. This argument is not valid because he does not admit any difference between them from the ontological point of view. If Brahman be not admitted to be knowable from the pragmatic standpoint, the false world-appearance would be without any substratum.[16] Hence the world is not a false appearance due to attribution.

Śrīpati further asks whether falsity of the world-appearance is its nonexistence or indefinability or liability to contradiction. It is not nonexistence since then the Vedas would not be authoritative being nonexistent. Nor is falsity indefinabilily, since it would lead to complete silence about the world. If the world is indefinable, nothing can be affirmed or denied of it. Nor is falsity liability to contradiction. Liability to contradiction is either being a counterentity of negation at all times or being contradicted by valid knowledge. It is not the first, since the world-appearance fulfils our practical purposes and gives scope for our actions. It is beginningless, and its existence in the past cannot be denied. Its existence at present cannot be denied, for it produces our pleasures and sufferings at present. Its existence in future cannot be denied, since it exists in God in a subtle state even during dissolution. Nor is falsity liability to contradiction by valid knowledge, since the wise who have acquired the knowledge of Brahman continue to experience the world. They are subject to hunger and thirst and appease them by eating and drinking. So their knowledge of difference is not destroyed. Hence the world-appearance is not false either in the sense that it is nonexistent or in the sense that it is indefinable or in the sense that it is sublated by the knowledge of Brahman. The doctrine of the world being a false appearance due to nescience is not found in the Upaniṣads. Brahman being the material cause of the world, it cannot be a false appearance since it is in the nature of Him. The world is not different from Him. It is the unfoldment of His power.[17] Even if God is said to be like a magician, and if the world is said to be His magical creation, He is admitted to be its cause. The Upaniṣads never speak of the world as produced by māyā or avidyā. The statements in the Purāṇas regarding the falsity of the world due to māyā or avidyā are certainly delusive. Deluded persons speak of the world as unreal, unfounded, and Godless. But in truth, the whole world is full of God, and this truth is realised when right knowledge dawns upon the mind. This is the true view in accord with the Upaniṣadas and should be entertained, and any other view about the falsity and Godlessness of the world should be rejected.[18]

The Śaṁkarites argue that the world appearance is false for it is seen or known. Śrīpati asks whether Brahman is known or unknown. If He is known, He must be false, like the world appearance. If He is not known, we cannot speak of Him and act upon the belief in His existence. He can be proved by knowledge alone. If Brahman is not known, nescience cannot be destroyed. Nescience of Brahman can be destroyed by the knowledge of Brahman alone. So what is seen or known is not reality as distinguished from the world appearance which has a pragmatic reality. If contradictedness consists in being contradicted by the knowledge of Brahman alone, and not by the knowledge of any other entity, then a first knowledge contradicted by a second knowledge cannot be said to be contradicted, and all other cases of contradiction would cease to be so. If what is not contradicted in three or four successive moments is considered to have a pragmatic reality, then a common illusion (e.g., illusion of a circle when a fire-brand is whirled around) would have pragmatic reality for it continues for a long time. The Śaṁkarites hold that the manifold world appearance has only pragmatic reality but no ontological reality.[19] Śrīpati asks about the nature of pragmatic reality. If it is knowability through pragmatic action, then Brahman also has pragmatic reality for He is known through pragmatic action in the form of instruction in the scriptural texts regarding His nature. Otherwise, a teacher cannot teach a pupil the nature of Brahman and a pupil cannot learn it from a teacher. The Śaṁkarites may argue that Brahman is not an object of pragmatic action, since It is indeterminate and differenceless. Śrīpati refutes the argument by observing that Brahman is not indeterminate and differenceless and that the Upaniṣads do not assert that Brahman is differenceless. Nor is pragmatic reality knowability through contradicted practical action, for it would apply to Brahman also. All practical actions are contradicted by the knowledge of Brahman because they are included in the world appearance. If what is contradicted be considered to be a pragmatic reality, then a common illusion (e.g., illusion of silver in a shell) would have pragmatic reality. But the Śaṁkarites regard it as an illusory reality.

Śrīpati avers that the falsity of the world is not taught by the Upaniṣads. What is the falsity of the world? It is either being contradicted by the knowledge of Brahman or being nonexistent in the past, the present, and the future. Śrīpati asserts that the world is not contradicted by the knowledge of Brahman. The Śruti "All this is indeed Brahman" asserts that all things of the world are of the nature of Brahman. The cognitions of different objects are not contradicted by the knowledge of Brahman, but they are eclipsed by the knowledge of them as of the nature of Brahman. The integral knowledge of all objects as of the nature of Brahman stops the knowledge of them as diverse and possessed of distinctive qualities. But the diverse objects are not sublated by the knowledge of Brahman. The world cannot be negated by the knowledge of Brahman because it is of the nature of Brahman. Hence the falsity of the world is irrational.[20] If the world is false, the knowledge of Brahman cannot lead to the knowledge of all. Janaka and others, who attained embodied release, lived like common people. Their knowledge of Brahman did not negate the world. To state that the world is a false appearance due to cosmic nescience (māyā) or individual nescience (avidyā) is to delude others. The 'Bhagavad Gītā' says, "The atheists say that the world is false and without any foundation". In fact, the world is true and founded in the Lord. Nor is the falsity of the world being negated in the past, the present, and the future. The Upaniṣads assert that the world is beginningless. It may be objected that the world was nonexistent before its creation since the Śruti says: "This was nonexistent before. Then it became existent". To this objection Śrīpati replies that 'nonexistence' of the world before means its existence in a subtle state because gross things did not exist at the time. "From nonexistence existence was born". Here existence means existence of gross things. If nonexistence meant absolute nonexistence, then a sky-flower would be the cause of the world. "Existence alone existed before". Here 'existence' means differenceless existence because the word 'before' occurs in the text. There is the Śruti "One Brahman alone without a second". Here the word 'one' shows that Brahman was the cause of the world. The words 'without a second' show that Brahman was the material cause and efficient cause of the world. Hence the world is not false in the sense that it was nonexistent before its creation.[21] Further, Śrīpati argues that the world is not false, like dream-cognitions, because it fulfils our practical needs, and because it is the field of our actions.[22] Bādarāyaṇa says, "The world is not nonexistent because it is perceived", "It is not false, like dreams, because of dissimilarity".[23] Thus Bādarāyaṇa asserts the reality of the world. Śrīpati argues that dreams are true during dream, and that they are not absolutely false, because they are created by God, because they are partly due to the revival of the residual impressions of the waking perceptions of real external objects, and because they sometimes foreshadow future good and evil, which turn out to be true. Hence the world cannot be false like dreams. If it were false, there would be the loss of earned merits and demerits and the acquisition of unearned merits and demerits.[24]

CRITICISM OF ŚAṀKARITES' CONCEPT OF ĪŚVARA.—Śaṁkara holds that God (Īśvara), a reflection of the indeterminate and attributeless Brahman in māyā, which is different from its substratum—Brahman, is the creator of the world. Śrīpati offers the following criticisms of this doctrine. 1. Śaṁkara admits that Brahman, the substratum of māyā, is indeterminate. Hence Brahman cannot create the world. Such indeterminate Brahman is unreal, like a hare's horn, because It cannot be known by any means of valid knowledge. 2. Brahman cannot be the substratum of Īśvara, since He is a phenomenal appearance according to Śaṁkara. 3. Brahman cannot be the substratum of souls and the world, because they also are false appearances according to him. 4. He denies the reality of two conscious entities, and so admits that Brahman becomes ignorant, like a soul, and is not omniscient. So the Śrutis declaring the omniscience of Brahman become meaningless. 5. Īśvara, being a phenomenal appearance, according to him, cannot reveal the Vedas, which are accepted by him as the highest authority. Thus he contradicts himself. If the Vedas are valid, Īśvara is an ontological reality.[25] 6. Perception is indeterminate and determinate. Determinate perception apprehends an object with its genus, quality, action, name and the like. Indeterminate perception apprehends an object endued with some quality, and cannot apprehend an object devoid of all qualities. (Cp. Rāmānuja). An entirely unqualified object can never be perceived. Inference is based on perception, and so cannot apprehend an unqualified object. Testimony is knowledge derived from the statement of a reliable person through words. Words can express determinate objects alone qualified by some qualities. Hence the so-called indeterminate and unqualified Brahman is unknowable, and therefore unreal.[26] Brahman is determinate and qualified and identical with Īśvara, Who is not a phenomenal appearance, and is the creator of the world. The world is real, a part of God's power. God as transcendent is the efficient cause, and as immanent, is the material cause, of the world. Creation is real, and not apparent, as Śaṁkara holds. Śrīpati regards the world as a real expression of a part of God's power. Power is nondifferent from the powerful beings, for they form an inseparable unity. (Cp. Somānanda). Divine power is nondifferent from God. The world, being a part of divine power, is nondifferent from God. Nondifference of an earthen pot from earth—its cause—must be admitted.[27] So Śrīpati advocates satkāryavāda, like Rāmānuja, and rejects Śaṁkara's vivartavāda, which regards an effect as a false appearance of its cause which is real, like the illusion of a serpent in a rope, and which regards the world as a false appearance of the indeterminate and unqualified Brahman. He rejects Madhva's doctrine of difference of the world from God, and Rāmānuja's doctrine of God and the world as related to each other as a soul and its body. He holds that the world is nondifferent from God, being the expression of His power, but that God is not identical with the world because He is transcendent of it. He is both transcendent of, and immanent in, it.

REFUTATION OF CĀRVĀKA MATERIALISM AND MĪMĀṀSAKA ATHEISM.—The Cārvāka puts forward the following arguments for materialism. There is no Brahman since He is not perceived through the sense-organs. Future life does not exist for no departed person returns from the next world and informs anybody of its existence. All material things are produced by the conglomeration of the four material elements—earth, water, fire and air. Life springs out of nonliving matter as beetles spring from cowdung. All unconscious things and conscious beings are produced from the material elements by their aggregation and destroyed by their disjunction and disintegration. A living being is not different from other material things. Life and consciousness spring from the aggregation of the material elements as red colour springs from the combination of turmeric, lime and honey. A soul is nothing but a body attended with consciousness which is a product of matter. The Mīmāṁsaka admits the reality of individual souls in addition to material elements, of future life and transmigration, and of Apūrva which regulates the fruition of merits and demerits and the distribution of rewards and punishments in accordance with them. He does not believe in the existence of God as the regulator of happiness and misery among the souls according to their merits and demerits. Hence enquiry into Brahman is not possible.

Śrīpati refutes these views. Enquiry into Brahman should not be entered upon because its end is absent or doubtful. If it is doubtful, either Brahman is doubtful or an individual soul is doubtful. Brahman is not doubtful for the Śruti says : "Brahman is truth, knowledge, and infinite". Thus Brahman, the supreme Lord, is undoubted. Nor is an individual soul doubtful, because it is known by 'I'-consciousness, and because the Śruti says : "The Lord and an individual soul are eternal ; the former is omniscient and omnipotent while the latter is ignorant and impotent". So an individual soul is known by 'I'-consciousness and from scriptural testimony. Brahman is known by perception, inference and scriptural testimony.[28] His existence is known by perception in an indirect manner. Those who are rich in wealth, assistants, talents, etc., are found to be unsuccessful in achieving their ends, and those who are lacking in them are found to achieve inconceivable ends. So God's favour is an indispensable condition of success. Gotama gives this argument for the existence of God. It is a popular argument.[29] Chariots, mansions, towers, ramparts and the like are built by intelligent persons. Similarly, ether and other insentient elements and sentient beings are produced by the supreme Lord. This is thought by the wise. It is unreasonable to hold that all insentient things and sentient beings are produced by the fortuitous combination of the four material elements—earth, water, fire and air.[30] Beasts, birds and other animals are not found to be produced by the four material elements. The distinctive qualities of beasts, men and the like are not found in the same kind of body. Life is hidden in cowdung, etc., so that beetles spring from them. Life cannot spring from nonliving matter. Unintelligent Apūrva cannot give the fruits of actions done by persons according to their merits and demerits. God, the Lord of the Law of Karma, can award them enjoyments and sufferings in accordance with their merits and demerits. So the atheistic doctrine of the Mīmāṁsaka is not reasonable. Unintelligent prakṛti also cannot produce the world. So the atheistic Sāṁkhya doctrine is refuted. Insentient atoms of earth, water, fire and air cannot produce the world. So the atheistic Vaiśeṣika doctrine also is refuted.[31]

GOD AND INDIVIDUAL SELF.—The Śruti about two beautiful birds expresses difference between a self and God. The Śruti about the identity of a self with God expresses identity between them. So both difference and identity between them should be admitted. The souls are parts of God, and nothing but His parts.[32] Some exponents of the Vedas hold that in the state of release a soul achieving similarity to Him is dependent on Him. Śrīpati does not accept this view. According to him, in the state of beondage a soul is an accessory of God Who is the principal, but in the state of release its dependnce on God, which is the cause of its fear, is inadmissible. The Śruti speaks of a released soul as identical with God. There is no contradiction between difference and identity between a soul and God. The Śruti admits both difference and identity between them, which Śrīpati regards as the highest authority.[33] He asserts that his view of difference and identity between a soul and God is supported by scripture, reason, and experience. The doctrines of nondualism or monism and qualified monism cannot reconcile the relevant scriptural texts adequately. They consider some texts to be principal and others to be subsidiary and unimportant. The Naiyāyikas, Madhva and others advocate the doctrine of difference, and cannot reconcile all scriptural texts. So their views are unreasonable and indefensible.

The Śruti says, "All creatures are one quarter of God". So individual souls are parts of God. The 'Bhagavad Gītā' says, "Souls are eternal parts of God". An individual soul is a part of God, as a ray of light is a part of a luminous thing,[34] as a white cow is a part of the genus of cow. A part is a qualification of a qualified object; a qualification is a part of a qualified object, which is a whole. Though the former is a part of the latter, there is difference in their nature. A ray of light is different from a luminous thing. Similarly, an individual soul is different from God. Yet it is nondifferent from God, because it cannot exist separately from Him. A soul as a qualification always exists as dependent upon God Who is the principal. The Śrutis expressing identity of a soul with God show that He is its Inner Controller. The Smṛti also says, "God is not affected by the joys and griefs of an individual soul, which are the fruits of its actions". Parāśara asserts that an individual soul is a part of God, as a ray of light is a part of a luminous thing, or as a power is a part of a powerful entity. God is superior to an individual soul in that He is devoid of merits and demerits and neither bound nor released, while it acquires merits and demerits, and is bound and released. So God is not affected by its happiness and misery.[35]

Although all individual souls are equally parts of God, yet some of them are pure and others are impure in connection with their bodies, as although all kinds of fire are equally parts of fire, yet fire in cremation grounds is impure and sacrificial fire in a Śrotriya's house is pure. Thus Brāhmaṇas, Kṣatriyas, Vaiśyas, and Śūdras possess different degrees of purity and impurity. Although individual souls are equally parts of God, yet they are atomic, different, and endowed with different bodies, and, consequently, do not share the experiences of one another. The souls released in embodied life, which have acquired the knowledge of God, being atomic and different from the other souls due to their being limited by their bodies till they attain disembodied release, do not share the experiences of the other souls. The bound souls' experiences of joys and sorrows are not intermixed with one another because of their atomic dimensions, difference, and being endowed with different bodies, although they experience the fruits of their actions due to the ripening of their merits and demerits which have begun to bear fruits. The released souls are pure because of their knowledge of God while the bound souls are impure and bound to embodied life and affected by pleasures and pains because of their ignorance of God.[36]

There are three kinds of individual souls. The bound souls are called 'paśu', have false conceit of 'I' in all actions, are not initiated by a competent teacher into a mantra of Śiva, and are devoid of devotion to Him. Pure suuls are endowed with the qualities of sense-control, mind-control, endurance, detachment, desire for release, devotion, and servitude to God, and initiated into a mantra of Śiva. The released souls are those whose mental modes are merged in Śiva. They are released in embodied life if they are entirely free of love and hate, and independent of the bodily experience of pleasure and pain. They transcend bodily life despite their being shackled with bodies. If they are affected by the frailties of their bodies, they have not attained disembodied release. Those souls have attained disembodied release, which are disembodied in their embodied life.[37] They have realised their disembodied souls.

There are four kinds of liberation, viz., residence in the abode of God, proximity to Him, community in nature with Him, and merging in Him. They are attained through sense-control, mind-control, endurance, abstention from sentient pleasure, detachment, desire for release, faith, devotion, servitude to God, meditation, and trance.[38]

An individual soul is a part of God, since the Śruti speaks of it as both different from, and identical with, God. It speaks of God as creator, controller, omniscient, independent, pure, endowed with auspicious qualities, and the Lord, and of an individual soul as created, controlled, ignorant, dependent, impure, endowed with inauspicious qualities, and a servant.[39] It also speaks of identity between them as shown above, and of God's pervading an individual soul. So its being a part of God must be admitted. Its being created, controlled, manifested, and maintained by Him, being contained in Him, being accessory to Him, worshipping Him, acquiring wealth, happiness, virtue, and release, and experiencing the fruits of its actions through His grace, shows its difference from, and dependence upon, Him. Otherwise, it cannot be established, since it cannot be perceived. Nor can a soul's identity with God of the nature of infinite, pure consciousness be proved by any other pramāṇa. The Śruti speaks of God's desire to become many, creating the elements and the world composed of them, entering into it as individual souls, and making it full of diverse objects. Thus souls perceive manifold objects, and experience happiness and misery because of the immanence of God in them as their Inner Controller, Who binds them to embodied life and releases them from bondage. So creation, bondage, and release are not false. A soul is not Brahman limited by a limiting adjunct, viz., nescience, since the Śruti speaks of its being controlled by God. Hence a soul should be admitted to be a part of God in order to reconcile difference and identity between them asserted by the Śruti.[40] The Smṛti also says, "God is real; the world is real; and individual souls are real by nature". Hence those who believe in the Vedas should admit that an individual soul is a part of God, being both different from, and identical with, Him in order to reconcile the 'difference'-texts with the 'identity'-texts, which are equally authoritative.

This is Śrīpati Paṇḍita's view. Some hold that the Śrutis expressing difference between an individual self and God either express conditional difference or attributed difference. Śrīpati urges that they cannot express conditional difference because if a soul be naturally nondifferent from God, it cannot worship God. Granting that a soul, though naturally identical with God, can worship Him, does God know the soul or not? If He does not know it, He ceases to be omniscient and becomes insentient. If He knows it, He knows its misery as His own misery since He is identical with it, and becomes tainted with its sins of omission and commission. Nor do the Śrutis expressing difference express attributed difference between a soul and God due to nescience. Does nescience exist in a soul or in God? A soul being really identical with God, cannot have nescience, because in that case it would cease to be of the nature of knowledge. Nor can God have nescience, because He is of the nature of self-luminous knowledge. He cannot be the Witness of nescience, and create the world through nescience. It cannot be argued that His manifestation is veiled by nescience, since the so-called veiling also is destroyed by His manifestation. Further, self-manifestation is His nature, and, if His manifestation is veiled by nescience, His nature is destroyed,—which is impossible. So His manifestation cannot be veiled by nescience. Therefore there is a natural difference between a soul and God.[41] A conscious soul attains identity with God through His grace, even as copper becomes gold through the influence of an elixir.[42] There are some Śrutis which express identity of a soul with God. There are some Śrutis which express natural difference between them also. Bādarāyaṇa advocates the doctrine of difference and nondifference or identity between them.[43] It is obvious in the 'Brahmasūtra'. It may be objected by Rāmānuja that difference and nondifference are contradictory to each other, that natural difference cannot be terminated, and that therefore qualified monism which reconciles difference with nondifference is reasonable. The souls are qualities of God Who is endowed with qualities. Śrīkaṇṭha has propounded qualified monism in his commentary on the 'Brahmasūtra'. To this objection Śrīpati rejoins that difference and nondifference are not contradictory to each other, and that the Śruti, the Smṛtis, and the Purāṇas advocate the doctrine of difference and nondifference. All experience that there is difference in waking state and dream, but that there is nondifference in deep sleep. Similarly, there is difference in creation, and there is nondifference in dissolution. A soul becomes God or Śiva through His grace through devotion. If God were the soul and if a soul were His body, as Rāmānuja holds, then God would be limited like a soul.[44] But He is unlimited and infinite, and a part of His power is manifested in the world. He is devoid of a body and sense-organs. So Rāmānuja's view is wrong. A soul discards its finitude, merits and demerits, and becomes identical with God, as rivers discard their names and forms and merge in an ocean. But a soul in bondage is not absolutely identical with God. Wood, stone, and iron are different from one another, although they are insentient and homogeneous in kind. Similarly, a soul and God are naturally different from each other, although they are conscious and homogeneous in kind. There are many Śrutis which assert natural difference between a soul and God. "The self and God both are unborn and eternal ; God is omniscient and omnipotent while the self has little knowledge and power". "God possesses the power of māyā, and creates the world with it ; a soul is overcome by māyā". "The one Lord enters into mutable prakṛti and immutable souls and controls them". "He is the Lord of prakṛti and souls". "He is eternal among the eternal souls, one among many, and fulfils the desires of many souls". If the souls were absolutely nondifferent from God, He would be tainted with their flaws. If they were absolutely different from Him, their difference would never be destroyed.[45] Hence a soul is both different and nondifferent from God.

The individual souls are real, many, eternal, and atomic. They are not illusory. They are of the nature of knowledge and knowers. They are active agents and experiencers of happiness and misery. They are not coextensive with one another and do not share the experiences of one another. The doctrines of unreality, and oneness of a soul, and of its identity with God are wrong.[46] If souls be Brahman limited by nescience, they are really one despite the difference of their limited adjuncts, and therefore they experience the joys and miseries of one another.[47] The souls cannot be reflections of Brahman in nescience or in internal organs produced by it, because the original and its reflection cannot exist in the same locus (e.g., the sun and its reflection in water), but a soul and Brahman are said to reside in the heart. The individual souls' merits and demerits also, which are causes of their limiting adjuncts, depend upon Brahman, and, consequently, cannot prevent the intermixture of their experiences. If their merits and demerits or limiting adjuncts can limit the one, indivisible Brahman, then they destroy Its nature. Further, the souls being ubiquitous according to Advaitavāda, they are present in all bodies, and, consequently, share the experiences of one another. Their merits and demerits cannot prevent the intermixture of their experiences. Hence the souls' atomic dimension, multiplicity, and natural difference in different bodies must be admitted.[48] If the Advaitist doctrines were true, there would be no distinction between some souls being possessed of love and others being possessed of hate. Desires are causes of love and hate. Merits and demerits are causes of desires. They cannot prevent the intermixture of souls' experiences of one another. It may be objected that Brahman makes some souls do right actions and others do wrong actions according to the Śruti, that therefore their experiences of happiness and misery due to their merits and demerits are really God's experiences, and that God urges the souls to do right actions in accordance with their merits and demerits, which are beginningless. To these objections Śrīpati replies, that the souls are not insentient like jars and the like, although they are not omniscient like God, that they are free agents of their voluntary actions, although they are dependent on and controlled by God, like the servants of a king dependent on him, and that therefore they must be the experiencers of the joys and sorrows, which are the fruits of their free actions in accordance with their merits and demerits. The Śruti unequivocally asserts that the souls have limited knowledge, limited freedom of volition and action, and are bound, and endowed with bodies from beginningless time. It undoubtedly advocates the souls' limited freedom of agency. They are conscious and free agents, although they are controlled by God. Their free will is limited by the divine will.[49] The denial of their limited freedom contradicts the Śruti, and is repugnant to reason and experience. There is no contradiction among the Śrutis which assert souls' free agency and those which assert God's controlling their actions, because souls are limited, being parts of God, and because parts are nondifferent from a whole.[50] Though they are nondifferent from God, He does not experience their joys and sorrows because He is devoid of merits and demerits, and because He does not perform their actions. The souls perform their actions with their limited freedom, and must therefore experience their fruits in accordance with their merits and demerits, although God controls their actions and impels them to do right or wrong actions according to their merits and demerits. They cannot escape from the fruits of their merits and demerits acquired by them by their free actions in the past. God does not constrain them to do their actions, but impels them to do certain actions in order to wear off their merits and demerits, which are innate predispositions of their past free actions. They can undo their merits and demerits by their free actions. God controls their actions as their Inner Controller. Śrīpati is not a pantheist, and does not advocate God's swamping human freedom in His absolute freedom.[51]

A liberated soul becomes supremely luminous Brahman, and shines in its own essential nature. Śripati holds that a soul that worships an image of Śiva attains gradual liberation, and that a soul that worships the formless Śiva attains immediate release, and becomes identical with Him. A soul attaining final release becomes omniscient, omnipotent, infinite being, knowledge and bliss, and identical with eternally pure and free Śiva. A bound soul's knowledge and action are limited by its merits and demerits, and so it is different from God in the state of bondage. But a liberated soul's knowledge and action are not limited by its merits and demerits, because they are destroyed at the time, and so it becomes identical with Him. Its natural nescience is destroyed by its knowledge of God, and so it attains identity with Him.[52] If a soul were essentially identical with Him, its attainment of essential identity could not be its highest good, since it is already attained. A soul that meditates on Śivatattva as formless, ubiquitous, supreme light of consciousness in the heart-ether destroys its subtle body, and attains identity with Him in embodied life. Śrīpati believes in embodied release. Although a soul and God are possessed of contradictory attributes from beginningless time, a soul can destroy its three kinds of impurities, become pure, and become identical with God. Difference and identity of a soul and God are clearly asserted by the Śruti. A bound soul is different from God, but a liberated soul is identical with Him in nature, and remains as both different from, and identical with, Him, like a river merged in an ocean.[53] Just as a river does not entirely lose its identity in an ocean, though it loses its distinctive characters, so a released soul does not entirely lose its identity in God, though it loses its limitations, and exists as inseparable from Him. The Śruti says, "A released soul becomes stainless and pure, and attains supreme equality with God"; "A released soul enjoys all objects of desire with God". Hence such difference as exists in the state of bondage between a soul and God cannot be admitted in the state of release.[54] In disembodied release a soul's existing inseparably and indistinguishably from God is supported by the Śruti. Śrīpati advocates identity of a soul with God in disembodied release but maintains that it does not lose its integrity in Him. Kauṇḍinya also, a Pāśupata Śaiva, regards sāyujya as intimate union of a soul with God without losing its identity in Him.[55] Śrīpati asserts that Vīra Śaivism advocates the doctrine of difference and identity between a soul and God, which is in conformity with the Vedas and the Upaniṣads, and which is the view of Bādarāyaṇa.[56]

AN INDIVIDUAL SOUL.—An individual soul is atomic, for the Śrutis declare it to depart from its body, move to other spheres of existence, and return.[57] Movement is movement to heaven to enjoy happiness and to hell to suffer pain. Return is return to the earth after exhausting enjoyment of happiness in heaven, and of misery in hell. So a soul is atomic. If it were ubiquitous, it would not be capable of movement, and be dissociated from its body. God is ubiquitous, but a self is atomic. The Śruti says, "This Self is great and unborn". Śrīpati avers that it refers to the Supreme Self or God. The Śruti says unambiguously, "This self is atomic and knowable through the illumined manas"; "The self is minute like the hundredth part of a hair". Śrīpati avers that these texts declare an individual soul to be atomic.[58] The Śruti says, "As rivers flow into an ocean and lose their names and forms in it, so a self, that has acquired the saving knowledge, is divested of its names and forms and attains to the Supreme Self." A self is the attainer, and God is to be attained. If the former were ubiquitous, it could never attain to the latter. One ubiquitous entity cannot attain to another ubiquitous entity. Further, if a self were ubiquitous, God would not be its Inner Controller. The atomic magnitude of a self is not due to the limiting adjunct of the internal organ, since it is unborn and eternal, and since it does not owe its existence to an internal organ which is produced after creation. Hence its atomic magnitude is natural to it. Śrīpati regards a bound soul as atomic and a released soul as ubiquitous.[59]

The self is of the nature of a knower.[60] It is not unconscious, and so not produced. Only insentient entities are produced. Is the self of the nature of knowledge as the Buddhist idealists, the Sāṁkhya and Śaṁkara maintain? Or, is it unconscious in its real nature but acquires consciousness as an adventitious quality as the Nyāya and the Vaiśeṣika maintain? Or, is it of the nature of a knower? Which of these views is rational and in conformity with the Śruti? If the self were of the nature of consciousness, it being ubiquitous would always and everywhere be conscious, and know objects, and its merits and demerits would be useless. But its consciousness is not perceived in deep sleep, swoon, and the like. In waking state knowledge of the soul is perceived, because the complement of its causes is present, while in deep sleep and the like its knowledge is not perceived, because its causal conditions are absent. Hence knowledge is not an essential quality of a self. Nor is knowledge its adventitious quality, which it acquires in conjunction with the manas and the body, because it is ubiquitous according to the Nyāya and the Vaiśeṣika, and so always in conjunction with the manas and the body. Hence it is of the nature of knowledge and a knower; it is neither unconscious nor mere knowledge, but of the nature of knowledge and a knower.[61] The Śruti says, "The self is full of knowledge, an internal light, a person"; "Who can know the knower"?; "This self is a seer, hearer, smeller, taster, thinker, doer, knowing person". Knowledge is the essential quality of an individual self while bliss is the essential quality of the Supreme Self.[62] A jīva's being a knower is sometimes manifested as in waking state and sometimes unmanifested as in deep sleep and the like. A released soul has knowledge. Hence a soul's minuteness and being a knower are not opposed to each other.[63]

Śrīpati next reproduces Rāmānuja's argument in exactly the same language. If a jīva were ubiquitous and of the nature of knowledge, it would either always have knowledge and absence of knowledge, or it would always have either knowledge or absence of knowledge, but it would not sometimes have knowledge, and sometimes not have knowledge. But, according to Śrīpati, a soul is atomic and has knowledge when endowed with a body and has no knowledge in other conditions. All souls being ubiquitous and, consequently, being connected with all sense-organs, their knowing at some times and their not knowing at other times would not be regulated by their merits and demerits also.[64]

Is the self an active agent or inactive ? Śrīpati reproduces Rāmānuja's arguments in the same language. Some hold that the self is inactive, that the insentient guṇas—sattva, rajas, and tamas—are active, and that their activity is attributed to the jīva. The 'Bhagavad Gītā' says : "Prakṛti is the cause of activity of a cause in producing an effect" ; "All actions are done by the guṇas of prakṛti" ; "The jīva thinks itself to be an active agent, being deluded by egoism" ; "The self is the cause of experiencing pleasure and pain". Thus prakṛti is active and the self is inactive.

Śrīpati refutes this view after Rāmānuja. The self is an active agent, since the scriptural injunctions and prohibitions are meaningful. It freely performs enjoined actions and abstains from committing prohibited actions, acquires merits and demerits, and experiences pleasures and pains as their appropriate fruits. If the self is not a free agent, the scriptural injunctions and prohibitions become meaningless. The scriptures produce the knowledge of right and wrong in the souls which are conscious, but they cannot produce it in prakṛti, which is unconscious. They enlighten conscious souls and impel them to perform right actions and refrain from committing wrong actions, for they alone can experience their fruits. The guṇas—sattva, rajas and tamas—are the causes of natural bodily actions alone, and not of voluntary actions which alone are moral or immoral. The 'Bhagavad Gītā' emphatically says : "The active self, the body, the sense-organs, various efforts, and daiva—merits and demerits—and divine will, are the causes of an action". It does not deny the freedom and activity of the self.[65] It can act in conjunction with insentient internal and external organs. Its power of action is restricted in the absence of internal and external organs. There is no contradiction in this view. The self cannot act at all times ; yet its activity is undeniable.[66]

The Advaita view, that the self is of the nature of knowledge and Brahman, that the internal organ alone is active, and that the internal organ being active its activity is not found in deep sleep because it becomes inoperative at the time, is unreasonable. The soul's power of action is not manifested in the absence of its body, sense-organs, manas, and vital forces ; yet its power of action cannot be denied, since the Śruti "Of the two beautiful birds in the same tree, the one eats its sweet fruit while the other merely looks on" ; becomes meaningless. Hence the view that the insentient internal organ is active is not reasonable.[67] It may be argued that buddhi alone is active because it is not found to have the power of knowing itself and other entities in deep sleep because of its absence. This argument is wrong, Śrīpati urges, because a soul's power is overcome by God's insentient power of māyā called 'tamas' in deep sleep. Its power of knowing itself and other entities is eclipsed by the supreme Lord's power of fettering it to bondage by contracting His power as the sun's rays are eclipsed by a cloud, or as the consuming power of a fire is eclipsed by a lunar gem, mantras, etc., or as coldness of water is eclipsed by the sun or by a fire.[68] So activity is an inherent attribute of the self with its other attributes. Further, if buddhi be active, the self cannot be the experiencer of the fruits of actions. If buddhi be active, it should be the experiencer of its actions. If it be the experiencer of its actions, there is no proof for the existence of the soul for the Sāṁkhya.[69] But he admits that the soul is an experiencer of the fruits of actions. So he should admit that the self is an active agent. In the world an active agent is found to act with the help of an instrument. If buddhi be an active agent, it should have an instrument. But it is not found to have an instrument. So it is not active. If buddhi be active without an instrument, then the Sāṁkhya admits that an entity without an instrument is active. So the self can be active without buddhi, which is its instrument. Further, if buddhi be active, it should also meditate. Meditation is a means of liberation, according to the Sāṁkhya, which is in the form "I am different from prakṛti". But buddhi is a modification of prakṛti, and cannot meditate in the aforesaid manner. Trance, the result of meditation, is the state in which the self merges in the supreme Lord. It is a state of superecstasy beyond ignorance, knowledge, and the world of difference, in which the Lord is revealed to the self, in which the body, sense-organs, internal organs, vital forces, and their functions cease, and which is replete with supreme bliss. In trance buddhi is modified into the form of the Lord.[70] Buddhi cannot be the agent of trance. So the self is an active agent. If it is not an active agent, it cannot acquire merits and demerits, and cannot meditate and have trance. Then it cannot attain liberation, which is attainable through faith, devotion, meditation, and trance. Buddhi cannot attain liberation. If it attained liberation, the Śrutis—"That thou art", and "The knower of Brahman becomes Brahman" would be meaningless. Liberation is the state of the self's becoming identical in nature with Brahman. In the state of liberation buddhi is destroyed because it is insentient. If buddhi attained liberation, self-destruction would become the nature of liberation.[71] The self acts with the sense-organs when it desires to do so, and it does not act, when it does not desire to do so, as a carpenter acts with an instrument when he desires to act, and he does not act when he does not desire to do so. If insentient buddhi were active, it would always be active, because it is devoid of any desire for enjoyment, which might regulate its action at times. So buddhi is not an active agent. Nor is prakṛti active, since desire is an attribute of a conscious entity. The conscious self alone is active, like a carpenter, and acts with its internal organs and external sense-organs in waking state when it desires to do so. It performs secular and scriptural actions, and experiences pleasures and pains. In deep sleep it experiences deep joy abiding in the Lord's power of binding called 'tamas' because the body and sense-organs are inoperative at the time. So it is proved that a conscious individual self alone is active.[72] But the self's activity is controlled by the will of God. It acts in accordance with its merits and demerits for experiencing their fruits in the form of happiness and misery. It is not conscious of its merits and demerits and cannot command their fruits despite its free activity. God alone is conscious of its merits and demerits, impels them to act accordingly, and associates its free actions with the fruits of its merits and demerits. Its freedom of will is subject to the divine will and limited by its merits and demerits acquired by it in the past by its free actions. If its actions were completely controlled by God, then the scriptural injunctions and prohibitions would be meaningless. If an individual self can perform enjoined actions and abstain from committing prohibited actions by its free will, then only is it morally responsible for its voluntary actions. Hence it is free to perform enjoined actions and commit prohibited actions. But the Śruti declares God to be all-pervasive, both inside and outside all beings, and their Supreme Self and Inner Controller. The 'Bhagavad Gītā' says, "God resides in the hearts of all creatures, and impels them to act." It is an individual self that acts, but its actions are controlled by God Who is different from it.[73] It is impelled but not compelled by God. If it is not free to do right actions or wrong actions, the scriptural injunctions and prohibitions become useless, and if its freedom of volition and action is not limited by God, its merits and demerits become useless. But both are necessary. Hence the self is free to will and act, and its freedom of volition and action is limited by God's will. He favours those souls which are favourably disposed towards Him, and induces them to act for the attainment of Him. He punishes those souls which are hostile to Him, and incline them towards those actions, which cause them sentient pleasures, and which are unfavourable to the attainment of Him.[74]

A soul experiences waking cognitions of external objects through the action of the external sense-organs and the internal organs with the gross body. God associates it with a gross body and the sense-organs by His power of binding, and makes its perception of external objects possible. It experiences dream-cognitions through its subtle body produced by the manas vitiated by sleep. They are contradicted by waking perceptions, which are not contradicted. Dreams are created by God, and so are true during dream state. The impressions of dreams persist in the waking state, and so dreams are remembered. Again, dreams also are due to the revival of the residual impressions of waking perceptions. Further, some dreams forecast future events, good or evil, which turn out to be true. So they are not absolutely false. A soul is not the creator of its dreams, because it cannot create the dreams which forebode its misfortune, and because it does not know its merits and demerits which are worn out by the experience of joys and sorrows in the state of dream. So dreams are created by God in accordance with its merits and demerits for its experience of their fruits.[75]

In dreamless sleep a soul experiences unconsciousness and a trace of bliss with its causal body of nescience. In waking state and dream it has the conceit of 'I' in the body and the sense-organs while in dreamless sleep it has no such conceit because it becomes completely unconscious of them. In deep sleep it sleeps in the heart in a region (purītat) full of tamas, which is a collocation of sattva, rajas, and tamas, and which is a part of God's power of consciousness, with its causal body.[76] It has no experience of waking cognitions or dream-cognitions, but it is bound by God's power of binding. Though it sleeps near the abode of God in the heart in deep sleep, it cannot experience Him, because it is fettered by His power of binding, and because it cannot know itself for the same reason. God creates deep sleep, by overcoming it endowed with a fragment of nescience with His power of cosmic nescience, and makes it experience a particle of His bliss in order to stop its waking cognitions and dream-cognitions and give it respite by making it enter a place near His abode in the heart.

Hence it does not experience God in deep sleep as a liberated soul does. Deep sleep is different from the state of release. A bound soul falls into deep sleep and awakes from it and remembers it. A released soul achieves liberation in the forms of residence in the abode of God, proximity to Him, and similarity of nature or form to Him, and becomes omniscient and omnipotent like Him. A bound soul, on the other hand, cannot have any knowledge, enjoyment and suffering in dreamless sleep because of the inactivity of the internal and external sense-organs, takes rest near God in the heart, and awakes again in order to experience the fruits of its merits and demerits.[77]

Deep sleep is a state of unconsciousness like swoon. In this state there is no conceit of 'I' in the body and the sense-organs while in swoon such conceit does not completely vanish. In swoon though there is no knowledge of external objects, there is the experience of internal pain, and therefore there is some conceit of 'I' in the body and the sense-organs. Swoon is different from waking state, because there is no knowledge of external objects in it. It is different from dream, because there is no knowledge of internal cognitions in it. It is different from waking state, dream, and deep sleep, because it is caused by a blow and the like. It is different from death wherein there is the cessation of the relation of vital forces with the body. In death the body is dead because vital forces cease to function while in swoon they operate feebly. God is the cause of a soul's waking state, dream, and dreamless sleep, and so its experience of these three states depends upon Him.[78]

BONDAGE AND LIBERATION.—Bondage consists in a soul's false conceit of 'I' and 'mine' in the manas, body, the sense-organs, and the vital forces. Liberation consists in its attainment of the nature of God, which is the result of the destruction of His power of māyā in the form of its bonds, due to the acquisition of the knowledge of itself and of Him in consequence of the ripening of its merits and demerits acquired in many births.[79] God is the cause of a soul's bondage in that He veils its knowledge by His power of māyā in the form of its bonds. He is the cause of its liberation in that He frees it from His power of māyā in the form of its bonds, and manifests its knowledge of itself as a spirit and of God. A soul cannot bind or liberate itself. It cannot be released from bondage without the grace of God or descent of His power. There are different degrees of descent of His power. (Cp. Abhinavagupta). A competent spiritual teacher infuses God's power into a disciple at the time of initiation. The inscrutable secrets of the nature of God, a soul, and its bonds are revealed to a person owing to the descent of His power in him. An aspirant awakens the dormant divine power called serpent power (kuṇḍalinī) in the mūlādhāra at the bottom of the suṣummā in the spinal cord, makes it ascend through it and pierce five centres,—svādhiṣṭhāna, maṇipura, anāhata, viśuddha, and ājñācakra, and unite with Śiva in the sahasrāra. Thus Śrīpati, an exponent of Vīra Śaivism, includes kuṇḍalinīyoga in spiritual discipline, like the Pratyabhijñā school of Śaivism. A soul can destroy its natural individuality by rigorous spiritual discipline, achieve identity with God, and be released.[80]

Śrīpati distinguishes between embodied release and disembodied release. All souls, which have acquired the knowledge of God, do not necessarily achieve embodied release. Those souls, which meditate on God with a form, and which have a desire for unalloyed happiness in the abode of God, assume auspicious spiritual bodies, and attain liberation in the forms of residence in His abode, proximity to Him, and similarity in nature or form to Him. Those souls which have acquired the virtues of sense-control, mind-control, endurance, abstention from sentient pleasures, detachment, and a strong desire for emancipation, on which God has bestowed His grace, and which meditate on formless God in the hearts, are merged in Him in trance, experience infinite bliss, and achieve embodied release. They retain their bodies until their merits and demerits, which have matured and begun to bear fruits, are worn out, and their bodies fall off. They achieve disembodied release after death of their bodies.[81] Those souls which go to the abode of God with spiritual bodies can achieve disembodied liberation by meditating on formless God. Those souls which worship God by performing their prescribed duties attain heaven. Those souls which worship God invested with a form achieve liberation in the forms of sālokya, sāmīpya, and sārūpya as described above with celestial bodies. Those souls which worship formless God achieve liberation in the form of mergence in Him. Those souls which have achieved embodied release destroy their subtle bodies here on earth while they are alive, and acquire identity with God. Their subtle bodies are destroyed because all their merits and demerits except those, which have begun to bear fruits in this life, are destroyed. When they are destroyed, their bodies perish, and they achieve disembodied release.[82] Thus Śrīpati recognizes gradual release and immediate release, embodied release and disembodied release, and four kinds of release : coresidence, proximity, similarity, and inseparable union. It should be noted that the intuitive knowledge of Brahman in the state of embodied release does not sublate the knowledge of the world, as Śaṁkara wrongly holds. The world exists at the time, and is not negated by the knowledge of God. A soul that has achieved embodied release experiences the supreme bliss of God in the state of trance, and loses the knowledge of itself and the world because it is merged in Him and becomes free of all mental modes. When it wakes from trance, it regains the knowledge of itself and the world. So the world is not a false appearance but real, and not sublated by the knowledge of Brahman.[83]

Śrīpati credits Bādarāyaṇa with the view that liberation is the attainment of the nature of God after the complete destruction of a soul's natural individuality and of the possibility of its rebirth.[84] Śaṁkara rejects the use of works for the attainment of liberation. The 'Pāśupatasūtra' does not regard the performance of the Vedic works appropriate to one's castes and stages of life as necessary for the attainment of release. But Śrīpati holds that the performance of the Vedic duties pertaining to one's castes and spheres of life without any desire for fruits, and offered to God, though not necessary for the emergence of the knowledge of God, is conducive to the achievement of emancipation, since it purifies the mind, and since it is not repugnant to the emergence of the knowledge of God. It is an indirect means to release.[85] All should perform prescribed duties till death without any desire for their fruits, inasmuch as they purify the mind. When the mind is purified, devotion to God arises. Undivided devotion produces the knowledge of God, which destroys nescience. So the performance of duties should not be given up at any stage of life. A yogin, who has acquired the knowledge of God, performs his obligatory and occasional duties, and who offers them to Him, is not affected by merits and demerits. He does not acquire these unseen potencies of actions, which produce happiness and misery. A yogin who has acquired the saving knowledge should perform actions for the good of mankind.

The prescribed works unmotived by any desire for fruits should never be discarded.[86] The merits and demerits produced by works are consumed by the true knowledge of God. Śrīpati admits that all duties,—prudential duties for the acquisition of desired objects, obligatory duties, and occasional duties,—duly performed and offered to God indirectly bring about the intuitive knowledge of God.[87] The householder should perform sacrifices, obligatory and occasional duties, for they are accessory to the acquisition of the true knowledge of God, and, conseqently, to the attainment of release. The students, the persons retired to forests, and the monks should perform their specific duties in order to achieve release.[88] All persons in different stages of life should cultivate the virtues of sense-control, mind-control, endurance, abstention from sense-pleasures, discrimination of the eternal from the noneternal, detachment and a strong desire for emancipation, for they are the internal means to the attainment of it, and directly generate the intuitive knowledge of God. All contrary desires and their potencies are exterminated by meditation on God through His grace when the mind is purified by the performance of the prescribed duties and by the cultivation of the inner virtues, which are accessory to the knowledge of Him.[89] All specific duties should be performed by those who have acquired the true knowledge of God and by those who have not yet acquired it.[90] The performance of works and the knowledge of God both are the prerequisites for the attainment of liberation,· since both are accessory to it, and all persons in different stages of life should resort to the combination of works and knowledge.[91] All should perform their specific duties, worship God, concentrate their minds on God, meditate on Him, bow to Him, hear of Him, and chant His name and glory with devotion throughout their lives. Hearing and reflection do not completely destroy the conceit of a caste and a stage of life. It is attenuated by them. Meditation on God tends to destroy it completely. It is the direct means to the attainment of the intuitive knowledge of God. An aspirant should practise silence, childlike simplicity, and wisdom after acquiring the knowledge of God.[92]

The persons in distress and sickness should practise good conduct, mutter God's name repeatedly, observe fasts on proper occasions, go on pilgrimage to holy places, perform charity, undergo penances, worship God, listen to instructions, reflect on them, and investigate His nature. They also are eligible for acquiring the knowledge of God. All are eligible for acquiring it whether they perform their respective duties pertaining to their stages of life or whether they do not do so only if they have a strong desire for release, since faith, devotion, and meditation are the principal means to the attainment of God.[93]

The ascetics should perform their specific duties till they die. Those who lapse from asceticism should atone for their sins, and then they become eligible for acquiring the knowledge of God. The sins of lapse are expiated by the performance of the 'cāndrāyaṇa', bathing in earth, pilgrimage, fasting, muttering God's name, and the like.[94] Thus Śrīpati considers the performance of duties, devotion, and knowledge of God to be the means of attaining liberation. (Cp. Nimbārka and Madhva).

[1] VSMRS., pp. 131-32.
[2] Gopinath Kaviraja Commemoration Volume, p. 137 ; VSMRS., pp. 135-36 ; DHIP., Vol. V, pp. 50-54 ; PO., pp. 204-15 ; CHI., Vol. IV, 1956, pp. 104-06.
[3] CHI., Vol. IV, pp. 106-07.
[4] ŚRBS., Vol I, pp. 1-3 ; i, 1, 4, & 30 ; ii, 1, 14 & 22 ; ii, 3, 40. DHIP., Vol. V, 1955, pp. 42-64, 173-90.
[5] ŚRBS., i, 1, 4, p. 45. [6] Ibid, p. 45. [7] Ibid.
[8] Ibid, i, 1, 4. p. 51. [9] Ibid, p. 52.
[10] Ibid, pp. 52-53.
[11] Ibid, i, 1, 2, p. 33.
[12] Ibid, pp. 32-33.
[13] Ibid, p. 30. [14] Ibid.
[15] Ibid, p. 31. [16] Ibid, i, 1, 4.
[17] Ibid, i, 1, 2, p. 31.
[18] Ibid. [19] Ibid, i, 1, 4, p. 48.
[20] Ibid, p. 47.
[21] Ibid, pp. 47-48.
[22] Ibid, i, 1, 1, p. 5.
[23] BS., ii, 2, 27-28.
[24] Ibid, ii, 2, 28 ; iii, 2, 6.
[25] Ibid, ii, 2, 39.
[26] ŚRBS., ii, 1, 32.
[27] Ibid, ii, 1, 14.
[28] Ibid, i, 1, 1, p. 4.
[29] NS., iv, 1, 19-21. HIP., Vol. I, p. 677.
[30] ŚRBS., i, 1, 1, p. 4.
[31] Ibid, i, 1, 1 ; HIP., Vol. II, pp. 463-73.
[32] ŚRBS., ii, 3, 40. [33] Ibid.
[34] Ibid, ii, 3, 43.
[35] Ibid, ii, 3, 44.
[36] Ibid, ii, 3, 46. Ibid, ii, 3, 45.
[37] Ibid, ii, 3, 46. [38] Ibid, ii, 1, 23.
[39] Ibid, ii, 3, 40. [40] Ibid.
[41] Ibid, ii, 1, 22. [42] Ibid.
[43] Ibid. [44] Ibid. [45] Ibid.
[46] Ibid, ii, 3, 42.
[47] Ibid, ii, 3, 47.
[48] ii, 3, 48. [49] Ibid.
[50] Ibid, ii, 3, 49.
[51] Ibid, ii, 3, 50.
[52] Ibid, iv, 4, 1. Ibid, iv, 4, 15.
[53] Ibid, iv, 4, 2-4.
[54] Ibid, iv, 4, 44.
[55] Ibid, iv, 4, 1-4.
[56] Ibid, ii, 2, 40.
[57] BS., ii, 3, 18. [58] ŚRBS., ii, 3, 18 & 21.
[59] Ibid, ii, 3, 28, p. 266 ; iv, 4, 15.
[60] Ibid, ii, 3, 17. [61] Ibid.
[62] Ibid, ii, 3, 27. [63] Ibid, ii, 3, 29.
[64] RBS., ii, 3, 32 ; ŚRBS., ii, 3, 30.
[65] ŚRBS., ii, 3, 31.
[66] Ibid, ii, 3, 34.
[67] Ibid, ii, 3, 34.
[68] Ibid, ii, 3, 35.
[69] HIP., Vol. II, pp. 40-41.
[70] ŚRBS., ii, 3, 36.
[71] Ibid. [72] Ibid, ii, 3, 37.
[73] Ibid, ii, 3, 38.
[74] Ibid, ii, 3, 39.
[75] Ibid, ii, 2, 28-29 ; iii, 2, 6.
[76] Ibid, iii, 2, 7.
[77] Ibid, iii, 2, 7 & 9.
[78] Ibid, iii, 2, 5 & 10.
[79] Ibid, iii, 2, 4.
[80] Ibid, iii, 2, 5. Cp. LY., pp. 17-19 ; ŚM., pp. 29-35.
[81] Ibid, iii, 4, 52.
[82] Ibid, iii, 4, 11.
[83] Ibid, ii, 2, 28 ; iv, 4, 1 & 4.
[84] Ibid, iii, 4, 1.
[85] Ibid, iii, 4, 12. Ibid, iii, 4, 9.
[86] Cp. BG., xii, 11-12 ; xviii, 2, 9 & 11 ; vi, 1 ; iii, 20.
[87] Ibid, iii, 4, 12-14, 16 & 26.
[88] Ibid, iii, 4, 26.
[89] Ibid, iii, 4, 27.
[90] Ibid, iii, 4, 32.
[91] Ibid, iii, 4, 33. Cp. Bhāskara.
[92] Ibid, iii, 4, 33—35 & 47.
[93] Ibid, iii, 4, 39. Ibid, iii, 4, 37-38.
[94] Ibid, iii, 4, 37-38, 40 & 42.

CHAPTER VII

PROBLEMS OF POST-ŚAMKARA ADVAITA VEDĀNTA

INTRODUCTION.—Śaṁkara (788-820 A.D.), the founder of the Advaita Vedānta, wrote 'Śārīrikabhāṣya' on the 'Brahmasūtra'. His philosophy was expounded in the second volume. Some problems of Post-Saṁkara Advaita Vedānta also were discussed. In the four chapters the most important problems will be discussed in greater detail, especially those which were criticized vehemently by Rāmānuja and Veṅkaṭanātha, Madhva, Jayatīrtha, Vyāsatīrtha, Rāmatīrtha, and Nimbārka and Vallabha's followers. Their criticisms will be given in the subsequent volumes which will be published successively. Padmapāda (900 A.D.), a disciple of Śaṁkara, wrote an elaborate gloss on 'Śārīrakabhāṣya', entitled 'Pañcapādikā', and commented on the first four sūtras only. Prakāśātman (1200 A.D.) wrote 'Pañcapādikāvivaraṇa', a subcommentary on it, and was called the Vivaraṇakāra. He was the founder of the Vivaraṇa school as distinguished from the Bhāmatī school. Vidyāraṇya (1400 A.D.) wrote 'Vivaraṇaprameyasaṁgraha', an important subcommentary on it. Vācaspati Miśra (900 A.D.) wrote 'Bhāmatī', a subcommentary on 'Śārīrakabhāṣya.' He wrote scholarly commentaries on important works in all the orthodox systems, and was the founder of the Bhāmatī school. Amalānanda (1300 A.D.) wrote 'Kalpataru', a subcommentary on 'Bhāmatī'. Appyayadīkṣita, (1600 A.D.) wrote 'Kalpataruparimala', a subcommentary on 'Kalpataru'. Ānandagiri or Ānandajñāna (1300 A.D.), a voluminous writer, wrote 'Tarkasaṁgraha' 'Upadeśasāhasrīvivṛti', and 'Gītābhāṣyavivecana'. Akhāṇḍānanda, a pupil of Ānandagiri, wrote 'Tattvadīpana', a commentary on 'Pañcapādikāvivaraṇa' of Prakāśātman. Govindānanda (1400 A.D.) wrote 'Ratnaprabhā', a subcommentary on 'Śārīrakabhāṣya'. Maṇḍana Miśra (800 A.D.), a disciple of Śaṁkara, wrote 'Brahmasiddhi' referred to by Vidyāraṇya in 'Vivarṇaprameyasaṁgraha'. Sūreśvara (800 A.D.), a disciple of Śaṁkara, wrote 'Bṛhadāraṇyakabhāṣyavārtika' and 'Naiṣkarmyasiddhi' and was known as the 'Vārtikakāra'. Some regard him as identical with Maṇḍana Miśra, formerly a Mīmāṁsaka, and converted by Śaṁkara to an Advaita Vedāntin. Others dispute their identity.[1] Sarvajñātman (900 A.D.), a disciple of Sureśvara, wrote 'Saṁkṣepaśārīraka' dealing with the fundamental problems discussed by Śaṁkara in his 'Śārīrakabhāṣya'. Vidyāraṇya's 'Pañcadaśī' is a popular manual on Advaita metaphysics and religion. His 'Jīvanmuktiviveka' is another work. Ānandabodha's (1100 A.D.) 'Nyāyamakaranda', Vādīndra's (1300 A.D.) 'Mahāvidyāviḍamabana', Rāmādvaya's (1300 A.D.) 'Vedāntakaumudī', an unknown author's 'Prakaṭārthavivaraṇa' (1200 A.D.), Vimuktātman's (1200 A.D.), 'Iṣṭasiddhi', Dharmarājādhvarīndra's (1600 A.D.) 'Vedāntaparibhāṣā' with its commentaries, 'Śikhāmaṇi' and 'Maṇiprabhā', Mahādeva Sarasvatī's 'Tattvānusandhāna' Mahādevānanda Sarasvatī's 'Advaitacintākaustubha', a commentary on it, and Gaṅgāpuri's 'Padārthatattvanirṇaya' are important works in Advaita Vedānta. Appyayadīkṣita's 'Siddhāntaleśasaṁgraha' is a very important digest of the different views of the Advaitavādins. Madhusūdana

Sarasvatī's (1600 A.D.) 'Advaitasiddi' and 'Siddhāntabindu' with their commentaries are very important works on Advaita metaphysics in conflict with the Mādhva system. Śrī Harṣa's (1200 A. D.) 'Khaṇḍanakhaṇḍakhādya' and Citsukha's 'Tattvapradīpikā' or 'Citsukhī' with their commentaries are the most important works on Advaita Vedānta dialectics. Sadānanda Vyāsa's (1500 A.D.) 'Vedantasāra' with its commentaries 'Subodhinī' by Nṛsiṁhāśrama Sarasvatī (1500 A.D.) and 'Vidvanmanorañjanī' by Rāmatīrtha is a popular manual used by the beginners in the study of the Advaita Vedānta. Sadānanda Kāśmīraka's (1800 A.D.) 'Advaitabrahmasiddhi' is another popular manual. Prakāśānanda's (1600 A.D.) 'Vedāntasiddhāntamuktāvalī', Nṛsiṁhāśrama's 'Bhedadhikkāra', and Raṅgojī Bhaṭṭa's (1650 A.D.) 'Advaitacintāmaṇi' are other works. These chapters are based on most of these works. They do not deal with the history of the Advaita Vedānta, but with the philosophical discussion of some important problems.

BRAHMAN : ESSENTIAL AND ACCIDENTAL CHARACTERISTICS.—Brahman etymologically means the greatest or infinite being. Existence, knowledge, and bliss are Its essential characteristics, since they constitute Its nature. Existence is not empirical existence limited by time, space and causality. It is spaceless, timeless and uncaused being. It is devoid of difference and plurality. It is above the distinctions of the phenomenal, empirical world. It is not conditioned by the intellect infected with the nescience (avidyā). It is not associated with māyā—cosmic nescience. It is not empirical, conditioned, attributed, or superimposed existence. It is transcendent, unconditioned, infinite, eternal existence. Knowledge is consciousness, awareness,—infinite, eternal, universal, transcendent, absolute consciousness. It is not a self's consciousness of a not-self. It is beyond the distinction of self and not-self, ego and non-ego. It is not involved in relatively and duality, change and becoming. In Brahman existence is consciousness, and consciousness is existence. Bliss is delight of existence, and delight of consciousness. It is delight of infinitude and universality and transcendence. Bliss is not produced, finite, limited pleasure or happiness due to the gratification of a desire. It is eternal, infinite, unlimited, universal. It is an index of perfection, self-fulfilledness, desirelessness. In Brahman consciousness is bliss, and bliss is consciousness. So Brahman is existence-consciousness-bliss. Existence, knowledge and bliss are not three different qualities of Brahman qualifying It. They constitute Its nature. So they are Its essential characteristics (svarūpalakṣaṇa). Amalānanda sets forth the argument that just as plulrality in being is due to limiting adjuncts, so the difference between existence and knowledge, and the difference between knowledge and bliss are due to limiting adjuncts, because knowledge and bliss devoid of existence are void, because existence devoid of knowledge is not manifested in consciousness, because being known without existence is imaginary, and because the witness (sākṣin) of the nature of existence and knowledge being an object of supreme love is of the nature of bliss. So Brahman is determined as of the nature of existence, knowledge and bliss as distinguished from the apparent plularity of individual forms. The Śrutis asserting existence, knowledge and bliss of Brahman do not signify determinate objects.[2] Vācaspati Miśra avers that the Śruti speaks of the attributeless (nirguṇa) Brahman, when it says, "Brahman is without sound, touch, colour, and infinite". The transcendent Brahman is devoid of all determinations due to adjuncts.[3] Vidyāraṇya opines that such Śrutis imply that Brahman is of the nature of universal transcendent consciousness. The detached Brahman is by nature nonphenomenal.[4] Vidyāraṇya explains the meanings of the essential characteristics of Brahman. Knowledge of an empirical self means a mode of mind with various modifications wherein universal consciousness is reflected. Its bliss is a mode of mind with pure sattva wherein universal conciousness is manifested as very agreeable feeling of felicity. Our knowledge and happiness are produced and transient. But knowledge and bliss in Brahman are eternal. So the modes of mind should be discarded to signify the essential characteristics of Brahman. The words 'knowledge' and 'bliss' in the Śrutis "Brahman is truth, knowledge and infinite", "Brahman is knowledge and bliss" should be taken in a secondary sense in regard to the mental modes, and they should be taken in a primary sense in regard to the remaining parts.[5] The words 'one', 'truth' and 'infinite' should be taken in a secondary sense to imply the absence of homogeneous difference, heterogeneous difference, internal difference, and falsehood.[6] Vidyāraṇya avers that truth, knowledge and bliss are not Brahman's attributes, for the relation of a substance to its attributes is inexplicable. It is neither difference nor nondifference. Further, the Śruti asserts Brahman to be attributeless (nirguṇa).[7] Truth, knowledge, bliss and infinitute are the nature of Brahman.[8]

Śaṁkara characterizes Brahman as of the nature of eternal, pure, conscious, free, omniscient and omnipotent being.[9] He includes essential and accidental characteristics of Brahman in the statement. Omniscience and omnipotence denote the knowledge of all and all powers, respectively. This statement refers to Brahman as transcendent (nirguṇa) and immanent (saguṇa). Vācaspati Miśra explains these characteristics of Brahman. Brahman is eternal, for It is undecaying. It is pure, since It is immaterial, bodiless and free of pain. It is conscious, for Its manifestation does not depend upon any other entity. It is self-luminous. Manifestation and bliss are non-different from each other.[10] It is eternally free from bondage. When a jīva is liberated, it realizes Ātman's purity and the like. It is, in its essence, devoid of birth, old age and death. Ātman is eternally free and transcendent, and appears to be bound because of avidyā. After showing the nature of Brahman unconditioned by an adjunct, Śaṁkara describes the attributes of Brahman as omniscience and omnipotence due to the adjunct of avidyā.[11] Īśvara, Brahman conditioned by avidyā, is the cause of the world, because He has omniscience and omnipotence. When an entity has knowledge and power, it has the power of producing an effect, and when it is devoid of them, it cannot be a cause.

Brahman's being the material cause and efficient cause of the world, its maintainer, and destroyer, being the moral governor of the empirical souls, and the Lord of the Law of Karma are Its accidental characteristics. They do not characterize Its nature, but are relative to Brahman as the foundation of the phenomenal world and empirical selves associated with māyā and avidyā, respectively. The world appearance and empirical selves are annulled when avidyā is completely destroyed by the intuitive knowledge of Brahman, and Its accidental characteristics disappear, and Brahman as infinite existence-consciousness-bliss blazes forth in consciousness.

The essential characteristics of Brahman are asserted by the Śrutis "Brahman is truth, knowledge, infinite"; "Knowledge is Bliss"; "What is infinite is bliss, there is no bliss in the finite".[12] Vidyāraṇya says, "Being the creator, maintainer and destroyer of the world is an essential characteristic of Īśvara, but an accidental characteristic of pure Brahman".[13] Īśvara is Brahman qualified by māyā—cosmic nescience. Raṅgojī Bhaṭṭa says, "Brahman's being the material cause and efficient cause of the world is Its accidental characteristic.[14] A material cause is a cause with which its effect is essentially identical. An efficient cause consists in possessing knowledge favourable to the production of an effect. Such knowledge is essential to Brahman.[15] An agent is possessed of volition and knowledge of the material of creation."[16] In the Śruti "That thou art" the word 'that' signifies the supreme Lord qualified by agency, etc., in a primary sense, and implies Brahman free of the attributes of agency and the like in a secondary sense.

Padmapāda opines that Brahman of the nature of bliss cannot be the cause of the world of the nature of non-bliss, that therefore the attributes of being the cause of the world, and the like are the indicating characteristics (upalakṣaṇa) of Brahman, and that they are the essential characteristics of the omniscient and omnipotent Īśvara.[17] Prakāśātman also regards Brahman's being the material cause and agent of the world as Its accidental characteristic.[18] Being of the nature of various kinds of effects and their actions and being of the nature of powers capable of producing them cannot be essential characteristic of pure Brahman to be known.[19] Vidyāraṇya avers that the nature of Brahman cannot be known through Its accidental characters alone without Its essential characters. Creation, maintenance and destruction of the world are the effects of Brahman, the cause. It is shown by Its essential and accidental characters. Creation and the like are related to Īśvara or Brahman, the cause, qualified by māyā, since they are not related to pure Brahman.[20] The Śruti says, "Brahman resolved, 'I shall become many' ". The first part of it proves Brahman to be the efficient cause, and the second part proves It to be the material cause of the world. Vācaspati Miśra says, "The world of which Brahman associated with avidyā is the material cause exists in Brahman, and is dissolved in Brahman".[21] Amalānanda avers that Brahman existing as the common factor in the individual jars produced by māyā, being characterized by Its existence does not leave existence, even as a reflection of the moon in water does not leave its identity with the moon, and that, similarly, Brahman does not leave knowledge and bliss in individual modes of knowledge and pleasure in which they are reflected, respectively.[22]

Vidyāraṇya criticizes Bhāskara's view. Bhāskara maintains that there is no substance devoid of attributes. Let there be no substance devoid of attributes. But Brahman is not a substance, for there is no evidence for it. The argument, that Brahman is a substance, because it is an inherent cause of the world, is invalid, since this view is the Nyāya view (ārambhavāda), which is rejected by the Advaita Vedāntin. The argument, that Brahman is a substance, because It is the material cause of the world, is false, since in that case a quality and the like would be the material cause of their properties of being known, being expressed by words, and the like. It is contended that the attribute (guṇa) is a property (dharma), and that there is no entity without a property. This contention is false, since the Advaitin admits the attribute of consciousness to be devoid of a property. If consciousness had a property, it would lead to infinite regress. So Bhāskara's denial of a substance devoid of attributes is nothing but intolerance of the Advaita Vedāntin's view. Hence

Brahman is of the nature of knowledge and bliss. This view is proved by Vedic testimony.[23]

Vācaspati Miśra says, "Activity is not an attribute of Brahman, because action, being the cause of a modification in its substrate, would make It mutable and, consequently, noneternal. Because Brahman is eternal, It cannot have action. If action subsists in another entity, the action cannot produce an aid in Brahman. Rubbing a mirror cannot make a gem pure.[24] Śaṁkara says, "Ātman is eternal, for It has no cause of destruction. It is immutable and eternal, since It has no cause of modification". Vācaspati Miśra avers that Brahman is devoid of modifications, of properties, of characteristics, and of states.[25] Śaṁkara says, "The Supreme Self cannot be imagined to be in conjunction with space, time and the like".[26] Space, time and causality are forms of intellect or buddhi.

Vidyāraṇya shows that Brahman is partless (niṣkala). If It has parts, he asks whether both parts and whole Brahman are self-manifest, or whether either of them is self-manifest. In the first alternative, both of them not being objects of each other's knowledge, neither can know Brahman to be composed of parts. In the second alternative, Brahman cannot be said to be a whole of parts, like the self and a jar. It is contended that Śrutis assert Brahman to be both devoid of parts and action and also possessed of action because of Its controlling the individual souls. The contention is false, because, though Brahman is really inactive, Its activity is due to māyā. So partless Brahman is not modified into the world, but appears to be the world appearance because of māyā.[27] The Śruti says, "Ātman is unborn, ubiquitous and eternal". Mutability is contradictory to eternality. Brahman is immutable, for It is partless.[28]

Vāçaspati Miśra avers that, Ātman or Brahman Itself is the ontological reality of all phenomenal appearances. The world appearance and empirical selves are shown by the beginniugless nescience.[29] They are ontologically unreal. It is contended that the Śrutis assert Brahman to be the omniscient, omnipotent cause of the world, Supreme Self of all, all-knowing, all-experiencing, all-desiring, all-tasting, all-smelling and the like, and that therefore the world is real. Vidyāraṇya urges that the contention is false, because all are conditioned by the adjuncts of false appearances and indefinable.[30] The immanent (saguṇa) Brahman as the Supreme Self of the world appearance is asserted by the Śruti to imply that the worship of such Brahman will ultimately lead to the immediate experience of the transcendent (nirguṇa) Brahman. The immanent Brahman as the omniscient and omnipotent cause of the world is the form attributed to the transcendent Brahman. The Śrutis regarding saguṇa Brahman do not conflict with those regarding nirguṇa Brahman, because the latter do not prove the existence of saguṇa Brahman.[31] The two sets of Śrutis do not contradict each other, because the Śrutis asserting Brahman invested with attributes are intended for those aspirants' worship of saguṇa Brahman, who are incapable of worshipping nirguṇa Brahman, and because they do not at all prove Its existence.[32] The words 'omniscience', 'omnipotence' and the like signify attributes limited by the adjuncts of phenomenal appearances, which are indefinable and unreal.[33] Śaṁkara says, "Though Brahman is attributeless, It is said to be invested with attributes due to names and forms for the sake of worship."[34]

IS BRAHMAN KNOWABLE ?—The Śruti says, "Brahman is different from being known, and from being unknown". So it denies the knowability of Brahman. But, though Brahman is unknownable, according to Vidyāraṇya, It is said to be knowable in a secondary sense by the intuitive knowledge produced by the Vedic testimony, associated with the consciousness manifested by a mode of the internal organ modified into the form of Brahman or infinite consciousness and bliss, which destroys avidyā and its effects. The Śrutis say, "Brahman ought to be seen or intuited by the manas alone"; "This subtle Ātman ought to be known"; "Know the Self declared by the Upaniṣads". These texts assert the knowability of Brahman by intending Brahman to be the object of the mental mode modified into the form of one infinite consciousness and bliss by Its mere proximity to the mode imparting Its form to it, as a jar imparts its form to a mental mode, which is modified into its form. An insentient object (e.g., a jar) can be invested with a peculiarity (atiśaya) in the form of manifestation produced by a pramāṇa and be an object of knowledge in this sense. But Brahman, being self-manifest, cannot be invested with a peculiarity in the form of manifestation produced by a pramāṇa. So Brahman is not the object of knowledge in the sense that It is not pervaded by the result of knowing. So the Śruti says, "Brahman is not expressed by words". But there is no absolute absence of the result of knowing in Brahman, because the consciousness of Brahman Itself through the limiting adjunct of manifestation by a mental mode is figuratively said to be the result of knowing. In a jar also the manifestation of the consciousness of Brahman through the adjunct of a mental mode modified into its form is said to be the result of knowing. Thus Brahman is not knowable in a primary sense, but It is knowable in a figurative sense.[35]

Padmapāda avers that Brahman known from the Vedas is not established by them as an object of the act of knowledge. When the immediate knowledge of the identity of the self with Brahman dawns, Brahman is not known as an object of knowledge. The distinction of a knower, a means of valid knowledge, valid knowledge, and an object of valid knowledge due to avidyā is simultaneously annulled, when the intuition of Brahman dawns. Yet the apprehension of Brahman as limited by this distinction is due to Vedic testimony.

THE CAUSE OF THE WORLD APPEARANCE.—1. According to some Advaitins Brahman is the cause of the creation, maintenance, and dissolution of the world, because the Śruti says: "These creatures are born out of Brahman, are maintained by It and are dissolved in It". Rāmādvaya, the author of 'Vedānta-Kaumudi' is the expotent of this view. 2. Some Advaitins regard Brahman as the material cause and efficient cause of the world, which are not different from each other. The world appearance merges in Brahman—the material cause. It is created and maintained by Brahman—the efficient cause. Brahman is the material cause of the world in the sense that It appears to be the world appearance, since the undifferenced, unchanging consciousness (kūṭastha caitanya) cannot produce the world as the atoms produce composite gross things. A modification is a change of an entity, which is its different state, but which has the same degree of reality. But an appearance is a change of an entity, which has not the same degree of reality. A nacre appears to be illusory silver, which has less degree of reality. The former has pragmatic reality while the latter has illusory reality. Similarly, Brahman has ontological reality while the world appearance has pragmatic reality, and is false. 3. Some followers of Sarvajñātman regard pure Brahman as the material cause of the world, since Bādarāyaṇa and Śaṁkara consider Brahman to be the material cause of the world, and since the Śruti says, "Ether is born out of Ātman or Brahman."[36] 4. According to Prakāśātman and his followers, the Vivaraṇa school, Īśvara invested with omniscience, omnipotence and other qualities, and associated with māyā, is the material cause of the world, for the Śruti says, "The world of names and forms was born out of Brahman—the omniscient and all-knowing Being—Whose penance consists in knowledge". Īśvara is the material cause of the world, because the world is a modification of māyā abiding in Īśvara. The nescience abiding in the souls is the cause of the internal organs and the like. Thus māyā and avidyā both are the material cause of the world. Māyā is cosmic nescience while avidyā is an individual nescience. Ether and the other elements are modifications of māyā abiding in Īśvara. So Īśvara is said to be the material cause of the world. The internal organs and the like are modifications of avidyā abiding in the jīva. So the jīva is said to be the material cause of the internal organ. This is the view of those Advaitins who distinguish between māyā and avidyā.[37] 5. Some Advaitavādins who do not draw any distintion between māyā and avidyā consider Īśvara to be the material cause of ether and the other elements, and consider the soul to be the material cause of the internal organ and the like, for it experiences identity with the latter. 6. Some Advaitists regard Brahman as the material cause of the entire world including the internal organs, and the soul as the material cause of illusions and dreams, since the Śruti says, "Vital force, manas, all sense-organs, earth, water, air, light and ether are produced out of Brahman". They advocate vivartavāda and maintain that Brahman creates the world appearance comprising the elements as the soul creates diverse dream-appearances. Some Advaitavādins advocating the doctrine of one soul think the soul to be the material cause of the world appearance including Īśvara. The soul itself is the cause of all, for it imagines all like dream-objects.[38] The Śruti says, "Prakṛti should be known as māyā". So māyā is insentient and common to a jar and other things. Thus māyā is experienced to be the material cause of the world. How, then, can Brahman be the material cause of the world? Gaṅgāpuri, the author of 'Padārthatattvanirṇaya' regards Brahman as the material cause of the world as existence, and māyā or avidyā as its material cause as insentience. Brahman appears to be the world while māyā is modified into the world.[39] 7. Some Advaitists define the material cause as common to the material cause of an appearance and the material cause of a modification. The material cause is that which produces an effect nondifferent from it. The world as an appearance is nondifferent from Brahman as existent. The world as insentient is nondifferent from nescience which is modified. The world appearance is nondifferent from Brahman in the sense that it is absent when Brahman is absent. Nondifference is not identity, but it negates difference. Śaṁkara and Vācaspati Miśra do not think the world appearance to be identical with Brahman. To regard it as identical with Brahman is a wrong conclusion according to Advaitavāda. Real nondifference or identity is negated. But the negation of identity does not prove real difference between Brahman and the world appearance. Brahman is the ontological reality, but the world is a false appearance. They have different degrees of reality. Real difference depends upon the reality of the distincts—the entity possessed of an entity and the entity possessed of its counter-entity. Because Brahman is the ontological reality and because the world-appearance is a pragmatic reality, there cannot be real difference between them.[39] There is no conflict between the experienced nondifference or identity of 'this' and 'silver' in the illusion "this is silver" and pragmatic difference between 'this' and 'silver'. The illusion has illusory reality (prātibhāsika sattā) while a nacre and silver have pragmatic reality (vyavahārika sattā). 8. According to Sarvajñātman Brahman Itself is the material cause of the world with the aid of māyā, since the changless consciousness cannot produce the world. Earth is not the direct cause of smoothness of a jar, but it is the indirect cause of the quality. Thus even what is not the material cause of an effect enters into it indirectly as its cause.[40] 9. In Vācaspati Miśra's view, Brahman, the object of the nescience abiding in the soul, by Itself appears to be the insentient world appearance, and so it is its material cause. Māyā or avidyā is a mere auxiliary cause. It is not an indirect cause as Sarvajñātman thinks. 10. According to the author of the 'Vedāntasiddhāntamuktāvalī' Brahman is not the material cause of the world, but the power of māyā is its material cause, since the Śruti says, "Brahman is without before, after and outside, and without cause and effect." But Brahman is figuratively called the material cause of the world, for It is the substratum (adhiṣṭhāna) of māyā—the material cause of the world.[41] 11. Some Advaitins maintain that Brahman endowed with the power of māyā, the archetype, is the cause of the world appearance, and that the jīvas each are bound to avidyā. Other Advaitins hold that pure, eternal Brahman reflected in māyā and avidyā is the cause of the world appearance, and that jīvas are bound to avidyā. In the first view, there is difference between māyā and avidyā, and Brahman is reflected in them. But in the second view, there is no difference between māyā and avidyā, and Brahman is not reflected in them. 12· According to Maṇḍana, the author of the 'Brahmasiddhi', each of the jīvas is deluded by its avidyā, which assumes the form of the world appearance in Brahman, and Brahman qualified by māyā, the archetype, or a reflection, is not the cause of the world appearance. The harmony among the world appearances perceived by the different jīvas is due to their similarity, like the illusory double moon perceived by many persons.[42] 13. Vimuktātman, the author of the 'Iṣṭasiddhi', maintains that one Brahman appears to be the world-appearance through Its avidyā, like dreams and the like. Brahman is said to be the cause of the world appearance, since It is by nature the substratum of the world-appearance.[43]

CRITICISM OF BRAHMAN'S MODIFICATION INTO THE WORLD (BHĀṢKARA).—The Advaitavādins regard Brahman as the material cause of the world. Vidyāraṇya asks whether Brahman discards Its previous form and is modified into another form or whether without discarding Its previous nature It appears to be the world. In the first alternative, after Brahman is modified into the world It will cease to exist as of the nature of knowledge and bliss. The opponent may contend that Brahman modified into the world at the time of creation is again modified into knowledge and bliss in the state of dissolution. This contention is false, because Brahman being of such a nature as to be modified into the world, a soul cannot attain release because of the absence of Brahman to be worshipped. Further, Vedic testimony about creation does not prove Brahman's being modified into the world. The Śruti "Atman is eternal, infinite, and unchanging" proves that Brahman is unmodifiable. What is unchanging is immutable. Brahman is unmodifiable, for It is partless. It is objected that a partless entity also is modified. Gold is modified into a necklace indirectly through its atoms in which it exists, as conjunction inheres in a part of a whole. So the conjunctions of the parts of a whloe produce a modification of it into another entity. Vidyāraṇya asks what modification is. A modification is either being made of parts lumped together owing to conjunctions of the parts, which are different from their previous conjunctions, as a lump of clay assumes the form of a jar, or being made of parts lumped together by the addition of other parts to its parts as milk is modified into curd by the addition of a sour coagulating substance, or assuming a different state like the growth of a young man to an old man, or assuming another form like the trunk of a tree assuming the form of a pillar, or conjunction with a different entity like an atom conjoined with another atom and becoming a dyad, or motion like water becoming a current in a river, or acquiring different qualities like a green mango becoming ripe, or producing a different substance tinged by its material cause. Vidyāraṇya urges that modification cannot be of the nature of any of these processes. The first and second alternatives are not possible, since a partless entity cannot have such modifications. The third and fourth alternatives also are not possible, because if Brahman is modified in such ways It connot become Brahman again, and so a soul cannot be released. An old man cannot become a young man again. A pillar cannot become the trunk of a tree again. The fifth, sixth and seventh alternatives are not possible, since the definitions of modification are too wide. Ether is conjoined with another substance, but is nôt modified. A bee moves, but is not modified. A cloth being dyed with a red dye is not modified into another entity. The eighth alternative also is not possible, because the modification of parts due to the modification of the whole is indescribable. Further, are the parts of gold modified into a necklace ? Or, are they modified into another substance appropriate to a necklace ? Or, do they assume another state appropriate to a necklace ? The second and third alternatives are not possible, since the parts are not perceived to become a substance differemt from a necklace, or to assume another state different from a necklace. The first alternative also is not possible, for a necklace is an effect of a whole lump of gold, and not of its parts. If it were produced by the parts of gold, the Nyāya doctrine of an effect as a new beginning, would be true. Śaṁkara's criticism of the Nyāya doctrine has already been given.[44] The contention that the parts of gold cannot enter into a necklace is invalid, since they can enter into it through the whole lump of gold. The contention that a whole abiding in its parts cannot be modified without a modification of the parts is false, because a dyad is produced and destroyed, though its component atoms are neither produced nor destroyed. Or, let there be a modification of the parts, yet their modification is due to the modification of the whole, and so it is not an example which proves the modification of Brahman.

What is the proof for Brahman's being partless on the strength of which It is said to be unmodifiable ? Vidyāraṇya replies that Vedic testimony is the proof for Brahman's being partless. Further, Brahman's being made of parts is indescribable. If Brahman consists of parts, either both the whole and the parts are self-manifest or either of them is self-manifest. In the first alternative, neither the parts nor the whole is known by the other, and so neither knows Brahman to be composed of parts. In the second alternative, the whole and the parts cannot be so related to each other, like a jar and self. A jar is known by self, but not by its part or whole. Hence Brahman is partless, and is not modified into the world, but appears to be the world appearance.[45]

CRITICISM OF SĀṀKHYA, NYĀYA, MĀDHYAMIKA AND CĀRVĀKA VIEWS.—Vidyāraṇya refutes the views of the Sāṁkhya, the Nyāya, the Mādhyamika, and Cārvāka in the following manner. The Sāṁkhya regards prakṛti as the material cause of the world. All effects are modifications of the material cause, which is common to them, as earthen pots are of the nature of earth as their material cause. All effects are modifications of sattva, rajas and tamas constituting prakṛti, the material cause, because they are limited, many, and of the nature of modifications, like earthen pots. Vidyāraṇya offers the following criticisms of the Sāṁkhya doctrine. Internal pleasure, pain, and delusion are perceived as different from external objects (e.g., a jar). So the reason of the inference is not proven. Īśvarakṛṣṇa describes sattva, rajas and tamas as pleasure, pain, and delusion, respectively. They are feeling-stuff. It is contended that the reason is proven, since the modifications like a jar and the like of the nature of pleasure, pain and delusion are causes of the experience of these feelings in the adjunct of consciousness (cit) which manifests them, as a face, an archetype, reflected in the adjunct of a mirror, is the cause of the experience of it. This contention is false, because if that were so one object would be experienced by a person as of a triple nature of pleasure, pain and delusion. It is contended that one object is perceived as of the nature of one guṇa because of the unseen principle (adṛṣṭa). This contention is false, since the unseen principle cannot regulate the capacity of an entity. It cannot make a stone soft. The Sāṁkhya argues that limitedness also is due to an entity. The argument is false, since in that case prakṛti and soul, which are eternal, would be limited and effects. But the Sāṁkhya regards them as unlimited and eternal. Similarly, manyness and modifications as reasons may be shown to be irregular. A rope made of two long and wide pieces of contracted cloth would not be an effect. So the Sāṁkhya view is wrong. Śaṁkara's criticism of the Sāṁkhya doctrine has already been given.[46]

The Nyāya holds that an effect is produced by substances of less dimension than its dimension, and that it is ultimately made of atoms. Vidyāraṇya refutes it by a counter-argument : the disputed dyad is produced by a substance made of parts, because it is made of parts, like a jar.

The Mādhyamika argues that an effect is preceded by an absence because its previous state is not perceived, though it is capable of being perceived, and so produced by the Void, like the self imagined by the opponents. Vidyāraṇya refutes it thus. The Mādhyamika's reason of the inference is unproven, since the previous state of a jar, a lump of clay, is perceived.[47]

Cārvāka holds that an effect is produced by nature. Vidyāraṇya refutes his view thus. He asks whether an effect is produced by itself, or whether it is produced without a cause. The first alternative is untenable, since it involves self-dependence. The second alternative also is inadmissible, since if an effect were produced without a cause, then a jar would simultaneously be existent and non-existent in that it does not depend upon gradual production. Cārvāka contends that if according to the Advaita Vedāntin gradual production by a cause is natural, then his doctrine also is naturalism, and that if it depends upon another cause, this view will lead to infinite regress. If gradual production by a cause is admitted to be due to difference in time, the order of time is natural, and so this view will be naturalism. If it depends upon another cause, it will lead to infinite regress. Vidyāraṇya urges that this contention is false for the following reasons. The capacitiy of entities in bringing about gradual production is independent of other causes, or its dependence on other causes is needless. The first alternative is admitted by the Advaita Vedāntin. In the second alternative, dependence on another cause is either not perceived, or is inexplicable, though it is perceived. The first alternative is untenable, for it is contradicted by perception. A potter's dependence on a wheel and a staff in producing an earthen jar is proved by perception. The second alternative also is inadmissible, because according to the Advaita Vedāntin inexplicability of all appearances is not a flaw, but a decoration. Further, Cārvāka maintains that earth, water, fire and air are the four elements, that perception is the only pramāṇa, and that naturalism is ontologically valid. In order to prove these theses he has to adduce reasons which have causes. If he does not adduce reasons, his theses are unproven. If they are held to be valid because they are experienced, he accepts the Advaitin's doctrine of indescribable (anirvacanīya) phenomena. So Cārvāka's view is false. Hence Brahman appears to be the world apearance.[48]

ĀTMAN IS SELF-MANIFEST.—The Śaṁkarite regards Self as self-manifest. The opponent refutes this view. 'Self-manifest' means either 'self' and 'manifest', or manifestation of self by itself, or not being manifested by an entity like itself, or being devoid of the absence of manifestation in regard to its being, or being manifest and being the cause of action in regard to it, or not being an object of a cognition, or being intuited without being an object of knowledge, or not being an object of knowledge, and yet being an object of action, or not depending on an entity like itself for an action in regard to itself, or being an object of immediate action without being an object of knowledge, or fitness for being so. He urges that all these alternatives are untenable. The first alternative is untenable, for a known cognition also is admitted by a Śaṁkarite to be self-manifest. Being known by a cognition and not being known by a cognition are contradictory to each other. The second alternative is not possible, since a knower knowing itself involves self-contradiction. The third alternative is not tenable, for the definition is too wide in that it applies to a lighted lamp and a jar. A lamp is not manifested by another lamp. But it is not self-manifest like consciousness according to a Śaṁkarite. A jar is not manifested by a jar. But it is not self-manifest. The fourth alternative is not admissible, since it is too wide in that it applies to pleasure and the like, which manifest their being. The fifth alternative is untenable, because it applies to a lighted lamp, which is the cause of action upon it, and which is manifest. The sixth alternative is not possible, because it cannot be proved by any knowledge produced by inference or testimony in that it is not an object of knowledge, and in that a desire for discussion in regard to it is not possible. The seventh alternative is not tenable, since the definition is too wide in that it applies to self according to Prabhākara, which in his view is known as a knower, but which is not known as an object of knowledge. The eighth alternative is untenable, because it is too wide in that it applies to illusory silver in a nacre according to Prabhākara, who regards it as the cause of action on it, but who does not regard it as an object of discrimination between perception and recollection. The ninth alternative is not admissible, since it is too wide in that it applies to a lighted lamp and a jar. A lamp does not depend upon another lamp for an action upon it, but it is not self-manifest like consciousness. A jar does not depend upon another jar for an action upon it, but it is not self-manifest. The tenth alternative is untenable, because if 'self-manifest' is not an object of knowledge, it cannot be known by inference or testimony, and so it cannot be an object of discussion, because the admission that it is an object of immediate knowledge is tantamount to the admission that it is an object of perception. The eleventh alternative also is not tenable, since fitness for being an object of immediate knowledge without being known is an attribute, and since self-manifest self or consciousness is devoid of an attribute according to the Śaṁkarite. If it is said to be its essence, self of the nature of consciousness being determinable by an action, it would have a counterentity. So 'self-manifest' cannot be defined. Nor is there any evidence for it.[49]

Citsukha refutes these arguments of the opponent of self-manifestness. The definition of it is not impossible. It is defined as fitness for the use of the word 'immediate' without being an object of knowledge. If it is an attribute, it is not a wrong conclusion according to the Śaṁkarite, for he admits the existence of an imaginary attribute in the state of bondage. Sureśvara avers that in the state of bondage an empirical self has attributes. Padmapāda avers that bliss, apprehension of objects, eternality, etc., are its attributes. In order to exclude insentient objects which are known, the adjective 'not being known' is added. This definition is faultless and proved by the inference : apprehension is self-manifest, for it is of the nature of apprehension ; what is not of the nature of apprehension is not self-manifest. It may be argued that apprehension is known, since it is an entity, like a jar. This kevalānvayi inference proves that apprehension is knowable. Citsukha urges that this argument is invalid, because if apprehension is known by another apprehension, it will lead to infinite regress. Self is self-manifest, since it is not an object of knowledge. If it were known, it would be an object of knowledge abiding in itself, and so would be subject and object of knowledge,—which is self-contradictory. The Śruti says, "Self is self-manifest".[50]

Vidyāraṇya avers that Self by itself is manifested. Being of the nature of consciouness (cit), it is not mediated by any other entity to manifest itself, like apprehension. Apprehension is not the manifestation of consciousness. It is Self that manifests consciousness, for there is nondifference between Self and apprehension.[51] Vidyāraṇya asks the opponent of self-manifestness of Self whether Self is immediately known as the abode of consciousness or whether it is known as merely related to consciousness or whether it is intuited as conditioned by consciousness or whether it is intuited as an object of consciousness. He shows that these alternatives are not possible. The first alternative is untenable, since Self is manifested without manifesting an object, like consciousness. In the experience "I know an object" Self is the subject or abode of consciousness. The second alternative is inadmissible, for it will involve an unwarranted stretch of a general rule : anything being merely related to consciousness (e.g., inferential knowledge) would be immediately known. The third alternative is untenable, since being conditioned by consciousness is not being the abode of consciousness, for an object, which is not an abode or subject of consciousness, would not be immediately known. Nor is being conditioned by consciousness either being the subject or being the object of consciousness, since the nature of an object cannot be ascertained. The fourth alternative also is not tenable, because consciousness of Self does not occur at a different time from that of consciousness of an object. If it occured at a diffenent time, the experience "This has been known by me" would not be possible, or the relation of the object to consciousness would not be known. Consciousness of Self and consciousness of an object cannot occur at the same time, for two cognitions of opposed entities—subject and object—cannot be produced simultaneously. So Self is intuited as self-manifest.[52]

Prakāśānanda also avers that Self is self-manifest, because it is asserted by the Śruti to be of the nature of a mass of knowledge and to be self-luminous. It is objected that Self's self-manifestness is contradicted by the fact that sometimes I experience "I know my self" and that sometimes I experience "I do not know my self", and that for this reason Self is both known and unknown. If I know my self, its knowness being an object of knowledge must be admitted. If it is an object of knowledge, it is not-self according to the Advaitist. So its self-manifestness is not proved. Hence what is self-manifest can never be an object of knowledge. If on the strength of the experience "I know my self" Self's being an object of knowledge is admitted, then it is not self-manifest. Self cannot simultaneously be manifest and unmanifest, for it involves self-contradiction. In fact, when it is manifested, it is not unmanifested. So how can Self be self-manifest ? Prakāśānanda obviates this difficulty by pointing out that Self is different from being known and unknown. The Śruti says, "Self is different from a known entity and an unknow entity." What, then, is the meaning of the experience "I know my self" ? Prakāśānanda replies that Self qualified by an adjunct is an object of knowledge, that indeterminate Self unqualified by an adjunct, reality in its pure nature, distinguished from nescience and pain, is not an object of knowledge, and that qualified Self is not self-manifest. Pure, unqualified Self alone is admitted to be self-manifest. The experience "I do not know my self" also proves Self to be self-manifest. It apprehends the nescience or ignorance of the Self. In the experience Self also is manifested. Otherwise, there would always be the experience "I do not know my self". The experience "I do not know my self" refers to self-manifest Self, and apprehends the nescience which veils its nature. So Self is both manifested and nonmanifested in the experience. This fact does not contradict Self's self-manifestness.[53] This view appears to be an original view.

ĀTMAN AND AHAṀKĀRA.—The opponent of Advaitavāda contends that an object alone can be superimposed on another object, and that ego (ahaṁkāra), an object, cannot be supesimposed on the Self, which is the subject. The Inner Self (pratyagātman) is of the nature of the subject. Padmapāda urges that this contention is false, since the Inner Self is not absolutely nonobjective in that it is the object of 'I'-cognition. The opponent contends that the Self, the subject, cannot become an object, because an object is external and apprehended as 'this' whereas the Self is internal and of the nature of 'not-this', and that two contradictory parts—'this' and 'not-this', object and subject—cannot coexist in one partless Self. This contention is invalid since ego of the nature of 'this' and 'not-this'—object and subject—is known by all as 'I'-cognition.

Kumārila opines that the self is a conscious substance, that as a substance it is an object of knowledge, that as conscious it is a knower, and that therefore it is both knower and known—subject and object. Padmapāda urges that this view is wrong, for the self is partless and inactive. In Prabhākara's view, the apprehension of an object is self-manifest; it manifests an object as 'this' and manifests self as 'not-this', and makes the act of knowledge inferable from apprehension; so ego is not of the nature of 'this'. He identifies ego or 'I' with Self. Padmapāda asks him whether Self manifests consciousness and apprehension manifests an insentient object, or whether apprehension also manifests consciousness, or whether apprehension itself manifests consciousness and Self is insentient. The first alternative is not justifiable, since the world would not be manifested to consciousness, if an insentient entity were the result of a pramāṇa. Prabhākara may contend that the knower being conscious apprehension manifests an object as 'this' and self as 'not-this', and that therefore the world is not unmanifested to consciousness. This contention is false, since the assumption of Self of the nature of consciousness being manifested by the knowledge of an insentient obiect is irrational. If Self be said to be manifested by the result of the act knowledge, as the light of a lamp manifests both the lamp and an object, then there will be infinite regress of the act of knowledge. In the second alternative, Self itself is manifested or it depends upon the apprehension of an object to be manifested. If Self be not self-manifest, although it is of the nature of consciousness, what is the reason of its not being manifested? It is not reasonable to hold that Self, being of the nature of consciousness, does not directly manifest itself, but that it is indirectly manifested by another entity, viz., apprehension of an object. In the third alternative, Self itself must be admitted to be the manifestation of consciousness, since there is no proof for the existence of any other result besides this. So Self is self-manifest, pure consciousness, and insentient ego of the nature of 'not-this' is superimposed on Self, and falsely known as 'I'. Ego is the cause of the apprehension of an object.[54] The knot of ego is called 'I'. 'I'-cognition is both of the nature of 'this' and consciousness, for Self of the nature of consciousness is reflected in ego of the nature of 'this'. Self becomes like an insentient object metaphorically. So 'I'-cognition is of the nature of 'this' and consciousness. Insentient ego is 'this' and pure transcendental consciousness or Ātman is 'not-this'. Self-manifest Inner Self (pratyagātman) by Its greatness is directly manifested. It is neither an object of acceptance nor of rejection. But ego can be superimposed on It.[55] Ego (ahaṁkāre) with the reflection of Self or pure transcendental consciousness is a knower, an agent, and an enjoyer or a sufferer. Self is not so, for It is the foundational consciousness transcending duality and plurality, distinction of knower, known and knowledge, of agent, object of action, and action, of enjoyer, enjoyed and enjoyment. Self's agency (kartṛtva) is due to its reflection in an internal organ, and false like redness of a crystal wherein a red flower is reflected. Self related to ego appears to be a knower (pramātṛ), an agent, and an enjoyer or a sufferer (bhoktṛ). It is not really so.[56]

Vidyāraṇya avers that the internal organ or its mode, ego (ahaṁkāra), superimposed on Self reflected in it is manifested as 'I'-cognition (ahaṁpratyaya). In the illusion "this is silver" silver superimposed on 'this' is manifested. In a red-hot iron ball iron is manifested as fiery, thongh it is not really so. Here a fire endued with the power of burning and iron are manifested. Similarly, Self endued with the power of apprehending and the internal organ or ego are manifested in the experience 'I know'. Ego is the apprended part, which is insentient, mutable, of the nature of pain, and distinct from objects and sense-organs, and Self is the apprehending part, which is lovable, immutable, witness, and consciousness common to objects and sense-organs. So 'I'-cognition is of the nature of 'this' and 'not-this'. Ego is of the nature of 'this', and Self is of the nature of 'not-this'. There is no distinction between Self and apprehension. So ego cannot be identical with Self. Self-manifest apprehension being eternal is the nature of Self. Self itself is said to be apprehended with an object as a limiting adjunct.[57]

Beginningless indefinable avidyā is the material cause of ego. Avidyā as directed by Īśvara is its efficient cause. The power of knowledge and the power of action are its nature. Transcendental, unchanging consciousness is its proof (pramāṇa). Agency, enjoyerhood and the like are its objects. Ego is not manifested in deep sleep, for it is of the nature of dissolution of the internal organ of which ego is a mode. Both the internal organ and ego are dissolved in deep sleep.[58] The opponent of idealistic monism contends that Self being conscious is a knower without ego being superimposed on it. Vidyāraṇya urges that this contention is false, because Self being detached (asaṅga), inactive and incapable of producing knowledge is not the agent of knowing or a knower. So it cannot be an agent and an enjoyer also.[59]

SĀKṢIN.—The witness (śākṣin) is different from the empirical self (jīva) according to the Advaitavādins. Appyayadīkṣita states Vidyāraṇya's view of the witness as propounded by him in the section of 'Kūsṭathadīpa' in 'Pañcadaśi'. The unchanging, immutable consciousness (kūṭastha caitanya), the substratum of the subtle body and the gross body, which are its limiting adjuncts, is called the witness (sākṣin), since it is their immediate knower. In the world also one that is a neutral perceiver is called a witness. Though the modes of the empirical self manifest its subtle body and gross body, they are insentient modifications of the internal organ, and can therefore manifest them slightly with the aid of the immutable consciousness limited by the bodies, which moves towards them. But the bodies are manifested by the immutable consciousness always. The mental modes issue out of the internal organ occasionally, in which the kūṭastha caitanya is reflected, and manifest them slightly. When the mental modes cease to exist in deep sleep, the two bodies are manifested by the kūṭastha caitanya.[60] It may be objected, that the assumption of the kūṭastha caitanya as the witness is unnecessary, and that the empirical self may be regarded as the witness. The objection is invalid, because the empirical self is an agent of secular and religious actions and an experiencer of their fruits, and because for that reason it is not an indifferent spectator. The Śruti asserts the sākṣin to be an indifferent spectator, and not an active agent and an enjoyer or a sufferer. Vidyāraṇya compares the sāksin to a lamp on the stage of a theatre, which illumines the master, the audience, and the dancer, and which shines by itself in their absence also. The empirical self is the ego (ahaṁkāra) invested with the reflection of the universal consciousness, has the conceit of experiencing joys and sorrows from the objects perceived by it, and undergoes many changes. In deep sleep the ego-sense vanishes. So it cannot be the sākṣin. But the kūṭastha caitanya persists in deep sleep as the substratum of the illusion of the empirical self, which is the ego invested with the reflection of the universal consciousness. So it is the sākṣin of its subtle body and gross body. The sākṣin thus distinguished from the empirical self is not of the rank of God, since He, the creator, maintainer and destroyer of the world, cannot be indifferent and an immediate knower of buddhi and the like. He knows them indirectly through the medium of the empirical self.[61] 2. Brahman invested with attributes and associated with cosmic nescience cannot be said to be pure, detached, and devoid of attributes. So Citsukha considers the pure Brahman that is the Inner Self of all empirical selves, which is identical in them, to be the sāksin.[62] 3. Rāmādvaya, the author of the 'Vedānta Kaumudī', regards God, the approver of the empirical selves' voluntary acts for the fulfilment of desires and acts of renunciation of the objects of pleasure, and yet a neutral spectator of their actions, as the sākśin, because the Śruti asserts one God hidden in all creatures, the Inner Self of all beings, their abode, the governor of their actions and merits and demerits, ubiquitous, conscious, detached, and devoid of the guṇas, to be the sākṣin. The sākṣin immediately knows the nescience existing in the empirical self in deep sleep, when causes and effects cease to operate. In this state it is called the prājña. God is the witness of deep sleep, and of departure of the empirical self, and so different from it.[63] 4. The author of the 'Tattvasuddhi' thinks the sākṣin to belong to the rank of Brahman, though it is manifested to consciousness as belonging to the rank of the empirical self, as in the illusion "this is silver" 'this' is really a nacre, though it is manifested to consciousness as silver.[64] 5. According to some Advaitavādins the empirical self conditioned by nescience is the sākṣin, since it is the immediate knower or seer. In the world also one who is a nondoer and an immediate knower or seer is called a witness. The sākṣin is not a form of God, since there is no evidence to prove it. The empirical self conditioned by nescience is indifferent. It is detached, indifferent, and of the nature of knowledge or manifestation. Agency is attributed to it, because it errroneously identifies itself with the internal organ. But it is really indifferent and inactive.[65] 6. If all internal organs were manifested by one sākṣin without any difference, the different knowers would not be necessary. So some Advaitavādins regard an empirical self conditioned by an internal organ, a limiting condition, as the sākṣin. Thus there are different sākṣins in different empirical selves. One jīvasāksin is not related to the other jīvasāksins ; nor is it capable of being related to them, and, consequently, not manifested to them. In deep sleep also a sākṣin conditioned by an internal organ, which exists in a subtle state, exists. There is a difference between a sākṣin and a knower (pramātṛ). In deep sleep a knower qualified by an internal organ does not exist, but a sākṣin or empirical self conditioned by an internal organ exists. There is a difference between a limiting qualification (viśeṣaṇa) and a condition (upādhi). The former enters into the constitution of the object qualified by it, while the latter does not do so but simply distinguishes it from the other entities. Dharmarājādhvarīndra regards the universal consciousness limited by an internal organ as an empirical self, and the universal consciousness conditioned by an internal organ as a jīvaśākṣin. A qualification is connected with an effect, and distinguishes it from the other entities. A limiting condition is present, distinguishes the object conditioned by it from the other entities, but is not connected with it.[66] 7. In Madhusūdana Sarasvatī's view, Ātman exists in deep sleep as its witness. Of the knower, the means of knowlege, and the object of knowledge, some may be absent in the waking state, dream and deep sleep. But Ātman, the witness of the existence and non-existence of any of them, exists in these states. It may be objected that the empirical self, the knower, is a doer and an enjoyer or a sufferer, that it knows or manifests itself and other objects, and that it does not depend upon a witness as a jar and other objects do. Madhusūdana urges that the objection is invalid, since the knowing self is mutable, and, consequently, cannot be the witness of its changes, because a known object cannot be a knower, and because a knower undergoes change in that it is known, and maintains that the one immutable consciousness is the witness of all. It may be objected that the sākṣin cannot invariably be present in the waking state, dream and deep sleep, because it is limited by nescience, and because it is therefore destroyed. Puruṣottama urges that the sākṣin is distinguished by nescience. The immutable consciousness is the witness.[67]

THE KNOWER, THE MEANS OF KNOWLEDGE AND VALID KNOWLEDGE.—Śaṁkara opines that the knower (pramātṛ), the means of valid knowledge (pramāṇa), valid knowledge (pramā) and the object of valid knowledge (prameya) are due to the superimposition of self and not-self on each other, called avidyā.[68] The opponent contends that the Inner Self (pratyagātman) does not depend upon other causes to cognize Itself, since It is of the nature of manifestation, that It is independent of any other entity, and, so not vitiated by its faults, that It has no parts, and that, consequently, Its one part cannot be cognized by another part. It is further contended that because It cannot be cognized and non-cognized by Itself simultaneously, there can be no superimposition in Its self-manifestness. Vācaspati Miśra urges that the contention is false, because, though It is partless and non-objective because of Its self-luminosity, It appears to be limited by a subtle body, a gross body, manas, buddhi and the like imagined by the indefinable, beginningless nescience. Though It is really unlimited by them, It appears to be different from them; though It is nondifferent from them, It appears to be a doer and an enjoyer or a sufferer; though It is really a nondoer and a nonenjoyer or a nonsufferer, It appears to be an object of 'I'-consciousness, and to assume the nature of an empirical self (jīva). Buddhi and the like being indefinable, the difference between them is indefinable.[69] Ātman is pure universal consciousness, and not a knower. If there were no body, sense-organs, buddhi, ahaṁkara and the like, the detached Ātmam would not be a knower of valid knowledge. If there were no knower, a means of knowledge would not operate. Perception, inference and scriptural testimony are means of knowing empirical objects (prameya), effects of the avidyā. Vacaspati Miśra avers that a knower is an agent of valid knowledge. Knowerhood is independence. It moves all means of knowledge to act. A pramāṇa is an instrument of valid knowledge. The unchanging, eternal Ātman of the nature of pure consciousness Itself does not act. So it acquires a semblance of activity from buddhi and the like because of their superimposition on It, and moves a pramāṇa to act. The pramāṇas are the objects of Ātman conditioned by the nescience supervised by the empirical self (jīva). The jīva is the knower. The organs of knwledge cannot perform their functions without being guided by the jīvātman, the knower. The detached, inactive Ātman cannot guide them. Valid knowledge is a mode of the internal organ inclined towards an object of knowledge. It is the nature of consciousness in an agent of knowledge. But a mental mode cannot be of the nature of consciousness, if Ātman of the nature of pure consciousness is not superimposed on it, for the internal organ is unconscious. The Ātman cannot be an agent of valid knowledge, if the active internal organ is not superimposed on it. So, because of superimposition of Ātmam and the internal organ on each other, resultant valid knowledge abides in Ātman limited by the adjuncts of buddhi and ahaṁkāra.[70] A pramāṇa is an instrument of valid knowledge. An agent of valid knowledge is a knower. It moves all causes of knowledge to act. It cannot move them to act, if it has no activity. Ātman of the nature of pure consciousness, which is immutable and eternal, is not in itself active, and is devoid of modifications. Its activity is due to the adjuncts, intellect and egoism, which are active. It can preside over the instrument of knowledge because of its superimposed activity. The empirical self limited by avidyā is the abode of the pramāṇas. The knower is free in its activity in regard to valid knowledge.[71] An empirical self (jīva) limited by avidyā is the abode (āśraya) of valid knowledge. An empirical object—an indefinable appearance due to avidyā—is an object of valid knowledge. Amalānanda avers that valid knowledge is partly conscious and partly unconscious, because it is an unconscious mental mode on which conscious Ātman is superimposed, that therefore the abode of valid knowledge also must be partly conscious and partly unconscious, because the empirical self (jīvātman), Ātman limited by the unconscious internal organ, intellect and egoism, is the agent of valid knowledge, and that this is not possible without superimposition of Ātman and buddhi and the like on each other.[72]

Vidyāraṇya explains the knower, the means of knowledge, and knowledge by referring to the three parts of the antaḥkaraṇa, which manifest one consciousness or Ātman. The part of the internal organ limited by the body is called an agent. Its function (vṛtti) intervening between the body and the object is called an act, a mental act. Its mode capable of manifesting an object is the other part. The internal organ is very transparent, and so consciousness of Ātman is manisested in its three parts. The knower is the consciousness of Ātman manifested in the agent-part. The means of knowledge is the consciousness manifested in the activity-part. Knowledge is the consciousness manifested in the mental mode which cognizes an object. A form of the internal organ is common to its three parts, which are related to one another as the knower, the means of knowledge, and knowledge. There is superimposition of consciousness of Ātman and internal organ on each other, and so their properties are attributed to each other.[73] Thus there is no intermixture of a knower, a means of knowledge, and knowledge. The contention, that there cannot be a knower, because egoism is unconscious, and because Ātman is unmodifiable, is invalid, since a knower is modifiable egoism qualified by the manifestation of consciousness.[74] The internal organ, the limiting adjunct of Ātman, is tinged by an object. If it is not tinged by an object, Ātman cannot manifest it, even as the light of a lamp can illumine an object with which it comes into contact.[75]

THE AGENT AND THE ENJOYER.—According to Vācaspati Miśra, though Ātman is a mass of pure consciousness and bliss, devoid of agency and nature of an enjoyer, and transcendent of all appearances due to avidyā, It appears to be an agent and an experiencer of pleasure, pain, grief and delusion because of Its being limited by the internal organ and egoism, and an object of 'I'-consciousness.[76] It is the one Inner Self (pratyagātman). The pratyagātman limited by the internal organ of the nature of 'this' and 'not-this' is an agent and an enjoyer, the abode of twofold avidyā, the object of 'I'-consciousness, the bound jīvātman due to the superimposition of Self and not-self on each other. The superimposition is beginningless. It is beginningless false knowledge, which is indefinable.[77] The empirical self (jīvātman) is the experiencer of all evils.[78]

Agency, etc., of the empirical self (jīva) cannot be inferred, since they are known immediately. Nor are they perceived through the external sense-organs, since the jīva, their substrate, is not their object. They are not perceived through the mind (manas), for there is no evidence to prove it. The double method of agreement proves the manas to be the material cause of agency of action and the like. It cannot prove that the activity of the manas is the cause of the activity of Ātman Itself, because it is doubltful. It is not determined whether nonmanifestation of activity in deep sleep is due to the nonexistence of the manas or due to the nonexistence of activity itself. Agency, etc., of the jīva are known by the witness-self, though they are ontologically false. The sākṣin is the knower of both truth and falsehood.[79] So the transcendent Brahman can be the Ātman of the empirical self with the empirical qualities of doerhood, enjoyerhood and the like.[80]

The Buddhists and the earlier Prābhākaras opine that agency of action, enjoyerhood, love, hate, pleasure, pain, etc., in the self are self-manifest. Vidyāraṇya refutes this view, and adduces the following arguments against it. If agency and the like are a substance or self, it is more rational to consider self to be self-luminous than to assume them to be so, since it does not violate the law of parsimony. If they are qualities, they cannot have the quality of self-luminosity, for a quality has no other quality. If agency and the like are the quality of self-manifestness, they cannot be produced as abiding in their substrate or self, like the light of the sun. They can be manifested in relation to the manifestation of the permanent self. It may be contended that agency and the like are true, for they are known by the witness-self (sāksin). This contention is false, because the sākṣin immediately knows both valid knowledge and invalid knowledge, and is neutral to the truth and falsity of the object of knowledge. If agency and the like are assumed to be true, the Śruti asserting Ātman to be detached is contradicted. So they are not self-manifest and true.[81]

THE EMPIRICAL SELF (JĪVA).—Vācaspati Miśra conceives of the jīva or jīvātman as Inner Self limited by the internal organ, buddhi and ahaṁkāra of the nature of 'this' and 'not-this', which is a conscious agent and experiencer of pleasure, pain and the like, which is the object of 'I'-consciousness, and which is bound.[82] Inner Self (pratyagātman) is one, a mass of pure consciousness and bliss, transcendent of phenomenal appearances, and devoid of agency of action and experience of pleasure and pain. It is not a knower, doer, and enjoyer, and not bound. Because Ātman of the nature of pure consciousness, though self-luminous, cannot distinguish Itself from Its limiting adjuncts, buddhi, ahaṁkara and the like because of superimposition of them on each other, It assumes the nature of an empirical self (jīva).[83] Ātman limited by the internal organ, buddhi and ahaṁkara is a knower, a doer, and an enjoyer or a sufferer, though the limiting adjuncts are not conscious. It is an object of 'I'-consciousness (ahaṁpratyaya). Though the jīva is not an object of knowledge, because it is self-luminous and of the nature of consciousness, it is an object of 'I'-consciousness as limited by the adjuncts.[84] Ātman of the nature of pure consciousness is self-luminous and realized by immediate experience. If It were not self-luminous, the world appearance would not be manifested, and there would be no practical life. The jīva divested of its limiting adjuncts—antaḥkaraṇa, buddhi and ahaṁkara—is Brahman.[85]

STATES OF AN EMPIRICAL SELF.—Dharmarājādhvarīndra describes the states of the jīva in the following manner. The waking state is the state of the cognitions produced by the external sense-organs. In the other states they become inoperative. The cognitions produced by the external sense-organs are modes of the internal organ. The universal consciousness, the only reality, is beginningless and eternal. Knowledge or cognition is not eternal. It is a mode of the internal organ modified into the form of an object. The state of dream is the state of the modes of the internal organ apprehending objects, but not produced by the external sense-organs. In order to exclude the waking state, the dream state is defined as not produced by the external sense-organs. In order to exclude deep sleep, dream is defined as a mode of the internal organ. Deep sleep is dreamless, in which there is no mode of the internal organ. Deep sleep is a mode of the nescience, which apprehends the nescience. In this state the internal organ is merged in the nescience, and so has no mode ; but the nescience has a mode which apprehends it. In the waking state and dream the mode in regard to the nescience is a mode of the internal organ, and not a mode of the nescience. So these two states are not covered by the definition of deep sleep. Some Advaitins state swoon and death as two other states of the jīva. Others include them in deep sleep.[86]

Mahādeva Sarasvatī gives the following account of the five states of an empirical self. The waking state is the apprehension of external objects (e.g., sounds) with the external sense-organs when the merits and demerits, which are the causes of pleasures and pains in this state, operate. In the state of dream the aforesaid merits and demerits cease to operate, and the external sense-organs cease to function. Dream is the state of the cognitions, which apprehend the objects arising from the residual impressions of the waking apprehensions. In deep sleep the merits and demerits, which are the causes of pleasures and pains both in the waking state and in dream, become inoperative, and particular cognitions cease because of the cessation of the jīva's conceit in the gross body and the subtle body, but the buddhi exists in a causal state in the form of the cessation of all particular cognitions. In deep sleep the internal organ merges in the nescience. Swoon is the state of the cessation of particular cognitions due to dejection consequent on a strike by a club and the like. Death is the state of mergence of the external sense-organs and the internal organs in the nescience due to the cessation of the merits and demerits, which were the causes of pleasures and pains in this birth, and the consequent cessation of the jīva's conceit in the gross body and the subtle body until it assumes another body in a future birth. Mahādeva Sarasvatī avers that dream is not a recollection but an internal illusion with a condition. It is a false perception. The internal organ tainted with the flaw of sleep and invested with the residual impressions of the objects and the sense-organs is modified into a chariot and other objects, and into the apprehending sense-organs, and into the mental modes in the form of the objects. Mahādevānanda avers that buddhi remains in the state of causal nescience in deep sleep while in trance the internal organ remains in its nature in waking state, although in both there is the cessation of particular cognitions.[87]

JIVA—THEORY OE SEMBLANCE (ĀBHĀSAVADA).—Sureśvara is an advocate of the theory of semblance. The Self (ātman) being conditioned by the root nescience (ajñāna), and attaining identification with the nescience is called the witness-self, the Inner Controller and the cause of the universe, because it cannot distinguish itself from its semblance (cidābhāsa) in the nescience. The Self being conditioned by the buddhi, and being identified with it is the empirical self, a doer, an enjoyer or a sufferer, and a knower, because it cannot distinguish itself from its semblance in the buddhi. Because the buddhi in each body is distinct, the semblance of the Self in it is distinct. So the Self which is not distinguished from the semblance in each intellect (buddhi) appears to be distinct. On the other hand, the nescience in all places being devoid of distinctness, there is no distinctness in the semblance of the Self in it. So the witness-self contained in it and not distinguished from it never appears to be distinct. This is the distinction between the semblance of the Self and the Witness-self. It may be objected that the Self or pure consciousness is free, that a semblance of the Self (cidābhāsa) is bound, that bondage and liberation subsist in different subtrates, and that one exerts oneself to bring about one's own destruction in that the Self is assumed to be bound by its semblance. This objection is unsound, since bondage means that the Self has a semblance, and since liberation means that the semblance has ceased to exist. This view is called the theory of semblance. Madhusūdana Sarasvatī states the view in this manner. It should be noted here that the pure Self is not identified with the root nescience, but that the semblance of the Self conditioned by the nescience is identified with the limitation, and that the semblance of the Self in the intellect is identified with the limiting adjunct, the intellect, since it cannot distinguish between the pure Self and its semblance limited by the intellect. The reflections are absolutely false according to the theory of semblance.[88]

JIVA—THEORY OF LIMITATION (AVACCHEDAVĀDA).—According to Vācaspati Miśra, the universal consciousness, which is the object (viṣaya) of nescience, is Īśvara, and the same consciousness, which is the abode (āśraya) of nescience is an empirical self. He admits many nesciences, which abide in many jīvas. Many individual souls are the abodes of many individual nesciences (tulāvidyā). But one Īśvara is the object of all nesciences. The world appearances differ in different individual souls because of their different nesciences. An individual soul itself as conditioned or limited by its nescience is the material cause of its world appearance. The individual souls recognize the world appearance to be the same owing to great similarity among their world appearances. Īśvara is figuratively said to be the cause of the universe for He is the substratum of the nesciences, the individual souls, and the world appearances. This account of the theory of limitation is given by Madhusūdana Sarasvatī.[89] The jīvas are limitations (avaccheda) of the pure Self by the individual nesciences. They are the creators of their different world appearances.[90] There is no transubjective common world appearance. Dharmarājādharīndra defines a jīva as universal consciousness limited by an internal organ according to the theory of limitation.[91]

JIVA—THEORY OF REFLECTION (PRATIBIMBAVĀDA).—Prakāśātman is an exponent of the theory of reflection. According to him, the universal consciousness, the prototype, conditioned by the root nescience is Īśvara, the Ruler of the universe, or Lord, and the same consciousness reflected in the nescience limited by the internal organ and the impressions and potencies in it is an empirical self. The reflections are real like the prototype. Prakāśātman was the author of the 'Pañcapādikāvivaraṇa' and called Vivaraṇakāra. Madhūsūdana Sarasvatī gives the account mentioned above.[92] Dharmarajādhvarīndra refers to the theory of reflection. The universal consciousness common to Īśvara and a jīva is the prototype. Īśvara-consciousness is its reflection in the māyā of the nature of nescience. Jīva-consciousness is its reflection in the internal organs. The former is like a reflection of the sun in the water of a tank. The latter is like a reflection of the sun in the water in a vessel. Īśvara is pervasive because the causal nescience, the adjunct, is pervasive. The jīvas are limited for the internal organs, the adjuncts, are limited. This theory is open to the objection that the flaws of the causal nescience, the adjunct, e.g., nonomniscience, etc., taint Īśvara, as a mirror, an adjunct, taints the reflection of a face on it with its dirtiness.[93]

So some Advaitists maintain that there is one universal consciousness (caitanya), that when it becomes the prototype it is called Īśvara-consciousness, and that when it is reflected in an adjunct its reflection is called jīva-consciousness. In the theory of one soul the nescience is the adjunct in which Īśvara-consciousness is reflected. In the theory of many souls many internal organs are the adjuncts in which Īśvara-consciousness is reflected. The distinction between Īśvara and a jīva is due to the distinction between the nescience and the internal organs in the latter theory. The defects of the adjuncts taint the reflections of Īśvara in them, but they cannot taint Īśvara, the prototype, since the adjuncts are found to taint the reflections alone on them. The distinction between Īśvara and a jiva, in this view, is like that between the sun and its reflection in water.

An objection is raised against the theory of reflection that Īśvara-consciouness does not exist in the internal organ in which it is reflected, even as a face does not exist in a mirror in which it is reflected, and that therefore Īśvara cannot be the Inner Controller in all souls. This objection is unsound, because though a limited prototype (e.g., a face) is not related to its adjunct (e.g., a mirror) wherein it is reflected, the pervasive ether reflected with its clouds and stars in water is related to water wherein it is reflected. Similarly, the unlimited universal consciousness is related to an internal organ wherein it is reflected. So Īśvara can exist as the Inner Controller in all souls. It is furthur objected that colourless Brahman cannot be reflected in an internal organ, for a coloured entity alone is found to be reflected in a transparent medium. This objection is invalid, for colour, which is colourless, is reflected. Colour is an attribute. An attribute is devoid of attributes. It is objected that a colourless substance can have no reflection. This objection is irrelevant, as Brahman or Ātman is not a substance. The Śruti says, "One Self appears to be many souls like the reflections of the moon in water." It contradicts the inference of the absence of a reflection from Brahman or Ātman.[94]

According to some followers of Prakāśātman, Īśvara is the prototype and a jīva is a reflection of Īśvara in the nescience. Īśvara being the the prototype is independent and a jīva being a reflection is dependent on Īśvara. The Smṛti says, "When the nescience will be absolutely destroyed, which creates all distinctions, who will make the unreal distinction between the self and Brahman ?" It implies that one and the same nescience is the adjunct of a jīva and Īśvara. So Īśvara is the prototype and a jīva is a reflection of Īśvara in the nescience. According to this view, Īśvara is not a reflection of the universal consciousness (cit) on the primordial nescience, but the prototype of a reflection on it.[95]

In Raṅgojī Bhaṭṭa's view, the empirical self is of the nature of consciousness, the witness of waking state, dream and deep sleep, distinct from the mind-body-complex. It is self-manifest, but not an object of consciousness. It is of the nature of bliss. Liberation is its highest good, because bliss constitutes its nature. It is the nature of bliss, because it is the object of supreme love. If joy were its attribute inhering in it, the self would not be the object of its supreme love. In release there can be no produced bliss. So bliss is the nature of the Self. Its bondage is due to egoism (ahaṁkāra). The empirical self of the nature of being, knowledge and bliss, the witness of the internal organ, is a reflection of Īśvara in the internal organ, a product of nescience.[96] Nescience, a positive entity, of the nature of sattva, rajas and tamas, is the adjunct of the reflection. This view is testified by the Śruti and supported by reasoning.[97] Endowed with egoism, the empirical self, is denoted by the word ‘thou' in the Śruti "That thou art" in a primary sense, but freed of egoism it is implied by the word 'thou' in a secondary sense.

Madhusūdana Sarasvatī states Sarvajñātman's view. The universal consciousness reflected in the premordial nescience is Īśvara ; the same consciousness reflected in the buddhi is an empirical self, and the same consciousness, conditioned by the nescience is the pure consciousness—the prototype (bimba). In both the views of Prakāśātman and Sarvajñātman, the plurality of the jīvas is due to the plurality of the buddhis. This view is the theory of reflection.[98] Appyayadīkṣita gives the following account of Sarvajñātman's view. Īśvara is the reflection of the universal consciousness (cit) in causal nescience, and a jīva is a reflection of the same consciousness in an internal organ (antaḥkaraṇa), which is an effect of casual nescience. The Śruti says, "The cause-nescience is the limiting adjunct of Īśvara, and the effect-nescience is the limiting adjunct of a jīva". An objection is raised against the theory of limitation, according to which, a jīva is the universal consciousness limited by an internal organ, as jar-ether is ether limited by a jar. In this theory, the region of the universal consciousness limited by a jīva in the next world differs from the region of it in this world. So there will be loss of earned merits and demerits and accrual of unearned fruits. But in the theory of reflection, the reflection of the pure Self in an internal organ does not differ in this world and in the next world. The internal organ remains the same in both worlds. The pure Self, the prototype (bimba), is attained by the liberated soul when the internal organ, the limiting adjunct, is destroyed.[99]

According to the author of the 'Prakaṭārthavivaraṇa' Īśvara is the reflection of the universal consciousness in māyā, which is the beginingless, indescribable origin of the physical elements, and which is related to the universal consciousness alone. The reflections of the universal consciousness in the nesciences possessed of the power of veiling and the power of projecting in innumerable limited regions of the māyā are the jīvas. Māyā is the primordial cosmic nescience. Avidyā is an individual nescience, a limited part of māyā. Īśvara is a reflection of universal consciousness or pure Self in māyā. A jīva is a reflection of pure Self in an individual nescience (avidyā). Appayadīkṣita gives this account of the aforesaid view.[100]

According to Vidyāraṇya māyā is of the nature of sattva, rajas and tamas, in which pure sattva unovercome by rajas and tamas predominates, and impure sattva overcome by rajas and tamas predominates in nescience (avidyā). Māyā and avidyā are two forms of the same entity. Īśvara is a reflection of the pure Self or universal consciousness in māyā. An individual soul is a reflection of the pure Self in nescience. One and the same root prakṛti is called māyā owing to the predominance of the power of projecting diverse appearances, and it is called nescience because of the predominance of the power of veiling the consciousness and bliss of the pure Self. Māyā is the adjunct of Īśvara. Nescience is the adjunct of a jīva. Though the root prakṛti is related to the pure Self alone, common to Īśvara and the individual souls, an individual soul alone has apprehension of nescience in the form 'I am ignorant', but Īśvara has no expérience of any relation to nescience. So the distinction between Īśvara and a jīva is established.[101]

Prakāśātman offers the following criticism of Vācaspati Miśra's doctrine of limitation. If Brahman were limited by nescience or an internal organ—an adjnnct, as ether is limited by a jar, Brahman being entirely limited in the state of a jiva, the unlimited Brahman would exist outside the jīvas, and would not be ubiquitous and controller of all, because the unlimited Brahman cannot exist in the limiting adjuncts by reduplicating Itself. It is contended that Brahman is immanent in all, and controls all, by Its nature, and not as existing outside all. This contention is false, because the Śruti asserts that is Brahman separate from the jīvas and enters into the mutations in proximity to the jīvas.

But, according to the doctrine of reflection, the jīva is a reflection of Brahman in nescience, or in an internal organ. Though ether (ākāśa) exists in water, ether in the reflection of the moon in water is perceived. So in the reflection of the moon both ether in water and ether in the reflection are perceived to exist. So ether reduplicates itself in the reflection. Similarly, ubiquitous Brahman exists outside and inside the jīvas, and controls them. There is no need of assuming that Brahman reduplieates Itself in the jīvas in order to control them. So the doctrine of refleetion is better than that of limitation.[102]

EKAJĪVAVĀDA : ONE SOUL IN ONE BODY.—Appyayadīkṣita states the doctrine of one soul thus. According to some Advaitavādins there is one soul with one body, and the other bodies are devoid of souls, like the bodies perceived in dream, and the entire world is imagined by the one soul, and its empirical life endures so long as its nescience endures. The soul being one, there is no real difference between bondage and release. The difference between a bound soul and a released soul is like one perceived in dream.[103] Mahādevānanda states the doctrine of one jīva as follows. Some Advaitavādins regard nescience as the limiting adjunct of a jīva. Nescience is one. So a jīva reflected in it is one. Bādarāyaṇa speaks of one semblance. So there is one jīva limited by one nescience. It is objected that if there is one jīva, there cannot be a distinction between bondage and release. The advocate of one soul replies that though there is one jīva, there are many knowers limited by many internal organs. A knower who has not yet acquired the saving knowledge is bound. Another knower who has acquired the saving knowledge is liberated. What is liberation? It is indeed the cessation of nescience, which includes the cessation of all effects of nescience, or of all false cognitions. Because causal or cosmic nescience continues, other illusory cognitions may be produced again. The destruction of some false cognitions is not the cessation of nescience. It may be argued that nescience is the power of veiling (āvaraṇaśakti), and that therefore a knower, that has acquired the knowledge of Brahman, is liberated, since his nescience, the cause of his bondage, is destroyed, and that a knower, that has not acquired the saving knowledge, is bound. This argument involves the assumption of many jīvas. It assumes that there are many nesciences, that they are the causes of bondage, and that there are therefore many jīvas. If there are not many jīvas, there cannot be a distinction between a bound soul and a released soul. It may be argued that release is the cessation of the root nescience (mūlāvidyā). This argument is invalid, since if the root nescience were destroyed, all souls would be released simultaneously. It is objected that if there be one soul, there cannot be a preceptor, who has acquired the knowledge of Brahman, and who can instruct an aspirant after release, and that consequently a bound soul can never be released. Further, if there be one soul, there cannot be a distinction between a soul eligible for the way of works and a soul eligible for the way of knowledge, which is made by the Advaitavāda. So the doctrine that nescience is one and that a jīva is one is unreasonable. Mahādevānanda replies that the Śruti speaks of one nescience, and the Smṛti speaks of one māyā of God, and of knowledge being veiled by nescience. So nescience is one and jīva limited by it is one. The distinction between bondage and release is imagined like one in dream.[104] Raṅgojī Bhaṭṭa gives a similar account of ekajīvavāda. The positive nescience being one, the reflection of Brahman in it or the jīva is one. It accounts for bondage and release by admitting difference among knowers (pramātṛ) limited by many internal organs (antaḥkaraṇa). The part of the nescience, which is the material cause of the internal organ, is destroyed through which a knower acquires the immediate experience of Brahman, and that knower is released, but the other knowers limited by the other internal organs are not released. The scriptures assert the embodied release of some souls. In order to conform with this scriptural testimony many parts of nescience have to be admitted. But the admission of many parts of nescience does not require that of many nesciences. Or, the Ekajīvavādins account for bondage and release in another way. The part of the power of veiling (āvaraṇaśakti) in the nescience is destroyed by the experience of Brahman, but the part of projecting the diverse world appearance (vikṣepaśakti) in the nescience is not destroyed by it, because prārabdha karmas hinder its destruction. So the admission of parts of the nescience is unavoidable. The objection, that if there were one soul, it would experience the pleasures and pains produced by other bodies, is invalid, because the pleasures and pains produced in an internal organ or mind are experienced by the knower limited by the internal organ. So the experience of pleasures and pains in different knowers depends upon the difference in the internal organs.[105]

Madhusūdana Sarasvatī advocates the doctrines of one soul and dṛṣṭisṛṣṭi. The one soul overcome by nescience is both the material cause and efficient cause of the world. All perceived objects are mere experiences. The illusion of different souls is due to the difference of bodies. The one soul is said to be released from bondage by acquiring the immediate knowledge of Brahman after listening to the scripture, reflection and meditation. The teacher from whom the person hears the scripture is imagined by him. The Śruti about

Śukadeva's release is mere eulogy. The word 'That' in the text "That thou art" implies the universal consciousness unconditioned by the nescience. Puruṣottama avers that one soul imagines many souls and objects in the waking state as it imagines them in dream. Desire, resolution, doubt and the like are modes of the insentient internal organ. There are many internal organs. So the one soul may imagine many souls and objects with the aid of the internal organs. In Madhusūdana's view, the distinction of soul and God is a creation of the one soul's buddhi. So the knowledge of nondual Brahman cannot be said to be annulled by the knowledge of duality. Madhusūdana Sarasvatī advocates the doctrine of Dṛṣṭisṛṣṭi which necessarily follows from it.[106]

EKAJĪVAVĀDA : ONE SOUL IN MANY BODIES.—Some Advaitavādins are not convinced of the truth of the aforesaid view because of its conflict with Bādarāyāṇa's aphorisms "God is the creator of the world" and "God is greater than a soul", and believe in one soul in many bodies. Hiraṇyagarbha is the principal jīva, a reflection of Brahman, and the other jīvas are the reflections of Hiraṇyagarbha like pictures painted in a scene, and enjoy empirical life of bondage and release in different bodies.[107] This view is open to the objections that there are different Hiraṇyagarbhas in different cycles of creatian, and that there is nothing to regulate which of them is the principal jīva of whom the other jīvas are reflections. So some Advaitavādins maintain that one jīva dwells in all bodies without any distinction, as a yogin creates many bodies and enjoys different kinds of pleasure through them by dint of his occult power due to meditation in the same way as he can perceive distant and hidden objects. This view is open to the objection that different bodies alone are not the causes of the different souls' experiences of different kinds of pleasures, but also their special merits. We cannot perceive distant and hidden objects because of the absence of special merit due to meditation. Yoga means the special merit produced by repeated meditation.[108]

THE DOCTRINE OF MANY JĪVAS.—The doctrine of one soul in many bodies cannot satisfactorily account for bondage and release. So some Advaitavādins believe in many jīvas. They are Brahman conditioned by many internal organs, which are the limiting adjuncts. An internal organ is produced by a nescience of a soul, and limits Brahman. So long as the nescience is not destroyed, the soul remains in bondage. When the nescience is destroyed, its effect—the internal organ, is destroyed, and the soul is liberated. So there are many souls.[109] Mahādevānanda adduces the following arguments of some Advaitists in favour of many jīvas. In some Advaitavādins' view, an internal organ is the limiting adjunct of a jīva, since an empirical self qualified by an internal organ is experienced to be an agent of action and subject to bondage, and since an effect is said to be the adjunct of a jīva. So an internal organ is the limiting adjunct of a jīva. This view is open to the objection that an internal organ, being an effect of nescience, is not independent, and consequently cannot distinguish between the Ātman and a jīva. So an internal organ is not the limiting adjunct of a jīva. But nescience is its limiting adjunct, since it is independent of an internal organ. There are many nesciences, and the jīvas are many, being reflected in many nesciences. The nesciences being limited, the jīvas also reflected in them are limited and distinct from one another. So their experiences of the fruits of their actions cannot be intermixed with one another. So there are many jīvas. Some Advaitavādins believe in many jīvas reflected in many nesciences with predominance of impure sattva.[110] Dharmarājādhvarīndra avers that one universal consciousness, as archetype, is Īśvara-consciousness, while as a reflection it is Jīva-consciousness, and that one nescience is the limiting medium of Īśvara's reflection in the doctrine of one soul while internal organs are the media of reflections of Īśvara in the doctrine of many souls.[111]

DOCTRINE OF DṚṢṬISṚṢṬI.—In some Advaitavādins' view, the objects of experience are created at the moment when they are perceived, and they do not exist before they are perceived. They are like the objects perceived in dream.[112] It is objected that there is no being, who imagines the entire empirical world of waking experience. The imaginer is either the unconditioned Ātman or the Ātman conditioned by nescience. The first alternative is not tenable, because in the state of release also the empirical world will continue because of the existence of the imaginer independent of any other condition, and because there will be no distinction between bondage and release. Nor is the second alternative tenable, because nescience being imagined, the imaginer will exist even before the imagination of nescience. In regard to this some Advaitavādins maintain that a being conditioned by a prior imagined nescience is the imaginer of the succeeding nescience, and that a series of imaginers imagining nesciences does not involve a vicious infinite, because the first imaginer is flawless. The world is created by one imaginer who imagines it.[113]

Prakāśānanda adduces the following arguments for the doctrine of Dṛṣṭisṛṣṭi. There is no evidence to prove the difference between cognitions and cognized objects. The world is known as mere experience, as in dream mere cognitions appear as cognitions and cognized objects. Similarly, the world is mere cognition. The moving and unmoving things of the world are mere experience of the Ātman. As a rope wrongly appears to be a serpent, so the Ātman or Brahman wrongly appears to be the world. The entire world with its reality is mere experience in the Ātman. It emerges, exists, and perishes again and again. The world is mere perception like reflections in the pure Ātman of the nature of supreme bliss devoid of sins and blemishes. It is said, "All perceptions of objects are reflected in the mirror of universal consciousness (cit) as the trees on the bank of a tank are reflected in its water". The world is the imaginary play of the Ātman and of the nature of perception.[114] Appyayadīkṣita states Prakāśānanda's view thus. Brahman's perception creates the world, since there is no proof for the difference of the perceived objects from the perceptions of them. The wise regard the world as of the nature of cognitions. The deluded persons erroneously think it to be of the nature of objects.[115]

UBIQUITOUS SOULS HAVE DIFFERENT EXPERIENCES.—It is objected that the Ātman being ubiquitous according to the Advaita Vedāntin he cannot account for different souls' experiences of joys and sorrows. Vidyāranya refutes this objection. He asks the opponent the meaning of his objection. Does he mean that when one person experiences pleasure, pain, etc., all others experience them because the consciousness of persons is one ? Or, does he mean that when a person perceives a jar, he perceives the entire world because his consciousness is ubiquitous ? The first alternative is untenable, because according to the Advaita Vedāntin consciousness alone is not the cause of the perception of an object, because it is veiled by avidyā, but consciousness manifested by a mode of the internal organ is the cause of perception. There are different internal organs in different persons. So there is no intermixture of the experiences of different persons. The second alternative also is inadmissible, since the internal organ of a person limited to him is not simultaneously related to the entire world, and because for that reason the consciousness manifested by its mode cannot make him perceive the entire world. It is contended that though the internal organ is limited, its mode may be all-pervading, like a ray of the limited sun. This contention is false, because the eyes, the ears, etc., modifications of the internal organ, are restricted to their proper objects in that merits and demerits, the cause of the modifications of an internal organ, can produce specific effects.[116] The opponent raises the following objection. Is the adjunct of an internal organ assumed in order to account for consciousness (caitanya) being tinged by an object, since consciousness being detached is by itself not tinged by an object? Or, is the adjunct of an internal organ assumed to account for the manifestation of an object, though consciousness is tinged by an object? The first alternative is untenable, because consciousness being detached cannot be tinged by an object even being limited by the adjunct of the internal organ. The second alternative also is inadmissible, since consciousness being related to an object can manifest it, the adjunct of the internal organ being needless. When the soul's internal organ, the adjunt, is destroyed, the ubiquitous consciousness being related to all objectes simultaneously can manifest them all. Vidyāraṇya refutes the objection in the following manner. The consciousness of the jīva being detached is not attached to other objects, but is by nature attached to the internal organ, as the genus of the cow, though all-pervading, is related to an individual cow endued with a dewlap and the like, but not to an individual horse or the like, or as a ray a light, though pervasive, manifests colour, and not taste, or odour. Similarly, the adjunct of the internal organ brings about the tinging of consciousness by an object.[117] If consciousness is not tinged by an object, the manifestation of consciousness cannot manifest objects, as the light of a lamp manifests an object with which it is connected. Brahman, being the material cause of the world, manifests it, which is nondifferent from Brahman, without being tinged by it through an adjnuct. But the jīva cannot manifest the world, since it is not the material cause of the world. Hence, though the detached witness-consciousness unveiled by avidyā is the jīva, it can manifest an object through a mode of the internal organ. The necessity of a mode of the inernal organ has been discussed elsewhere.[118]

A soul being a reflection of Brahman in an internal organ, which is its limiting adjunct, can manifest an object through the internal organ. Different souls are different reflections of Brahman in different internal organs, and perceive different objects through them. Though the apprehension of an object be of the nature of Brahman-consciousness, it is not in conflict with its being of the nature of the jīva-consciousness, because a mode of the internal organ, the adjunct of the jīva, does not pervade an object, and is not manifested. Though Brahman is related to the internal organ, the jīva has not always the knowledge of Brahman because of the absence of a mode of the internal organ modified into the form of Brahman. The mere nature of the internal organ does not manifest an object, but its modification into the form of the object manifests it. Otherwise, the properties of the internal organ also would be manifested. The jīva also is manifested in the internal organ modified into the form of the jīva as a mode of egoism, and not in the mere nature of the internal organ. The jīva is not apprehended in deep sleep owing to the absence of a mode of egoism. Hence the jīvas being reflections of Brahman in the internal organs can account for their experiences being limited to themselves and not being intermixed with one another in ubiquitous Brahman-consciousness.

The Advaita Vedāntists, who regard the jīvas as limitations of Brahman by the internal organs, can account for the limitation of their experiences to themselves because of the veiling power of the internal organs. They are the effects of avidyā. An effect has the power of veiling its material cause. A scorpion is an effect of cow-dung, and can veil the latter. The latter is not found in the former. A tree is an effect of earth, and can veil the latter. The latter is not found in the former. So the experieuces of the different souls are not intermixed with one another.[119]

BRAHMAN, ĪŚVARA AND JĪVA.—According to Vācaspati Miśra the empirical self (jīva) is Inner Ātman or Brahman limited by the internal organ, intellect and egoism, the abode of avidyā of two kinds, a conscious doer and enjoyer.[120] He advocates the theory of limitation (avaccheda). The jīva devoid of the limiting adjuncts is Brahman of the natnre of eternal pure consciousness.[121] Brahman is self-luminous light of consciousness devoid of all limiting adjuncts. Pure Ātman is the sākṣin of Its limited form—the jīva.[122] Īśvara is Brahman limited by avidyā, and omniscient and omnipotent. He is the cause of the world. Etenality, purity, consciousness, and freedom are the essential form of Brahman, not due to limiting adjuncts.[123] But omniscience and omnipotence are the adventitious form of Brahman due to the limiting adjunct (avidyā). Īśvara's omniscience and omnipotence are due to the beginningless avidyā.[124] He is the source of the Vedas. Īśvara is "all-acting, all-desiring, all-tasting, all-smelling". These determinate qualities are due to the limiting adjuncts, and are superimposed on Brahman.[125] Brahman is indeterminate, uniform, homogeneous consciousness and existence. Its determinate qualities are really indetermitate, but are attributed to It because of its limiting adjuncts.[126] Īśvara is Brahman limited by avidyā, and has determinate qualities. Brahman is indeterminate and attributeless. The determinate form of Īśvara is superimposed on Brahman because of the limiting adjuncts for meditation or prayer.[127] Omniscient and omnipotent Īśvara is the creator of the world, which is an effect limited by objects in the nature of names and forms or appearances, that are neither real nor unreal but indefinable, and that are, in reality, unlimited, indeterminate Brahman.[128] Īśvara is omniscienct because He is bodyless, and because there is no obstacle to His knowledge. He is omnipotent because there is no obstruction to His activity. He is not subject to bondage. But the jīva has a body-mind-complex, and is subject to bondage. So its knowledge, though eternal, is obstrueted by avidyā, which is the cause of its body. It has limited knowledge and power of activity. Īśvara is devoid of avidyā, body, and bondage.[129] Because the jīva is embodied and limited by antaḥkaraṇa, buddhi and ahaṁkāra due to avidyā, it undergoes transmigration and suffers. Its innate omniscience and omnipotence are concealed by its false identification of itself with its body.[130]

In Vidyāraṇya's view, Īśvara is a reflection of Brahman is cosmic nescience (māyā) abounding in pure sattva while a jīva is a reflection of Brahman in individual nescience (avidyā) abounding in impure sattva. Brahman is pure consciousness, being and bliss, neither knower or known, inactive, and detached, while Īśvara is the omniscient, omnipotent, creator, maintainer and destroyer of the world, Inner Controller, and Moral Governor. Īśvara endowed with māyā creates the world. Creation is imagined by Īśvara.[131] In Dharmarājādhvarīndra's view, Īśvara is Brahman limited by māyā while Īśvarasākṣin, Divine Witness, is Brahman conditioned by māyā. Māyā is a limiting adjunct (upādhi) of Īśvarasākṣin, which does not enter into the nature of the latter, while māyā is an attributive (viśeṣaṇa) of Īśvara and enters into His nature and qualifies Him. Thus he represents the view of the theory of limitation. Īśvara is a reflection of Brahman in māyā while a jīva is a a reflection of Brahman in an internal organ according to the theory of reflection. Māyā being pervasive, Īśvara reflected in it is ubiquitous while an internal organ being limited, a jīva reflected in it is limited.[132] According to Mahādevānda, Īśvara is a reflection of Brahman in māyā wherein the power of projecting appearances (vikṣepa) predominates, while a jīva is a reflection of Brahman in avidyā wherein the power of veiling (āvaraṇa) predominates. Brahman conditioned by avidyā is Īśvara while Brahman reflected in avidyā is a jīva.[133] In Sadānanda's view, Brahman conditioned by collective nescience is called Īśvara Who is omniscient, omnipotent creator and governor of the world and Inner Controller.[134] According to Sarvajñātman, Īśvara is a reflection of Brahman in casual māyā while a jīva is a reflection of Brahman in an interual organ. According to the author of the 'Prakaṭārthavivaraṇa', Īśvara is a reflection of Brahman in the beginningless, indefinable māyā, the material cause of the elements related to Brahman. In some Advaitists' view, Īśvara is imagined by a jīva because Brahman assuming the state of a jīva imagines by its avidyā the false world appearance as a dream-object.[135] According to some Advaitins of the Vivaraṇa school a jīva is a reflection of Īśvara, the archetype, the former being dependent and the latter being independent in that a reflection always depends upon the original. In some Advaitists' view, a jīva is a reflection of Īśvara Who is pure consciousness limited by an internal organ, an adjunct of a jīva. Īśvara Himself is the Inner Controller of a jīva.[136]

Bhāskara holds that Īśvara Himself is denoted by the word 'Brahman', and that Brahman or Īśvara is the creator, since the Inner Self is not perceived to create the world. Vidyāraṇya asks whether Īśvara is different or nondifferent from the cause of the world. If He is different, either prakṛti or atoms are the cause of the world. But they have been shown by Śaṁkara not to be its cause. If He is nondifferent, He is either prakṛti or atoms. Though common people do not perceive the Inner Self to be the cause of the world, experts in Śruti, Smṛti and reasoning perceive It to be so. Vidyāraṇya thinks Īśvara Himself to be the Inner Self.[137] Brahman is attributeless (nirguṇa) and transcendent while Īśvara is invested with attributes (saguṇa) and immanent in jīvas and the world.

TURĪYA BRAHMAN, ĪŚVARA, HIRAṆYAGARBHA, VAIŚVĀNARA, PRĀJÑA, TAIJASA AND VIŚVA.— Sadānanda distinguishes the transcendent consciousness (turīya caitanya) or Brahman, God (Īśvara), Hiraṇyagarbha, Sūtrātman, or Prāṇa, and Vaiśvānara from one another, on the one hand, and the transcendent consciousness, prājña, taijasa, and viśva from one another, on the other. The nondual existence-consciousness-bliss is Brahman—the only ontological reality. Nescience is indefinable, neither being nor nonbeing, of the nature of sattva, rajas and tamas, a positive entity, opposed to knowledge. The collection of nesciences is said to be one. Its adjunct is excellent, and it abounds in pure sattva. The one universal consciousness conditioned by cosmic nescience is God (Īśvara), the omniscient Lord of all, the Inner Controller of all, the ruler of all beings, and the cause of the world. An individual nescience is an inferior adjunct, and abounds in impure sattva. The universal consciousness conditioned by an individual nescience is endowed with limited knowledge and limited power, and is called prājña. It has an indistinct adjunct, manifests an individual nescience, and a limited number of objects. Īśvara conditioned by the cosmic or collective nescience is not different from prājña conditioned by an individual nescience, even as ether limited by a forest is not different from ether limited by a tree, or as ether reflected in the water of a tank is not different from ether reflected in a drop of water. The universal consciousness, which is not conditioned by cosmic nescience or an individual nescience, the substratum of Īśvara and prājña is called the transcendent or fourth consciousness (turīya caitanya), even as ether unlimited by a forest or a tree or unreflected in the water of a tank or in a drop of water is called all-pervasive ether.

The subtle bodies are taken together, and form a collection. The universal consciousness conditioned by the collection of them is called Hirṇyagarbha, Sūtrātman, or Prāṇa. It is called Sūtrātman because it interpenetrates all subtle bodies. It apperceives the five unquintupled elements, and is endowed with the power of knowledge, the power of volition, and the power of action. The universal consciousness conditioned by an individual subtle body is called taijasa, since the luminous internal organ is its limiting adjunct. The subtle body is subtle compared with the gross body. The vital sheath, the mental sheath, and the intellectual sheath constitute the subtle body. It is full of the dispositions (vāsanā) of the waking experiences, and the cause of dream. The gross body merges in it. Sūtrātman and taijasa experience subtle objects with subtle mental modes in sleep. They are nondifferent from each other as Īśvara and prājña are nondifferent from each other.

The universal consciousness conditioned by the collection of gross bodies is called Vaiśvānara or Virāṭ, since it exists in various ways in it, and has a conceit in it. It experiences gross objects for it has conceit in them. The universal consciousness conditioned by an individual gross body is called viśva, since it discards its conceit in its subtle body, and enters into its gross body in the waking state. The physical sheath constitutes the gross body, and is the vehicle of its experience of gross objects. Vaiśvānara experiences sound, touch, colour, taste, and odour, in the form of the Deities presiding over the cognitive sense-organs. Viśva experiences them through the cognitive sense-organs. Vāiśānara is nondifferent from viśva as Sūtrātman is nondifferent from taijasa, since the former is conditioned by the collection of gross bodies, and since the latter is conditioned by an individual gross body.

The universal, unlimited, unconditioned consciousness is called Turīya Caitanya. It is the substratum of the consciousness limited by the collection of adjuncts, and of the consciousness limited by an individual adjunct. It is of the nature of inner bliss. Turīya Caitanya, prājña, taijasa, and viśva interpenetrate one another like a fire and iron in red-hot iron. Īśvara, Hiraṇyagarbha, and Vaiśvānara are identical with the unlimited universal consciousness—Turīya Brahman, Which is their substratum. Turīya Brahman is Turīya Caitanya, and the only ontological reality.[138]

Madhusūdana Sarasvatī gives the following account of prājāa, taijasa and viśva. The universal consciousness conditioned by nescience invested with the potencies of an internal organ, devoid of conceit in an internal organ and a gross body and unconditioned by them, and the knower of deep sleep is prājña. The same consciousness conditioned by nescience and an internal organ, devoid of conceit in a gross body, and the knower of dream is taijasa. The same consciousness limited by nescience, an internal organ, and a gross body, and the knower of the waking state is viśva. The empirical self (jīva) assumes three forms. The fourth or transcendental consciousness, common to all, the knower of all, is homogeneous and and uniform, and is the witness (sākṣin). Ātman or Brahman is the only ontological reality or consciousness. It is always of one form, and becomes threefold according as its adjuncts differ. Conditioned by the causal nescience, it assumes the form of Īśvara. Conditioned by nescience and limited by an internal organ invested with potencies, it assumes the form of an empirical self. In some Advaitavādins' view, the Ātman or universal consciousness is the archetype, and Īśvara is its reflection in nescience. According to them the Ātman, the archetype consciousness, is the sākṣin. In some Advaitavādins' view, Īśvara is the archetype and an empirical self is a reflection of Īśvara in nescience. According to them the consciousness common to Īśvara and a jīva, which is the immediate knower of all, is the sākśin, of the nature of bliss. In Sureśvara's view, Īśvara Himself is the sākṣin, the universal consciousness being twofold—Īśvara and jīva. Īśvara is threefold : Brahmā, Viṣṇu and Rudra or Śiva. Īśvara conditioned by rajas of the causal nescience is Brahmā—the creator. Hiraṇyagarbha also is sometimes called Brahmā, since He creates the gross elements. Īśvara limited by sattva of the causal nescience is Viṣṇu—the maintainer. Īśvara limited by tamas of the causal nescience is Rudra or Śiva—the destroyer. Ātman, Brahman, or one universal consciousness, is imagined to have these forms for the worship by the aspirants.[139]

ADVAITA VEDĀNTA ABSOLUTE IDEALISM AND YOGĀCĀRA VIJÑĀNAVĀDA.—It is objected that the Advaita Vedānta view that all known objects are false appearances of the universal consciousness and cannot exist apart from Brahman is identical with the Yogācāra Vijñānavāda. Vidyāraṇya urges that the objection is groundless, because though there is partial resemblance between the two views, they are not identical with each other in all respects. According to the Vijñānavādin there are many momentary cognitions, and the objects of cognitions are identical with cognitions. But, in the Advaita Vedāntin's view, Brahman, Reality, is one eternal consciousness, and objects are superimposed on It, and capable of producing different practical actions, and their permanence is not contradicted until the intuition of Branman dawns. Consciousness is one, since it is identical in all cognitions in that it is recognized as one and the same in the cognitions of different objects. The difference in the cognitions of a jar, a cloth, etc., is due to the adjuncts (upādhi) of different objects, and cognition of difference is not natural to consciousness. Consciousness is eternal as it is one without a second. A cognition and its object are not identical with each other, because a cognition is internal while an object is external, and because consciousness is common to all cognitions while objects are different from one another. The capacity of different objects for producing different practical actions is known by experience. Their permanence is known by recognition. The different jīvas are superimpositions of different egoisms (ahaṁkāra) on one, eternal, universal consciousness. So the Advaita Vedānta Absolute Idealism is not to be confused with the Yogācāra Vijñānavāda.[140] Vidyāraṇya discusses subjective idealism advocated by some Yogācāras.

CRITICISM OF THE DOCTRINE OF DIFFERENCE AND NONDIFFERENCE.—Vācaspati Miśra refutes the doctrine as follows. Some opine that an entity is both nondifferent and different. A serpent is nondifferent as a snake and different as its coiled state. Vācaspati asks them whether the property of a snake and the property of a coil are different from the snake or whether they are nondifferent from the snake. If they are different from the snake, then the latter should be said to be different from them, and it should not be said to be both different and nondifferent from them. One entity cannot be said to be different and nondifferent because of the difference and nondifference of other entities, since it would involve an undesired contingency. If the property of a snake and the property of a coil are not different from the snake, then there is no difference in objects of difference and nondifference, because they being nondifferent from the entity, there is nondifference between them. It may be contended that though they have the same object, they are always experienced to be different, and that therefore there is no conflict between difference and nondifference. This contention is false, because there can be no conflict between any two entities, if there is no conflict between two entities, which are contradictory to each other in their nature. It is contended that what is always experienced may be real, though it be unreasonable. This contention is false, because, if that were so, the sense of the soul's identity with the body would be true inasmuch as it is always experienced. But this sense of identity has been proved to be false. So the difference of the empirical self from Ātman or Brahman is due to the beginningless nescience, and is not real. When the nescience is destroyed by the knowledge of Brahman, the jīva is released. If its difference from Ātman were real, the nescience would not be destroyed by the true knowledge. There is no other means to release than the knowledge of Ātman or Brahman. So the doctrine of difference and nondifference is false. Amalānanda observes that the property of a snake is common while the property of a coil is distinctive. So they are different and should be said to inhere in the same entity. But, in reality, the entity is not both different and nondifferent. There is natural conflict between being and nonbeing. If there is no conflict between them, then there can be no conflict between any two entities.[141]

CRITICISM OF BHARTṚPRAPAÑCA'S DOCTRINE OF DIFFERENCE AND NONDIFFERENCE.—Satcidānandendra Sarasvatī avers that Sureśvara refutes Bhartṛprapañca's view of difference and nondifference in 'Naiṣkarmyasiddhi'. Some conceive of Brahman as both different and nondifferent from the individual self (jīva). Sureśvara adduces the following arguments in refuting this view. The view that Brahman is different from the jīva cannot be propounded without refuting nondifference between them. If this is not admitted, Brahman's being different and nondifferent from the jīva cannot be proved by any pramāṇa.

If Brahman different and nondifferent from the jīva is admitted, though It is without any proof, then Brahman being nondifferent from the jīva shares in its misery, which is endless. A released soul being identical with Brahman becomes identical with all jīvas, and suffers from their untold misery.[142]

CRITICISM OF BHĀSKARA'S DOCTRINE OF DIFFERENCE AND NONDIFFERENCE.—Bhāskara maintains that the individual soul is both different from, and identical with, Brahman. Vidyāraṇya refutes this doctrine by adducing the following arguments against it. The jīva is not related to Brahman as an individual to a genus, or as a quality of a substance, or as an effect of a cause, or as a qualified state of an essence, or as a part of a whole, because there is no evidence for it. Difference and identity are nowhere to be found in the absence of these relations. The 'Bhagavad Gītā' asserts the jīva to be a part of God. But this view is contradicted by the Śruti "Brahman is partless". The Śruti "All creatures are a quarter of Brahman" shows the finitude of the souls. Otherwise, Brahman, a whole, would be produced by Its parts, the souls. Bhāskara may argue that Brahman is really partless, but that Brahman limited by the adjuncts of buddhi and the like comes to have parts. This view also does not make the difference between the jīva and Brahman real, for partless ether cannot be cut into parts by the stroke of a sword. If it be argued that the limiting adjuncts of the internal organ and the like can really divide Brahman into parts or jīvas, then why should Brahman create the limiting adjuncts and bring about an evil? Brahman cannot create the internal organs for the sake of the jīvas, for the division of It into jīvas is not possible before the creation of the internal organs and the like. Nor can merits and demerits, potencies of the nescience, divide Brahman into the jīvas, since Bhāskara admits the internal organs, etc., alone to be the limiting adjuncts of Brahman. Bhāskara may argue that difference between the jīva and Brahman is natural, like that between 'blue' and 'yellow', and that identity between them is due to their belonging to the same genus. Then the words 'self' and 'Brahman' in the Śruti "This Self is Brahman" would not have the same meaning. Bhāskara may argue that difference between the jīva and Brahman is neither accomplished nor beginningless but due to a limiting adjunct, and is manifested in Brahman. Then difference between them is an illusion, an attribution of what does not exist in Brahman. Bhāskara's contention, that difference proved by a valid pramāṇa cannot be an illusion, is false, since difference between the jīva and Brahman cannot be proved by perception and inference, and because Vedic testimony does not prove difference. On the contrary, Vedic testimony proves identity between the jīva and Brahman, and denies difference between them, since the Śruti has it—"Ātman, the Inner Controller, is immortal"; "There is no other Knower". Bhāskara may contend that bondage of the jīva and Brahman's freedom from bondage prove difference between them. This contention is invalid, since Bhāskara admits identity also between them, and cannot, therefore, explain bondage and liberation. Further, Brahman, being identical with the jīva, cannot escape from being tainted by its bondage, as ether enclosed in a jar cannot escape from being tainted by smoke in it. Bhāskara may contend that difference being stressed makes the distinction between bondage and liberation possible. Then bondage may as well be due to relation of Brahman to the nescience, and release may as well be due to the destruction of the relation of Brahman to the nescience as the Advaita Vedāntin maintains. Bhāskara may contend that the existence and the nonexistence of a relation of the nescience to the same entity—Brahman—is self-contradictory. This contention is false, for Bhāskara himself admits that difference and identity exist together in the same entity. Bhāskara may contend that identity is not the absence of difference, but that it is some other property. The contention is false, since even then difference and identity are contradictory to each other, as they negate each other. If Bhāskara is afraid of contradiction between relation of avidyā to Brahman and the destruction of its relation to Brahman, he should not admit both difference and identity between the jīva and Brahman. If he admits difference and identity between them, he should not be intolerant of the Advaitist's doctrine that the jīva is a reflection of Brahman, the archetype, in the nescience related to It. Further, there is no example to prove that the jīva, a part, being bound, Brahman, a whole, remains unbound. When a part of a cloth is polluted by the touch of an impure thing, the whole cloth is polluted and washed. So Brahman, being identical with the jīvas, cannot remain free from bondage, and must be tainted by the flaws of all souls according to Bhāskara. So the attainment of such tainted Brahman cannot be the supreme end of life, and scriptural instructions become useless. The limiting adjuncts of some souls are partly annulled by their knowledge and meditation, but all limiting adjuncts cannot be annulled in this way So Brahman cannot be dissociated from all blemishes of the souls. According to the Advaita Vedāntin Brahman is flawless. Dirtiness of a reflection does not taint its archetype. Liberation is attained by a soul when its avidyā is destroyed, as all objects imagined in the state of dream are destroyed on waking from sleep. Bhāskara may argue that both difference and identity between the jīva and Brahman must be admitted, because if the jīva were identical with Brahman, the words 'that' and 'thou' in the Śruti "That thou art" would be useless. This argument is false, because, if that were so, bondage to the body and the senses would not be destroyed by the knowledge of the meaning of this text. Is bondage destroyed by reasoning or by scriptural testimony? The first alternative is not possible, because according to, Bhāskara difference and identity between the jīva endowed with a body, etc., and Brahman are real, and because for that reason bondage to a body and the like cannot be destroyed by reasoning about the Śruti "That thou art". Nor is the second alternative possible, because the Śruti is a mere eulogy in that it declares identity between the jīva and Brahman. Bhāskara may argue that the purport of Vedic testimony here refers to the cessation of bondage to the body and the like in the state of release. Yet if the difference between the jīva and Brahman does not cease in the state of release, the adjunct of the body, the senses and the internal organ must be admitted to account for continuity of bondage to them in the state of release. Then this state of release does not differ from bondage. If the difference-part of the jīva ceases in the state of release, then also it is not terminated by the knowledge of the Reality, because it cannot terminate its object. Bhāskara regards difference also as the object of the knowledge of the Reality. Nor can works terminate the knowledge of the difference-part of the jīva, because it contradicts Vedic testimony, and because Bhāskara admits that Vedic testimony proves difference and identity between the jīva and Brahman at all times. Nor can Bhāskara's doctrine of difference and identity explain the meanings of the words 'that' and 'thou' in the Śruti "That thou art".

Is the jīva denoted by the word 'thou' the whole made of the parts 'difference' and 'identity', or a collection of the two parts, or two parts themselves? In the first alternative, if the identity-part is Brahman, then Brahman becomes a part of the jīva, and the jīva becomes a whole composed of parts. If the identity-part is not Brahman, then there is absolute difference between the jīva and Brahman. The second alternative is not possible, since the jīva would then be a nonentity in that a collection different from its members cannot be ascertained. In the third alternative, the jīva is either the identity-part itself, or it is the difference-part itself, or it is each of the two parts. If it is the two parts, they are either nondifferent from each other, or both different and nondifferent from each other. The first subalternative is not possible, because, if that were true, Brahman Itself would become the jīva. The second subalternative is not possible, since in that case the jīva would be absolutely different from Brahman. The third subalternative is not possible, because in that case each jīva would become two. The fourth alternative is not possible, since in that case Brahman Itself would become the jīva, and bondage and release would not be possible. The fifth alternative is not possible, because it will lead to infinite regress of difference and identity, and because scriptural instruction will become useless. The identity-part cannot be tainted by the flaw of avidyā, because it is of the nature of Brahman. So it does not require scriptural instruction. Nor does the difference-part require scriptural instruction, because it cannot experience "I am Brahman". In the state of release the difference-part cannot be related to Brahman by identity, for difference-part cannot have identity in that difference and identity are contradictory to each other. The difference-part cannot be tainted by the flaw of avidyā, for difference does not exist before the creation of the adjuncts. Bhāskara may contend that the jīva is by itself a different part or whole independently of its limititing adjuncts. The contention is false, because that part being destroyed the jīva is destroyed, and none remains to be instructed by the scripture. The identity-part or Brahman being eternally released, it does not require scriptural instruction. If release also be said to be both different and nondifferent from Brahman, then this view contradicts the Śruti "The knower of Brahman becomes Brahman Itself", and release does not differ from bondage. Both difference and identity between the jīva and Brahman are not necessary to account for heaven and hell, bondage and release. They can partly be explained by difference. Difference and identity both cannot exist together in the state of release in the same entity. Difference exists in distinct entities possessing difference, and cannot exist in one and the same nondifferent entity. Vedic testimony establishes identity between the jīva and Brahman, denies difference between them, and does not prove both difference and identity. Hence the doctrine of difference and identity between them is false.[143]

ĀTMAN IS SELF-PROVED AND UNPROVABLE.—Sureśvara avers that the knower (pramātṛ), the means of knowledge (pramāṇa) and the object of knowledge (prameya) are concerned with external objects alone, and cannot prove the existence of the Inner Self or Spirit.[144] Perception and other pramāṇas are directed towards external objects, and so cannot prove the existence of Ātman—Inner Self.[145] It can be proved by the scriptural sentence "That thou art" or the like. It is known as the eternal witness (sākṣin) of all changing mental modes. The eternal Ātman is the presupposition of all cognitions of objects. Ātman is different from all objects of knowledge.

It is known from scriptural testimony alone, which destroys nescience (avidyā), the cause of all evils—the distinction of the knower, knowledge, the means of knowledge, and the object of knowledge, as the manifester of the real nature of things.[146] The knowledge of Ātman is not produced after the extinction of avidyā. It depends upon the scripture, which points to the existence of Ātman, the supreme Reality, the true knowledge of which destroys avidyā and its products—the knower, the means of knowledge, knowledge, and the object of knowledge.[147] Ātman is self-proved, and cannot be proved. So It must be admitted to be real.[148] It is the presupposition of all proofs. Scriptural testimony merely reveals the nature of the self-existent Ātman.[149] It cannot be perceived even by gods as another object. It is self-existent and self-proved. It is self-luminous. It is the inner light of eternal consciousness. It transcends intellect and its modes, and is eternally free. Śaṁkara says "Ātman is self-proved, for It is the unchanging, eternal consciousness of pramāṇa and the like, and independent of any pramāṇa. It is of the nature of eternal, self-luminous consciousness. The knowledge of an object of knowledge depends upon a pramāṇa. But the witness of all is self-provid."[150]

ĀTMAN IS UNPRODUCED, ETERNAL AND IMMUTABLE.—Vidyāraṇya proves Ātman to be without an origin by the following arguments. After birth of a body a child feels pleasure and pain. So a soul existed before birth as the agent of merits and demerits, which are the causes of pleasure and pain, respectively. A soul is not noneternal, since its destruction cannot be determined. It cannot be destroyed by itself. It cannot be destroyed without any cause. If it were so destroyed, all entities would be destroyed without any cause. It cannot be destroyed by any other cause, since it being an incorporeal entity cannot be related to any cause of its destruction. Even if it were related to an entity, its destruction would not be possible. Relation of an entity to another entity is brought about by an action. An action requires the existence of an entity to produce its result in it. It does not require the destruction of the entity. So it is proved that Ātman is associated with and dissociated from many bodies, and undergoes many births and deaths. It is neither produced nor destroyed. Because Ātman—an unchanging entity devoid of activity—cannot enjoy and suffer, and because a modification is admitted to be a result of an action, an empirical self (jīva) can be an active agent. Ātman being inactive and immutable cannot be an enjoyer or a sufferer. So an empirical self is an enjoyer or a sufferer. It is an active agent and experiences pleasure and pain. It undergoes birth and death. It is bound and liberated. Ātman is changeless, eternal and immutable.[151] A mutable entity is limited, and, consequently, not-self. Activity cannot be an attribute of Ātman, since it is neither different nor nondifferent from Ātman.[152] It is unlimited, inactive, and immutable.

ĀTMAN IS OF THE NATURE OF COGNITION OR CONSCIOUSNESS.—Ānandabodha proves that Self is of the nature of cognition. Consciousness constitutes the nature of Ātman. It is contended that a cognition being momentary cannot be the nature of Self. This contention is false, because momentariness of a cognition is not proved. When blue is cognized, yellow is not cognized. From this fact it is not proved that a cognition is momentary. Though blue and other objects are not cognized, apprehension of essential being or conseiousness cannot be eliminated.[153] Śaṁkara admits that indeterminate perception apprehends being (sat), which is identical with consciousness. Ānandabodha argues that it is is not right to hold that individual cognitions, like the cognition of blue, the cognition of yellow, etc., are produced and destroyed. There cannot be apprehension of difference among cognitions unless there is the conscious Self. The Self alone, that is conscious, can apprehend their difference. Thus the knowledge of different cognitions presupposes the Self, which is of the nature of consciousness.[154] No other entity can apprehend the difference between them. The difference between cognitions also is indeterminable.[155] The Advaitist holds that Ātman or Brahman is of the nature of one, eternal, universal consciousness, which apprehends different cognitions and different objects projected by avidyā. They are imaginary or indeterminable. The concept of Ātman of the nature of consciousness is flawless. Because Ātman is consciousness, It is self-luminous.[156] Citsukha avers that though consciousness conditioned by blue, yellow and the like adjuncts is not apprenended, essential consciousness is apprehended. So cognition or consciousness is not momentary.[157] Ātman is eternal consciousness. Rāmatīrtha elaborates on Śaṁkara's arguments, and shows that Ātman has eternal consciousness as its essential characteristic. Ātman, being of the nature of consciousness, is self-luminous. If Its self-luminousity were not admitted, the world would not be manifested, and practical life would cease.[158]

ĀTMAN IS OF THE NATURE OF SUPREME BLISS AND THE OBJECT OF SUPREME LOVE.— Sureśvara avers that Ātman is of the nature of the highest bliss and good unrelated to evil. Evil is of the nature of not-self. Ātman is of the nature of consciousness and bliss, and cannot, therefore, be evil or misery.[159] Ātman is the ontological psychic principle underlying the empirical self (jīva). Brahman is the ontological cosmic principle underlying the world appearance. Ātman is Brahman. "May I have good ; may I have no evil". This is false knowledge, which is the cause of voluntary action. I am by nature good, and devoid of evil. There is no pain in my nature. I am, in my real nature, supreme bliss and good and eternal knowledge and consciousness.[160] Ānandabodha avers that Ātman, being of the nature of supreme bliss, is manifested as the object of supreme love.[161] Its blss is eternal, infinite and not limited by any adjuncts. So it is not an object of love as a means, like a piece of sandal or a woman. All empirical objects of joy are really objects of love for the sake of Ātman underlying them. If they are loved for the sake of Ātman, It is undoubtedly an object of supreme love for Itself. Hence it is proved that Ātman is the object of supreme love, since It is of the nature of supreme bliss.[162] Object-pleasure is sentient, and a mere semblance or reflection of the infuite bliss of Ātman. It is objected that none will endeavour for the achievement of liberation, if Ātman is of the nature of supreme bliss and an object of supreme love. Ānandabodha rejoins that the knowledge of the real nature of Ātman is veiled by avidyā, which is destroyed by vidyā. Love for Ātman is unconditional. When avidyā is destroyed by vidyā, the supreme bliss of Ātman is manifested.[163] Liberation is eternally realized. But in the state of bondage the bliss of Ātman is manifested indistinctly because of the obstruction of various names and forms—mind-body-complex and objects created by avidyā. It is distinctly manifested when vidyā dawns on the mind of an aspirant.[164] In the state of liberation the immediate experience of Ātman destroys all impurities due to avidyā, and the pure, supreme bliss of Ātman is distinctly manifested. This is the difference between bondage and release.[165] Raṅgojī

Bhaṭṭa argues that liberation would not be the supreme good of the self, if bliss were not its nature, since produced happiness is not possible in the self. The absence of pain cannot be the supreme end of a person desirous of release. It is coveted by him, because it produces pleasure. It is objected that if the self is an object of love because happiness inheres in it, then it is an object of hate because pain inheres in it. The objection is unsound, because Self is of the nature of infinite and eternal bliss. Pleasure and pain, happiness and misery, are produced and noneternal. They are attributes or modes of the internal organ or manas, and not attributes of Self. Bliss is the essence of Self. So it is the object of supreme love. Madhusūdana Sarasvatī also confirms this view. Puruṣottama Sarasvatī avers that joy, grief, anger, greed, delusion and the like are attributes or modes of egoism (ahaṁkāra). Ātman is an object of supreme love, because It is of the nature of bliss.[166]

ĀTMAN, COGNITION AND OBJECT (SUREŚVARA).—Sureśvara gives the following account of the relation between Ātman or Self and cognitions. The momentary cognitions in the forms of sounds and other objects are cognized by one, eternal, nonsuccessive Self. The cognitions are momentary while the cognizing Self is eternal. The former are successive while the latter is nonserial. The former assume the forms of objects due to the nescience, while the latter is of the nature of unconditioned consciousness. Ātman is one eternal consciousness, while cognitions of objects due to avidyā are superimposed on It.[167] The cognitions are successive—past, present and future, but Ātman cognizes them simultaneously. It is never devoid of consciousness, and does not make any effect.[168] It is inactive and desireless. It is devoid of pleasure, pain, delusion, aversion, imagination and recollection. It is formless while cognitions are invested with forms of objects. It is nontemporal, and cognizes cognitions, which are past, present and future. It is unchanging, and cognizes changing, momentary cognitions.[169] It is independent, and cognizes dependent cognitions. It is inward-looking and one, while cognitions are outward-looking and cognize external objects.[170] Ātman is unchanging because It is the witness of all cognitions. Ātman or Self is the witness (sākṣin) of the empirical self (jīva), which suffers and acts. The suffering empirical self is not the witness. The witness also does not suffer.[171] A being suffers since it undergoes change. A being that does not undergo change cannot suffer. A being suffers since it undergoes change. A being that does not undergo change cannot suffer. Ātman is the witness of the changes of cognitions, and so it is unchanging. The changing empirical self cannot be the witness.[172] Ātman is of the nature of consciousness, and, consequently, does not undergo any variation.[173] (Cp. T.H. Green). Cognitions cognize objects with which they come into contact, and are modified into their forms. Ātman cognizes the cognitions invested with the forms of objects without undergoing any change. The production and destruction of cognitions cannot be proved without the existence of unchanging Ātman of the nature of consciousness. It is the witness of momentariness of cognitions.[174] The eternal, nontemporal Self of the nature of consciousness cognizes changing, mutable cognitions of objects.[175] Cognitions are never uncognized by the unchanging, eternal self-manifest Ātman of the nature of consciousness.[176] The cognitions, which cognize objects, differ from one another. But the Self that cognizes cognitions is one and unchanging.[177] Ātman, one light of consciousnss, cognizes the cognitions of the objects of the world.[178] They are manifested by Ātman. Ātman cognizing the cognitions of objects cannot be cognized. Who will know the knower of cognitions?[179]

Sureśvara indicates the relation of cognitions to their objects also in the above account. Cognitions cognize objects to which they are related, and assume their forms. Sureśvara opines that the cognition of an object or not-self presupposes the Self, which cognizes its knowledge. If there is no knowing Self, an object cannot be known. Self and not-self are established by perception and other means of valid knowledge in the world. An object or not-self is known only when Ātman is already known. The knowledge of an object presupposes that of Ātman.[180] Both an external object and 'I' (aham) are not-self, and known by Ātman, which is without outside and inside, and which is the inward-looking eternal, universal consciousness.[181] Ātman is the prius of the knowledge of an object. Sureśvara says, "Objects do not exist without knowledge, but knowledge exists without them."[182] So objects cannot exist without being known by the self. This is the dictum of idealism. So Ātman which cognizes valid knowledge and its object is not an object of knowledge.[183] It is one, eternal, universal consciousness, which manifests the universe and knowledge of manifold objects due to avidyā. Self (ego) and not-self (not-ego), I and object, are superimposed on Ātman

An external object with a form is known by knowledge. Knowledge is determinate knowledge, 'I' (aham) am the knower. The empircal self (jīva) is 'I'. Eternal Ātman is the witness (sakṣin). It is neither the knower, nor knowledge, nor the known. It is beyond this distinction. It is devoid of acceptance or rejection, and the witness of them. It is one undivided, nondual, universal, eternal consciousness.[184] It is the witness of the empirical self or 'I'. It is inactive and eternal. It is not an agent, knower, and enjoyer or sufferer. Because It is of the nature of eternal knowledge or consciousness, It is not an agent and the like.[185] Cognitions are known and proved by the unchanging, eternal consciousness, Ātman. which is self-existent and self-proved.[186] External objects are known and proved by cognitions, which are noneternal. Eternal Ātman does not require any proof from any other entity. It is self-proved and independent. Cognitions depend upon, and are known by, Ātman.[187] The knower is tinged by the known ; the known object is tinged by 'I'-notion. When 'I'-notion is destroyed, nonduality of Ātman is intuited. 'I'-notion is false.[188] Inactive Ātman appears to be an enjoyer or a sufferer owing to false 'I'-notion.[189] Egoism is due to superimposition of self and not-self on each other. Superimposition is due to avidyā.[190] As clouds suddenly appear in the sky, overcast it, and then disappear, so the world appearance due to avidyā appears in Brahman or Ātman, veils Its nature, and then disappears.[191] Brahman is the substrate and the object of avidyā.

COGNITION IS SELF-MANIFEST.—Ānandabodha proves that a cognition is self-manifest or self-aware. Some (e.g., Nyāyā) opine that a cognition manifests or cognizes an object, but that it is not self-manifest. Ānandabodha asks whether an unmanifest cognition cognizes an object, or whether a manifest cognition cognizes an object. An unmanifest cognition does not cognize an object. If it did so, there would be a doubt as to whether an object (e.g., a jar) has been cognized, or whether it has not been cognized by a person. But he who has cognized a jar has never any doubt. So it is proved that a cognition is manifested at the time when it cognizes an object because no doubt arises after the cognition of the object.[192]

It is contended that a cognition is manifested by another cognition, when it cognizes an object. This contention is false, since it leads to infinite regress. But an endless series of cognitions does not exist, when an object is cognized by a cognition. It is contended that a cognition, which cognizes a cognition, is a mental cognition. Ānandabodha asks whether the conjunction with manas, which produced the cognition of an object, will produce the cognition which will cognize the cognition of an object, or whether another conjunction with manas will produce it. The same conjunction with manas cannot produce both the cognitions, for they do not arise simultaneously. It may be said that it produces them successively. But one instrument (karaṇa) is not found to produce two effects successively. Two successive cognitions can be produced by two noninherent causes, e.g., two conjunctions with manas. Otherwise, recollections of things would be produced simultaneously. If causes are not successive, their effects cannot be successive. If causes are simultaneous, the succession of their effects is uncaused and accidental. It is conteded that one conjunction with manas produces both cognitions successively, because the conjunction of manas with the different sense-organs and the conjunction of the sense-organs with different objects are successive. This contention is false, because manas, guided by Ātman, conjoined with the different sense-organs, which are conjoined with different objects, can produce different cognitions simultaneously.[193] The second alternative also is not justified. The cognition of the cognition of an object is not produced by another conjunction with manas, since then there will arise an undesired contingency. At the time of the cognition of an object, there is an act in manas; then there is separation from manas; then there is destruction of the previous conjunction; then there is production of the next conjunction with manas; then another cognition is produced. So there is an appreciable interval of time between the cognition of an object and the cognition of the cognition. So the second cognition cannot cognize the first cognition of an object as present. So it is better to hold that a cognition of an object is self-manifest or self-aware than to hold that the second cognition cognizes a past cognition by eliminating the other hypotheses.[194] Further, a pitcher and the like are insentient, and, consequently, not self-manifest. Nor are they manifested by one another. If a cognition is insentient, it also cannot manifest itself. It is contended that a cognition, though insentient, manifests an object, like the eyes, which, though insentient, manifest a visible object. This contention is false, because the alternatives involved in it are not admissible. Manifesting is producing manifestation. The manifestation produced by a cognition is either nondifferent from the object of the cognition, being different from the cognition, or it is different from the object of the cognition.[195] It is not the nature of the object, since an insentient object and manifestation cannot be identical with each other, like a liquid and a solid, and since the momentary manifestation cannot be identical with a stable object.[196] Nor is the manifestation different from the object, since the former is an attribute of the latter produced by a cognition.[197] Kumārila holds that a cognition produces cognizedness (jñātatā), or manifestness (prākaṭya) in an object. This view is wrong, since cognizedness cannot be produced in a past object and in a future object, but since they are manifested by cognitions. If the manifestation of an object is held to be internal, a cognition itself is the manifestation of an object. If the cognition be insentient, it cannot manifest the object.[198]

An object also cannot manifest itself, for it is not-self. So the whole world becomes blind or unmanifest. Hence a cognition is self-manifest, and manifests an object.[199] It is contended that a cognition does not cognize itself, for it involves self-contradiction : a cognition cannot be a cognizer and a cognized object. This contention is false, since a cognition manifests itself, like light. A light manifests itself, and is not manifested by another light. Similarly, a cognition manifests itself without being manifested by another cognition. Just as there is no self-contradiction in light manifesting itself, so there is no self-contradiction in a cognition manifesting itself. Hence a cognition is self-manifest.[200]

COGNITION AND OBJECT.—The Sautrāntika infers an external object from its reflection in a cognition, because it is manifested in a cognition, which is not an object. Vidyāraṇya asks whether the inferential cognition directly manifests the object without its reflection in the cognition or whether it manifests its object through its reflection in the cognition. In the first alternative, the reason is irregular or variably concomitant with the probandum. In the second alternative, an inference will not be produced, because its object is not manifested through its reflection in the cognition. So direct apprehension of an object cognized cannot be denied.[201] Perception of invariable concomitance of a probans with a probandum is a precondition of inference. So the Sautrāntika view is wrong.

The Yogācāra Vijñānavādin opines that external objects being nonexistent, objects in the form of cognitions are directly apprehended. Vidyāṇya rejects this view as wrong, because external objects also, which are not cognitions, are directly apprehended or perceived.[202] If they were illusory, they would be contradicted. But they are not contradicted. So an object of knowledge (e.g., a jar) is perceived as an object, and not as a cognition. A cognition is not perceived, because it is self-manifest.[203] The Self of the nature of cognition is self-manifest. So a cognition also is self-manifest.

The Buddhists opine that a cognition itself is a means of knowledge and its result. Vidyāraṇya rejects this view as wrong, because it involves self-contradiction in that the same cognition is a means or cognitive act and a result or resultant cognition. It is argued by the Buddhists in defence of their view that though a knower has no casual activity (vyāpāra), yet the fourfold intercourse of the self, manas, a sense-organ, and an object is a means of knowledge, and figuratively said to be a knower's causal activity. But cognition, which is invariably present, cannot produce variable results such as appropriation, rejection and indifference. So a congition is not a means of knowledge (pramāṇa) and its result (phala).[204]

THE NATURE OF COGNITION.—Prakāśātman gives the following accounts of the views of cognition. According to the Jaina and the Cārvāka consciousness (caitanya) of the self itself is a cognition. Prakāśātman refutes this view by urging that if unconditioned consciousness of the self itself manifested an object, it would always manifest all objects. Because consciousness is produced by the body according to some Cārvākas, the casual operation of the body in producing consciousness is inferred from consciousness. The Nyāya, the Vaiśeṣika and Prabhākara identify a cognition, a means of knowledge, with consciousness, its result. They regard the fourfold intercourse between the self and manas, manas and a sense-organ, and a sense-organ and an object as the cause of the cognition, and dispense with a knower's causal operation. The Buddhists also identify a cognition with consciousness. But they do not regard the self as permanent, but as a series of momentary cognitions. They infer casual operation of the preceding cognitions from the succeeding cognitions. According to the Sāṁkhya a mental mode is a cognition as a means of knowledge and consciousness as its result. Prakāśātman urges that a result in the form of consciousness cannot be produced without a knower's casual operation in the permanent self. It is objected that because the self cannot have causal operation in the form of motion, a cognition is produced by the cause, which is said to produce a knower's causal operation. Prakāśātman asks whether the production of a result by an agent's causal operation is known by perception or whether it is known by inference. If it is not known by perception, it cannot be known by inference also, because invariable concomitance between the probans and the probandum is not perceived. So the agent's causal operation is not known everywhere. But an agent's causal operation is known in the world. It is contended that an agents' causal activity is perceived in the world as the cause of a result. Then the self's causal activity is inferred on the strength of invariable concomitance between an agent's causal activity and a result. It is objected by the Vaiśeṣika and others that the self's causal activity in the form of a modification is not necessary, because a cognition emerges from the fourfold intercourse as an effect, which is a new beginning (ārambha). Prakāśātam urges that then let a cognition be the result of the activity of voluntary effort, because a result is invariably preceded by an agent's causal activity. It is objected that a cognition is produced by the self's conjunction with manas, its noninherent cause, without the self's causal activity, and that an agent's causal activity cannot produce a result without the agent's conjunction with an instrument. This objection is groundless, because in cooking, the result depends upon a cook's causal activity without which nothing can be cooked. So an agent's causal activity cannot be denied in producing a result. Even the Buddhists, who deny the reality of the permanent self, admit cognitions to be produced by causal activity of the preceding cognitions. It is objected that the ubiquitous and incorporeal self conceived by the Advaita Vedāntin cannot have motion or modification, and, consequently, can have no causal activity. To this objection Prakāśātman replies that the self interpenetrating the internal organ, a product of avidyā, is modified into a cognition.[205] A cognition is a mental mode intelligized by the self because of its superimposition on the internal organ. Consciousness is not a modification of the self, because it is eternal. Hence a particular mode of the internal organ, an adjunct of eternal consciousness or self to manifest an object, is called a cognition as a means of knowledge and consciousness as its result, which is the manifestation of an object.[206] The self is the eternal consciousness and devoid of causal activity, but its limiting adjunct, the internal organ, a product of avidyā, is active, and is modified into a cognition. The internal organ is insentient, but is intelligized by the self which interpenetrates it owing to superimposition on it, or which is reflected in it, and a mental mode or a cognition manifests an object. This is the Advaita Vedānta view. According to Sureśvara the knower's causal activity which produces consciousness is a cognition.[207]

Vidyāraṇya gives the following accounts of the nature of cognition. According to the Sāṁkhya cognition or consciousness is the nature of the self. The self is a substance. So cognition is a substance. Vidyāraṇya interpretes the Sāṁkhya view in this way, and refutes it. If cognition be a substance, it is either of atomic magnitude or ubiquitous or of intermediate magnitude. In the first alternative, a cognition would manifest a limited part of an object, like a fire-fly. In the second alternative, a cognition would manifest all objects everywhere. In the thire alternative, a cognition would consist of parts and depend upon them, and would not depend upon the self. If a cognition be said to depend upon the self as a jar depends upon the ground, then the self and its cognition must be admitted to be non-different from each other, like a lamp and its light, because the self cognizes as a lamp illumines. Cognition is similar to illumination. Vidyāraṇya expounds Prakāśātman's arguments.[208]

According to Nyāya, Vaiśeṣika, and Prabhākara, a cognition is the result of a means of knowledge (pramāṇa), and a quality of the self. Vidyāraṇya refutes the view. If it is a quality of the self, it is like brightness of a lamp, and cannot be produced, if its substrate, the self, be not produced. The self is admitted to be eternal ; a cognition cannot be produced in it. So a cognition is an eternal quality of the self. Because it is eternal, it is always present in it. Then the cognition of an object would be cognized as the self itself. It is contended that the self cannot be a cognition, because the self is proved by a cognition. The contention is invalid, because, if the self were proved by a cognition of an object, it would be not-self, like a jar. It is argued that the cognitions of blue, yellow and the like being different from one another are not of the nature of the self. The argument is false, since the cognitions are not experienced to be different from oue another in their nature inasmuch as there is no evidence for assuming their difference. Production and destruction of cognitions are not causes of assuming their difference. If their production and destruction depend upon their difference, then there is mutual dependence : their production and destruction depend upon their difference ; their difference depends upon their production and destruction. Production and destruction of cognitions are unnecessary for explaining their difference, because the relations of one consciousness to different objects are produced and destroyed.[209] The Advaita Vedānta explains different cognitions in the self in this way. So a cognition is not a quality of the self.

The Buddhist opines that there is real difference among cognitions, but that the difference is not known because of similarity, as different flames are not distinguished from one another owing to similarity. This view is wrong, since cognitions are self-manifest, and cognize their difference while flames are cognized by another being. The Buddhist may cite the example of self-luminous Brahman, That is unknown, in his favour. Vidyāraṇya urges that Brahman is concealed by avidyā, which is proved by perception and inference, and that, consequently, It is unknown. So there is one cognition or consciousness without an origin. It is devoid of origin, because its prior nonexistence is not known. Sureśvara argues that an effect is perceived by all to be preceded by prior nonexistence, that prior nonexistence is cognized by the witness (sākṣin) or consciousness, but that there no prior nonexistence of consciousness. Hence self-manifest cognition is the nature of the Self because of its eternity.[210] This view is not contradicted. The Self itself is called a cognition, when it is related to an object—its adjunct, and it is called the Self when its relation to an adjunct is not considered.

Kumārila regards cognition as an act of the self, which is inferred from its result, manifestness (prākaṭya) or cognizedness in its object. Manifestness is perceived by another cognition through conjunction and inherence. Cognitive act inheres in the self and manifestness is conjoined with the object. Vidyāraṇya adduces the following arguments in refuting Kumārila's view. Because Kumārila admits another cognition to perceive manifestness of an object, the first cognition exists at the time when it is produced and at the time when the second cognition is produced. Kumārila contends that simultaneity of a result, which is being destroyed, and of a result, which is not being destroyed, is admitted by him. Yet Vidyāraṇya urges that magnitude of the self and taste of the object also should be perceived by the second cognition, because magnitude of the self inheres in it, and because taste of the object inheres in it. If they are not perceived, conjunction of manifestness with the object and inherence of the first cognition in the self cannot be apprehended. Kumārila contends that the cognition which perceives manifestness of the object has no capacity for perceiving magnitude of the self and taste of the object. Even then manifestness of the object is not perceived by another cognition, like the object, because it is never found in its being without manifestation, and because it is self-manifest.[211] Nor can it be said that manifestness produced in a jar by the self's cognitive act called a means of knowledge (pramāṇa) is perceived by another cognition, like colour of the jar. Vidyāraṇya asks whether the self's causal act is a motion or a modification. He replies that the self cannot have motion, because it is ubiquitous. If the self's causal act is a modification of it, manifestness produced by it will exist in the self, and not in the object, as a jar, a modification of earth, exists in earth. Kumārila contends that a modification of the self produces manifestness in an object, as a modification of hair, like greyness, produces old age in the body. Vidyāraṇya asks whether the abode of manifestness is conscious, or whether what produces manifestness is conscious, or whether the abode of causal activity called cognition, which produces manifestness, is conscious. In the first alternative, a jar will be conscious, for it is the abode of manifestness. In the second alternative, the eyes will be conscious, since they produce manifestness in the jar. In the third alternative, the self is the abode of cognitive act, because it is related to the result produced by it, as Devadatta is satisfied as the result of his eating. But the self is not related to manifestness in the object, produced by its cognitive act. Kumārila has to infer the self's being the abode of cognitive act. The reason for the inference is unproven, for the self is not related to the result of its cognitive act, e.g., manifestness. Kumārila contends that the self's relation to the result of its cognitive act is known by such experience as "The jar is apprehended by me". The contention is false, since this experience contradics Kumārila's view that the result 'manifestness' abides in the object, and not in the self. Hence Kumārila's view should be rejected and self-manifestness of manifestness, the result of cognitive act, should be preferred.[212] Vidyāraṇya has expounded Prakāśātman's arguments.

CRITICISM OF THE CĀRVĀKA VIEWS OF ĀTMAN.—Some Cārvākas conceive of Ātman as a conscious body composed of earth, water, light and air. The body cognizes different objects, and experiences pleasure and pain. Vidyāraṇya asks whether the elements of the body individually or collectively cognize objects. In the first alternative, the elements cannot simultaneously cognize them. Because they act individually, they cannot be related to one another as principal and subordinate, and cannot combine with one another and act collectively. So they cannot collectively cognize different objects and experience pleasure and pain. If they can do so without combining with one another, then they being external to a body also can do so. The elements cannot cognize objects successively, for they are combined in a body. The Cārvāka argues that earth, water, light and air in a body cognize odour, taste, colour and touch, respectively, and that therefore they do not cognize objects successively. If all cognizable objects are present at the same time, the elements in a body cannot cognize them successively. Nor can the elements in a body collectively cognize different kinds of objects, for the different elements have no separate corsciousnesses. Because they have no separate consciousnesses elsewhere, they do not exist in a body, which is their aggregate. It is contended that though the elements singly do not produce consciousness, they can collectively produce it. The contention is false, because there is no cause for their collection. The collection is not due to the future experience of different objects, because the experience being subordinate to the elements, the elements, which are principal, being devoid of the relation of principal and subordinate, cannot produce an aggregate. Experience of different objects cannot be principal, for it is experienced by a soul. So there cannot be collection of the elements in a body. Collection is not coexistence of an experiencer and experience in the same place. If it were so, then the elements existing everywhere, experience of different kinds of objects would exist everywhere. Nor is the whole produced by the elements as their aggregate. If it differs from the four elements, it is the fifth element, which is denied by the Cārvāka. If it is not different from them, it cannot be their aggregate, because it is nothing but the elements, and because the doctrine of difference and nondifference is not admitted. It is contended that the whole being dependent on the elements is not the fifth element. The contention is false, because then water depending on earth, there would be four elements. Nor is an aggregate the object of the cognition of one substance. In fact, the cognition of one substance in many entities is a mere illusion. Nor is an aggregate simultaneous relation to an action realizing one purpose, because in that case water heated by a fire produced by fuel and kindled by air would be an aggregate of earth, water, fire and air. Nor is an aggregate interpenetration like that of a fire and an iron ball, because air cannot interpenetrate a body, and because water heated by a red-hot iron ball and conjoined with air would be an experience. Nor can one element alone experience different kinds of objects, because its experience in the presence of all elements is not determined. Some Cārvākas opine that the sense-organs cognize objects, or that the body combined with the sense-organs cognizes objects. This view also is false on the same grounds.[213]

The Self is not insentient, for it is known to be self-luminous by perception, inference and scriptural testimony. It is perceived to be self-manifest in deep sleep. Its self-luminosity is proved by the inference : the Self is self-luminous, because It is devoid of existence apart from manifestation in its being, like a lighted lamp, or like a cognition, because It is the manifester of an object, like a lighted lamp, or because It is the abode of manifestation of an object, like a light, or because It is known by immediate knowledge, being not known through the sense-organs, like a cognition, or because It has the quality of manifestation, being devoid of the quality of manifestation produced in a substance having an attribute, like the sun. The Self is known to be self-luminous from the scripture which says,

"This Self is self-luminous". So the body, vital force, the sense-organs, and the internal organ, which are insentient, are not the Self. Sureśvara calls them not-self, since they are objects of the witness (sākṣin) or Ātman. They are objects of changing cognitions while the Self is unchanging, eternal consciousness.[214]

CRITICISM OF THE BUDDHIST VIJÑĀNAVĀDIN'S VIEW OF ĀTMAN.—The Buddhist Vijñānavādins conceive of Ātman or Self as a series of momentary cognitions. Recognition of its identity is due to similarity of cognitions succeeding in a psychic continuum.[215] Similarly, David Hume says, "What we call a mind, is nothing but a heap or collection of different perceptions, supposed to be endowed with a perfect simplicity and identity." "Successive perceptions only constitute the mind." "The identity which we ascribe to the mind is only a fictitious one". "Resemblance of our perceptions makes us ascribe to them an identity."[216] Action, knowledge, bondage and release are explained by a series of cognitions related to each other as cause and effect.[217]

Vidyāraṇya gives the following criticism of the Vijñānavādin's view. A series of momentary cognitions is not capable of performing actions, which are successive. Every person first knows an agreeable object, then desires it, then makes an effort, then acquires it, and then experiences pleasure. If many momentary cognitions ignorant of one another can do such actions successively, different souls or series of cognitions can do the same series of actions. But it is found to be impossible. In order to avoid such an absurd contingency we must admit a permanent self to perform a series of actions. There is no experience "I am a cognition". But there is the experience "This is my cognition". This experience is not false, for it is not contradicted. So the self is not a series of momentary cognitions ; it knows them. But the experience of 'I' is due to superimposition of egoism (ahaṁkāra), which is not-self, on Ātman.[218] Further, recognition of personal identity proves the existence of a permanent self. It is not an illusion due to the perception of similarity of successive cognitions. Separate lights are perceived in a flame on close observation. But in the recognition of the same self there is no perception of many souls. So there is one self-luminous Ātman.[219] Śaṁkara argues that similarity is uncaused, for its substrate is non-existent. Rāmatīrtha explains the argument thus. Similarity is due to the possession of common parts, or of common qualities. Momentary cognitions are devoid of common parts or common qualities. Of two momentary cognitions said to be similar to each other one being nonexistent, similarity between them is not cognized. So the perception of similarity of the succeeding momentary cognitions is not the cause of recognition of identity of the self.[220] So there must be a permanent self to cognize similarity between an antecent momentary cognition and a succeeding momentary cognition. But the Vijñānavādin does not admit it, for it contradicts the doctrine of momentariness.

CRITICISM OF THE MĀDHYAMIKA VIEW OF ĀTMAN.—The Mādhyamika opines that Ātman is void, because no cognitions are experienced in deep sleep. If there were cognitions in deep sleep, there would be cognitions of objects too, since cognitions are never without objects. It is contended that waking cognitions and dream cognitions alone cognize objects, but that cognitions in deep sleep do not cognize objects. The contention is false, since there is no difference between them. The cognitions in deep sleep cognize objects, because they are cognitions like waking cognitions and dream cognitions, which cognize objects. It is contended that a person never remembers objects experienced in deep sleep on waking from it, and that therefore cognitions do not cognize objects. The contention is false, because, if that were true, there would be no cognitions in deep sleep, because they are not remembered on waking from it. The Mādhyamika argues that as determinate cognitions of objects are produced by indeterminate cognitions prior to them, so existent cognitions are produced by the nonexistence of objects or void. Similarly, the cognition "I exist" is produced by the nonexistence of the cause of the immediately preceding cognition. So void is reality.[221] Vidyāranya gives this account of the Sūnyavādin's view of Ātman.

He refutes the doctrine by adducing the following criticism. Void is not capable of 'I'-cognition.[222] If void had 'I'-cognition, the son of a barren mother also would have it. So void cannot be Ātman. In deep sleep Ātman cognizes the nescience (avidyā) in which the internal organ is dissolved for the time being. So there is recollection "I slept happily so long" on waking from it. The recollection is due to the Self's cognition of avidyā during deep sleep. This is the Advaita Vedāntin's view. Rāmatīrtha offers the following criticism of the Mādhyamika view by elaborating Śaṁkara's arguments. Void is not cognized by buddhi, or by a mental mode in the form of a cognition, since buddhi or a cognition is immediately known by the witness (sākṣin). The witness is a seer or immediate knower. It is not void. So Ātman manifested as the seer even in deep sleep prior to determinations of buddhi must be admitted. Otherwise, there can be no recollection of it from waking from sleep. So Ātman is not void.[223] Śaṁkara regards deep sleep as the existence of buddhi in the state of its causal nescience. Buddhi is merged in causal nescience on the cessation of all cognitions.[224] So there is no void in deep sleep.

CRITICISM OF THE JAINA VIEW OF ĀTMAN.—The Jaina conceives of the Self as different from the body, the sense-organs, buddhi and the like, but coextensive with its body. Rāmatīrtha argues that the soul coextensive with the body cannot be Ātman, for it is limited. According to the Advaitist Ātman is ubiquitous Brahman, and cognizes all objects. All cannot be imagined in limited Ātman coextensive with its body, for there is no imaginer of all. Incorporeal Ātman is not really associated with any adjunct, and so appears to be limited. Its limits are imaginary.[225] It is imagined to cognize all objects, since they are due to avidyā. Further, what is limited is noneternal, because it is modified. But Ātman is eternal, because It is immutable. So the Self cannot be coextensive with its body.

CRITICISM OF THE NYĀYA-VAIŚEṢIKA VIEW OF ĀTMAN.—Rāmatīrtha asks whether consciousness is Ātman's essential characteristic or accidental characteristic. In the first alternative, it is a constant, inalienable characteristic of the Self, like odour of earth, since It is not distinct from Its essential characteristic. So It cannot have cognition as an impermanent quality. If cognition is an impermanent quality of the Self, what is its essential characteristic different from that of the not-self? None other than consciousness can be Its essential characteristic. So the self must be admitted to be unchanging, undifferentiated consciousness.[226]

This Advaita Vedānta view of the Self disproves the Nyāya-Vaiśeṣika view that the Self acquires consciousness from its conjunction with manas and that consciousness is its adventitious quality.

The Nyāya-Vaiśeṣika opines that a cognition is cognized by another cognition. This view is wrong, for it leads to infinite regress. The other difficulties in this view have been discussed already in connection with Ānandabodha's exposition of self-manifestness of a cognition.

The Nyāya-Vaiśeṣika opines that pleasure, a quality of the self, is manifested by a cognition, another quality of it. Pleasure is cognized by a cognition, since they exist in the same substrate—the self. This argument is invalid, since heat of a fire is not manifested by light, though both qualities exist in the same substrate—a fire. There is no general rule that a cognition and its object must exist in the same locus. If there were such a rule, there would be no such distinction as "This is a cognizer" and "This is cognized." A cognition cannot cognize a pleasure not only because they exist in the same substrate—the self, but also because they do not coexist in the self simultaneously. A pleasure and a cognition do not coexist in the same self, since the Vaiśeṣka admits that the self's conjunction with manas is the noninherent cause of a quality of the self. So when a pleasure is destroyed owing to the destruction of the self's conjunction with manas, which is its noninherent cause, it cannot be cognized by a cognition produced by another conjunction of the self with manas, which is its noninherent cause. The Nyāya-Vaiśeṣika denies simultaneity of the qualities of the self. Further, the Advaitist denies inherence admitted by the Nyāya-Vaiśeṣika according to which qualities inhere in a substance. The Advaitist's criticism of inherence will be given later. Further, both manas and self being partless cannot be conjoined with each other. Even if conjunction of them be possible, the self being ubiquitous cannot be separated from manas, and cannot therefore have another conjunction with manas. Because another conjunction of the self with manas cannot be produced, a cognition cannot be produced, and a pleasure cannot be cognized by a cognition. For similar reasons, pain, desire, aversion and volition also cannot be cognized by a cognition. They also being different from one another, and being distinct in their nature, they are not produced at the same time. They are produced by different conjunctions of the self with manas. So pleasure, pain, etc., are not cognized by a cognition. It cannot be argued that pleasure, etc., are qualified by a cognition, because they inhere in the same self. This argument is invalid, because there are distinct cognitions such as cognized pleasure, cognized pain and the like. Cognition is self-cognized.[227] Cognition, pleasure, pain, desire, aversion and volition are cognized by Ātman as witness (sākṣin). Even according to the Vaiśeṣika pleasure and the like cannot be the qualities of the self. The self is admitted by it to be immutable. Because it is immutable, it cannot have mutations, like pleasure and the like. Because the self is admitted by it to be ubiquitous, it is eternal. An eternal substance cannot have noneternal qualities. Further, according to the Vaiśeṣika, a subtance and its quality are entirely different from each other. So a particular pleasure cannot be definitely stated to be a quality of a particular self. Because of entire difference between a quality and a substance, a particular pleasure may be a quality of another self, or of manas, which is different from the pleasure.[228] Pleasure and the like may be qualities of manas, which is active, corporeal, and invariably concomitant with them.

The Nyāya-Vaiśeṣika opines that the self has noneternal cognition as its quality. Madhusūdana Sarasvatī urges that a cognition is not a quality of the self, because the relation between a substance and its quality is not determinable as will be shown later. The assumption of Ātman as one eternal cognition is better than that of the self having many noneternal cognitions as qualities. It is needless to assume many individual cognitions, their prior nenexistence, posterior nonexistence, inherence, genus and the like. The assumption of the Self as one eternal cognition does not violate the law of of parsimony of hypotheses. The different cognitions are one consciousness limited by and related to different objects as adjuncts due to avidyā. The experiences of their production and destruction are due to the relation of one consciousness to its different objects which limit it. If they were experienced without relation of consciousness to its objects, ether, time and space also would be many, because they are experienced as many. The Nyāya-Vaiśeṣika admits ether, time and space each to be one and eternal appearing to be many in relation to the adjuncts. Similarly, cognition or consciousness is one and eternal appearing to be many in relation to its objects, which are its limiting adjuncts. The Self is of the nature of one, eternal cognition.[229]

The Nyāya opines that the self is an object of mental perception. Vidyāraṇya rejects the view as false, because it is not substantiated by a proof. The self is proved independently of the manas. It can be known as the substrate of the cognition of an object, as Prabhākara holds. Therefore the assumption of another cognition (e.g., mental perception) is redundant.[230] The Nyāya-Vaiśeṣika regards consciousness, cognition, or manifestation as a quality of the self. Prakāśātman urges that if it is the self's essential quality, the self is self-manifest, and not manifested or cognized by another cognition. Because cognition is its essential quality, the self can never be divested of it, as the sun cannot be divested of light—its essential quality. Cognition cannot be produced in the self, its substrate, because the self is of the nature of cognition or manifestation. So the self is of the nature of consciousness or manifestation.[231]

CRITICISM OF KUMĀRILA'S VIEW OF ĀTMAN.—Kumārila opines that the self is a conscious substance, that as conscious it is a knower, that as a substance it is known, and that it is an object of 'I'-consciousness. The self is of the nature of 'not-this' or subject and 'this' or object. The former is a knower while the later is known. Padmapāda urges that this view is wrong, since the self is partless and unmodifiable.[232] Vidyāraṇya adduces the following arguments in refuting Kumārila's view. The substance-part of the Self cannot be the self, for it is insentient. If its consciousness-part is the object of knowledge, it involves contradiction between the knower and the known, and between the principal and the subordinate. Consciousness cannot be modified simultaneously into the knower and the known, for it is partless. If the self were known as an object, it would be not-self like a jar.[233]

Kumārila opines that the self is an object of mental perception or 'I'-cognition (ahaṁpratyaya). Vidyāraṇya refutes this view. Though the self is not an object of this cognition either entirely or partly because it is not an object and because it is partless, yet the internal organ superimposed on the self is manifested as 'I'-cognition in which the self is reflected. 'I'-cognition is a mental mode in which the self is reflected. The self endowed with the power of cognizing and the internal organ in which the self is reflected appear to be two—the knower and the known, as a fire endowed with the power of burning and iron heated by it appear as two. "'I'-cognition cognizes the self" is an appearance, as "iron burns" is an appearance. 'This'-part, which is cognized, is the internal organ, because it is insentient, modifiable, different from external objects and sense organs, and full of pain, and 'not-this' part is the self, because it is immutable, witness, an object of love, and consciousness common to external objects, the sense-organs and the like. So 'I'-cognition is of the nature of 'this' and 'not-this'.[234] This is the Advaitin's view of 'I'-cognition. So the Self is not an object of 'I'-cognition.

CRITICISM OF PRABHĀKARA'S VIEW OF ĀTMAN.—Prabhākara opines that a cognition is self-cognized, and that it manifests the self as the knower and an object as known. Padmapāda asks whether the self is manifested by consciousness (caitanya) and an insentient object is manifested by a cognition (anubhava), or whether a cognition also is manifested by consciousness, or whether a cognition is manifested by consciousness and the self is insentient. The first alternative is inadmissible, since if the insentient self were manifested by consciousness, the world would not be manifested by Ātman, and practical life would cease. It is contended that a self-cognized cognition manifests the self as a knower and an object as known, and that the world is not therefore unmanifested. Padmapāda urges that this contention is false, because it is not reasonable to hold that a cognition, which is conscious in itself, aided by an insentient object and a pramāṇa, is manifested. Further it is contended that a cognition aided by consciousness, the result of a cognitive act, menifests the self and an object, as the light of a lamp manifests the lamp and an object. The contention is false, for it will lead to an infinite series of the acts of manifestation. In the second alternative, either the self is manifested by itself, or it depends upon the cognition of an object for its manifestation. If it be held that the self, though of the nature of consciousness, is not self-manifest, the view is unreasonable. It does not stand to reason that the self, though of the nature of consciousness, is unmanifest in itself, and is made manifest by another entity. If the self and its cognition both are self-manifest, like two lamps, the self cannot depend upon its cognition to manifest it, as one lamp is not manifested by another lamp. In the third alternative, the self itself must be admitted to be of the nature of consciousness and self-manifest, for there is no proof for the existence of any other result of cognition. If a cognition is produced by a means of knowledge, it manifests its object with its distinctive character (viśeṣa). Consciousness is common to different cognitions of objects. Its distinctive characters are due to different objects. It cognizes different objects through its distinctive characters. So Ātman is of the nature of consciousness and self-manifest. The self is not insentient and manifested by a cognition as Prabhākara maintains[235]

Vidyāraṇya offers the following criticism of Prabhākara's view of Ātman. Prabhākara argues that cognition admitted by the Advaita Vedāntin and himself is self-manifest, and that, consequently, the assumption of the self-manifest self is redundant. So Prabhākara's view that the cognition of an object cognizes the self as its substrate and an object as known is better than the Advaitin's view. The cognition of an object, which is self-luminous, manifests the self as its substrate. Vidyāraṇya asks whether the self alone is manifested by cognition, or whether the cognition also is manifested by cognition, or whether the cognition alone is manifested by cognition. In the first alternative, the cognition manifests an insentient self. Vidyāraṇya asks whether the cognition unmanifested like the eyes manifests an object, or whether the cognition manifested like a light independent of any other homogeneous luminous entity manifests an object. The first subalternative is inadmissible, because the eyes produce a cognition distinct from them, but because a cognition manifests an object without depending on a cognition distinct from itself. In the second subalternative, a cognition without depending on any other cognition distinct from itself manifests an object. So a cognition characterized as manifestation of consciousness by its nature manifests an object. There is similarity among a cognition, the eyes and a light in manifesting an object. But there is dissimilarity also among them. A cognition manifests an object, because it is opposed to ignorance of an object; it is a conscious manifestation. A light manifests an insentient object, since it is opposed to darkness, which conceals it. The eyes are an instrument of the knowledge of an unknown object, because they are the immediate means of producing the cognition of it.[236] It is contended that it is not right to argue that a cognition does not depend upon a homogeneous entity, like a light, since a light is manifested by the eyes, which are of the same kind. Vidyāraṇya urges that this contention is false, because either the eyes destroy darkness in light or produce a cognition. The first alternative is untenable, since light has no darkness. In the second alternative, light is manifested by a cognition produced by the eyes. So a cognition independent of a homogeneous entity is manifested by consciousness. If it manifested the insentient self, the world would not be manifested by the latter before the cognition. It is contended that the knower's consciousness (pramātṛcaitanya) manifests all objects through the cognition of the insentient object. This contention is false, because if the cognition of an insentient object is the cause of the self's consciousness being related to an object, then it is a mode of mind (buddhi), and this is admitted by the Advaitavādin. The cognition of an object is a mental mode in which the Self is reflected according to the Advaitist. It is contended that the cognition of the insentient object is the cause of the manifestation of the self. This contention is obviously false, since the self of the nature of consciousness cannot be manifested by the cognition of an insentient object.[237] Then let the cognition of an object manifest the object alone. It is not the Advaitavādin's view. If another cognition produced by the cognition of an insentient object, different from the self's consciousness, be said to manifest an object, then it will lead to infinite regress. Nor is the second main alternative, that the self and the cognition both are manifested by consciousness, admissible, because they can be proved independently of each other. If both were manifested by consciousness, by what would their relation be known? They are ignorant of each other, and so cannot cognize their relation to each other. It is contended that the self is not manifested by itself, because it is of the nature of consciousness, like another self's consciousness, and is, therefore, manifested by a cognition. This contention is invalid, because, if that were true, a cognition also would be manifested by another cognition. It is argued that a cognition being immediate awareness is self-manifest. The argument is equally true of the self as well. So the self, being of the nature of consciousness, and being immediate awareness, like apprehension, is manifested by itself.[238] The cognition spoken of already is apprehension or immediate knowledge. The third alternative that cognition itself is manifested by consciousness is invalid, because the self itself must be admitted to be self-luminous consciousness inasmuch as there is no difference between the self and cognition.[239] Because self-luminous eternal cognition is the nature of the self, Prabhākara's view that the self is manifested by the cognition of an object, and that insentient ego (ahaṁkara) of the nature of 'I' is the self is wrong. Prabhākara regards the self as insentient endowed with the quality of cognition, which is adventitious, and of the nature of 'I'. So Vidyāraṇya interprets the self conceived by him as insentient ego. The self conceived by the Advaita Vedānta is one eternal self-luminous consciousness. Prabhākara contends that in the experience "I see a jar" ego is experienced as the seer, and that, therefore, ego as the seer is the self. Vidyāraṇya urges that, if it were true, ego or 'I' would be manifested as the self in deep sleep, but that it is not so manifested. So ego is not the self.[240]

CRITICISM OF THE SĀṀKHYA VIEW OF ĀTMAN.—The Sāṁkhya does not conceive of the self as an active agent. The soul is incorporeal and ubiquitous and cannot have action characterized by modification of motion. Its action is not intrinsic to its nature, because, if it were so, it would never be devoid of action, like consciousness. Nor is its action adventitious, since it cannot be tinged with the cause of action. The Sāṁkhya considers buddhi to be active, and holds that its activity is attributed to the self. Vidyāraṇya urges that there is no error according to the Sāṁkhya, which advocates the doctrine of akhyāti. So the activity of buddhi cannot be attributed to the inactive self.[241] So the self is not active. If it is active, it must be an experiencer of joys and miseries. Bhoga is not relation of the self to joys and miseries. If it were so, it would sometimes not have these emotions, like activity. The Sāṁkhya conceives of the self as an enjoyer (bhoktṛ) in the sense of being the seer of known objects, being of the nature of consciousness.[242]

The Sāṁkhya infers the self from its reflection in the insentient internal organ, as a face is inferred from its reflection in a mirror. The self of the nature of consciousness can never be directly known. Vidyāraṇya urges that this view contradicts the direct apprehension of the self as 'I'-consciousness.[243] If the self be said to be inferred from its reflection in the internal organ in order to convince others of its existence, there is no objection. But direct apprehension of the self cannot be denied.

THE ADVAITA VEDĀNTIN'S VIEW OF ĀTMAN, MENTAL MODE, AND OBJECT.—According to Advaita Vedāntin Ātman or Self is one, eternal, universal consciousness. It is self-manifest. Ātman limited by an internal organ is a knower (pramātṛ). Limited by a mode of an internal organ It is a means of knowledge or a cognition (pramāṇa, jñāna). Limited by an external object It is object-manifestation. In reality, all these are consciousnesses—knower-consciousness (pramātṛ-caitanya), knowledge-consciousness (pramāṇa-caitanya), and object-consciousness (viṣaya-caitanya). An internal organ is an adjunct of an empirical self (jīva), which is a knower, since the internal organ is active while the Self is not active. The internal organ as a modification (vṛtti) issues out of a sense-orifice to an external object, and is modified into it. The internal organ is related to an object through its mode, which assumes the form of an object. The internal organ is transparent because of the excess of sattva in it. The Self is reflected in it, and intelligizes it, as a fire interpenetrates a piece of iron and makes it red-hot. The Self cannot be directly related to an object. It can be related to an external object through a mode of the internal organ in which It is reflected, and which assumes the form of the object, and is thus related to it.[244] The Self thus related to a particular object through a mental mode is manifested as object-consciousness in a particular form. Ātman, universal consciousness, is self-manifest. But It is veiled by the nescience (avidyā), and so is not manifested everywhere. It is manifested by the internal organ, in which It is reflected and which It interpenetrates, in its particular mode related to a particular object.[245] It is objected that consciousness limited by a knower may manifest a mode of the internal organ, which assumes the form of an object, but that it cannot manifest and cognize an object. To this objection Prakāśātman replies that consciousness limited by a knower, which pervades the activity of an internal organ, acquires the capacity for overcoming insentience of the object from its relation to the mode of the internal organ. The internal organ produces the capacity for manifesting consciousness in the object to which it is related, as it produces the capacity in itself.[246] Consciousness limited by the internal organ is the knower, and immediate apprehension of an object is the result.[247] The knower's consciousness becomes identical with knowledge-consciousness or consciousness limited by a mental mode, and knowledge-consciousness becomes identical with object-consciousness. Thus the knower's consciousness becomes identical with object-consciousness.[248] Though Ātman or universal consciousness is ubiquitous, its manifestation is veiled by avidyā, and, consequently, its manifestation of a particular object depends upon a mode of a limited internal organ related to the object.[249] A knower cannot manifest a particular object without a mental mode (antaḥkaraṇavṛtti), which is called a cognition (jñāna). A particular cognition is a mental mode, and not a quality of the Self or Ātman, That is pure consciousness (caitanya). It is eternal and universal consciousness unrelated to an internal organ and its modes, which are produced by avidyā. One knower's consciousness cannot manifest all objects, because it can manifest an object, which is related to a mode of an internal organ, and because it cannot manifest other objects.[250] Consciousness limited by a particular object is manifested as identical with a particular knower's consciousness as stated above. It is not manifested as identical with another knower's consciousness. So a particular knower's consciousness does not manifest all objects.[251] Manifestation is overcoming a veil of avidyā,—not an excess produced in the nature of an object.[252]

CRITICISM OF MANY INDIVIDUAL SOULS.—Ānandabodha refutes the existence of many individual souls (ātman) by adducing the following arguments. The theistic Vedāntists think of a soul to be atomic (aṇu) in magnitude. If it were atomic, it would not experience sensations in all parts of its body. The Jaina conceives of a soul as coextensive with its body. If it were so, it would consist of parts, and, therefore, be noneternal. The Naiyāyika and others think of a soul as ubiquitous. If it is so, one soul can experience different cognitions, feelings and volitions in different bodies as limiting adjuncts, as one ubiquitous ether (ākāśa) can produce sensations of sound as limited by the earholes, and the assumption of many souls is needless. The so-called ubiquitous souls occupy the most extensive space and the unlimited time. So their multitude is unnecessary. One ubiquitous supreme soul,

Ātman, can have different experiences through different bodies as adjuncts. Some contend that other souls are inferred in the following manner. My voluntary actions in my body are preceded by volitions of my soul. So voluntary actions in other bodies are preceded by volitions of other souls, because they are voluntary actions, like mine. So other souls are inferred from their voluntary actions. Ānadabodha ūrges that this contention is false, because the opponent proves another soul not as a knower like his self, but as not-self known by his self.[253] The opponent formulates his inference in another form. As voluntary actions in my body are perceived to be preceded by my volitions, so voluntary actions in another body are not perceived to be preceded by my volitions. A volition inhering in my soul is perceived ; but a volition favourable to a voluntary action in another body is not perceived by me ; so another soul with such a volition is inferred by me. Ānandabodha urges that the assumption of real individual souls to account for perception and nonperception of volitions in oneself and another is not justifiable.[254] One real ubiquitous Self may produce voluntary actions in different bodies through Its different adjuncts, viz. internal organs. Different empirical selves (jīva) are one Self limited by different internal organs or reflected in them. They are not ontologically real. So different souls in different bodies cannot be proved.[255] On the other hand, one Ātman is proved by the Upaniṣads, Smṛtis, and Purāṇas. Some infer that individual souls are many, since they are substrates of the genus of soul (ātmatva), inferior to the genus of substance. Ānandabodha refutes it by the counter-inference that Self is not many, because It is eternal, ubiquitous, and incorporeal, like ether.[256] Some infer that individual souls are many, because they are substrates of the genus of soul, inferrior to the genus of substance, and of special qualities imperceptible through the external sense-organs. Ānandabodha urges that this inference is invalid, because the reason is unproven. The Advaitavādin does not admit that Self has special qualities.[257] The knowing Self cannot have the qualities of the known. An eternal entity cannot have noneternal qualities. Cognitions, feelings, volitions, impressions, merits and demerits are noneternal, and are not qualities of the eternal Self.[258] Ether (ākāśa) endued with noneternal sound is not eternal, but produced by Ātman. It is noneternal, for it is insentient. Atoms are noneternal, as they are insentient. So there are not many souls.[259]

Kaṇāda argues that there are many souls, because they account for their different experiences. Some are happy while others are miserable ; some are bound while others are released. If there were one Self, one soul being happy, the others would be happy, and one soul being released, the others would be released.[260] The Advaita Vedāntin does not deny the empirical, phenomenal reality of many empirical selves (jīva). They are not ontologically real. Some of them are bound while others are released. Their experiences do not coalesce with one another. They are either semblances (ābhāsa), or reflections (pratibimba), or limitations (avaccheda) of one Ātman. The advocates of this view quote different Śrutis in favour of their views.[261] The Advaitavadins' criticisms of many real individual souls advocated by the Theistic schools of Vedānta are weak and unconvincing and repugnant to morality and religion.

[1] DHIP., vol. II, pp. 82-83 ; P. C. Divanji's Introduction to Siddhāntabindu, p. xcii ; V. A. Ramasvami Sastri's Introduction to 'Tattvabindu', p. 41.
[2] VKT., i, 1, 2, p. 95. [3] VPS., p. 98. [4] Ibid, p. 90.
[5] Ibid, p. 229. [6] Ibid. [7] Ibid, p. 217.
[8] Ibid, p. 215. [9] ŚBS., i, 1, 1. [10] Bhām., i, 1, 1, p. 80.
[11] Ibid. [12] VPS., pp. 195 & 216.
[13] Ibid, pp. 194-95. [14] ACM., p. 40. [15] Ibid, p. 41.
[16] Ibid, p. 43. [17] PPD., p. 81. [18] PPV., p. 205.
[19] Ibid. [20] VPS., p. 195. Ibid, pp. 194 & 197.
[21] Bhām., i, 1, 2, p. 95. [22] VKT., i, 1, 2, p. 94.
[23] VPS., p. 217. [24] Bhām., i, 1, 4, pp. 126-27.
[25] Ibid, p. 135. [26] ŚBS., iv, 3, 14, p. 998.
[27] VPS., p. 206. [28] Ibid, p. 204.
[29] Bhām., i, 1, 4, p. 134-35. [30] VPS., p. 217.
[31] Ibid, p. 97. [32] Ibid. [33] Ibid, p. 229.
[34] ŚBS., i, 2, 14, p. 248. [35] VPS., p. 244.
[36] SLS., 58-60, 65-68, 71-73.
[37] Ibid, pp. 72-74, 81-82, 84-85. [38] Ibid, pp. 87-88.
[39] Ibid, pp. 89-90. [40] Ibid, pp. 87-92 & 95.
[41] Ibid, pp. 96-99. [42] VPS., p. 224. [43] Ibid, p. 225.
[44] HIP., Vol. II, pp. 542-44. [45] VPS., pp. 204-05.
[46] HIP., Vol. II, pp. 467-70. [47] VPS , p. 209.
[48] Ibid, pp. 208-11 ; HIP., Vol. II, pp. 471-73, 477-85.
[49] TPD., pp. 3-6. [50] Ibid, pp. 25-26. [51] VPS., p. 57.
[52] Ibid, p. 85. [53] VSM., pp. 129-37.
[54] PPD., p 17. [55] Ibid, p. 29.
[56] Ibid, pp. 20-21. [57] VPS., pp. 53, 57-58.
[58] Ibid, p. 62. [59] Ibid, p. 88.
[60] SLS., pp. 234, 236-37. PD., viii, 48 & 56.
[61] SLS., pp. 240-42 ; SLSV., p. 243.
[62] SLS., p. 243. [63] Ibid, pp. 245-48.
[64] Ibid, pp. 248-49. [65] Ibid, pp. 249-50. [66] Ibid, p, 253 ; VP., pp 102-03 ; IPC., Vol. I, pp. 373-74.
[67] SB., p. 12.
[68] ŚBS., i, 1, 1, p. 40. [69] Bhām , i, 1, 1, p. 38.
[70] Ibid, p. 42. [71] Ibid, p. 41.
[72] VKT., i, 1, 1, p. 42. [73] VPS., p. 72 ; Ibid, p. 71.
[74] Ibid. [75] Ibid. p. 75. [76] Bhām., i, 1, 1, p. 46.
[77] Ibid, p. 45. [78] Ibid, p. 45.
[79] VPS., p. 98. [80] Ibid, p. 97. [81] Ibid, p. 98.
[82] Bhām., i, 1, 1, p. 45. [83] Ibid, p. 38.
[84] Ibid, p. 39. [85] Ibid, p. 58.
[86] VP., pp. 387 & 394. [87] TA., pp. 89-90 ; ACK., pp. 89-91. [88] SB., pp. 26-27. SNS., ii, 51.
[89] Ibid, p. 29. [90] Bhām., i, 1, 4, p. 126.
[91] VP., p. 102. [92] SB., p. 28. [93] VP., p. 381.
[94] Ibid, p. 382. [95] SLS., pp. 130 & 132.
[96] ACM , pp. 30 & 38. [97] Ibid, pp. 32, 35 & 38.
[98] SB., p. 28. [99] SLS., p. 103. [100] Ibid, p. 99.
[101] Ibid, pp. 101-02 ; PD., i, 16 ; vi, 155.
[102] PPV., pp. 65-66.
[103] SLS., pp. 160-61. [104] ACK., pp. 40-43.
[105] ACM., pp. 36-37. [106] SB., 29-30 ; SBBS., p. 30 ; TPD., pp. 375-77.
[107] BS., ii, 1, 32 ; ii, 1, 22 ; SLS., p. 162.
[108] SLS., pp. 163-65 ; SLSV., p. 165.
[109] SLS., pp. 165-66.
[110] ACK., pp. 38-40 ; TPD., pp. 375-77.
[111] VP., p. 381. [112] SLS., pp. 467-77.
[113] Ibid, pp. 477-78. [114] Yogavāśiṣṭa, VSM., pp. 103-06.
[115] SLS., p. 484.
[116] VPS., p. 72. [117] Ibid, p. 73.
[118] Ibid, pp. 73-74. [119] Ibid, p. 74.
[120] Bhām., i, 1, 1, p. 45. [121] Ibid, p. 58.
[122] Ibid, i, 1, 4, p. 134.
[123] Ibid, i, 1, 2, p. 80 ; ŚBS., i, 1, 2, pp. 79-80.
[124] Bhām., i, 1, 3, p. 99. [125] Ibid, iii, 2, 11, p. 709.
[126] Ibid, p. 710. [127] ŚBS., iii, 2, 12, p. 708 ; Bhām.
[128] Bhām. i, 1, 5, p. 166. [129] Ibid, pp. 171-72.
[130] Ratnaprabhā, iii, 2, 6. [131] PD., vi, 132, 155, 160, 164, 182, 196-97 & 223. [132] VP., p. 381.
[133] TA., p. 38. [134] VS., p. 9. [135] SLS., pp. 103, 99&159.
[136] Ibid, pp. 132 & 139. [137] VPS., pp. 190-91.
[138] VS., pp. 8-13, 20-21, 23-25 ; ACK., pp. 85-86, 88&93.
[139] SB., p. 53 ; ACK., p. 88. [140] VPS., pp. 74-75.
[141] Bhām. & VKT., iii, 2, 27.
[142] SNS., i, 78, p. 102. Ibid, i, 68-78. Introduction, p. 15.
[143] VPS., pp. 242-46. [144] SNS., iii, 42.
[145] Ibid, iii, 45. [146] Ibid, ii, 1. [147] Ibid, i, 36.
[148] Ibid, i, 89. [149] Ibid, i, 98. Ibid, iii, 41-42.
[150] US., ii, 93, p. 80. [151] VPS., p. 183.
[152] SB., pp. 18-19. [153] ĀNM., p. 144.
[154] Ibid, pp. 144-45. [155] Ibid, pp. 144-45.
[156] Ibid, p. 145. [157] NMV., pp. 143-44.
[158] USPY., xvi, 57, p. 270 ; SB., p. 19.
[159] SNS., i, 30. [160] Ibid. [161] ĀNM., p. 173.
[162] Ibid, p. 175. Ibid, pp. 172-74. [163] Ibid, p. 176.
[164] Ibid, pp. 176-77. [165] Ibid, pp. 177-78.
[166] ACM., pp. 25-26 ; SBBS., p. 11. SB., p. 19.
[167] SNS., ii, 69. [168] Ibid, ii, 71. [169] Ibid, ii, 74.
[170] Ibid, ii, 75. Ibid, ii, 71-74. [171] Ibid, ii, 76.
[172] Ibid, ii, 77. [173] Ibid, ii, 78.
[174] Ibid, p. 191. Ibid, ii, 81.
[175] Ibid, ii, 82. [176] Ibid, ii, 83. [177] Ibid, ii, 86.
[178] Ibid, ii, 89. [179] Ibid, ii, 92. [180] Ibid, iv, 3.
[181] Ibid, iv, 6 ; iv, 8. [182] Ibid, ii, 97.
[183] Ibid, ii, 98, p. 204. Cp. IEP., pp. 189-201.
[184] SNS., ii, 107 ; ii, 108. [185] Ibid, ii, 113.
[186] Ibid, ii, 115. [187] Ibid, ii, 110. [188] Ibid, ii, 53.

[189] Ibid, ii, 63. [190] Ibid, ii, 100-02.
[191] Ibid, ii, 68. [192] ĀNM., p. 138.
[193] NMV., p. 140. [194] ĀNM., p. 141.
[195] NMV., p. 141. [196] ĀNM., pp. 142-43.
[197] Ibid, p. 142. [198] Ibid. [199] Ibid.
[200] Ibid, pp. 137-43. IPC., Vol. I, pp. 219-21.
[201] VPS., p. 54. [202] Ibid. Cp. ŚBS., ii, 2, 28.
[203] VPŚ., p. 55. [204] Ibid, p. 56. Cp. PPV., p. 50.
[205] PPV., p. 175. [206] Ibid.
[207] Ibid, p. 174. Ibid, pp. 174-75.
[208] VPS., p. 57. PPV., p. 53.
[209] VPS., p. 58. Ibid, pp. 57-58.
[210] VPS., p. 58. PPV., p. 53. [211] VPS., p. 55.
[212] Ibid. Cp. PPV., p. 51.
[213] VPS., pp. 184-85. VS., p. 26. USPY., xi, 1-3, pp. 243-44. IPC., Vol. I, p. 223.
[214] VPS., pp. 189 & 185 ; SNS., ii, 89.
[215] VPS., p. 182. US., xvi, 23, p. 253.
[216] A Treatise of Human Nature, Vol. I, E.M.L., 1951, Part IV, pp. 200, 240 & 245. [217] VPS., p. 182.
[218] VPS., p. 183. Ibid, pp. 182-83. [219] Ibid, p. 189.
[220] US., xvi, 26, p. 254 ; USPY., Ibid, pp. 254-55. IPC , Vol. I, pp. 223-24.
[221] VPS., p. 182. [222] Ibid. [223] USPY., xvi, 16, p. 249.
[224] PK., p. 2. [225] USPY., xvi, 22, p. 252.
[226] Ibid, xvi, 57, p. 270. [227] Ibid, xvi, 51-54, pp. 266-68. SNS., ii, 76-78, 81-82.
[228] Ibid, xvi, 55, pp. 268-69. [229] SB., p. 19.
[230] VPS., p. 54. [231] PPV., p. 52. [232] PPD., p. 17.
[233] VPS., p. 54. [234] Ibid, p. 53. [235] PPD., p. 18.
[236] VPS., p. 56. [237] Ibid, p. 57. [238] Ibid, p. 57.
[239] Ibid. [240] Ibid, p. 58. [241] Ibid, p. 189.
[242] Ibid, p. 190.
[243] Ibid, p. 54. PPV., p. 50. IPC., Vol. I, pp. 247-56.
[244] PPV., p. 70. [245] Ibid. [246] Ibid. [247] Ibid.
[248] Cp. VP., p. 59. TA., pp. 133-34. IPC., Vol. I, pp. 128-39. [249] PPV., p. 71.
[250] Ibid. [251] Ibid. [252] Ibid. [253] ĀNM., p. 27.
[254] Ibid, p. 28. [255] Ibid, p. 29. [256] Ibid, p. 30.
[257] Ibid, p. 19. [258] Ibid, pp. 19-20. [259] Ibid, pp. 4-20.
[260] Ibid, p. 4. Vaiśeṣika Sūtra, iii, 2, 20.
[261] ĀNM., pp. 24-25.

CHAPTER VIII

WORLD

MĀYĀ AND AVIDYĀ.—Sureśvara defines nescience (avidyā) as neither existent nor nonexistent, nor both, neither different nor nondifferent from Ātman, neither composed of parts nor partless nor both. It is unmanifest and undifferentiated into concrete names and forms. It is the cause of the subtle body and the gross body. It is the causal body of an empirical self (jīva). It is a semblance of Ātman or one universal, eternal consciousness. It is the cause of the false world appearance. It is annulled by the suprarational intuition of the identity of Ātman, the psychic principle, with Brahman, the cosmic principle.[1] Ānandagiri describes the Inner Self (pratyāgātman) as of the nature of existence, consciousness and bliss, and Brahman as of the nature of truth, knowledge, and infinitude. Avidyā is not existent, like Brahman. Nor is it absolutely nonexistent, since it has the power of producing effects, which are capable of producing practical actions, and since there is such an experience as "I am ignorant." Nor is it both existent and nonexistent, for it is self-contradictory. It is not different from Ātman, because difference either as nature or as a property is not determinable as will be shown later. Nor is it nondifferent from Ātman, for then it will be an eternal existent, like Brahman. It cannot be both different and nondifferent from Ātman, since it is self-contradictory. But though, it is neither existent nor nonexistent nor both, and neither different nor nondifferent from Ātman nor both, it is the root cause of the world appearance, and, consequently, its undifferentiated and unmanifest seed. It is not composed of parts, for they are not yet differentiated from it as effects. Nor is it partless, since it is insentient and modified into manifold objects. Nor is it both composed of parts and partless, as it involves self-contradiction.[2] It is indefinable (anirvacanīya).

Vācaspati Miśra regards the world as a false appearance of Brahman associated with indefinable twofold avidyā.[3] Amalānanda explains two kinds of avidyā thus. One avidyā is a beginningless, indefinable, positive entity. The other is a series of potencies of previous confusions. It is indefinable, because it is neither real nor unreal.[4] According to Vācaspati Miśra Brahman is the independent creator of the world, and avidyā is its instrument, which does not compromise Its independence. Evidently, avidyā is the beginningless, insentient, indefinable, positive entity underlying the world appearance. It is something like subtle matter. Later Advaitists call it māyā—cosmic nescience. Avidyā as a series of potencies (vāsanā) of confusions in empirical selves (jīva) is psychological. The poteneies are dissolved in the indefiable, beginningless, insentient, positive avidyā in dissolution. They are again revived at the next creation of the world appearance, and produce the mind-body-complexes of empirical selves. During dissolution the internal organs of the jīvas are merged in their cause—indefinable avidyā—and exist with the impressions of confusions as subtle powers.[5] Later Advaitists called nescience in the jīvas avidyā—individual nescience.

Brahman That knows and resolves with beginningless, indefinable avidyā is the material cause of the world.[6]

Padmapāda regards the knowledge of Brahman as the cause of destruction of all evils, and the nescience as the cause of all evils. Avidyā is the cause of an empirical self's false knowledge of being a knower, a doer, and an enjoyer or a sufferer. It is the cause of superimposition of the self and the not-self on each other. Vidyā is opposed to avidyā. It is the true comprehension of the nature of reality or Brahman.[7] Avidyā veils the nature of reality, and makes it appear to be what is different from it. Vidyā rends the veil, and manifests the true nature of reality. Avidyā is the cause of superimposition (adhyāsa). Vidyā destroys superimposition.

Prakāśātman defines the power of nescience as a positive entity abiding in Ātman or Self, which is the material cause of a stream of illusory experiences of false appearances. It is proved by perception, inference and presumption. 1. The immediate experience or perception "I am ignorant, and do not know me or anything else" proves nescience to be a positive entity. The opponent objects that this experience cognizes the absence of knowledge. Prakāśātman urges that this objection is invalid, since nescience is experienced as a positive entity, like the experience "I am happy", and since negation is cognized by nonapprehension according to the Bhāṭṭa. Even according to him the absence of knowledge in self is not possible. In the experience "knowledge does not exist in myself" the knowledge of the self, which is the abode and the object of the knowledge, exists ; so there can be no experience of the absence of knowledge. But according to Prakāśātman, who advocates the perception of nescience as a positive entity, witness-consciousness experiences all objects either as known or as unknown. It experiences an object as known through valid knowledge. It experiences an object as unknown in a general way or in a particular form or as excluding nescience. So the experience of witness-consciousness proves the perception of positive nescience in Self. 2. Inference also proves nescience as a positive entity. Just as a ray of the light of a lamp manifests an object which was unmanifested before in darkness, so knowledge manifests an object, which was unmanifested before, by removing the nescience, which veiled its object before in the same place, which is different from its prior negation. So the positive nescience of an object is inferred from the knowledge of it. 3. Presumption also proves nescience as a positive entity. If there were no nescience, the illusory experiences of false appearances would not be possible. The illusory experience of silver in a necre must have a material cause. If its material cause were real, the illusory experience would be true. So its material cause must be positive nescience. If its material cause had an origin, it would lead to a vicious infinite. So its material cause must be without an origin. The beginningless, positive, false nescience related to Ātman can be the material cause of all false appearances.[8] It is itself a false superimposition, and the material of other false superimpositions, because effects are not produced without causes.

The Śruti says, "Bondage is terminated by the knowledge of Brahman". It indicates that prior nescience abides in Brahman as the cause of relation to superimpositions. Otherwise, bondage due to superimpositions cannot be terminated.[9] So avidyā is proved by presumption.

The nescience is cognized by the witness-consciousness, and shown to be a positive entity distinguished from the absence of knowledge by the means of valid knowledge.[10] It does not depend upon difference between its substrate (āśraya) and its object (viṣaya) for its existence, but it performs two functions in the same entiy—Brahman, viz., subsisting in It, and making It its object. Avidyā subsists in Brahman, and produces ignorance of It. Brahman is both the substrate and the object of avidyā, as darkness abides in a pot and conceals its nature, which is devoid of activity and a veil.[11] Avidyā veiling the nature of its substrate does not conflict with its abiding in the same substrate. A cloud conceals the sky, and abides in it. The nescience does not conflict with Braham or self-lumionous consciousness, its substrate, because the witness-consciousness manifests it.[12] Prakāśātman, like Padmapāda, regard the beginningless avidyā as the cause of the beginningless distinction of empirical selves and Brahman, and a stream of false superimpositions. The nescience abiding in Brahman and being related to Its nature alone creates the phenomenal difference between an empirical self and Brahman.[13] Prakāśātaman proves that avidyā does not abide in a jīva or in an internal organ.

Vidyāraṇya identifies māyā with prakṛiti, since the Śruti says, "Māyā should be known as prakṛti, and Īśvara as endowed with the power of māyā." He proves avidyā to be devoid of origin, since the 'Bhagavad Gītā says, "Know prakṛti and puruṣa to be without origin". Because avidyā is beginningless, a jīva's bondage is beginningless. Vidyāraṇya identifies māyā with avidyā.[14] But he distinguishes between them elsewhere, and treats māyā as an adjunct (upādhi) of Īśvara, and avidyā as an adjunct of an empirical self (jīva). Prakṛti invested with sattva, rajas and tamas related to the reflection of Brahman full of consciousness and bliss is twofold. Māyā is manifested by Īśvara. Avidyā is manifested by a jīva. Pure sattva unovercome by rajas and tamas predominates in māyā. Impure sattva overcome by rajas and tamas predominates in avidyā. Māyā and avidya are the two forms of the root prakṛti. Īśvara reflected in māyā dominates it, and is omniscient. The jīva, a reflection of Brahman in avidyā, is dominated by it, and is ignorant. Avidyā is the jīva's causal (kāraṇa) body. Māyā with tamas predominating in it is modified into the elements. Brahman associated with māyā with pure sattva is the efficient cause, and associated with māyā with tamas is the material cause, of the world. Māyā is the limiting adjunct of Īśvara while avidyā is the limiting adjunct of the jīva. The Supreme Brahman transcends the limiting adjuncts of māyā and avidyā.[15] Space, time and objects are constructions of māyā, and do not lin it Brahman. The Śruti says, "Īśvara has the power of māyā. Māyā is prakṛti." Māyā, a power of God, has the power of creating the world and the power of deluding the jīvas. Māyā is the material cause of the world. God guiding māyā is the effiicient cause of the world. Māyā is said to be of the nature of tamas in the 'Gopālatāpanī Upaniṣad.' It is insentient and unconscious. From the ontological standpoint it is nonexistent. From the empirical standpoint it is neither existent nor nonexistent but indefinable. From the popular standpoint it is real and experienced by all. It is dependent for it is not experienced without self-manifest consciousness. It is independent for it makes detached transcendental consciousness appear different from it as the diverse world. It makes Brahman appear to be Īśvara and jīvas. It has the inconceivable power of making the changeless, pure Ātman or Brahman appear as the manifold world appearance.[16]

Māyā has the power of projecting the world of diverse phenomena (vikṣepaśakti) pre-eminently. Avidyā has the power of veiling the nature of the self-luminous Brahman. It makes the self-manifest Brahman or Ātman unmanifest. It has the power of superimposing the mind-body-complex on the Ātman—pure transcendental consciousness.

Padmapāda considers avidyā to be the cause of superimposition of the not-self on the Self, which is the root of all evils. Knowledge is the comprehension of the Reality. Bondage is due to avidyā or the jiva's ignorance of being of the nature of Brahman. Avidyā is assumed to exist in the jīva, which conceals the manifestation of Brahman to it. If the jiva knew itself to be identical with Brahman, the scriptural instruction for acquiring the knowledge of its identity with Brahman would be infructuous. The Śruti declares Brahman to be manifested to many jīvas limited by the beginningless avidyā.[17] The later Saṁkarites regard māyā as cosmic nescience, and avidyā as individual nescience. Māyā is modified into the world, which is an appearance of Brahman. Avidyā is the cause of the jīva's bondage.

Citsukha states the opponent's denial of avidyā, and refutes his view. The opponent refutes the concept of indefinable nescience in the following manner. He identifies nescience with negation or absence of knowledge. No nescience different from it is known or reasonable, since the people experience nescience either as prior negation or posterior negation of knowledge. Nescience means no-science or absence of knowledge. Science means knowledge. So nescience means negation of knowledge, or what is opposed to knowledge, or what is other than knowledge. In the first alternative, the absence of knowledge is not indefinable, like the absence of the known object. In the second alternative, doubt, illusion and the like, which are opposed to knowledge—contrary or false knowledge, are not indefinable, since they are positive in their nature. In the third alternative, all except nescience would be nescience. Nescince can neither be defined nor proved. Nescience is not what is removable by knowledge, because, in that case, prior knowledge also which is destroyed by posterior knowledge would be nescience. It may be contended that nescience is originless but that prior knowledge is not originless, and that therefore it is not nescience. This contention is invalid, since an originless positive entity, like self, is eternal and therefore not destructible by knowledge. Nescience cannot be defined as originless and indefinable. This definition is faulty, for an indefinable entity cannot be different from being and nonbeing. Nescience cannot be defined as the material cause of an illusion. This definition is too wide, because it applies to the self also for it is the material cause of illusion. It may be contended that the self is not the material cause of an illusion, because if the self were its material cause, an illusion would be true, like the self. This contention is false, because an illusion is true *as* illusion. The experience of the existence of its object proves that the illusion is false, but it does not disprove the existence of the illusion. If the illusion did not exist, there would be no such experience as "the illusion existed so long". Supposing nescience with a charaeteristic, which cannot be comprehended, exists, what is its proof? The monist argues that the experience "I am ignorant" proves its existence. The opponent urges that nescience is the negation of knowledge and experienced as such. The experience does not prove that nescience is originless and positive in nature. Nor does the experience of a person waking from deep sleep "I did not know anything so long," "I was ignorant so long" prove the existence of nescience as a positive entity, since the monist admits that the witness-self knows the absence of knowledge also and so can recognize it on waking from deep sleep. But, according to the opponent, the absence of knowledge is inferred by a person on waking from deep sleep and cannot be recognized. The monist may object that the absence of knowledge cannot be cognized by indeterminate consciousness during deep sleep, because it depends upon the knowledge of its counterentity, which is not possible in the state. This objection is groundless, for difference is cognized by indeterminate perception indistinctly as it is distinctly cognized by determinate perception. So the absence of knowledge is indistinctly cognized by indeterminate perception and distinctly perceived by determinate perception. The Viśiṣṭādvaitavādin infers the absence of knowledge during deep sleep after waking from sleep. He maintains that the absence of knowledge is indistinctly cognized by indeterminate perception in deep sleep and distinctly cognized by a person on waking from sleep. The absence of knowledge is inferred from the absence of the collocation of causes of knowledge as the probans of inference.

Citsukha adduces the following arguments to prove nescience to be an originless positive entity, which is destroyed by the intuitive knowledge of Brahman. Being originless, it is a positive entity, and capable of being annulled by the true knowledge of Brahman. This definition is not too narrow, since all nesciences have these three characteristics. The Self is not included in the defiinition of nescience, since It is an originless positive entity, and since It is not destructible by true knowledge. So the definition is not too wide. The atoms are not admitted by the Advaitavādin to be originless. Their nature also is not admitted by the monist. So they are not included in the definition of nescience. Nescience is not impossible, because it is different from being and nonbeing and figuratively called a positive entity in that it is different from a nonentity, and in that it cannot be inferred to be an originless, positive entity, like the Brahman, indestructible by true knowledge of It.[18] It is proved to be a positive entity by the experience "I am ignorant of the nature of the object", which cannot be explained without admitting positive ignorance. The experience cannot be explained by the absence of valid knowledge by the Viśiṣṭādvaitavādin, because he admits that the experience "I have no valid knowledge", which is a knowledge qualified by an object, is a valid knowledge, and that therefore the object also is known as a qualification of the knowledge. Thus the opponent's statement involves self-contradiction. The opponent may contend that the object is known by valid knowledge in a general way, but that it is not known in detail, and that therefore his statement is flawless. This contention is invalid, since the knowledge or ignorance of the special characteristics of the object cannot remove the defect stated above. The opponent may object that the Advaitavādin admits nescience, though positive in nature, to be removable by true knowledge, but that it cannot account for the experience "I do not know the object." This objection is invalid, because, according to the monist, positive nescience is known by witness-self, and not known by valid knowledge. Nescience is the object of witness-consciousness, which precedes the production of valid knowledge.[19] Some Advaitavādins maintain that all objects are the objects of witness-consciousness, either as known or as unknown.

The Śruti says, "There was darkness" before creation. The word 'darkness' does not mean negation of knowledge. The Śruti says, "There was no nonbeing". Therefore 'darkness' means positive nescience, and not the absence of knowledge. The Smṛti says, "Those who take refuge with God cross māyā". So nescience is removable by knowledge.

Further, nescience is defined as the material cause of an illusion. The definition does not apply to the Self, since It is detached, unchanging, and not the material cause of any effect. If a real entity were the material cause of an illusion, the illusion would be true, though an illusion also is indefinable, and is experienced as different from nonbeing. If an illusion were true, it could not be recognized as "it existed so long". Therefore the material cause of an illusion is not real, and it is proved that an illusion is positive nescience.[20]

Sadānanda Yogīndra defines nescience as a positive entity, indefinable, different from being and nonbeing, of the nature of sattva, rajas and tamas, and opposed to true knowledge, because of the experience "I am ignorant" and the Śruti "Brahman conceals Its powers by its guṇas". Nṛsiṁha Sarasvatī explains this definition as follows. It is not a being, as it is unreal, like a hare's horns. Nor is it a nonbeing, as a nonbeing cannot be a cause. But nescience is the cause of the false world appearance. It is not definable as a being or as a nonbeing. So it is indefinable. But, if it were indefinable, it would be incapable of being known, and so would be nonexistent. In order to distinguish it from such an unknowable nonentity, it is said to be of the nature of sattva, rajas and tamas. The Śruti speaks of nescience as originless and of the nature of sattva, rajas and tamas. If nescience were existent like the pervasive ether, the false experience of the world appearance would never cease. So nescience is said to be opposed to knowledge, and terminated by the intuitive knowledge of Brahman. The Nyāya regards nescience as the absence of knowledge. This view is wrong. Nescience is a positive entity. But, though it is of the nature of three guṇas, they cannot be distinguished from one another. It is an indistinguishable mass of them. It is an indefinable entity capable of doing what cannot be done.

Rāmatīrtha explains Sadānanda Yogīndra's definition of nescience as follows. If nescience were existent, it would not be annulled, like Brahman. If it were nonexistent, it would not be an object of immediate experience, and it would not produce phenomena. Because its experience and annulment are known to be nescience, it is said to be indefinable. It is not false knowledge, which is a quality of an empirical self. In order to distinguish it from false knowledge, it is defined as of the nature of three guṇas. The guṇas and the possessor of them being nondifferent from each other, nescience is said to be of the nature of the three gunas indistinguishable from one another. Nescience is not the absence of knowledge. It is a positive entity (bhāvarūpa). Rāmatīrtha asks whether the knowledge, which is the counter-entity of nescience, is witness-consciousness, or whether it is a mode of mind, or whether it is a quality of an empirical self. Witness-consciousness is eternal, and is not a counter-entity of the absence of knowledge. A mode of mind is called knowledge in a figurative sense. So nescience is not the absence of a mental mode. Rāmatīrtha asks whether nescience is the absence of a particular knowledge, or whether it is the absence of knowledge in general. The first subalternative is untenable, since the experience "I am ignorant" or "I do not know any thing", which is not the ignorance of a particular thing also is experienced as nescience. So nescience is not the absence of a particular knowledge. The second subalternative is inadmissible, because in the absence of the knowledge of a particular thing there is no knowledge in general. Because there is no particular knowledge or no knowledge in general, there can be no absence of knowledge. So nescience is not the absence of knowledge. Nescience is not an ontological reality, though it is a positive being. Nescience is not definable as existent or nonexistent or both, or as composed of parts or devoid of parts or both, or as different, or nondifferent or both. So it is indefinable (anirvacanīya). The experience "I am ignorant" does not cognize the absence of knowledge.[21]

THE ABODE AND THE OBJECT OF NESCIENCE.—Sureśvara proves that Brahman or Ātman is the abode and the object of avidyā. Not-self is insentient by nature. What is devoid of knowledge by nature cannot be related to nescience. Supposing nescience exists in not-self, it cannot produce any excess (atiśaya) in itself. Nor can not-self acquire knowledge, whose negation is nescience, because not-self is produced by nescience.[22] Nor does not-self exist already, and then becomes devoid of knowledge, and then becomes the locus of nescience, because it is devoid of any nature without nescience. So not-self canot be the object of nescience.[23] Nor is it the locus of nescience. Being unconscious, it cannot have nescience. So Ātman is the locus of nescience.[24] Ātman is not of the nature of nescience, because Its nature is consciousness. It can have a peculiarity (atiśaya) in the form of lapse of knowledge. It can also acquire knowledge. Ātman is unchanging in nature. It is independent of nescience (ajñāna) and self-existent. Ātman Itself becomes ignorant owing to lapse of knowledge. It becomes ignorant of Itself. It becomes ignorant of Its real nature.[25] The objection, that Ātman being of the nature of knowledge, and having no other entity besides Itself, cannot acquire nescience from knowledge, is unsound, because the distinction of Ātman and knowledge is due to nescience, like a rope appearing to be a serpent.[26]

Ānandabodha also agrees with Sureśvara that Brahman is both the abode and the object of avidyā. The jīva cannot be the abode of avidyā, since the jīva owes its apparent existence to avidyā. If the jīva is regarded as the abode of avidyā, the view involves vicious interdependence. If the jīva is beginningless, like Brahman, it is not a reflection of Brahman in avidyā, because a reflection comes into existence after its original (bimba). If the jīva is without an origin, the distinction between it and Brahman cannot be said to be due to avidyā. Hence Brahman Itself devoid of origin and end is the abode and object of avidyā.[27]

Like Maṇḍana Miśra, Vācaspati Miśra regards an empirical self (jīva) as the abode of avidyā, and Brahman as its object. Avidyā is indefinable, and does not abide in Brahman That is eternal and pure.[28] A jīva is Brahman limited by beginningless, indefinable avidyā. Identified with the subtle body, the gross body and the sense-organs it is the object of 'I'-consciousness.[29] Amalānanda endorses this view. Appyadīkṣita regards the Inner Self (pratyagātman) limited by the internal organ and the like, of the nature of 'this' and 'not-this', conscious doer and experiencer of pleasure and pain, or empirical self, as the abode of avidyā as cause and effect.[30] Prakāśānanda states Vācaspati Miśra's view as follows. The great knowers of the truth maintain that a jīva is the abode of avidya, and that Brahman is the object of nescience.[31]

Ānandabodha's criticism of Vācaspati Miśra's view has already been given. Prakāśātman offers the following criticism of Vācaspati Miśra's view that Ātman or Self limited by the internal organ, an empirical self (jīva), is the abode of avidyā. The view is wrong, for there is no proof for it. The opponent argues that the experience "I am ignorant" proves that the nescience abides in a jīva. This argument is false, because, if it were true, the experience "I do not apprehend" would prove that a jīva is the abode of manifestation of consciousness (caitanya). The opponent argues that the internal organ appears to be conscious because of the relation of the internal organ and consciousness to the Self, even as iron appears to burn because of the relation of iron and burning to a fire. Prakaśātman urges that, similarly, it may be argued that a jīva has the experience "I am ignorant" because of the relation of the internal organ and the nescience to the Self, and not because of the relation of the internal organ to the nescience. The experience "I am ignorant" can be explained without assumption of the relation of the internal organ and the nescience to the Self. Further, the relation of the nescience to the Self in deep sleep is admitted, because the internal organ is merged in the causal nesience in this state.[32] The opponent objects that the nescience is assumed to abide in a jīva or Self qualified by an internal organ, because its abiding in the nature (svarūpa) of the Self is inexplicable. The objection is groundless, because relation to the nature of the Self is present in a jīva or Self qualified by an internal organ also.[33] If an internal organ, an insentient entity, were the abode of the nescience, it would be the abode of false knowledge and valid knowledge also.[34] (Cp. Sureśvara). But it cannot be their abode. So it cannot be the abode of the nescience. The opponent objects that the abiding of the nescience in the nature of Brahman is inconclusive. Prakāśātman urges that the opponent's view assumes two inconclusive elements, viz., the abiding of the nescience in the nature of Brahman and its abiding in Brahman qualified by an internal organ. Prakāśātman's view assumes one inconclusive element, viz., the abiding of the nescience in Brahman or Ātman. So his view is better than Vācaspati Miśra's view. In deep sleep Ātman has relation to the nescience. Bondage is the relation of Ātman to the nescience. Liberation is destruction of the relation of Ātman to the nescience. Avidyā abides in the Self in bondage. It ceases to abide in It in release. So Ātman is the abode of avidyā.[35]

Vidyāraṇya elaborates on Prakāśātman's arguments. He asks Vācaspati Miśra whether the distinction between a jīva and Brahman is real, or whether it is due to the nescience. In the first alternative, a jīva is either limited by an internal organ, or it is by nature different from Brahman, or it is a real part of Brahman—the whole. The first subaltermative is inadmissible, since an internal organ, which is produced, cannot limit originless Brahman. An internal organ is not beginningless, because it does not exist in deep sleep. It is merged in the nescience in this state. If it be said to exist in a subtle state, what is a subtle state? It is either partlessness, or loss of parts, or existing in the causal state, or existing as a trace of impression or potency (saṁskāraleśa). The first subalternative is untenable, because partlessness of an entity composed of parts is tantamount to its destruction. The second subalternative is unjustified, since the internal organ with the remaining parts would not have any effects, and would not be destroyed. If all its effects have been produced, there would be no deep sleep but there would be waking. In the third subalternative, either the cause of the internal organ or nescience exists or nescience as well as the internal organ, the effect, exists. In the first subalternative, the nescience alone will exist, and the internal organ will not be present. In the second subalternative, there will be experience in deep sleep. In the fourth main alternative, a trace of impression of an internal organ connot limit Brahman, and so a jīva would be released in deep sleep. The opponent contends that an internal organ cuts Brahman into fragments, as an axe cuts a piece of wood into bits. The contention is false, because the incorporeal, universal consciousness or Brahman cannot be cut into fragments. According to Vidyāraṇya the nescience is the stuff of the limitation of Brahman ; duality of Brahman and a jīva exists in the nescience itself, and is attributed to Ātman.[36] An internal organ, an effect of the nescience, limits Brahman through the nescience, and not directly. So there is no fault in this view. The second alternative is inadmissible, because a jīva cannot really differ by nature from Brahman in that the distinction between them is due to the nescience and so unreal. The third alternative also is illegitimate, since incorporeal, partless Brahman is by nature devoid of parts. So the distinction between a jīva and Brahman is due to the nescience. Vidyāraṇya admits it. Avidyā related to the pure consciousness or Brahman creates the distinction between a jīva and Brahman, disregards the nature of Brahman, becomes partial to a jīva, and generates its bondage, even as a mirror related to the nature of a face creates the distinction between the face and its reflection, and produces a peculiarity in the reflection. It is objected that in the experience "I am ignorant" avidyā abiding in Ātman qualified by egoism (ahaṁkāra) is manifested, and that avidyā abiding in Ātman is not manifested. The objection is unsound, because avidyā and the internal organ or egoism related to Ātman are manifested in the experience, as iron appears to burn, because iron and burning are related to a fire, and not because the internal organ is the abode of avidyā. Otherwise, there would be interdependence : the internal organ would be inferred from its relation to avidyā ; the relation of avidyā to the internal organ would be inferred from avidyā abiding in Ātman qualified by the internal organ. The relation of avidyā to Ātman unqualified by the internal organ in deep sleep is admitted.[37] So avidyā does not abide in Ātman qualified by avidyā. It is objected that detached pure consciousness (caitanya), Ātman, cannot be the abode of avidyā, and be related to it, and that, consequently, Ātman qualified by the internal organ is assumed to be the abode of avidyā. The objection is groundless, since when Ātman qualified by the internal organ is the abode of avidyā, Ātman also is the abode of avidyā in that Ātman is included in qualified Ātman.[38] Ātman is qualified by the internal organ and its relation to avidyā. If another entity be said to be qualified by them, it cannot be the abode of avidyā, for it is insentient. (Cp. Sureśvara). Otherwise, false knowledge, true knowledge and liberation would abide in an insentient entity, because it is the abode of avidyā. Hence avidyā abiding in Ātman or pure consciousness being partial to a jīva is said to abide in a jīva. Avidyā abiding in Ātman does not compromise Its detachedness.[39] The difficulty in avidyā abiding in Ātman arises from the fact that the opponent thinks of it as something real. It is indefinable. Its relation to Ātman also is indefinable. So there is no difficulty in the Advaitavādin's view.

Vidyāraṇya refutes the view that Brahman cannot be the object of avidyā. The opponent contends that Brahman is self-luminous, and that therefore It cannot be the object of the nescience. He further contends that a jar is not said to be unknown, when it is cognized. Vidyāraṇya urges that the contention is false, because an object cognized through a means of valid knowledge is not an object of the nescience in that a pramāṇa terminates the nescience of the object. A jar perceptible by the witness-consciousness (sākṣin) is nothing but consciousness (caitanya). It is object-consciousness. It may be the object of nescience. The witness-consciousness does not terminate the nescience ; rather, it cognizes the nescience, and proves it. Otherwise, it cannot be proved to be opposed to all means of valid knowledge and reasonings.[40] So it is said, "This nescience is opposed to all reasonings, without an object, incomprehensible by reason, and veils self-luminous Brahman, as darkness veils the sun. The nescience is of the nature of ignorance. It is not comprehensible by reason. If it were so, it would be a real entity." That this incomprehensible nescience can veil the self-luminous Ātman is not questionable.[41] No empirical self or object can transcend it. It is a false appearance due to avidyā. It exists, as if it were the Supreme Self, disregarding a pramāṇa and reality. Yet it is not real. Experience cannot be denied. All reasoning is based on apprehension. If it were not based on apprehension, it would be baseless. Even self-luminous Ātman is experienced as distinguished from the mind-body-complex or veiled by the nescience.[42] So the Brahman is the object of the nescience ; or it veils self-luminous Ātman. It does not veil an empirical self or an empirical object, which is an unreal entity. The beginningless, indefinable avidyā cognized by witness-consciousness (sākṣin) veils Brahman or Ātman, and creates the distinction between a jīva and Brahman.

Prakāśānanda refutes Vācaspati Miśra's view that a jīva is the abode of avidyā, and that Brahman is its object. Brahman or Ātman is self-luminous, and so cannot be the object of avidyā or ignorance. It is objected that the word 'ātman' means a jīva, that it is the abode, but not the object of avidyā, and that Brahman is its object. Jīvas are many ; otherwise, the distinction of a bound soul and a released soul cannot be accounted for. So nesciences are assumed to be many.

The soul which has acquired the immediate experience of its identity with Brahman is liberated ; and that which has not acquired it is bound. Otherwise, if there is one nescience, the nescience and all its effects are destroyed. So the perceived world would cease to be perceived. If none has attained liberation yet, there will be no desire for hearing, and there will be no emancipation. If there are many nesciences abiding in many jīvas with Brahman as their object, then Ātman or a jīva is not the object of nescience. When the words 'jīva' and 'Brahman' are used, do they express one entity or two entities ? If they express one entity, Prakāśānanda's view is right, and the opponent's view is wrong.[43] Or, the words 'jīva' and 'brahman' both express Ātman, or the word 'jīva' means Ātman, and the word 'brahman' means some other entity than Ātman. In the first alternative, Ātman is the object of nescience as the word 'Brahman' means Ātman. It is objected that if Ātman is the object of nescience, or if It is not known, It cannot be manifested, for It is veiled by the nescience, even as a jar veiled by darkness cannot be seen. This objection is invalid, since Ātman as mere consciousness is manifested, Which is not the object of the nescience, but since Ātman as nondual bliss is the object of the nescience. Otherwise, even the nescience would not be established. It is objected that the nature of nondual bliss is nondifferent from mere consciousness of Ātman. Prakāśānanda admits that in reality there is no difference between them. How, then, can Ātman be the object of the nescience ? Prakāśānanda replies that Ātman is the object of the nescience because It is related to the beginningless nescience. Ātman is assumed to be the object of the nescience on the strength of the illusory experience that there is a false difference between the pure consciousness and the nondual bliss of Ātman, that the latter is the object of the nescience and so not manifested to consciousness, and that the former is manifested to consciousness. The experience is due to the imagined difference between the two characteristics of Ātman. In fact, Ātman is manifested in Its nature as self-manifest supreme bliss. Why should the experience be regarded as illusory? Prakāśānanda replies that Ātman, the object of supreme love, is manifested as of the nature of bliss. Still the difference between the abode and the object of the nescience has not been determined. Prakāśānanda replies that it is true. If the nescience has an object, which is not different from its abode, it abiding in Ātman makes itself the object, even as darkness within a room has the place in the room as its object.[44] The nescience does not depend upon anything else to make Ātman its object. If Ātman is different from Brahman, the difference between them is either natural or conditional or due to a condition or adjunct. If Brahman were naturally different from Ātman, It would be insentient, the Śruti "Brahman is knowledge and bliss" would be contradicted, Brahman would not be the object of the nescience, since It would be known as an insentient object, and Brahman being different from Ātman would be not-self like a jar. In the second alternative, being conditional is being produced by a limiting condition, or being known by it, or being dependend on it. The nescience is the limiting condition of the difference between a jīva and Brahman, since an effect of the nescience being occasional or produced at a particular time cannot produce the difference between them. Being conditional is not being produced by a limiting condition, because prior to the production of difference between a jīva and Brahman the nescience exists in pure Ātman, because the nescience does not depend upon the difference, and because another independent nescience is not admitted. So the first alternative is not admissible. Being conditional is not being known by the limiting condition, since the nescience being insentient cannot manifest or know anything. So the second alternative is untenable. Dependence is found to be of three kinds in the world as being produced by an entity, as abiding in an entity, and as being manifested by an entity. Dependence as any of these cannot be due to the nescience. So the third alternative is inadmissible. It may be argued that the difference between a jīva and Brahman depending upon the nescience is like the relation of Ātman to the nescience. This argument is invalid, since relation depends upon the relata while difference does not depend the distincts. Hence it is established that the nescience abiding in Ātman devoid of the distinction between a jīva and Brahman makes Ātman its object. Pure consciousness devoid of distinction is both the abode and the object of nescience.[45]

Bhāskara opines that an internal organ is the abode of the nescience. Prakāśātman adduces the following arguments against this view. He asks the advocate of the view whether the Self is the knower of all or whether It is the knower of some entities. In the second alternative, the opponent admits that the Self is ignorant of certain entities. So the nescience abides in the Self. The opponent contends that though the Self is the abode of nonapprehension and false knowledge, an internal organ is the abode of the nescience as a positive entity. What is the nature of positive nescience? If it is different from knowledge, Prakāśātman does not object to it, since ocular diseases (e.g. dim vision, jaundice, etc.) are different from knowledge, and abide in not-self. If the nescience be said to be opposed to knowledge, the contention is false, because there is no conflict between knowledge and ignorance of the same object in different persons. The opponent contends that the nescience abiding in an internal organ conflicts with the knowledge abiding in a knower. The contention is false, for there is no evidence to prove it. When another person is in deep sleep, and when his internal organ is merged in the casual nescience, my inference of an action of his internal organ does not destroy the nescience in his internal organ. The opponent contends that the nescience abides in the internal organ as a defect (doṣa) as the cause of false knowledge. The contention is false, because, if it were true, the nescience would abide in the visual organ also. The opponent contends that the visual organ, which is produced, cannot be the abode of the beginningless nescience. The argument holds good of an internal organ also; it is produced, and so cannot be the abode of the beginningless nescience. Only conscious beings, which have knowledge, and which do not apprehend something, can be veiled by the nescience. So an insentient internal organ cannot have nescience. It can abide in conscious Ātman. This is Sureśvara's argument reiterated by Prakāśātman.[46]

IS NESCIENCE ONE OR MANY?—Like Sarvajñātman, Prakāśānanda maintains that the nescience is one. The nescience is proved by scriptural testimony or by ordinary perception or by presumption. It is not proved by scriptural testimony. The part of the Vedas dealing with religious rites conducive to the production of certain desired fruits on earth or in heaven are not concerned with the nescience. The Upaniṣads dealing with Brahman of the nature of supreme consciousness and bliss as the supreme end are not concerned with the nescience. Nor is the nescience the object of ordinary perception, since there would be no controversy about it if it were an object of perception. Hence the nescience is assumed, to account for the construction of diverse objects of pleasure and pain, to exist in Ātman or Brahman of the nature of eternal bliss, That is detached, indifferent and self-contented. The assumption of one nescience possessed of manifold powers is adequate to explain the manifold world, since it satisfies the law of parsimony, and since one flaw of sleep is found to produce various dreams.[47]

According to the advocates of one soul there is one nescience, which limits Ātman, and makes It one soul. The Śruti says, "One unborn soul experiences one unborn nescience made of sattva, rajas and tamas, sleeps, and is bound. It awakes from sleep, discards it, and is released". So the nescience is one and the cause of the world appearance, since it is made of sattva, rajas and tamas. It is unproduced. The soul is not produced, for it is unborn. It is one. But many souls are perceived in the world. How, then, can the soul be said to be one? The Śruti asserts the soul to be identical with Brahman. Brahman is one. So the soul is one. It is objected that the soul being identical with self-manifest Brahman cannot become different from it. Prakāśānanda replies that the soul following the nescience sleeps, as it were, and that its knowledge is eclipsed as it is veiled by the nescience. The sleeping soul experiences the effects of the nescience, and is bound, like a dreamer. It is objected that the nescience is beginningless and so imperishable, and that therefore the soul can never destroy it and be liberated. Prakāśānanda urges that the soul awakes from the sleep of nescience, discards it, and it released. It is objected that the soul being limited by the nescience, and the nescience entering into its nature, the soul can never discard it. Prakāśānanda replies that the nescience does not enter into the nature of the soul, because the soul is conscious while the nescience is insentient, and because the nescience is admitted to be a limiting adjunct of the soul. The distinction between bondage and release is like one in dream. Thus Prakāśānanda recognizes one nescience.[48] The doctrine of one soul is discussed elsewhere. He is an advocate of one soul (ekajīva) and creation due to apprehension (dṛṣṭisṛṣṭi).

According to the advocates of many souls (Vācaspati Miśra) there are many nesciences existing in many souls. The souls, which have not yet acquired the direct knowledge of Brahman, are bound. Those which have acquired the saving knowledge are released. The existence of the nescience in a soul is its bondage, and the destruction of nescience in a soul is its liberation.[49]

Sometimes a distinction is made between the root nescience (mulājñāna) and the phases of nescience (avasthājñana). Some Advaitins maintain that there are as many instances of nescience as there are instances of knowledge, because nesciences are like the prior negations of the instances of knowledge. The knowledge of a jar destroys the veil created by the nescience of a jar. Thus the root nescience is one, but its phases are many. Madhusūdana Sarasvatī refers to this view.[50]

FALSITY OF THE WORLD APPEARANCE.—Ānandabodha argues that the world appearance is constructed by avidyā. It is false, because it is insentient (jaḍa) and seen (dṛśya) or known.[51] An insentient entity is not-self, unmanifest, noncognition, and ontologically nonexistent.[52] A seen or known entity invariably depends on another conscious being for being known and used. It depends upon a knower, that manifests or cognizes it, because it is a limited, known object. Ātman knows it, but It does not know Itself, as a sword does not cut itself. Ātman is self-luminous. Ānandabodha states his inference thus : the world is false, because it is seen or known ; whatever is known is false ; the world is known ; so it is false, like illusory silver in a nacre. The reason is not unproven, because knowness is definitely known to exist in the world.[53] Again he states his argument thus : the world is projected by avidyā, because it is insentient and seen or known as an object, like illusory silver or a dream-object.[54] The world is false, for it is known ; whatever is known is false ; the world is known ; so it is false. The reason, knownness, is known for certain to exist in the world. The reason is not contradicted, since it is not pervaded by the contradictory of falsity, or truth. Nor is the reason irregular, because it has no variable concomitance with the probandum, e.g., falsity, in that knownness does not exist in Ātman or Brahman inasmuch as It manifests Itself without depending on any other entity. So the inference is valid.[55]

Madhusūdana Sarasvatī states the following definitions of a false entity in order to show that the world appearance is false. Padmapāda defines a false entity as indefinable and not the locus of existence and nonexistence. Brahman is existent for It is not liable to be contradicted in the past, the present, and the future. A hare's horn is nonexistent, since it is contradicted in all times, and since it is not cognized anywhere. The world appearance is neither existent, like Brahman, nor nonexistent, like a hare's horn. But it is cognized, and serves our practical purposes till the true knowledge of Brahman dawns. So it has pragmatic (vyavahārika), empirical, relative reality.[56] It has no ontological reality. Nor is it a fleeting series of momentary ideas. Prakāśātman defines a false entity as a counterentity of contradiction in three times in a place where it appears. It is an entity which appears in a place where it really did not exist, does not exist, and will not exist. It is not absolutely real, for it is contradicted by the true knowledge of Brahman. It is not absolutely unreal, like a hare's horn, as it appears to exist in a place. The opponent raises the question whether the negation of the world appearance is real or whether it is unreal. He argues as follows. If the negation of the world appearance is real, it is an entity other than Brahman, and so monism is abandoned. If such negation be held to be illusory, the opponent also admits it to be illusory. If such negation be held to have a pragmatic reality, then that being contradicted would make the world appearance the positive counterentity of negation or real. If a negation is negated, its positive counterentity is affirmed. Madhusūdana refutes this objection. The negation of the world appearance is real ; it is identical with Brahman, the locus of such negation. So the reality of such negation does not compromise monism.[57] Nor is the positive counterentity of such real negation, the world appearance, real, for illusory silver, the positive counterentity of the real negation of illusory nacre-silver, is not real. The negation of the world appearance is indeed unreal. But though it is unreal, it is not illusory but pragmatic. Though a pragmatic reality is liable to contradiction, yet such negation does not make the world appearance its positive counterentity or real, for in dream the illusory negation of an illusory object does not make its positive counterentity, the illusory object, real. If a negation is contradicted, it does not necessarily make its positive counterentity real. But when a negation possesses a less degree of reality than its positive counterentity, it cannot oppose the reality of its positive counterentity. Here both the world appearance and its negation have the same degree of reality in that both have pragmatic reality. Such negation does not establish the absolute reality of the world appearance. Both the world appearance and its falsity are known, and false and liable to contradiction.[58]

Prakāśātman defines a false entity as that which is liable to be terminated by true knowledge of Brahman (jñānanivartya). The opponent raises an objection against this definition. The preceding knowledge is destroyed by the succeeding knowledge. According to this definition the former should be considered to be false, but it is not false for that reason. A jar is destroyed by the blow of a club. It is a pragmatic reality, and so false, but it is not destroyed by true knowledge. Madhusūdana refutes this objection by pointing out that an entity which is a counterentity of the absence of existence in general is liable to be terminated by true knowledge. Existence is of two kinds : existence of an entity in its nature and existence in the form of its material cause according to Satkāryvāda. When a jar is destroyed by the blow of a club, it exists in the form of its material cause, earth, though it does not exist in its nature. So the destruction of a jar is not the negation of its existence in general. The second knowledge does not destroy the existence in general of the first knowledge. Prakāśātman says, "There is the experience of termination of a nescience with its effect present or merged in it by a true knowledge." The nescience of a jar is terminated by the true knowledge of a jar. The former is an effect of nescience. Sureśvara says, "The nescience with its effect is destroyed by the direct knowledge of Brahman arising from the hearing of the Śruti "That thou art." The nescience, the material cause of illusory nacre-silver, with its effect, illusory silver, is terminated by the direct knowledge of its substratum (e.g., a nacre). The probandum is not absent from the example, illusory nacre-silver, because difference among the nesciences, the material causes of the different cases of illusions is admitted. After the direct knowledge of the substratum the nescience of silver and illusory nacre-silver do not exist. In fact, terminability by true knowledge means terminability by the direct knowledge of the substratum of a false entity. So the third definition is valid.[59]

Citsukha defines a false entity as that which is the positive counterentity of the absolute negation coexisting with the object in the same locus. It appears to be in the locus of its absolute negation or absence. It is really absent in the place where it appears to be.[60] Madhusūdana Sarasvatī expounds his view thus. The opponent argues that a jar inheres in its component parts, its material cause, when it is produced, and that its absolute absence from the latter is not possible. This argument, Madhusūdana urges, is false, because as a jar and its absolute absence can exist at the same time, so they can exist in the same place. A jar exists in its component parts, and its absence exists on the ground at the same time. The prior negation of a jar exists in its component parts before it is produced. There is no conflict between it and the component parts of a jar, which are the material cause of the jar. Similarly, the prior negation and the absolute negation of a jar coexist in its component parts. They are the material cause of the jar for its prior negation exists in them. The opponet argues that the prior negation of an object cannot exist in the locus of its absolute negation. Madhusūdana urges that the inference of falsity of the world appearance is based on the Śruti "There is no plurality here." There is no conflict between the presence and the absence of entities of different degrees of reality. A jar has pragmatic reality, but its absence is absolute. So a jar and its absence can coexist in its component parts, since they posses different degrees of reality. The law of contradiction holds good between two entities of the same degree of reality. Though the world-appearance is absolutely absent in its locus, yet it appears to exist in it, and is not as unreal as a hare's horn, since the latter does not appear to exist in its locus.[61]

Ānandabodha, defines a false entity as that which is distinct from the existent (sat). What is existent is established by a means of valid knowledge. A means of valid knowledge is an instrumental cause of valid knowledge not tainted with a flaw (doṣa). So a false entity is established as an entity different from what is proved by a means of valid knowledge, like a dream. Or, what is proved by a pramāṇa is being pervaded by uncontradictability. Here also the adjective 'appearing to exist', should be added to the definition of a false entity in order to exclude the attributeless Brahman from its scope, since Brahman being attributeless is devoid of existence as an attribute, and also to exclude an absolutely nonexistent hare's horn, since it does not appear to exist. What does the word 'existence' in the phrase 'distinct from the existent or real' mean ? It means either the locus of the genus 'beinghood' or the uncontradicted, or of the nature of Brahman. The first alternative is not tenable, since the genus of jar due to nescience is admitted to exist in a jar. So it is existent (sat) or real. But it is a pragmatic reality devoid of ontological existence. In the second alternative, contradictability ends in falsity. In the third alternative what is sought to be proved is already proven (siddhasādhana) or admitted. The world appearance is distinct from Brahman.[62]

FALSITY OF THE FALSE WORLD APPEARANCE.—The Advaitin regards the world appearance to be false, but does not regard its falsity to be true, for in that case he would accept dualism. The opponent argues that the falsity of the world appearance is false, and that therefore the world appearance becomes true. Madhusūdana Sarasvatī urges that this argument is invalid, since the falsity of the world appearance does not establish its truth. Two entities of the same degree of reality can be contradicted by the same contradicting knowledge. The world appearance and its falsity both are pragmatic realities, and can, therefore, be contradicted by the direct knowledge of Brahman, as illusory nacre-silver and an entity different from a nacre are contradicted by the knowledge "This is a nacre". But the illusory nacre-silver and its absence have different degrees of reality. Illusory silver has illusory reality, but its absence has pragmatic reality. The knowledge "This is a nacre" contradicts the illusory nacre-silver but does not contradict its absence there. There is no conflict between two entities of different degrees of reality, though they are of the nature of mutual absence. What is pragmatically false is not pragmatically true, but may be illusorily true. The same entity can be both true and false as having differing degrees of reality. The world appearance is pragmatically true but ontologically false. Nacre-silver is illusorily true, but pragmatically false. So the falsity of the false world appearance does not establish its ontological truth.[63]

Citsukha states the view of the opponent of the falsity of the world appearance as follows. Falsity is either incognizability by a means of valid knowledge, or cognizability by a knowledge which is not produced by a means of valid knowledge, or cognizability by false knowledge, or being different from an existent entity, or being different from an existent entity and a nonexistent entity or nonentity, or being either nescience or its effect, or being destructible by true knowledge of Brahman, or being the object of denial in an object of experience, or being subject to annulment, or being experienced as existing in a locus with its absolute negation. The first alternative is untenable, because, if it were true, Brahman also would be false, since It is self-manifest and not cognizable by any means of valid knowledge according to the Advaitin. The second alternative is inadmissible, since an illusory object (e.g., silver) is experienced as an object of false knowledge, a particular nacre being experienced as a particular piece of silver, since the opponent admits the empirical objects to be real, momentary and effects of Brahman, and since the objects of recollection, which is invalid, would be objects of false knowledge. The third alternative is untenable for the reason stated above. The fourth alternative is inadmissible, since a hare's horn and the like also are not false, though they are different from existent entilies inasmuch as both a hare and horns are existent, though a hare's horn is nonexistent. The fifth alternative is untenable, because what is different from an existent entity is nonexistent, because what is different from a nonexistent entity is existent, and because no other intermediate entity is possible. The sixth alternative is inadmissible, since indefinable nescience is not known, since nescience in the form of nonperception and false knowledge is real, and since its effects—residual impressions and voluntary actions—are real. The seventh alternative is untenable, because knowledge, pleasure and the like, though destructible by the knowledge of Brahman, are real, and because all objects, though real, are admitted by the opponents to be destructible by the knowledge of God. The eighth alternative is inadmissible, since what is experienced in an object through a means of valid knowledge cannot be denied there, for otherwise there would be an unwarranted stretch of a general rule to cases to which it is not applicable. The Nyāya and the Vaiśeṣika admit that what is attributed to an object of illusion here exists elsewhere. Silver attributed to a nacre here exists in a shop elsewhere. The ninth alternative is untenable, because a nacre and the like also are admitted to be annulled by a sublating knowledge, and because a prior knowledge is admitted to be destroyed by a sublating knowledge. But a nacre continues to exist, and is not an object of sublating knowledge and not destroyed by it. The tenth alternative also is inadmissible, since though conjunction, disjunction, sound, and special qualities of a soul, which subsist in particular regions of their substrates, are experienced as existing in the loci of their absolute negations, they are admitted by the opponents to be real.[64]

Citsukha proves the falsity of all empirical objects by adducing the following arguments. 1. Falsity is not uncharacterizable. All existents being admitted to be substrates of their being counterentities of their absence prove their falsity. Threads are the counterenties of the absence of a cloth ; it did not exist before in them, but comes into being later when they are conjoined in a particular way. So it does not always exist. Hence it is false. All entities except Brahman are effects, and exist in their material causes. They are superimposed on Brahman in the state of empirical existence, their material cause, as silver is superimposed on a nacre, and are therefore false. But Brahman is true, since It does not exist in a substrate, and is not the counterentity of Its absence. 2. The text "earth itself is true and its three forms are true" does not convey the ontological truth of earth and its forms, since the Śruti says, "All this is indeed Brahman." So Brahman alone is true. 3. Inexplicability of the relation of the knower and the known contradicts the inference of the truth of empirical objects. 4. Inexplicability of an empirical object being known due to inexplicability of the relation of a cognition to an object contradicts the truth of an empirical object.[65]

FALSE EMPIRICAL OBJECTS CAN PRODUCE PRACTICAL ACTIONS.—The opponent of Advaitavāda objects that all these objects of experience are nonexistent. Padmapāda replies that they are false and of the nature of beginningless indefinable avidyā, but that they are not nonexistent.[66] The opponent objects that false objects cannot produce practical actions necessary for worldly life. Appyayadīkṣita replies that they produce practical actions like dreams. It is objected that bathing and the like produced by dream-water are false, but that bathing, etc., produced by water in the waking state are true. Some Advaitins reply that the power of producing practical actions of the same drgree of reality is common to both dream-water and water in the waking state. Dream-water, which has illusory existence, can produce illusory bathing while water in the waking state, which has empirical existence, can produce empirically real bathing. So they both produce practical actions. Some Advaitins opine that dream objects not only produce the practical actions which are contradicted by waking perceptions, but that they produce also feelings and emotions and their bodily effects, which are not contradicted by waking cognitions. The dream of a beloved woman produces pleasure which persists on waking. The dream of a serpent produces fear and trembling which persist on waking. Pleasure and fear and their bodily effects are not contradicted by waking perceptions. Other Advaitins opine that the nature of water and the like can produce practical actions like drinking, bathing etc., and that their truth is not their cause, since their truth and being a determinant of practical actions are absent. It is contended that if the truth of a dream-object were not the cause of its producing a practical action, then illusory water in a mirage and illusory silver in a nacre also would produce practical actions like empirically real water and silver, which are perceived. This contention is false, the author of 'Tattavaśuddhi' urges, because there is no genus of water in illusory water in a mirage, and because there is no genus of silver in illusory silver in a nacre, which are necessary for producing the respective practical actions, and because the illusion of water is produced by the residual impression of water perceived in the past. Hence illusory water in a mirage cannot produce practical actions because of the absence of the genus of water in it. But empirically real water, though false from the ontological standpoint, can produce practical actions in worldly life. Empirically real objects have relative, pragmatic existence. They have a higher degree of reality than illusory water and illusory silver. They are contradicted and annulled by the firmly established intuitive knowledge of Brahman, Which alone has ontological reality.[67] The Advaita Vedānta does not deny the empirical reality of external objects and their producing practical actions.[67]

WORLD APPEARANCE AND ĀTMAN.—Ānandabodha avers that the manifold world appearance is not really nondifferent from Ātman of the nature of pure consciousness, but that it is neither different nor nondifferent nor both, but a projection of the beginningless nescience. If it were nondifferent from Ātman, self-luminous Ātman would be many.[68] It is objected that real Ātman is of the nature of manifestation, that manifold forms attributed by avidyā not being identical with manifest Ātman are unmanifest, and that, consequently, they cannot be manifested by Ātman. This objection is groudless, because one Ātman appears to be the manifold world appearance. Diverse forms are manifested as false appearances of one Ātman attributed to It by avidyā. They cannot be nondifferent from self-manifest Ātman. It is contended that unmanifest insentient objects are manifested by Ātman, and so are real, like Ātman. Ānandabodha urges that the contention is false, because the relation between them is due to avidyā. There is no real relation between them. Relation distinct from the relata or non-distinct from them is indeterminable. If the relation be distinct from the relata, it will lead to infinite regress.[69] If it be nondistinct from the relata, they alone exist, and there is no relation. There is no conjunction between an insentient object and conscious Ātman, because sentient consciousness is not a substance. Conjunction is possible between two substances. Nor is there inherence between conscious Ātmam and a cognized object, because they exist separately from each other. No other relation called subject-object-relation (viṣaya-viṣayi-bhāva) is determinable. Its indeterminability will be shown later. If there were a subject-object-relation, past and future objects could not be known by Ātman, because they and Ātman could not be related to each other as subject and object. If there be no relation between consciousness and a cognized object, one of them cannot determine the other. Hence one Ātman or pure consciousness appears to be many false appearances of the nature of not-self under the influence of beginningless avidyā. Avidyā projects indefinable false appearances. Avidyā creates apparent difference between a jīva and Brahman, and manifold world appearance. Avidyā is false knwledge of duality and difference. Vidyā is suprarational intuition of the identity of Ātman. Avidyā is the cause of bondage. Vidyā is the cause of liberation. It is the complete destruction of āvidyā and its effects.[70]

SUPERIMPOSITION (ADHYĀSA).—Śaṁkara defines superimposition as attribution of an object known by 'this'-consciousness to Self, known by 'I'-consciousness, and of the nature of pure consciousness, because they cannot be of the nature of each other in that they are possessed of contradictory natures, like light and darkness. Common people confuse the true and the false, Self and not-self, with each other, and say, "I am this" and This is mine". The superimposition of not-self on Self is free from self-contradiction. Padmapāda defines superimposition as apprehension of an entity as what it is not, which is false. Vidyāraṇya defines it as apprehension of an entity in what it is not. He observes that though Self and not-self are equally superimposed on each other, yet Self is not superimposed in its essential nature (svarūpa) on not-self, but that it is superimposed on not-self as related to another entity whereas not-self is superimposed in its nature on Self. This is the reason for its falsity. Self is true ; not-self is false ; they are superimposed on each other. The true and the false are falsely identified with each other, in the experiences "I am endowed with a body and the sense-organs", and "the body and the sense-organs are mine". Self and not-self are not related to each other as a qualified substance and a quality, like cloth and whiteness, in which both difference and identity are known, because superimposition is admitted to be illusion of absolute oneness of two entities of contradictory characters. It is contended that adhyāsa is not superimposition of identity but superimposition of oneness. Vidyāraṇya urges that this contention is false, because we speak of 'my body' as we speak of whiteness of a cloth. Thus we speak of the difference of Self and body like that of cloth and whiteness. It is contended that nonapprehension of difference being destroyed by apprehension of difference, superimposition prevaded by nonapprehension of difference is destroyed. Vidyāraṇya urges that this contention is false, for apprehension of difference is not admitted. Though common people speak of 'my body' they do not apprehend difference between Self and body without proper spiritual discipline. So on the strength of experience adhyāsa is certainly superimposition of oneness. On the strength of the usage of the common people adhyāsa may be said to be superimposition of identity. It is contended that oneness is identity. This contention is false, as they are distinct from each other in that indentity is contradictory to mutual negation while oneness is contradictory to difference. An empirical self (jīva) and Brahman are realy one, but their identity is spoken of depending on their difference imagined by the nescience. There is no conflict between their ontological oneness and empirical difference. It is contended that oneness of Self and body is real, for it is so experienced, as jīva and Brahman are really one. This contention is false, for real oneness of self and not-self, the true and the false, entirely distinct entities, is not possible. Hence oneness of them is superimposed.[71]

Śaṁkara regards the beginningless, indefinable, positive nescience to be the material cause of superimposition. The contention, that beginninglessness of its effect, superimposition, does not stand to reason, is false for the following reason. Superimposition is attribution of the flaw of being an agent of action, being an experiencer of pleasure and pain, and of having attachment and aversion to Ātman. Attribution of being an enjoyer or a sufferer to Self depends on attribution of being an agent of action to Self, since a nondoer cannot enjoy or suffer. Attribution of agency of action to Self depends on attribution of having attachment and aversion to Self, for one devoid of attachment and aversion cannot be an agent of action. Having attachment and aversion depends on being an enjoyer or a sufferer, as one who has not experienced pleasure and pain cannot have attachment and aversion. So there is a beginningless series of attribution of agency of action and the like, like a beginningless series of seeds and sprouts.[72] This argument refutes the objection that attribution depends upon the experience of the false world appearance, and that the experience of the false world appearance depends upon attribution, for nescience being beginningless, the prior nescience is the cause of the succeeding attribution. The body and the like exist in the form of potencies, and produce the succeeding superimpositions.[73]

The opponents of monism object that superimposition does not stand to reason. Self and not-self are devoid of identity with each other, because they are always devoid of the nature of each other, like light and darkness. In this inference the reason (hetu) is not nonexistent, because Self and not-self are devoid of identity, because they are possessed of contradictory natures, like light and darkness. Nor is the reason unproven. Self and not-self have contradictory natures, because they are the objects of 'I'-consciousness and 'this'-consciousness, respectively, like Devadatta and his enemy. Common people regard the aggregate of the body and consciousness as self, and regard a stone and the like as not-self. Their oneness and superimposed oneness are not admitted by the Advaitavādin. Nor is contradiction between them always experienced. Prabhākara and the Nyāya-Vaiśeṣika regard the insentient substratum of knowerhood, enjoyerhood, doerhood and the like as Self, and consider the body, the sense-organs and things of the world as not-self. According to the Advaitist, egoism (ahaṁkara) the substratum of knowerhood, doerhood, enjoyerhood and the like, insentience, and its cause—nescience are not-self. So Self and not-self are not admitted by all to be superimposed on each other or to be identical with each other, or contradictory to each other. The Advaitist regards Self as flawless, and of the nature of pure consciousness, and all other entities as not-self. Is one of them the object of 'I'-consciousness and 'this'-consciousness both? Or, is Self the object of 'I'-consciousness, and is not-self the object of 'this'-consciousness? Is it stated as the reason for the inference of superimposition? In the first alternative, the reason is unproven. In the second alternative, the reason is partly unproven, because the body, the sense-organs, vital forces, and the internal organ, of the nature of not-self, are not objects of 'Thou'-consciousness or 'this'-consciousness. So superimposition cannot be proved by inference.

Vidyāraṇya refutes this objection. Superimposition is proved by the Advaitist by inference. The reason is not partly unproven in regard to Self. Though Self is self-manifest, egoism may be said to be an object of 'I'-consciousness in a figurative sense because of its fitness for being a more distinct object of usage. Though Self and not-self are possessed of contradictory natures, they are related to each other as subject and object.[74]

The opponents of monism ask whether there is identity of seer or knower with the seen or known, or whether there is identity of the seen or known with the seer or knower. In the first alternative, the identity is not natural, for a knower of the nature of consciousness alone cannot be known. If the knower were known, the former's identity with the latter would not be possible, because a knower or subject cannot be known or object. If the identity is adventitious, the knowing self by itself is modified into the known object, or it is modified with the aid of a cause. Both alternatives are inadmissible, for the knower is partless. Partless ether itself or with the aid of a cause cannot be modified into an entity composed of parts. If a known object has identity with a knower, its being known is either natural or adventitious. If its knownness is natural, it cannot be a knower. If a known object is held to be partly known, it is both a knower and known,—which is self-contradictory. It its being a knower is adventitious, either it itself is modified into a conscious knower, or it transfers consciousness of Self to itself. The first alternative is not tenable, for an effect produced by an insentient entity cannot be a conscious knower. A jar, a modification of insentient earth, is not found to be of the nature of consciousness. The second alternative also is not admissible, since Self, which is all-pervading and of the nature of consciousness, cannot enter into anything. So superimposition cannot be inferred. Let there be no superimposition of two entities invested with attributes on each other. Still there may be superimposition of the relation of the attributes of Self on Self. It may be argued that Self of the nature of pure consciousness cannot have attributes. The argument is invalid, since it has apprehension of objects, bliss, eternality and the like. Though they are its essence, they are manifested to consciousness as many in the mental modes, and so they may be figuratively said to be Self's attributes. It is contended that an attribute leaving the entity invested with it cannot be independently superimposed on another entity. The contention is invalid, for in the illusion of a red crystal redness of a red japā flower is found to be superimposed on a crystal. This contention is invalid, since attributes are never independent of a substance. Redness is not supirimposed independently of a red japā flower on a crystal. In a crystal redness abiding in a japā flower reflected on a crystal is perceived, not independently of it. So there is no superimposition of the relation of mere attributes apart from the substances, in which they abide, on another entity. Superimposition of a substance and an attribute on another substance being refuted, superimposition of cognitions also, which invariably accompany objects, on another entity is refuted. Hence superimposition is not reasonable.[75]

Vidyāraṇya refutes this objection. He asks whether the objector seeks to prove the unreality of superimposition because of its being opposed to reason or whether it is denied by him. The first alternative is not tenable, for the Advaitist, who belives in indefinable nescience, admits both the irrationality and unreality of superimposition. Superimposition of Self and not-self on each other is opposed to rational arguments. So its indefinability is admitted. Otherwise, its reality would be admitted. It may be objected by the opponent that he denies the existence of superimposition, and argues that superimposition of self and not-self on each other does not exist, because there is no cause for its existence. In common experience of the illusion "This is silver", similarity between the substratum (e.g., a nacre) and the superimposed entity (e.g., silver) in an attribute (e.g., brightness) or in parts is the cause of superimposition. But Self is devoid of attributes and parts. So not-self cannot be superimposed on Self; nor can it be superimposed on not-self. It may be argued that in the illusion of a red crystal there is no similarity between redness and a crystal, and that yet redness is superimposed on a crystal. The argument is invalid, for the illusion is due to a condition, which does not depend upon similarity. Redness of a proximate japā flower is the cause of the manifestation of redness in a crystal. Similarity is not the cause of illusion in this case. It may be objected that agency and the like are superimposed on Self with egoism, their substrate, as a condition. Let there be somehow superimposition of agency and the like on Self with egoism as an adjunct ; but there can be no superimposition, at all, of egoism, an entity within the body, devoid of an adjunct, on Self because of the absence of similarity between them. This objection is groundless, for an odour devoid of an attribute and parts is perceived to be similar to another odour, and one is superimposed on the other. So not-self may be superimposed on Self owing to similarity as an entity. It may be argued that no attribute can really exist in Self, which is of the nature of pure consciousness, and that therefore there is no similarity between Self and not-self. Let similarity not be the cause of an illusion devoid of an adjunct. But there are illusions even without similarity. There is no similarity in the illusion of a yellow conchshell, which is devoid of an adjunct. It may be argued that the bile is the cause of this illusion. Vidyārṇya urges that the nescience is the cause of illusion or superimposition of not-self on Self. It is objected that it is better to deny the existence of superimposition than to admit the nescience to be the cause of superimposition, since its being the absence of knowledge or being a positive entity is disputed. Vidyāraṇya urges that this objection is invalid, since perception of the beginningless nescience as veiling Self's consciousness and bliss cannot be denied in that it depends upon the existence of Inner Self alone, which is its sustainer. If the nescience were denied, Inner Self also would be denied. Hence superimposition of Self and not-self on each other is undeniable.[76]

The opponent of Advaitavāda objects that superimposition is not possible, for either not-self is superimposed on Self or Self is superimposed on not-self. The first alternative is not possible, for Self, being devoid of common and particular characters, similarity and the like, and always manifesting itself, cannot be the substratum of superimposition of not-self. The second alternative also is not admissible, for not-self is admitted by the Advaitist to be false. If a false entity be the substratum of superimposition, the Advaitin would accept the Mādhyamika doctrine of Śūnyavāda. If not-self be admitted to be true, it cannot be annulled by the right knowledge of Brahman, and so liberation cannot be attained. What is true can never be annulled. Further, the Śrutis assert not-self to be false. It is also inferred to be false from its being known, like illusory silver in a nacre. Not-self is proved to exist only when Self is superimposed on it. There is the possibility of flaws, similarity and the like in Self because of superimposition of not-self on it. Thus the fault of self-dependence arises. This reasoning removes the objection that there is no room for alternatives arising from superimposition of Self and not-self on each other imagined by the nescience, because the existence of the nescience in self-manifest Self cannot be proved. For the nescience also is either superimposed or not superimposed. In the first alternative, the fault of self-dependence arises. In the second alternative, the nescience cannot be destroyed, and so liberation cannot be attained. Further, since all have their root in superimposition, there can be no distinction between illusion and valid knowledge. Further, one and the same self cannot be the knower, the known, the means of valid knowledge, and valid knowledge. One being many involves self-contradiction. If it does not involve self-contradiction, the Advaitavāda becomes Vijñānavāda.

Madhusūdana Sarasvatī refutes this objection. "I am a man"; "I am a doer"; "I am an enjoyer or a sufferer." These experiences are common to all. They are not recollections, because they are immediate apprehensions, and because they are preceded by nonapprehension of difference. Nor are they valid knowledge, since they are contradicted by the Śruti and by valid arguments. The Śruti asserts Self to be a nondoer, a nonenjoyer, a nonsufferer, and of the nature of supreme bliss. The arguments are the following : the body, the sense-organs and the like are modifiable, because they are limited by time and space. They are, consequently, not-self, and cannot know themselves. If they are assumed to know themselves, that will involve self-contradiction, since the known cannot be a knower. Further, a substance cannot be related to an attribute either as different or as nondifferent from each other. If knowledge be held to be impermanent, too much will be proved if each individual knowledge is assumed to have an individual difference, destruction, prior nonexistence, inherence, genus and the like, and too little will be proved if they are assumed to be the same in each case, since the difference between the knowledge of a jar and the knowledge of a cloth can be experienced by referring to their limiting adjuncts (e.g., a jar and a cloth). If the experience of difference between one jar and another jar were possible in itself without consideration of the limiting adjuncts, ether, time, and space also would be many. If doerhood and the like be assumed to be really existent in Self, they will never cease, and so liberation will never be achieved. If Self is assumed to be not self-luminoius, the world will cease to exist. Because Self is an object of supreme love, It is of the nature of bliss. Hence Self is devoid of attributes, eternal, self-manifest, and of the nature of bliss.[77]

According to Vācaspati Miśra superimposition is pervaded by nonapprehension of difference. Apprehension of difference is contradictory to it. It terminates nonapprehension of difference and superimposition pervaded by it.[78] Attribution of the attributes of two opposed entities to each other is false superimposition. It is indefinable. Inner Self is pure consciousness and bliss. Buddhi and ahaṁkara are unconscious, active, and painful. They are opposed to each other. But because of nonapprehension of difference between them, their attributes are superimposed on each other. Superimposition of not-self on Inner Self is the root of all evils. It is the nescience (avidyā). Because of this superimposition the pure, blissful Inner Ātman appears to suffer misery. The nonapprehension of difference is terminated by the apprehension of difference between them through hearing, reflection and meditation. Then the comprehension of the nature of Reality—the true knowledge (vidyā) of Ātman of the nature of consciousness dawns, which removes superimposition.[79]

THE SUBSTRATUM OF DREAM-PHENOMENA.—In some Advaitīsts' view, dream-objects superimposed on the unlimited jīva-consciousness, or on the consciousness limited by egoism, or on the consciousness devoid of individual phases of the nescience, which are contradicted and annulled by the intuition of Brahman alone, which terminates the nescience — their material cause, are illusory because they are produced by the flaws of sleep and the like in addition to the root nescience, which is their material cause. The Advaitists speak of the root nescience called deep sleep as the cause of both dreams and waking perceptions. The dream-objects are not illusory because they are produced by phases of the nescience.[80] In some Advaitists' view, dream-objects are illusory because they are contradicted by waking perceptions, and because they are experienced as false, like false waking perceptions, and because they are contradicted by knowledges other than the intuition of Brahman. If dream-objects were contradicted by the intuition of Brahman, they would not be contradicted by waking perceptions. Śaṁkara asserts that dreams are contradicted by waking perceptions.[81] According to some Advaitists, a phase of the nescience (avasthājñāna) in the form of sleep as distinguished from the root nescience is the cause of dream-objects. It veils the empirical self, a reflection of Brahman in the nescience, the knower of the empirical world, and also the empirical world, on the cessation of the operation of merits and demerits of the empirical self, which are the causes of pleasures and pains in its waking state. Sleep is proved to be a phase (avasthā) of the root nescience, which is produced at the time, and which veils the empirical self and the empirical world, because the empirical self, which is not veiled by the root nescience, has false conceits "I am a tiger", "I am a Śūdra", "I am the son of Yajñadatta" in sleep, as it has false conceits "I am a man", "I am a Brāhmaṇa" and "I am the son of Devadatta" in the waking state.[82]

According to Bhāratītīrtha, as in the state of waking the nescience abiding in the consciousness (caitanya) limited by the part 'this' corresponding to a nacre manifested by a mental mode produced by the intercourse of the visual organ with an object, aided by the subconscious impression of silver, is modified into illusory silver, so in the state of dream the nescience abiding in the consciousness manifested by a mode of the internal organ inside the body, tainted by the flaw of sleep and the like, and aided by various subconscious impressions revived by the empirical self's merits and demerits, is modified into dream-objects.[83] According to some Advaitists, the unlimited jīva-consciousness, not manifested by mental modes, is the substratum (adhiṣṭhānā) of dream-phenomena. The jīva-consciousness unlimited by egoism and the like, which is self-intuited, is their substratum. It knows dream-objects immediately. The pure Brahman and Īśvara-consciousness are known from the scripture alone. Mental modes (vṛtti) cannot arise in them, which are unlimited archetype-consciousness. Mental modes in the form of 'I' can arise in the consciousness limited by egoism and the like. So the jīva-consciousness unlimited by egoism and the like is the substratum of dream-objects.[84] According to Sarvajñātman, illusory perceptions are immediate cognitions of objects. Dream-cognitions also are illusory, and immediate cognitions of mental objects, which subsist in the jīva-consciousness unlimited by egoism and the like.[85] In some Advaitists' view, the jīva-consciousness limited by egoism (ahaṁkāra) is the substratum of dream-objects. Egoism, being a qualification, does not enter into the jīva-consciousness, which is its substratum. But the jīva-consciousness, a reflection of Brahman in the nescience, unlimited by egoism is the substratum of dream-objects. So there is no experience "I am an elephant" in dream.[86] According to some Advaitists, the archetype-consciousness is the substratum of dream-objects. They are perceived by the empirical self whose nescience is the material cause of the dream-objects, and not by any other. So there are divergent Advaitist views as to the substratum of dream-objects.[87]

ILLUSORY SILVER IS INDEFINABLE (ANIRVACANĪYA).—Dharmarājādhvarīndra, a Śaṁkarite, regards illusory silver in a nacre as indefinable and having illusory existence, a lower degree of reality than the empirical reality of silver in the world appearance. Illusory silver and the illusion of silver both are modifications of avidyā. Illusory silver is produced by avidyā aided by the residual impression of silver, revived by the perception of 'this' or brightness in a nacre, and by a defect of the visual organ in contact with a nacre through a mental mode issuiug out to it through the eye. A mental mode in the form of 'this' or brightness is produced by the contact of the visual organ tainted by a defect with a nacre present to it. Consciousness determined by 'this' or 'this'-consciousness is reflected in the mental mode. Owing to the issuance of the mental mode to the nacre 'this'-consciousness, consciousness determined by the mental mode, and consciousness determined by the internal organ become identical with one another. Then avidyā in the form of a nacre abiding in 'this'-consciousness identified with the knower-consciousness aided by the residual impression of silver revived by the perception of similarity (e.g., brightness), and by a defect of the visual organ is modified into illusory silver and the illusory cognition of silver.[88] Illusory silver is not real, for it is contradicted by the sublating knowledge "this is not silver". Nor is it unreal, since it is perceived, and since it evokes a responsive action (e.g., picking up). It is not real and unreal both as it involves self-contradiction. So it is indefinable, indescribable, and inexplicable. It has illusory existence. It is not unreal, like a hare's horn. It is not real, like a jar, which has empirical reality, and which can contain water. The world appearance persists until it is sublated by the intuition of Brahman, Which alone has ontological reality in that It is not contradicted in the past, the present, and the future. Indefinable illusory silver persists until it is contradicted by the sublating knowledge "this is not silver." Brahman has ontological reality (pāramārthika sattā). Real silver in a jeweller's shop has empirical reality (vyavahārika sattā). Illusory silver has illusory reality(prātibhāsika sattā). These are the three degrees of reality according to the Advaita Vedānta.

The opponent of Advaita Vedānta asks whether indefinability is the absence of description or whether it is the absence of the cause of description. The first alternative is not tenable, since illusory silver is described as "this is silver" during illusion. The second alternative is not admissible, for the subalternatives involved in it do not stand the test of reason. The cause of description is either a cognition or an object. The first subalternative is not tenable, since the Advaitavādin admits the cognition of silver to be the cause of description. The second subalternative also is not justifiable, because if an existent object were absent, there would be apprehension of a nonexistent object, because, if a nonexistent object also were absent, there would be apprehension of an existent object, and because the absence of both an existent object and a nonexistent object would be inexplicable in that they are contradictory to each other and in that the negation of the one leads to the affirmation of the other, there being no intermediate possibility. So an indefinable entity is not distinct from an existent entity and a nonexistent entity or nonentity. Nor is an indefinable entity sublatable by a sublating knowledge. If 'sublatable' be admitted by the Advaitin to be 'terminable', a prior cognition or a residual impression being destroyed by a posterior knowledge would be indefinable, and the world appearance being destroyed by the knowledge of Īśvara would be indefinable, and so the definition of sublatability would be too wide. If 'sublatability' be admitted by the Advaitin to be the object of a sublating knowledge, then a nacre, the substratum of illusory silver, would be sublatable, for it is the object of the sublating knowledge "this is not silver", and Brahman, the substratum of the false world apperance, would be sublatable, for It is the object of the sublating knowledge "the world appearance is not true". So the definition of 'sublatibility' would be too wide. If sublation be the object of negation of an entity in the past, the present, and the future, and if sublatability be the object of such sublation, the definition is too narrow, because illusory silver, a modification of avidyā, present to the visual organ, is not admitted by the Advaitin to be the object of such negation, and because the empirically real silver being admitted to be the object of such negation would be indefinable, and because the definition of sublatibility would be too wide. A similar reasoning disproves the view that indefinability is being the object of negation in an object of experience, since the experienced silver present to the visual organ is not an object of such negation as "this is not silver", and since it is merged in the avidyā whereof it is a modification when its substratum, a nacre, is known by the sublatiug knowledge.

Further, what does an existent (sat) entity mean? Is it endued with existence? Or, is it unsublatable? Or, is it the nature of Brahman? The first alternative is not tenable, since an empirical object endued with existence being admitted to be sublatable by the Advaitin, the invariable concomitance 'whatever is unsublatable is existents' is not proved. The second alternative is not justifiable, since in that case 'what is unsublatable is unsublatable or existent', and since there is no distinction between the probans and the probandum. The third alternative is not admissible, for it proves what is already proved or admitted by the Advaitin.

What is the proof for the indefinable illusory silver? It may be said to be proved by presumption. Illusory silver is apprehended and yet sublated later. It is assumed to be indefinable to account for these inexplicable facts. A nonexistent entity (e.g., a man's horn) is not apprehended, and an existent entity, Brahman, is not sublated. But illusory silver is both apprehended and sublated later. So presumption proves indefinable illusory silver. The opponent of Advaita Vedānta urges that such presumption cannot be its proof, since silver existing in some other place is perceived, since real silver is nonexistent here, since it may be sublated later, and since it can be accounted for otherwise. Further, the argument that a nonexistent entity cannot be apprehended is invalid, for it is apprehended through the word 'nonexistent'. Otherwise, the word would be meaningless. So an indefinable entity cannot be proved by presumption.[89]

Let it be proved by the inference: the disputed entity is distinct from existent and nonexistent, because it is apprehended by perception produced by a defect in a sense-organ, like identity of silver with a nacre proved by illusion. This inference is invalid, since the example is devoid of the probandum. The identity is not distinct from existent and nonexistent. The identity of silver with a nacre is not admitted by experts to be distinct from existent and nonexistent. It is not admitted by both the disputants. So it cannot serve as an example. Further, being perception produced by a defect in a sense-organ is either being an object of knowledge produced by a defect of a sense-organ or being the substratum of manifestness produced by a defect of a sense-organ. The first alternative is not tenable, since the cognition being one, the cognition of the substratum, a nacre, is not produced by a defect of a sense-organ. The second alternative also is not admissible, because for the opponent it is unproven. Silver existing in some other place cannot be the substratum of manifestness produced by a knowledge generated by a defect in a sense-organ ; nor is it admitted by the opponent. Furthermore, an indefinable entity is not favourable to an illusion ; nor is it in conformity with the sublating knowledge. The illusion apprehends silver, and an indefinable object. The sublating knowledge "this is not silver" apprehends the nonexistence of silver. In the illusion "this is existent silver" 'this' is manifested to consciousness as existent, and in the sublating knowledge "this is not silver" the nonexistent silver is manifested to consciousness. Moreover, the word 'silver' in an indefinable object is not due to the genus of silver, since the genus is absent. If the genus of silver were present, indefinable silver would not be sublated, like real silver. Besides, if the object of the illusion "this is silver" were indefinable, it would not be apprehended as silver. Even if it were apprehended as silver, the apprehension would be due to a vitiated sense-organ, or to a residual impression, or to a witness-consciousness. The first alternative is not admissible, since the apprehension being a mere experience or manifestation to consciousness cannot be in contact with a sense-organ. The second alternative is not tenable, because there can be no residual impression of an unapprehended object. The third alternative also is not justifiable, since what is cognizable by the witness-consciousness alone is not cognized through a sense-organ.[90]

Citsukha refutes the opponent's criticism by adducing the following arguments. 1. He defines an indefinable entity as what cannot be thought as existent, as nonexistent, and as both. Pratyagrūpa defines an indefinable entity as being endued with the absence of the counterentity of existence, of nonexistence, and of both together.[91] This definition does not suffer from the fallacies of nonpervasion (avyāpti) and overpervasion (ativyāpti), since all objects apprehended by illusions are covered by it. The opponent's arguments about the absence of description or the absence of the cause of description are entirely irrelevant to disprove the indefinabily of an object of illusion, because the experience, the cause of description, and its object cannot be admitted to be ascertained as existent, or nonexistent, or both and spoken of as such, though they are objects of speech and action. Nor is the collective negation of both existence and nonexistence, which are contradictory to each other, unreasonable because of the rule that the negation of one of the contradictories implies the affirmation of the other, there being no scope for an intermediate possibility, since collective negation of existence and nonexistence both is not admitted to be a real entity. What is unascertainable by nature cannot have any real nature. If it had a real nature, the unascertainable entity would be existent. Nor does the negation of existence or nonexistence necessarily imply the affirmation of nonexistence or existence, respectively, according to the Advaitin, who advocates indefinable illusory existence, because the invariable concomitance between the probans and the probandum is not proven. 2. Or, what is sublated by a knowledge, is indefinable. The definition is not vitiated by overpervasion, for it does not apply to a prior knowledge or to a residual impression, because though they are destroyed by knowledge, they are not sublated by a posterior knowledge. Sublation consists in producing the knowledge of the absence of an object of illusion. The absence of neither a prior knowledge nor of a residual impression is made known by a posterior knowledge in an object of experience, as the absence of illusory silver is made known by the sublating knowledge "this is not silver". An empirical object, e.g., a jar, is destroyed by the knowledge of God or by a blow of a club, but the latter cannot produce the knowledge of the absence of a jar in its locus. So there is no overpervasion. This reasoning refutes the argument that a nacre and Brahman are indefinable, because they are the objects of the sublating knowledges "this is not silver" and "the world appearance is not true". Some Advaitins opine that sublation is the negation of existence in the past, the present, and the future, and sublatability is being the object of such negation. The definition does not suffer from nonpervasion or overpervasion, because the sublating knowledge "this is not silver" produces the knowledge of the absence of silver at the present time, and, consequently, at three times, and becauss it cannot produce the knowledge of the absence of empirical silver in some other place in that it is known to exist there. The contention that the sublating knowledge "this is not silver" produces the knowledge of the nonexistence of silver in the past, the present, and the future in a nacre is false, since it is not possible in the present case. It produces the knowledge of the nonexistence of silver at the present time. It is contended that the possibility of an appearance of silver is the possibility of such an entity. This contention is false, because there is no experience "this is an appearance of silver", and because there is the experience "this is silver". It may be argued that the sublating knowledge "this is not silver" negates silver in the object of experience, and that it is ascertained later to be an appearance of silver. Then the definition is not tainted by nonpervasion, since the opponent admits such negation in the object of experience. Therefore, empirical silver known in some other place is not the counterentity of such negation, since that is not the object of the illusion of silver. Otherwise, there would be no empirical silver in the world, which has pragmatic reality. So empirical silver here is the counterentity of the negation "this is not silver", and its existence is denied by the sublating knowledge "this is not silver" in this place. The illusion of silver prompts a person to pick it up, because he perceives it as identical with empirical silver. The sublating knowledge convinces him that it cannot be empirical silver at three times. This being true, an illusion cannot be the apprehension of an object as different from it. Like relation the two relata also must be admitted to be distinct from existent and nonexistent, because apprehension of them and sublation of them later cannot be otherwise explained. Therefore the aforesaid definition is not tainted by overpervasion. It is contended that apprehension and sublation of illusory silver are explained by the existence of silver in another place and its nonexistence here. This contention is false, since the existence of silver in another place is not the cause of the perception of silver here, and since if there be no perception of illusory silver, it cannot be sublated. It is contended that if a nonexistent entity be not apprehended, the word 'nonexistent' would be meaningless. This contention is false, because the nonexistence of immediate knowledge is sought to be affirmed here, and because mediate knowledge is not refuted. Nor is the invariable concomitance "whatever is existent is unsublatable" unproven, since what the opponent regards as existent the Advaitavādin regards as existent in the empirical world. Nor can apprehension and sublation be otherwise explained.

Existence and nonexistence alone lead to apprehension and sublation, or nonsublation and nonapprehension, respectively. The assumption of any other entity as their condition violates the parsimony of hypotheses. It is contended that existence and nonexistence do not lead to apprehension and sublation, respectively, because the Advaitavādin admits an empirical object (prapañca) also endued with existence to be sublated by the intutive knowledge of Brahman, and because a nonexistent entity also is apprehended through the word 'nonexistent'. This contention is false, since an empirically existent object is not sublated in empirical life according to the Advaitin, and since immediate knowledge of an existent object is intended here by him. An objection is raised that existence and nonexistence leading to nonsublation and nonapprehension, respectively, what is distint from existent is sublated and what is distinct from nonexistent is apprehended, and the assumption of any exception to the rule violates the law of parsimony, that the assumption of existence and nonexistence leading to apprehension and sublation, respectively, does not violate the law of parsimony. This objection is unsound, because the opponent's assumption of an exception to the rule equally violates the law of parsimony, and because the opponent also admits that what is distinct from existent and nonexistent leads to nonapprehension and nonsublation, respectively. On the other hand, the opponent cannot account for the apprehension of a nonexistent entity in an illusion. It cannot be maintained that an attributed entity (e.g., silver) is apprehended because of its existence, because an attributed being does not exist here, and because if an existent entity were apprehended, an illusion and its sublation would not be accounted for. Further, a nonexistent entity cannot be perceived. An indefinable entity (e.g., silver) is proved by the inference: the disputed object of illusion is indefinable, because it is sublated ; what is not so, is not so, for example, Ātman. It is contended that the sublation of silver is unproved because its relation to a nacre is sublated. This contention is false, because if the relation alone between two distinct entities (e.g., two trees), were negated, after its being sublated, both the distinct entities would be apprehended here. So the relation between silver and a nacre is not sublated, but indefinable silver is sublated. It is contended that if indefinable silver be the object of the illusion "this is silver", it contradicts the perception "this silver is existent". This contention is invalid, since the relation of the indefinable silver to existence also, like its relation to 'this', the substratum, is apprehended in the illusion. Further, the admission of illusory (prātibhāsika) silver does not contradict the perception "this silver is existent", though Brahman, the ontological reality, and empirical silver are absent. Nor does the sublating knowledge "this is not silver" contradict the perception of existence, because existence is denied here in the sense that it is not capable of producing a fruitful practical action. Nor is an indefinable entity unfit to be spoken of as silver, because the object of the illusion of silver is produced by the residual impression of the determinate perception of silver. It is contended that an indefinable entity cannot be perceived as silver. The contention is unjustified, since illusory silver, as already shown, is a modification of avidyā abiding in the consciousness of self determined by a nacre, superimposed on the consciousness, and capable of being perceived as silver. It is objected that a superimposed entity cannot be perceived because of the absence of its contact with a sense-organ. The objection is groundless, since a superimposed entity does not depend upon contact with a sense-organ in order to be perceived. Otherwise, according to the opponent also, silver and its relation would not be perceived. Hence an indefinable entity is the object of an illusion.[92] It has illusory reality (prātibhāsika sattā) as distinguished from the empirical reality (vyavahārika sattā) of external real objects.

STATUS OF OBJECT.—Śaṁkara rejects Vijñānavāda by urging that the nonexistence of an external object cannot be proved, because it is perceived. External objects, e.g., a post, a wall, a jar, a cloth and the like are perceived. What is perceived cannot be denied.[93] The Vijñānavādin contends that no one perceives anything other than perception. The contention is false, because an external object distinct from perception must be admitted, since it is perceived.[94] No one perceives a post, or a wall as a perception. So an object of perception is external, perceptible, and empirically real according to Śaṁkara. The Vijñānavādin argues that waking perceptions are cognitions like dreams. Śaṁkara urges that they cannot be like dreams, because dreams are contradicted by waking perceptions. But waking perceptions of posts and the like are not contradicted. So Śaṁkara does not deny externality of an object of perception.[95] He does not advocate subjective idealism, and reduce an external object to a mere cognition or idea. Nor does he deny its empirical, pragmatic reality. It is capable of producing practical actions in empirical life. But he denies its ontological reality. As dreams and illusions are ontologically unreal, so the world characterized by duality or difference is ontologically unreal.[96] The ontological reality is devoid of the distinction of knower, knowledge and known object.[97] Vācaspati Miśra follows Śaṁkara faithfully in admitting externality of an object of perception. He avers that the witness (sākṣin) perceives an apprehension as apprehending an external object, which as different from an internal cognition cannot be denied. A cognition cannot cognize itself as an object, since it involves self-contradiction. It cognizes an object distinct from itself. A knower knows an object (e.g. blue) through knowledge. It does not know knowledge through another knowledge. Nor is knowledge a knower. So Vācaspati emphatically asserts the existence of an external object.[98] The Vijñānavādins admit immediate apprehension of an object, because they identify an object with a cognition. Prakāśātman refutes it by urging that what is immediately apprehended is its object, and not a cognition.[99] He follows Śaṁkara in recognizing externality of an object distinct from a cognition. Vidyāraṇya also argues that an external object is perceived, and that therefore its perceptibility cannot be denied.[100] The Vijñānavādins contend that what are perceived are cognitions. Vidyāraṇya urges that the contention is false, because an external object also, which is not a cognition, is immediately apprehended or perceived.[101] This is a mere repetition of Śaṁkara's arguments.

But Prakāśānanda strikes a discordant note, and regards the world of diverse objects as mere cognitions in universal consciousness or Ātman—a mere mental play. Some Advaitins argue that a cognition cognizes an object, because there is invariable concomitance between them. Prakāśānanda urges that the argument is invalid, because the invariable concomitance of a cognition and object is not proved, and because their coexistence in the same locus is not possible, since they exist in different places, and since they do not exist at the same time in that a cognition cognizes a past object or a future object. Hence the difference between a cognition and an object is not proved by a pramāṇa. The entire world is manifested as mere experience.[102] The difference between a cognition and an object is a false appearance like that in dream. As a rope appears to a person with false vision to be a serpent, so Ātman appears to a soul infected with avidyā to be the manifold world. It is a mere experience in Ātman Itself.[103] The diverse objects of the world are reflections in the mirror of Its universal consciousness. The world is a mere mental play of the universal mind.[104] The nescience veiling Ātman and abiding in It is imaginary. It is not real. Here Prakāśānanda emphasizes the ontological unreality of objects of cognitions, and does not deviate from Śaṁkara's ontological position. But he appears to deny the externality of an object to a cognition from the empirical standpoint. The majority of Śaṁkarites admit that an object is external, presentable and empirically real, but ontologically unreal. Advaita absolute idealism is different from Vijñānavādin's subjective idealism.

DEGREES OF REALITY.—Śaṁkara admits three degrees of reality. The nondual Ātman or Brahman is the ontological reality. A rope is the substratum of an illusory serpent, has empirical or pragmatic reality, and exists in the past, the present and the future. An illusory serpent has an experiential (prātibhāsika) reality, and lasts as long as the illusion lasts. There is no illusion without a substratum. All names and forms, empirical objects, have pragmatic (vyavahārika) reality, and continue till the dawn of the immediate realization of Brahman. The world appearance is more real than illusory objects. Brahman of the nature of existence, knowledge and bliss unlimited by space, time, causality and adjuncts, transcendent of duality and plurality, and taintless and absolutely pure is the ontological reality.[105] It is the substratum of the world appearance, which is due to avidyā. Both empirical objects and illusory objects are unreal from the standpoint of the ontological reality of Brahman. To emphasize this truth sometimes Śaṁkara compares the world appearance with illusory objects.[106] Ether and other empirical objects are produced by māyā like illusory serpent, mirage, dream and the like. They are unreal, because they did not exist in the past and will not exist in the future. They fulfil our practical purposes; food gratifies hunger; water appeases thirst. But dreams and illusions do not fulfil our practical needs. Empirical objects are less real than Brahman while illusory objects are less real than empirical objects. They also are false, for they have origin and end.[107] Illusory objects are grounded in empirical objects. But hare's horns are pure figments of the imagination, and absolutely nonexistent. So the former are not like the latter.[108] Padmapāda also emphatically declares that the world is not absolutely nonexistent like a hare's horn, but is of the nature of the beginningless, indescribable avidyā. Vācaspati Miśra admits Ātman or Brahman to be the ontological reality of the world appearance due to avidyā, which has only empirical reality.

Dharmarājādhvarīndra opines that an empirical object (e.g., a jar) does not exist in Brahman as an ontological reality, but that its pragmatic reality is not negated in Brahman. It is an object of perception, which has empirical validity. Rāmakṛṣṇa opines that from the pragmatic standpoint the perception of a jar is valid, but that the illusion of silver in a nacre is invalid. Ontological reality is not contradicted in the past, the present and the future. Pragmatic reality is not contradicted in the state of bondage. Illusory reality is not contradicted so long as the illusion lasts.[109]

The earlier Advaita Vedāntins recognized three degrees of reality : ontological, pragmatic and illusory. Prakāśānanda denies the pragmatic reality of unknown objects. When they are not perceived by bound souls, they are experiences in Ātman. He admits only two degrees of reality : the ontological reality of Ātman and illusory reality of nacre-silver, rope-serpent and the like. The so-called unknown empirical or pragmatic objects are not proved by perception or other pramāṇas, since they will be shown to have no validity. They are not proved to be indescribable (anirvacanīya), for indescribability has not been proved already. So ether and the like are not proved to be indescribable, for there is no example to prove the inference. If it be argued that the illusion of a serpent in a rope is proved, then ether and the like have illusory reality, like illusory serpent. If they be held to be unkown also, then an illusory serpent will not serve as an example. Prakāśānanda opines that there may be a distinction between the real and the unreal even in dream. So even in the realm of experienced reality a distinction may be made between the real and the unreal, so that a person may cry when his near and dear ones die.[110] (Cp. Berkeley). In dim light many persons simultaneously have the illusion of a serpent in a rope. There is agreement (saṁvāda) among their experiences. They recognize the rope to be a serpent, though each of them has a different experience, and cannot experience another's illusion. They recognize the rope as one serpent because of nondiscrimination. Similarly, in the waking state a person perceives an empirical object, falls asleep, wakes, and perceives an empirical object, but recognizes it to be the same object owing to nondiscrimination. In deep sleep the empirical objects vanish, but the Ātman continues with Its consciousness. There is no second reality at the time. So there is no empirical world. Recognition of the same object after waking is due to nondiscrimination, because it is another object.[111] So all effects—knowledge and known object—are due to avidyā. The being of all entities is experiential.

The opponent contends that there is a difference between the knowledge of an illusory serpent and the knowledge of ether. The former is produced by avidyā whereas the latter is due to perception or some other pramāṇa. A serpent does not exist before the illusion of a serpent is produced by avidyā. But an empirical object (e.g., a jar) exists before it is perceived, since its perception is produced by the intercourse of a sense-organ with the object. So the existence of an empirical object unknown by a soul must be admitted. Otherwise, the distinction between an illusory serpent and a real rope cannot be explained. Prakāśānanda replies that the sense-organs are not the cause of the knowledge of an empirical object. If they are so, they are the cause, of valid knowledge alone, or of knowledge common to valid knowledge and illusion, or of illusion alone. They are not the cause of valid knowledge alone, because this involves vicious interdependence. The validity of knowledge produced by the sense-organs is proved by its cognizing an object different from that of an illusion. An illusion is proved to cognize an object different from that of knowledge produced by the sense-organs. It is wrong to argue that being an object of valid knowledge is the cause of the truth of the object, because the valid knowledge "this silver is false" cognizes a false object, and because it is not proved that it is contradicted. The sense-organs are not the cause of knowledge in general, because Ātman devoid of attributes is not known through the sense-organs. They are not the cause of the knowledge of Ātman. The Advaitins themselves admit that an illusion is caused by avidyā. So the sense-organs are not necessary for the production of an illusion. As the presence or the absence of the sense-organs is necessary in dreams, so their absence or presence is necessary for producing empirical objects. All empirical objects are effects of avidyā, and mere experiences. So there are two degrees of reality. Brahman is the ontological reality. All objects—not-self—are due to avidyā and apprehensional in nature.[112] From the ontological standpoint there is no difference of being, since Realily is one Brahman. Nṛsiṁhāśrama Muni rightly observes that if there be real difference in being, being will be unreal, and that being cannot be qualified by being.[113]

CRITICISM OF SUBSTANCE.—A substance is defined as the substrate of a quality. Śrīharṣa refutes this Vaiśeṣika view thus. This definition is too wide, since colour and the like have the quality of number. The experience of number of colours is not illusory, because it is not contradicted. The Vaiśeṣika contends that a quality being devoid of qualilies, colour cannot be the substrate of qualities. This contention is false, since colour cannot be ascertained to be a quality of a substance.[114]

Citsukha refutes the definition thus. The Vaiśeṣika admits that at the first moment of its production a substance is devoid of qualities. So the definition is not applicable to a substance in such a state. So it is too narrow. The Vaiśeṣika admits qualities to be twenty four in number. So they are substrates of the quality of number. Thus the definition is too wide. The experience of qualities having number is not contradicted, and is therefore valid.[115] The Vaiśeṣika admits difference in the number of substances and that of qualities. He admits nine substances and twenty four qualities. He defines a substance as the material or inherent cause of an effect. This definition is too wide, since colour and other qualities also are the material cause of effects. The Vaiśeṣika defines a substance as the substratum of the genus of substance. This definition is invalid, because there is no manifester of the genus of substance, and because there is no pramāṇa by which we can know it.[116] The advocate of a genus must admit a manifester of it, but he cannot ascertain it. If an entity endued with a quality manifests the genus of substance, then a quality also which is the attributive (viśeṣaṇa) of a substance is the manifester of the genus of substance, and therefore it is a substance. Similarly, an inherent cause also cannot manifest the genus of substance. If what is independently perceptible be said to be the manifester of the genus of substance, then what is independence ? It is either perceptibility without the perception of its substrate or not subsisting in any other entity. The first alternative is not legitimate, since a sound is perceptible without its substrate—ākāśa—being perceived. So sound is a substance. But the Vaiśeṣika admits it to be a quality. The second alternative also is not admissible, because, if it were true, a whole subsisting in its parts would not be a substance. But the Vaiśeṣika admits it to be a substance. So what does not subsist in any other entity cannot be the manifester of the genus of substance. So the definition of substance is invalid.[117]

Raṅgojī Bhaṭṭa criticizes the definition of substance after Śrīharṣa and elaborates his arguments. A substance is defined as the substratum of quality and action. This definition applies to colour, and makes it a substance, because colour has number, distinctness, nearness, distance and the like. "There are many colours" ; "colour is distinct from taste" ; "this colour is near" ; "that colour is distant". All have such experiences. They are not illusory, since they are not contradicted. If colour be not admitted to have number, a jar cannot be proved to have number, although it is perceived to be one. The argument, that if a quality be admitted to have a quality, this will lead to infinite regress, is invalid, because infinite regress is flawless if it does not hinder the production or cognition of an entity. A substance may be defined as having a quality through a particular relation, and colour being not related to number through that relation may be said to be not a substance. What is that relation ? If it be inherence, there is inherence of number in colour. If the relation be other than inherence, it is natural state (svarūpasambandha). Svarūpasambandha also exists between colour and number. So the definition is too wide and so invalid.[118]

CRITICISM OF QUALITY.—Śrīharṣa refutes quality in the following way. The Vaiśeṣika defines a quality as an entity having a genus and being devoid of a quality. This definition is invalid, because its being devoid of a quality has not been proved, and because a quality (e.g., colour) is experienced to have number. The Vaiśeṣika contends that the experience of qualities having number is false, because a quality is qualityless. This contention is false, since the argument involves interdependence : a quality is devoid of qualities because the experience of number in colour is false ; the experience of number in colour is false, because a quality is devoid of qualities. The Vaiśeṣika contends that his argument does not involve interdependence, because the experience of number in colour is contradicted inasmuch as colour being a quality is proved by some other reason (hetu). Colour is a quality, because it has a genus without being an action, like a sound. This argument does not involve interdependence. Śrīharṣa urges that this contention also is invalid, because sound, the example of the inference, has number, and is therefore a substance, and cannot be proved to be a quality. The Vaiśeṣika contends that number is the example in favour of his argument, because number is devoid of number in that it will lead to infinite regress. This contention also is invalid, because number having distinctness, it is a substance, and cannot serve as an example.[119]

Citsukha refutes the category of quality in the following manner. A quality is defined as having a generality but being devoid of a quality. This definition involves interdependence : a quality is known to be a quality, if its being devoid of a quality is known ; its being devoid of a quality is known, if a quality is known.[120] Śrīdhara defines a quality as an entity having a generality, being devoid of a quality, not being the cause of conjunction and disjunction, being neutral in them. This definition also involves interdependence as shown above.[121] Vallabha, a Nyāya-Vaiśeṣika syncretist, the author of the 'Nyāyalīlāvatī' defines a quality as an entity having a generality, being not a motion, and not being an inherent cause. This definition also is invalid, since a colour, which is a quality, is the inherent cause of number which inheres in it as shown already. A quality is defined as an entity having a generality, being devoid of touch, subsisting in a substance, and being distinct from a motion. This definition also is invalid, because a quality being distinct from a motion has not been proved.[122]

CRITICISM OF ACTION.—Citsukha refutes action thus. An action or motion is defined as an entity, which is the cause of conjunction and disjunction, and which does not depend upon any other cause. Citsukha refutes it. This definition is invalid, because an action is not the cause of conjunction and disjunction without depending upon a cause inasmuch as it depends upon the inherent cause, God's volition, time, space, and merits and demerits of souls.[123] God's volition, time, space, and soul's merits and demerits are the general causes of all effects. They are produced for souls' enjoyments and sufferings. Raṅgojī Bhaṭṭa refutes motion thus. An action or motion existing in a whole substance cannot be proved, since a cloth is perceived to move in a particular region. "The tree is conjoined with a substance". This experience is possible if there is conjunction of a substance with a part of the tree. Like conjunction, an action or motion also exists in a part of a substance, which is limited in space and time.[124] It does not pervade a whole substance.

CRITICISM OF GENERALITY : GENUS (JĀTI).—The Vaiśeṣika defines a genus as an eternal, entity inhering in many individuals. The genus of cow is one and eternal, and inheres in many individual cows. Citsukha offers the following criticism of generality. The perception of the same form in many individuals cannot prove its existence, since the alternatives involved in this concept are not legitimate. Such perception is either the apprehension of the same form (e.g , cow) in one individual as in another individual, or the apprehension of the same nature (svabhāva) of cow in individual cows, or the apprehension of individual cows as having the same attribute (dharma). The first alternative is inadmissible, because there may be apprehension of the same form in many individuals without apprehending the genus as one moon is perceived in many reflections of it in vessels of water. An individual may be perceived as a cow because of its having a dewlap and the like. The second alternative is untenable, since one nature of cow in all individual cows is not ascertained. Even if it is ascertained, the assumption of genus is unnecessary. The third alternative also is unreasonable, because there is no experience "this individual is endued with the genus of cow." It may be argued that there is the apprehension of the one attribute, viz, being endued with a dewlap and the like, in all individual cows. This attribute may be the ground of the experience of one common character in them, and the assumption of genus is unnecessary. Further, the Vaiśeṣika must admit a manifester of a genus. Where does the manifester exist ? If it exists in an individual in which a genus exists, this involves interdependence. How is the manifester of a genus manifested ? If another manifester is admitted to manifest the previous manifester, then this will lead to infinite regress. If both the genus and its manifester do not exist in the same individuals (e.g., cows), they exist in all individuals. Then all genera will exist in all individuals ; the genus of cow will exist in horses, and the genus of horse will exist in cows. Thus there will be intermixture of genera (jātisāṁkarya). If the manifester of a genus be said to exist in an individual in which it is experienced, then the assumption of a manifester is needless. If experience proves the existence of an entity, then ākāsa is blue. But the Vaiśeṣika thinks it to be colourless. Moreover, the Vaiśeṣika who admits a genus must seek for a common property other than a genus (upādhi) to account for the experience "this is a genus", "this is a genus" and the like. If he admits such a common property other than a genus, let that be the ground of the experience of commonness of individuals, and the assumption of a genus is useless. So a genus cannot be proved by perception. Further, either a genus exists in all individuals, or it exists in its proper individuals. Both the alternatives are unjustified. The existence of a genus in all individuals is either through conjunction, identity, inherence, or some other relation. A genus is not a substance, and therefore cannot be conjoined with individual substances. Nor can it inhere in them, because if did so, then all individuals would be experienced as of the nature of all. A genus cannot exist in all individuals through any other relation. If any other relation were admitted, more than six categories would be admited. Nor can a genus exist in its proper individuals. The genus of cow existing in some other individual cannot be related to a new-born cow.[125] It cannot jump and enter into the new-born cow, since it is devoid of action. If it leaves the former individual, that cannot be called a cow. Nor can the genus of cow exist partly in both individuals, since it is partless. When a cow is produced by the collocation of her causes, she may be said to be produced as being connected with the genus of cow. But this is not possible, because the genus of cow does not exist there. If it is said to exist there, then all genera exist in all individuals, and when all individuals will be destroyed at the time of dissolution, all genera will be destroyed. But the Vaiśeṣika considers a genus to be eternal. When all proper individuals are destroyed, a genus may be said to exist in its nature (svarūpa). This is not possible, since a content cannot exist when its substratum is destroyed. If a content existed, though its subtratum was destroyed, a colour would exist even after a coloured substance was destroyed. So a genus cannot exist either in all individuals or in its proper individuals.[126] The Advaita Vedāntist's criticism of the Nyāya-Vaiśeṣika view of a genus is very similar to the Buddhist's criticism of it.[127]

Citsukha refutes generality (sāmānya) thus. What is generality? It is either the cause of the experience of an entity being common to many iudividuals, or the pramāṇa or means of its knowledge, or being common to many individuals, or inhering in many individuals while being eternal, or being eternal, one, and inhering in many individuals. The first four definitions are invalid, because they are too wide, and the fifth definition is invalid, because the meaning of the word 'many' cannot be ascertained.[128] The first definition is too wide, since it is applicable to a part of the collocation of the causes of such experience, which also produces it. The second definion is too wide, because it is applicable to the cause of such experience inasmuch as the experience can be inferred from its cause. The third definition is too wide, since being common to many individuals exists in conjunction, disjunction and the like also. The fourth definition also is too wide, because it applies to atoms which are eternal, and which exist in many effects produced by them. But the Vaiśeṣika does not think atoms to be generalities. The fifth definition is invalid, since the nature of 'many' is indeterminable. Inhering in many individuals is not inhering in entities, which are the substrata of the number—duality and the like, because quality and action are not substances, and so cannot be the substrates of the number—duality and the like. Yet the Vaiśeṣika admits the generality of quality and the generality of action. A generality or genus cannot be eternal because of its indestructibility. The destruction of the genus not being well-known, it cannot be said to the counter-positive entity of its destruction. The Vaiśeṣika contends that the Advaitists regard Brahman as eternal, and that therefore he should not deny eternality of a genus. Citsukha replies that Brahman being devoid of attributes, It is not the substrate of the attribute of eternality. Brahman is considered to be eternal, because destruction is unascertainable. The Vaiśeṣika contends that a jar and the like also are eternal, because their destruction is unascertainable. Citsukha replies that anything other than Brahman is indefinable and unreal, but that ontological reality underlying it is Brahman. A generality is other than Brahman, and therefore indefinable and unreal, and not eternal, like Brahman.[129]

CRITICISM OF PARTICULARITY (VIŚEṢA).—The Vaiśeṣika defines particularity (viśeṣa) as existing in eternal substances and distinguishing them from each other. Citsukha criticizes this definition, and denies the existence of particularity. According to the Vaiśeṣika a soul and a manas are eternal. The genus of soul and the genus of manas abiding in a soul and a manas, respectively, would be particularities. So the definition is too wide. The Advaitin does not admit the eternality of manas and the reality of the genus of Ātman in that It is Brahman and one. So viśeṣa is not a distinct category.[130]

Raṅgojī Bhaṭṭa urges that the argument of the Vaiśeṣika, that the eternal atoms endued with the same qualities and actions would not be distinguished from one another without particularities (viśeṣa) inhering in them, is false, since, if that were true, viśeṣas also would require other viśeṣas to be distinguished from one another. The Vaiśeṣika argues that they are distinguished from one another by their nature. Then on the same ground the aforesaid atoms also can be distinguished from one another by their nature (svarūpa), and the category of viśeṣa is an unnecessary assumption.[131]

REFUTATION OF INHERENCE (SAMAVĀYA).—Citsukha refutes the concept of inherence. The Vaiśeṣika, Praśastapāda, defines inherence as the relation between two inseparable entities, which are related to each other as the substrate and the content, and which is the cause of the cognition "here it exists". Separable entities are those which can exist apart from each other. Inseparable entities are those which cannot exist apart from each other. Inherence is the relation between them. A cloth inhers in its threads. Though threads abide in their parts which produce them, a cloth abides in the threads which produce it. It cannot exist apart from them. But they can exist apart from the cloth. So they are not inseparably related to each other. These two noneternal entities exist in separable substrates. Separable existence is opposed to inseparable existence. The capacity for separate movement of eternal entities is their separable existence. So the incapacity for separate movement is inseparable existence. Ether and the genus of substance, which are inseparable, would be inherence, since they are incapable of separate movement. Merit, the cause, would be related to pleasure, the effect, by inherence. In order to preclude this contingency, inherence is defined to be a relation between a substrate and a content. Pleasure does not subsist in merit. So they are not related to each other by inherence. The relation of ether and the word 'ether'—the denoter-denoted-relation—would be inherence, for they are inseparable. In order to prelude this possibily inherence is defined as the cause of the cognition "here it exists". The word-object relation does not produce such a cognition, as a word does not exist in its object. If inherence were defined as the relation of a content to its substrate, which produces the cognition "here it exists", the relation of a plum to a hand in which it exists would be inherence. In order to preclude this possibility, inherence is defined as the relation between two inseparable existents. Śrīdhara objects that the three characteristics combined together do not define inherence, because if they did the relation of the absence of a jar on the ground would be inherence, since the absence of a jar does not subsist except on the ground, although the ground exists in its parts, since the absence of a jar is a content while the ground is its substrate, and since the relation between them produces the cognition "here it exists". But the relation of the absence of a jar on the ground is not inherence. In order to exclude the relation of a negation to its substrate, inherence is defined as the relation between an attribute and its substance, an effect and its material cause, a whole and its parts, a genus and an individual, and a particularity (viśeṣa) and an eternal individual. Citsukha urges that this definition is too wide, since it applies to the relation of the qualification and the qualified to each other. Citsukha asks for the proof of the reality of inherence. It is neither perceived nor inferred. The Vaiśeṣika contends that a cloth is perceived to exist *in* the threads. Citsukha urges that the alternatives involved in this supposition are not admissible. Inherence produces either the cognition of a substrate, or the cognition of a content, or the cognition of both. None of the alternatives are admissible, since the threads and the cloth both produce the cognitions of the substrate, the content, and both. The Vaiśeṣika contends that a genus and an individual are related to each other, and that there is another experience "here it exists". This contention is false, for the alternatives involved in it are unprovable. Citsukha asks whether inherence is perceived by this experience, as belonging to this experience, or as belonging to another, or as its essence. The first alternative is not admissible, since inherence being perceived as depending on another relation of belonging to it would lead to a vicious infinite. The second alternative is not tenable, because, if that were true, inherence would be perceived as belonging to another. The third alternative also is inadmissible, since, if it were true, inherence would not be perceived as a relation in that a relation subsists between two relata and cannot be the essence of either of them. The Vaiśeṣika contends that even in the absence of a relation belonging to the experience, it is proved by the experience. This contention is false, because, if that were true, in the absence of a genus and the like 'belonging to that' would be experienced, and there would be the apprehension of a nonentity. Even if in the absence of a relation the nature of the two relata were determined, then a genus would be related to an individual without any relation in order to be perceived as belonging to it, and inherence would be needless. So inherence cannot be proved by perception. Nor can it be proved by inference, for there is no mark (liṅga) from which it can be inferred. The Vaiśeṣika argues that the cognition "here it exists" is inferred to be caused by the relation of inherence, because it is an uncontradicted experience, like the experience of plums in a dish. This argument is invalid, because the relation of a content to a substrate, the relation of a qualification to the qualified, and the like are admitted, and because the inference thus proves what is already admitted or proven. The Vaiśeṣika contends that the relation of a content to a substrate and the like depending upon inherence is not already proven. This contention is false, since there is no inherence in the relation of the absence of a jar to the ground, although the absence of a jar is a qualification of the ground which is qualified by it. So inherence cannot be proved by inference.[132]

THE NATURE OF COESSENTIAL IDENTITY.—The Advaitavādin regards the so-called inherence as coessential identity (tādātmya). Raṅgojī Bhaṭṭa explains its meaning. A material (e.g., earth) is a cause having identity with its effect (e.g., an earthen jar). Earth is the material cause of an earthen jar.[133] Tādātmya is not identity and difference, because they in regard to the same being are contradictory to each other. Nor is it absolute identity, because, if it were so, a material cause would not produce an effect. Though they are identical with each other in essence, they are not absolutely identical with each other. Tādātmya is difference which does not separate the being of two entities, and which does not contradict the cognition of their relating to the same object. Whiteness and a white substance refer to the same object. The difference between them does not separate their being, and prevent them from referring to the same object.[134]

REFUTATION OF NEGATION (ABHĀVA.)—Citsukha criticizes the concept of negation in the following manner. Negation is either other than being, or the nonlocus of being, or contrary to being, or close proximity to a being in its nature, or the object of the cognition of nonexistence, or being determined by dependence on its counterentity (pratiyogin), or not the object of the cognition of existence, or not the object of indeterminate knowledge, or being devoid of the characteristics of a being. The first definition is faulty, as a being also is other than another being. It is too wide. The second definition involves self-dependence (ātmāśraya), since the word 'nonlocus' means the negation of locus. So negation is defined as negation. The third definition is too wide, because contrariety to some being also is contrariety to being, although it is not negation. If contrariety to all beings be said to be negation, it is not possible. The negation of a jar is not contrary to all beings, since, if it were so, in the absence of a jar the world would be absent. If contrariety means the negation of identity, it exists in a being also. The absence of a jar exists in a cloth, which is a positive entity. The fourth definition is too wide, since inherance also has close proximity to a being in its nature. The fifth definition is too wide, because a jar and the ground also are the objects of the cognitions of qualified negations such as "a jar does not exist on the ground", although they are positive entities. The sixth definition is faulty, for length, shortness and the like, though positive entities, depend on each other as counterenties. The seventh definition is not possible, as a negation also is the object of the cognition of existence : "the absence of a jar exists". The eighth definition is too narrow, since the genus of a Brāhmaṇa is not the object of an indeterminate cognition. The opponent admits it to be the object of a determinate cognition. The ninth definition is circular, because the words 'being devoid of' mean absence. Further, positive entities also are partly devoid of the characteristics of other positive entities, but they are not negations. If a negation means not being the locus of the characteristics of all beings, each positive entity is devoid of the characteristics of all beings. So the definition is too wide. Thus negation is uncharacterizable and indeterminable.[135]

Raṅgojī Bhaṭṭa argues that all cognitions and practical actions are explicable by the absence of objects related to particular times, and that therefore the assumption of prior negation and posterior negation is unnecessary. The Vaiśeṣika contention, that in the absence of prior negation the experience "a jar will be produced" is inexplicable, is false, because production in future is not the object of prior negation. Further, that a jar will be produced is known from the fact that it does not exist in the potsherd. So prior negation is nothing but the potsherd in which prior negation of a jar is said to exist. Similarly, posterior negation is nothing but the fact that a jar is destroyed at sometime. The experience "a jar is destroyed on the ground" is a fact. The posterior negation of a jar consequent on its destruction is needless.[136] (Cp. Rāmānuja and Madhva).

REFUTATION OF DIFFERENCE.—Ānandabodha refutes difference in 'Nyāyamakaranda', and Citsukha explains his arguments in his commentary on it. He elaborately refutes difference in 'Tattvapradīpikā'. Ānandabodha asks whether perception cognizes difference alone, or whether it cognizes objects also, which are different from each other. If it cognizes objects as well, he asks whether perception cognizes objects first and then cognizes difference between them, or whether it cognizes both simultaneously. The first subalternative is inadmissible, because it cannot cognize difference first without cognizing the objects, which differ from each other. The second subalternative also is untenable, since a momentary cognition has no succession of causal operation, and so cannot apprehend objects and their difference simultaneously. Maṇḍana Miśra says, "The production itself of a cognition is its causal operation, and cognition is of the nature of the apprehension of an object."[137] Ānandabodha argues that perception cannot cognize different objects and their difference simultaneously, because perception of difference depends upon the perception of the distinguished entity and distinction, which cannot occur simultaneously. It is not right to argue that the cognition of difference depends upon the cognition of the distinguished entity, but that the former is not produced by the latter, because, if it were so, dependence of the former on the latter would not be determined. If an effect depends upon something arising from a cause, it depends upon the cause. If the production of the effect does not depend upon its cause, the former cannot depend upon the latter.[138] Citsukha argues that all discerning persons must admit that the cognition of difference does not depend upon the cognition of different entities in manifesting or apprehending its object (e.g., difference), that the cognition of difference depends upon the cognition of different entitities, because the former is produced by the latter, and that, therefore, the cognition of the cause and the cognition of the effect cannot occur at the same time.[139]

Some opine that all entities are of the nature of differences. They are perceived as of the nature of distinctions from one another. Perceptions also cognize them as distinct from one another. Ānandabodha refutes this view by adducing the following arguments. Without the perception of yellow its nature as distinct from blue is not cognized. The perception of an object cognizes its nature, and does not cognize its distinctness from another object.[140] The perception of blue cognizes the nature of blue; it does not cognize blue as of the nature of distinction from yellow and the like.[141] Nor does perception first cognize the being of blue, and then cognize it as of the nature of distinction from yellow and the like. Nor can difference distinct from the different entities be determined. If it were so, the difference being distinguished by another difference it would lead to infinite regress. It is contended that the difference is not distinguished by another difference, because it is difference by nature. The contention is false, because, if it were so, the difference would be nothing but the different entities according to the law of parsimony.[142] But it is wrong to argue that a jar and other entities are distinguished by a difference, but that a difference is by nature so. Difference distinguishes an entity from other entities. If it were of the nature of an entity, no entity would be one. Oneness which means nondifference contradicts difference. Even an atom is not one entity. An aggregate of atoms also is not one. Nor is it of some other kind. Oneness and manyness, which are contradictory to each other, are not of the same kind. Of them if one is negated, the other is affirmed, like 'eternal' and 'noneternal'. So the world would be void in reality.[143] The opponent contends that the form of blue is of the nature of difference, which is dependent on yellow and the like, that it does not depend upon blue, that it is not one as of the nature of blue, that it is different because it depends upon another entity, and that, therefore, his view is flawless. This contention is false, because difference due to its cause, depending on other entities cannot be determined.[144] If it did depend upon other entities, its own nature independent of other entities would be contradicted, and its own nature and the nature of a contradictory entity would exist together,—which is impossible.[145] So difference in its nature does not depend upon other entities. Further, if blue and difference were one, we could not use such expressions as "blue is different", and "the difference of blue", speaking of blue as a substantive (viśeṣya) and as an attributive (viśeṣaṇa), and therefore perception would not cognize difference itself, because difference is not of the nature of being.[146] The opponent contends that he does not regard difference to be of the nature of being (bhāva), but that he admits difference to be different from entities, which are different, but that the admission of another difference between different entities does not lead to endless regress, because this fault does not occur owing to the absence of the destruction of the knowledge of the first difference.[147] Ānandabodha urges that this contention is false, because the first difference is not proved inasmuch as it depends upon the other differences. When a difference is known as a substantive or an attributive (e.g., 'difference of a pitcher from a post' or 'a pitcher is different from a post'), it cannot be known as a substantive or an attributive without cognition of another difference. So the cognition of another difference must be admitted, and that difference, again, will depend upon another difference, and so on. So there is the fault of infinite regress. The opponent contends that indeterminate perception cognizes an entity and its difference simultaneously as unrelated to each other, and that determinate perception, which follows it, cognizes difference between them. This contention is false, because indeterminate perception also cannot cognize difference without cognizing its counterpositive entities, because it is perception, like determinate perception. This inference is flawless. Indeterminate perception also is preceded by perception of entities, which are different. So this involves vicious interdependence. Hence it is proved that perception cannot cognize difference.[148] Inference depends upon perception of difference between a probans and a probandum. So inference cannot prove difference. Testimony depends upon perception of difference between a word and the object denoted by it. So testimony also cannot prove difference. Hence difference cannot be proved by any pramāṇa.[149] The cognition of difference cannot be proved by a pramāṇa, because its proof has not been determined, or because it is a cognition of difference, like the cognition of difference in dream.[150] All difference is a false appearance projected by the beginningless avidyā and its impressions.[151]

Difference is false, because it is difference, like difference between reflections of a face in mirrors.[152] When the false appearances of different entities are annulled, void does not remain. They are false appearances in the existent Brahman, That exists in each of them. So when they are annulled, Brahman remains. The different entities, a jar and the like, are imagined in the existent Brahman, since each of them is interpenetrated by It. As each of the reflections of the moon in water is interpenetrated by the form of the moon, so each of the empirical objects is interpenetrated by the existent Brahman. In the illusion "this is silver" illusory silver is attributed to 'this', which is the substrate of illusory silver. It is interpenetrated by 'this'. Similarly, false appearances of empircal objects are interpenetrated by Brahman wherein they are imagined.[153] Brahman is the substrate of the world appearance. Nṛsiṁhāśrama Muni also avers that the diverse world appearance is of the nature of Ātman, and nondifferent from It. Śrīharṣa adduces the following criticisms of the concept of difference. The difference, which is perceived is either the nature of an entity, or mutual negation (anyonyābhāva), or dissimilarity, or some other entity. If nature is difference, the nature of a jar is its difference from a cloth, and the nature of a cloth is its difference from a jar. So when the nature of a jar is perceived, a cloth also enters into its nature, a cloth and a jar become identical, and their identity is known by the perception which cognizes the difference between them. But this is contrary to experience. It may be objected that if the nature of a cloth were its difference from a jar, the identity of a jar and a cloth would not be cognized, because the difference between them is not cognized. Śrīharṣa replies that identity is ontologically real, but that difference is a false appearance due to nescience. Without cognizing the nature of a jar and a cloth the difference between them cannot be cognized. But without cognizing the difference between them their nature can be cognized. So the cognition of nature or identity is the sustainer of the cognition of difference. The former is the principal while the latter is subordinate to it. The knowledge of nature is valid while the knowledge of difference is false.[154] If a counterentity of difference also were the nature of difference, then the former would not be able to determine the nature of difference. There is no evidence to prove that difference has no counterentities. Difference is always determined by its counterentities, and is of their nature. It is absurd to argue that the nature of a cloth, which does not depend upon any other entity, is determined by its counterentity—a jar, and then becomes different from a jar. What is blue by nature is not determined by yellow, and then becomes yellow. Further Śrīharṣa asks whether the nature of a counterentity of a cloth is the nature of a jar, or whether it is an attribute of a jar. In the first alternative, the nature of a counterentity of a cloth being the nature of a jar, the nature of a jar includes the nature of a cloth, and so there is identity between them. There is no evidence to prove that a counterentity does not depend upon or differ from any other entity. The nature of a counterentity is always determined by the nature of another entity from which it differs. When a jar is said to differ from a cloth, the nondifference of the cloth from the jar in part is admitted. The second alternative is not tenable. The nature of a counterentity cannot be a certain attribute. A jar being a counterentity of a cloth or differing from it, a cloth also would enter into its nature, and there would be identity of a cloth with the jar. If a cloth aequired the attrihute of a jar, a jar also would acquire the attribute of a cloth. They would subsist in each other and be the substrates of each other, and thus they would be the substrates and attributes of each other. But the object of a valid cognition is never a cloth with a jar as its substrate or attribute or a jar with a cloth as its substrate or attribute. Further, if an attribute were not related to a substrate, there would be an unwarranted stretch of a general rule: two absolutely unrelated entities would be related to each other as a substrate and an attribute. If an infinite number of relations be assumed to exist between a substance and an attribute, there would be a vicious infinite. If natural relation (svarūpasambandha) were assumed between them, they would become identical with each other. Similarly, a jar is identical with its attribute. It is not different from its attribute. The perception which cognizes difference in nature cognizes identity.[155] It it objected that when a jar is perceived as independent of any other identity, it is perceived as a jar alone, but that when a jar is perceived as different from a cloth, its difference from a cloth is perceived. Śrīharṣa urges that this objection is invalid, because the perception of a jar differs from the perception of its difference from a cloth. The former cognizes the jar alone, but can become the perception of its difference from a cloth. A cloth is not manifested or cognized by the perception of a jar. This is the difference between the perception of a jar alone and the perception of its difference from a cloth which differs from the perception of 'a jar and a cloth' also. The perception of a jar and a cloth and the pertion of the difference of a cloth from a jar never cognize the same object. In order to perceive a jar and a cloth no one perceives that a cloth differs from a jar. So the determination of the nature of a jar does not depend upon the perception of a cloth.[156]

Citsukha practically reiterates Śrīharṣa's criticism of difference as the nature of an entity. Difference is not the nature of an entity, because, if it were so, it would not depend upon its counterentity. A is different from B. A's difference from B depends upon B—its counterentity. If A's difference were its nature, the difference and its counterentity being included in its nature, B also would be included in its nature and be identical with A. It may be argued that a counterentity—B—is not included in the nature of an entity—A, but is indifferent and yet determines the difference, and that therefore B does not become identical with A. This argument is invalid, because although a counterentity is not included in the nature of difference, the difference constituting the nature of an entity would not be determined by any other condition, like the nature of an entity. B being a counterentity of A, would enter into its nature; A being a counterentity of B, would enter into its nature. Thus A and B would be identical with each other.[157] So difference cannot be the nature (svarūpa) of an entity.

Śrīharṣa then criticizes the concept of difference as mutual negation (anyonyābhāva). A is not B. B is not A. There is the negation of B in A, and there is the negation of A in B. There is mutual negation of A and B in each other. Mutual negation also involves difference of an entity from a counterentity. So the counterentity also is included in its nature. Thus there would be identity between an entity and a counterentity.[158] Further, the identity between two entities is the counterentity of mutual negation. If it is not at all desired, then mutual negation qualified or distinguished by identity also cannot be cognized by valid knowledge. We speak of the negation of identity. So identity is admitted to be the counterentity of negation. This assumption is open to objection. The identity between a jar and a cloth is absolutely unreal. So in the experience of negation, which is the counterentity of identity, identity cannot be an attribute or a distinctive mark of the negation. There cannot be an experience of mutual negation at all. Even if there is an experience, it cannot be valid. An entity qualified or distinguished by a hare's horn cannot be an object of valid knowledge. So a valid knowledge cannot cognize identity qualified or distinguished by absolutely nonexistent mutual negation. It is objected that identity is not the counterentity of mutual negation, but that a cloth and the like are its counterentities, and that therefore the experience of mutual negation is not absolutely nonexistent. This being so, the negation of a cloth abiding in a jar is absolute negation itself, and not the negation of identity. Then, what is the difference between relational negation and mutual negation ? Just as the opponent admits that the negation of a jar is related to a cloth and that therefore the negation of relation to a jar abides in a cloth, so he must admit that the negation of a jar abides in a cloth. So identity and relation being the counterentities of absolute negation and relational negation, respectively, the difference between absolute negation and relational negation must be admitted. This being so, identity must be admitted to be the counterentity of absolute negation. If mutual negation of a jar and a cloth means that the nature of a cloth does not exist in a jar and that the nature of a jar does not exist in a cloth, the nature of a jar and the nature of a cloth as distinct attributes being not admitted, they cannot be denied of each other, and if both be assumed to be identical with each other, the nature of a cloth would exist in a jar, and the nature of a jar would exist in a cloth. If that is denied, both become devoid of the nature of a jar and the nature of a cloth. Dissimilarity and difference in nature being not possible, mutual negation of a jar in a cloth cannot be an object of valid knowledge, because it cannot cognize a substrate and a negation abiding in it.[159]

Citsukha shows that mutual negation is not difference by adducing the following arguments. Mutual negation subsists either in a different substrate or in a nondifferent substrate. It cannot subsist in a different substrate, because if it did so, an infinite number of differences would have to be admitted between them. They would be gradually related to the substrate. The substrate being produced at a particular time, it cannot be related to the differences. If they could be gradually related to the substrate in the past and the future, the substrate (e.g., a jar) would be beginningless and endless. It may be argued that all differences are simultaneously related to the substrate. The argument is invalid, because then differences cannot subsist in a different substrate in that it cannot be different, if it is not already related to difference. A substrate is different only in relation to difference. There being nothing to determine which difference will exist in which substrate qualified by difference, no single difference can exist. The assumption of an infinite number of differences would be useless to account for the succeeding differences by the preceeding differences. Nor can difference subsist in a nondifferent substrate. If difference subsists in a nondifferent substrate, the substrate cannot be one. Since one substrate does not exist, many substrates also cannot exist. Citsukha reiterates Śrīharṣa's argument.[160]

Then Śrīharṣa criticizes the concept of difference as dissimilarity (vaidharmya). Dissimilarity also cannot be perceived as difference. It contradicts the Śrutis asserting identity. If another dissimilarity is admitted to subsist in a dissimilarity, the admission will lead to infinite regress. If another dissimilarity is not admitted to subsist in a dissimilarity, two dissimilarities become identical with each other. Further, Śrīharṣa asks whether two dissimilarities, which are differences, subsist in a substrate different from a jar and a cloth, or whether they subsist in a substrate nondifferent from them, because the two differences being opposed to each other cannot have any other different forms, like difference-cum-non-difference in that they being opposed to each other cannot be produced together. In the first alternative, Śrīharṣa asks whether the difference, which makes the dissimilarities different from each other, subsists in a different substrate, or whether it subsits in a non-different substrate. In the first subalternative, there would be a vicious infinite. The opponent may assume an infinite number of differences. Śriharṣa urges that infinite differences cannot exist, because gradually they cannot be related to their substratess which are limited by time. The opponent may coutend that the differences are related to their subssrates, which are produced simultaneously, and that the former may subsist in the latter at the same time. There is no opposition among jarness, earthness and substanceness, because they are produced simultaneously. But, Śrīharṣa urges, the question whether a difference subsists in a different entity or whether it subsists in a nondifferent entity remains unanswered. If a number of preceding and succeeding differences are admitted, an immediately preceding difference accounting for an immediately succeeding difference, then a difference occurring before and then disappearing later cannot subsist in an entity, like one who hears something and then forgets it.[161]

It may be held that the nature itself of two entities distinguishing them from each other is their difference. Then the two entities distinguishing them from each other become devoid of any nature, because their nature is difference. It may be objected that though their special natures distinguish them from each other, their nature in itself does not distinguish them from each other, and that therefore they do not become devoid of their nature. Śrīharṣa urges that since their special nature distinguishes them from each other, their nature in itself remains undistinguished and is identical. The opponent contends that he does not admit that a nature is common to the individuals, but that it abides in particular individuals, which has various meanings. This contention is false, since then the genus of a cow cannot be proved in that there is no generic nature. Further, if nature were difference or distinguishing attribute, then there would be no doubt as to whether when a substrate is perceived its nature is perceived, or whether when a substrate is perceived its nature is not perceived. If a difference were held to subsist in a nondifferent entity, then one individual would be perceived as many, and in the absence of one there would be the absence of many. If a jar and a cloth, though nondifferent from each other, were different, then an individual jar, though nondifferent, would be different, and there would be no one individual, and there being no one individual, there would not be many individuals. Hence no difference subsists in a different entity or in a nondifferent entity, and therefore it does not subsist in a neutral entity, which is neither different nor nondifferent.[162] Citsukha offers the following criticism of difference as dissimilarity. Difference is not dissimilarity, since if dissimilarity had another dissimilarity, it would lead to a vicious infinite. If dissimilarity had no other dissimilarity, two dissimilaritie would be identical, and their substrates also would be identical, and this would leads to monism.[163]

Then Śrīharṣa criticizes the concept of difference as distinctness. Because difference is neither nature, nor mutual negation, nor dissimilarity, it is not distinctness, which is another attribute. Distinctness also cannot subsist in its substrate, which is different and nondifferent as shown above. If difference is assumed to subsist in its substrate, because it cannot be identical with its substrate, then there arises the difficulty of self-dependence. If difference subsists in its substrate, then there is another difference to distinguish them from each other, and this leads to a vicious infinite. If difference is not assumed to subsist between difference and its substrate, then there is identity between them, and thus ultimately there is identity alone. It may be contended that though nature, mutual negation and dissimilarity are not difference, there is no identity because distinctness subsists in an individual entity, which is difference. This contention is false, because distinctness also cannot exist in a different or nondifferent entity, which is its substrate. It is objected that the Identity-texts are contradicted by the cognitions of difference, which are the sustainer, and which sustain the differences among letters, words and the like, since the sustained entity is dependent on the sustainer. Śrīharṣa urges that this contention is false, because the Advaitavādin denies the ontological reality of difference but does not deny its empirical reality due to the nescience (avidyā), which serves as cause and effect.[164] The Identity-texts prove the ontological identity of Brahman. The knowledge of ontological identity cannot be contradicted by the knowledge of empirical difference or plurality. Ontological identity can be contradicted by ontological difference but not by empirical difference due to nescience. The sustainer or independent cannot be contradicted by the sustained or subsidiary. So there is no ontological difference.[165] Citsukha refutes the concept of difference as distinctness as follows. Distinctness has no other distinctness. So distinctness would be identical with its substrate. Further, distinctness is a quality. Qualities are devoid of qualities. So distinctness cannot subsist in qualities, and therefore there can be no difference in qualities. It may be contended that the existence of difference between two qualities is due to their mutual negation. This contention is invalid, because, if that were true, the experience of difference between two substances also would be due to their mutual negation. There is no need of distinctness, since there is no proof for its existence. So difference is not distinctness.[166]

Citsukha criticizes the concept of difference as contrariety (vailakṣaṇya). Difference is not contrariety, since it involves self-dependence. Contrariety consists in plurality of characteristics. Plurality is difference which has not been proved. Furthermore, it is difficult to ascertain the nature of contrariety. Six substances are assumed to have various characteristics. A substance is defined as the substrate of qualities. This definition is too narrow and too wide. At the moment of its production a substance is devoid of qualities according to the Vaiśeṣika. So the definition is too narrow. Qualities are admitted by the Vaiśeṣika to be the substrates of number. They are admitted to be twenty four in number. So the definition is too wide. Thus contrariety being indeterminable, it is not difference.[167]

CRITICISM OF NYĀYA DEFINITION OF CAUSE.—Citsukha adduces the following criticisms of of the concept of cause. A cause is either an antecedent, or an invariable antecedent, or what has no effect due to the absence of the auxiliary causes, or what belongs to the class of entities the presence and absence of which are followed by the presence and absence, respectively, of its effect, or what occurs in a part of space with the aggregate of conditions, or what has causal operation, or what not being admitted leads to the contingency of eternal existence or eternal nonexistence. The first definition is not valid, because an ass, an antecedent, would be the cause of smoke according to it. The second definition is wrong, since time would not be a cause according to it, because time is one, and has no other time, and is not an antecedent. Priority and posteriority are not due to conditions associated with them (e.g., the position of the sun), as it involves interdependence : priority and posteriority of time depend on priority and priority of conditions ; priority and posteriority of conditions depend upon priority and posteriority of time. The third definition is not reasonable. What is an invariable antecedent ? It is either what existing only an effect comes into being, or what is an unconditional antecedent, or what exists in prior time as being favourable to the production of its effect, or what existing at the prior moment, an effect must come into existence. The first subalternative is untenable, because an ass, an invariable antecedent of a particular case of smoke would be its cause, although it is not an invariable antecedent of all cases of smoke. The second subalternative is inadmissible, because, if it were true, an ass and ether (ākāśa) also being invariable or unconditional antecedents would be the cause of a particular smoke. Ether is eternal and ubiquitous. The third subalternative is untenable, since anything other than prior existence is not determined to be favourable to the production of an effect. The fourth subalternative also is not admissible, since then a seed would not be a cause of a sprout in that a seed exists prior to a sprout, which may not be produced. The third main alternative is not tenable, because a cause not being determined, its auxiliary causes cannot be determined. A cause is an aggregate of the principal cause and the auxiliary causes. If an aggregate is not a cause, the abseuce of an effect cannot be due to the absence of auxiliary causes. If an auxiliary cause is another cause which assists a cause, then the former would depend upon itself (ātmāśraya) inasmuch as a cause is not determined. The fourth main alternative is untenable, because an ass would be the cause of a particular smoke in that when as ass is present, a smoke is present, and when an ass is absent, a smoke is absent, and because ether would not be a cause in that it cannot be present and absent, being eternal and ubiquitous. The fifth main alternative is inadmissible, since an aggregate not being determined, an entity existing in a part of it cannot be determined. An aggregate is either a collection of entities or a collection of causes. The first subalternative is untenable, since, if that were so, a collection of noncauses would be an aggregate. The second subalternative also is inadmissible, because a cause not being determined, an aggregate of causes would depend upon itself. Further, a collocation of causes is either the nature of the cause or different from it. In the first subalternative, an effect would be produced by the members of the collection singly. In the second subalternative, if the collection were an eternal entity, the effect would always be produced. Even if the collection were noneternal, the individual causes singly being the cause of the collection, and the collection always existing, an effect also would always be produced. If the individual causes collectively were the cause, it would involve self-dependence or infinite regress. If the main effect without the other consequences were produced by the individual causes producing the collection, the latter would be useless. On the same ground an aggregate cannot be what consists of members determined by each other. Nor is an aggregate the proximity of causes, for the nature of proximity has not been determined. Proximity is not existing at one time, for it does not exist in time. Nor is proximity existing in one point of space, for proximity does not exist in space. Proximity exists in a substance. Nor is proximity existing in one part of space and at one point of time for the reasons stated above. Nor is proximity conjunction and inherence, since in that case they would be causes. Nor is proximity being the cause of the same effect, since it would involve self-dependence in that the relation of cause and effect is not yet known. Nor is the last causal operation of the causes an aggregate of causes, because the individual causes singly, or their collection producing the causal operation would be vitiated by the aforesaid defects. Further, the causes are endued with causal operation or not endued with it in producing a causal operation. In the first subalternative, there is infinite regress. In the second subalternative, let the causes produce the effect, and an intermediate causal operation is needless. If a causal operation requires another causal operation to prodnce an effect, it will lead to infinite regress. If a causal operation produces an effect without a causal operation, let the causes themselves produce an effect, and causal operation is unnecessary. If that after which an effect is certainly produced were an aggregate, then disjunction would be a cause. The conjunction of the causes is destroyed, and they are disjoined from one another before the effect is produced. So disjunction would be the cause of an effect. But disjunction is not regarded as its cause. The sixth main alternative is untenable, because, if it were true, the last causal operation would not be a cause, for it is devoid of causal operation. Further, it would involve self-dependence ; a causal operation is defined as produced by a cause, and producing an effect which is produced by the cause.[168] So causal operation involves self-dependence, because it is defined by including a cause in its definition. Being endued with a causal operation is either inhering in a causal operation or producing a causal operation. In the first subalternative, the performance of a sacrifice would not be the cause of the attainment of heaven, since it does not inhere in Apūrva, which is the causal operation intervening between the cause and the effect in that a sacrifice is destroyed before Apūrva is produced. So it is untenable. The second subalternative also is untenable, for it involves self-dependence. The seventh main alternative also is inadmissible, because prior negation, though uncaused, has neither eternal existence, nor eternal nonexistence, and because a hare's horn, though uncaused, has no eternal existence.[169]

CRITICISM OF EFFECT.—Citsukha adduces the following criticisms of the concept of effect. An effect is either what acquires its nature from its cause, or what is related to beinghood (sattā), being marked by prior negation, or what is a counterentity of prior negation, or what has prior negation, or what was nonexistent before and is related to future time. These definitions cannot he proved. The first definition is unjustified, since a cause not being defined an effect cannot be defined. The second definition is unreasonable, since destruction devoid of beinghood would not be an effect. The third definition is not valid, because a counterentity means what cannot coexist in the same point of space with an entity. An effect and its prior negation cannot coexist in the same point of space. If a counterentity means what cannot coexist at the same time, time also is an effect, since time cannot coexist with its prior negation at another time in that it is nonexistent. The self also is an effect, since it does not coexist with its prior negation. It is eternal and devoid of prior negation. The fourth definition is not reasonable, for 'having' means 'being the locus of'. According to this definition the self is an effect, because it is the locus of the prior negation of pleasure and the like, which are effects. The fifth definition is not valid, for future time would not be an effect according to it inasmuch as it is not related to future time. It may be contended that future time is not an effect for it is eternal. This contention is false, since in that case prior negation also would be an effect in that it has no prior existence and in that it is related to future time, depending on some conditions. It may be contended that prior nonexistence means prior negation. This contention is false, since the word 'having' being not determined, the phrase 'related to future time' is meaingless. On the same ground an effect cannot be defined as what always exists at a future moment, since the invariable existence at the future moment cannot be defined, because a cause in relation to which an effect always exists at the next moment is not defined, and because time also has not been defined. Hence a cause is not what existed at the preceding moment, and an effect is not what will exist at the next moment ; causality cannot be determined.[170]

CRITICISM OF KNOWER-KNOWN-RELATION.—Citsukha shows that the relation of a knowing self and a known object is not possible. The relation between them cannot be due to relation of an object to a sense-organ, or the internal organ, since God's cognition apprehends an object, although it is not produced by a sense-organ, since a yogin's cognition cognizes past and future external objects in the state of trance, though it is not produced by the internal organ related to them, and since external objects are not cognizable through the internal organ, since our sensory hallucinations also, though not produced by the sense-organs, manifest external objects, and since our recognition 'this is that Devadatta' is admitted to be perception, though the cognition of 'that' is not produced by a sense-organ in that it is past. It may be argued that 'that' is perceived through the relation of united qualification (saṁyukta-viśeṣaṇatā) with a sense-organ. The argument is false, because if a relation other than inherence were perceived without sense-object-intercourse in the inference 'the hill is fiery', fieriness would be perceived, through the relation of united qualification. So the relation of a knowing self to a known object is not possible. An object is superimposed on the self or false.[171]

CRITICISM OF COGNITION-OBJECT-RELATION.—It may be argued that the relation of a knower to a known object is the relation of a cognition (viṣayi) to an object (viṣaya). The argument is false, since such a relation has not yet been determined. An object of a cognition is not the substrate of the result produced by the cognition in it, nor does a cognition produce a result in its object, because the alternatives involved in them are not justifiable. The result is either cognizedness or action. The first alternative is not tenable, for cognizedness is not produced in past and future objects, which would cease to be objects of a cognition. The second alternative also is not admissible, since no action is produced in the self, though it is cognized. It may be argued that what is manifested in a cognition is the object of that cognition. This argument is invalid, for the alternatives involved in it are not justifiable. The phrase 'in the cognition' means either that the cognition is the locus of manifestation of the object, or that the cognition is merely related to the object, or that the cognition is produced by the object. The first alternative is not tenable, since an internal cognition cannot be the locus of an external object. The second alternative is not admissible, because, if it were true, a jar being related to a cognition would be subject, and a cognition would be an object. The third alternative also is not justifiable, since, if it were true, a sense-organ and merits also would be objects of a cognition in that they produce it. It may be argued that a sense-organ and merits are not objects of cognitions, because an object is manifested in a cognition, and that this qualification precludes them from being objects of cognitions in that they are not manifested in cognitions. This argument is invalid, since the nature of 'being manifested' has not yet been determined. It may be argued that an object is the cause which imparts its form to a cognition. This argument is false, because all causes of a cognition would be its objects inasmuch as there is no difference between a cognition and its form. It may be argued that what is known and imparts its form to a cognition is its object. This argument is false, since the nature of 'being known' is not yet determined. Nor is the objective case of the act of cognition an object, since, if it were true, past and future things would not be objects of cognitions, and since God's knowledge would not be an object of knowledge in that it is not produced by an act of knowledge. It may be argued that what is a qualification of a cognition is its object, and that what is qualified is its cognition without depending on any other relation. This argument is false, since though there is a relation of a qualification and a qualified entity between inherence in my self and cognition of colour, the former is not cognized by the latter. So the relation of a cognition to its object is not determinable.[172]

CRITICISM OF BEING (BHĀVA).—Citsukha refutes being or existence. Being is either the object of the cognition of "it exists", or not the object of the cognition "it does not exist", or determination of an object as not depending on its counterentity, or an object cognized by indeterminate cognition, or being characterized by the charactesritics of six categories—substance, quality, action, generality, particularity and inherence, or being characterized by the characteristics of any one of the categories. Being is not the object of the cognition of "it exists", because negation or nonexistence also is the object of the cognition "it (e.g. nonexistence of a jar) exists". So the definition is too wide. Being is not the object of the cognition "it does not exist", because, if the definition were true, the object of the cognition of "a jar does not exist in the ground" would be the being or existence of a jar. Being is not the determination of an object as not depending on a counterentity (pratiyogī), because, if it were true, 'short' and 'long' depending on each other would not be being. Being is not cognized by indeterminate cognition, since a jar and the like exist before and after indeterminate cognitions of them. Being is not characterized by the characteristics of the six categories, because each of the six categories is devoid of the characteristics of all six categories. Being is not characterized by the characteristics of any one of the categories as shown already. So being is indeterminable.[173]

CRITICISM OF MANAS.—Vidyāraṇya criticizes the Naiyāyika concept of manas as an eternal, partless and atomic substance. Manas is not eternal, for it is limited, like a jar. The contention that manas is eternal, since it is a partless substance, like a self, is invalid, for the probans is unproven. Vidyāraṇya opines that manas has parts, because it is an instrument (karaṇa) of knowledge, like the visual organ. It has no impact with a coporeal substance, for it does not go out of the body while it is alive. In the state of death even the visual organ and the like, which are admitted to have parts, have no impact with other corporeal substances. Manas is not atomic, because it is composed of parts, and because it has conjunction and disjunction, like a jar. The Pātañjala opines that manas is ubiquitous. Vidyāraṇya refutes this view. Manas is not ubiquitous, because, if it were so, it would be omniscient owing to its conjunction with all sense-organs at the same time. Manas is of intermediate magnitude according to the Advaita Vedānta. This concept is flawless. Manas can enter into a small body by decrease of parts; and can enter into a large body by increase of parts.

The Buddhist idealists opine that manas is the immediately preceding cognition (samanantarapratyaya), because it is the instrument of the succeeding cognition. Vidyāraṇya criticizes this view. The preceding cognition alone without depending on invariable concomitance cannot produce the succeeding cognition, because the cognition of a probans depending on invariable concomitance is found to produce the cognition of the probandum. It is contended that verbal cognition without depending on invariable concomitance produces the cognition of an object. This contention is false, because the Buddhists include verbal cognition in inference, and because inference depends on invariable concomitance. It is contended that a cognition of a qualification without depending on invariable concomitance produces a determinate cognition of a qualified object. This contention is false, because a determinate cognition is produced by sense-object-intercourse. The Buddhists argue that a cognition immediately preceding a cognition does not produce a succeeding cognition, but that it imparts its form to the cognition. This argument is invalid, because a form and what has a form are not different from each other, and because a form being natural to what has a form does not depend on any other cause. So manas is different from an immediately preceding cognition.[174]

Raṅgoji Bhaṭṭa refutes the Vaiśeṣika concept of manas as the internal organ. There is no proof for the existence of manas. The Vaiśeṣika argues that attention to one sensible object to the exclusion of others is inexplicable without manas. This argument is invalid, since it can be explained by merits and demerits (adṛṣṭa) of an individual soul, or by the desire to know a particular sensible object.[175] Otherwise, when manas is conjoined with the visual organ, why it is not conjoined with the auditory organ is inexplicable. If a soul's merits and demerits regulate the fact, they may as well regulate attention to a particular sensible object. The Vaiśeṣika argues that manas is inferred from the perception of pleasure, pain and the like, which are not perceived through the external sense-organs, and that they are perceived through manas. The argument is false, since there is no proof for the existence of many external sense-organs, and since one sense-organ limited by the eyes, the ears and the like can perceive colour, sound and the like, respectively.[176] Or, let the visual organ, subject to contraction and expansion, issue out of the eyes, and perceive colour, being limited by the ear-hole perceive sound, pervading the whole body perceive touch, being limited by the nose perceive odour, being limited by the tongue perceive taste, and being unlimited perceive pleasure, pain and the like.[177] The assumption of many sense-organs is unnecessary, for the contracting and expanding visual organ alone endowed with force can perceive all kinds of sensible objects. The Vaiśeṣika himself admits that one sense-organ of touch being limited by the visual organ perceives the touch of smoke. It is contended that if one sense-organ being limited by different sense-organs can perceive all kinds of sensible objects, a person born blind will be able to perceive colour, and not perceive touch. The contention is false, because the Vaiśeṣika admits that a deaf person fails to perceive sound because of the absence of the ear-hole aided by special merits and demerits, and because, similarly, a born blind person can perceive touch, but cannot perceive colour because of the absence of the eyes aided by special merits and demerits. So a wise person should assume one sense-organ capable of perceiving all kinds of sensible objects through the limiting conditions of different sites.[178]

The Vaiśeṣika infers the atomic magnitude of manas from the nonsimultaneity of the special qualities of the self—cognition, pleasure, pain, desire, aversion, and volition, But Raṅgojī Bhaṭṭa urges that there is no proof for their nonsimultaneity, because we experience pleasure in the hands and pain in the feet simultaneously. Their simultaneity is not illusory, since it is not contradicted.[179]

CRITICISM OF TIME.—Citsukha refutes time by the following arguments. Time is not proved by perception. A substance is perceived by the visual organ and the tactual organ. The former cannot perceive a substance devoid of colour, and the latter cannot perceive a substance devoid of touch. The manas cannot perceive anything independently of the external sense-organs. So time cannot be perceived by the external sense-organs or by the manas. Nor can it be known by inference, for there is no mark of inference (liṅga) invariably related to time. Priority, posteriority, simultaneity, nonsimultaneity, quickness, and lateness are not marks of inference individually or collectively, because they have no distinctive marks without being associated with some condition (upādhi) such as the motion of the sun. If they depend upon the conditions, the latter are the distinctive marks of priority and the like, and the assumption of time is needless.[180]

CRITICISM OF DIRECTION (DIK).—Citsukha refutes direction or space. It is not perceived by the sense-organs. Nor is it inferred, because there is no mark (liṅga) invariably accompanied by direction. The cognitions of east, west, north, south, north-east, north-west, south-east, south-west, up and down are not marks of inference, since they are not marks without being associated with any condition (upādhi). Without any fixed point of reference, which is a condition, any object may be in any direction from another object.[181] Pratyagrūpa asks whether direction associated with a condition or unassociated with a condition is the object of the cognitions of east and the like. If direction unassociated with a condition is their object, he asks whether it is one, or whether it is many. If direction is one, it cannot account for the cognitions of east and the like. If ten directions are assumed, Citsukha urges that the assumption contradicts

Kaṇāda's doctrine of nine substances. Further, if ten directions are assumed to account for the cognitions of the east and the like, many ākāśas should be assumed to account for various kinds and degrees of sounds. If many directions are assumed, like many ākāśas, the assumption contradicts Praśastapāda's assertion that direction, like ākāśa and time, is one, because there is no genus of each of them. If the cognitions of east and the like are said to be due to direction associated with the first conjunction, etc., of the moving sun with mount Meru, then these conditions may account for the various cognitions, and direction is needless. If they depend upon direction associated with the conditions, then there is interdependence: direction associated with the conditions is proved by the cognitions of east and the like; the cognitions of east and the like are proved by direction associated with the conditions. If direction is inferred from the conditions as a mark of inference, the cognitions of east and the like are needless. If these cognitions depend upon the conditions unassociated with direction, direction is unnecessary. It is contended that the existence of direction is proved by the fact that conditions existing in the sun and the objects situated in the east and the like being not associated with any other objects in their nature, direction is necessary to account for the relation of the objects to the conditions. Citsukha urges that time can account for the relation between them, and that therefore direction is useless. Raṅgojī Bhaṭṭa opines that omnipotent God performs the functions of ākāśa, time and direction. So they are unnecessary.[182]

CRITICISM OF ETHER (ĀKĀŚA).—The Vaiśeṣika infers the existence of ākāśa as the inherent cause of sound. Sound is a special quality. It is not a special quality of earth, water, light and air. Therefore, it is a special quality of ākāśa in which it inheres, and is perceived through the ear. Raṅgojī Bhaṭṭa urges that omnipotent God, the general efficient cause of sound, should be admitted to be the inherent cause also of sound. He performs the functions of ākāśa, time and direction (space), which are supposed to be performed by them. They are not different from Him. This view accords with the law of parsimony. Padmapāda regards ākāśa and direction as mental constructs in which all empirical objects appear to subsist.[183]

CRITICISM OF CONJUNCTION.—Citsukha refutes conjunction. Conjunction is either contact of two substances which were not joined before, or noneternal relation, or specialized by being produced, or being specialized by existing in a substance limited in time and space, or having a genus inferior to the genus of quality existing in a noninherent cause of a substance. The first definition is invalid, because it involves self-dependence (ātmāśraya: 'not joined before' means the absence of conjunction. If the words mean the absence of any relation, the definition is too wide inasmuch as it applies to the relation between threads and a cloth. But the Vaiśeśika thinks it to be inherence. Before a cloth is produced, no relation exists between threads and a cloth, because a cloth, a relatum, does not exist. It is contended that inherence of a cloth in threads exists between threads and a cloth, for inherence is eternal. The contention is false, since, if it were true, the inherence would exist even before threads and a cloth are produced, and they would not be produced at some time. If the definition were true, it would not apply to the conjunction of eternal substances. It is contended that there is no conjunction between two eternal substances. Citsukha urges that the inference "ākāśa and the like are joined with self, because conjunction exists in them, like a jar" is valid. The second and third definitions are invalid, for they are too narrow inasmuch as they do not apply to conjunction of two eternal substances. They are invalid, also because they are too wide inasuch as they apply to the relation between an owner of a substance purchased by him. The substance was not obtained (aprāpta) by him before, and later it is obtained (prāpta) by him by purchase. The fourth definition is invalid, for it is too narrow inasmuch as it does not apply to conjunction of two eternal substances. Partless and eternal substances have no parts. So they cannot have conjunction in their limited regions. The fifth definition also is invalid, because noninherent causes of a substance and a genus being indeterminable, being specialized by them cannot be determined. So conjunction is indefinable.[184]

CRITICISM OF DISJUNCTION.—Citsukha refutes disjunction. It is either absence of contact of two substances which were conjoined before, or a quality opposed to conjunction, or having a genus lower than the genus of quality existing in what exists in direction, and existing in a noneternal substance, and not existing in conjunction. The first definition is invalid, since its subalternatives are untenable. The word 'noncontact' is neither disjunction nor the absence of a relation. If it means disjunction, the definition is circular and involves self-dependence. If it means the absence of a relation, the definition is too wide inasmuch as it applies to destruction of conjunction also. The second definition is faulty, for a quality opposed to conjunction is indeterminable. If opposition means nonexistence in the same place, the definition is not possible, because the Vaiśeṣika admits the non-coexistence of a destroying substance (e.g. a club) and a destroyed substance (e.g. a jar) in the same place. If 'opposed' means what removes, the definition applies to merits and demerits of a soul and God's volition, which are the general causes of removal. If a remover means a a quality which removes coujunction being in the same locus, it applies to merits and demerits of a soul, which remove conjunction of manas with a self. It is contended that disjunction is a quality opposed to conjunction, which exists in a locus in which an action exists. This contention is false, since action is not proved in that conjunction and disjunction are not proved. The Vaiśeṣika admits that action is the noninherent cause of conjunction and disjunction. Because conjunction is not proved, a quality opposed to it also is not proved. Because action destroys prior conjunction, the assumption of disjunction is unnecessary. The Vaiśeṣika asks how an action which produces a conjunction destroys it. Citsukha replies that a conjunction produced by a prior action is destroyed by a succeeding action. The third definition also is faulty, because the qualifications are not well-known. Conjunction has been refuted. Qualities have been shown to be indefinable. Genus also is indeterminable. The definition is cumbrous. So disjunction is indeterminable.[185]

CRITICISM OF NUMBER.—The Vaiśeṣika holds that number twoness, threeness, or manyness is produced by diseriminative intellect (apekṣābuddhi) which combines the perceptions of oneness in different objects. Each object is one. There is no twoness or threeness in objects of perception. Discriminative intellect does not supply the 'a priori' category of number from within as Kant holds. Oneness exists in each object. Discriminative intellect produces twoness in objects by comparing onenesses in objects and combining them together. The Vaiśeṣika is an empiricist, and not an apriorist or rationalist. Citsuka refutes twoness as follows. "These are two". It is neither known by perception nor by inference. The perception "these are two" cognizes "this is one", "this is one". No other cognition can cognize twoness. The following objection is made by the opponent. The perception cognizes either the aggregate alone or its particular feature. It cannot cognize the aggregate alone, because the aggregate having no variety cannot be cognized as twoness, threeness and the like. Nor can the perception cognize the particular feauture of the aggregate, because the alternatives involved in it are untenable. The perception cognizes either the difference in the oneness of the aggregate or the difference in the altrubutes of the aggregate. The first alternative is not possible, for oneness is the same everywhere. The second alternative also is not possible, since there is no difference in the attributes of the aggregate inasmuch as either real or attributed twoness, threeness and the like numbers are not admitted. This objection is unsound, because if twoness, threeness and the like are produced and cognized by discriminative intellect (apekṣābuddi), the alternatives involved in it are vitiated by the same defects. If discriminative intellect cognizes the aggregate of the quality of oneness, it is not proved to produce the difference in the numbers twoness, threeness and the like inasmuch as the aggregate is the same everywhere. The opponent contends that discriminative intellect, which cognizes the aggregate of oneness specialized by twoness, threeness and the like, produces twoness, threeness and the like. The contention is invalid, because if such discriminative intellect produced the cognitions of twoness, threenes and the like, the assumption of its producing them would be needless.[186] The opponent contends that a quality attributed to an entity always presupposes its truth somewhere. The contention is false, since the relation of silver to a nacre, though not real anywhere is an object of illusion. The inference "the magnitude of a dyad is produced by its noninherent cause (e.g. twoness), which is produced, because it is an effect, like a cloth", is invalid, beeause a dyad and its magnitude are not admitted by the Advaitin, and because the example, a cloth, is devoid of the probandum inasmuch as the Advaitin does not admit that a cloth is produced by the noninherent cause of the conjunction of theads. Nor is twoness the aggregate of the number oneness, because oneness other than the nature of an object is indeterminable. The contention that the natures of objects being different, there can be no common cognition "this is one" in different objects, is false, because even if the number oneness is admitted, it is different in different substances. If a substance is said to be one because it is cognized as qualified by the number oneness, then in colour or the like the number oneness cannot be cognized, since colour is not qualified by the number oneness. Colour is a quality, and so cannot have the number oneness, which is a quality. A quality is devoid of quality according to the Vaiśeṣika. If the number oneness is cognized in colour as its nature, it is so cognized in a substance also. Inherence of oneness in a substance qualified by the number one leads to infinite regress. So a substance of such a nature in which the number oneness is assumed to inhere may be cognized as one, and the assumption of number is needless. The denial of the genus of one is not an undesired contingency for the Advaitin. The cognition of oneness in a substance does not prove the existence of number, since oneness exists in qualities also, and since its existence in them is not contradicted by valid knowledge. Though number does not exist, twenty four qualities, five motions, and two kinds of genus, higher and lower, are cognized. The use of number in regard to them is not in a secondary sense, because its use in a primary sense is not contradicted by valid knowledge. So the definition of twoness as a genus lower than the genus of number, which is lower than the genus of quality existing in the noninherent cause of the magnitude of a dyad is invalid, since there is no proof for the existence of number twoness. So number is indefinable.[187]

Prabhākara regards number as a distinct category. Citsukha avers that his criticism of similarity applies to number. It is not a substance, for it exists in qualities. Nor is it a quality, because it exists in qualities. Nor is it an action, since it exists in actions. Nor is it generality, particularity and negation, for it exists in them. Nor is it power, because power is imperceptible while number oneness it perceptible. Nor is it inherence, because inherence is eternal while number is noneternal, and because oneness exists in one entity while inherence is a relation between two inseparable entities.[188]

CRITICISM OF MAGNITUDE.—Citsukha refutes magnitude in the following manner. Magnitude is either the cause of the use of measure, or has a genus lower than the genus of quality existing in the noninherent cause of twoness, or has the genus lower than the genus of quality existing in an entity which does not exist in an entity with an eternal form, which is not the locus of a noninherent cause, or has the genus of magnitude. The first definition is invalid, since it applies to merits and demerits of a soul, and God, that are general causes of measure, but since they are not magnitudes. It is too wide. It is contended that magnitude is the cause of the cognition and use of measure, being their object. This contention is false, since the definition applies to the genus of magnitude, which also is their object. It is contended that the addition of the qualification 'having a genus' makes the definition valid. The contention is false, because a substance also has a genus. It is contended that the addition of the qualification 'having the genus of magnitude' makes the definition valid. The contention is invalid, because such characteristics can account for the cognition and use of measure, and make the assumption of magnitude useless.[189] The second definition is invalid, because twoness and its inherent cause have been refuted. Being endued with a qualified genus being known, the cause of its cognition and use should be stated. It should be known as existing in all individuals implied by it through a common property which exists in all individuals; otherwise, it will not apply to all individuals. Because the common property accounts for the cognition and use of magnitude, the cumbrous definition is useless.[190] The third definition also is invalid for it is vitiated by the same fault. The fourth definition is invalid, since the manifester of the genus of magnitude cannot be determined. If it is determined, the definition is vitiated by the aforesaid defect. So magnitude is indefinable. Magnitude cannot be proved. The use of measure is not rightly defined, and so cannot be its proof. Measure means either a span or a cubit, or atomic magnitude or large magnitude, or nonubiquity or limitedness. These definitions are false, because they are too narrow. Atomic magnitude and large magnitude are not proved. So the cognitions and uses of them are not proved, and nonubiquity may be cognized and used as nonpervasiveness.

The weight of ten lavas is called limited and also heavy. The Vaiśeṣika holds that atomic magnitude inheres in particular substances, and that large magnitude inheres in other particular substances. They can account for the cognitions and uses of different magnitudes. So the assumption of magnitude is needless. It violates the law of parsimony.[191]

CRITICISM OF SIMILARITY.—Kumārila thinks similarity to be a distinct category for the following reasons. It is not a substance, for it exists in qualities. But a substance does not exist in qualities. Similarity is not a quality, since it exists in qualities. Nor is it an action, because it exists in actions. Nor is it a genus, a particularity, or nonexistence for similar reasons. Nor is it number, for it exists in numbers. "This oneness is similar to this oneness." "This twoness is similar to this twoness." We speak such sentences and perceive them. Similarity is cognized by determinate perception. "This is similar to this." Similarity is perceived between two entities, which are similar to each other.

Citsukha offers the following criticism of Kumārila's view. He asks whether similarity is endued with touch, or whether it is not endued with touch. If it is so endued, it is a substance. If it is not endued with touch, it exists either in one entity or in many entities. If it exists in one entity, it is either a quality, or an action, or a particularity. If it exists in many entities, it is either generality or inherence.[192]

BRAHMAN, ĪŚVARA, MĀYĀ AND POWER.—The author of 'Prakaṭārthavivaraṇa' avers that Ātman or Brahman is devoid of power, because It is partless, or because It is ubiquitous, like ether.[193] Pratyabhijñā school of Śaivism regards Śiva as possessed of divine power or Śakti, both being inseparable from each other, and forming an indissoluble unity. Śaṁkara considers various powers producing various effects in nature under the influence of time, space and cause to be neither real nor unreal but indescribable and imagined by māyā or avidyā. But Brahman in Its ontological nature transcends all phenomenal appearances.[194] The Advaita Vedānta regards power as māyā. Vidyāraṇya considers the whole world to be pervaded by parts of prakṛti or māyā, a power of Īśvara. Rāmakṛṣṇa avers that prakṛti or māyā is the material cause, and that Īśvara is the efficient cause, of the world. Māyā is God's power of constructing the world, and avidyā is His power of deluding an empirical self.[195] Dharmarājādvarīndra describes Īśvara as endowed with māyā, which contains unlimited and undetermined powers, with which He creates the empirical world of names and forms with the aid of the souls' merits and demerits.[196] So unqualified Brahman is devoid of power, but Īśvara limited by, or reflected in, māyā is endowed with unlimited powers, which are neither real nor unreal but indescribable.

The Śruti says, "Īśvara endowed with māyā creates the world", "God's powers are various and spontaneous ; they are knowledge, strength and action."[197] The 'Śvetāśvatara Upaniṣad' is a theistic Upaniṣad, and all theistic Vedāntists identify Brahman with Īśvara, and consider His powers to be real. The Śruti says, "One God conceals Himself with the effects of avyakta." Śaṁkara evidently interprets the powers of prakṛti as indescribable powers of māyā.[198] Īśvara manifests māyā and its effects as their supervisor. Īśvara is Brahman limited by māyā.

CRITICISM OF NYĀYA-VAIŚEṢIKA ATOMISM: WHOLE AND PART.—Śaṁkara's criticism of atoms was given in the second volume. The criticisms of his followers are given here. The Vaiśeṣika holds that two atoms of the same kind joined together produce a dyad of the same kind. Three dyads of the same kind are joined together, and produce a triad of the same kind. Large substances are the aggregates of triads. An atom is partless, and has atomic magnitude. A dyad also has atomic magnitude. A triad has large magnitude. The atomic magnitude of an atom and the atomic magnitude of a dyad are not the causes of large magnitude of a triad, because a magnitude of a kind produces a larger magnitude of the same kind. The atomic magnitude of a dyad is not a larger magnitude than that of an atom. The magnitude of a triad is not of the same kind as atomic magnitude. So number twoness in atoms is the noninherent cause of the magnitude of a dyad, and the number threeness in atoms is the noninherent cause of large magnitude of a triad. The Nyāya-Vaiśeṣika thinks atoms to be the material or inherent cause of the world, and God to be its efficient cause.

Citsukha adduces the following arguments in refuting atomism. Atoms do not exist, for there is no proof for their existence. They are not perceived. The inference, that degrees of small magnitude must stop at atoms, the smallest and indivisible units of the world, like degrees of large magnitudes stopping at the largest magnitude, is false, since atoms are non-existent, since their atomic magnitudes are nonexistent, since there are no degrees of magnitude, and since atoms, the loci of the probans, are unproven (āśrayāsiddha). If the degrees of small magnitude must stop somewhere, the triads may be the lowest limit.[199] The Vaiśeṣika contends that a triad is composed of parts, because it is visible while having large magnitude and action, and that therefore decrease of large magnitude cannot stop at a triad. Large magnitude of a triad is produced by manyness of its causes. Citsukha urges that atoms are visible to the yogins and yet partless and indivisible, and that, similarly, triads, though visible, are partless and indivisible. The qualification 'having large magnitude' is meaningless, for atoms are not proved.[200] Partless atoms cannot have conjunction with each other; so two atoms cannot be conjoined to produce a dyad as its inherent cause as the Vaiśeṣika maintains. The conjunction of two atoms to produce a dyad cannot be inferred from their being substances, since atoms are not admitted by the Advaitin, and since composite substances made of parts have conjunction according to the Vaiśeṣika. A triad is not produced by three dyads, because its large magnitude is due to manyness of atoms, because the process of the production of a dyad is not proved as already shown, and since a triad may be produced by atoms also. The Vaiśeṣika contends that if a triad were produced by atoms, it would not have large magnitude, since the atomic magnitudes of atoms being eternal cannot produce an effect, and since partless atoms cannot have loose conjunction (pracaya). This contention is false, because the large magnitude of a triad may be produced by manyness of its causes or atoms. If it be argued that number manyness in atoms cannot produce large magnitude of a triad, then number twoness in atoms cannot produce atomic magnitude of a dyad. But the Vaiśeṣika holds that the magnitude of a dyad is produced by number twoness in atoms.[201] No composite substance can be produced by atoms. The Vaiśeṣika contends that a composite substance is proved by the valid cognition of one gross blue object. The contention is false, since if such parts, as are assumed to produce a composite object, can produce the cognition of one gross blue object, the assumption of a whole produced by parts is unnecessary.[202]

The Nyāya and the Vaiśeṣika maintain that a whole is made of parts, which is different from them, and which inheres in them. Inherence is refuted elsewhere. Citsukha criticizes the concept of a whole in the following manner. If a whole exists in its entirety in its parts, it will continue to exist, if some parts are destroyed, even as a genus continues to exist, if some individuals are destroyed. The Vaiśeṣika contends that a whole cannot exist without its inherent cause—the parts. The contention is false, because though a whole exists in its entirety in each part, it exists with all its parts, the inherent cause, in each part, because for this reason a horn of a cow will serve the function of her udder in that the whole qualified by its parts exists in each part, and because all parts will be perceived in each part.[203]

It may be argued that a whole being an effect, it exists simultaneously in many parts, and that so it will become many, like colours. Nor can a whole exist partly in its parts, for it has no parts different from those parts, which produced it. If it had its own parts different from those which produced it, it would have an infinite number of parts, and therefore a mountain and a mustard seed would have the same magnitude, and the parts and whole would be distant from each other. This argument is false, because one whole cannot be said to have entirety or parts, and because many entities alone can have entirety or parts. Further, the question whether a whole exists entirely or in parts is based on invariable concomitance or proved by the Vaiśeṣika or by his opponents. The Buddhists do not admit it, since all are momentary according to them, and so no entity can be the substrate of another entity. The Advaita Vedāntists hold that an effect is imagined in a cause; therefore they do not admit the existence of a whole or effect in its parts or cause, since an effect is a false appearance.[204] The Vaiśeṣika does not prove the invariable concomitance on which the question is based. The question whether a whole exists entirely or partly in its parts does not arise, since the Advaitist does not admit a whole. One whole existing in many parts being refuted, its conjunction, disjunction, number twoness, distinctness, genus and the like are refuted.[205] The argument, that many objects cannot produce the cognition of one object, is false, because many threads can produce the cognition of one cloth because of their producing the action of covering a body, and because many letters can produce the cognition of one word signifying one object. Similarly, many parts can produce the cognition of one object without producing a whole different from its parts. The Vaiśeṣika contends that atoms being imperceptible, they cannot produce the perception of one object. The contention is false, because imperceptible atoms are not proved.[206] The whole cannot be the same as parts, for they have opposite attributes; a cloth can cover a body, but its parts cannot do so; a cloth moves, but its threads do not move. The Vaiśeṣika contends that its parts do not move, and cannot cover, but that the whole (e.g., a cloth) can move and cover. The contention is false, because, if it were true, the parts and the whole would have separable existence. Separable existence is indefinable. A jar and a cloth are said to have separable existence, because they do not inhere in each other. Similarly, a whole and its parts may have separable existence. The Vaiśeṣika contends that if a whole and its parts had separable existence, they would not be known as a whole and its parts. The contention is false, because though a word is not a whole with letters as its parts, letters produce the cognition of one word, and because though a sentence is not a whole with words as its parts, words produce the cognition of one sentence. Similarly, parts can produce the cognition of one object, and the so-called whole and its parts have separable existence.[207] The Advaita Vedānta does not think a whole to be necessary at all for the explanation of an aggregate of parts.

CRITICISM OF YOGĀCĀRA VIJÑĀNAVĀDA.—The Buddhist Vijñānavādin does not believe in the existence of external objects, but admits the existence of many momentary cognitions, the objects of which are non-different from them.[208] The Advaitin, on the other hand, admits the reality of one, eternal consciousness on which objects are superimposed. They are capable of producing effects and practical actions, and their stability is uncontradicted. They are phenomenal appearances, and have empirical reality. They are annulled when an empirical self (jīva) realizes its nature as one, eternal, universal consciousness or Brahman.[209] The Vijñānavādin sets forth the following arguments in favour of his view. 1. There is nondifference between blue and the cognition of blue, because they are always perceived together.[210] If blue were different from its cognition, it would not be manifested in the cognition. 2. Why is blue manifested in the cognition? Why are not all objects manifested in it? No relation between blue and its cognition, which regulates the former being manifested in the latter, is found. Its producing the cognition cannot be the regulating relation, because, if it were true, the sense-organs also would be the object of the cognition of blue in that they produce the cognition of blue. So there is nondifference between blue and its cognition. 3. The opponent contends that in the apprehension "I know this" the cognitions of 'I', knower, 'this', object, and 'know', knowledge, with their different natures related to one another are apprehended. This contention is false, since momentary cognitions cannot be related to one another. But the Vijñānavādin amends this position and adjusts it to the doctrine of momentariness. At first there is the cognition of 'I', then there is the cognition of 'this'; then there is the cognition of 'know'; the three cognitions invested with their forms are successively produced; the third cognition perfumed by the residual impressions (vāsanā) of the first and the second cognitions produces another cognition. This momentary cognition assumes the form of the object. Otherwise, no relation between a cognition and its object being determined, an object would not be apprehended by a cognition. Momentariness of cognitions is indisputable. 4. Just as the cognition of blue produces the knowledge of blue being different from yellow, so it produces the knowledge of its being present as different from past and future. So the momentariness of a cognition is perceived.[211]

Vidyāraṇya offers the following criticisms of Vijñānavāda. 1. A cognition is not momentary, for it is not perceived to differ at every moment. The Buddhist contends that the difference is not perceived because of close similarity between the cognitions at the different moments. The famous Western empiricist, David Hume, says, "The smooth passage of the imagination along the ideas of the resembling perceptions makes us ascribe to them a perfect identity".[212] This contention is invalid, since the difference is either an attribute (dharma) of a cognition cognized by another cognition or the nature (svarūpa) of the cognition cognized by the cognition itself. In the first alternative, the difference between the cognition (dharmin) and its difference (dharma) not being cognized by another cognition, the difference between one cognition and another will not be cognized. If the difference between the cognition and its difference were cognized, then the cognition, its difference, and difference between them would be imagined in the cognition of difference, and the imagined entity would be nondifferent from them. In the second alternative, the difference which is the nature of the cognition is not manifested because of similarity. This means that the cognition itself is not manifested. If the cognition is not manifested, this will result in the collapse of practical life or world-blindness (jagadāndhya). 2. The Vijñānavādin contends that difference between momentary cognitions is admitted to account for similarity between them. This contention is invalid, since similarity is not proved by any pramāṇa, and since it is opposed to the manifestation of identity.[213] Similarity is proved to be indeterminable elsewhere. 3. The Vijñānavādin contends that the manifestation of identity in consciousness is illusory and so not opposed to similarity, that rather the illusion of identity itself is not possible without similarity among the different momentary cognitions, and that it is the cause of the assumption of similarity among cognitions at different moments. This contention is invalid, since it involves vicious interdependence : when cognitions are proved to be different from, and similar to, one another, the manifestation of identity in consciousness is proved to be illusory ; the manifestation of identity in consciousness being proved to be illusory, the difference and similarity among cognitions are proved.[214] 4. The Vijñānavādin contends that the Advaitist's argument also involves interdependence : the knowledge of identity is proved to be valid, when similarity is not proved by any pramāṇa, and when it is proved to be opposed to a pramāṇa ; similarity is not proved by any pramāṇa, and is proved to be opposed to a pramāṇa, when the knowledge of identity is proved to be valid. This contention is false, since the Advaitist admits recognition, which apprehends the identity of an object as self-evident.[215] It does not require any other proof. So the doctrine of Vijñānavāda is false. Śaṁkara's criticism of Vijñānavāda was given in the second volume. The Advaita Vedānta advocates absolute idealism as distinguished from subjective idealism of some Yogācāras. But all Yogācāras were not subjective idealists. Maitreyanātha, Asaṅga and Vasubandhu were Absolute Idealists.

CRITICISM OF NATURALISM AND ALLIED DOCTRINES.— The 'Śvetāśvatara Upaniṣad' mentions time, nature (svabhāva), destiny (niyati), chance (yadṛcchā), material elements, an individual soul (puruṣa), or conjunction of persons as the cause of the world. Śaṁkara explains these terms. Time is the cause of the modifications of all material elements. Nature is powers inherent in things, e.g., heat of fire. Destiny is merits and demerits, virtues and vices, which produce good and evil, respectively. Chance is accidental happening of an event. The material elements are ether (ākāśa), air, light, water and earth. Puruṣa is an individual soul, which is conscious and intelligent. They are the source (yoni) of the world. Śaṁkara refutes them. They are either individually or collectively the cause of the world. Each of them is not its cause, for it contradicts perception. The collection of them is not its cause, since it is a means to the end of an individual soul which is present, since it is not independent, and since it cannot be an instrument of the creation, maintenance, dissolution and regulation of the world. Because it is endowed with limited power and dependent, it cannot be the cause of its creation. It is dependent, because it depends upon its merits and demerits (karma) acquired in past births, which produce its happiness and misery in this birth, which it cannot avoid. So it is powerless to create the world. Or, being of limited power, it cannot create the world of objects, which are the causes of its happiness and misery.[216]

Prakāśātman states and criticizes naturalism (svabhāvavāda). Some Cārvākas are naturalists. According to the naturalists an effect is not produced by a cause. The opponent asks whether an entity is its own cause, or whether it is devoid of a cause. The naturalist replies that an entity is devoid of a cause. The opponent objects that if an entity is uncaused, a jar exists and does not exist at the same time, because it is independent of a cause, which produces an effect gradually. The naturalist replies that if a cause produces its effect gradually owing to its nature, it involves naturalism. If a cause depends upon another cause in producing its effect gradually, this will lead to infinite regress. If the order of succession in time in the production of an effect by a cause is natural, this involves naturalism. If it depends on another cause, this will generate infinite regress. Hence all effects are various, are produced gradually, and are produced owing to their nature as they are perceived. The capacities of causes for producing effects are self-existent and natural. The cause-effect relation among entities, the former being a condition favourable to the prodution of an effect, and the latter being favoured by the former, is proved by perception.[217]

Vidyāraṇya offers the following criticism of naturalism advocated by the followers of Bṛhaspati. He asks the meaning of infinite regress involved in the assumption of a cause in producing its effect. It means either that the capacity of entities for producing their effects is uncaused or that the search for the causes of their capacity for producing their effects is useless. The first alternative is admitted by the Advaitin. The second alternative means either that dependence of entities on other causes is not perceived, or that though it is perceived, it is indefinable in nature. The first subalternative is not true, since it contradicts perception. A potter making an earthen jar out of clay with the aid of a staff and a wheel is perceived. The second subalternative is admitted by the Advaitin, who thinks all experienced entities to be indefinable appearances. It is not a fault, but an adornment for him.[218] If the naturalist states any reasons (hetu) for his theses that earth, water, light and air are real, that perception is the only pramāṇa, and that naturalism alone is valid, he admits that an effect depends upon a cause. If he does not state any reasons for his theses, they are unproven. If he thinks a cause and effect as mere experiences, he admits the Advaita doctrine of the world as a false appearance.[219] So omniscient and omnipotent God Himself is the cause of the world.

The 'Bhagavatgītā' says, "Persons of demoniac disposition state the world to be founded in untruth, unfounded in reality, and devoid of God, and persons are born out of the sex-union of their parents alone for the gratification of their desires."[220] Śaṁkara observes that this is the view of the Lokāyatas, and explains it as follows. As we are false, so the world is not founded in truth. Virtue and vice are nonexistent. The world has no firm foundation. It is not created and governed by God according to the moral law of karma. Madhusūdana Sarasvatī also regards this view as that of the Lokāyata. According to him variety in the world is natural. This view is false as shown above.[221]

CRITICISM OF THE BUDDHIST DOCTRINE OF MOMENTARINESS.—Vidyāraṇya expounds the Buddhist doctrine of momentariness in the following manner. All entities are momentary, because they produce effects, unlike a hare's horn.[222] It is nonexistent, for it does not produce any effect. The opponent of the doctrine of momentariness argues that a stable entity alone in conjunction with auxiliary causes, which is different from an effect, can exercise causal efficiency and produce an effect, and that a momentary entity cannot produce it. The Buddhist asks whether a stable entity produces only one effect, or whether it produces many effects simultaneously or successively. If it produces one effect at once, it is momentary. If it produces many effects simultaneously, then also it is momentary. If it is capable of producing many effects, its effectuation cannot be delayed. So entities produce their effects at one moment.[223]

Vidyāraṇya adduces the following arguments in refuting this doctrine. The nature of producing effects (arthakriyā) as conceived by the Buddhists is indeterminable. Vidyāraṇya applies the doctrine to cognitions. Their producing effects cousists in producing cognitions, which cognize them as their objects at the same moment, or in producing cognitions at some other moment. In the first alternative, they produce such cognitions in their own stream of cognitions, or in some other stream of cognitions, or in the omniscient stream of cognitions. The first subalternative is inadmissible, because it is not possible inasmuch as cognitions are self-aware or self-manifest. In the second subalternative, a cognition of Devadatta, though self-aware, produces a cognition in Yajñadatta's stream of cognitions, which cognizes the former. This view is wrong, since how a perceptual cognition produces a cognition, which cognizes it as an object, cannot be described. A cognition in one person is nowhere perceived to produce a cognition in another person, which cognizes it. Nor does an inferential cognition produce a cognition in another person, which cognizes it as an object, because the Buddhist admits perceptual cognition alone to be produced by an object. The third subalternative also is unjustified. If cognitions in all bound persons produce a perceptual cognition in the omniscient stream of cognitions, which cognizes them, then the latter will be tainted with the impurities of the former, because according to the Buddhist idealists cognitions and their objects are identical with each other.[224] The Buddhisht idealist contends that though the omniscient stream of cognitions is tainted with the impurities of the bound persons' streams of cognitions, the impurities are destroyed by the latter's knowledge of the truth. This argument in defence of the Buddhist idealist's position is unavailing, because the impurities cannot be destroyed at the same moment when they are produced. Nor can some other cognition in the omniscient stream reproduce the impurities and then destroy them, because the impurities of the preceeding cognitions are not the objects of a succeeding cognition. Even if they are cognized by the latter, the latter will be tainted with the impurities of the former, and cannot destroy them. Nor can the cognitions of the bound persons leave aside their impurity-part, and enable their cognition-part to produce a cognition in the omniscient stream, which cognizes them. Even if it were possible, the omniscient stream ignorant of the impurities of the bound persons' cognitions would not be able to instruct them. The main second alternative also that arthakriyā is producing an effect at some other moment is illegitimate, because in this process the last moment will be nonexistent in that it does not produce an effect. The last moment is that of the stream of cognitions in the state of bondage. It does not produce an effect, and is, therefore, nonexistent. Similarly, the preceding cognitions also are nonexistent. If at the last moment a cognition of a bound person produces a cognition in the omniscient stream which cognizes it, then the çognition of the last moment and the cognition of the omniscient stream both being pure and of the same nature will belong to the same stream, because a cause and an effect of the same nature belong to the same stream. Because the two streams become one and nondifferent, there can be no release of a bound person. If entering into the omniscient stream be said to be release, then also the cognition at the last moment of a bound person's stream of cognitions being the object of a cognition in the omniscient stream is indeterminable. So the cognition at the last moment of a bound person's stream of cognitions cannot produce a cognition in the omniscient stream of cognitions. If there is difference between the two streams, a cognition in the former can be the object of the latter's cognition. But here there is no difference. A cognition does not differ from another cognition. If it did so, a cognition from which it differs would be a non-cognition in order to be different. Nor does a cognition differ from another cognition in its form, because, if it did, the cognition which is invested with a form would be non-cognition. So a cognition at the last moment of a bound person's stream of cognitions producing a cognition in the omniscient stream of cognitions and thus determining its existence cannot be established.[225] Even if such producing an effect is assumed, it proves the existence of its cause or the existence of the experience of its cause. The first alternative is inadmissible, since a cause exists before its effect, and since, otherwise, it would not be a cause. In the second alternative, the effect manifested by its effect will prove the existence of the experience of its cause, and thus will lead to infinite regress. If it be argued that a cognition manifests itself, and that therefore it does not lead to infinite regress, then the view that producing an effect (arthakriyā) is the cause of experience is given up. If a cognition is said to exist because it produces itself, it involves self-dependence (ātmāśraya). Hence existence does not consist in producing an effect, but is a natural property of an entity.[226] So a stable entity exists, produces an effect at one moment, and then becomes inactive. The contention, that a stable entity cannot successively produce many effects, beause an entity able to produce them cannot delay production, is invalid, since such an entity is perceived to produce them successively depending on the aids of the auxiliary causes.[227]

Some Buddhist realists opine that soil, water and other auxiliary causes produce a peculiarity (viśeṣa) viz, swollenness in a seed, and tha. then the seed produces a sprout. Otherwise, the seed would not depend upon soil, water and the like. This argument is invalid for the following reasons. The seed is either capable of producing the peculiarity in itself or it is not so capable. If it is not capable, it cannot produce the peculiarity, even if it is aided by a thousand auxiliary causes, and then it cannot produce the sprout. If a seed is capable of producing a peculiarity in itself, and if it produces swollenness in itself when it is aided by the auxiliary causes, then this will give rise to infinite regress. If a seed can produce swollenness in itself without their aid, then it is able to produce a sprout without the peculiarity. The Buddhists contend that the production of a sprout is preceded by swollenness, and that swollenness is produced by the seed aided by the auxiliary causes, because these are perceived. The contention is false, because, if that were true, a cause able to produce an effect by itself would depend upon the auxiliary causes, which do not render any aid to it. This contingency will contradict the Buddhists' own view. So this view of some Buddhists does not stand the test of reason.

Some Buddhists opine that a cause is not aided by the auxiliary causes, but that an effect produced by a momentary principal cause depends upon auxiliary causes, because an effect is produced by many causes. In the opponent's view also, an effect is produced by a stable cause aided by the auxiliary causes. But, in his view, a stable cause must produce its effects at once, because there is nothing to restrict its production of effects, and because the entire cause is present. The relation of the principal cause to the auxiliary causes does not regulate its production of effects, since the relation also exists so long as the relata exist. The relation does not depend upon another relation, for this will lead to infinite regress. The opponent may argue that in the Buddhists' view also an effect is not produced at the moment when a cause exists, because then a cause and an effect would occur at the same moment, and that the production of an effect by a cause at another moment will not be regulated by any condition. This argument is invalid, because the preceding moment when a cause exists regulates the production of an effect at the succeeding moment. So the doctrine of momentariness is preferable to the doctrine of a stable cause.

Vidyāraṇya urges that everywhere the cause-effect relation should be determined by invariable concomitance. According to the Buddhists, the invariable concomitance between an effect and a cause (e.g., smoke and fire) is either between an individual smoke and an individual fire, or between a smoke-series and a fire-series. The first alternative is not possible, because a momentary smoke and a momentary fire cannot exist at the time of the knowledge of agreement in presence and agreement in absence. In the second alternative, a fire in the state of a charcoal will produce a smoke, because the members of the same series do not differ from one another. It may be argued that smoke cannot be produced because of the absence of wood. The argument is false, because a charcoal also belongs to the wood-series. Nor is there the absence of a relation between wood and charcoal. Because the series is continuous, the relation also is continuous. If the relation is said to be not continuous, because it is preceded by another relation, then there will be infinite regress. The Buddhist cannot deny that the method of agreement in presence and agreememt in absence establishes that an effect is aided by an auxiliary cause, which renders an aid to it, because it is indispensable. Both the views admit that double method of agreement establishes the relation of favourer and favoured between an auxiliary cause and an effect. The Buddhists admit that a momentary fire with the assistance of a different auxiliary cause and with the difference of place produces many effects simultaneously ; for example, a momentary fire produces another fire in its place, smoke above, ashes below, and a cognition in another person. Similarly, the Advaitavādin admits that a stable cause with the assistance of different auxiliary causes and with the difference of time produces many effects at different times.[228] Successive production of many effects by a stable cause with the assistance of auxiliary causes is reasonable. An auxiliary momentary cause cannot render an aid to a principal momentary cause. A momentary cause cannot produce many effects at different times. So the doctrine of momentariness is wrong.[229]

[1] PKV., 39-41. [2] PKVV., pp. 54-60.
[3] Bhām., i, 1, 1, p. 1. [4] VKT., i, 1, 1, p. 3.
[5] Bhām., i, 3, 30, p. 333. [6] Ibid, i, 1, 5, p. 167.
[7] PPD., p. 30. [8] PPV., p. 13. [9] Ibid, p. 14.
[10] Ibid, p. 43. [11] Ibid. [12] Ibid. [13] Ibid, p. 45.
[14] VPS., p. 49. [15] PD., i, 15-18, 44-48.
[16] Ibid, ii, 38 ; iv, 2 ; vi, 23, 25-30, 32-35. SLS., pp. 101-02. [17] PPD., pp. 30, 14-15. VPS, pp. 13-14.
[18] TPD., pp. 54-57. [19] Ibid, p. 60.
[20] Ibid, pp. 57, 59-61. [21] VS., p. 11, VM., pp. 86-90.
[22] SNS., Ch. III, p. 226. [23] Ibid. [24] Ibid, p. 227.
[25] Ibid. [26] Ibid. [27] ĀNM., p. 313.
[28] Bhām., i, 1, 4, p. 126. [29] Ibid, p. 127.
[30] VKT., i, 1, 4, p. 126 ; KTP., p. 127.
[31] VSM., 3, p. 11. [32] PPV., p. 45. [33] Ibid.
[34] Ibid. [35] Ibid. [36] VPS., p. 47. [37] Ibid, p. 48.
[38] Ibid. [39] Ibid. [40] VPS., p. 50. [41] Ibid. [42] Ibid.
[43] VSM., 3 & 5, pp. 11, 13 & 17. [44] Ibid, 6, p. 23.
[45] Ibid, pp. 18-30. [46] PPV., p. 46.
[47] VSM., pp. 30-35. 'Vācaspati Miśra on Advaita Vedānta', p. 203. [48] VSM., pp. 33-39.
[49] AcK., p. 41 ; SLS., p. 172. 'Vācaspati Miśra on Advaita Vedānta', p. 200.
[50] SB., p. 36. [51] PM., p. 11. [52] Ibid, p. 13.
[53] ND., p. 1. [54] ĀNM., p. 128. [55] NDA., pp. 1-4.
[56] AS., pp. 48-51 ; PPD., p. 4. [57] Ibid., pp. 96-97.
[58] Ibid, pp. 100-05. [59] Ibid, pp. 160-63 ; 164-71 & 78.
[60] Ibid ; Ibid, pp. 182-83. [61] Ibid, pp. 182-86, 189-90. TPD., p. 33.
[62] Ibid, pp. 195-203 ; SPMS., pp. 25-33. Cp. VP., pp. 217, 220-21.
[63] AS., pp. 207, 210, 212, 216-17, 220-22.
[64] TPD., pp. 32-34. [65] Ibid, pp. 39-40, 44 & 47.
[66] PPD., p. 13. [67] SLS., pp. 489-90, 492-94 & 497.
[68] ĀNM., p. 302. [69] Ibid, p. 303. [70] Ibid, pp. 305-06.
[71] VPS., p. 14. [72] Ibid, p. 13.
[73] ŚBS., i, 1, 1 ; PPD., p. 4 ; VPS., pp. 241 & 14.
[74] VPS., p. 10. [75] Ibid, p. 12. [76] Ibid, pp. 12-13.
[77] SB., pp. 16-19. [78] Bhām., i, 1, 1. [79] Ibid.
[80] SLS., p. 281 ; SLSV., p. 451.
[81] ŚBS., ii, 2, 28 ; SLS., p. 452. [82] Ibid, pp. 454-55.
[83] Ibid, p. 460. [84] Ibid, p. 461. [85] Ibid.
[86] Ibid, pp. 464-65. [87] Ibid, p. 466.
[88] VP., pp. 136-37. IPC., Vol. I, pp. 273-306. IEP., pp. 74-120.
[89] TPD., pp. 75-76. [90] Ibid, pp. 77-78.
[91] Ibid, NPS., p. 79. [92] Ibid, pp. 79-83.
[93] ŚBS., ii, 2, 28, pp. 547-48. [94] Ibid, p. 548.
[95] Ibid, ii, 2, 29, p. 555. [96] MKŚB., ii, 31.
[97] Ibid, iv, 1. [98] Bhām., ii, 2, 28, pp. 549-50 & 551.
[99] PPV., p. 50. [100] VPS., p. 54. [101] Ibid.
[102] VSM., 18, p. 103. [103] Ibid, 22, p. 104.
[104] Ibid, p. 105. Ibid, pp. 103-06.
[105] MKŚB., i, 1 ; i, 6.
[106] Ibid, i, 18. Ibid, i, 27 ; ii, 6, 7 & 32.
[107] Ibid, ii, 7. [108] Ibid, i, 7. PPV., p. 13. Bhām., i, 1, 4, p. 115 ; i, 1, 5, p. 139. VP., p. 223 ; ŚM., p. 224.
[109] ŚM., p. 224. [110] VSM., pp. 59-60. [111] Ibid, p. 62.
[112] Ibid, p. 73. Ibid, pp. 66-73. [113] BD., p. 116.
[114] KKK., p. 579. [115] TPD., p. 175. [116] Ibid, p. 178.
[117] Ibid, pp. 175-76, 178-79. [118] ACM., pp. 4-5.
[119] KKK., pp. 579-80. SMV., p. 580.
[120] TPD., p. 181. [121] Ibid. [122] Ibid, pp. 181-82.
[123] Ibid, p. 184. [124] ACM., p. 13. [125] TPD., p. 303.
[126] Ibid, p. 305. [127] HIP., Vol. I, pp. 321-33.
[128] TPD., p. 190. [129] Ibid, pp. 190-92.
[130] Ibid, pp. 193-94. [131] ACM., pp. 13-14.
[132] TPD., pp. 198-99, 201-03. Cp. Bhām., ii, 2, 13.
[133] ACM., p. 41. [134] Ibid. [135] TPD., pp. 272-74.
[136] ACM., pp. 16-18. [137] ĀNM., p. 35.
[138] Ibid, pp. 32-36. NMV., pp. 35-36. [139] NMV., p. 36.
[140] Ibid, p. 44. [141] ĀNM., p. 44. [142] Ibid, p. 45.
[143] Ibid, p. 46. [144] Ibid, p. 47. [145] Ibid. [146] Ibid, p. 49.
[147] Ibid, pp. 49-50. Cp. BD., pp. 101-04.
[148] ĀNM., p. 53. [149] Ibid, p. 55. [150] Ibid.
[151] Ibid, p. 56. [152] PM., p. 7. MKŚB., ii, 6.
[153] PM., p. 7. Cp. BD., p. 116. [154] KKK., i, 18, p. 113.
[155] Ibid, p. 117. [156] Ibid, p. 118. [157] TPD., pp. 166-67.

[158] KKK., p. 119. [159] Ibid & SMV., pp 118-21.
[160] TPD., pp. 174-75 ; KKK., p. 124.
[161] KKK., & SMV., pp. 123-24 ; i, 19 ; SMV., p. 124.
[162] Ibid, pp. 125-28.
[163] TPD., pp. 172-73. Cp. VSM., pp. 221-24.
[164] KKK., p. 129. [165] Ibid, pp. 127-30, 132-33.
[166] TPD., p. 173. [167] TPD., pp. 175-76. BD., pp. 79-116. VSM., pp. 234-39. [168] TPD., p. 318.
[169] Ibid, pp. 313-19. [170] Ibid, pp. 319-20.
[171] Ibid, pp. 44-45. [172] Ibid, pp. 45-47.
[173] Ibid, p. 274. [174] VPS., p. 188. [175] ACM., p. 7.
[176] Ibid. [177] Ibid. [178] Ibid, p. 8. [179] Ibid, p. 9.
[180] TPD., pp. 320-21. [181] Ibid, p. 324.
[182] Ibid, pp. 323-25. NPD., p. 324. ACM., p. 6.
[183] ACM., p. 6. [184] TPD., pp. 294-95.
[185] Ibid, pp. 296-98, 299-300. [186] Ibid, p. 300.
[187] Ibid, pp. 300-01, 302-03. [188] Ibid, p. 251.
[189] Ibid, pp. 309-10. [190] Ibid, p. 310. [191] Ibid.
[192] Ibid, p. 251. [193] PĀV., i, 1, 1, p. 17.
[194] ŚBS., ii, 1, 27. [195] PD., vi, 23 ; iv, 12 ; PDV., vi, 23.
[196] VP., pp. 353-54. [197] Śvet. Up., iv, 9-10 ; vi, 8.
[198] Ibid, ŚB., vi, 10 ; iv, 9-11. [199] TPD., p. 283.
[200] Ibid, pp. 288-89. [201] Ibid, p. 285. [202] Ibid, 290.
[203] Ibid, p. 292. [204] Ibid, p. 287. [205] Ibid, p. 293.
[206] NPD., p. 290. [207] TPD., pp. 290-91. Cp. Bhām., ii, 2, 11-12, pp. 502-11.
[208] VPS., p. 74. [209] Ibid. [210] Ibid, p. 75. [211] Ibid, p. 75.
[212] 'A Treatise of Human Nature', Vol. I, p. 198. (E.M.L)
[213] VPS., p. 76. [214] Ibid, p. 76.
[215] Ibid. Cp. Bhām., ii, 2, 28-31, pp. 541-58. Cp. HIP., Vol. II, pp. 376-90, 482-85.
[216] ŚB. on Śvet. Up., i, 2. AUT., p. 30.
[217] PPV., p. 218. [218] VPS., p. 211. [219] Ibid.
[220] BG., xvi, 8. [221] MSBG., xvi, 8. ŚBBG., xvi, 8. HIP., Vol. I, pp. 229-76.
[222] VPS., p. 78. [223] Ibid. [224] Ibid, p. 79.
[225] Ibid, p. 80. [226] Ibid. [227] Ibid. [228] Ibid, pp. 81-82.
[229] VPS., pp. 78-80, 81-82. PPV., pp. 78-79.

CHAPTER IX

LIBERATION

BONDAGE.—Śaṁkara opines that a jīva has innate omniscience and omnipotence, but that they are concealed by false conceit of its identity with its body, sense-organs, manas, buddhi and ahaṁkāra—its limiting adjuncts. Its false conceit is due to avidyā. Īśvara is the cause of its bondage and release. Its bondage is due to the ignorance of the nature of Īśvara, and its release is due to the true knowledge of the nature of Īśvara.[1] Vācaspati Miśra opines that a jīva's bondage is due to the apprehension of difference between itself and Īśvara because of its being limited by the mind-body-complex. It is contended that Ātman being self-luminous by nature cannot have false knowledge of its identity with Its adjuncts—the mind-body complex, though ether of the nature of not-self can be limited by a jar and the like. The contention is false, for a jīva has false conceit, which is beginningless and indefinable. Though a jīva has innate eternal knowledge, it is conceated by avidyā, false conceit, love, hate and the like.[2] Avidyā is beginningless and indefinable, and the root of bondage. True knowledge (vidyā) of the real nature of a jīva as Ātman or Brahman destroys avidyā, and manifests its eternal freedom or release. A jīva's bondage is beginningless, like its cause—avidyā, but it is terminated by vidyā.[3] Liberation is not produced by vidyā.

According to Vācaspati Miśra avidyā abiding a jīva depends upon Īśvara, Who is its cause and object, but not its abode, because it cannot abide in Brahman of the nature of true knowledge.[4] Īśvara is the source or cause of avidyā. He binds a jīva. Vācaspati is not an advocate of one soul and one avidyā as some wrongly think. He unequivocally asserts that he does not advocate one avidyā in all jīvas, but many nesciences in many jīvas. The jīva whose avidyā is destroyed by the intuition of Brahman is liberated, and not any other jīva. So the release of one soul does not lead to the release of all souls.[5] There is no conflict between one soul's avidyā and another's vidyā. So some souls are bound, and others are released. Vācaspati advocates both theories of limitation and reflection. He says, "According to Śruti jīvas are reflections of Brahman in the mirror of avidyā.[6] A reflection does not differ from its archetype in reality ; but it acquires impurity from a mirror, the medium of reflection. So a jīva imagined by avidyā, an adjunct, is like a reflection of Brahman or Supreme Ātman."[7] When it achieves an immediate experience of Brahman, its nescience and its effects, all afflictions, are exterminated, and it realizes its identity with Brahman. Brahman is not tainted by the impurites of Its reflections in avidyā in the state of bondage, as the moon is not tainted by the impurities of its reflections in impure water. When a mirror is destroyed, a reflection becomes its archetype. When avidyā is destroyed, a jiva, a reflection of Brahman in it, acquires the nature of Brahman.[8] Govindānanda also advocates the theory of reflection.[9] The theory of limitation advocated by Vācaspati has already been explained.

Ānandabodha avers that when the nescience is annulled, no regulation of bondage and release in Brahman is necessary. The distinction between bondage and liberation cannot be proved by a means of knowledge without the nescience, because a pramāṇa itself is due to the nescience as shown already. If it is proved by a pramāṇa, this will involve vicious interdependence.[10] The others cannot explain the nature of release and bondage. The distinction between a teacher and a disciple also is due to avidyā. When it is annulled, there is no distinction. When vidyā is produced, no teacher's instruction is necessary. Though there is no real distinction between a teacher and a disciple, there is an empirical distinction between them due to avidyā.[11] The objection, that a teacher who has achieved the true knowledge of Ātman is devoid of avidyā, and cannot teach a disciple, is unsound, because a teacher is constructed by a disciple's avidyā. The objection, that a teacher constructed by a disciple's imagination due to avidyā is insentient and so cannot acquire true knowledge, is unsound, since a teacher who has acquired true knowledge is imagined by a disciple owing to avidyā.[12] All distintions are due to avidyā, and unprovable by pramāṇas. One Brahman devoid of all differences perceives all different forms constructed by avidyā and is bound.[13] One universal consciousness or Ātman, whose avidyā has been completely annulled by the true knowledge (vidyā) produced by the knowledge of an imaginary teacher, and who has washed off all differences, is released. So Brahman Itself is bound by Its avidyā, and is released by Its avidyā. Brahman Itself is the abode of avidyā, and a jīva is not its abode.[14]

The Naiyāyika contends that intelligence (buddhi) is knowledge, which is an attribute of Ātman, and that it is not the internal organ as the Advaitin opines. Vidyāraṇya urges that this contention is false, because the detached Ātman would never be bound to embodied life, if the internal organ, an effect of avidyā, did not limit It, false bondage could not be attributed to It, as redness of a japā flower is attributed to a crystal.[15] Bondage is of the nature of nescience. It is terminable by the knowledge of Brahman. So it is not ontologically real.[16] (Cp. Somānanda). A jīva's being a knower, a doer, and an enjoyer or a sufferer is bondage. It is the seed of misery, and, consequently, suffering. Is bondage real or unreal? If it is real, it cannot be destroyed by the knowledge of Brahman.

Some opine that real bondage is destroyed by the knowledge of Brahman. Vidyāraṇya asks them whether such knowledge produces a peculiarity (atiśaya) called termination in its object, or whether it produces a peculiarity in its abode. In the first alternative, he asks them whether such knowledge terminates the bound self, or whether it terminates attributes in the bound self, or whether it terminates the bound self's agency of action and the like, which are opposed to its being infinite bliss knowable by it, or whether it terminates unknownness in its object. The first, second and third alternatives are untenable, since the knowledge of blue colour of a multicoloured mango does not terminate its object, or taste which inheres in the mango, or yellow colour opposed to blue colour. The fourth subalternative is the Advaitin's veiw. In the second alternative, Vidyāraṇya asks whether such knowledge terminates its abode, or whether it terminates the attributes in its abode, or whether it terminates the attributes related to both its abode and object. The first subalternative is inadmissible, since the self wherein such knowledge abides would be destroyed every moment, if it were true. The second subalternative is illegitimate, because the knowledge of a jar does not destroy the attributes in the self. The third subalternative is unjustified, since the knowledge of one's body does not destroy the self's relation to its body. The contention, that real bondage is terminated by the knowledge of Brahman because of the Śruti "Knowing Brahman one attains immortality," is false, because the Śruti is indifferent to the reality or the unreality of bondage. Hence bondage is of the nature of nescience and unreal.[17]

LIBERATION.—Maṇḍana Miśra says, "Liberation is the destruction of the nescience. Bondage is the nescience".[18] Sureśvara regards beginningless nescience (avidyā) as the root of the tree of embodied life of bondage. It is the source of untold misery. The nescience is destroyed by the immediate experience of the Reality or Brahman.[19] Sureśvara defines avidyā as nonapprehension of the reality of one Ātman.[20] It is an object of apprehension. Ānandabodha defines liberation as the manifestation of the eternal, infinite bliss characterized by the complete destruction of pain.[21] It is the destruction of avidyā. One Brahman or Ātman of the nature of the highest bliss, which is not manifested by any other entity, though without a second, appears to be with a second called the empirical self (jīva) defiled by empirical attributes. So the beginningless avidyā itself is the embodied life. Its destruction is caused by the dawn of the true knowledge of the pure Brahman transcending all determinations due to avidyā.[22] Liberation is the complete destruction of avidyā. Reality is nondual Ātman. It is determined by reflection on many scriptural monistic sentences. Meditation on them produces the intuition of one Ātman. It exterminates avidyā by repeated practice. Avidyā and vidyā are contradictory to each other. The illusion of silver in a nacre is contradicted by the true knowledge of the nacre. Similarly, the true intuition of one Ātman contradicts the false knowledge of empirical difference and plurality.[23] An objection is raised that the omniscient Brahman cannot be the abode of avidyā, because it involves self-contradiction. The omniscient Being cannot be ignorant. The Advaitists, who opine that Brahman Itself is bound through Its nescience, and is released through Its knowledge, cannot account for the fact that some are bound while others are released. They cannot account for the distinction between a teacher and a disciple. If a teacher's true knowledge (vidyā) is produced, there cannot be a disciple, because all difference has been destroyed by the teacher's vidyā. If his vidyā has not been produced, he cannot be a teacher. Without a teacher a disciple's vidyā cannot be produced, for the Śruti says, "One with a teacher knows Brahman". It may be argued that the distinction between a teacher and a disciple is generated by māyā. The argument is invalid, because if a teacher, who has acquired vidyā, is associated with māyā, he cannot teach a disciple, and because if a teacher is imagined by avidyā in a disciple, he is insentient, cannot acquire vidyā, and so cannot be a teacher. Ānandabodha replies that so long as the nescience continues bondage and release happen as in dream.[24]

LIBERATION AS ETERNALLY REALIZED.—Śaṁkara defines liberation as of the nature of eternal, pure Brahman. It is a jīva's becoming Brahman. It is not producible, modifiable, purifiable, and attainable. It is eternal and intrinsic to the essence of the self. Ātman is the essence of the empirical self. It is eternal, pure, enlightened and free. Freedom is essential to Ātman, and eternal. Śaṁkara's arguments are elaborated by his followers. Liberation is eternal according to the Śruti. Brahman or Ātman is eternal and so devoid of action. If It were related to any action, It would be noneternal. Eternality of Brahman cannot be disproved by reasoning. Reason cannot override the Śruti. The Śruti, "the knower of Brahman becomes Brahman" proves that the intuition Brahman immediately generates liberation. It destroys the nescience, which is the cause of bondage. The Śruti declares that the immediate knowledge of Brahman and becoming Brahman are synchronous. There is no action intervening between them.[25] The immediate experience of Brahman and becoming identical with all occur simultaneously, and so there is no intermediate action between them.[26] Becoming all does not require any other voluntary action except the immediate experience of Brahman.[27] False knowledge (avidyā) is knowledge of difference. It is destroyed by the immediate experience of Identity. Removal of false knowledge is generated by the experience of identity of self with Brahman, and not by an action.[28] The Śruti "The knowledge of Brahman shows a person, whose taints have been destroyed, Brahman beyond darkness" proves that false knowledge is the barrier between a bound person and release. As soon as false knowledge is removed, release is experienced. It does not prove that liberation is accomplished by an action. The knowledge of Brahman does not depend upon any action of a person, like wealth and the like, but depends upon the nature of Brahman untouched by appropriation or rejection, like knowledge produced by perception and the like.[29] Hence liberation is nothing but the destruction of false knowledge. It is known from the Vedas and justified by reasoning.[30] The objection that Brahman is an object of the act of knowledge is unsound, because Brahman is not an object of the act of knowledge, but knowable from the Vedas alone. If Brahman were an object of the act of knowledge, It would not be knowable from the scripture alone as Bādarāyaṇa asserts. The eternal, free Ātman is revealed by the Vedas, and realized by a self, whose nescience has been destroyed. Brahman or Ātman is eternally free and pure. Liberation is the immediate experience of Its nature, and, therefore, eternal.[31] Brahman reveals Its nature to immediate knowledge when the nescience is destroyed. Liberation is not generated by the knowledge.

Vidyāraṇya proves eternality of liberation in the following manner. Liberation is without origin and end. It cannot be accomplished by the act of worship of God, because the Śrutis "A released soul is released"; "Being Brahman Itself, a jīva attains Brahman". prove that emancipation is without an origin. The Śrutis "A jīva enjoys immortality (amṛta) through true knowledge", "A jīva abiding in Brahman attains immortality" prove that release is indestructible. If it had an origin, it would have an end. If it had an end, a released soul would be bound again. If liberation were accomplishable by an action, like earthly prosperity, it would be related to a body, sense-organs and the like, and it would be subject to increase and decrease. The contention that liberation is achieved in a disembodied state, because the fruits of karmas are various, is false, because disembodied state is intrinsic to a soul, and because it is not produced by an action. A soul is partless, and cannot, therefore, have conjunction with a body. Nor can a soul inhere in a body, since it is not the inherent cause of a body. Nor is a soul identical with a body, because it has a nature contradictory to that of a body. Because there is no real relation between them, disembodied state is natural to it, and its embodied state is caused by its false knowledge.[32] False knowledge cannot be destroyed by actions. Disembodied release cannot be modified by actions, since the immutable Ātman cannot be modified.[33]

Padmapāda proves that liberation is not attainment (prāpti) of Brahman, since it is always effected by an action. Brahman is ubiquitous, and so always has contact with a jīva. Its attainment of Brahman does not depend upon an action. The contention that attainment of Brahman in a region free from modifications depends upon an action is false, because even in the region of modifications ubiquitous Brahman is not touched by modifications. It is contended that Brahman does not exist in a region of modifications, but exists in a region devoid of modifications, and that the attainment of It depends upon an action. Then the attainment of Brahman in that region is either the jīva's becoming identical with Brahman, or its existence in the region in its own form. In the first alternative, the jīva's nature is destroyed, and its liberation is self-destruction. In the second alternative, it will be separated again from Brahman, since conjunction always ends in disjunction. But the Śruti declares that a liberated self is not bound again.[31]

Prakāśātman proves that liberation is not attainment of Brahman in the following manner. The Vedas assert ubiquity of Brahman and Its being untouched by modifications. The contention, that Brahman's ubiquity is asserted by the Vedas in a figurative sense and that Its existence in a special region devoid of modifications is asserted by them in a primary sense, is false, because, if that were true, Brahman would be of intermediate magnitude and consist of parts, like earth and the like. If Brahman is Inner Self, a jīva cannot become Brahman, and Brahman also cannot become a jīva, because both are impossible. Nor can a jīva and Brahman become another substance, because, if they became so, ubiquitous Brahman would have parts and be destroyed. Nor is there a relation called essential identity (tādātmya), because there is no other relation than conjunction between two different substances. Nor can an atomic jīva acquire the nature of ubiquitous Brahman because of self-contradiction. If a jīva loses its atomic magnitude, its nature is destroyed. So liberation is not attainment of Brahman in a region devoid of modifications.[35]

Vidyāraṇya elaborates on the afore-said arguments, and proves that liberation is not attainment of Brahman. The Śruti says, "A knower of Brahman attains the supreme Brahman." Some interpret it in the sense that a released soul attains Brahman in a distant region. Vidyāraṇya avers that attainment of Brahman is not becoming Brahman, which he has criticized elsewhere, and that it is not production of another substance by a jīva and Brahman, because then liberation would be destructible. Because liberation is eternal, because Brahman is ubiquitous and partless, another substance cannot be generated by a jīva and Brahman. Attainment of Brahman cannot be a relation between a jīva and Brahman, because no relation between them is possible. It cannot be identity, since an atomic jīva and ubiquitous Brahman cannot be identical with each other. Nor can it be inherence or any other relation, for two different substances cannot have any other relation than conjunction. Conjunction always ends in disjunction. So a released jīva would be separated from Brahman, and be bound again. But the Śruti says, "A released soul is not bound again." So a released soul cannot be separated from Brahman. The Śruti says, "A released soul after attaining Brahman becomes the Lord of itself (svarāt)." This will lead to the undesirable contingency that there will be many Gods. So Vidyāraṇya interprets the Śruti asserting a released soul's attainment of Brahman as the manifestation of Brahman, its essential nature, on the destruction of its nescience.[36] This is the best interpretation from the standpoint of Absolute Monism. Further, a jīva associated with its adjunct of nescience, or internal organ, cannot go to Brahman in a region free of modifications. A jīva is nothing but Brahman limited by nescience or internal organ. If a jīva goes to Brahman, the region will be free of Brahman, and Brahman in the transcendent region conjoined with the jīva will be increased. So its going to Brahman in an upper region is an illusion due to the upward movement of an adjunct (upādhi). An adjunct also cannot go to Brahman, because its stuff, Brahman, is devoid of Brahman. A jar cannot move, for its stuff, earth, cannot move. Hence a jīva's movement to Brahman in a region without modifications is illusory, like movement in a dream. So the attainment of Brahman preceded by action is not possible.[37]

Padmapāda proves that liberation is not purification of Ātman, because no excellence can be generated in It, and because no taints can be removed from It. Nor can existing Ātman be manifested by an action, even as a mirror is manifested by rubbing out its dirt, since Ātman is devoid of action, and since being Inner Spririt It is not the object of action of another entity.[38] It is objected that a taint of Ātman is removed by meditation on God, as darkness in a jar is removed by the light of a lamp. Padmapāda asks whether the taint is real or of the nature of nescience. If it is real, it cannot be removed without a modification of Ātman. But Ātman cannot be modified, as the Śruti asserts It to be unmodifiable. If the taint is of the nature of nescience, it cannot be removed without intuitive knowledge of Ātman. It cannot be removed by meditation on God, ablution and the like. Only 'this'-part of the ego can be purified by such acts. So liberation is not purification of Ātman. Prakāśātman sets forth the following arguments to prove that Ātman is not purifiable, and that liberation is not Its purification. If purification means removal of taints, it is either removal of taints in Ātman or removal of taints in some other entity. Partless Ātman cannot be purified, because It is devoid of action, and, consequently, incapable of motion and modification. It is Inner Self (pratyagātman), and cannot be conjoined with active substances ; so no excellence can be produced by them in It. There are no flaws in Ātman, which can be removed by meditation on God or by the acts of ablution and the like. The objection that the Śruti speaks of purification of Ātman in the form of production of excellence in It by Vedic rites is groundless, since the ego (ahaṁkāra) is purified by them. It moves the body, the sense-organs and the manas, and is a doer, enjoyer, and sufferer, and is purifiable. Associated with universal consciousness the ego continues till the termination of bondage. The accretion of merits and demerits is produced in the modifiable ego, but not in the unmodifiable Ātman.[39] It is not amenable to purification. Vidyāraṇya elaborates on these arguments. Ātman is eternally pure and free of taints, and cannot be purified by acts. If Its taint is due to nescience, it cannot be removed by actions, since It is inactive inasmuch as It is partless and ubiquitous. It cannot be removed by the action of other substances, for they cannot act upon It because of their conjunction with It. If the taint is of the nature of nescience, it can be removed by true knowledge of Brahman, and not by an action.[40] The internal organ with its taints, love and hate, merits and demerits, is purified.

by meditation on God and other such acts. But the Self unassociated with an adjunct, which does not perform virtuous or vicious actions, which has no taints, merits and demerits, cannot experience their fruits, and cannot be purified by the aforesaid acts. So purification of the eternally pure Ātman is not possible.[41]

CRITICISM OF RIVAL VIEWS OF LIBERATION.—Ānandabodha refutes the rival views of liberation. The Mādhyamika holds that the extinction of the series of momentary cognitions tainted by love, hate, delusion and impressions (vāsanā) of the forms of objects is liberation. It is like the extinguishing of a lighted lamp. Ānandabodha refutes this view by adducing the following arguments against it. Destruction of the self cannot be the supreme good of a person. He asks whether release in the nature of destruction of the series of cognitions is the good of the members of the series or whether it is the good of the series. He argues that the members of the series are produced and then destroyed, and so are not related to liberation, and that destruction of the series of cognitions cannot be the good of the series itself, because self-destruction cannot be one's good. One is dear to oneself, and one's destruction cannot be sought for by one. Further, there is no series distinct from its members, which may have bondage and release. Nor are the members of a series themselves a series, for they do not know that they are members of a series. Nor is a series causal relation among the members, the preceding member being the cause of the succeeding member, because the causal relation is not known by them. Perception cannot cognize the relation, since each momentary member of the series knows its nature alone, and not its relation to other members. Perception is immediate knowledge, and apprehends specific individuals (svalakṣaṇa). Each member's self-awareness alone is perception; it cannot apprehend the relation between a preceding member and a succeeding member.[42] So perception cannot cognize the causal relation among the members. Nor can the causal relation be cognized by inference, because invariable concomitance between the probans and the probandum is not perceived. So the series is imaginary, and neither real nor unreal but indefinable. If this imaginary series be said to be bound and released, then there may not be its extinction in liberation as there is no extinction of it in bondage. If the cessation of a series be release, what realizes an end is absent, and, consequently, the end cannot be realized by it. There can be no voluntary action, which is not directed towards the realization of an end. So the Mādhyamika view of release is irrational.[43]

The Yogācāra Vijñānavādin opines that the emergence of a series of pure cognitions acquired by excellence in meditation (bhāvanā) is liberation. Ānandabodha offers the following criticism of this view. Even if a series of pure cognitions is produced, the series of impure cognitions being destroyed, its supreme good is not realized. If a series of pure cognitions itself be said to be release, then the series of impure cognitions, which endeavours to achieve release, does not realize its end. If a series be imagined in liberation, continuance of afflictions also in this state is unavoidable. Imagination is due to impressions (vāsanā) of false knowledge; impressions are destroyed by meditation on momentariness. If meditation cannot destroy impressions of bondage, it can far less destroy love, hate and delusion. So bondage continues in release. Hence the Yogācāra view of liberation is unjustified.[44]

The Nyāya-Vaiśeṣika regards liberation as the soul's abiding in its essential nature and the destruction of all specific qualities. Cognition, pleasure, pain, desire, aversion, volition, impression, merit and demerit are its specific qualities. They are destroyed in release, but its general qualities, e.g., ubiquity, etc., are not destroyed. Ānandabodha refutes this view by adducing the following arguments. The destruction of all special qualities, especially pleasure, cannot be the supreme good of a soul. If absolute negation of pain be said to be release, mere extinction of pain is never found to be the end of voluntary actions. Drawing out thorns not only removes pain, but also generates pleasure. So the acquirement of pleasure is the end of voluntary actions. Further, absolute negation of pain is not experienced in release, because when all special qualities of a soul are destroyed, there is no consciousness. So liberation does not differ from a state resembling swoon.[45] If the experienced absence of pain be said to be release, like the absence of pain in deep sleep, it is not right, because there is no evidence for the absence of consciousness in deep sleep. If the absence of some other entity be said to be cognized by consciousness, then what cognizes the absence of consciousness ? If it is cognized by consciousness, then there is no absence of all consciousness at the time. In the absence of all consciousness the relation of a probans to a probandum cannot be cognized at the time. So the absence of all cognitions in deep sleep cannot be inferred by a sleeping person from a mark (liṅga) of inference. Further, a sleeping person admits pleasure and its cognition during sleep from his recollection "I slept happily" on a previous day. So the experience of pleasure, and not mere absence of pain, is good in deep sleep. So deep sleep does not serve as an example for the Nyāya-Vaiśeṣika argument. It is contended that the absence of the experience of pain is inferred from the nonexperience of the recollection of pain during deep sleep, that the knowledge "I slept without pain" is acquired from it, and that this meaning is implied by the statement "I slept happily". This contention is invalid, because the absence of apprehension cannot be inferred from the absence of recollection, because the probans has variable concomitance with the probandum, and because sublating cognition is not absent.[46] So even in deep sleep unperceieved absence of pain is not good, but experienced happiness is good in the state. So the absence of the experience of pain is not the supreme good. Intelligent persons do not endeavour to bring about self-destruction resembling a state of swoon.[47] Absolute nonmanifestation of existence does not differ from negation or nonexistence. Hence complete destruction of the special qualities of the soul cannot be its liberation.[48]

The Jaina conceives of liberation as the continuous upward movement of a soul to supramundane space on the destruction of its intermediate magnitude. Ānandabodha refutes this view. When its body is destroyed, its magnitude coextensive with the body is destroyed, and the soul is destroyed. An entity with atomic magnitude and a ubiquitous entity alone are indestructible, since they are partless. If the soul is eternal and ubiquitous, it cannot continuously move upward. Further, even if it can do so, movement cannot be liberation, since it entails much fatigue. It is rather an evil, which should be shunned.[49]

The Vaiṣṇavas regard liberation as the acquirement of an imperishable body. Ānandabodha refutes this view. A body is noneternal, like our body. It is produced, and, consequently, perishable. What is produced can never be imperishable.[50]

The Sāṁkhya considers liberation to be a soul's abiding in its essential nature of pure, eternal consciousness due to discrimination between prakṛti and a soul. Ānandabodha offers the following criticisms of this view.[51] 1. A soul's abiding as eternal, pure consciousness is not its supreme good, because anything but the immediate experience of bliss does not deserve to be so. The Sāṁkhya does not admit a soul to be of the nature of bliss. So it cannot regard the manifestation of its bliss as liberation. 2. One, who is bound, is released. Bondage of a soul is due to false knowledge or nondiscrimination. Love, hate and the like are due to nondiscrimination. They are admitted by the Sāṁkhya to be modes of buddhi, and not qualities of a soul. These modes of buddhi cannot bind a soul. The discriminative knowledge of buddhi cannot release a soul. A saint should not be punished for a thief's crime. A thief should not be released from prison for a saint's merit. 3. The Sāṁkhya contends that bondage and release of prakṛti are attributed to a soul. This is not possible, for there is no cause of false attribution. According to the Sāṁkhya a soul is completely indifferent, and so cannot be master of prakṛti, which is supposed to act as a servant for its experience of joys and sorrows and cease to act for its emancipation. A servant renders some service to his master. But prakṛti or buddhi cannot render any service to a soul, which is absolutely pure by nature.[52] 4. The Sāṁkhya contends that prakṛti or boddhi shows its activities to a soul, and produces its enjoyments and sufferings, as a dancing woman shows her dances to a spectator in order to produce joys in him. This contention is invalid, since buddhi cannot produce any feelings and emotions in a soul in that it is devoid of them according to the Sāṁkhya.[53] 5. A dancing woman cannot show her dances to a person, who does not desire to see them. A person, who desires to see dances, disires to obtain joys from them. One who repeatedly exercises one's eyes to see dances, cannot be indifferent to them. There cannot be an indifferent spectator of a sight worth seeing. If a soul has capacity for seeing the acts of prakṛti, it will always see them, and will never be released, if its capacity does not cease. If its capacity is destroyed, it cannot see them. The cessation or noncessation of the capacity of prakṛti for showing its activities and modifications to a soul does not depend upon a particular soul, because there is contradiction in their natures.[54] Capacity is related to an effect. It is capacity for producing a particular effect. Buddhi cannot produce an effect in a soul, which is pure by nature. So prakṛti, or buddhi, its evolute, cannot be seen by a soul, because it is not capable of being experienced by it. Because service rendered to a soul by prakṛti is not determinable, the relation between them as master and servant is not possible.[55] 6. The relation between prakṛti and a soul is not determined to be either different or nondifferent from them. So their relation cannot be servant-master relation. It is not different from prakṛti and a soul, since the Sāṁkhya does not admit it. It admits prakṛti and souls only. If the relation of servant and master is nondifferent from them, it cannot be destroyed, like prakṛti and souls. So there can be no liberation. Further, the relation between the seer (draṣṭṛ) and the seen (dṛśya) also is indeterminable. If prakṛti acts for the experience and release of a soul, it ought to desist from its activity by producing the experience of one quality (e.g., a sound) because it has fulfilled its end, and should not act for its experience any more. If it goes on producing its endless modifications for the soul, the latter can never be released.[56] Then prakṛti acts only for a soul's experience of joys and sorrows, and not for its release. It is absurd to argue that prakṛti acts for a soul's release, as a cow's milk oozes out for the nourishment of a calf. There being no difference in the souls, why should not prakṛti act either for the experience of all souls or for their liberation? There is no reason why it should act for the experience of some souls and for the release of others. If insentient prakṛti act for some souls' enjoments and sufferings and for others' emancipation, it may bind released souls also sometimes, because there is no rule to regulate its unintended, accidental acts.[57] So the Sāṁkhya view of liberation is unjustified.[58]

Appyaya Dīkṣita refutes the Mādhva's view. The Mādhva maintains that a released soul cannot acquire the nature of God, because the difference between them is eternal, and that it can acquire sinlessness and other qualities like those of Him is false, because a released soul acquires sinlessness and the like qualities in that it has the characteristics of Brahman innate in it, and because it contradicts Bādarāyāṇa's aphorism that a released soul's essential nature of pure consciousness is manifested. In release a soul does not acquire adventitious qualities, but is accomplished in its essential nature. Sinlessness and the like are eternally existent in a soul; they are concealed by God in bondage and manifested in release. If a soul is eternally sinless and pure, it cannot be related to and tainted by sin, and it cannot be an agent, an enjoyer, and a sufferer, and its bondage is not real. Thus nondifference or identity between a soul and Īśvara (Brahman) is indisputable.[59] Bondage opposed to identity is not real. Otherwise, Bādarāyaṇa's aphorism asserting the suppression of sinlessness, truthful resolve and the like qualities in bondage would be unmeaning. Sinlessness and the like are eternally realized without any hindrance in God. But they are concealed in a bound soul, because it cannot experience its identity with God. Concealment of its eternal purity prevents it from realizing its identity with Him. 'Īśvara' here implies Brahman. It is objected that bondage is not false because of a soul's being eternally self-realized sinlessness in that sinlessness is not the absence of sin but being endowed with a power, which hinders the generation of sins even by the commission of prohibited or unrighteous actions. Similarly, truthful resolve also can be described as being endowed with a power; it does not prove identity of a soul with God. Appyaya Dīkṣita replies that there is no proof for assuming such powers denoted by the words.[60] In the state of bondage the Advaitin admits that sins are generated by the commission of sinful actions. So there is no need for assuming the existence of a power hindering the generation of sins. Bādarāyaṇa asserts that until the true knowledge of Reality (vidyā) emerges there is separation from the greatness of vidyā, but that when the true knowledge is achieved, the past sins are destroyed and future sins do not accrue. Hence in the state of release there is freedom from sins, and the assumption of power in release is needless. Bondage is due to avidyā, when a soul's divine qualities are concealed. Liberation is due to vidyā, when its supreme bliss and other divine qualities are manifested, and it attains identity with the supreme Lord (īśvarabhāvāpatti).[61]

EMBODIED LIBERATION.—Bādarāyaṇa admits embodied release. He asserts that karmas other than prārabdha karmas are destroyed by the immediate knowledge of Brahman, and that prārabdha karmas are worn out after producing their fruits.[62] Śaṁkara explains Bādarāyaṇa's view, and adduces arguments in support of it. The merits and demerits accumulated (sañcita) in the past births and in this birth are destroyed by the saving knowledge, but those, which have begun to bear fruits, and which have produced the present body are destroyed after its owner has experienced their fruits—joys and sorrows. As false knowledge of the double moon, though it has been sublated by the valid perception of one moon, continues for some time owing to the force of its impression (saṁskāra), so false knowledge of duality continues for some time owing to the impression of avidyā, which sustains prārabdha karmas.[63]

Vācaspati Miśra also holds the same view. The immediate experience of Brahman quickly destroys the accumulated (sañcita) and future (āgāmi) karmas, but cannot destroy prārabdha karmas, which have become mature, active and fruitful. These are stronger than others, which are dormant and inactive.[64] It is objected that the body of a released soul cannot continue owing to the impression of avidyā, because avidyā is not real. A real entity can leave an impression behind. Merits and demerits are constructed by māyā, which is unreal. So when avidyā is destroyed, merits and demerits are destroyed. An impression of avidyā is not real, and so cannot continue. It is not right to argue that fear and trembling are due to the illusion of a serpent in a rope, and continue even after the illusion is contradicted by the valid perception of a rope, because though a serpent is known not to exist, the knowledge of a serpent continues, and because fear and trembling continue for this reason. But here there is no avidyā (māyā), no impression of it, no object of it, and so nothing continues. Vācaspati Miśra replies that avidyā is indescribale and that its effects also are indescribable. There is nothing unreasonable in this view. The production and destruction of merits and demerits are indescribable.[65] Maṇḍana Miśra objects that a person whose wisdom is firm (sthitaprajña) has not experienced Brahman. Vācaspati Miśra replies that such a person is self-realized and perfect, and has achieved embodied release.[66]

Prakāśātman gives the following account of embodied liberation. Most Advaitins admit embodied release after the immediate knowledge of Brahman. The opponent objects that there cannot be the knowledge of duality in embodied life after the destruction of avidyā and its effects—merits and demerits. Prakāsātman replies that because the body, the sense-organs and the internal organ continue to exist after the immediate experience of Brahman, their cause—appropriate merits and demerits (karma)—must exist. It is objected that the experience of the identity of a soul with Brahman and the experience of duality cannot coexist with each other after the destruction of avidyā and karmas. Prakāśātman replies that sometimes there is the experience of the identity of a soul with Brahman in superconscious trance, and that sometimes there is the experience of duality due to the flaw of prārabdha karmas.[67] The Śruti asserts that the knowledge of Brahman has not the power of destroying prārabdha karmas, which have begun to bear fruits. It is objected that a living person endowed with a body cannot acquire the immediate knowledge of Brahman, that its power of destroying all past karmas and future karmas except prārabdha karmas is not admitted, and that all karmas are destroyed by the immediate knowledge of Brahman. Prakāśatman replies that the Śruti and the Smṛti assert that Vyāsa and others achieved immediate knowledge of Brahman in embodied life due to prārabdha karmas, and attained embodied liberation.[68] A knower of Brahman has a semblance of the experience of duality, for his actions are not motived by attachment, aversion and desire.[69] It is objected that avidyā cannot have an impression (saṁskāra). Prakāśatman replies that avidyā is false knowledge, and that it has an impression, like odour, a quality, which has an impression. We have already stated Vācaspati's view that all effects exist as potencies in causal nescience in the state of dissolution. Knowledge has an impression. False knowledge (avidyā) also has an impression. Ātman is the abode of avidyā and its impression. Avidyā is the material cause of all effects other than an impression of avidyā. Though Ātman is not the material cause of an impression of avidyā or false knowledge, It is the abode of an impression of avidyā, as it is the abode of avidyā. There is no opposition between Ātman being the abode of an impression of avidyā and not being its material cause, as there is no opposition between Ātman being the abode of avidyā and not being its material cause. The continued experience of Brahman gradually destroys the impression of avidyā, and when it completely destroys the impression, the body falls and disembodied liberation is achieved.[70] Vidyāraṇya also maintains that the experience of the identity of a soul with Brahman and the perception of duality are not simultaneous but successive in the state of embodied liberation. The knowledge of Reality has made accrual of sins in future impossible. Even if it be possible, they are destroyed by daily experience of Reality.[71]

Vidyāraṇya discusses the question whether a soul's relation to a body is due to merits and demerits (karma) or whether it is due to avidyā. If it be due to karmas, they are either natural to Ātman or due to the body. They are not natural to Ātman, because It is devoid of action. They are not due to the body, because this view will involve interdependence : karmas depend on the body ; the body depends on karmas. If a stream of a series of karmas and a series of bodies be admitted in order to avoid interdependence, this view will amount to the concept of a series of blind persons leading another series of blind persons. If it be urged that there is no opposition between them as between a series of seeds and sprouts, then there will be no difference between a body and Ātman, which is well known. So Ātman's relation to a body is not due to karmas, but to avidyā. It is destroyed by the knowledge of Reality. A knower of Brahman is not bound again. Though the knowledge of Reality destroys avidyā, which is the material cause of karmas, it cannot destroy prārabdha karmas, because the knowledge is produced through a body due to karmas.[72] In fact, karmas are modes of the internal organ, and do not belong to Ātman.

Citsukha gives the following account of embodied liberation. The opponent objects that a trace (leśa) of avidyā is either a part of avidyā or another form of avidyā. It is not a part of avidyā, since it is not admitted to have parts. Nor is it another form of avidyā, because avidyā being destroyed, a form of it cannot continue. Let, then, a trace of avidyā be an impression (saṁskāra) of avidyā or false knowledge of duality or difference. When the illusion of a serpent is destroyed by the perception of a rope, trembling due to fear is found to continue. This also is not possible, because when avidyā is destroyed, its impression —its effect—is destroyed. If an impression of avidyā be not its effect, and if it continue, duality becomes true. If an impression of avidyā be false, its material cause, avidyā, must be positive false knowledge (bhāva) ; otherwise, it would be without an abode. Ātman cannot be its abode, because It is detached and devoid of avidyā. Ātman devoid of avidyā cannot be the abode of its impression. Nor is one whose wisdom is firm (sthitaprajña) and who has transcended the guṇas—sattva, rajas and tamas (guṇātīta)—is released while alive. He is an aspirant after release in a higher state. Citsukha refutes the objection by adducing the following arguments. A trace of avidyā means another form of delusion (moha) due to false knowledge. Prārabdha karmas are a hindrance to the immediate knowledge of Brahman. Because a trace of avidyā continues, its effects—prārabdha karmas—continue. One, who has achieved the immediate knowledge of Ātman, is released in embodied life.[73] The author of 'Nyāyasudhā' opines that though avidyā, the cause of bondage, is one, it has many forms; that one form is the cause of the false knowledge of the reality of the world appearance; that a second form imagines appearances of empirical objects capable of producing practical actions; that a third form imagines objects of false perceptions or illusions; and that the certain knowledge of nondual Reality destroys all imaginary forms of duality or plurality. The forms of cosmic nescience (māyā) capable of producing practical actions, which are effects of māyā, are destroyed by the immediate experience of Reality. But a jīvanmukta person's trace of māyā, which is the cause of apparent objects capable of being perceived, continues. In the state of superconscious trance it is concealed; at other times it produces the appearance of the body and the world; it is destroyed when the fruits of prārabdha karmas have been experienced by him. Thus the experience of the identity of a soul with Brahman and the experience of duality do not coexist at the same time. The trace of māyā is not destroyed by the opposite knowledge of Reality because of the obstacle of stronger prārabdha karmas.[74] It is contended that this view involves interdependence: continuance of a trace of avidyā depends on the continuance of prārabdha karmas obstructing the power of the knowledge of Reality; the continuance of prārabdha karmas depends on the continuance of a trace of avidyā. The contention is false, because the Śruti says, "Again at the end there is the cessation of cosmic nescience". It means that two forms of avidyā are destroyed; a trace of cosmic nescience continues after the immediate knowledge of Brahman, and embodied release is generated by it. The Śruti says, "At the end the cosmic nescience is destroyed."[75] It is also experienced that when prārabdha karmas are destroyed by the experience of all their fruits, which obstructed the power of the knowledge of Brahman, it completely destroys avidyā owing to the absence of the obstacle. The contention that a trace of avidyā, which is a form of avidyā, is destroyed when avidyā is destroyed, is false, because when a particular form of an entity is destroyed, the entity in general may continue. It is admitted by experts. A person whose wisdom is firm, and who has transcended sattva, rajas and tamas, is not an aspirant for release, because none can be free from all desires except one who has experienced Brahman.[76] So such a person has achieved embodied release.

Raṅgojī Bhaṭṭa maintains that the immediate experience of Brahman destroys avidyā's power of veiling It, but that it cannot destroy its power of projecting the world appearance. Its part of projecting the world appearance continues, and makes embodied release possible.[77] Its destruction is obstructed by prārabdha karmas. This view does not differ from Citsukha's view discussed above. It is objected that avidyā has no parts, that the immediate knowledge of Brahman due to hearing cannot destroy a trace of cosmic nescience later, because it ceased long ago, and that a knowledge is not found to be obstructed by an obstacle in producing its fruit. The objection is groundless, because the admission of parts in indescribable avidyā cannot be disproved by any valid reasoning,[78] because the Mādhva admits that a beginningless soul has parts, though it is of atomic magnitude, and because the Naiyāyika admits that ether (ākāśa), though partless, has conjunction with a substance in a particular region of it. A trace of avidyā can be destroyed later in the absence of the knowledge of Brahman arising from hearing a monistic text, because a woman or a Śūdra's avidyā is destroyed by pilgrimage to holy places, fasting, muttering God's names and the like. Knowledge is found to be obstructed by an obstacle in producing its fruit. Knowledge produces an action, which is found to be hindered by an obstacle. Hence when prārabdha karmas are exhausted by producing their fruits, the immediate knowledge of Brahman due to hearing a monistic text destroys avidyā's power of projecting the world appearance, and a soul becomes Brahman of the nature of infinite being-knowledge-bliss.[79]

Mahādeva Sarasvatī regards a person devoid of love and hate, free from all desires, egoless, contented with Ātman, beyond sattva, rajas and tamas, and destitute of karmas as released in embodied life. Embodied liberation can be achieved by the practice of the knowledge of Reality, the destruction of emotional dispositions (vāsanā), and the destruction of mind. Love and hate are emotional dispositions.[80] Destruction of mind is its inactivity due to the destruction of love, hate and desire. When prārabdha karmas are worn out, the present body falls, and a jīvanmukta soul exists in the state of the infinite bliss of Brahman.[81] A knower of Brahman achieves disembodied liberation (videhamukti) after death of the body. Others opine that disembodied liberation is nonproduction of a future body.[82] Mahādevānanda opines that when cosmic avidyā with its power of projecting the world appearance is destroyed by the destruction of prārabdha karmas, a knower of Brahman is not endowed with a future body. The destruction of his accumulated karmas and the nonaccrual of his future karmas were effected already by his immediate knowledge of Brahman.[83] They occurred simultaneously with the experience of Brahman. The non-production of a future body also was synchronous with this experience.[84]

Mahādeva Sarasvatī opines that embodied release is accomplished by the knowledge of the Reality, destruction of emotional dispositions, and destruction of mind. Though destruction of dispositions and destruction of mind are the pre-requisites for the knowledge of the Reality, they are the subordinate duties of a monk desirous of the knowledge of Brahman, and the practice of hearing and the like is his principal duty. But the practice of the knowledge of Brahman is the subordinate duty of a monk who has acquired the knowledge, and destruction of dispositions and destruction of mind are his principal duties.[85] These are continuing processes, which are firmly established by prolonged practice and constant vigilance.

Even persons released in embodied life should practise the preservation of knowledge, the absence of disharmony, termination of sufferings, and manifestation of supreme bliss. 1. Preservation of knowledge consists in stopping production of doubts and illusions again and again, which are obstacles to release, like the nescience. They can be stopped by the practice of embodied release. 2. Penance is the concentration of mind. Absolute mental concentration of a jīvanmukta person is generated by complete arrest of all mental modes. 3. The absence of disharmony in the extraverted state of a jīvanmukta person consists in his absolute tranquillity of mind despite the presence of grave provocations. 4. Termination of all sufferings in earthy life is brought about by destroying false knowledge by true knowledge, by arresting all mental processes by the practice of yoga, and by concentrating the mind on Ātman and modifying it into Its form. Sufferings in future life are prevented by destroying the nescience (ajñāna) and accumulated karmas, and by preventing accrual of karmas in future through the knowledge of Brahman. 5. The supreme bliss of Brahman is completely manifested by terminating the nescience and its veiling power and projecting power by the practice of yoga and saving knowledge in the absence of hindrances.[86] Sarvajñātman denies the possibility of embodied liberation, and regards the assertion of the scripture about it as eulogy, because even a trace of avidyā cannot continue after the immediate experience of Brahman is achieved. Vimuktātman severely criticizes the arguments for embodied release, and yet grudgingly acquiesces in it. Some Advaitists maintain that the scripture has no need of proving embodied liberation, because avidyā with its effects and impressions (vāsanā) are destroyed by the immediate experience of Brahman generated by meditation, and that there is no embodied release.[87]

Prakāśānanda also does not believe in embodied release. He offers the following criticism of it. Vidyā overpowers avidyā and its effects, the body falls at once, and disembodied release is achieved. The fall of the body cannot be arrested by prārabdha karmas, since they also are effects of avidyā and are destroyed by vidyā. If they can prevent the fall of the body, vidyā cannot terminate avidyā, since the body is an effect of avidyā. It is wrong to argue that vidyā terminates all effects of avidyā except prārabdha karmas, and that it can destroy them in future, because an entity cannot have two natures. It is also wrong to argue that vidyā terminates avidya's power of concealing the nature of Brahman, but that it cannot terminate its power of projecting the world appearance, because there are not two nesciences. The same avidyā cannot have two powers. One nescience cannot exist and not-exist at the same time. It is wrong to argue that power of the nescience is terminated, but that the nescience is not terminated, because power and powerful nescience are nondifferent from each other, and because if they were different from each other, the nescience would not be terminated. The contention that the nescience is terminated when prārabdha karmas are worn out, is invalid, because there is no evidence to substantiate their being exhausted. The contention, that the knowledge of Brahman (vidyā) after the exhaustion of prārabdha karmas being not obstructed by them terminates the nescience, is false, because there is no knowledge after the destruction of prārabdha karmas and the fall of the body, and because the prior knowledge of Brahman was obstructed by the prārabdha karmas. The contention, that a residual impression of avidyā called a trace of avidyā continues and keeps the body alive, is false, because it is an effect of avidyā. If a trace of avidyā were mere avidyā, the use of the word 'impression' would be futile. The contention, that the body continues after embodied liberation is achieved, because the Śruti and the Smṛtis bear testimony to the truth, is false, because the scriptures have no purpose to prove embodied emancipation.[88] Prakāśānanda's arguments against embodied liberation closely resemble those of the theistic Vedāntins against it, which will be discussed in the fourth and fifth volumes.

DISEMBODIED LIBERATION.—Mahādeva Sarasvatī avers that a person, who has worn off prārabdha karmas by appropriate enjoyments and sufferings, attains disembodied liberation on the death of his body. According to other Advaitins nonproduction of a future body is disembodied release, which occurs simultaneously with the emergence of the immediate experience of Brahman. When the immediate knowledge of Brahman destroys the nescience and accumulated merits and demerits (sañcita karma), it prevents the accrual of future merits and demerits, and makes the production of a future body impossible owing to the exhaustion of prārabdha karmas due to the experience of their fruits; the nonproduction of a future body occurs simultaneously with the knowledge. A soul which has attained disembodied release continues to experience the supreme bliss of Brahman. It does not depart from the body but becomes Brahman here.[89] (Cp. Abhinavagupta).

SARVAMUKTI.—It is objected that when the nescience of one empirical self is destroyed by the intuitive knowledge of Brahman, not only that jīva is liberated, but that all jīvas are liberated, since there is one nescience in all jīvas. Some Advaitins uphold this view, and do not regard it as an undesired contingency. So Advaitists admit many nesciences as the Śruti says, "Indra assumes many forms through many māyās." There are different nesciences in different jīvas, so that when one nescience is destroyed by a jīva, it is liberated, but the other jīvas remain bound. Other Advaitins recognize one nescience with different powers of veiling Brahman, so that when the nescience endued with a distinct power of veiling is destroyed by one jīva, it alone is liberated, and the others remain bound.[90]

SELF-FULFILLEDNESS (KṚTAKṚTYATĀ).—Vidyāraṇya describes the state of self-fulfilledness in the following manner. Supreme fulfilment is the ultimate result of spiritual discipline. It is the state of supreme satisfaction untainted by pain due to desire for any object of sentient pleasure, for it is the state of supreme delight. A self-fulfilled person has completely destroyed all desires for worldly enjoyments. He has no duties to perform, since he has transcended all duties. Though others attribute bondage to him because he lives a bodily life, he is not entangled in bondage. He does not practise hearing, reflection and meditation, since he is firmly established in the immediate experience of Brahman. One who has not acquired the knowledge of Brahman ought to practise hearing. One who is tormented by doubts ought to reflect. One who has false knowledge ought to meditate. A self-fulfilled person has completely destroyed the false sense of identity of his self with the body, and is not troubled by doubts and errors. But sometimes he experiences "I am a person" owing to the influence of prārabdha karmas. This false experience cannot be destroyed by repeated meditation, but only when prārabdha karmas are completely worn out and when the body perishes. A self-fulfilled person does not practise meditation and trance, for he has completely arrested his mental modes. One who is agitated by mental modes should practise them. A fulfilled person always experiences his identity with Brahman, supreme bliss and fulfilledness. He is inactive and detached, and not affected by his secular and religious actions due to the influence of his prārabdha karmas, since he is devoid of the sense of being an agent and enjoyer and sufferer. Though he is completely fulfilled, he acts for the good of mankind. He automatically performs ablution, worship, japa, meditation, and begs alms for his livelihood. He does not perform these actions under any moral or religious obligation. He does dot voluntarily perform any secular or religious actions, nor does he persuade others to do any action, for he always experiences his self to be the eternal, pure Sākṣin of the nature of consciousness. He does not wrangle for he experiences his self as the detached Sākṣin while one who acts voluntarily identifies one's self with one's body, and is concerned with intellect and speech. Neither nescience nor egoism—its product—can hinder the knowledge of a fulfilled person, because his knowledge of Brahman has destroyed them. He being firmly established in the knowledge of Brahman is neither affected by pravṛtti nor by nivṛtti. Actions for the preservation of life are pravṛtti while renunciation and the like are nivṛtti. The only duty of a fulfilled person is to awaken true knowledge in ignorant persons. He is always conscious of his having realized the supreme end, of his freedom from moral obligation, and of his supreme self-delight. He is conscious of his experience of the bliss of Brahman, of his freedom from suffering from bondage and nescience. He acquires the state of transcending good and evil, and duties and virtues. He achieves the state of dutilessness (naiṣkarmya).[91]

KNOWLEDGE ALONE IS THE MEANS TO RELEASE.—Sureśvara elaborately discusses the different views about the means to liberation, and concludes that knowledge alone is the means to liberation. The Mīmāṁsakas, upholders of works (karmavādin), opine that works are the means to liberation. Nonperformance of prudential duties (kāmya karma) results in nonattainment of heaven. Nonperformance of prohibited duties (niṣiddha karma) results in nonattainment of hell. The performance of daily obligatory duties (nitya karma), and of occasional duties (naimittika karma) prevents the accrual of the sins of ommision. Prārabdha karmas which initiated the body and have begun to bear fruits will be worn out by appropriate enjoyments and sufferings. Any endeavour for the achievement of the true knowledge of Ātman is useless. The performance of duties will lead to release. The Śruti says, "Performing your duties on earth, desire to live for a hundred years".[92] Liberation is achieved by persons in all stages of life by performing duties—physical, verbal and mental—to the best of their abilities. There is no other means to release.

Sureśvara refutes the Karmavādin's view thus. Liberation can never be achieved by the performance of works. Abandonment of prudential and prohibited works is not possible. Prārabdha karmas can be worn out by proper enjoyments and sufferings. Demeritorious works, which have not yet begun to bear fruits, can be worked out by expiations. Earned merits and demerits can be exhausted by the knowledge that the self is not the agent of actions. But the Karmavādin does not admit that the true knowledge of the self, which alone destroys the aforesaid knowledge, is a means to release. The karmas, the fruits of which have not been experienced, and which have not begun to bear fruits, cannot be exhausted by any means whatsoever. The karmas also, which have begun to fructify, cannot be discarded, because an agent is free to perform actions (pravṛtti) for the fulfilment of desires or to abstain from doing such actions (nivṛtti) and cultivate dispassion.[93] Voluntary actions, which are not completed, can be abandoned. But completed voluntary actions are incapable of being discarded. Nor can a person make a resolve that he will not perform any prudential action or commit any prohibited action. Even the most discerning and virtuous persons had to suffer for their subtle sins. There is no Śruti asserting that an aspirant for release should perform daily obligatory duties and occasional duties, and discard prudential duties and prohibited actions, and that the karmas, which have begun to fructify, can be worn out by appropriate enjoyments and sufferings. Embodied life of bondage is beginningless. Endless merits and demerits have been earned by a soul in numberless births. They can never be exhausted by the performance of prudential duties and prohibited actions. Daily obligatory duties cannot destroy the demerits due to prudential actions, because they do not produce any positive fruit. There are Śrutis which prove that sins are destroyed by atonements. But there is no Śruti which proves that daily obligatory duties destroy merits and demerits due to prudential duties. Sins are not destroyed by sins; merits are not destroyed by merits; prudential duties produce merits, and so cannot be destroyed by prudential duties, because they are not opposed to each other. So works cannot generate emancipation; they produce desires alone. They can never bring on liberation. The Śruti inculcates renunciation of actions and acquisition of the right knowledge of Ātman as the only means to release.[94] So whole-hearted performance of specific duties in all orders of life does not lead to liberation, but knowledge alone achieves the supreme end. It is suprarational intuition of Ātman.

Sureśvara adduces the following arguments also against the Karmavādin's view. Destruction of nescience alone is release, which can be achieved by true knowledge of Ātman. The performance of prescribed works is not a means to release. Works are of the nature of nescience, and so cannot destroy it. They produce nescience, as darkness produces darkness.[95] (Cp. Śaṁkara). Even if works are a means to liberation, either one work or all works together generate release. If each work generates it, the other works are useless. If all works together produce release, they become one work, since they produce one result. This view is not reasonable, for works are heard to produce different results. The performance of daily obligatory duties (e.g., ablution, prayer thrice, etc.) destroy sins. The performance of prudential religious works leads to the attainment of heaven. The Śruti never speaks of works directly generating release. The performance of daily obligatory duties does not produce any positive fruit. Both upholders of works and knowledge enjoin the nonperformance of prudential works and prohibited works. So works are not a means to emancipation.[96] Works spring from the nescience (ajñāna), false knowledge of the mind-body-complex as the Self. So they cannot destroy delusion due to the nescience. True knowledge of Ātman is opposed to the nescience, as the sun is opposed to darkness. This knowledge due to scriptural testimony is not contradicted. It does not depend upon any other condition to produce its fruit. It is quite sufficient to destroy the nescience, the cause of bondage. Works cannot destroy it.[97] An empirical self (jīva) is born because of the nescience, desire and action, being bound by the nescience, and dies with sorrow. The nescience is the cause of desire; desire is the cause of action. The nescience is the cause of bondage. Bondage is destroyed by the destruction of the nescience.[98]

Some opine that works indirectly lead to release. The performance of daily obligatory duties, and of occasional duties, and of specific duties offered to God purify the mind and produce dispassion for heaven. So the mind is inclined towards the Inner Self (pratyagātman). When the mind is purified of all desires, an aspirant visions the Inner Self. Works are fulfilled by producing purity of mind, and then are discarded. So those, who are desirous of knowledge of Ātman and release, should perform daily obligatory duties and occasional duties for purification of mind. Works are indirectly the cause of destruction of the nescience. They are not a means to emancipation, because it is neither producible, nor attainable, nor modifiable, nor purifiable, as Śaṁkara says.[99] Śaṁkara admits that disinterested performance of duties purifies the mind.[100] Maṇḍana Miśra and Sarvajñātman also hold this view.

Some opine that knowledge combined with works (jñānakarmasamuccaya) leads to liberation. Sureśvara refutes it by adducing the following arguments. Knowledge combined with works cannot destroy the nescience, for works donot coexist with the destruction of the nescience. Works are due to the nescience, and so cannot coexist with its destruction. But knowledge is destruction of the nescience. The nescience is false knowledge of reality. Knowledge is true knowledge of reality. Works are the nescience. So knowledge and works cannot be combined with each other, like the sun and dark night.[101] One who has acquired the knowledge of Ātman looks upon the body and action as not-self, whereas a victim of the nescience erroneously identifies his self with his body, and is engaged in action. False knowledge is combined with works, but true knowledge is never combined with them. True knowledge of Ātman destroys the false knowledge of the distinction of the agent, action and fruit without which no action is possible. When true knowledge of Ātman is acquired, false knowledge is at once destroyed. So knowledge cannot be superior or subordinate to action, which depends upon false knowledge.[102] The advocates of knowledge combined with works must admit this truth, because knowledge cannot arise without destroying the nescience. Knowledge is suprarational intuition of Identity or Ātman; the nescience is perceptual or rational knowledge of difference. So knowledge cannot be combined with works, either as superior, or as subordinate, or as equal to them.[103] Knowledge and action are opposed to each other in their causes, natures, and effects. A means of knowlege is the cause of knowledge while the nescience is the cause of action. Knowledge manifests the nature of Reality while action conceals the nature of Reality. Knowledge leads to abiding in eternal, unchanging consciousness while action produces an effect. So they cannot combine with each other.[104] Before Śaṁkara and Sureśvara some were upholders of the doctrine of combination of knowledge with works as means to release. Śaṁkara has refuted the doctrine. Criticism of Bhāskara's doctrine by Vidyāraṇya will be given later.[105]

Among the Advaita Vedāntins some are advocates of combination of knowledge with meditation (bhāvanā), and are called Bhāvanāsañcayavādins, and some are exponents of knowledge combined with repeated practice, and are called Prasaṁkhyānavādins. Hearing a scriptural text produces the knowledge "I am Brahman", but it does not destroy the nescience. Daily practice of meditation for a very long period of time generates proficiency in meditation, which destroys the nescience without leaving any trace. The Śruti says "Becoming a god, one attains divinity". Other Advaitins hold that knowledge acquired from a scriptural sentence cannot comprehend the real nature of Ātman, because it is relational knowledge derived from a verbal statement. When this knowledge is repeatedly practised for a long period of time, it comprehends the real nature of Ātman, and uproots the nescience. This knowledge is nonrelational and immediate. The Śruti says, "A Brāhmaṇa should cultivate suprarational intuition after acquiring the knowledge of Brahman". Sureśvara refutes both these views. True knowlede of Ātman or nondual eternal consciousness destroys the nescience or knowledge of the distinction of an agent and action. So knowledge of Identity cannot be combined with knowledge of difference.[106]

CRITICISM OF BHĀSKARA'S DOCTRINE OF JÑANAKARMASAMUCCAYA.—Vidyāraṇya criticizes Bhāskara's doctrine of the combination of knowledge and works as the means to release. Works result in the attainment of Brahmaloka and other higher worlds. The works prescribed for the monks (e.g., meditation, etc.) assist the emergence of knowledge, and do not produce a different fruit. According to Prabhākara daily obligatory duties do not produce any fruit. According to Kumārila they produce heavenly happiness. According to the Advaita Vedāntin they produce disposition or potency and inclination towards the Inner Self and desire to know it (vividiṣā). Works can never produce release.

The identity of the jīva and Brahman is not the effect of the combination of works and knowledge, for it is an accomplished reality, and cannot be accomplished. Nor is the termination of avidyā and its effects the effect of the combination, since it is the effect of knowledge. The Śruti says, "The knower of Ātman crosses grief." The effect of knowledge, according to Bhāskara, is the destruction of the adjuncts necessary for works, or the destruction of false superimposition or illusion, or the destruction of the series of false superimpositions, or the destruction of the potencies of false knowledge, or the manifestation of the nature of Brahman. The first alternative is not tenable, since the adjuncts necessary for works being real cannot be destroyed by knowledge. The second alternative is not admissible, because false illusions being momentary themselves cease to exist. The third alternative is untenable, since a series of false illusions cannot be destroyed, unless a false illusion is destroyed by knowledge. The fourth alternative is inadmissible, because the impression of the illusion of silver in a nacre is not found to be destroyed by the knowledge of the nacre. If the impression (saṁskāra) of the repeated knowledge of a nacre destroyed the impression of the illusion of silver, then the impression of knowledge would be the cause of release, and knowledge would not be its cause. This view would contradict the Vedic testimony, which asserts knowledge to be the cause of release. The fifth alternative is untenable, for Brahman is self-manifest.[107]

KNOWLEDGE AND ACTION.—Vidyāraṇya opines that liberation is the immediate knowledge of idenity of the self with Brahman attainable by knowledge, and not by action. The objection, that knowledge also, like meditation, is a mental act, is groundless, since knowledge and action are different from each other as to their causes and results. The manifestation of an object is the result of knowledge. The Ātman being the object of knowledge, It cannot be produced. No result of knowledge is produced. The nature of Ātman is manifested by a mode of the internal organ (antaḥkaraṇa), which is the adjunct of the manifestation. But the result of meditation on the god Garuḍa is the destruction of poison, which is production of a nonexistent result. Meditation on a god results in subjection or persecution of a foe. The existence of an object is not the cause of meditation, but it is a volition of a person preceded by a desire under the direction of a superior person or a scripture. A person meditates on a nonexistent fire or a woman. But knowledge is produced by a means of valid knowledge and an object of valid knowledge, but not produced by a desire and a volition of a person. A foul odour is smelt by one against one's will. Inferential knowledge and verbal knowledge of a past object, or of a future object, are produced by a probans and a statement of a reliable person, respectively, because a past object and a future object are nonexistent. But these cognitions are not produced by a person's desire and volition.[108] An act of meditation depends upon a person's desire and volition. The contention, that knowledge is a mental act, because it is a modification of the internal organ, is invalid, since knowledge is different from an action, which executes a command, and since knowledge does not depend upon a person's desire and volition, like an act of meditation. A person can meditate on an existent or a nonexistent fire according to his volition, or meditate on an existent fire as something else, or nonexistent. But a person cannot but perceive a fire in intercourse with his visual organ. He cannot make it, unmake it, or make it otherwise as an object of perception. He turns towards it in order to perceive it. He turns away from it in order not to perceive it. These acts are the causes of perception and nonperception, respectively. He is free to do or not to do these acts. But his knowledge or absence of knowledge does not depend upon his free will, but upon the object of knowledge.[109] If knowledge were produced by a person's volition, the second cognition, the third cognition and the like in a series of cognitions would not be produced, because the first cognition alone is immediately preceded by a person's volition. In a series of acts (e g., the revolving of a wheel) the first act produced by a volition produces force (vega), which produces the second act and so on. But in a series of cognitions the first cognition does not produce a residual impression, which produces the second cognition and so on. If it did so, the second cognition and the succeeding cognitions would be recollections. If they were recollections, they would not depend upon sense-object-intercourse. But a series of perceptual cognitions depends upon sense-object-intercourse. So the second and the third cognitions and the like in a series of perceptual cognitions are produced by their objects in intercourse with the sense-organs, and not upon a person's volition. Similarly, recollection also does not depend upon a person's volition, but upon the revival of a residual impression.[110] A person is found to remember an undesired object without an effort of volition on the revival of a residual impression by the perception of a similar object or owing to an unseen force (adṛṣṭa). Sometimes an effort of volition is found in recollection. It focuses the mind only, and revives a residual impression, which produces recollection. So volition is not the direct cause of recollection. Hence knowledge is not an action.[111]

CONTEMPLATION, MEDITATION, RECOLLECTION AND KNOWLEDGE.—Vidyāraṇya shows that contemplation (bhāvanā) differs from knowledge. Sometimes scripture enjoins contemplation of a god for whom an oblation is made to a sacrificial fire. The mediate knowledge of a particular figure of a god is produced by words in scripture uttered without any volition of a person. Contemplation of a particular figure of a god in a fire before a person is not knowledge, because it does not exist. Scripture does not prove the existence of the figure of the god in the burning charcoals of a fire. If it did, it would contradict perception. But it proves that contemplation of an object, though nonexistent, produces a particular result. The relation between the means and the result is not false. Scripture is not invalid, because the object of enjoined contemplation is nonexistent. The Advaitists admit contemplation to be dependent on a person's volition, because it is of the nature of the act of meditation.[112]

The objection, that meditation also depends upon apprehension, which is a kind of knowledge, because it is a series of recollections, is groundless, because there can be no recollection of an unperceived object.[113] But meditation on a fire as a woman is prescribed. A woman has never been perceived to be made of a fire. The act of manas imparts a particular form to the object of meditation.[114] Meditation is a series of mental acts endued with the forms suggested by a sentence in scripture, and not a series of recollections.[115] It is contended that meditation on a perceived black round stone (sālagrāma) as Viṣṇu with four hands enjoined by scripture does not differ from a series of recollections. This contention is false, because meditation on Viṣṇu is not recollection in that the Deity was not perceived before. Recollection of perceived objects also is different from meditation.[116] A person focuses his mind with an effort of volition on a perceived sentence in scripture studied in childhood, and remembers the succeeding sentences in the same order in which he learned them. This is recollection. But the person's volition is not its cause. The sentences, which he perceived, are its cause. The remembered sentences cannot be altered by him. Sometimes he cannot remember a thing in spite of an effort of volition. Sometimes a sentence in scripture suddenly flashes in memory after an act of uncleanliness without a volition. So recollection depends upon the revival of a residual impression produced by the perception of an object in its real nature. It cannot be made, unmade, or altered by a person's volition.[117]

MEDITATION, IMAGINATION, AND KNOWLEDGE.—Meditation is unrestricted imagination of the attributes of a perceived or unperceived, existent or nonexistent object. A person does not depend upon an object in it. He does not depend upon any other means except his volition and mind.[118] Imagination cannot be restrained by the command of a king or by scripture. But meditation on an object prescribed by scripture yields the prescribed fruit. Scripture regulates the relation between a prescribed means and an unperceived end. It is unchallengeable in this matter, because its power and greatness are inconceivable. Otherwise, offering oblations to a sacrificial fire and attainment of heaven in future as its fruit cannot be related to each other. Scripture is the authority in regard to supersensible objects. A person's valid knowledge depends upon its object. He can bring about the collocation of causes of knowledge, but knowledge is produced by the proper means of knowledge and the object of knowledge. It is not produced by a person's volition.[119] But meditation is not like knowledge. It is produced by a person's volition. It is not produced by a collocation of causes brought together by a person's volition, because it does not depend upon any other collocation of causes than a person's volition.[120] Meditation can be directly done, undone, or altered by a person's volition without any other means. But knowledge produced by a pramāṇa cognizes an object. It does not produce any result, and does not depend upon a person's volition, whereas meditation does not depend upon an object, produces a result, and is produced by a person's volition alone. Thus, though knowledge and meditation are equally mental, they differ from each other as to their results, objects and causes.[121] So the knowledge of Brahman cannot be achieved by action, since it does not depend upon a person's volition. Hence it is not capable of being enjoined by the Vedas : there can be no Vedic injunction (vidhi) in regard to it. The Śruti "The Ātman should be seen" means that It is worthy of being seen. The Śruti, "One should see Ātman in Ātman by Ātman" simply indicates the means of intuiting Ātman. Vidyāraṇya does not admit the possibility of a Vedic injunction in regard to the knowledge of Ātman.[122]

Vidyāraṇya elaborates on Prakāśātman's arguments to show that the knowledge of Ātman cannot be acquired from a Vedic injunction (vidhi), which is of the nature of a command (niyoya). A command is an intention of a superior person to move an inferior person to perform an action. This is not possible in the Veda, which is impersonal (apauruṣeya). It is objected that a command moves a person to act, and that an object known from the cognition of what ought to be done (kārya) moves a person to act. Vidyāraṇya asks what ought to be done means. It is either what is related to a volition, or what can be accomplished by a volition, or a transcendent object different from the agent and action and capable of being accomplished by a volition. The first alternative is inadmissible, because volition is a person's act of will while what ought to be done is an effect of volition. What is related to a volition cannot be an effect of volition. The argument partly involves vicious self-dependence (ātmāśraya). The second alternative is unjustified, because what is conducive to pain would move a person to act in that it ought to be done inasmuch as it is capable of being accomplished by a volition. The third alternative also is untenable, because an object unknowable through pramāṇas cannot be known from scripture in that its meaning is not known. But Prabhākara's view is not the right view of what moves a person to act, because what is conducive to the good of a person and capable of being accomplished by his volition moves him to act.[123] The rise of the moon is a means to a person's good, but it is not capable of being accomplished by a person's volition. So it does not move a person to act. The Advaitin admits that what is conducive to one's good and capable of being accomplished by one's volition is what ought to be done by him.[124] The same object ought to be done, for it is capable of being accomplished by a volition, and is conductive to one's good for it realizes one's good.[125] Eating food and drinking water were known to be conducive to good in the past. Their being conducive to good at present is inferred from the past similar actions. Hence a scriptural injunction conveys what is capable of being accomplished by one's volition and is conducive to one's good, and it does not convey a command.[126] The highest good inculcated in the Vedānta is liberation characterized by the destruction of the nescience. The immediate knowledge of the identity of self with Brahman is the means to liberation, as the knowledge of a nacre destroys the ignorance of it. Prabhākara objects that a Vedic injunction always relates to an action which ought to be done, and not to an existent object. This objection is groundless, since the Śruti "Ātman ought to be heard, reflected and meditated on" means existent (siddha) Ātman, since It is not accomplishable by a volition (kārya) inasmuch as there is neither any pramāṇa for it nor any end to be realized by the action. In order to know the meaning of a sentence, its invariable concomitance with an action is not necessary. So authoritativeness of the Vedānta consists in its expounding the nature of Brahman.[127]

AN ACTION AND BRAHMAN BOTH ARE NOT DENOTED BY A VIDHI.—Some opine that a sentence in the Vedānta denotes an action in a primary sense, but that it denotes the existent Brahman as subsidiary to an enjoined action. Vidyāraṇya offers the following criticism of this view. A command (niyoya) and Brahman both cannot be proved by a sentence in the Veda, because a command is to be accomplished, and because Brahman is an existent reality. Nor can a command alone be proved by a sentence in the Veda, because what ought to be done is not determined. Nor is the knowledge of Brahman through hearing the Vedānta texts what ought to be done, because the knowledge of Brahman can be acquired from the study of the Vedānta, but because Its nature is determined by deliberation. Nor is a series of recollections of Brahman known from the Veda what ought to be done, because, if it were true, liberation produced by actions would be noneternal, like the attainment of heaven produced by prescribed sacrifies. It is contended that a series of recollections of Brahman is what ought to be done, for it produces the immediate knowledge of Brahman. Vidyāraṇya asks whether a series of recollections directly produces the immediate knowledge of Brahman, or whether it produces such knowledge through an unseen force (adṛṣta), or whether it produces such knowledge through another knowledge. The first alternative is inadmissible, since a series of recollections, which are mediate cognitions, cannot produce the immediate knowledge of Brahman. If it could do so, a series of inferences would produce the perception of an inferable object. In the second alternative, the unseen merit alone produced by a series of recollections is not able to produce the immediate knowledge of Brahman, because immediate knowledge is produced by a pramāṇa. A pramāṇa aided by the unseen merit mentioned above does not produce the immediate knowledge of Brahman, since a pramāṇa alone can produce it, and since the unseen merit is needless. The third alternative also is not justified, because another knowledge itself, or through an unseen merit, produces such immediate knowledge. Both subalternatives are vitiated by the difficulties mentioned above.[128]

It is objected that meditation on Brahman known from the Vedas is what ought to be done. Meditation is not a series of recollections, since a series of recollections cognizes an object, but since meditation may be on an attributed object.[129] Meditation on Brahman brings about the immediate knowledge of Brahman. A dead son may be perceived by a person after repeated meditation on him. Similarly, the immediate experience of Brahman may be produced in a person after repeated meditation on It. But it cannot be said to be false like the perception of a dead son. It may agree with scriptural testimony, because sometimes an object perceived in dream agrees with a waking cognition. Vidyāraṇya urges that this objection is unsound, because it contradicts self-validity of Vedic testimony.[130] The perception of an object in dream is not possible without the operation of the visual organ, but agreement of a perception in dream with a waking perception is due to similarity. It is contended that though a series of recollections of, and meditation on, Brahman are not enjoined by the Veda, another transcendent knowledge, which results in the immediate knowledge of Brahman should be brought about by a person desirous of liberation through hearing of, and reflection and meditation on, a Vedānta text such as "That thou art". This contention is false, because the assumption of validity of knowledge of Brahman Itself is better than the assumption of validity in the transcendent knowledge to be effected to prove the validity of a Vedānta text, because the former is in harmony with the law of parsimony.[131] What is related to a Vedic injunction is not the cause of validity, but what produces valid knowledge is the cause of validity. Valid knowledge of Brahman is produced in regard to Itself, and not in regard to a Vedic injunction. So what ought to be done in regard to Brahman cannot be determined.

CRITICISM OF PRABHĀKARA'S VIEW OF NIYOGA.—The opponent argues that the Vedic injunction "Ātman ought to be worshipped" or "Ātman ought to be seen" is a command to see Ātman. Sureśvara, like Śaṁkara, urges that the knowledge of the real nature of Ātman does not depend upon the action of a person.[132] Ātman is eternally existent, and so cannot be accomplished by the act of seeing. Ātman is worshipped by nonperception of the not-self.[133] Ātman is of the nature of eternal knowledge, unprovable by pramāṇas, of the nature of Inner Self (pratyagātman), devoid of physical qualities, and so cannot be perceived, and is yet indubitable. So Ātman cannot be an object of the act of vision. One who has achieved the immediate knowledge of Ātman at once abides in It, and does not require any action to realize It. So the Śruti "Ātman ought to be seen" is not an imperative (niyoga) for action.[134]

Prabhākara opines that a moral imperative moves a person to act in order to execute it. It transcends time, is knowable from the Vedas alone, and conveys that an action ought to be done.[135] Ānandabodha states Prabhākara's view thus, and refutes it by adducing the following arguments. Where there are explanatory repetitions (anuvādaka) in prescribing actions in the Vedas, their consistency with the prescriptive sentences should be known by inference, because their differentiating criteria are not laid down by the Vedas. Nor is a moral imperative knowable from the Vedas alone. In a child's voluntary action of sucking the mother's breast there is no scope for a Vedic injunction. The act is motivated by the desire to realize one's good.[136] Sucking the breast is a means to the realization of the child's good. It is presumed here that the child voluntarily realizes his good in sucking his mother's breast. A command, which transcends the past, the present and the future, is unreal, like a sky-flower, and cannot move a person to act.[137] It cannot be a source of moral obligation. Nor is there any other independent being, who imposes a command upon a person. An independent person does not follow social customs in his voluntary actions. A command is always imposed on a person by another person. A person is never independent in carrying out a command. So a Vedic command also is an attribute of a being.[138] But whose command it is cannot be determined. Prabhākara does not believe in God Whose command it may be said to be. In what sense, is a command distinct from time past, present and future? It is distinct from time in regard to its object (artha) or in regard to words (śabda). If it is distinct from time in regard to its meaning, it is unreal, like a horn of an ass. Being distinct from time is pervaded by relation to time.[139] Relation to time more pervasive than a command, which is nontemporal, and distinguished from it, distinguishes the being of a command pervaded by it, as a fire pervades smoke. If a command is distinct from time in regard to words, it does not differ from a jar and the like, which exist in time. Hence a Vedic sentence does not convey a command to perform a particular action, but is related to eternally accomplished Brahman, since the Veda is a pramāṇa, like perception.[140]

HEARING, REFLECTION AND MEDITATION.—According to some Advaitins, (e.g. Maṇḍana Miśra) hearing a monistic text produces undoubted mediate knowledge. It can never produce immediate knowledge. Hearing aided by reflection and meditation as auxiliaries produces the immediate knowledge of Brahman, as the sense-organs aided by subconscious impressions produce recognition. Hearing which by itself can produce mediate knowledge, aided by prolonged and intense meditation, can produce immediate knowledge, even as hearing about a beloved woman aided by prolonged and intense thought of her produces the immediate knowledge of her in a loving person. Hearing produces momentary, mediate knowledge, but meditation produces immediate knowledge of eternal Ātman.[141] In some Advaitists' view, hearing is not the cause of the immediate knowledge of Brahman, since the Śruti says, "Brahman should be intuited by the illumined mind alone". The teachers of the Advaita Vedānta speak of the mind purified by sense-restraint, mind-control and the like as the cause of the vision of Ātman. Śaṁkara has propounded this view in his commentary on the 'Bhagavad Gītā'. Some Advains maintain that hearing is the cause of undoubted mediate knowledge of Brahman. So there is a definite injunction (niyamavidhi) about hearing in the Vedas, which ought to be observed. According to some Advaitists, there is a definite scriptural injunction that "Ātman ought to be seen or intuited." The immediate knowledge of Ātman is stated to be the fruit of hearing. Hearing is not admitted to be the direct cause of the immediate knowledge of Ātman, but to be its cause through the medium of manas, which is the instrument of the immediate knowledge of It. Hearing being of the nature of hypothetical reasoning (tarka) is not intrinsically valid, and cannot independently produce immediate knowledge. Manas is the organ of the immediate knowledge of Ātman. So hearing through the instrumentality of manas can produce the immediate knowledge of It.[142] In some Advaitins' view, mediate knowledge or immediate knowledge of Brahman is not the fruit of hearing the Vedānta, because it is the fruit of scriptural testimony as a pramāṇa, and because hearing is a particular mental mode of the nature of reasoning favourable to the ascertainment of the nature of nondual Brahman. It may be argued that hearing itself is scriptural knowledge qualified by the ascertainment of the import of the Vedānta texts by reasoning, and that the knowledge of Brahman is its fruit. This argument is wrong, since there can be no injuction in regard to knowledge, and because hearing is the mental act of reasoning in the nature of exclusion of the not-self. The knowledge of Brahman is not the result of reasoning either by ascertaining the import of the monistic texts or by removing obstacles to the production of the knowledge of Brahman in a person in the form of illusions and the like, because the knowledge of the import of a monistic text is not admitted to be the cause of scriptural knowledge, because the absence of counteracting conditions is not admitted to be a cause, and because for these reasons they cannot be the media through which hearing can produce the mediate or immediate knowledge of Brahman. Further, if the knowledge of Brahman were produced by reasoning in addition to scriptural testimony, the validity of this knowledge would be extrinsic and due to extraneous causes. But the Advaitins advocate the doctrine of intrinsic validity of knowledge. So there is a definite injunction in regard to hearing, which is in the nature of reasoning conducive to the knowledge of Brahman either by ascertaining the import of a monistic text or by removing blemishes in a person desirous of the knowledge of Brahman in the form of illusions. "The Ātman ought to be seen" This text is not the statement of the fruit of hearing but a mere praise of Ātman as worthy of being intuited. This is the view of Sarvajñātman.[143] In Sureśvara's view, the Śruti "The Ātman ought to be heard" is an injunction as a specific enumeration (parisaṁkhyāna vidhi). It is aimed at preventing a person from indulging in discussing irrelevant matters besides ascertaining the nature of Brahman. "One abiding in Brahman attains to immortality." This Śruti shows that abiding in Brahman is the only means to liberation, and that there is no other means. "Know one Ātman alone, and abandon discussion about other matters." This Śruti prohibits indulgence in discussions of irrelevant matters. A definite injunction or rule in regard to meditation is admitted, for if there were no such rule, a person thinking himself to have done all his duties after acquiring verbal knowledge of scriptural testimony from hearing monistic texts would not make any effort to meditate on Ātman conducive to the immediate knowledge of It, which can terminate the nescience. So a specific rule is possible, which may result in the removal of the nescience. So there is a definite injunction "Ātman ought to be intuited" as well as a specific injunction "The not-self ought not to be perceived."[144] In Vācaspati Miśra's view, reasoning about the nature and knowledge of Brahman is based on the rule of studying the Vedas (adhyayana vidhi), like reasoning about the duties prescribed by the Vedas, because there is no rule in regard to hearing. Reflection and meditation do not depend upon injunctions. Reflection is of the nature of reasoning favourable to the ascertainment of the real nature of the reality. Reasoning is the cause of determining the real nature of its object. Meditation, being in the nature of repetition of the thought of Brahman, is the cause of the clarity of the knowledge of Brahman. Just as there is no injunction in regard to reflection and meditation, so there is no injunction in regard to hearing. Just as reflection and meditation are in the nature of knowledge, so hearing also is in the nature of knowledge. So there is no injunction in regard to hearing. But there is a rule of study of the Vedas.[145]

According to Mahādeva Sarasvatī the thought of the impossibility of the reality of Brahman alone and the contrary thought of the reality of the world are destroyed by hearing, reflection, and meditation. Mahādevānanda Sarasvatī explains his view as follows. The thought of impossibility relating to the pramāṇa is overcome by hearing. The thought of impossibility relating to the object of knowledge is overcome by reflection. The contrary thought is overcome by meditation. When the thought of impossibility and the contrary thought are destroyed by hearing and the like, and when there are no other hindrances, the immediate experience of Brahman in the form "I am Brahman" is produced by the Śruti "That thou art." Vidyāraṇya explains contrary thought as thinking of something as different from its real nature. Thinking of the Self as the mind-body-complex is contrary thought. Thinking of the world as true is contrary thought. These contrary thoughts are overcome by constant reflection on the reality of Brahman alone, and on the falsity of the world appearance.[146]

MEDITATION.—Vidyāraṇya discusses two interesting questions about the nature of meditation and the validity of the immediate knowledge of Brahman produced by it. Meditation is not recollection. Recollection is the exact reproduction of an object perceived in the past due to the revival of the subconscious trace of the past perception. It cannot be made, unmade, or altered by the voluntary effort of a person. Though sometimes a person can voluntarily recollect an abject, his recollection mainly depends upon the object. But meditation is unrestricted constructive imagination of an attribute, existent or nonexistent, in an object perceived or unperceived in the past, and independent of the nature of an object, but dependent on the will of a person. It does not require any means other than a person's mind and volition. Productive imagination cannot be restricted by scripture and by a royal command. But meditation in conformity with scripture produces a particular result declared by it. Scripture regulates the relation between a particular means and a particular end realized by it, which is supersensible. The contention, that meditation prescribed by scripture cannot produce a particular result, if it is not based on a real object, is false, since scripture having inconceivable powers is unchallengeable. The performance of a sacrifice on earth resulting in the transport of a soul to heaven after death is inexplicable. It is objected that meditation depends on apprehension, since it is a series of recollections. This objection is invalid, for meditation is not a series of recollections as shown above. It is objected that meditation is not a means of valid knowledge, and that therefore the immediate knowledge of Brahman generated by it is not valid knowledge. The objection is groundless, since Vedic testimony being the most authoritative pramāṇa produces the valid immediate knowledge of Brahman. Meditation is a subsidiary aid to hearing Vedic texts, though it is not a pramāṇa.[147]

VERBAL KNOWLEDGE AND IMMEDIATE KNOWLEDGE OF BRAHMAN.—The Advaitists hold that the nescience is destroyed by the immediate knowledge of Brahman. It is the intuitive knowledge of the identity of the jīva with Brahman. A mediate false knowledge is destroyed by a mediate true knowledge. An immediate false knowledge is destroyed by an immediate true knowledge. According to some Advaitins, the immediate knowledge is produced by the Vedic sentence "That thou art" or the like; verbal knowledge generates immediate knowledge. According to other Advaitists, the immediate knowledge is produced by manas purified by reflection and meditation. In the earlier Advaitists' view, the immediate knowledge is not due to a particular organ, but due to a particular object of knowledge. The knowledge produced by the sentence "That thou art," which cognizes the identity of the jīva with Brahman, is immediate.[148] According to other Advaitins, immediateness of knowledge is due to a particular organ of knowledge, and not due to a particular object, since a subtle object is perceived by an acute sense-organ, and since it is not perceived by a nonacute sense-organ. Since immediateness of knowledge is due to its being produced by a sense-organ, knowledge produced by a sentence or testimony is not immediate, but the knowledge of Brahman produced by manas purified- by reflection and meditation is immediate. The Śruti says, "Brahman ought to be intuited by the mind alone." The mind is purified by hearing and reflection. When the Śruti speaks of incomprehensibility of Ātman by the mind, it refers to the unpurified mind.[149] Thus hearing, reflection and meditation are the means of achieving knowledge. The Śruti says, "Ātman ought to be seen", "Ātman ought to be heard, reflected and meditated on." Thus it inculcates hearing, reflection and meditation for the intuition of Brahman. Hearing consists in mental activity favourable to the comprehension of nondual Brahman intended by the Vedānta. Reflection consists in mental activity which produces hypothetical reasoning favourable to the removal of all doubts arising from other pramāṇas as to the meaning of the monistic texts. Meditation consists in mental activity favourable to the stable concentration of the mind on Ātman withdrawing it from external objects drawn towards them because of beginningless evil dispositions (vāsanā). Meditation is the direct cause of the immediate knowledge of Brahman. Reflection is the cause of meditation. A person, who has not reflected on an object, is unable to firmly grasp its meaning, and he who is devoid of firm comprehension of an object, is incapable of meditating on it. So reflection is an indispensable condition of meditation. Hearing is the cause of reflection. Without hearing the purport of the Vedānta its meaning cannot be ascertained. In the absence of its ascertainment there is the absence of verbal knowledge. In the absence of verbal knowledge there can be no reflection favourable to the determination of reasonableness or unreasonableness of the reality knowable from the Vedānta. According to some Advaitins all the three—hearing, reflection and meditation—are the causes of the immediate knowledge of Brahman.[150]

According to Prakāśātman hearing is the chief cause of the immediate knowledge of Brahman, and reflection and meditation, which succeed it and assist it in producing the immediate knowledge, are its auxiliary causes. Hearing is the principal cause, and reflection and meditation are the auxitiary causes of the immediate knowledge of Brahman, just as a lump of clay is the principal cause of an earthen vessel, and a wheel and a staff are its auxiliary causes. Prakāśātman says, "The comprehension of a word invested with the power of denoting an object is the immediate cause of the knowledge of its object, since a pramāṇa is the immediate antecedent of the knowledge of its object. But reflection and meditation are the mediate causes of the intuition of Brahman through the mediation of concentration of mind rich with the dispositions of a favourable inclination of the mind towards the Inner Self. So verbal knowledge or hearing is the immediate cause, and reflection and meditation are the mediate causes of the immediate knowledge of Brahman."[151] Prakāśātman avers that reflection and meditation are subordinate to hearing.[152] The repeated hearing of a scriptural monistic text attended with reasoning produces immediate knowledge of Brahman. It is due to the Śruti, which is an authoritative pramāṇa. Hearing culminates in the immediate knowledge, which is valid. Reflection produces fitness of the mind for being concentrated on the identity of the self with Brahman by removing the thought of its impossibility (asambhāvanā). Contemplation or meditation removes the opposite thoughts (viparītabhāvanā) and impressions of the illusion of the self's identity with the mind-body-complex. Hypothetical reasoning (tarka) also is auxiliary to valid knowledge, because it is not certain knowledge, but the thought of the possible and the impossible.[153]

Vidyāraṇya elaborates on Prakāśātman's arguments, and expresses his view emphatically. Though Brahman is self-manifest, hearing scriptural testimony is capable of producing the immediate knowledge of Brahman. It is hindered by the thoughts of impossibility of the identity of the self with Brahman due to sins and by the contrary thoughts of the identity of self with the mind-body-complex. So the immediate knowledge of Brahman does not become firm and steady. Sins are destroyed by the performance of specific duties pertaining to one's order of life. Contrary inclinations of the mind are destroyed by sense-restraint, mind-control, endurance of heat and cold, and the like internal means. Thoughts of impossibility of the identity of the self with Brahman are eliminated by reflection in the form of the hypothetical reasoning (tarka). Opposite thoughts of identity of the self with the mind-body-complex are eliminated by meditation, which generates one-pointedness of mind, and enables it to comprehend subtle objects. Then the immediate knowledge generated by scriptural testimony becomes steady.[154] Brahman is immediate or intuitable. Mediate knowledge of It is not possible. Hearing the Vedānta is the cause of the immediate knowledge of Brahman.[155] So hearing produces immediate knowledge at the outset, which becomes firm after the destruction of hindrances. It is objected that meditation is the principal cause of the immediate knowledge of Brahman, and that hearing and reflection are its auxiliary causes, because the immediate knowledge is produced just after meditation. This objection is unsound, because meditation is not the instrumental cause (karaṇa) of immediate knowledge, and because meditation is not a pramaṇa, which may produce immediate knowledge. But hearing, which is in the nature of comprehension of the denotative power of the words in a scriptural sentence, is the instrumental cause of the immediate knowledge, and reflection and meditation are its subsidiary causes.[156] Reflection eliminates impossibility in regard to the object, and dispels doubts in the mind. Meditation eliminates contrary thoughts, and generates one-pointedness of mind. They remove hindrances, and render assistance to the generation of the immediate knowledge. Thus, according to the Vivaraṇa school, hearing is the principal cause, and reflection and meditation are the auxiliary causes, of the immediate knowledge of Brahman.[157]

According to Vācaspati Miśra hearing a Vedic text generates undoubted knowledge of Brahman, because the Veda is the only pramāṇa in regard to It. Hearing results in certain knowledge of It ultimately.[158] Reflection is reasoning in conformity with the Veda, and not in conflict with it.[159] Just as Brahman cannot be intuited without hearing, so It cannot be intuited without reflection and meditation. Their presence is a means to the intuition, and their absence leads to its absence.[160] Immediate knowledge is a mental mode, which is the intuitive realization of Brahman, which removes the nescience and brings about the revelation of the nature of Brahman. It is the result of hearing a Vedic text, which is a pramāṇa.[161] The mind purified by the residual impressions of meditation on Brahman preceded by hearing and reflection is the instrumental cause (karaṇa) of the immediate experience of Brahman.[162]

But there are no injunctions as to reflection and meditation. Meditation is the cause of the residual impressions, which are capable of producing the immediate experience through the purified mind. The experience of Brahman is a particular mental mode assuming Its form produced by the mind purified by the residual impressions of hearing, reflection and meditation. It is valid since the Veda is a pramāṇa.[163]

OBSTACLES TO LIBERATION.—Mahādeva Sarasvatī mentions three kinds of obstacles to liberation relating to the present, the past, and the future. The obstacles relating to the past are repeated recollections of the objects of enjoyment experienced in the past, which engross the mind. They can be stopped by the constant thought of Brahman limited by them as adjuncts. The adjuncts are false, but Brahman limited by them is true. The obstacles relating to the future are the remnants of prārabdha karmas, which have not yet borne fruits, and desire for happiness in heaven. Prārabdha karmas are of two kinds: those which are motivated by the desire for fruits, and those which are pure. The former are destroyed after producing their fruits. The latter destroy sins, and produce the knowledge of Brahman. Until the remnants of prārabdha karmas are destroyed by appropriate enjoyments and sufferings, hearing and the like cannot produce the knowledge of Brahman. Desire for happiness in heaven is an obstacle to the immediate knowledge of Brahman. The obstacles relating to the present are attachment to objects of enjoyment, dullness of intellect, vain reasoning, and false conceit of one's agency. Mahādeva Sarasvatī mentions the means of counteracting them. Attachment to objects of enjoyment is overcome by sense-restraint, mind-control and the like. Dullness of intellect is overcome by hearing the scripture. Vain reasoning is overcome by reflection. False conceit of one's agency is overcome by meditation.[164]

MEANS TO LIBERATION : WORKS.—The Advaita Vedāntins regard knowledge as the only means of liberation. Śaṁkara's view has already been given in the second volume. Is not the performance of prescribed duties necessary for liberation? According to Vācaspati Miśra and his followers the performance of prescribed duties—sacrifices, charity, and penance—is preparatory to the emergence of knowledge, since it produces the desire to know Brahman (vividiṣā). These duties ought to be performed till this desire is generated. They are the external means. Sense-control, mind-control, etc., are proximate to the emergence of knowledge. The performance of daily obligatory duties and occasional duties in many births produces faith in the attainment of Brahman. But despite the presence of a strong desire to know Brahman there are hindrances to the acquisition of knowledge due to the accumulated sins of many births, which generate strong inclination towards the objects of enjoyment. Knowledge means the saving knowledge of Brahman. So until interest in hearing and the like is produced, prescribed duties ought to be performed after removing obstacles.[165]

According to Prakāśātman and his followers, Vivaraṇa school, the prescribed duties ought to be performed, which purify the mind, until inclination towards the Inner Self in the form of the desire to know Brahman (vividiṣā) arises, then they should be renounced, and then knowledge arises from works and their renunciation.[166] What is the difference between the view that works are necessary for knowledge and the view that works are necessary for the desire to know Brahman? According to the second view, even when works have produced the desire to know Brahman, and when works are renounced, hearing, reflection, and meditation, which are necessary for dispassion for worldly enjoyments ought to be practised under the guidance of competent teachers until knowledge emerges. According to the first view works fulfil their purpose when they generate the strong desire to know Brahman through hearing and the like, and works are not necessary for the emergence of knowledge.[167]

Which works are necessary for knowledge? According to some Advaitins the duties relating to the different stages of life (āśramakarma) are necessary for knowledge. The students acquire knowledge, by studying the Vedas, the householders, by performing sacrifies and charity, the persons retired from the householder's life, by undergoing penances, and the monks, by meditation on Brahman. According to Amalānanda the duties pertaining to stages of life are not necessary for knowledge, but those relating to castes are necessary for it. Prudential duties for the fulfilment of empirical desires result in the attainment of earthly and heavenly happiness. They cannot generate knowledge. It depends upon the performance of daily obligatory duties, for they destroy sins. Knowledge dawns upon a pure mind, free of sins.[168] But, in Sarvajñātman's view, both daily obligatory duties and prudential duties ought to be performed as subsidiary to knowledge.[169] In Sureśvara's view, the Brāhmaṇas, the Kṣattriyas and the Vaiśyas are eligible for knowledge. They perform daily prayer thrice regularly, and are so eligible for knowledge. According to other Advaitins the Śūdras are eligible for the works conducive to knowledge. They should perform japa or mutter God's names, practise charity, and undergo penances to attain knowledge. Sick persons should practise japa, charity and the like for the attainment of knowledge. They are born in higher castes as a result of the performance of these duties, and then engage in hearing and the like to attain knowledge as the higher castes attain gradual release. They attain heaven by the worship of qualified Brahman, and then attain liberation by worshipping unqualified Brahman.[170]

Let the householders perform prescribed works, purify their minds, and acquire knowledge. But how can the ascetics, who have renounced all works, acquire knowledge? According to some Advaitins, sins hindering the emergence of knowledge being innumerable, some are destroyed by the performance of sacrifices, and some are destroyed by merits produced by renunciation of works or asceticism (sannyāsa), and so renunciation also is conducive to knowledge through purification of mind. The householders do not acquire knowledge in this life, but acquire it in a future birth through renunciation of works, and through hearing and the like. Janaka, a house-holder, acquired knowledge because of his renunciation of works in a previous birth. In some Advaitins' view, a Brāhmaṇa ascetic who has acquired knowledge should practise child-like simplicity, erudition in scriptures, and abstention from speaking. Renunciation of works is included in withdrawal of the sense-organs from their objects, which is an inner means to liberation. A person alone who has renounced all works, and who has become a monk, and who is eligible for hearing and the like, can acquire knowledge. So knowledge is produced by the merits born of renunciation of works or asceticism alone. According to other Advaitins, asceticism being a subordinate part of hearing and the like and resulting in knowledge of Brahman, hearing, etc., produce knowledge directly, and there is no need of assuming merits produced by asceticism.[171]

Vidyāraṇya avers that liberation is not accomplishable by works, for it is known by reasoning and from Vedic testimony to be eternal. If the worship of Brahman were a mental act like daily prayer, liberation would be dharma, like heavenly happiness, the fruit of sacrifices, and would be an object of scriptural injunction. Then an embodied soul would enjoy liberation. But the Śruti says, "Good and evil, pleasure and pain, do not touch a disembodied soul". So a disembodied soul achieves liberation. The disembodied state of Self is not an effect of dharma, because it is the natural state of Self. So the disembodied state called liberation, which is different from the fruit of dharma is established as natural and eternal. It cannot be said to be partly an effect of dharma, because, if that were so, liberation would be noneternal, like heavenly happiness. So liberation is not accomplishable by works. If it were so, Brahman would be an object of action. But the Vedic testimony emphatically denies Brahman's being active and an object of action. The Śruti "The knower of Brahman becomes Brahman" shows that the knowledge of Brahman and becoming Brahman occur simultaneously. So the knowledge of Brahman is not an object of action. The Śruti forbids an action intervening between knowing Brahman and becoming Brahman. Becoming all or Brahman does not depend upon any action but upon the immediate knowledge of Brahman. Liberation is known by the knowers of the Vedas from Vedic testimony. It is not noneternal, because it is revealed by the Vedas.[172]

DEVOTION.—Śaṁkara defines worship (upāsana) as approaching the Deity (upa) and sitting (āsana) before Him with continuous thoughts about Him without interruption of dissimilar thoughts. For persons with false conceit of self in the mind-body-complex the worship of unqualified Brahman is extremly difficult. A true devotee is devoid of false conceit of self in the mind-body-complex, and devoid of desires for objects of enjoyment. He is egoless and devoid of enmity. His intellect is fixed on eternal Brahman. He is a true jñānin endowed with the knowledge of the supreme reality. Śaṁkara identifies devotion with the knowledge of Brahman, like a Śaiva of Pratyabhijñā school. The qualities of ascetics, who have destroyed all desires, and who have acquired firm knowledge of the Reality are mentioned by the 'Bhagavad Gītā' as the qualities of true devotees.[173]

Īśvara is Brahman invested with qualities by the intellect infected with the nescience for the sake of worship. He is a phenomenal appearance. He is lower Brahman limited by māyā. The worship of Him with devotion leads to the attainment of Brahmaloka. His grace gives His devotee the power to acquire the knowledge of the unqualified Brahman. Thus devotion brings on gradual release (kramamukti). But knowledge brings about immediate release (sadyomukti). So devotion is inferior to knowledge.[174] Śaṁkara avers that a worshipper of Īśvara, qualified Brahman, easily can make his mind devoid of modes and acts, and can acquire the knowledge of Brahman. Prakāśātman avers that the worship of qualified Brahman purifies the mind so that self-manifest unqualified Brahman may manifest Itself to the purified mind. It enables the mind indirectly to the intuition of the identity of self with Brahman. Śaṁkara admits that the performance of the prescribed duties pertaining to one's caste and order of life, penance and worship of Īśvara with devotion generates detachment, discrimination, sense-restraint, mind-control, withdrawal of the senses from their objects, endurance, faith in scripture and the preceptor, concentration of mind, and desire for emancipation. Madhusūdana also identifies supreme devotion with the immediate experience of Brahman after the Inner Self is experienced.[175]

WORSHIP.—Worship of qualified Brahman consists in meditating on an image of a Deity, muttering a mantra and the like. When the mind is purified by meditation on Brahman, and when a greater power of concentration is acquired by it, an aspirant is enabled to meditate on Brahman unconditioned by an adjunct (avidyā). Meditation on a qualified Deity facilitates meditation on unqualified and unconditioned Brahman. But the intuitive knowledge of Brahman cannot be acquired without hearing, reflection and meditation. The worship of qualified Brahman cannot generate the intuitive knowledge of unqualified Brahman, the substratum of empirical self, and so cannot terminate the nescience. It generates superhuman powers in Brahmaloka. It cannot remove all hindrances to release. It cannot annul the nescience and its effects. But through the grace of Īśvara an aspirant meditates on attributeless Brahman after hearing, reflection and meditation, annuls the nescience and its effects, and realizes his identity with Brahman. He realizes his nature as infinite consciousness and bliss. This is Madhusūdana's view.[176] In Vidyāraṇya's view, the worship of qualified Brahman purifies the mind, and indirectly brings about the intuition of Brahman. It is a means to gradual release (kramamukti) and not to immediate release (sadyomukti). The scripture inculcates the worship of qualified Brahman, for it engenders concentration of mind. But it can be generated by the worship of unqualified Brahman also without that of qualified Brahman or Īśvara.[177]

The worship of unqualified Brahman, in Vidyāraṇya's view, is meditation on "I am Brahman, infinite bliss." Meditation on attributeless Brahman alone ripens and results in indeterminate trance. The 'Māṇḍūkya Upaniṣad' idenifies 'Om' with Brahman. Meditation on 'Om' is often the worship of unqualified Brahman. 'Om' should be meditated on in the heart-cavity as identical with unqualified Brahman. 'Om' is represented as higher Brahman and lower Brahman both. But 'Om' should be meditated on as attributeless Brahman of the nature of infinite being-knowledge-bliss. Greater stress should be laid on infinite bliss as the nature of Brahman. Worship is a mental act of the nature of thinking. Thinking is never without an object. The repetition of the knowledge about unqulified Brahman is worship of It. So long as the knowledge continues to be mediate, it is called worship. When it generates the intuitive experience of unqualified Brahman, it is called knowledge. Knowledge of Brahman is always immediate and intuitive. Worship is thinking attended with the idea of a name, but knowledge is not attended with the idea of a name. Knowledge is the manifestation of the nature of Brahman alone. Thinking of unqualified Brahman, discussing about It with experts, comprehending Its nature, and meditating on It daily constitute the practice of the worship of unqualified Brahman.[178]

THE INTERNAL MEANS TO LIBERATION.—When all hindrances are removed by proper spiritual discipline the following internal means should be practised for the emergence of the immediate experience of Brahman. Mind-control consists in the restraint of the internal organ. Sense-restraint consists in the control of the external sense-organs. Endurance consists in bearing heat and cold, joy and grief, etc. Withdrawal of the external sense-organs from their objects (uparati) consists in renunciation of worldly life. Faith is faith in the preceptor, and in the Vedānta. Concentration is mental concentration on hearing, reflection and meditation. The Śruti says, "After practising mind-control, sense-restraint, renunciation, endurance, and concentration one ought to see Ātman in oneself." These internal means must be practised as the necessary propaedeudic to the immediate experience of Ātman. These are the internal means conducive to it.[179]

KNOWLEDGE.—Govindānanda regards knowledge as the only means to release. He regards liberation as the highest state of perfection incapable of any increase. So its means is the knowledge of the Reality, which is of the same kind. Liberation is nondifferent from Brahman, and, consequently, unchanging. Because it is immutable, it is not attainable through dharma. It is not a result of works, because it is opposed to the fruits of dharma, because it is supersensible, because it is free from grief, and because it is not enjoyable through a body. Works in conformity with dharma are inculcated by Vedic injunctions. But liberation is not produced by a Vedic injunction, because it differs from fruits of enjoined works, like Ātman. It consists in the cessation of the nescience. Its fruit is known, and so not capable of being accomplished by a command. It is the intuitive knowledge of Ātman. It is identical with Brahman, the supreme Reality, and so not accomplishable and not capable of being done under a Vedic prescription. Brahman is neither acceptable nor avoidable. It gives neither pleasure nor pain, and so is not an object of voluntary actions for acquirement of pleasure or avoidance of pain. Brahman is knowledge, and attainable through knowledge alone.[180] Ānandagiri also avers that the knowledge of Brahman, the only ontological reality, which rejects all names and forms and actions, is the means of achieving immortality. So it does not exist in a person, who performs enjoined works, and who is related to works.[181]

Vidyāraṇya shows how knowledge is the only means to liberation. Constant thought of the objects of desire produces attachment to them. Attachment generates a desire for them. When a desire is thwarted, anger arises. Afflictions are generated by desire, anger, greed, delusion and envy. They can be conquered by sense-restraint, mind-control, endurance, concentraion of mind, and meditation on Brahman. Meditation culminates in trance. Trance is at first determinate (ṣavikalpa), and then it becomes indeterminate (nirvikalpa). The former is conscious while the latter is superconscious. Muttering 'Om' for a long period of time destroys passions and thoughts of their objects. When passions are conquered, the mind becomes devoid of modes (vṛtti) and acts. Complete inactivity of mind is called destruction of mind. The certain knowledge, that known objects are not real but false appearances, makes the mind objectless. When the mind becomes objectless and inactive, it is immersed in supreme tranquillity. It is a state of supreme enlightenment (nirvāṇa) and absorption in bliss. The supreme status cannot be attained without renunciation of desires and culture of silence. The mind is distracted by actions, which bring about enjoyments. Its distraction can be conquered by destroying all desires for pleasures and stopping all actions. The sages regard a person whose mind is not at all distracted as identified with Brahman. He not only knows Brahman but becomes Brahman. He realizes his identity with Brahman, and abides in one, infinite consciousness and bliss. He transcends the distinction between the world and jīva, jīva and Īśvara, and Īśvarā and Brahman. This state is embodied release.[182]

Vidyāraṇya mentions two ways of acquiring knowledge : sāṁkhya and yoga. Sāṁkhya consists in hearing assisted by reflection and meditation, which generates knowledge (vidyā). Yoga consists in worship of, or meditation on, unqualified (nirguṇa) Brahman. Meditation on the mystic syllable 'Om' in the heart-cavity results in the intuition of Brahman. Meditation is the means and intuition is the end. 'Om' is unqualified Brahman for meditation. Brahman as infinite truth, knowledge and bliss, essential characteristics, should be meditated on in the form. "I am Brahman, infinite bliss". Such meditation results in the immediate experience of unqualified Brahman. A person, whose sins have been destroyed, quickly experiences Brahman through hearing, reflection and meditation. A person, who meditates on unqualified Brahman as 'Om' in the heart-ether, experiences It later. (Cp. Pāśupata). So the first method is better than the second.[183]

YOGA.—Śaṁkara describes the following eight parts of spiritual discipline. Detachment (vairāgya) is disinclination to objects of enjoyment. Discrimination is distinction between eternal Ātman and noneternal objects of knowledge. Sense-control (dama) is the restraint of the external senses. Mind-control (śama) is the eschewal of desires. Abstention (uparati) is the withdrawal of the senses from their objects. Endurance (tilikṣā) is bearing all sufferings without flinching. Faith (śraddhā) is reverence for scriptures and instructions of a teacher. Concentration (samādhāna) is one-pointedness of mind on a good end. Desire for release (mumuksutva) is firm knowledge about the means to release from bondage. These are mentioned by Śaṁkara as subsidiary means to emancipation.[184]

He mentions fifteen acts as subsidiary to meditation. Sense-control (yama) is the restraint of the sense-organs due to the knowledge that all are Brahman. It should be practised again and again. Moral observance (niyama) is acquirement of supreme delight arising from continuous thought of Brahman and elimination of dissimilar thoughts. Renunciation (tyāga) is rejection of the world appearance as false after knowing its real nature as pure consciousness (cit). Silence (mauna) is absorption in indescribable and incomprensible Brahman. Indescribable Brahman cannot be described. The world appearance is indefinable (anirvacanīya). It is neither real nor unreal. Silence is the real nature of the Self. But mere abstention from speaking is silence for the ignorant. Space (deśa) is what is always pervaded by Brahman, and where no living being ever existed, exists, or will exist. Time (kāla) is one, nondual, integral bliss, which is the source of all creatures. Posture (āsana) is the position of the body which facilitates continuous thinking of Brahman with ease. Fixation on origin (mūlabandha) is concentration of mind on Brahman, the origin of all creatures. It ought to be practised by pursuers of rājayoga. Bodily equipoise (dehasāmya) is the state of the body in which the mind is merged in uniform Brahman. It is not erect posture of the body like a dead tree. Fixed vision (dṛksthiti) is the vision of the world as full of Brahman. It is vision full of knowledge. It is not fixing the eyes on the tip of the nose. Fixed vision is vision fixed on Brahman above the distinction of seer, seen and seeing. Breath-control (prāṇāyāma) is the arrest of all mental modes due to contemplation of all mental modes due to contemplation of all existents, mental and external, as Brahman. Inhalation (pūraka) is the mental mode "I am Brahman." Exhalation (recaka) is the negation of the world appearance. Retention (kumbhaka) is the fixation of the mental mode "I am Brahman". Abstention (pratyāhāra) is the immersion of the mind in Brahman after intuiting It in objects. It should be practised by aspirants after release. Fixation (dhāraṇā) is fixation of mind on Brahman after intuiting It in all objects to which the mind is naturally drawn. Meditation (dhyāna) is the mind abiding with a mental mode "I am Brahman" without an object, which gives supreme delight. Trance (samādhi) is the intuitive experience of Brahman through the mental mode "I am Brahman", which does not undergo any change, and which then disappears. There is manifestation of Brahman without a mental mode. Then an aspirant is fulfilled (siddha), and dispenses with spiritual discipline. His nature becomes Brahman. This state of a self-realized person cannot be comprehended by mind and described by words.[185] Śaṁkara interprets parts of yoga in a monistic sense, like advocates of Pratyabhijñā school of Śaivism.

KUṆḌALINĪYOGA.—The 'Prapañcasāra' is attributed to Śaṁkara. It is a Śākta Tantra. He and his followers were not unaware of kuṇḍalinī yoga. By this yoga we mean concentration of mind at certain centres of mystic consciousness referred to in connection with Pratyabhijñā Śaivism and meditation on Brahman or the Divine. Breath-control and contemplation of spicific letters of alphabet on the petals of the different lotuses or centres (cakra) may be dispensed with as Śrī Aurobindo did. It is a very powerful method of spiritual discipline. But why spiritual powers are awakened by the practice of this method cannot be explained by reason. The scripture is the only authority in regard to supersensible things. The incontrovertible truth is the result of experiments by yogins for centuries in sādhana. Śaṁkara quotes the Śrutis in his commentary on the 'Brahmasūtra'. "Heart-cavity is in the middle of the chest. It is a lotus and the seat of inner ākāśa or Brahman". "It is called the abode of Brahman (brahmapura)". "The controller of all, of the nature of pure consciousness, resides in the internal heart". "The internal heart is Ātman, That is sinless, immortal, devoid of hunger, thirst, and grief, and Whose desire and resolve are truthful". "This Brahman is also attributeless".[186] Śaṁkara avers that a yogin concentrates his mind at the heart after closing all doors of the senses, and ascends through the nerve to the centre of the head, and meditates on Brahman. Ānandagiri avers that brahmanāḍī runs through the spinal cord (suṣumnā), heart, throat, middle of the eyebrows, and forehead to the centre of the head. A yogin's soul attains the highest state after departing through brahmarandhra.[187] Śaṁkara says, "A soul favoured by Brahman residing at the heart meditated on by it acquires identity with Brahman, and departs through a nerve at the centre of the head. It acquires immortality". Vācaspati Miśra says, "The luminous brahmanāḍī rises from the heart, penetrates the root of the palate, reaches the centre of the head, and enters into the solar orb. A soul meditates on Brahman there for a long time, and then departs through the nerve". Govindānanda says, "The nerve called suṣumnā issues from the heart, runs through the right side of the palate, throat, the middle of the nose, and reaches the centre of the head. A soul gathers the solar rays there, and departs through brahmarandhra".[188] Nṛsiṁha Sarasvatī distinctly mentions kuṇḍalinīyoga for the realization of unqualified Brahman. He says, "A yogin should sit with folded legs, press the lower part of his body above the anus, rouse dormant divine power (kuṇḍalinī) coiled and dormant at the basic centre (mūlādhāra) at the root of the spinal cord (suṣumnā), raise it through the abdominal centre (svādhiṣṭhāna), the navel centre (maṇipūra), the heart-centre (anāhata), the throat centre (viśuddha) and the eye-brow centre (ājñā) to the thousand-petalled centre (brahmarandhra) at the top of the head called nirvāṇa. A soul experiences the bliss of the Supreme Soul or Brahman by uniting with It there".[189] Nīlakaṇṭha refers to the basic centre (mūlādhāra), the heart-lotus (hṛdayapuṇḍarīka), the eye-brow centre (ājñācakra), and brahmarandhra, and speaks of the order of conquering the stages of mystic consciousness (bhūmikājayakrama). Evidently, here he refers to the dormant divine power (kuṇḍalinī) being roused, and rising from the basic centre, piercing the higher centres gradually, and uniting with Brahman at the highest centre.[190] So it is evident that the Advaita Vedāntins practised kuṇḍalinīyoga for the realization of qualified Brahman or Supreme Divine Person and attributeless Brahman.

PURE AND IMPURE EMOTIONAL DISPOSITIONS.—A disposition consists in the reception of things desired by a person without firm deliberation of pros and cons. Dispositions are of two kinds: pure and impure. An impure disposition is the cause of birth and death. A pure disposition is the cause of the destruction of birth and death. An impure disposition is fraught with strong nescience and intense egoism. A pure disposition ceases to be a seed of rebirth, and remains as a fried seed in the mind to sustain the present body to wear off prārabdha karmas, because the aspirant has experienced Brahman, the infinite bliss. It is the cause of liberation. A disposition is an emotional disposition or potency. There are many kinds of impure dispositions: a disposition to enjoy bodily pleasures, a disposition to experience happiness on earth and in heaven, and a disposition to study the scriptures. Mahādeva Sarasvatī gives this account of the nature of the different kinds of impure dispositions after Śaṁkara. Mahādevānda Sarasvatī divides śāstravāsanā into three kinds: passion for the study of the scriptures, passion for comprehending their meanings, and passion for performing the acts prescribed by them. They are impure, for they can never be completely satisfied. The knowledge of Reality cannot be acquired merely by studying the scriptures. They are impure for they are hindrances to the acquisition of knowledge. All bodily dispositions are impure, since they are hindrances to the acquisition of knowledge and causes of rebirth. Desires for women, sons and the like are impure. Boast, pride, conceit, anger, cruelty, ignorance and other evil passions are impure dispositions. Mahādeva avers that the practice of attenuation of impure dispositions consists in conquering them by discrimination, discernment of faults, discarding the company of the vicious, and cultivating the opposite pure dispositions. The practice of knowledge consists in deep attachment to the bliss of Brahman for the attenuation of love and hate, consequent on the knowledge of the falsity of the world appearance. The practice of knowledge contributes to the gradual destruction of evil dispositions. Dispositions cease when the Self is known to be detached, when the will-to-be is abandoned, and when the destructibility of the body is firmly impressed on the mind.[191]

KNOWLEDGE OF REALITY, DESTRUCTION OF DISPOSITIONS, AND DESTRUCTION OF MIND.—Mahādeva Sarasvatī opines that the knowledge of the Reality, attenuation of dispositions, and arrest of mental modes or destruction of mind are interdependent on one another. When the knowledge of the Reality has been acquired, dispositions in the form of love and hate are attenuated owing to the absence of external objects. In the absence of the knowledge of the Reality the objects of love and hate continue to exist, and produce dispositions of love and hate. So the knowledge of the Reality is the cause of the gradual destruction of dispositions. So the attenuation of dispositions is the cause of the knowledge of the Reality. When love and hate are attenuated by discrimination, discernment of faults, and opposite dispositions, the knowledge of the Reality dawns upon the purified mind in the form "All this is Ātman, and there is nothing else." In the absence of attenuated dispositions the mind is tainted by love and hate, and inclined towards external objects, and the knowledge of the Reality is not produced owing to the absence of sense-restraint and mind-control, and owing to the nonpractice of hearing, reflection and meditation. So the attenuation of dispositions is the cause of the knowledge of the Reality. They are the causes of each other.

Similarly, the knowledge of the Reality and nonproduction of mental modes (manonāśa) are the causes of each other. When the knowledge of the Reality dawns, the world appearance is known certainly to be false, and so the mind is not attracted towards it, and Ātman being determined to be the only Reality and being incomprehensible by the mind, it does not make any effort to know it, and so the mind ceases to function, and becomes devoid of mental modes. In the absence of the knowledge of the Reality, the knowledge of the truth of the world appearance does not cease, and the mental modes continue to be produced by external objects, and so there can be no cessation of the mind. Thus the cessation of the mind is the cause of the knowledge of the Reality. Again, when the mind ceases, all mental modes regarding plurality cease in the absence of the limiting adjunct (upādhi), and the immediate experience of Brahman emerges. So the cessation of the mind is the cause of the knowledge of the Reality.

Similarly, the attenuation of dispositions and the cessation of the mind are the causes of each other. In the absence of the attenuation of dispositions in the form of love and hate the mind continues to be attracted towards external objects. So there can be no cessation of the mind. But when dispositions are destroyed, mental modes cease to be produced in the absence of their seeds or motives, and the mind ceases to function. Similarly, when the mind ceases to function, mental modes are not produced, and dispositions are destroyed. In the absence of the cessation of the mind, it continues to experience joys and sorrows under the influence of prārabdha karmans, and emotional dispositions of love and hate continually arise in the mind. So the destruction of dispositions and the destruction of the mind are the causes of each other. Hence the destruction of dispositions, the destruction of the mind, and the knowledge of the Reality should be practised simultaneously. Then embodied release is attained.[192]

Those who are eligible for adopting the method prescribed by the Vedas are of two classes: principal and subordinate. The former are those who have worshipped qualified Brahman or God (īśvara), who have discerned the faults of the empirical world appearance, who have acquired detachment, and who are engaged in hearing and the like to acquire the knowledge of the Reality. They can attain the knowledge and embodied release finally by God's grace, since they have acquired concentration of the mind by the practice of yoga. They need not practise attenuation of dispositions and cessation of mental modes. The latter are those who have not worshipped qualified Brahman, who have not practised sense-restraint, mind-control and the like, who are reccently engaged in hearing and the like with a desire to know Brahman. They will acquire the knowledge of Brahman after practising hearing and the like for a long time. But they have to practise attenuation of dispositions and cessation of mental modes, because in the absence of these steps, their knowledge of the Reality cannot destroy their nescience, since they are shaken again and again by their innate desire for enjoyments due to their prārabdha karmas.[193]

Evil dispositions are destroyed by cultivating the opposite good dispositions. Friendship for happy beings, compassion for distressed creatures, joy for virtous persons, and indifference to vicious persons are good dispositions. These should be assiduously cultivated in order to destroy love, hate, envy, pride, malice and other evil passions, and generate tranquillity of mind.[194] The demoniac qualities or vices are destroyed by the godly qualities or virtues. Fearlessness, purity of mind, knowledge of the Self, concentration of mind, charity, sense-restraint, study of the scriptures, penance, simplicity, spiritedness, forgiveness, patience, purity of body and mind, nonkilling, absence of conceit, non-injury, truthfulness, absence of anger, tranquillity of mind, absence of wickedness, compassion for creatures, absence of greed, tenderness, moral discrimination, and steadiness are virtues. Boast, pride, conceit, anger, cruelty, ignorance or moral non-discrimination, lust, greed, delusion, love of power, ambition, insatiable thirst for enjoyments, egotism, physical strength, hate for God, and the like are vices. Vices should be conquered by the cultivation of virtues.[195]

Then the disposition to think of the pure, transcendental consciousness or Brahman alone should be practised. The world appearance of names and forms or phenomena being imagined by nescience in the pure transcendental consciousness, devoid of reality in itself, is manifested, when the being of the consciousness is manifested. "I am Brahman" should be repeatedly meditated on after firmly knowing the world appearance to be false. The disposition to think of the pure transcendental consciousness alone (cinmātravāsanā) is of two kinds : the thought preceded by the recollection of the subject, the object, the sense-organ, and the thought of one pure transcendental consciousness without the recollection of the subject, the object, and the sense-organ. The first takes the form "I think of the world, which is nothing but one pure consciousness". It results in conscious trance (śamprajñāta samādhi). The second takes the form "I am one pure consciousness" without the distinction of the subject, the object, and the sense-organ. It results in superconscious trance (asamprajñāta samādhi). When the disposition to think of one pure consciousness is repeatedly practised and firmly established, all evil dispositions are destroyed. This is called the practice of the destruction of dispositions.[196]

DESTRUCTION OF MIND.—The mind is composed of sattva, rajas and tamas. Sattva produces pleasure. Rajas produces pain, for it is restlessness. Tamas produces delusion. Lust, anger, greed, delusion, pride, envy, etc., are modifications of sattva, rajas, and tamas of the mind. They are mental modes. The mind agitated by the mental modes becomes gross and unfit for the intuition of Ātman. So the process of making it subtle by arresting the mental modes is called the destruction of the mind (manonāśa). The means to it are the acquisition of the knowledge of Brahman, keeping the company of the saints, destruction of dispositions, and the practice of yoga. All mental modes are restrained by the practice of breath-control, since the arousal of mental modes depends upon the operation of vital forces. Naturally the Self identifies itself with external objects, and so the mind is modified into the form of the not-self. But when these mental modes in the form of external objects are arrested by the practice of meditation on the Self, the mind is modified into the form of the Self. The mental modes are arrested by practice, detachment, and concentration of mind, and meditation on the Self results in trance. Trance is of two kinds : conscious and superconscious. Conscious trance is a stream of cognitions of one pure consciousness alone without thought of the thinker, the object of thought, and the mind. It is the result of the intense practice of meditation. Restraints, moral observances, bodily posture, breath-control, and withdrawal of the sense-organs from their objects are the external means of conscious trance. Fixation of the mind at the six centres of mystic consciousness in the body on the Inner Self (pratyagātman) alone, meditation or continuous stream of the thought of the Inner Self, and trance are the internal means of conscious trance. Meditation consists in a stream of cognitions of the Inner Self unmediated by dissimilar thoughts. Trance consists in a stream of cognitions of the Inner Self uninterrupted by dissimilar thoughts. Trance is of two kinds described already.[197] When the external means are firmly established, the internal means should be practised. The repeated muttering (japa) of the mystic syllable 'Om' attended with the thought of its meaning or Brahman facilitates the achievement of trance. It is the abbreviation of 'so'ham' or "I am He" or Brahman. The practice of arrest of mental modes and knowledge or discrimination are the two means of destruction of the mind. Thus the knowledge of the Reality, the destruction of dispositions, and the destruction of the mind repeatedly practised lead to embodied ralease.[198]

There are the following obstacles to the achievement of conscious trance : mergence, distraction, taint, and relish. Mergence is sleep. Distraction is repeated recollection of the objects of enjoyment. Taint is stupefaction of the mind by love, hate and the like. Relish is the enjoyment of determinate bliss in the initial stage of trance. In sleep rouse the mind to consciousness by breath-control. Control the distracted mind by discerning the faults of the objects of distraction and by fixing the mind on Brahman. Conquer the stupefied mind by knowing the motives. Do not allow the mind fixed on Brahman to be diverted by hostile emotions. Abstain from relishing the determinate bliss of meditation, and become detached by cultivating supreme wisom (prajñā) or higher knowledge of Brahman. When the mind becomes tranquil by the practice of conscious trance unhindered by obstacles, supreme wisdom replete with truth (ṛtambharā prajñā) emerges.[199] It is yogic perception of the past, future, remote, hidden, and subtle objects. The restraint of conscious trance being repeatedly practised generates supreme dispassion for objects composed of sattva, rajas and tamas. Even after complete detachment is achieved the practice of trance should be continued. When all mental modes are arrested, superconscious trance is achieved. It is achieved by supreme detachment and meditation on God. Brahman is immediately experienced by the mind rendered subtle by the practice of superconscious trance.[200]

WHAT TERMINATES THE NESCIENCE.—Some Advaitists maintain that the knowledge of identity of a soul with Brahman produced by a scriptural monistic text like "That thou art" terminates the causal nescience (mūlājñāna), because the latter is the object of the former, and because the latter is not the object of the universal consciousness in its nature (caitanyasvarūpa). If the causal nescience were not terminated by the knowledge of identity of a soul with Brahman, it would be terminated by the knowledge of a jar. The knowledge of identity of a soul with Brahman alone terminates the causal nescience. So the knowledge of a jar, which is not the knowledge of identity of a soul with Brahman, does not terminate the causal nescience.[201] The identity of a soul with Brahman is not an entity additional to the universal consciousness. If it were so, it would contradict monism. If the identity of a soul with Brahman were not real, the Vedānta text "That thou art" would not convey the ontological reality of Brahman alone. If mere consciousness were the identity, the knowledge of a jar or the like also would cognize it. The knowledge of Brahman is not admitted to cognize any relation called identity between a soul and Brahman. So in the sentence "That thou art" the subject and the predicate convey the same meaning, or denote the same reality—Brahman.[202] It is objected that the knowledge of Brahman also, like the knowledge of a jar or the like, does not terminate the causal nescience, because an effect is found to coexist with its material cause in the world. Appyaya Dīkṣita urges that, though no opposition between an effect and a material cause is found elsewhere, there is opposition between ignorance and knowledge of the same object, and that sometimes opposition between an effect (e.g., the burning of a cloth) and a cause (e.g., conjunction of the cloth with a fire) is found. Hence the immediate knowledge of Brahman produced by hearing a monistic Śruti terminates the causal nescience.[203]

THE CESSATION OF NESCIENCE.—Sureśvara opines that the true knowledge of Ātman terminates the nescience, and that the cessation of the nescience (avidyā nivṛtti) is liberation [204] Ānandabodha discusses the nature of the cessation of the nescience. It is either true or false. In the first alternative, it is either Ātman Itself or an entity different from It. If it is Ātman Itself, the cessation of the nescience is eternal. The beginningless Ātman cannot cease. Cessation is preceded by a being which has cessation. If it is so, then Ātman cannot be beginningless. The cessation of the nescience is brought about by true knowledge (vidyā). Then the cessation of the nescience cannot be identical with Ātman, because, if that were so, Ātman would be brought about. If this be admitted, Ātman cannot be the abode of the nescience from the beginningless time. The nescience also is admitted to be beginningless. If the second alternative be true, monism is abandoned and dualism is admitted. Citsukha urges that if Ātman has a beginning, It cannot be the abode of the beginningless nescience, or that the nescience has an origin.[205] Ānandabodha asks the opponent the meaning of falsity. If it means indefinability, it does not differ from the nescience and its effects. If it is an effect of the nescience, its cause, the nescience, being unsettled, liberation cannot be achieved. The nescience itself being the cessation of the nescience is inconceivable. If falsity be said to be nonbeing, then what is absolutely nonexistent (tuccha) cannot be a cause and have causal operation. If falsity be distinct from absolute nonexistence and be of the nature of negation (abhāva), then it is definable, and amounts to dualism, and leads to nonattainment of release. The negation of a being is its cessation, and the negation of a nonbeing is a positive entity.[206] The nescience cannot be either being or nonbeing, since it is admitted to be indefinable. Nor is the cessation of the nescience either being or nonbeing. Nor is it known to be another kind of cessation; nor can it be imagined to be so. If the cessation of the nescience be said to be a false positive entity, it is real, like Ātman. So emancipation is not the cessation of the nescience. But it is known to be so. Its nature cannot be determined by various determinate concepts. For this reason the cessation of the nescience is indefinable, like illusory silver in a nacre. This doctrine does not contradict the doctrine of monism or make the achievement of liberation impossible, because the cessation of the nescience is not admitted to be of the nature of being, because it is indefinable, and because its stuff is nonnescience.[207] The opponent asks how the absence of the indefinable nescience can be brought about. What is neither existent nor nonexistent is indefinable. This is the distinctive mark of the indefinable. So the cessation of the nescience is indefinable.[208] The distinctive mark of the indefinable is very extensive.

Some Advaitists opine that the Supreme Ātman Itself is the cessation of the nescience. A sage says, "Ātman Itself is the cessation of the nescience".[209] Ānandabodha rejects this view. If it were true, there would be eternal cessation of the nescience, or Ātman would have a beginning as stated above. The Vedas do not assert that Ātman Itself is the cessation of the nescience. Other Advaitists opine that the doctrine of indefinability of the cessation of the nescience is vitiated by the following difficulties. Both the nescience and the cessation of the nescience being indefinable, one becomes the other; the cessation of the nescience becomes the nescience. Because the nescience continues, release cannot be achieved. Ānandabodha urges that indefinability of the cessation of the nescience is not vitiated by the aforesaid difficulty, because though the nescience and its cessation both are indefinable, indefinability has no natural obstacle to it while the cessation of the nescience is limited by the condition that it has no other cessation.[210] If the cessation of the nescience had a cessation, it would give rise to infinite regress. The objection, that if the indefinable nescience had cessation, its noncessation would be real, like Ātman, is unsound, since Ātman cannot cease inasmuch as It exists by nature. Hence the indefinable being characterized as different from the existent and the nonexistent, all difficulties are obviated.[211] But if the indefinable be characterized as sublatable (bādhyatva), then the cessation of the nescience cannot be sublated. But the Advaitists do not admit this characteristic of the indefinable. Some scholars opine that Ānandabodha was a pupil of Vimuktātman. So probably he borrowed his doctrine from his teacher. In Vimuktātman's view, the cessation of the nescience is neither real nor unreal nor both nor indescribable but something of the fifth kind.[212]

Citsukha gives the following account of the cessation of the nescience. It is not real, because, if it were so, it would be an entity in addition to Ātman, and this view would contradict monism. If the cessation of avidyā were not distinct from Ātman, it would be of the nature of Ātman, and would always exist, and so there would be no experience of bondage and suffering. If the cessation of avidyā were of the nature of Ātman, Ātman would not exist before the cessation of avidyā, because It would be produced by avidyā, and therefore avidyā would be independent. Nor is the cessation of avidyā unreal, because, if it were so, it would be absolutely nonexistent, like a hare's horn, and would not be generated by the true knowledge of Brahman. If the cessation of avidyā were nonexistent, it would be describable, and this view would be dualism. If it were indescribable, its cause would exist, and liberation would not be achieved. The nonexistence of an existent entity is its cessation, and the existence of a nonexistent entity is its cessation. But the nonexistence of avidyā, which is neither existent nor nonexistent, cannot be its cessation.[213] Nor is the cessation of avidyā indescribable, because, if it were so, avidyā would be its effect, and its effect would be avidyā in that both are indescribable. Ānandabodha opines that the cessation of avidyā has no cessation, and that therefore its indescribability is different from that of avidyā. If the cessation of avidyā had cessation, there would be infinite regress. If destruction had destruction, there would be an infinite series of destructions, and the Śruti asserting nonreturn of a released soul would be contradicted, because the cessation of the cessation of avidyā is the re-emergence of avidyā. Hence if the cessation of avidyā be indefinable, avidyā will be its effect, and its effect will be avidyā. Nor is the cessation of avidyā of a fifth kind, because it is indescribable inasmuch as it is different from the existent and the nonexistent, and inasmuch as what is neither existent nor nonexistent is admitted to be indescribable.[214] Nor is the cessation of avidyā Ātman Itself, as Maṇḍana Miśra opines, because, if it were so, it would be eternal, like Ātman, and there would be no bondage, and Ātman, like the cessation of avidyā, would be generated by the true knowledge of Reality as shown already.[215] It is contended that Ātman as known is the cessation of avidyā, and that Ātman by its nature is not so. This contention is false, because knowledge being an attributive (viśeṣaṇa) of Ātman, and being eternal, an internal organ would exist in the state of release also, because the knowledge of Brahman is acquired through a mental mode, a modification of the internal organ. If the cessation of avidyā were noneternal, release also would be noneternal. So the cessation of avidyā is not explained. Citsukha defines the cessation of avidyā with its effects—the world appearance including the mind-body-complex—as Brahman characterized by truth, knowledge, bliss, infinitude and nonduality opposed to duality characterized by falsity, insentience, pain and not-self, reflected in a mental mode identified with the from of Brahman produced by hearing a monistic Śruti. Hence Ātman as known by a soul, that has achieved the immediate knowledge of It is the cessation of avidyā with its effects.[216] So the known Ātman is the cessation of avidyā with its effects.[217]

Appyaya Dīkṣita gives the following account of the cessation of avidyā. He discusses the views of Maṇḍana Miśra and Ānandabodha, and then states his own view. The cessation of avidyā is indescribable, since it is the modification of an entity at the moment just after the emergence of the immediate experience of Brahman superimposed on Ātman, like a jar, which has indescribable production, existence and destruction. So the cessation of avidyā being indescribable is flawless.[218] It does not continue in the state of release, for it is momentary. It is objected that, the cessation of avidyā being momentary, liberation cannot be stable. The objection is unfounded, because the cessation of avidyā itself is not the highest good. It is generated by the knowledge of Brahman, because it is different from happiness and misery. Avidyā is the cause of all evil, because it veils the infinite bliss of Brahman. When avidyā is destroyed, the infinite bliss is manifested. When it is manifested, the misery of bondage is destroyed. The knowledge of Reality is the means to the realization of the highest good.[219] The destruction of the sufferings due to bondage, like the cessation of avidyā, is not the highest good, but the achievement of the infinite bliss of Brahman is the supreme end in itself in the state of release. It is beatitude.[220]

Raṅgojī Bhaṭṭa gives the following account of the cessation of avidyā. It is either of the nature of Ātman, its abode, or additional to It. It is objected that, if it is of the nature of Ātman, it cannot be produced by the knowledge of Reality, for Ātman is eternal. The objection is unsound, because the prior nonexistence of a future obstacle, which is beginningless, is produced by the utterance of God's name, because the prior negation of future sufferings is produced by atonement, and because, according to the Mādhva, the manifestation of bliss, which is essential to the self, is produced by the grace of God. Similarly, the cessation of avidyā, which is beginningless, can be destroyed by the knowledge of Reality, even as the prior negation of a jar is destroyed by a potter, clay, a wheel, a staff and the like. In the absence of the knowledge of Reality there is the absence of the cessation of avidyā. So beginningless avidyā is destroyed by the knowledge of Reality. Or, the cessation of avidyā is distinct from Ātman, and real. The Śruti "There is no plurality here" means that the destruction of, plurality due to avidyā, or of avidyā, is not false. This view does not overthrow monism, because monism admits the reality of one positive being. But the cessation of avidyā is not a positive entity (bhāva).[221] It is contended that the cessation of avidyā is false, because it is seen or known (dṛśya). This contention is false, since a known positive entity is pervaded by falsity, but because the cessation of avidyā is not a positive entity.[222] So the cessation of avidyā is distinct from the abode of avidyā.[223] Some Advaitins hold that the cessation of avidyā is its essencelessness, and that it can be brought about by the knowledge of Reality.[224] It is objected that essencelessness is either destruction or distinct from it. It is not destruction, because this alternative is not different from what has already been refuted. Nor is it distinct from destruction, because it cannot be determined. This objection is groundless, since the opponent also, who does not admit the falsity of the world appearance, must admit essencelessness to be distinct from destruction.[225] If it were not distinct from destruction, there would be the perception of a jar even after its destruction. It is contended that a jar is not perceived, for it is destroyed. The contention is false, since, in that case, after the destruction of a jar some other entity is produced. But it does not account for the nonperception of a jar. It is contended that a jar does not exist at the time, and that, therefore, it is not perceived. What is the meaning of the statement "a jar does not exist"? It means either that its essencelessness is produced, or that its destruction is produced. In the first alternative, the opponent admits essencelessness. In the second alternative, the production of another entity called the destruction of a jar cannot account for the nonperception of the jar. The production of one entity cannot explain the nonperception of another entity. The production of a jar cannot explain the nonperception of a staff. It is contended that the destruction of a jar is an obstacle to the perception of a jar. Then the destruction of a jar is an obstacle to the perception of an existing jar or to that of a nonexisting jar. The first alternative is untenable, because at the time of the destruction of a jar its counterentity, a jar, cannot exist. The second alternative also is not justified, because the nonexistence of an entity distinct from essencelessness is indeterminable. So the opponent must admit that an entity is destroyed by becoming essenceless, and that there is no entity distinct from it, called destruction.[226] Essencelessness is unreality of essence (svarūpa). Avidyā can be destroyed by the knowledge of Reality. Brahman is absolute reality. So the immediate knowledge of Brahman destroys avidyā, and Brahman alone, the absolute reality, remains.[227]

Prakāśānanda discusses the nature of the cessation of avidyā as follows. The opponent contends that it is either destruction of avidyā, or produced by knowledge, or another entity, or the nature of Ātman, and shows that it is none of them. The cessation of avidyā is not like the destruction of a jar by the blow of a club. If the second alternative were true, the destruction of an antecedent knowledge by a succeeding knowledge would be the cessation of avidyā. It is not the destruction of all knowledge, for the immediate knowledge of Brahman is not destroyed. It is neither another entity nor the nature of Ātman for reasons stated above. Hence the annulment of avidyā not being determined, liberation cannot be achieved by terminating avidyā and its effects. Prakāśānanda refutes these objections. Sublation (bādha) is certain knowledge of the nonexistence of the world appearance superimposed on Brahman just after the immediate knowledge of its substratum —Brahman. Sublation is the certain knowledge that the world appearance did not exist in the past, does not exist at present, and will not exist in future. It is proved by a released soul's experience. Sureśvara gives this definition of sublation.[228]

The opponent raises an objection. Avidyā is annulled by vidyā because of opposition between them. Opposition is either the absence of co-existence at the same time, or the absence of co-existence in the same locus, or the nature of destroyer and destroyed, or the nature of being and nonbeing. The first alternative is untenable, for vidyā co-exists with avidyā at the same time in that vidyā destroys avidyā; otherwise, vidyā would be needless. The second alternative is unjustified, since there is no opposition between my avidyā and your vidyā, and since they must exist in the same soul. In the third alternative, the nature of destroyer and destroyed should be determined. If the annulment of avidyā be its destruction, destruction is either an entity different from avidyā, which is to be destroyed, or its attribute. If it be a different entity, it is not related to avidyā, and so there cannot be destruction of avidyā. If it be an attribute of avidyā, it will continue avidyā, its substratum. Otherwise, it will cease to be an attribute of avidyā, for an attribute cannot exist without a substratum. Thus in the third alternative vidyā will continue avidyā, and there will be no opposition between them. The fourth alternative is untenable, because both vidyā and avidyā are positive in nature (bhāvarūpa), and because avidyā has no prior nonexistence in that it is beginningless. Otherwise, they would not coexist at the same time. So the nature of opposition between them being not determined, vidyā cannot annul avidyā. If vidyā annul avidyā without any opposition between them, avidyā may as well annul vidyā.

To this objection Prakāśānanda replies that vidyā overpowers and annuls avidyā (upamardaka), and that avidyā is overpowered and annulled (upamardya) by vidyā. They are opposed to each other, like light and darkness.[229] This is their nature. It is irreversible. Avidyā cannot overpower and annul vidyā. If avidyā were not annulled by vidyā, vidyā would never be generated. The difficulties about destroyer and destroyed do not arise, because after vidyā is generated, avidyā is annulled at once. Ānandajñāna also opines that the knowledge of differenceless Brahman overpowers the knowledge of the empirical self as a knower, agent and enjoyer, which are opposed to each other.[230]

SENTIENT PLEASURE AND BLISS OF BRAHMAN.—Vimuktātman opines that Ātman is of the nature of bliss. Ātman is infinite, and so Its bliss is infinite. Ātman is identical with infinite bliss. There is no conflict between identity and bliss. The knowledge of difference between Brahman or Ātman and bliss is false.[231] Bliss is eternal. It is of the nature of unchanging Ātman. Infinite and eternal bliss of Ātman appears to be various, noneternal, impure pleasures of sensible objects through mental modes, which are effects of avidyā. In a pure mental mode the pure Ātman of the nature of bliss is reflected, but in an impure mental mode It is not reflected, or It is imperfectly reflected as impure pleausre. Purity of pleasure depends upon the purity of mind. Degrees of purity of pleasure depend upon degrees of purity of mind, the reflecting medium, although the bliss of Ātman is one, uniform, and universal.[232] Degrees of purity of pleasure depend upon degrees of desirelessness or absence of desire for sentient pleasure. If Ātman were not of the nature of bliss, liberation would not be the supreme end of life, because it is devoid of pleasure. Ātman is supreme bliss ; other objects are pleasant for the sake of Ātman. Pleasure is not a means to any other end, but all objects are means to pleasure.[233] Ātman is dear to one for Ātman Itself, but all objects are dear to one for the sake of Ātman. So Ātman Itself is bliss. Its being of the nature of bliss is undeniable on the strength of scriptural testimony, reasoning and experience. The experience of Ātman is replete with plenitude of bliss.[234]

Vidyāraṇya distinguishes between sentient pleasure and bliss of Brahman. The sentient pleasure of objects (viṣayānanda) is an infinitesimal particle of the infinite bliss of Brahman. The Śruti says, "The creatures enjoy a particle of Brahman's infinite bliss". Mental modes are calm (śānta), restless (ghora) and deluded (mūḍha). Detachment, forgiveness, generosity and the like are calm mental modes. Craving, affection, love, hate, greed and the like are restless mental modes. Delusion, fear and the like are deluded mental modes. Brahman's nature of consciousness is reflected in all mental modes. Brahman's consciousness and bliss are manifested in calm mental modes. Brahman's bliss is not reflected in restless and deluded mental modes because of their impurities. But Brahman's consciousness is manifested in all mental modes because of their slight transparence. Both consciousness and bliss of Brahman are reflected in calm mental modes because of their greater transparence. Rajas predominates in restless mental modes, which prevents Brahman's bliss from being reflected in them. Pain arises from fear lest the desire for a particular object should not be fulfilled. If the desire is not gratified, hate and anger arise, which prevent pleasure from arising. If hate and anger are not satisfied, pain arises. Anger, greed, hatred and the like cause great pain. Not the least pleasure can arise from them. If a desired object is attained, joy arises, which is a calm mental mode. Great pleasure arises from the enjoyment of a desired object. The greatest happiness arises from aversion to all objects of enjoyment. It is called the happiness of wisdom (vidyānanda). Forgiveness, generosity, conquest of anger and greed, and the like generate great happiness due to the reflection of Brahman's bliss in calm mental modes. Being, consciousness and bliss are the characteristics of Brahman. Its being alone is manifested in insentient things. Its being and consciousness are manifested in restless and deluded mental modes. Its being, consciousness and bliss are manifested in calm mental modes. This state is called the knowledge of mixed Brahman or Brahman with phenomena. The knowledge of pure, unmixed Brahman arises from the cultivation of knowledge and yoga prescribed by the Advaita scripture. The pain in restless and deluded mental modes is due to māyā. The happiness in calm mental modes is the knowledge of mixed Brahman, since the sattva of māyā produces the reflection of Its bliss in them. Being alone in insentient things should be meditated on, discarding their phenomenal appearances. Being and consciousness alone should be meditated on in restless and calm mental modes, discarding pain in them. Being, consciousness and bliss should be meditated on in calm mental modes. A person who is not eligible for meditation on unqualified Brahman should meditate on mixed Brahman. So the nature of the pleasure of objects is discussed to induce an aspirant to meditate on mixed Brahman. Meditation on mixed Brahman generates indifference to three kinds of meditation on mental modes. Then meditation on Brahman without mental modes, called happiness of pure dispositions (vāsanānanda), should be practised. Mental concentration being acquired by meditation, the knowledge of Brahman becomes firm. It becomes identical with the infinite, undivided, complete bliss of Brahman (akhaṇḍaikarasa). No difference arises in the integral bliss of Brahman because of the absence of limiting adjuncts. When the differentiating adjuncts are destroyed by yoga and discrimination, the self-luminous, unconditioned, nondual Brahman is manifested without the distinction of the enjoyer, the enjoyed, and the experience of bliss. This undifferentiated state is called the bliss of infinitude (bhūmānanda). Dharmarājādhvarīndra recognizes two kinds of pleasure : relative and absolute. Sentient pleasure produced by objects through the sense-organs is relative and limited. The highest pleasure or bliss is the supreme bliss of Brahman—the supreme end.[235]

THE BLISS OF BRAHMAN IS ATTAINABLE.—According to the Advaita Vedānta the infinite bliss of Brahman is attainable. It is objected that the infinite bliss of Brahman is innate in the Inner Self, and so eternally achieved. Some Advaitins reply that though the infinite bliss of Brahman is eternally achieved, it is veiled by avidyā and made, as if it were nonexistent, in the state of bondage, and that, consequently, a bound soul feels unfulfilled. When its nescience is annulled, its power of projecting the world appearance including the mind-body-complex is destroyed, and a soul realizes its innate infinite bliss, as a person recovers a gold necklace already round his neck. Other Advaitists reply that the imaginary absence of the infinite bliss of Brahman from a bound soul due to avidyā continues until it is destroyed. When avidyā is destroyed, the imaginary absence of the bliss of Brahman is destroyed, and at the next moment the bliss of Brahman is realized by a released soul.[236] Other Advaitists opine that the infinite bliss of Brahman exists in a bound soul, but that it is not experienced in the state of bondage, and that what is not knowable cannot be the end of our voluntary actions. So the infinite bliss of Brahman is not the supreme end. The infinite bliss of Brahman cannot be said to be immediately experienced by a soul's essential knowledge (svarūpajñāna) in the state of bondage. The infinite bliss of Brahman being always nondifferent from a soul's essential bliss, it is not immediately experienced by a knowledge through a mental mode (vṛttijñāna) invested with the form of Brahman even in the state of release. Mere nondifference of an object-consciousness with a knower's consciousness is not immediate experience. If it were so, when consciousness limited by a jar was manifested, its odour also would be immediately experienced. But a jar-consciousness being identified with a knower's consciousness through the consciousness limited by a mental mode, the odour of the jar also would be immediately experienced, because it is identified with the jar-consciousness. But the identity of an object-consciousness not veiled by a nescience with a knower's consciousness is immediate experience.[237] When the veil of a jar-consciousness by the nescience of a jar is removed by a mental mode (vṛtti) assuming its form, and when the jar-consciousness (viṣayacaitanya) is identified with a knower's consciousness (pramātṛcaitanya) through the consciousness limited by the mental mode (pramāṇacaitanya), there is the immediate experience of the jar. (Chapter X). Similarly, the immediate bliss of Brahman innate in a soul is veiled by avidyā in the state of bondage, and, consequently, is not immediately experienced. When the veil of avidyā is destroyed by the knowledge of Brahman in the state of release, the innate bliss of Brahman is immediately experienced by a soul, and it becomes Brahman. So the immediate experience of the highest bliss, the supreme end, is attainable through true knowledge (vidyā).[238] Other Advaitists hold that the identity of an object-consciousness with the knower's consciousness favourable to empirical use is immediate experience as explained above. Yet there is no immediate experience of the infinite bliss innate in a soul, as there is no immediate experience of another person's consciousness in the state of bondage, because the difference between a soul's bliss and Brahman's bliss, like the difference between a soul and Brahman, is superimposed on Ātman by the nescience (ajñāna). When the nescience is destroyed by vidyā, illusory difference between them is destroyed, and the infinite bliss of Brahman is immediately experienced.[239]

THE KNOWER OF ĀTMAN IS DEVOID OF PRAVṚTTI AND NIVṚTTI.—Sureśvara avers that a person, who has achieved the knowledge of Ātman, is neither engaged in actions for the acquirement of pleasure (pravṛtti), nor abstains from worldly enjoyments (nivṛtti), because he has transcended the knowledge of difference, and is established in the knowledge of identity of Ātman.[240] He discarded external objects of enjoyment and refrained from all actions prompted by love and hatred, and from negative actions of renunciation to achieve the saving knowledge of Ātman. True knowledge of Ātman negates pravṛtti and nivṛtti both. Pravṛtti is positive action for sentient pleasures. Nivṛtti is negative action of renunciation of enjoyment. Avidyā is annulled by vidyā. Vidyā is true knowledge of Ātman. Once produced, it destroys all knowledge of difference involved in enjoyment and renunciation. It is objected that the knowledge of Ātman cannot destroy the merits and demerits due to actions done in the past births and the present birth, and to be done in the future births, because avidyā produces time, space and causes, which are endless, because the knowledge of Ātman, the witness of all time, space and causes, is not yet produced, and because all nescience is not destroyed. Sureśvara replies that the objection is groundless, since the true knowledge of Ātman destroys the nescience and its effects completely, and since one, who has achieved this knowledge, has no duties to perform.[241]

Some Advaita Vedāntins believe in embodied release. They opine that a person, who has achieved the immediate knowledge of Ātman, and destroyed his nescience completely, does not discard actions, as a person, who has acquired the true knowledge of a rope, which appeared to be a serpent, does not cease to tremble owing to fear. His nescience, the root of his bondage, being destroyed, he practises renunciation so long as his body lasts. A person, who has acquired the immediate knowledge of Ātman (jñānin), is incapable of committing sins. Vice produces ignorance, which produces immoral actions. A jñānin's ignorance has been destroyed; so he cannot commit prohibited actions. Nor does he perform prescribed actions, since he has no desire for virtue. Even a person desirous of release does not perform actions as he pleases, not to speak of a liberated person. One, who has renounced desires for happiness here and hereafter, who is desirous of release, cannot engage in actions for sentient pleasures. One who is oppressed with hunger never desires to take poison. Similarly, one who is an aspirant for liberation never commits immoral actions. Attachment to pleasure, an effect of ignorance, arises in the state of the acts of mind. But when ignorance is destroyed, and when the mind becomes desireless and inactive, there can be no action for the fulfilment of desires for pleasures. A jñānin's mind is turned towards Ātman and completely withdrawn from the external objects of enjoyment; so he abstains from vices spontaneously, and does not exert any effort for doing so.[242]

It is objected that a person, who has achieved the immediate experience of Brahman, does whatever he pleases, because he is not subject to the injunctions of the Vedas. To this objection Prakāśātman replies that actions are motivated by the acquirement of good and avoidance of evil, but that a knower of Brahman, who has experienced the infinite bliss of Ātman, which destroys all evil, is not motivated by the aforesaid ends, and that so he cannot act as he pleases. He has no attachment and aversion, because they have been destroyed by the knowledge of Brahman. Prārabdha karmas are exhausted by producing their fruits. So a released person cannot act as he pleases.[243]

WHAT DESTROYS THE MENTAL MODE WITH THE FORM OF BRAHMAN.—The immediate knowledge of Brahman is a mental mode, which assumes Its form. It is knowledge through a mental mode (vṛttijñāna). It terminates the causal nescience. But what terminates this last mental mode? It is objected that there is nothing to destroy it. Some Advaitins hold that the immediate knowledge of Brahman through a mental mode, which is a product of avidyā, superimposed on Brahman destroys all appearances of empirical entities superimposed on It, and then destroys itself, as dust in conjunction with water destroys all other dust, and then destroys itself.[244] Other Advaitins opine that the immediate knowledge of Brahman through a mental mode destroys the causal nescience, and then destroys itself, even as water poured on red-hot iron destroys its heat, and then itself. Others cite the example of a heap of dry grass burnt by a fire; it destroys a heap of dry grass, and then itself. Other Advaitists opine that the immediate knowledge of Brahman through a mental mode cannot terminate the causal nescience and its effect—the world appearance, because the nescience is always destroyed by knowledge or manifestation, and because it cannot be destroyed by a mental mode, which is insentient. The means is insentient; so a mental mode is insentient. It cannot destroy nescience or ignorance. But consciousness intelligizing a mental mode destroys nescience. So consciousness intelligizing the last mental mode, which assumes the form of Brahman, destroys the nescience. The universal consciousness is the witness of the causal nescience by its nature, but cannot destroy it. But when it intelligizes the mental mode invested with the form of Brahman, and when it is manifested by the mental mode, it destroys the root nescience.[245] The universal consciousness manifested by the last mental mode as the highest state of trance destroys the world appearance, effect of the root nescience, and then the nescience itself.[246] So the destruction of the last mental mode is not inexplicable. Other Advaitins hold that the knowledge of Brahman destroys the root nescience itself, since knowledge and nescience are directly opposed to each other.[247] The world appearance is destroyed, when its material cause, the root nescience, is destroyed. The knowledge of Brahman through a mental mode (vṛttijñāna) is included in the world appearance, because it is insentient. It may be contended that the world appearance cannot be proved to be false, if it is not directly destroyed by the knowledge of Brahman. The contention is invalid, because the falsity of the world consists in its being directly or indirectly destroyed by the destruction of the causal nescience brought about by the knowledge of Brahman, although the world appearance is not directly destroyed by the knowledge of Brahman.

Śaṁkara mentions the method of acquiring a mental mode invested with the form of Brahman. A cause exists in its effect; earth exists in a pitcher; but an effect does not exist in its cause. When an effect ceases to exist, a cause also ceases to be a cause. The pure reality is indescribable by words. The continued practice of such contemptation results in a mental mode assuming the form of Brahman. Then the knowledge of Brahman through such a mental mode arises in a person of pure mind. A person should at first perceive a cause alone apart from its effect, then perceive it in its effect, then discard the effect, and then cease to perceive the cause. Then the person remains as a sage devoid of cause and effect. A person who contemplates an object of certain knowledge for a long time is absorbed in it. A wise person should contemplate all things as imperceptible being of the nature of Ātman or pure infinite consciousness everyday. He should contemplate the perceptible world to be imperceptible Brahman, and abide in perennial delight with a mind replete with knowledge and bliss. When he is established in such knowledge and bliss, he achieves isolation from the empirical world.[248]

THE STATE OF RELEASE.—When the true knowledge of Brahman dawns on an empirical self, does it acquire the nature of Īśvara, or does it abide in the nature of pure universal consciousness alone on the destruction of its adjuncts (upadhi)? Appyaya Dīkṣita states the different views. According to the advocates of the doctrine of one soul (ekajīvavādin), when the difference between a jīva and Brahman, and the whole world appearance imagined by one nescience is destroyed by the knowledge of Brahman, the released soul exists as undifferenced consciousness.[249] According to the advocates of many souls (anekajīvavādin) some souls are bound and others are released; when the knowledge of Brahman dawns on a soul, the world appearance constructed by its nescience is annulled, but the world appearance including the difference between a jīva and Īśvara constructed by the nescience of the bound souls continues. A jīva is a reflection of Īśvara in an effect-nescience (avidyā). Īśvara is a reflection of Brahman in the causal nescience (māyā). A released soul exists in the state of universal pure consciousness as archetype.[250] The exponents of the doctrine of many souls do not favour the doctrine of limitation (avaccheda), because a released soul may be limited by another internal organ on the destruction of its internal organ in the state of bondage, and thus be bound again. But the Advaitavādins, who conceive of a soul as a reflection of Īśvara in an effect-nescience, both Īśvara and a jīva having universal pure consciousness as common to them, think of a released soul as acquiring the nature of Īśvara invested with omniscience, omnipotence, rulership of all, truthful resolve and the like, until all souls are liberated.[251] When one Brahman-consciousness is reflected on many adjuncts—nesciences in many souls, when one adjunct is destroyed by one soul's knowledge of Brahman, it is released, and exists in the state of its archetype, because it is a reflection of Brahman-consciousness in an effect-nescience in bondage.[252] When the reflection is destroyed on the destruction of the nescience, the released soul must exist as its archetype-consciousness. It is objected that a released soul is devoid of the nescience, and that so it cannot acquire the nature of Īśvara invested with truthful resolve, rulership of all and other qualities, because all are imagined by the nescience. The objection is unsound, because the world appearance is imagined by the nesciences of the other bound souls, though the released soul's nescience has been destroyed.[253] Īśvara's rulership of all and other qualities are not due to His nescience because of His stainlessness, but are imagined by the nesciences of the bound souls.[254]

It is objected that if the bliss of Brahman is knowable, it is an object of the act of knowledge. The relation of an agent and object is not possible without an action and an instrument of action. Thus the knowability of the bliss of Brahman involves dualism. So the Śruti "Bliss is Brahman" is false. If the bliss of Brahman is not known, it cannot be the supreme end of human endeavour, and unknown bliss is as good as nonexistent. To this objection Maṇḍana Miśra gives the following reply. The bliss of Brahman is not unknowable. If Brahman were unknowable, all entities would be unknowable, since they are created and manifested by It. Nor is Brahman knowable, for It is not the object of an act of knowledge. If It were so, the knowledge of It would produce some other fruit, which is not experienced, and generate a vicious infinite. So Brahman is knowable, since It is self-manifest. It is not knowable in the sense that It is not an object (viṣaya, karma) of the act of knowledge. If It were so, It would differ from subject or Self, and become not-self. Its being knowable consists in Its being self-manifest. Hence the bliss of self-luminous Brahman of the nature of bliss is not knowable, because it is not an object. Nor is it unknowable, because It is self-manifest.[255] Brahman is self-luminous and of the nature of supreme bliss. Ātman is of the nature of bliss, because It is the object of supreme love.[256] Bliss is positive delight, and not a negation of pain. Knowledge and bliss are not attributes, but the essence of Brahman. There is no difference between them.

BRAHMAN AND PRAMĀṆA.—Vimuktātman shows how scriptural testimony manifests self-manifest Brahman. A means of valid knowledge (pramāṇa) manifests an object. What is not manifested by a pramāṇa, is not an object. Brahman is self-manifest, and not manifested by a pramāṇa. Though Brahman is self-manifest, the ignorant think It to be nonexistent and unmanifest.[257] A cognition is self-manifest as existent. A pramāṇa also proves it to be self-existent. So a cognition is an object of a pramāṇa, and a self-manifest entity also is manifested by a pramāṇa.[258] Nonmanifestation of it is nescience (ajñāna), and annulment of the nescience is manifestation of it by a pramāṇa. Unmanifestability of a self-manifest entity by a pramāṇa is tantamount to its being unmanifest.[259] So scriptural testimony removes the nescience of self-luminous Brahman, and manifests It in this sense. Vimuktātman's view of knowability of Brahman, though not an object of knowledge, has already been stated.[260] A pramāṇa removes the nescience, and manifests Ātman. The nescience being not-self, destruction of it does not affect Ātman.[261] The end of a pramāṇa is the termination of the nescience of its object. Insentient entities are not-self and devoid of nescience. So a pramāṇa cannot remove their nescience. The nescience exists in self-luminous Ātman of the nature of infinite consciousness. So Ātman is capable of being proved or manifested by scriptural testimony. The knowledge of Brahman has validity in this sense. So the Inner Self alone is the ontological reality, and there is no other reality. Ātman is Brahman knowable through the Upaniṣads.[262] Ātman alone is the object of the utmost valid knowledge, being the manifester of all pramāṇas.

Maṇḍana Miśra shows how Brahman is not provable by perception and the like, but by scripture alone in the following way. It is not proved by perception, which cognizes difference alone opposed to Its identity. Nor is It proved by inference, since it depends upon perception. Nor is It proved by comparison (upamāna), because it cognizes similarity, which presupposes difference. Nor is It proved by presumption, for it reconciles two inconsistent facts perceived, and so presupposes difference. These pramāṇas presuppose difference between a knower and a known object. Brahman, a positive being, cannot be cognized by nonapprehension. Nor can perception and other empirical pramāṇas prove the negation of the false world appearance, because so long as they exist, the world appearance cannot be negated inasmuch as they also are false appearances.[263] Verbal statement of a reliable person also cannot prove Brahman, because it depends upon another pramāṇa, viz., perception. Nor can independent verbal testimony of a reliable person prove Brahman, because it is either affirmation or denial. So long as they exist, Brahman devoid of all difference cannot be proved. Brahman devoid of all difference is proved by the Vedas alone. The nature of Brahman can be ascertained by negation of the false world appearance of difference.[264]

ŚABDĀDVAITA.—Śaṁkara rejects this view. But Maṇḍana Miśra is in favour of Bhartṛhari's doctrine of monism of Śabda (Logos). The Śruti "Om is higher (para) and lower (apara) Brahman" shows that the mystic sound 'Om' (akṣara) is Brahman, because it is not modifiable (kṣara) in that a modification is losing the prevous attributes. So Brahman is identical with the sound 'Om'. The Śrutis "Meditate on Om as Ātman" and "Be united with Om" show that 'Om' is identical with Brahman. The Śrutis "Om is Brahman" and "Om itself is all this" unequivocally identify the sound 'Om' with Brahman and the world. The Śruti

"Meditate on the Supreme Person by means of this (Om) alone" should be interpreted in the primary sense. It proves the identity of Brahman with 'Om'. It should not be interpreted in a figurative sense as eulogy. In the Śruti "Om is all this" both 'this' and 'all' are known from the scripture; all are not perceived. There is no contradiction between them. A knower of all as Ātman or Brahman is instructed to meditate on It as 'Om'.[265] A Śruti says, "All worlds are speech itself." It identifies all with speech or sound. The Sūkta on speech shows that speech is the nature of all, and the ruler of all. Logos as Reality is transmuted into the world. All things are forms of speech and conducive to positive and negative actions.[266] Consciousness is the power of speech. When words are withdrawn, power of speech, or inner speech, continues. The knowledge of an object is entirely dependent on speech. So all objects of knowledge are known to be attended with speech. So they are either transformations or appearances of speech.[267] The doctrine of Śabdādvaita anticipates the modern Behaviourist's doctrine of thinking as inner speech.

CRITICISM OF ŚABDĀDVAITA.—Vimuktātman, following Śaṁkara, severely criticizes Bhartṛhari's doctrine. He adduces the following arguments against it. 1. Sound is not Brahman, because there is no evidence to prove it. The scripture declares Brahman to be devoid of sound. A sound is not Brahman, since it is perceived through the auditory organ, as a colour is perceived through the visual organ. An internal sound also is indeed perceptible through the auditory organ, because it is like an external sound. If it is perceptible throuh the intellect (buddhi), it is not Brahman, like an external sound. If an internal sound is admitted by the Śabdika to be perceptible through the intellect and yet not self-manifest, it is not proved. If it is admitted to be self-manifest, it is nothing but Ātman. But Ātman is not sound, because a sound is known, and because Ātman is a knower, and is not known.[268] A known object (eg., a sound), like a jar, cannot be a knower. A sound is known. An unknown object cannot be a sound. A known object, like a jar, is not Brahman. So Brahman is not a sound. There is no Śruti asserting a sound to be Brahman. If Brahman were a sound, It would not be Brahman. The Śrutis "Brahman is what is not uttered by speech, but by what speech is manifested," "Brahman is what does not hear through the ear", and "Brahman is devoid of sound and touch" unequivocally declare Brahman not to be a sound, or like a sound. 2. The world is a false appearance of Brahman, and neither a modification nor a false appearance of sound-principle (śabda tattva). The Śruti emphatically says, "Brahman Itself is this" and "Ātman Itself is this", and proves that Brahman is signified (vācya) by 'Om' (vācaka), and that the eternal sound is not both signifier and signified. So the doctrine of monism of sound is not proved to be true. 3. The Śābdika raises the following objection. The Advaitavādin's argument does not prove that Ātman is the nondual reality (ātmādvaita), because Ātman is not Brahman. Ātman is known as 'I'. The ego ('I'), an agent, is known, like a jar. But the Advaitin does not consider Brahman to be known as an object. So Ātman is not Brahman. This objection is groundless, because Ātman is pure knowledge while the ego is known, and because Ātman is not really 'I' while the ego is 'I'. Ātman is egoless transcendent knowledge. The Śrutis "That thou art", "I am Brahman", "This Ātman is Brahman" identify Ātman with Brahman. The scripture does not assert Ātman not to be Brahman. It is well-known that Ātman is a knower, and that It is not known as an object. One partless Ātman cannot be known simultaneously or successively to be a knower and a known object.[269] If it were known, It would be known by another person, It would not a knower, and It would be not-self, like a jar. Because It is a knower and self, It is not known as an object. A sound is not known to be a knower or a self, and so cannot be proved to be unknowable. A sound being Brahman is contradicted by perception, because it is known. But Ātman's being Brahman is not contradicted by perception, because It is not perceptible.[270] 4. Brahman is Ātman. Ātman is the Inner Self (pratyak) or Subject. But a sound is an external (parāk) object. If sound were Brhman, It would not be asserted to be an inner principle. An insentient sound being an external object cannot know Brahman to be the Inner Self.[271] If the eternal sound were Brahman, It would not be an Inner principle, but would be an external object, It would not be called Ātman, there would be no knowledge "I am Brahman", there would be the knowledge "Not-self is Brahman", and the Śruti "I am Brahman" would be contradicted". So monism of Ātman is proved, and monism of sound, like monism of a jar, is not proved. Thus Vimuktātman condemns the doctrine as absurd and ridiculous.[272] (Cp. Somānanda and Utpaladeva).

BHĀVĀDVAITA.—Maṇḍana Miśra is an exponent of the doctrine of bhāvādvaita, which posits the ontological reality of Brahman as existent along with the negation of the world appearance (prapañcābhāva) and the annulment of the nescience (avidyānivṛtti). The former does not come into conflict with the latter. They are compatible with each other. Tradition ascribes the doctrine to Maṇḍana, and is called Maṇḍanamata. He says, "The annulment of the nescience is the knowledge of Brahman, That is nondual and noumenal."[273] The cessation of avidyā is the intuitive knowledge of Brahman, if avidyā is nonapprehension, because a positive being itself is the negation of negation. If avidyā is misapprehension, the emergence of a contradicting knowledge itself is the cessation of a nescience.[274] The Śruti says, "One who knows Brahman becomes Brahman". So the knowledge of Brahman and becoming Brahman occur simultaneously. It is objected that simultaneity is inapplicable to one and the same entity. Maṇḍana urges that one entity also is spoken of as a positive entity and a negation.[275] "When a jar will be destroyed, it will become potsherd". Maṇḍana says, "The negation of the world appearance is known from the scripture". It is known from the nagative texts such as "This is not so ; this is not so" and the like.[276] Maṇḍana does not use the word 'bhavādvaita'.

[1] ŚBS., iii, 2, 5 ; RP., iii, 2, 6. [2] Bhām., i, 1, 5.
Ibid, i, 1, 4. [3] Ibid, i, 1, 4. [4] Ibid, i, 4, 3, p. 378.
[5] Ibid, iv, 1, 9, pp. 377-78. [6] Ibid, i, 1, 4, p. 939.
Cp. BRS., p. 12. [7] Ibid, ii, 2, 18, p. 502.
[8] Ibid, ii, 3, 44, p. 623. [9] RP., ii, 3, 45. BRS., p. 12.
[10] ĀNM., pp. 324-25. [11] Ibid, p. 326.
[12] Ibid, pp. 326 & 327. [13] Ibid, p. 328.
[14] Ibid, p. 331. Ibid, p. 336. [15] VPS., p. 63.
[16] Ibid, p. 8. [17] Ibid, pp. 7-8.
[18] ĀNM., p. 271. NMV., p. 271. PM., pp. 20-21.
[19] SNS., ii, 103. [20] Ibid. [21] ĀNM., p. 271.
[22] Ibid, pp. 288-89. [23] Ibid, p. 289. [24] Ibid, p. 314.
[25] PPD., p. 89. [26] Ibid, pp. 89-90. [27] Ibid. [28] Ibid.
[29] Ibid, p. 91. [30] Ibid. [31] Ibid, p. 91.
[32] VPS., p. 239. [33] Ibid. [34] PPD., p. 92.
[35] PPV., pp. 267-68. [36] VPS., p. 246. [37] Ibid, p. 248.
[38] PPD., p. 92. [39] PPV., p. 271. [40] VPS., 248. [41] Ibid.
[42] ĀNM., pp. 272-73. [43] Ibid, pp. 269-70 ; 271-74.
[44] Ibid, p. 275. Ibid, p. 270. [45] Ibid, pp. 276-77.
[46] Ibid, p. 279. [47] Ibid.
[48] Ibid, p. 281. Ibid, pp. 270, 275-81.
[49] ĀNM., NMV , pp. 270 & 281. [50] Ibid, p. 281.
[51] Ibid, p. 271. [52] Ibid, p. 284. [53] Ibid.
[54] Ibid, p. 285. [55] Ibid, p. 286. [56] Ibid, p. 287.
[57] Ibid, p. 288. [58] Ibid, pp. 271, 282-88.
[59] SLS., p. 741. [60] Ibid, p. 743. [61] Ibid, pp. 738-44.
[62] BS., iv, 1, 15 & 19. [63] ŚBS., iv, 1, 15 & 19.
[64] Bhām., iv, 1, 15, p. 958. [65] Ibid.
[66] Ibid, VKT., iv, 1, 15. [67] PPV., p. 284. [68] Ibid.
[69] Ibid. [70] Ibid, p. 105. Ibid, pp. 105-06.
[71] VPS., p. 263. [72] Ibid, p. 263. Ibid, pp. 262-63.
[73] TPD., p. 385. [74] Ibid, pp. 385-86. [75] Ibid, p. 386.
[76] Ibid, p. 387. BRS., iii, 107, p. 130.
[77] ACM., p. 74. [78] Ibid, p. 75. [79] Ibid p. 76.
[80] TA., p. 358. Ibid, pp. 355-57.
[81] Ibid, pp. 413-14. Ibid, p. 348.
[82] Ibid, p. 349. [83] ACK., p. 349.
[84] TA., pp. 350-51 ; ACK., pp. 349-51.
[85] ACK., pp. 358, 362-63. Cp. VCM., pp. 139-44.
[86] TA., pp. 406-09, 411-13.
[87] SLS., p. 683. IS., pp. 74-78.
[88] VSM., p. 274. Ibid, pp. 270-73.
[89] TA., pp. 345, 348-51 ; 413-14. Cp. PS., 96.
[90] VP., pp. 436 & 438.
[91] PD., vii, 153-61, 164-65, 169, 171-72 ;
ACK., pp. 333-34.
[92] SNS., i, 10-13 ; i, 18. Is. Up. 1. SNS., i, 18.
[93] SNS., i, 81, p. 106. [94] Ibid, i, 81-85, 87 & 89.
[95] SNS., i, 24. Ibid, i, 21. Cp. BBV., iii, 2, 37.
[96] SNS., i, 25-28. [97] Ibid, i, 35-37.
[98] Ibid, i, 43. Ibid, i, 42. [99] Ibid, i, 53.
[100] ŚBG., iii, 19. BRS., p. 36. SŚR., iii, 347.
[101] SNS., i, 56 ; i, 53-55. Cp. BRS., p. 28.
Ibid, pp. 32-33.
[102] SNS., Ibid, i, 64. Ibid, i, 58-59, 61-62.
[103] Ibid, i, 65. Cp. BBV., iii, 3, 69.
[104] SNS., i, 66. NSKA., i, 66. Cp. ĀNM., pp. 344-52 ;
BBV., iii, 3, 70. [105] ŚBG., Introduction, Ch. III.
[106] SNS., i, 67 ; Bṛ. Up., iv, 1, 2 ; iv, 4, 20.
Cp. US., xiii, 9-18.
[107] VPS., p. 166. HIP., Vol. II, pp. 588-97.
[108] VPS., p. 249. [109] Ibid, p. 251. [110] Ibid. [111] Ibid.
[112] Ibid, pp. 251-52. [113] Ibid, p. 252. [114] Ibid.
[115] Ibid. [116] Ibid, p. 253. [117] Ibid. [118] Ibid.
[119] Ibid, p. 256. [120] Ibid. [121] Ibid. [122] Ibid, pp. 250-56.
[123] Ibid, p. 237. [124] Ibid, p. 238. [125] Ibid. [126] Ibid.
[127] Ibid. [128] Ibid, p. 236. [129] Ibid. [130] Ibid, p. 237.
[131] Ibid. [132] SNS., i, 88, p. 113. [133] Ibid.
[134] Ibid, iii, 47-48 ; iv, 69. [135] ĀNM., p. 230.
[136] Ibid, p. 231. [137] Ibid, p. 242. [138] Ibid.
[139] Ibid, p. 255. [140] Ibid, pp. 256-57.
[141] BRS., p. 134 ; BRSV., p. 266 ; SLS., pp. 30-31.
[142] SLS., p. 32 ; SLSV., p. 33. [143] SLS , p. 36.
[144] Ibid, pp. 38-40. [145] Ibid, pp. 52-53 & 57.
[146] TA., ACK., p. 302 ; PD., vii, 67-68.
[147] VPS., pp. 252-53. Cp. VCM., 379-83.
[148] VP., pp. 412-14. [149] Ibid, pp. 415-16.
[150] VP., p. 424. [151] Ibid, pp. 424 & 428. [152] PPV., p. 4.
[153] Ibid, p. 101. [154] VPS., pp. 102-03. [155] Ibid, p. 103.
[156] Ibid. [157] Ibid. [158] Bhām., i, 1, 1.
[159] Ibid, i, 1, 2, p. 89. [160] Ibid, i, 1, 4, p. 153.
[161] Ibid, i, 1, 2, p. 89. [162] Ibid, i, 1, 4.
[163] Ibid, i, 1, 4, p. 89.
[164] TA., ACK., pp. 304-08. Cp. VCM., 78-88.
[165] SLS., pp. 549-51, 553-54. [166] Ibid, p. 557.
[167] Ibid, pp. 557-58. [168] Ibid, pp. 560-61, 563-64.
[169] Ibid, p. 565. [170] Ibid.
[171] ŚBS., iii, 4, 47. SLS., pp. 586-89. [172] PD., iv, 43-53.
[173] ŚBG., xii, 3, 5, 13-14, 19-20. Cp. RKBG., xviii, 54,
p. 393.
[174] ŚBS., iii, 2, 12, 24, 31 & 37. Cp. VCM., 196-208.
[175] ŚBS., iii, 2, 12, 24 & 33. APR., 3-9 & 144. PPV.,
p. 106. MSBG., xii, 11.
[176] MSBG., xii, 6-7 & 20. [177] PD., ix, 51-52, 138 & 143.
[178] PD., ix, 63, 68, 70, 73, 126, 139-40, 146-48 & 150.
[179] ŚBS , iii, 4, 27 ; TA , ACK., pp. 309-10.
[180] RP., i, 1, 4, p. 61, 62, 63, 65 & 76. [181] AUT., p. 16.
[182] PD., PDV., iv, 60-69. BG., ii, 62.
[183] PD., ix, 34-38 ; SLS., pp. 609-12, 617-18.
Cp. PSS , V. 24-25.

[184] APR., 3-9. [185] Ibid, 100-12, 114-24 & 126. Cp. Supra, p. 61.
[186] ŚBS., iii, 3, 12 & 39 ; iv, 2, 17.
[187] ŚBG., viii, 12 ; ĀGBG., viii, 13.
[188] ŚBS., Bhām., RP., iv, 2, 17. [189] SBD. on VS., p. 47.
[190] NKBG., viii, 10, p. 88.
[191] TA., ACK., pp. 366-67, 369-71. Cp. VCM., 268-77, 430-32 & 444. Adhyātma Up., 12-13 ; Śāṇḍilya Up , 41-42 ; Annapūrṇā Up., V, 78-83 & 86.
[192] TA., pp. 358-60. Cp. VCM., 268-77, 314-20, & 430.
[193] TA., pp. 360-65 ; ACK., pp. 364-65.
[194] TA., p. 376. [195] BG., ŚBG., Ch. xvi.
[196] TA., ACK., 379-80 & 82. VCM., 268-77.
[197] Ibid, pp. 379-80. HIP , Vol. II, pp. 161-66 ; ŚM., pp. 30-32, 49-51.
[198] TA., ACK., pp. 382-94, 400-05. [199] TA., pp. 296-67.
[200] Ibid, pp. 395-402. [201] SLS., p 662. [202] Ibid, p. 669.
[203] Ibid, p. 670. [204] SNS , i, 36. [205] NMV., p. 353.
[206] ĀNM., p. 354. [207] Ibid, p. 356. [208] Ibid.
[209] Ibid, p. 357. [210] Ibid, p. 358. [211] Ibid, p. 359.
[212] IS., p. 85. ISV , p. 452. Introduction, p. xiii.
[213] TPD., p. 380. [214] Ibid, p. 381. [215] Ibid, p. 382.
[216] Ibid. [217] Ibid, p. 383. [218] SLS., pp 696-97.
[219] Ibid, pp. 697-98. [220] Ibid, p. 701. [221] ACM., p. 71.
[222] Ibid. [223] Ibid, p. 72. [224] Ibid. [225] Ibid, p. 73.
[226] Ibid. [227] Ibid, p. 74.
[228] VSM., pp. 257-60. Ibid, p. 265. AUT., p. 27.
[229] Ibid, verse, 41, p. 268. [230] Ibid, pp. 265-70. AUT., p. 22.
[231] IS., p. 27. [232] Ibid, p. 28. [233] Ibid, p. 29 & 30.
[234] Ibid, p. 31. [235] PD., xv, 1-5, 13-33 ; VP., p. 407. Cp. VCM., 122, 142 & 154.
[236] SLS., p. 702. [237] Ibid, p. 704. [238] Ibid.
[239] Ibid, p. 705. [240] SNS., iv, 54.
[241] Ibid, iv, 55-58. Ibid, iv, 59. BVB., i, 4, 1455.
[242] Ibid, iv, 55-63, 65, 67-69.
[243] PPV., p. 284. Cp. AUT., p. 20. [244] SLS., p. 672.
[245] Ibid, p. 678. [246] Ibid, p. 679. [247] Ibid.
[248] Ibid, pp. 679-80. APR., 135-42 & 144.
[249] SLS., p. 706. [250] Ibid, p. 707.
[251] Ibid, p. 709. Ibid, pp. 708-09. [252] Ibid, p. 709.
[253] Ibid, p. 710. [254] Ibid. [255] BRS., p. 4. Ibid, pp. 3-4.
[256] Ibid, p. 5. Ibid, pp. 4-5. [257] IS., i, 9, p. 71.
[258] Ibid. [259] Ibid, p. 72. ISV., p. 442. [260] IS., p. 72.
[261] Ibid, i, 156, p. 216. [262] Ibid, pp. 216-17.
[263] BRS., pp. 22-23. [264] Ibid, i, 3, p. 23. [265] Ibid, p. 17.
[266] Ibid, p. 18. Ibid, pp. 16-19. [267] Ibid, p. 19.
[268] IS., i, 75, pp. 172-73. [269] Ibid, p. 175.
[270] Ibid. [271] Ibid, pp. 175-76.
[272] Ibid, p. 176. Ibid, pp. 173-76.
[273] BRS., iii, 106, p. 119. [274] Ibid, pp. 121-22.
[275] Ibid, p. 122. [276] Ibid, iv, 3, p. 157. BRS., Introduction, pp. xl-xli.

CHAPTER X

POST-ŚAMKARA ADVAITA EPISTEMOLOGY

VALID KNOWLEDGE (PRAMĀ).—Sureśvara defines valid knowledge as the knowledge of an object, which was not known before. Knowledge cognizing an object known before is invalid. So he excludes recollection from valid knowledge. Novelty is a characteristic of valid knowledge.[1] Vācaspati Miśra defines valid knowledge as uncontradicted, undoubted knowledge of an object, which was not known before. Pramāṇas produce valid knowledge.[2] It is valid in itself. Its validity is not proved by adventitious circumstances.

INTRINSIC VALIDITY AND EXTRINSIC INVALIDITY OF KNOWLEDGE.—Prakāśātman, a Śaṁkarite, discusses the different views on the validity and invalidity of knowledge in the following manner. The Śāṁkhya holds that validity and invalidity both are intrinsic to knowledge. Prakāśātman urges that the same knowledge connot be both valid and invalid, for it is self-contradictary. If the Sāṁkhya holds that some cognitions are valid while other cognitions are invalid, it is true, but the former are valid because they agree with their objects, and the latter are invalid because they disagree with their objects. So the validity of the former is not intrinsic to them, and the invalidity of the latter is not intrinsic to them. But the Sāṁkhya does not admit it. Knowledge is common to valid knowledge and invalid knowledge. It is not known from the nature of knowledge what knowledge is valid, and what knowledge is invalid. So valid knowledge cannot produce appropriation of its object, and invalid knowledge cannot produce rejection of its object. The distinction between valid knowledge and invalid knowledge is not known by perception. But the distinction between them is known from their harmony or disharmony with their objects as stated above. Hence the Sāṁkhya doctrine is not tenable.[3]

The Nyāya holds that both validity and invalidity are produced and known by extraneous conditions. Prakāśātman refutes this view thus. Validity and invalidity are not due to extraneous conditions because the nature of the knowledge devoid of validity and invalidity is not known. Nor can validity of knowledge or its capacity to manifest the nature of its object be known from the knowledge of the proficiency of its cause, since it involves infinite regress. The validity of a knowledge is known from the knowledge of the proficiency of its cause, and the validity of tne latter knowledge is known from the knowledge of the proficiency of its cause, and so on to infinity. Nor is validity of a knowledge produced by a cause, which is different from the organs of the knowledge itself. Knowledge is momentary; so validity cannot be produced in it by some other cause. There being no distinction between valid knowledge and false knowledge as they are experienced, the validity of a knowledge cannot be ascertained before its being produced by the proficiency of the sense-organ concerned is known, and consequently, it cannot produce a practical action. The validity of a knowledge cannot be ascertained unless it's being produced by the proficiency of its cause is known, which is different from the proficiency of the sense-organ that produces the knowledge in which validity abides. There being no distinction between a valid knowledge and an invalid knowledge as they are manifested to consciousness, the validity of a knowledge cannot be ascertained from the knowledge of its being produced by the proficiency of its cause. Copresence and coabsence between the validity of a knowledge and the proficiency of the cause of a knowledge depends upon the absence of defects which hinder its validity. So the proficiency of the cause of a knowledge is not an unconditional and necessary antecedent of a valid knowledge. A knowledge and its validity are not produced by the proficiency of the cause of the knowledge unless the defects of the sense-organs are absent. The validity of a knowledge cannot be known from the knowledge of a successful action, or from the knowledge of its harmony with its object, since it leads to infinite regress.[4] If the validity of a knowledge is known from the knowledge of its harmony with its object, or from the knowledge of a successful action, then the validity of the latter knowledge also depends upon the knowledge of its harmony with its object, or from the knowledge of another successful action, and so on to infinity. The defence may be made that the validity of a knowledge as a means to a practical action is known from its harmony with a practical action, but that the validity of the knowledge of a practical action is not known from the knowledge of another practical action, since the latter is absent, and that therefore there is no infinite regress. Then the validity of a knowledge as a means to a practical action also is known from the knowledge itself for the same reason.[5] Otherwise, there will be mutuai dependence : the validity of a knowledge would depend upon a successful action produced by it; and a successful action would depend upon a valid knowledge. A person does not perform a successful action in order to ascertain the validity of a knowledge. But when he knows a cognition to be undoubted and valid, he performs an action to appropriate its object. A valid knowledge prompts a successful action. But successful action does not determine the validity of a knowledge. To regard the former as a proof of the latter is to commit the fallacy of hysteron proteron (putting the cart before the horse). The first cognition itself is intrinsically valid and known to be valid, and removes the doubtfulness or invalidity of the successive cognitions of harmony with its object or of harmony with a practical action. Hence as soon as a knowledge is produced, its validity is known, and it prompts a successful action ; it is known to be valid as soon as it is produced, and its agreement with its object is known ; its validity or determination of the nature of its object is known from the knowledge itself. But the invalidity of a knowledge is produced by its causes vitiated by defects, and is known by its sublating cognition. So it is reasonable to hold that invalidity is extrinsic and due to extraneous causes.[6] It may be argued that the invalidity of a knowledge cannot be produced by extraneous causes because it is nothing but the prior nonexistence of validity. This argument is invalid, since doubt, false knowledge, etc., are positive knowledge. It may be objected that a knowledge, which is intrinsically valid, cannot be extrinsically invalid, because intrinsic validity and extrinsic invalidity are contradictory to each other. This objection is baseless, since a fire which is naturally hot is felt as cold due to the presence of a counteracting condition, viz., a medicine counteracting heat. Similarly, a knowledge is intrinsically valid, but can be made invalid by the defects of its cause, which counteract its validity. So there is no contradiction between intrinsic validity and extrinsic invalidity of a knowledge. A knowledge, which is intrinsically valid, gives rise to an action until defects of its cause are known. Hence it is proved that a knowledge independent of any other knowledge of the proficiency of its cause, or of the knowledge of its validity, or the like is, by its very existence, the cause of the ascertainment of its validity and a practical action.[7]

Vidyāraṇya refutes the opponents' views more elaborately. He refutes the Sāṁkhya view that both validity and invalidity are intrinsic to knowledge. The same knowledge cannot be valid and invalid, since it is self-contradictory. The Sāṁkhya cannot hold that some cognitions are valid, and that others are invalid, since he does not state the cause of valid knowledge and the cause of invalid knowledge, and since both are of the nature of knowlede.[8] The Sāṁkhya cannot attribute validity and invalidity to different causes, for he admits that they are intrinsic to knowledge.

Vidyāraṇya refutes the Nyāya view that both validity and invalidity are extrinsic to knowledge by pointing out that just after its production a knowledge would be devoid of validity and invalidity for some time, since the cause of its validity or the cause of its invalidity is not yet known. But common experience does not testify to the existence of such knowledge as is neither valid nor invalid.

Vidyāraṇya offers the following criticism of the Buddhist view that invalidity is intrinsic to knowledge, and that validity is extrinsic to knowledge. He asks whether validity of knowledge is produced or known by extraneous conditions. It cannot be produced by any other cause than that of the knowledge itself, since momentary knowledge produced by the sense-organs cannot endure for some time until its validity is produced by some other cause. The Buddhist may argue that at first a knowledge is produced by its cause (e.g., a sense organ), and that afterwards its validity is produced by the proficiency of its cause, and that thus validity of the knowledge is produced by other conditions. This is not possible, since the knowledge is momentary and cannot endure for more than one moment. Hence validity is not produced by the proficiency of the cause of a knowledge. The Buddhist may argue that if it is not possible, validity cannot be present when the proficiency of the cause of a knowledge is present, and validity cannot be absent when the proficiency of the cause of the knowledge is absent. This argument is wrong, since validity is present when defects of the cause of a knowledge are absent, and since validity is absent when the defects are present. The absence of defects is the so-called proficiency. No proficiency of a sense-organ is perceived except the absence of any defect. When the entire collocation of the causal conditions is present, and yet an effect is not produced, a counteracting condition is present, and hinders its production. A defeciency is not present when all defects of the cause of a knowledge are absent. Hence the validity of a knowledge is not produced by any other cause than that of the knowledge itself.[9] Nor can the validity of a knowledge be known from the knowledge of extraneous conditions. The validity of a knowledge is its capacity for ascertaining the real nature of its object. It is either known by the knowledge of its being produced by the proficiency of the cause of the knowledge, or it is known by the knowledge of its harmony with the action prompted by it.[10] The first alternative is not tenable because, if it were true, even when a jar is known, an action would not be performed because the cognition of the jar cannot ascertain the real nature of its object, until its being produced by the proficiency of the cause of the knowledge is known. It may be argued that the knowledge of a jar does not prompt an action, but that the subsequent knowledge of its being produced by the proficiency of the cause of the knowledge prompts an action. This argument is wrong, since it would lead to infinite regress. The knowledge of being produced by the proficiency of the cause of the first knowledge also would be useless, like the knowledge of a jar, before the knowledge of the knowledge which ascertains its validity is produced, and so on to infinity. The second alternative also is untenable for the same reason. If the validity of a knowledge be known by the knowledge of its harmony with an action prompted by it, then the validity of the knowledge of its harmony also will be known by another knowledge of harmony with another action, and so on to infinity. In order to avoid such infinite regress it must be admitted that the validity of knowledge is known by the same knowledge. It may be argued that the validity of the knowledge of a means (e.g., eating) is known from the knowledge of its harmony with the realisation of its end (e.g., satisfaction of hunger), but that the validity of the knowledge of the result of an action (e.g., satisfaction) is known by itself, and that therefore there being no other action, there is no infinite regress. This argument is wrong because the knowledge of a means is intrinsically valid because it is knowledge, like the knowledge of an action prompted by it. The opponent's defence involves mutual dependence : a person performing an action determines the validity of a knowledge from the knowledge of its harmony with the successful action ; and a person who determines the validity of a knowledge performs an action ; or, the determination of the validity of a knowledge depends upon the knowledge of successful action ; and successful action depends upon the determination of the validity of a knowledge.[11] It may be argued that the validity of a knowledge is determined by the knowledge of other extraneous conditions because gold is tested by various tests in order to determine its nature as gold. This argument is plausible because the knowledge of the tests does not determine the validity of the knowledge of gold, but merely removes doubts which hinder the validity of the first knowledge of gold. Hence it must be admitted that validity of a knowledge is produced by the cause of the knowledge itself, and not by any other extraneous conditions, and that it is known by the knowledge itself, and by no other knowledge, and that the invalidity of a knowledge is produced by deficiency in the cause of the knowledge, and that it is known by a sublating cognition.[12] It may be objected that invalidity is not produced by other conditions, since it is the absence of validity, like the prior nonexistence of validity. This objection is unsound, because it is without any valid reason (hetu). Nescience, doubt, and error are said by Kumārila to be invalid knowledge. These are not mere absence of valid knowledge, but are positive knowledge. Nescience (ajñāna) is not the absence of knowledge, but the knowledge of some other object. Even intrinsic validity of a knowledge becomes invalid owing to the presence of some defeciency in the cause of the knowledge. There is no contradiction in this view.[13] Fire is hot by its nature, but is perceived to be cold owing to the presence of a counteracting condition (e.g., incantations). Hence it is proved that validity of a knowledge is intrinsic to it. Vidyāraṇya sums up his view thus. It must be admitted that validity of a knowledge is intrinsic to it both in regard to its origin and apprehension in the sense that it does not depend upon any other extraneous conditions than what produces the knowledge and what apprehends the knowledge. But invalidity of a knowledge is produced by defects in the causes of the knowledge, and is known by a contradicting knowledge. Citsukha defines intrinsic validity of knowledge as being produced by the collocation of the causal conditions of knowledge and as not being produced by any other cause.[14]

Mahādeva Sarasvatī states his view thus. Validity of a knowledge is determined by itself. Validity consists in the knowledge of an object as it really is, and not as different from what it is. Validity of a knowledge is known by what apprehends the knowledge. Knowledge is a mental mode (vṛtti), and is apprehended by the witness consciousness (sākṣicaitanya). So validity of the mental mode or knowledge also is apprehended by the witness consciousness, which apprehends the knowledge. Hence validity of a knowledge is intrinsic to it.[15]

Dharmarājādhvarīndra states his view thus. Validity consists in the knowledge of an object in its real nature conducive to a fruitful action. This definition is common to apprehension and recollection. Validity is produced by the complement of causal conditions of the knowledge, and does not require any additional proficiency (guṇa) in them, since there is no proficiency common to all kinds of valid knowledge. It is objected that according to this view invalid knowledge also is included in valid knowledge, because it is produced by common causal conditions of knowledge. Dharmarājādhvarīndra replies that the absence of defects also is a causal condition of valid knowledge, and that it does not make validity of a knowledge extraneous for extraneousness depends upon adventitious positive conditions. Intrinsic validity of a knowledge in regard to its apprehension consists in its being apprehended by what apprehends the knowledge. A knowledge, a mental mode, is the substrate of validity. It is apprehended by the witness consciousness. So validity of the knowledge also is apprehended by the witness consciousness. Dharmarājādhvarīndra agrees with Mahādeva Sarasvatī in this respect. Invalidity of a knowledge is produced by defects in the causes of the knowledge. Witness consciousness cannot apprehend invalidity of a knowledge, since the knowledge (vṛttijñāna) cannot present its disagreement with the nature of its object to consciousness, which constitutes its invalidity. Invalidity of a knowledge is inferred from unfruitful action as a mark.[16]

But the Advaita Vedānta view of intrinsic validity of knowledge is not the same as the Bhāṭṭa Mīmāṁsaka view. According to Kumārila, at first the cognition "this is a jar" is produced ; then the cognition "I know the jar" or the cognition of cognizedness (jñātatā) of the jar is produced ; and then the cognition or cognitive act is inferred from the cognition of cognizedness. Thus the validity of the knowledge, or its knowing an object as it really is, is inferred from the cognizedness of the object. The Bhāṭṭa means by the determination of the validity of a knowledge the inference of its validity from the cognizedness of the object. Mahādevānanda refutes this view by pointing out that there is no proof for the existence of cognizedness besides an object's being known by a knowledge. When it is known that a jar is cognized, it is cognized as an object of knowledge. If cognizedness were produced in a jar when it was known, seenness would be produced in it when it was seen, and destroyedness would be produced in it when it was destroyed. Further, if cognizedness were produced in an object of knowledge, past and future objects could not be known since they are nonexistent at present. The Bhāṭṭa may reply that cognizedness would be proved in a past object when the cognition "a past object is known" is produced. Mahādevānanda urges that cognizedness cannot exist without a substrate, since it is an attribute, and since an attribute cannot exist without a substrate. Furthermore, the doctrine of cognizedness will lead to infinite regress. Cognizedness of an object will be known from another cognizedness produced in the first cognition, and so on to infinity. Hence cognizedness is unproven, and the validity of a knowledge cannot be inferred from it. Thus the Bhāṭṭa doctrine of the determination of the validity of knowledge is wrong.[17]

Prabhākara holds that the self-manifest cognition "I know a jar" manifests 'I' as its substrate or knower, and a jar as its object, and apprehends itself and its validity. He takes the determination of the validity of knowledge in this sense. Mahādevānanda refutes this view by pointing out that there is no proof for the self-manifestness of a produced cognition.[18] The Advaita Vedāntin holds that the witness consciousness alone is self-manifest, but that a mental mode or a produced cognition is not self-manifest.

According to Murāri Miśra, at first, a determinate cognition "this is a jar" is produced by the sense-object-intercourse, then the representative cognition (avuvyavasāya) "I know the jar" is produced. The second cognition apprehends the first cognition. The cognition of an object is called a determinate cognition. The cognition of the relation of the knowing subject and the known object is the self-appropriated cognition. The latter apprehends the validity of the former. Mahādevānanda denies the existence of the so-called representative cognition. If a cognition is known by a representative cognition or after-cognition, then the latter will be known by another after-cognition, and so on to infinity. A determinate cognition is apprehended by the witness consciousness. There is no proof for the existence of a representative cognition.[19] Hence a representative cognition cannot know the validity of a determinate cognition. There can be no mental perception of a cognition. The manas is not a sense-organ. There can be no conjunction of the self with it. Hence Murāri Miśra's view is unreasonable. The Advaita Vedāntin concludes that the validity of a produced cognition is known by the witness self, which apprehends the knowledge in which the validity abides.[20] The Advaita Vedāntin's view of the determination of the intrinsic validity of knowledge differs from the Mīmāṁsaka views of Kumārila, Prabhākara and Murāri Miśra.

THE JAINA CRITICISM OF INTRINSIC VALIDITY OF KNOWLEDGE.—Prabhācantra, a Jaina, refutes the doctrine of intrinsic validity of knowledge. He asks whether all cognitions are intrinsically valid in being produced, or in being known, or in producing effective actions, there being no other alternative. In the first alternative, what is the meaning of the validity of a cognition by being produced by itself? Is it produced without a cause? Or, is it produced by the aggregate of its causal conditions? Or, is it produced by the collocation of the causal conditions of the cognition in which it abides? There is no other alternative. The first subalternative is not possible. If validity is uncaused, it cannot give rise to an effective action. A particular cognition is valid for it agrees with a particular object in a particular place at a particular time. Otherwise, it cannot give rise to an effective action. The second subalternative is useless, since it proves what is already proved. Everything is known to be produced by the complement of its causal conditions. The third subalternative is untenable, because a specific effect (e.g., validity) cannot be produced by a nonspecific or common cause (e.g., the cause of a cognition). Validity is caused by a specific cause, because it is a specific effect, like invalidity.[21] As invalidity of a cognition is produced by a sense-organ vitiated by defects (e.g., jaundice), so validity of a cognition also is produced by a cause endowed with some proficiency. Nor is validity of an initial cognition known by itself, because it is infected with the doubt whether it is valid or invalid. Both validity and invalidity of a habitual cognition are known by themselves.[22] Nor does validity by itself produce an effective action on its object, because it depends upon the knowledge of its validity, like invalidity. Validity depends upon the knowledge of the validity of the cognition or its correspondence with its object in order to produce an effective action in the form of appropriation of its object, as invalidity depends upon the knowledge of invalidity of the cognition or its noncorrespondence with its object in order to produce an effective action in the form of rejection of its object. If validity is not known, mere validity does not prompt an effective action. Hence the validity of an initial cognition is neither produced by itself, nor known by itself, nor does it produce an effective action by itself. Hence the Mīmāṁsā and the Vedānta doctrine of intrinsic validity of knowledge is wrong. Prabhācandra rejects it. Citsukha criticizes this view.

NECESSITY OF ISSUANCE OF A MENTAL MODE.—The opponents of the Advaida Vedānta contend that issuance of a mental mode (vṛtti) to an object is not necessary because all objects are manifested by the witness self (sākṣin), that the admission of issuance of a mental mode to an object to account for the production of an impression of an object on the mental mode is unnecessary, and that an object of perception is manifested by the Sākṣin limited by a nonissuing mental mode, as an object of inference is manifested by the Sākṣin limited by a nonissuing mental mode. The former mental mode is perception while the latter mental mode is inference. Perception is immediate knowledge while inference is mediate knowledge. This view does not remove the distinction between mediate knowledge and immediate knowledge, because the mental modes differ as their instruments differ. Verbal knowledge is produced by the knowledge of the statement of a reliable person. Inference is produced by the knowledge of a reason. Perception is produced by the intercourse of a sense-organ with an object. 1. According to some Advaitins, in perception the object-consciousness or the consciousness limited by an object being the substratum of the object, issuance of a mental mode is necessary for the manifestation of the object-consciousness owing to the absence of svarūpasambandha or any other relation between a cognition and its object, though a direct relation in the form of identity is possible. In inference the jīva-consciousness limited by a mental mode not issuing out to distant object (e.g., a fire) manifests and cognizes it, since no way through which it may issue out to the object is perceived. 2. In some Advaitists' view, the jīva-consciousness directly manifests egoism, pleasure, pain and the like related to it, the consciousness related to an object (e.g., a jar) is the cause of the immediate knowledge of it, and issuance of a mental mode to the object is necessary for the manifestation of the object-consciousness. The identity of the jīva-consciousness with the Brahman-consciousness which supports the object is manifested by a mental mode issuing out to the object.[23] 3. In some Advaitists' view, the perception of vividness (spaṣṭatā) of an object perceived consequent on the removal of nescience of it proves issuance of a mental mode to it. The object of perception is vivid whereas the object of verbal knowledge is not vivid. The unique sweet taste of a mango perceived is vivid whereas the taste of it known from verbal testimony is not vivid. The perception of vividness of an object perceived due to the manifestation of identity of the knower's consciousness (pramātṛcaitanya) with the Brahman-consciousness in which the object subsists can terminate a desire to know the object further. The issuing out of a mental mode to the object is the cause of the perception of its vividness. The absence of vividness in an object of verbal testimony is due to the absence of identification of the knower's consciousness with the Brahman-consciousness which supports the object. Pleasure and pain directly known by the Sākṣin are vivid. There is no vividness in Brahman known from scriptural testimony prior to reflection and meditation owing to nondestruction of the nescience. But there is vividness in Brahman intuited by immediate knowledge after reflection and meditation due to destruction of the nescience. 4. According to some Advaitins, issuance of a mental mode to an object is necessary for the destruction of the nescience of an object by the knowledge of it. A nescience of an object is destroyed by the knowledge of it. Issuance of a mental mode to an object is necessary for the destruction of its nescience which veils the object. 5. In some Advaitists' view, as external light is perceived to destroy external darkness in the same locus, so the knowledge of an object destroys the nescience of it in the same locus, and issuance of a mental mode to an object is necessary for the destruction of its nescience in the same locus. 6. According to some Advaitins, issuance of a mental mode to an object is not necessary for destroying the veiling of an object by a nescience of it, but it is necessary for manifesting the identification of the knower's consciousness with the Brahman-consciousness, which manifests the object or for tinging the knower's consciousness by the object. The identity of the jīva-consciousness with the Brahman-consciousness, which is manifested by a mental mode issuing out to an object, is emphatically asserted by the Advaita Vedānta.[24]

RELATIVE SUPERIORITY OF PERCEPTION AND SCRIPTURAL TESTIMONY.—The Advaita Vedānta regards Vedic testimony in respect of the reality of nondual Brahman as the highest pramāṇa. The opponent objects that scriptural testimony about the reality of Brahman alone is contradicted by perception, which apprehends the reality of difference. The Advaitin urges that this objection is unsound, since the world appearance apprehended by perception is known to be false. It is objected that belief in the falsity of the world appearance cannot be produced by Vedic testimony and reasoning, because they are contradicted by the existence of a jar and the like. To this objection the author of the 'Tattvaśuddhi' replies that perception neither apprehends a jar, a cloth and the like, nor their existence, but that it apprehends beinghood alone common to them, and that therefore perception is favourable to the establishment of one Brahman as of the nature of being. Perception which apprehends mere indeterminate being is favourable to the establishment of one Brahman.[25] The author of the 'Nyāyasudhā' urges that though a jar and the like are perceived through the sense-organs, their being (sattā) also, which is common to them and their substrate, is perceived by them, and that therefore there is no contradiction between the perception of different objects and the perception of their being, which is their substrate.[26]

According to Sarvajñātman, although perception apprehends the being of a jar and the like, it apprehends external objects, and cannot be a valid pramāṇa for the reality of Brahman, and so no doubt can arise that perception contradicts scriptural testimony about the reality of one Brahman alone. A pramāṇa produces the knowledge of an object, which is not known. A jar and the like being insentient are not objects of nescience (ajñana), as they cannot be veiled by it. They are objects of perception, but were not unknown. The self-manifest Brahman alone is an object of nescience, for It is veiled by nescience. So Vedic testimony is a valid pramāṇa for the existence of Brahman. The Śruti "Ātman ought to be seen or intuited" shows that Ātman is an object of valid knowledge. It means that Ātman is worthy of being intuited.[27]

Other Vedāntists maintain that where there is a conflict between perception of the truth of the world appearance and Vedic testimony about its falsity, the latter is stronger than the former, since the latter is not vitiated by any doubt while the former is vitiated by a doubt.[28]

It is objected that if Vedic testimony is stronger than perception, then in the Śruti "The person on whose behalf a sacrifice is made is a stone" the word 'stone' should not be taken in a secondary sense, but that it contradicts perception, since a person is not a stone. To this objection Vācaspati Miśra replies that the Vedic texts, which have monistic import only, are strong and authoritative, but that the other Vedic texts, which are mere eulogies, are not so. The Vedic testimony is superior to perception because of its being flawless and posterior to perception. Where there is a conflict between perception and Vedic testimony, perception is contradicted by Vedic testimony, but Vedic testimony is not contradicted by perception. Vedic testimony is stronger than perception, because it is flawless.[29] But though perception is contradicted by Vedic testimony, it has empirical validity, since it apprehends an object. If it did not apprehend its object, it would not be possible, as there is no objectless cognition. Perception capable of producing a fruitful action is assumed to apprehend a pragmatic object, though it is contradicted by Vedic testimony about monism, and though it cannot produce the knowledge of Brahman. Thus the antecedent perception of a jar and the like is contradicted by the subsequent knowledge of their falsity by Vedic testimony about the reality of Brahman alone.[30] It is objected that perception is the sustainer of Vedic testimony, and that for this reason the former is stronger and more authoritative than the latter sustained by it, that between an interruption of perception and a Vedic text the former is not the sustainer of the latter, but the former is contradicted by the latter, but that here the perception of letters and words is the sustainer of the Vedic testimony about the falsity of the world appearance, and that therefore it contradicts the Vedic testimony. The Advaitin replies that the objection is groundless, for the Vedic text "There is no plurality here" and the like communicates the knowledge of the absence of the world appearance of empirical objects (e.g., letters, etc.) by nature. Other Advaitins reply to the above objection that the perception of letters and words is common to true testimony and false testimony alike. So Vedic testimony about the reality of one Brahman alone is sustained by the perception of letters and words constituting the Vedic sentence. But Vedic testimony refutes their nature as true. So there is no contradiction between Vedic testimony and perception which sustains it. Other Advaitists reply to the above objection that though the Śruti "There is no plurality here" declares the ontological nonexistence of plurality, it does not contradict the perception of plurality which is its sustainer because empirical reality, different from a nonentity and capable of producing a fruitful action continues till the intuitive knowledge of Brahman dawns. Otherwise, perception and other empirical pramāṇas would be devoid of objects. The knowledge "this is not silver" contradicts the knowledge "this is silver". But until the latter is contradicted by the former, illusory silver different from a nonentity is admitted to exist along with its substrate, a nacre. A similar reasoning refutes the view that the denial of the ontological reality of the world appearance proves that it is a nonentity like a hare's horn. Other Advaitins reply to the above objection that the Śruti "There is no plurality here" denies the truth of the world appearance, but does not deny its nature. The denial of it by nature, being unable to contradict it, cannot nagate it. If it contradicts the world appearance by nature, it contradicts perception. So perception without conflicting with Vedic testimony apprehends a pragmatic reality in the form of a semblance of truth. In the bare locus of negation or absence, its counterentity cannot exist. In Brahman, the substrate of the world appearance, the absence of the world appearance cannot be known by Vedic testimony declaring its negation. Other Advaitins reply to the above objection that the three grades of reality—the ontological reality of Brahman, the empirical or pragmatic reality of the world appearance, and the illusory reality of nacre-silver and the like need not be assumed, because the ontological being of Brahman, the substrate of the world appearance, which permeates the existence of empirical objects (e.g., a jar, etc.) can account for the false conceit of their existence, and because for that reason the assumption of a semblance of existence is not proved by any pramāṇa. If the semblance of being of the world appearance is not possible without the ontological being of Brahman, how does the Advaitin explain the illusion of silver in a nacre without assuming the truth of silver in a distant place ? The Advaitin replies that distant silver being not in intercourse with a sense-organ is not immediate or perceived, and so cannot produce the immediate perception of illusory silver. Vedic testimony does not contradict the perception of letters and words in order to prove the falsity of the world appearance. Hence Vedic testimony is stronger than perception.[31]

PRAMĀṆAS DO NOT CONTRADICT THE REALITY OF ONE ĀTMAN.—The world appearance is due to māyā—cosmic nescience. Perception and other means of knowledge have empirical or pragmatic validity, because they belong to the realm of phenomenal appearances. But scriptural testimony in regard to the reality of one Brahman has ontological validity. It is not contradicted by any sublating cognition.[32] Perception and other pramāṇas prove difference, which is contradicted by scriptural testimony asserting the reality of one Brahman. Difference is an indeterminable appearance. So the pramāṇas except scriptural testimony about one Brahman are empirically valid. But scriptural testimony about one reality is ontologically valid. It is contended that though a pramāṇa other than scriptural testimony about one Reality is a phenomenal appearance, some knowledge is in harmony with its object while some other knowledge is not in harmony with its object. Ānandabodha urges that this contention is invalid, because though the knowledge of a ray of a gem and the knowledge of a ray of a lighted lamp are equally false from the ontological point of view, there is a difference between them in regard to their practical effects (arthakriyā). The knowledge of the ray of a gem leads to the attainment of a gem, which is mistaken for a lamp. The knowledge of the ray of a lighted lamp leads to the attainment of a lamp. Thus an empirical knowledge of an object is valid, while another empirical knowledge of an object is invalid. A knowledge, which is in harmony with its object, and which leads to its attainment, is empirically valid. But a knowledge, which is not in harmony with its object, and which does not lead to its attainment, is invalid. It is contended that Vedic testimony about the reality of one Brahman is invalid, because it contradicts earlier perception, which was proved to be valid, and because it depends upon the latter. The contention is invalid, because there is no conflict between empirically valid perception and ontologically valid Vedic testimony, though difference proved by perception is contradicted by identity or oneness proved by Vedic testimony.[33] Though the valid knowledge of silver arises after the illusory knowledge of silver, it contradicts the illusion. The prior knowledge is contradicted by the later knowledge. Vedic knowledge is valid in itself, and proves the ontological reality of one Brahman. It does not depend upon perception in proving its validity. The later Vedic testimony is stronger that earlier perception.[34] Though all are known to be appearances due to māyā, practical actions follow from false cognitions of appearances until the reality of one Brahman is immediately experienced. The false knowledge of all appearances is annulled, when the Reality is intuited. The apparent objects due to māyā have empirical reality, and contradict illusory reality (e.g., silver). The intuition of Brahman, though of the nature of avidyā, destroys other manifestations of avidyā, and then destroys itself, and establishes the reality of pure Ātman. The intuition of Brahman is a state of the empirical self (jīva), and so a manifestation of avidyā.[35]

Citsukha says, "The means of knowledge are ontologically unreal, and so cannot contradict the ontotogical reality of one Brahman".[36] So, though perception and the like pramāṇas have empirical validity in the realm of phenomenal appearances due to māyā, they do not disprove the ontological reality of one Brahman. Even the scriptural sentences are appearances due to māyā ; yet they prove the reality of one Brahman.[37] Scriptural testimony asserting the reality of one Brahman should be interpreted in a primary sense, and not in a secondary or figurative sense.[38]

THERE IS NO CONFLICT BETWEEN PRAMĀṆAS.—Sureśvara says, "I have repeatedly said that a pramāṇa, which produces valid knowledge, is not contradicted by another pramāṇa."[39] Where there is apprehension of conflict between scriptural testimony of one Brahman and perception of difference, there is no real contradiction, but a person under delusion thinks that there is a contradiction. Perception is subordinate to scriptural testimony.[40] I see colour with my eyes. There is no scope for scriptural testimony in this matter. Scipture proves the ontological reality of the Inner Self (pratyagātman) while perception proves the empirical reality of external (parāk) objects.[41] So there is no conflict between them. Different pramāṇas give the knowledge of different objects. So there is no conflict among them. Perception is not scriptural testimony; scriptural testimony also is not perception. In perception there is perceptual illusion. In testimony there is false testimony. Pramāṇas produce the knowledge of their proper objects with their powers without any aid of the other pramāṇas.[42]

AKHAṆḌĀRTHATĀ OR SĀMĀNĀDHIKARAṆYA.—Akhaṇḍārthatā means having the same meaning. It is sāmānādhikaraṇya or the state of relating to the same object. Vidyāraṇya interprets the meaning of the secular sentence "that is this Devadatta" thus. The word 'that' primarily means Devadatta qualified by the past time. The word 'this' primarily means Devadatta qualified by the present time. But they secondarily mean Devadatta unqualified by the past time and the present time, so that the sentence means the identity of Devadatta, which is cognized by recognition. Vidyāraṇya interprets the meaning of the Vedic sentence "That thou art" thus. It means the identity of the jīva and Brahman by leaving out agency and the like from 'thou' (jīva) and meaning by it the witness consciousness alone, and by discarding mediateness and the like from 'that' and meaning by it the one transcendental consciousness alone. The Vedic sentence "That thou art" has an undivided meaning because it refers to the same object different from a cause and an effect and the like, because it relates to the same object, like the sentence "that is this Devadatta." Vidyāraṇya interprets the Vedic sentence "Brahman is truth, knowledge and infinite" thus. It means the same reality—Brahman, since it expresses the essential characters of Brahman, like the sentence "the moon is of excellent illumination." The first sentence does not express any relation between Brahman and Its essential characters—truth, knowledge and infinitude. The second sentence does not express any relation between the moon and excellent illumination. Yet the words 'truth', 'knowledge', and 'infinitude' exclude falsity, insentience, and finitude as the word 'illumination' excludes clouds, and the word 'excellent' excludes stars and the like, and, consequently, they are not useless. So the Vedic sentence has the same meaning, though its component words are different.[43]

Mahādeva Sarasvatī clearly explains the meaning of 'akhaṇḍārthatā' or 'sāmānādhikaraṇya'. In the senternce "That thou art" the subject and the predicate mean the same universal consciousness, which is the substantive (viśeṣya) qualified by the attributes (viśeṣaṇa)—'endowed with infinite knowledge and power', and 'endowed with finite knowledge and power.' The sentence cannot produce the knowledge of a relation, or of a qualified entity, or of identity of a qualified entity with an attribute or qualification, since it is contradicted by perception. It means one and the same universal consciousness. Undividedness or sameness consists in being devoid of heterogeneous difference, homogeneous difference, and internal difference. It is devoid of heterogeneous difference, because the world appearance being different from Brahman is false in that it is imagined by nescience. It is devoid of homogeneous difference, since the jīva and Brahman are absolutely identical. It is devoid of internal difference, for it is one homogeneous being. Or, undividedness consists in being devoid of three kinds of difference, since it is ubiquitous. It is unlimited by space, as it is eternal. It is unlimited by time, for it is of the nature of all. It is unlimited by objects, since they are nonexistent. Or, undividedness consists in unqualifiedness, being manifested by many nonsynonymous words in a sentence. In the sentence "That thou art" the word 'that' primarily means omniscient and omnipotent God, and the word 'thou' primarily means empirical self (jīva) endowed with limited knowledge and power; but the word 'that' secondarily means the universal consciousness, and the word 'thou' secondarily means the inner self, the substrate of the consciousness limited by an individual nescience. The sentence means the universal undifferentiated consciousness, though the words 'that' and 'thou' primarily mean mediately known God and immediately known self, respectively. Dharmarājādhvarīndra interprets the meaning of the sentence "That thou art" in the same manner. Though there cannot be identity between the qualified entities, omniscient God and ignorant jīva, primarily meant by the words 'that' and 'thou', they secondarily mean or imply the unqualified Brahman, so that the sentence means one and the same object.[44]

THE PRAMĀṆAS.—Śaṁkara recognizes perception, inference, scriptural testimony, comparison, presumption, and non-apprehension as the sources of valid knowledge. Dharmarājādhvarīndra also enumerates six kinds of pramāṇas, which yield empirical truth.[45]

(1) Perception.—There is one eternal consciousness. It is Brahman. When it is determined by the internal organ (antaḥkaraṇa), it is called the subject-consciousness (pramātṛcaitanya). The empirical self (jīva) is the subject-consciousness. When the eternal consciousness is determined by mental modes, it is called the knowledge-consciousness (pramāṇa-caitanya). When it is determined by an empirical object, it is called the object-consciousness (viṣayacaitanya). In external perception the mind goes out to an empirical object through a sense-organ, and is modified into its form. This mental mode assuming the form of the object is called vṛtti. So the knowledge-consiousness (pramāṇa-caitanya) or consciousness determined by the mental mode coincides with the object consciousness (viṣaya-caitanya). There is identification of the apprehending mental mode with the object. The mental mode conforms to the empirical object. The mental order conforms to the given order. In external perception the mental mode and the object occupy the same position in space. This mark distinguishes perception from inference. The perceptive process and the object occupy the same point of time. They occupy the present time. The memory of pleasure is not perception. Memory is a present mental mode. But pleasure remembered is past. The aprehending mental mode and the apprehended object occupy different time-positions. The object should be capable of being perceived. Fitness (yogyatva) for being perceived is a mark that distinguishes perception from scriptural testimony, which apprehends supersensible objects like merit (dharma) and demerit (adharma). In the bare perception of an object there is only identification of the knowledge-consciousness (pramāṇa-caitanya) with the object-consciousness (viṣaya-caitanya). But in the perception of the object as object there is not only identification of the knowledge-consciousness (pramāṇa-caitanya) with the object-consciousness (viṣaya-caitanya) but also identification of the knowledge-consciousness (pramāṇa-caitanya) with the subject-consciousness (pramātṛ-caitanya). The apprenending mental mode is referred to the empirical self and identified

with it.[46] In internal perception of pleasure the apprehending mental mode is identified with the mental mode of pleasure, or the knowledge-consciousness (pramāṇa-caitanya) coincides with the object-consciousness (viṣaya-caitanya).

Perception is indeterminate (nirvikalpa) or determinate (savikalpa). Indeterminate perception is non-relational apprehension. "That thou art". This verbal knowledge is indeterminate perception. There is no subject-predicate relation in it. Determinate perception is relational apprehension. "I know the jar". This is determinate perception. There is subject-predicate relation in it. Perception is either sensuous or non-sensuous. Perception through the sense-organs is sensuous. Mental perception is non-sensuous, since the manas is not a sense-organ. In sensuous perception the mind goes out to an external object through a sense-organ, and is modified into its form. In mental perception the mind does not go out to an object. Mental modes of pleasure, pain, and the like are perceived in it. Perception, again, refers to an object (jñeya) or a cognition (jñapti). An object is perceived through the medium of a mental mode (vṛtti). A cognition is directly perceived by the self without an intervening mental mode. Perception is, again, divided into perception of the Witness Self (jīvasākṣin) and perception of the Divine Witness (īśvarasākṣin). The eternal consciousness (Brahman) limited by the internal organ is the jīva. When it is conditioned by the internal organ, it is the jīvasākṣin. The eternal conciousness limited by māyā is Īśvara. When it is conditioned by māyā, it is Īśvarasākṣin.[47]

ILLUSION.—In the illusory perception "this is silver" the visual organ perverted by a defect comes into contact with a nacre, and generates a mental mode in the form of 'this-consciousness'. The consciousness of 'this' is perception. There is identification of 'this-consciousness' with the knowledge-consciousness and the subject-consciousness. The mental mode goes out through the visual organ to the bright object ('this'), and is modified into its form. This is perceptive process. Then avidyā in the form of a nacre in the object-consciousness which is identified with the subject-consciousness, is transformed into the objective illusory silver and the subjective illusion of silver with the aid of the impression of silver revived by the perception of brightness, which is common to the nacre and the silver, and a defect in the visual organ. The illusory silver, which is a modification of avidyā, exists in 'this-consciousness' subsisting in avidyā. All effects are modifications of avidyā, and subsist in it. The consciousness of 'this' is valid perception. The consciousness of 'silver' is a memory image. But illusion fuses them into a unitary psychosis, which is perceptual. Illusory silver has illusory reality (prātibhāsika sattā), while real silver has empirical reality (vyāvahārika sattā). Illusion is contradicted by right perception. Illusory silver is neither existent nor non-existent, but indefinable (anirvacanīyakhyāti). Maṇḍana Miśra recognizes two kinds of error, viz., nonapprehension and misapprehension.[48]

The Mādhyamika maintains that in an illusion a nonexistent thing (e.g., silver) is apprehended as existent. This doctrine is called Asatkhyāti. An illusion without foundation in an object is not possible. The illusion of an imaginary city has its foundation in the sky. An illusion without any substrate is inconceivable. An absolutely non-existent thing cannot be apprehended as existent. The Śūnya cannot be the substrate of the illusion of silver. If it were so, the illusion would be apprehended as "the Śūnya is silver", and not as "this is silver".

Further, when the illusion is sublated, the Śūnya would be apprehended. But it is not apprehended. So the doctrine of Asatkhyāti is not tenable.[49]

The Yogācāra maintains that in an illusion a subjective idea is apprehended as an external object. There are no external objects. There are only ideas (vijñāna). The internal idea of silver appears to be a real external object. This doctrine is called Ātmakhyāti. The Sautrāntika ascribes perception to four causes. The auxiliary cause (sahakāri pratyaya), e.g., light, is the cause of distinctness of perception. It is not the cause of the perception of silver. The dominant cause (adhipati pratyaya), e.g., the eye, is the cause of visual perception. It is not the cause of the perception of silver. The immediately preceding cause (samanantara pratyaya), e.g., the immediately antecedent cognition, is not the cause of an illusion. The antecedent cognition of a jar cannot produce the cognition of silver. An external object (ālambana pratyaya) is not the cause of the illusion of silver, since the Vijñānavādin denies the existence of external objects. If the cognition of silver be said to be due to the impression (saṁskāra) of it, the impression is either permanent or momentary. If it is permanent, the Buddhist doctrine of momentariness is undermined. If it is momentary, the momentary impression being known, it contradicts the doctrine of the existence of mere cognitions (vijñānamātravāda). If the illusion of silver be said to be a cognition of silver in the series of beginningless cognitions, appearing to be an external object, is the silver unproduced or produced? If it were unproduced, the illusory cognition of silver would not be apprehended as an emergent cognition. If it is produced, it is produced by an external object or a cognition. It cannot be produced by an external object, since it does not exist. It cannot be produced by a pure cognition, since it is of the nature of liberation. If it is said to be produced by an impure cognition due to a vitiated cause, either the cognition of the cause itself apprehends illusory silver or some other cognition apprehends it. The cause and the effect are momentary, and exist at different times; so the antecedent cognition of the cause cannot perceive the succeeding illusory silver. Some other pure cognition cannot apprehend illusory silver. If it could, any cognition would apprehend any object. If some other impure cognition apprehends it, it is either produced by silver or not produced by it. If it is produced by silver, silver must exist as an external object, since it prompts activity. If it is not produced by silver, it cannot apprehend silver, since that is the object of a cognition, which imparts its form to it. So silver cannot be apprehended in the illusion of silver. The doctrine of Ātmakhyāti is not tenable.[50]

Prabhākara advocates the doctrine of Akhyāti or Vivekākhyāti. He maintains that in the illusion "this is silver" there are two cognitions, the perception of 'this' and the recollection of 'silver', that there is non-apprehension (akhyāti) of the distinction (viveka) between them, and that non-discrimination between the given element and the ideal element due to obscuration of memory (smṛtipramoṣa) constitutes the illusion. Prabhākara maintains that all apprehension is valid, and that there is no logical error. Truth depends on practical efficiency. Error depends on practical inefficiency. A cognition in itself is valid. But if it prompts fruitless activity, it is invalid. In cognitions as such there is no error.[51] Vidyāraṇya criticizes the Prābhākara doctrine of Akhyāti. What is non-apprehension (akhyāti)? It is either mere absence of apprehension, or cognition of a person seeking one object prompting activity in respect of another object, or cognition of many objects as undistinguished from one another. On the first view, there would be illusion in deep sleep only, and there would be no illusion in waking and dream. On the second view, there would be no illusion where there is no activity owing to quick sublation or laziness. On the third view, distinction, the counter-entity of non-distinction, is either apprehension of difference (bhedagraha) or non-apprehension of non-difference (abhedāgraha). It is not apprehension of difference, since in the illusion "this is silver" there is apprehension of difference between the general (sāmānya) and the particular (viśeṣa), and therefore there cannot be non-distinction between them. It is not non-apprehension of non-difference, since there is apprehension of difference, and, consequently, there is no non-apprehension of non-difference, and therefore there can be no non-distinction. The Prābhākara urges that non-discrimination (aviveka) is non-apprehension of non-relation (asaṁsargāgraha), and that illusion consists in not cognizing the presentation of 'this' and the memory image of 'silver' to be non-related. Non-apprehension of non-relation cannot be as between apprehension and momory, since in that case "I am a man" would not be an illusion. But, in fact, it is an illusion, in which there is non-apprehension of non-relation between two apprehensions. Non-apprehension of non-relation cannot be as between any two things, since in that case "the cloth is white" would be an illusion as there is non-apprehension of non-relation in it, while it is a valid cognition. Non-apprehension of non-relation cannot be as between two things devoid of knowledge of relation, since it involves the same defect. Therefore the doctrine of Akhyāti is not tenable.[52]

The Naiyāyika and the Bhāṭṭa Mīmāṁsaka maintain that in the illusion "this is silver" there is misapprehension of a nacre as silver. They advocate the doctrine of Anyathākhyāti. One object, e.g., a 'nacre' is apprehended as otherwise (anyathā) i.e., as 'silver' which exists in some other place. Vidyāraṇya asks whether otherwiseness belongs to the cognition, or to the result, or to the object. If it belongs to the cognition, the cognition of silver has for its basis or object a nacre. Then, is the nacre the object of the cognition of silver, because it imparts its form to the cognition, or because it is the object of activity prompted by the cognition? The first alternative is untenable. A nacre cannot impart its form to the cognition of silver. The second alternative also cannot be maintained. The perception of a tiger prompts the use of a sword. But the sword is not the object of the cognition of a tiger. Otherwiseness cannot belong to the result or manifestation, which is common to valid knowledge and illusion. There is no difference in the manifestation brought about by valid knowledge and illusion. Otherwiseness cannot belong to the object. Is otherwiseness in the object identity of a nacre with silver? Or is it transformation of a nacre into silver? If it is identity of a nacre with silver, is there absolute difference between them, or difference and non-difference? They cannot be absolutely different, since absolutely different things cannot be identical. They cannot be different and non-different, since in that case "this is silver" would not be an illusion like the cognition "the cow is short-horned". If a nacre is modified into silver, there can be no sublation. Therefore the doctrine of Anyathākhyāti is untenable.[53]

(2) Inference.—Inference is produced by the knowledge of invariable concomitance (vyāpti) of the middle term with the major term as such. The knowledge of vyāpti is its instrumental cause (karaṇa). The residual impression of it is the intermediate function

(vyāpāra) which generates inference. The Nyāya regards the knowledge of the existence of the probans pervaded by the probandum in the subject of inference (tritīyaliṅgaparāmarśa) as the instrumental cause (karaṇa) of inference. But the Advaita Vedānta does not regard it as a cause of inference, far less an instrumental cause. Vyāpti is the co-existence of the probans or the middle term and the probandum or the major term in all the substrates of the middle term. It is known by observation of concomitance of the middle term with the major term, and non-observation of their non-concomitance. The number of instances is not material to inference. Concomitance may be observed once or many times. Observation of concomitance alone is the ground of inference.[54] Vyāpti does not depend upon the agreement in absence between the middle term and the major term. Inference is of one kind. It is Anvayi. It depends upon the agreement in presence between the middle term and the major term. It is founded on their positive concomitance. It is not Kevalānvayi like the inference "this pot is knowable, because it is nameable". The Navya Nyāya calls it a Kevalānvayi inference, because there is no agreement in absence (vyatirekavyāpti) between the middle term (e.g., 'nameable') and the major term (e.g., 'knowable'). Concomitance between 'not-nameable' and 'not-knowable' cannot be ascertained, because the terms do not stand for existents. All attributes abide in Brahman, since every attribute is the counter-entity (pratiyogi) of its absolute negation (atyantābhāva), though Brahman is devoid of attributes. There is absolute negation of all attributes in Brahman.[55] There is no Anvaya-vyatireki inference, which is said to be based on agreement in presence and agreement in absence between the middle term and the major term, since knowledge of vyatirekavyāpti, agreement in absence, is not a cause of inference. There is no Kevalavyatireki inference, since knowledge of negative concomitance of the absence of the major term and the absence of the middle term cannot generate inference. "Where there is no fire, there is no smoke". This is vyatirekavyāpti. Concomitance of the absence of a fire and the absence of smoke cannot produce the inference of the existence of a fire from the existence of smoke. What is called Kevalavyatireki inference is presumption (arthāpatti).[56] Thus the Advaita Vedānta rejects the three kinds of inference, Kevalānvayi, Kevalavyatireki, and Anvaya-vyatireki recognized by the Navya Nyāya. There are two kinds of inference, inference for oneself (svārtha) and inference for others (parārtha). The former is generated by the impression of vyāpti. The latter consists of three members only, proposition (pratijñā), reason (hetu), and example (udāharaṇa), or example, application (upanaya), and conclusion (nigamana). Three members can show vyāpti and existence of the middle term in the subject of inference. The two other members of the Nyāya syllogism are redundant. The Nyāya states a demonstrative syllogism thus : (1) "the mountain is fiery (pratijñā); (2) because it is smoky (hetu); (3) whatever is smoky, is fiery, as the kitchen (udāharaṇa); (4) the mountain is smoky (upanaya); (5) therefore, it is fiery (nigamana)". The Advaita Vedānta agrees with the Mīmāṁsā in advocating the three-membered syllogism. Bhaṭṭa Vādīndra explains different kinds of crooked or irregular syllogisms called 'mahāvidyā' and criticizes them.[57]

(3) Comparison (upamāna).—Comparison is the means of the knowledge of similarity. A person, who has perceived a cow in a town, goes to a forest, and perceives a wild cow. He has an apprehension "this animal is similar to a cow" owing to the intercourse of of his eyes with the animal. Then he has an apprehension "my cow is similar to this animal".

This knowledge of similarity of a cow to a wild cow is acquired by comparison. The knowledge of similarity existing in a wild cow to a cow (gavayaniṣṭhagosādṛśyajñāna) is the instrumental cause (karaṇa). The knowledge of similarity existing in a cow to a wild cow (goniṣṭhagavayasādṛśyajñāna) is the result. This knowledge of similarity cannot be acquired from perception, since the cow is not present to the eyes. Nor can it be acquired from inference, since similarity existing in a wild cow to a cow cannot serve as a mark of inference (liṅga) as follows : "my cow is similar to this wild cow ; because she is the correlate of similarity existing in this wild cow ; whatever is the correlate of similarity to another thing is similar to it, as Caitra, the correlate of similarity existing in Maitra, is similar to Maitra." The Advaita Vedānta contends that the reason or mark (liṅga) must exist in the minor term (pakṣa), but that the reason 'similarity existing in a wild cow to a cow' does not exist in the minor term 'my cow'. Therefore, it cannot prove the existence of the major term 'similarity existing in my cow to a wild cow'. Therefore the knowledge of similarity existing in my cow to a wild cow cannot be acquired from inference. It is acquired from comparison, which is neither perception nor inference, but a distinct means of valid knowledge.[58] A presented suggests its similar B. Then we have the knowledge that A is similar to B. The similarity of B to A is apprehended (anubhavasiddha). It is not inferred through the function of vyāpti. It is not perceived, since A alone is perceived.[59]

The Advaita Vedānta view of comparison is similar to the Mīmāṁsā view. Kumārila and Prabhākara regard comparison as the knowledge of similarity of a perceived object (e.g., a wild cow) in a remembered object (e.g., a cow). Comparison is the knowledge of similarity of the remembered cow to a perceived wild cow. It depends upon the knowledge of similarity of the wild cow to the cow.[60] The Nyāya, on the other hand, holds that comparison is the knowledge of similarity of an unfamiliar object (e.g., a wild cow) to a familiar object (e.g., a cow).[61]

(4) Presumption (arthāpatti).—It is the assumption (āpatti) of a fact (artha) to account for another inexplicable fact. The postulation of a hypothesis to explain the inexplicable fact is called arthāpatti. It is presumption, postulation, or implication. The knowledge of the fact to be explained (upapādyajñāna) is the instrumental cause (karaṇa). The knowledge of the fact that explains (upapādakājñāna) is the result (phala). A person is known not to eat in the day time, and yet gets stout. His stoutness is to be explained (upapādya). It cannot be explained without postulating his eating at night. In the absence of his eating at night his stoutness cannot be explained. Eating at night explains the unintelligible fact (upapādaka). This assumption (kalpanā) of a hypothesis is called (arthāpatti). It is the supposition of a cause. The effect is given. The cause is assumed.[61]

The Advaita Vedānta agrees with Kumārila's view that arthāpatti is assumption of some unperceived fact to account for some inconsistency in perceived facts.[62] Prabhākara maintains that there must be an element of doubt as to the truth of the two inconsistent facts perceived. Presumption removes the element of doubt. We know that a person is alive, and perceive his absence from his house. This perception generates a doubt whether he is alive or dead. The doubt is removed by the presumption of his living somewhere else.[63] This view is wrong. If the person's living be doubtful, his going out of his house cannot be assumed. If his living is certain, then only the presumption is made.

Presumption cannot be regarded as an inference, since the universal major premise cannot be based on positive concomitance (anvayavyāpti). Negative côncomitance (vyatirekavyāpti) is not admitted by the Advaita Vedānta. The Kevalavyatireki inference based on negative concomitance is nothing but presumption.[64]

(5) Non-apprehension (anupalabdhi).—Non-existence (abhāva) is known by non-apprehension or non-cognition. It cannot be known by the other pramāṇas. Non-apprehension is the unique pramāṇa which cognizes negation or non-existence.[65] The non-existence of a jar on the ground is known by non-apprehension. When the jar is removed from the ground, we perceive the ground, the locus (adhikaraṇa) of the non-existence of the jar, but wė do not perceive the non-existence itself. We know the non-existence by non-apprehension. Though the locus of non-existence is perceived, the non-existence itself is not perceived. Non-existence is known by non-apprehension. It can never be known by perception. The perceptive process is directed only to the locus of the non-existence, but not to the non-existence itself. The non-existence is known by appropriate non-apprehension (yogyānupaladbhi). The object of abhāva must be capable of being perceived. The object, which is absent, must be fit for being perceived. If it is not capable of being perceived, its non-existence cannot be known by non-apprehension. A jar is capable of being perceived. If the jar had been present, it would have been perceived. Merit (dharma) and demerit (adharma) are supersensible. They cannot be perceived. So their non-existence cannot be known by non-apprehension. The thing that is absent, must be of the same order of reality as its locus which is perceived. The negation must not be absolute negation, but it must be the negation of something perceptible.

Prabhākara maintains that the non-existence of a thing is non-different from its bare locus (adhikaraṇa). The non-existence of a jar on the ground is nothing but the bare ground. When we perceive a jar on the ground, we perceive the ground as related to the existence of the jar. But when the jar is absent, we perceive the bare ground only.[66] The Sāṁkhya also holds that non-existence of a thing is identical with its bare locus.[67] Perception of the mere locus is erroneously called non-apprehension. Perception of the bare ground is a positive cognition. It is not non-cognition. The Advaita Vedānta, like Kumārila, contends that if the non-existence of a jar on the ground were identical with the bare ground, it would be perceived even when the jar is present on the ground.[68] The Advaita Vedānta regards non-existence as non-different from its locus. It considers the world appearance to be non-different from Brahman, its locus. But it maintains that non-existence is known by non-apprehension, and that it is not known by the perception of its locus. But Dharmarājādhvarīndra admits four kinds of non-existence : prior non-existence, posterior non-existence, mutual non-exirtence, and absolute non-existence recognized by the Nyāya-Vaiśeṣika. The Naiyāyika advocates the adjectival theory of non-existence. He considers non-existence to be an attribute of the locus. The ground is qualified by the non-existence of a jar. The non-existence of the jar on the ground is perceived through the visual organ which is in conjunction with the ground qualified by the non-existence of the jar. Non-existence is perceived through the sense-object-intercourse called viśeṣaṇatā. The Advaita Vedānta rejects this view, since viśeṣaṇatā cannot be a mode of sense-object-intercourse. If it were so, there would be the cognition of the non-existence of a jar on the ground which is hidden by a wall, since it is qualified by the non-existence of the jar.[69] All pramāṇas except scriptural testimony have pragmatic validity. If they conflict with practical actions, or lead to unsuccessful actions, they are invalid. They give empirical truths. But the Vedānta gives the ontological truth. It conveys the reality of Brahman.

(6) Testimony (āgama).—A sentence refers to an objective relation. That sentence is a valid source of knowledge, which refers to an objective relation, which is not contradicted by any other means of valid knowledge.[70] A sentence must fulfil four conditions in order to convey a meaning. It must have syntactical connection (ākāṅkṣā) among its essential parts. A verb must demand a subject, a transitive verb, an object, and the like. A sentence must have fitness (yogyatā) or compatibility of meaning among its parts. The objective relation conveyed by a sentence must be free from contradiction. It must be harmonious. "He wets the ground with a fire". This sentence is meaningless. The objective relation conveyed by it is self-contradictory. A sentence must have proximity of its parts (āsatti). If the words 'bring', 'a', and 'cow' are uttered at the interval of one hour each, they do not form a sentence, and convey any meaning. They must be uttered in close succession to form a sentence. A sentence must have an objective intention (tātparya). 'Saindhavam ānaya'. It means either 'bring a horse' or 'bring salt'. If a person utters the sentence while taking his meal, it obviously means 'bring salt'. Fitness (yogyatā) is the formal compatibility of meaning. Intention (tātparya) is compatibility in a material reference. It is correspondence of the subjective intention of the speaker with the objective relation conveyed by the sentence.[71]

A sentence is composed of words. The Nyāya maintains that a word denotes an individual (vyakti), connotes a genus (jāti), and suggests a configuration (ākṛti), or that a word denotes an individual endued with a genus and a configuration. But the Advaita Vedānta maintains that a word denotes a genus (jāti), and not individuals, since individuals are infinite in number. How, then, can it denote an individual? The genus and the individual are apprehended by the same cognition produced by a word at the same time.[72] Śaṁkara admits the existence of universals which are not born, while individuals are born and die. Words are related to universals, not to individuals, since individuals are infinite in number. There is an eternal relation between words and their meanings.[73]

Words are composed of sounds. Sounds are not created, but only manifested. When a letter is uttered, it is not created anew but only manifested in an audible form. The sound-form is eternal, but its manifestation alone is in time. The word is eternal. It existed in all previous cycles. It is remembered by Īśvara, and manifested to us. The Veda is eternal. It embodies eternal truths. It is revealed by Īśvara in the beginning of each cycle.[74] The Vedas are self-evident. Their authoritativeness is independent of other conditions. They are eternal. They embody eternal truths. The entire Vedānta is concerned with Brahman including false attributions (adhyāropa) and refutation (apavāda) of them. It also proves the negation of the false world appearance (prapañcābhāva). The positing of Brahman and the negating of the world are compatible with each other. When there is a conflict between scriptural testimony and other pramāṇas, the former is stronger and valid.

ŚRUTI (INTUITION) AND REASON.—Śruti embodies the intuitions of seers. In regard to supersensible and suprarational matters Śruti is the only authoritative source of knowledge. The existence of God, or Brahman, future life or immortality of the soul, liberation and the like are supersensible. Śruti is the only unimpeachable authority in respect of these topics. Reason should be in harmony with intuition. Intuition overrides reason, but reason cannot overthrow intuition.[75]

Perception, inference and the other pramāṇas are concerned with empirical (vyāvahārika) objects. They have empirical validity, but not ontological validity. Śruti gives the ontological truth of the reality of Brahman, That is nondual and indeterminate. When there is conflict between Śruti and perception, the former should be accepted as valid. Perception and inference should not conflict with practical actions, because they deal with empirical objects. They should correspond to external objects and relations among them.[76]

TESTS OF TRUTH.—Vācaspati defines a pramāṇa as what generates uncontradicted, and undoubted knowledge, not acquired in the past. A true knowledge must be novel, and not a reproduction of past knowledge. It must be undoubted. It must be uncontradicted by valid knowledge. Noncontradiction or coherence with a system of true judgments is the test of truth according to the Advaita Vedānta. It agress with Bradley and Bosanquet, Western Idealists, on this point. When a judgment is contradicted by other valid judgments, it is false. When it is not contradicted by other valid judgments, it is true. Novelty is a test of truth. It implies correspondence of a judgment with given facts, which have empirical reality. The Advaita Vedānta advocates the representative theory of perception according to which a cognition represents its object. A cognition is a mental mode which is modified into the form of its object. The consciousness of the Self is reflected in the insentient mental mode, and enables it to cognize the object. So there is correspondence between them. The invalidity of an illusion (e.g., silver in a nacre) is known by an unfruitful action (visaṁvādipravṛtti) (e.g., nonattainment of silver). So a valid knowledge is known by a fruitful action (saṁvādipravṛtti).[77] According to Maṇḍana Miśra empirical validity is known by correspondence with fruitful action ; empirical pramāṇas cannot enlighten us on the ontological reality of Brahman ; they are not independent of one another in their nature, and they are characterized by correspondence with fruitful practical actions. Noncontradiction (abādhitatva) stated above holds good of the empirical world until mystic intuition of Brahman is achieved. The root nescience, the cause of illusions, is contradicted by the realization of Brahman.[78] Mahādeva Sarasvatī defines valid knowledge as apprehension which cognizes the real nature of an object. Apprehension is knowledge other than recollection. It is of two kinds, true and false. Apprehension of the real nature of an object is valid. Apprehension of an object contradicted by a valid knowledge is invalid.[79] Mahādeva regards correspondence and coherence both as tests of truth. Vimuktātman avers that the knowledge, which sublates an illusion, is empirically true. The knowledge of a nacre sublates the illusion of silver, and has empirical truth. From the ontological standpoint it is false. Empirical pramāṇas give only empirical truths. Empirical objects are neither real, nor unreal, nor both, but indescribable and inexplicable (aniravacanīya), because they are effects of inexplicable cosmic nescience (māyā).[80] They have empirical reality, and are capable of leading to practical actions (arthakriyā). True empirical objects lead to effective actions, while false empirical objects lead to ineffective actions. The Advaita Vedānta does not deny externality, empirical reality, presentability, and practical efficiency of true empirical objects. It has been elaborately explained already in the eighth chapter.

SUBLATION.—Vidyāraṇya discusses the nature of sublation (bādha) by which falsity of an illusion is ascertained. Sublation is not the arrest of the voluntary action of a person to get illusory silver by the perception of a nacre, because a person devoid of attachment does not exert himself to get silver. Sublation may be said to be the arrest of a voluntary action preceded by attachment to get an illusory object. If it were true, then a person perceiving illusory water at a distance in a desert in the hot sun, and desisting from proceeding at the sight of a thief or a serpent, would have sublation. But his illusion of water (e.g., a mirage) is not destroyed, and so it is not sublated. Sublation is not the destruction of the capacity for a voluntary action to appropriate an illusory object, because a person can perform a voluntary action in the same place at some other time to get illusory silver in a nacre because of the nondestruction of the capacity. If sublation is discrimination of what are perceived as nondistinct, either the attribute of difference first exists and then is perceived, or difference being the nature of the objects is perceived at the same time. If the first alternative were true, everywhere the cognition of an object being that of an undiscriminated thing, the knowledge of difference would be the sublator (bādhaka). If the second alternative were true, there would be no nondiscrimination when an object was perceived. Sublation is not the knowledge of mutual nonexistence of objects, which are perceived as identical, because if they are entirely different from each other, or if they are different and nondifferent from each other, the perception of difference (e.g., whiteness of a jar) after first perceiving identity (e.g., a white jar) would be the sublator of the first cognition. Sublation is not the destruction of a false cognition, because a cognition being momentary is destroyed by its nature. Sublation is not the destruction of the object of false knowledge, because an object is real, and so cannot be destroyed by a cognition. Nor is sublation the destruction of the defect of the object of false knowledge, because the defect is real, and so cannot be destroyed by a cognition. But sublation cannot be denied, because it is well-known. Vidyāraṇya avers that sublation is the termination of a nescience with its effect, present or past, by a true knowledge.[81] The knowledge of a nacre is the sublator of the illusion of silver. Or, the knowledge "this is not silver" is the sublator of the illusion "this is silver". Thus falsity of an illusion is ascertained.

ADVAITA VEDĀNTĀ SCEPTICISM: CRITICISM OF VALID KNOWLEDGE.—Śrīharṣa refutes the Nyāya definitions of valid knowledge and the different kinds of valid knowledge recognized by it and Kumārila Bhaṭṭa, viz , perception, inference, comparison, testimony, presumption and nonapprehension. The criticism of the categories has already been given.

Śivāditya defines valid knowledge (pramā) as apprehension of the real nature of its object.[82] Śrīharṣa urges that the meaning of 'real nature' (tattva) cannot be determined. Nothing exists which may be denoted by the words 'real nature'. Brahman alone is real; everything else is an unreal appearance. It is contended that an object related to apprehension is manifested to awareness and exists in buddhi, and is called real nature. This contention is false, for a nacre, which is not silver, is manifested to consciousness as silver as its object. So a valid cognition cannot be distinguished from a false cognition. Apprehension has always an object. So valid cognition is the apprehension of the attributes of its object. If a substantive thing endued with attributes be said to be not reality, then the definition of valid cognition will not apply to that part of the substantive (dharmin), and so the direct apprehension of the substantive will not be a valid cognition.[83] It is contended that the fault shown in the definition is due to breaking a thing into parts, e.g., the substantive and the attributes, but that reality means nature (svarūpa) alone. This contention is false, because the genus of nature or a common property other than the genus can neither exist in nature nor be absent from it. The nature of one thing is confined to it, and cannot apply to other things. The words 'real nature' cannot exclude erroneous cognitions. The cognition of the quality of silver in a nacre also is certainly the cognition of its nature. It is not reasonable to say that the substantive (e.g., a nacre) or the quality of silver is not its nature. Nor is it reasonable to say that the relation between them, which is manifested to consciousness, is not its nature. Inherence of the quality of silver in a nacre also is manifested to consciousness, and so that also is its nature. It is contended that though inherence is nature, yet the quality of silver does not inhere in the individual nacre. This contention is false, since, though the quality of silver does not exist in the individual nacre, nature cannot be excluded from it. It is contended that mere nature is not the reality of an object of cognition, but that the nature of a thing, which is apprehended as related to a particular part of space and time, is the reality of the thing. This contention is false, because, if that were so, the right cognition of a thing would be invalid in the part of its relation to time and space.[84] It is contended that the real nature of thing is as it is apprehended. This contention also is false, because, if what is apprehended with a nature at a time remains with the nature at some other time, the apprehension of the thing with the same nature at some other time is not false. An earthen jar is dark when it is unbaked, and it becomes red when it is baked. But even when it is dark in its unbaked condition, it is perceived as red by a person with eyes affected by red bile. So the cognition of it is valid according to the definition. But the cognition is false. So the definition is faulty. Further, the apprehension of a thing being qualified by time is invalid, because being qualified by time cannot be related to some other time.[85] Furthermore, the nature of apprehension has to be ascertained. It is either a species of the genus of knowledge or knowledge different from memory, or knowledge devoid of the characteristic of memory, or knowledge produced by an uncommon cause at the time immediately prior to memory. The first alternative is unjustified, for one genus of apprehension cannot be proved, because there are no cognitions like "I apprehend", "I apprehend", in perception, inference, comparison and testimony, which are different from memory. Further, perception, inference, comparison, testimony and memory will be shown to be indeterminable.

Udayana defines valid knowledge as proper determination.[86] Śrīharṣa refutes it thus. This definition is invalid, because the word 'proper' cannot mean having the real nature (tattva) of a thing for its object, or agreement of a cognition with its object for the reasons stated above.[87] If the word 'proper' means entirety, it means either a cognition cognizing an object with all its parts or a cognition cognizing an object with all its qualities. The first alternative is inadmissible, since the determination of a partless object would not be valid, if it were true. The second alternative also is untenable, because, if that were true, determinate cognitions of all nonomniscient persons would be invalid. Only omniscient God has determinate cognition of all the qualities of an object. If the word 'proper' means an object with its distinctive qualities, then valid knowledge is the determination of an object with its distinctive qualities. This definition is invalid, since then the illusion of silver in a nacre will be valid, for a person seems to perceive the distinctive qualities of silver in a nacre.[88] It is contended that in the valid perception of a thing its special distinctive marks are perceived whereas in the illusory perception of an object its special distinguishing features are not perceived, that the former is not contradicted while the latter is contradicted, and that if this distinction be not admitted, the real nature of an object cannot be distinguished from its unreal nature. This contention is false, because the special nature of the distinctive marks cannot be determined, by knowing which an illusion can be known as false.[89] It is difficult to determine which special distinctive characters are real, and which are unreal. A dreamer perceives all distinctive features of things, and thinks them to be valid. If special distinguishing marks are taken in a general sense, then in illusory perception of silver in a nacre the distinctive mark of being before the eyes is present in the nacre. If special distinguishing marks mean all special distinctive marks, then no definition including all of them is possible inasmuch as they are endless in number. If special distinguishing features of an object be said to be known by the perception of an object, which is not contradicted, that is not possible, because the later contradicting cognition is vitiated by the same fault as vitiated the contradicted cognition. The nature of valid knowledge has not yet been ascertained.[90] Contradicting cognition and contradicted cognition are contradictory in their nature ; they cognize objects contradictory to each other. So the former cannot determine the latter. Moreover, determination is apprehension, and is vitiated by the faults of apprehension already shown.[91]

Valid knowledge is defined as undeviating apprehension.[92] If 'undeviating' means 'in harmony with the real nature of an object apprehended,' then the definition has already been shown to be false. If 'undeviating' means 'not existing without its object' it means either the cognition existing in the place where its object exists, or the cognition existing at the time when its object exists, or the cognition corresponding with its object in all its features. The first definition is invalid, since it does not apply to valid cognitions of objects nonexistent in the place. The second definition is invalid, for it does not apply to inference of past and future objects. The third definition is invalid, since complete correspondence of a cognition with its object in all its features cannot be determined according to the realist who admits difference between them, and since an illusion also will correspond with its object in all respects according to the Buddhist subjective idealist who admits identity between them, and the qualification 'undeviating' will be needless. If correspondence means correspondence of a cognition with particular aspects of its object, then the definition was already shown to be faulty when valid knowledge as apprehension of the real nature of an object was refuted.[93]

The Buddhists (e.g., Dharmottara) define valid knowledge as apprehension, which is not inconsistent with its object.[94] This definition is false, because noninconsistency of a cognition with its object cannot be ascertained. If it means a cognition agreeing with another cognition cognizing the object with a similar nature, then a series of illusions continuing for some time will be valid, because they are not contradicted so long, and because they are in agreement with their objects. If noninconsistency means not being known by another cognition which cognizes the object with a contradictory nature, then the definition will apply to an illusion which has not yet been contradicted by a sublating cognition, and such a wrong cognition will be valid. Further, the cognition of a white conchshell by a person with normal eyes contradicted by the cognition of a yellow conchshell by a person with jaundiced eyes will be invalid. If noninconsistency means a cognition not being contradicted by a cognition produced by a nonvitiated sense-organ, then that should be the definition of valid knowledge. Further, until the nature of vitiated condition of a sense-organ is known, the nature of its unvitiated condition cannot be known. If valid knowledge be defined as cognition which is not wrong cognition, that is not possible, for wrong cognition cannot be determined until valid cognition is determined. If noninconsistency means the cognition of an object with the same nature as it exists, it means either as it exists in a general way or as it exists with its distinctive features. In the first alternative, the dream-cognition of a fire with smoke or the cognition of an object produced by the testimony of an unreliable person will not be wrong, because they cognize objects as they exist in a general way. In the second alternative, the cognition of an object with its distinctive features means its causal efficiency (arthakriyā) or the cognition of an object with the collocation of its causes. Both the alternatives are vitiated by faults already shown. If a cognition cognizing an object with its particular features means its causal efficiency, real causal efficiency is not determinable, and so the cognition is not capable of evoking a responsive action. If causal efficiency means mere experience, then wrong cognition also, being experience, will be valid.[95] If noninconsistency means cognition of an object having causal efficiency, and if causal efficiency is taken in a general way, then even wrong cognition will be valid. If noninconsistency means a cognition having causal efficiency as experienced, then it cannot be ascertained.[96] If causal efficiency as experienced be said to be known from the cognition of causal efficiency of its object, this is false, because even without the cognition of the cousal efficiency of its object, causal efficiency of a cognition can be experienced.[97] If causal efficiency be said to be valid cognition or desire to speak of an object, this is not possible, since valid cognition is not yet determined, and since a dream-cognition, which is consistent with intention to speak, will be valid. Noninconsistency with causal efficiency at some other time also is indeterminable.[98]

Valid knowledge is defined as cognition, which is fit for bringing about the attainment of the object cognized.[99] This definition of Dharmottara also is refuted by the reasoning stated above. It is invalid, for what object is to be attained is not certain. Silver is perceived in the illusion of silver in a nacre, but silver is not attained. It is not certain when the object is to be attained. If the object is attained at a future time, it continues for more than one moment, and this contradicts the doctrine of momentariness. The object is not attained at the moment when it is cognized. The production of a cognition and the attainment of an object do not occur at the same moment.[100]

Valid knowledge is defined as apprehension, which is uncontradicted.[101] If uncontradicted apprehension means that what is not contradicted at the time when it is produced, then an illusion is a valid cognition, for it is not contradicted at the time. If uncontradicted apprehension means apprehension, which is not contradicted at a future time, it cannot be ascertained. If uncontradicted apprehension means a person's apprehension of an object, which is not contradicted in his experience, then an illusion is valid until it is contradicted. If uncontradicted apprehension means apprehension, which is not contradicted in all persons' experiences, it is indeterminable.[102]

Valid knowledge is defined as the experience, which is distinct from hypothetical reasoning, doubt, illusion and memory.[103] This definition is invalid, for hypothetical reasoning and the like and distinctness from them are unascertainable. Valid cognition is defined as the cognition, which is the substrate of the genus of valid cognition.[104] This definition is invalid, because if the genus of valid knowledge being known is the cause of the knowledge of valid knowledge, there will arise no error and doubt as to valid cognition. If valid cognition be said to be related to the genus of valid cognition attended with the absence of flaws, the mere knowledge (jñānamātra) wherein error and doubt have not yet arisen would be vitiated by the same difficulty. When this characteristic of valid cognition is known, how will this characteristic be known to exist in mere knowledge ? It cannot be known by mental perception. If it were known by mental perception somewhere, a cognition would never be invalid, and error and doubt would never arise in regard to it, because when a cognition will be cognized by mental perception, its validity also will be cognized by it. If the validity of mere cognition be said to be cognized by mental perception through some other sign, the sign itself being the characteristic of valid cognition may produce the knowledge of it. If the characteristic be said to be many, they are indeterminable. Further, knowledge is intrinsically valid : its validity does not depend on extraneous conditions as shown already. So valid cognition is not the substrate of the genus of valid cognition. This reasoning refutes the definition of valid knowledge as cognition related to a particular power, for it cannot be determined.[105] Hence valid knowledge is indefinable.

CRITICISM OF PRAMĀṆA.—A pramāṇa is defined as a means of right apprehension.[106] The author of 'Prakaṭārthavivaraṇa' criticizes the definition in the following way. Right apprehension is either manifestation of a real object or manifestation of an unknown object or knowledge distinct from appearance of valid knowledge. The first definition is too wide, for it applies to recollection, which cognizes a real object. It is contended that recollection is produced by a residual impression alone whereas apprehension is produced by a cause (e.g., a sense-organ), which is different from an impression. This contention is false, since recollection also is produced by conjunction of a soul with manas, which is a sense-organ. Further, apprehension being different from recollection is proved by a pramāṇa or not proved by a pramāṇa. If it is proved by a pramāṇa, this involves interdependence. When a pramāṇa has been defined, apprehension may be proved to be different from recollection, and then the definition of a pramāṇa may be proved. If apprehension being different from recollection is not proved by a pramāṇa, then the rule that the nature of an entity is proved by a pramāṇa is violated. Otherwise, the definition of a pramāṇa applies to recollection. If the second alternative were true, a serial perception would not be apprehension, because it cognizes what was cognized before. But the serial perception 'this is a jar' is regarded as valid apprehension. It is contended that even in a serial perception an object qualified by the next moment is unknown. The contention is false, since, according to the Nyāya, time is not perceived. Further, when a jar is known, its unknowness before cannot be known because of contradiction between knowing it and not knowing it. When it is not known, its being unknown cannot be known. Let then a jar being unknown before be known at the time when it is known. But its mere being known does not prove that it was unknown before. There is no apprehension of an object, when it is known by recollection. Nor is an object known by valid knowledge an object of apprehension, since this will involve interdependence. When an established object is unknown, its being known by a pramāṇa is established ; on the strength of this its being unknown before is established. If its being unknown before is proved by a pramāṇa, then a pramāṇa cannot be dispensed with. Because an object being unknown before is not determined, manifestation of an object unknown before is not right apprehension. The third definition distinctly involves interdependence. When right apprehension is proved to be valid knowledge, its appearance (ābhāsa) is proved ; when an appearance of valid knowledge is proved, right apprehension is proved to be valid knowledge. Further, right apprehension is either an instrument (karaṇa) or a mere cause (kāraṇa) of valid knowledge. In the first alternative, the definition will not apply to God's knowledge. In the second alternative, the definition will apply to time, which is a general cause of right apprehension. Further, if right apprehension is the characteristic of a pramāṇa in general, then the definition is too narrow, because generality is not a means, and because it has no dissimilar instance. If the definition be said to be the general characteristic of individual pramāṇas, then it involves interdependence. When individual pramāṇas are characterized by general characteristics, they are proved to be pramāṇas. When they are proved to be pramāṇas, the general characteristics are proved to be common to them. So the definition is false. Again, a pramāṇa is defined as 'yathārtha' knowledge. 'Yathārtha' means either existing without transcending an object or cognizing an object. The first definition is too narrow, because knowledge exists in a soul, which transcends an object. The second definition is too wide, since it applies to illusion which cognizes an object. Knowledge is that by which an object is cognized. So a pramāṇa is not 'yathārtha' knowledge. Hence a pramāṇa is indeterminable.[107]

CRITICISM OF PERCEPTION.—Akṣapāda defines perception as cognition produced by the intercourse of a sense-organ with an object and not contradicted.[108] Śrīharṣa offers the following criticisms of this definition. If it is so defined to distinguish it from other similar cognitions or perceptions, it fails to do so. Until it distinguishes itself from other perceptions, it is not distinct from them. If it is admitted to be distinct from them, though it does not distinguish itself from them, it does not apply to other perceptions. But a definition is always of a class-concept; an individual cannot be defined. If perception is defined to distinguish itself from other perceptions, it is not a definition of perception. If perception is so defined to distinguish itself from inference, comparison and testimony, which are dissimilar cognitions, the word 'dissimilar' is inadmissible, since perception is similar to them as objects of valid knowledge. Further, the production of perception by sense-object-intercourse is not perceived, because a sense-organ is imperceptible, and because its intercourse with an object is imperceptible. Perception is not experienced as qualified by sense-object-intercourse.[109] The production of perception by sense-object-intercourse is said to be inferred from its effect as a probans (liṅga), because the effect cannot be explained without a cause. This argument is invalid, since sense-object-intercourse in general is inferred as a cause of the effect, but being produced by an object with a special form is not proved in that a form common to all objects of perception is not proved. If being produced by sense-object-intercourse be inferred from immediate knowledge, then there is interdependence: the production of perception by sense-object-intercourse is inferred from immediate knowledge; immediate knowledge is inferred from sense-object-intercourse.[110] If there be some other mark of inference of the production of perception by sense-object-intercourse, let that be the definition of perception, since that being absent, immediate knowledge is absent, and since that produces the experience of being present before a sense-organ. Where there is no mark (liṅga) applicable to all instances of perception, there can be no inference of perception being produced by a sense-organ, and so it cannot be said to be immediate knowledge. Further, a sense-organ has intercourse with an object and with a self, but an object alone is perceived, but a self is not perceived. So a specific condition must be present in sense-object-intercourse, which prevents perception of the self. A perception produced by the intercourse of a sense-organ with an object with a manifested form is in the form "This is a jar". It is contended that a means of valid knowledge (pramāṇa) always produces valid knowledge of an object. So a valid perception produces the immediate knowledge of an object with its distinguishing features. Otherwise, a jar would be perceived as "this is a cloth". Because the visual organ is not in intercourse with a cloth, it is not perceived. The self is not perceived, since it does not belong to the object. If it is so, then is the cognition of a jar indeed perceived in the self, being produced by the intercourse of a sense-organ with the self? If the self is said to be not perceived, because it is not manifested, the contention is wrong, since the self is manifested somewhere by some cognition; otherwise it would not be knowable.[111]

Citsukha adduces the following arguments in refuting the Nyāya definition of perception. Uncontradictedness of perception cannot be determined. It cannot be known from its being produced by a collocation of causes unvitiated by faults, because faultlessness of its causes cannot be perceived. Nor can it be inferred from mere knowledge as a probans, since, if that were true, faultlessness in the causes of illusion also would be known, and it would be valid. Nor is faultlessness of the causes of perception inferred from uncontradicted knowledge, since it involves interdependence: uncontradictedness of knowledge is inferred from its being produced by a faultless instrument (karaṇa) of knowledge; being produced by a faultless instrument of knowledge is inferred from uncontradicted knowledge. Nor is uncontradictedness of knowledge inferred from its not being sublated by a sublating knowledge, because it is contradicted either by the experiences of all persons or by the experience of the perceiver. A nonomniscient person cannot know that a cognition is not contradicted by the experiences of all persons. The perceiving person may not have a sublating cognition because of his going to another place or because of his death. A person's perception of nonexistent water in a desert illumined by the rays of the sun may not be contradicted because of his receding from the place or because of his death. Nor is uncontradictedness of a cognition inferred from its capacity for producing an effort in the perceiver, because it is incapable of being determined. Effort is either desire to act, or a physical effort, or relation to the result (e.g , water). It is argued that the capacity for producing an effort (pravṛttisāmarthya) being inferred from a mark (liṅga) produces the knowledge of uncontradictedness. If the argument were valid, the capacity for producing an effort being inferred from knowledge in general would produce the knowledge of its uncontradictedness, and therefore illusion and dream also would be uncontradicted, because they also produce efforts to act. Or, the capacity for producing an effort to act produces the knowledge of uncontradictedness. This argument involves interdependence : the capacity for producing an effort is inferred from uncontradictedness ; uncontradictedness is inferred from the capacity for producing an effort. Vācaspati Miśra argues that the disputed cognition is in agreement with its object, because it produces an effective action (samarthapravṛtti). This argument is wrong, since a person mistakes a ray of a gem for a gem, makes an effort to pick it up, and gets it. Here an erroneous perception produces an effective action. The reason is contradicted.[112] Further, relation to a fruit is either the obtainment of the object manifested in consciousness, or obtainment of a similar object. The object manifested in consciousness (e.g., water) cannot be obtained because of the disjunction of its parts by the action of a cow or the like in it. When a star is perceived, either the star perceived or a similar star is not obtained. Furthermore, uncontradictedness of a cognition is not a genus of valid knowledge (pramātva). If it were the genus of valid knowledge, there would be intermixture of genera (jātisaṅkara), because it is said, "All illusory cognitions are valid in regard to the substantive (dharmin) and erroneous in regard to its attribute (prakāra) manifested in consciousness". So in the illusion "this is silver" 'this'—part is valid, and 'silver'—part is erroneous. So there is intermixture of genera of valid knowledge and invalid knowledge.

Citsukha observes that if perception were produced by sense-object-intercourse, divine perception, yogic perception of atoms, and recognition would not be perception. God's perception is eternal, and so is not produced by sense-object-intercourse. The manas also is a sense-organ, and so inference produced by it would be perception. Yogic perception of atoms and the like is not produced by the intercourse of a sense-organ with atoms. So it would cease to be perception. Recognition (e.g., "this is that Devadatta") is regarded as perception. But 'that'—part of it is not produced by sense-object-intercourse. So it would not be perception. So perception is indeterminable.[113]

CRITICISM OF DETERMINATE AND INDETERMINATE PERCEPTION.—The Nyāya recognizes two kinds of perception : determinate (savikalpa) and indeterminate (nirvikalpa). Determinate perception is produced by a cause and refers to the relation between a name and an object signified by it. Inderminate perception apprehends a mere object without a name and an object signified by it. The author of 'Prakṭārthavivaraṇa' criticizes these definitions in the following manner. The relation of a name to an object named is either apprehended by determinate perception, or produces determinate perception. In the first alternative, the so-called determinate perception is not perception, since it is apprehended by the visual organ. The eye cannot apprehend the relation between a name and an object. In the second alternative, it is known elsewhere, because it produces the knowledge of the relation of a name to an object elsewhere, and because determinate perception involves that knowledge, or recollection. The relation between a name and an object is not known by manas alone, because recollection is due to the revival of a residual impression. But the relation between them is not invariable. So determinate perception is not always produced by the relation of a name to an object.[114] A person with eyes wide open and with an attentive mind would not have determinate perception of an object in spite of the sense-object-intercourse, because the name of an object is not perceived through the eyes, because the object signified by the name is not perceived, and because the residual impression of the name cannot be revived without the perception of the object. Determinate perception is defined as knowledge different from indeterminate perception. This definition also is false, because difference is proved when its counterentities are proved, and because difference which is proved already has counterentities, and because this involves interdependence.[115] So determinate perception is a false appearance, like the false appearance of the difference between a reflection of the moon in water and the moon. Indeterminate perception is defined as apprehension of a mere object. It means either apprehension of generality of an entity or apprehension of an undetermined entity. The first alternative is not justified, because generality depends upon its being common to many individuals, and because being common to many individuals depends upon difference among them being proved. But difference cannot be apprehended by opening the eyes at the first moment. The second alternative also is untenable, because being not determined by a condition depends upon the knowledge of a condition. Further, the sense-object-intercourse cannot produce the apprehension of an undetermined object, because intercourse (e.g., conjunction) is found to exist between a sense-organ and a limited object distinguished from other objects, and because a sense-organ cannot have intercourse with an unlimited and undistinguished object. So both determinate perception and indeterminate perception are indeterminable.[116]

CRITICISM OF INFERENCE.—Citsukha adduces the following arguments in refuting inference. It is not knowledge produced by the consideration of a probans invariably concomitant with the probandum existing in the subject of inference, since it has no causal operation (vyāpāra). An instrument has always a causal operation through which it can produce a result. A probans invariably concomitant with the probandum is not the instrument of inference, since invariable concomitance is indeterminable. It is defined as uniform co-absence of the probandum with the probans, or natural relation between them, or unconditional relation between them.[117] The first is defined as wherever there is the absence of the probandum, there is the absence of the probans. Such invariable concomitance between individual cases of the probandum and those of the probans cannot be perceived because of their infinite number. We are not omniscient, and so cannot perceive all individual instances of both. If all individual cases of both be said to be perceived through association with their generalities (sāmānya-lakṣaṇa-pratyāsatti), then all knowable things can be perceived through association with their generality, and all persons will be omniscient. Further, there is no effort to infer unless a uniform relation between the probans and the probandum is proved ; unless individual cases of both are perceived, the uniform relation between them cannot be proved. So all individual cases of both with their distinguishing features must be perceived at the time of perceiving invariable concomitance between them. But this is not possible, since a person perceiving invariable concomitance between knowability and nameability will be omniscient. Further, uniform co-absence of the probandum with the probans (avinābhāva) is not invariable presence of the probandum with the presence of the probans, because in a kevalānvayi inference this characteristic of invariable concomitance is not present. If the probans is present in other places than in the subject of inference, the inference is not kevalavyatireki. Avinābhāva is not the uniform absence of the probans with the absence of the probandum, since this characteristic of invariable concomitance is not present in a kevalānvayi inference. The uniform relation is not both, because this characteristic of invariable concomitance is not present in an anvyavyatireki inference. For similar reasons invariable concomitance is not natural relation between the probans and the probandum, because the relation between the genus of the probans and the genus of the probandum, or between the individual cases of the former and those of the latter cannot be perceived, and because natural relation cannot be determined. Nor is invariable concomitance unconditional relation, since the relata between which it obtains are unascertainable, and since this involves interdependence. A condition (upādhi) (e.g., wet fuel) invariably accompanies the probandum (e.g., smoke), but does not accompany the probans (e.g., fire).[118] So a condition is proved by invariable concomitance ; invariable concomitance is proved by a condition.[119] Further, invariable concomitance between inference and invariable concomitance depends upon invariable concomitance. So this involves self-dependence (ātmāśraya) or begging the question.[120] Where there is invariable concomitance, there is inference, and where there is no invariable concomitance, there is no inference. Furthermore, invariable concomitance is not known by perception, because it is impossible. Nor is it known by inference, since this will lead to infinite regress. Nor is it known by comparison, testimony, presumption, and nonapprehension, which are indeterminable. So invariable concomitance is indefinable and unprovable.

The subject of inference (pakṣa) is defined as that substantive (dharmin) in which the attribute—existence of the probandum—is doubtful. In a debate neither the proponent nor the opponent entertains any doubt. If they have any doubt, they cannot engage in a debate. The neutral judges also do not have any doubt, for they know the truth of the subject of debate. Further, without a doubt a person about to infer a fire after perceiving smoke in a hill can do so ; but if he has a doubt in the existence of a fire in the hill, he cannot do so. Because the subject of inference is indefinable, a probans invariably concomitant with the probandum existing in it is indefinable. In the absence of the existence of such a probans in the subject of inference there can be no inference. The subject of inference cannot be defined as an object endued with an attribute which has to be inferred for another person. This definition does not apply to inference for oneself, since no attribute is inferred for another person in it. The subject of inference is not endued with a property which is desired to be proved, since there is an inference of a property which is not desired to be known. So neither invariable concomitance, nor the existence of a probans invariably concomitant with the probandum in the subject of inference can be determined. So inference is indefinable. Inference for another person depends upon inference for oneself, and is therefore indefinable.[121]

Inference is defined as a means of apprehension on the ground of invariable concomitance between a probans and a probandum. "The hill is fiery, because it is smoky, like a kitchen." The author of 'Prakaṭārthavivaraṇa" asks whether inference is a means of apprehension of fieriness alone, or whether it is a means of apprehension of fieriness limited by the hill (e g., "the hill is fieriy"). In the first alternative, inference is not a means of apprehension of fieriness alone, because it is already known by perception, and because inference generates recollection of the fact. So the definition is too narrow. The second definition also is too narrow, because fieriness of the hill is apprehended without apprehending the invariable concomitance of smokiness and fieriness. But, according to the definition, it cannot be apprehended without apprehending the invariable concomitance of them. This criticism disproves Udayana's view that both invariable concomitance (vyāpti) and a probans pervaded by a probandum existing in a subject of inference (pakṣadharmatā) are necessary for inference, because general invariable concomitance between a probans and a probandum is proved on the strength of invariable concomitance, and because its application to a special instance (e.g. a hill) is proved on the strength of the knowledge of the existence of the probans (e.g., smokiness) in the subject of inference (e.g., the hill). Further, Udayana's view is false, because the characteristic does not apply to each part of the definition, and because one characteristic cannot be of two natures. The absence of a smoke with the absence of a fire is invariable concomitance. Such co-absence of a probans and a probandum cannot be proved by a pramāṇa. Further, the two attributes, smokiness and fieriness, cannot be proved to be different or nondifferent from each other, because difference is indeterminable as shown already. It is contended that invariable concomitance and the existence of a probans in the subject of inference collectively are the means of inference as sense-object-intercourse and a residual impression collectively are the means of recognition. This contention is false, because, if that be true, each is not a characteristic of inference, and because they collectively are not the means of inference in that the opponent does not regard the aggregate to be an entity different from its units, and in that the recollection of invariable concomitance and apprehension of the existence of the probans in the subject of inference occur successively, and in that a residual impression is not perceived, and in that the knowledge of the presence of the probans in the subject of inference together with the residual impression of invariable concomitance is not perceived. So they cannot prove inference.[122]

Inference is defined again as knowledge derived from a mark or probans (liṅga) qualified by its invariable concomitance with a probandum and by its existence in the subject of inference. This definition is vitiated by interdependence. Invariable concomitance also is indeterminable. It is defined as natural pervasion of a probans by a probandum. It is of two kinds: invariable co-presence (anvaya) and invariable co-absence (vyatireka). The former is pervasion of a probans in general by a probandum in general. The latter is pervasion of the absence of the probandum in general by the absence of a probans in general. Natural pervasion is unconditional. A condition (upādhi) is what is nonpervasive of a probans but co-extensive with a probandum. This definition is vitiated by interdependence. When invariable concomitance is proved, a condition is proved. When a condition is proved, unconditional invariable concomitance is proved. So inference is indeterminable.[123]

CRITICISM OF COMPARISON (UPAMĀNA).—An inhabitant of a town hears from a forester "a wild cow (gavaya) is like a cow", goes to a forest, perceives a strange animal like a cow, and knows it to be a wild cow. This knowledge is upamiti, and the means of its knowledge is comparison (upamāna) according to the Naiyāyika. Upamiti is the knowledge of the meaning of a testimony of a reliable person after perceiving a strange object. This knowledge is not produced by testimony, because if it were produced by testimony, a person would have this knowledge without perceiving a wild cow. The contention that the fact is indeed known in a general way from testimony is false, because though it is known in a general way, an individual animal is not known to be a wild cow. Otherwise, a person knowing from a reliable person that wherever there is smoke, there is a fire, would have the knowledge of the existence of a fire in a hill. It is contended that the knowledge that an individual animal is called a wild cow is derived from perception. This contention is false, because, if it were true, a person would have this knowledge even without hearing from a forester that a wild cow is like a cow. It is contended that perception aided by the residual impression of testimony is indeed the cause of the knowledge. The contention is false, because namability is not perceptible. Even its being called a jar is not known by perception in a jar. Nor is its namability known by inference, since similarity to a cow exists in another cow also, which is a dissimilar instance (vipakṣa).

Akṣapāda defines comparison as proving the existence of an unknown entity from a well-known similarity.[124] Uddyotakara explains it as the knowledge of similarity, which depends upon the recollection of a testimony due to the revival of its residual impression.[125] Some Naiyāyikas define comparison as the knowledge of the relation between a name and a namable object. If these definitions were true, the inference "this earth is called earth because it has odour, because what has no smell, is not earth" would be comparison, because it is the result of the relation between a name and a namable object.[126] So comparison is indefinable.

CRITICISM OF TESTIMONY (ŚABDA).—The Mīmāṁsaka defines scriptural testimony as the knowledge of an object not present before a sense-organ, which is derived from the knowledge of a scriptural sentence.[127] This definition is too wide, since it applies to the inference of a particular speaker, who is not present before a sense-organ, from his words as a probans. From the words of a speaker outside a room, the speaker is inferred. The definition is too wide, for it applies to the inference of a fire from smoke signified by the word 'smoke'. Further, what is 'śabda', which produces the knowledge of an object not present before a sense-organ? It is not a word, since it does not by itself produce the knowledge of such an object. It is simply a reminder of what is already known. Nor is 'śabda' a sentence, since its nature is not defined. A sentence is either a mere aggregate of words with different meanings, or a collection of words conveying one meaning, or words possessing proximity, expectancy and compatibility. The first definition is not true, because according to it 'cow', 'horse', 'man' would be a sentence. The second definition is not true, since words conveying one meaning are not explained. Oneness is either being endued with the number 'one', or nondifference, or nature. It is not the first, since, if it were true, the words 'cow', 'horse', 'man' would be a sentence inasmuch as each word being endued with the number one, the aggregate would be so. The second and third definitions of oneness are false, because of the words 'cow', 'horse', 'man' each is nondifferent from itself, and because each of them has a nature. But they do not form a sentence. Further, being determined by having oneness of being may be said to be being qualified by it. Then it is being related to a qualification (viśeṣaṇa). If being related be said to be qualified by a relation, this involves self-dependence. If it be said to be the substrate of the relation distinguished from a qualification, this also involves self-dependence, for the word 'distinguished' means 'qualified'. Moreover, qualification and qualified each would be qualified. Then there is the absence of being qualified in a relation, since there is no other relation. If some other relation exists, this will involve infinite regress.[128] Nor are words having proximity, expectancy and compatibility a sentence, because expectancy, an attribute of a person, does not exist in words. Expectancy is desire to hear another word in order to complete the meaning of a sentence. Compatibility is not fitness of words for being used together, for in the sentence "irrigate the land with a fire" also the words are used together. Nor does compatibility mean fitness of words for conveying a connected meaning of depending on each other, since the words in a false sentence also have such fitness. In a deceiver's false sentence "fruits exist on the bank of a river" also the words convey a connected meaning. It they had no such fitness, the words of a valid sentence also would not have such fitness. It is contended that in a false sentence the component words have no fitness for conveying a connected meaning, because it is in conflict with another pramāṇa. This contention is false, since in the absence of a relation also fitness for being related is not contradicted.[129]

Moreover, a sentence is a pramāṇa for the knowledge unqualified by its meaning or for the knowledge qualified by its meaning. It is not a pramāṇa for the knowledge unqualified by its meaning, for such knowledge would not produce a practical action. It is not a pramāṇa for the knowledge qualified by its meaning, because the meaning, the qualification, is not known by perception inasmuch as the existence of fruits on the bank of a river are not present before a hearer's sense-organ. Nor is it known by inference, because there is no probans invariably concomitant with it. Nor is it known by memory, since it was not apprehended before. Nor is it known by conjecture, for it is not included in perception or inference. Nor is it doubt, since it is devoid of two alternatives. Nor is it illusion, because if it were illusion, an object would never be obtained. If it is known by testimony, this involves interdependence, and inference is useless.[130] If the meaning, the qualification, is not known, the knowledge qualified by the meaning cannot be known. If a qualification is not known, the entity qualified by it cannot be known. If a sentence is a pramāṇa for its meaning, it is not possible, since there is no agreement between a sentence and its meaning in that a word and its object do not always exist in the same place and at the same time. The relation between a word and its object signified by it is said to be that of signifier and signified—name and named. A name produces the knowledge of its object. A named entity is the object of the knowledge produced by it. If a word can produce the knowledge of a particular object without a relation, perception and inference also can apprehend the object without a relation, and so the assumption of a relation between a word and its object is needless.[131] Moreover, a word signifies a genus or an individual or an individual qualified by a genus. It does not denote a genus, because if it did so, an individual would not be spoken of or acted upon. Further, if a word always denoted a genus, time, ākāśa, and direction would not be denoted by words, because they each being one individual have no genus. A word does not denote an individual also, since there are innumerable individuals. A word does not denote an individual qualified by a genus, since such an individual also is distinguished from other individuals, and so cannot be denoted by a word. If being qualified by a genus be said to be common to all individuals qualified by a genus, then also the difficulty in a genus being denoted by a word is not obviated. Furthermore, how is it known that a particular word signifies a particular object? The Naiyāyika thinks it to be known by convention. This view is wrong, because a convention also cannot account for the relation between a word and a genus, or an individual, or an individual qualified by a genus.[132] Hence the definition of scriptural testimony as the knowledge of an object, which is not present before a sense-organ, produced by a sentence is invalid.[133]

The Naiyāyika defines testimony as a sentence uttered by a reliable person. This definition is invalid, since a reliable person is indeterminable, and since a sentence uttered by such a person is found to be false. A reliable person is not one who says what he perceived, for his report may be incorrect through inadvertence. He is not a person who states what he actually perceived, since his statement may partly state what he actually perceived and partly state what he did not actually perceive. A reliable person is not devoid of love and hate, because sometimes reliable persons are found to be tainted with these passions. A reliable person is not a person, who is untainted with love and hate in regard to a particular matter, because such a definition does not apply to all individuals. A class-concept alone is defined, but individuals are indefinable. Hence the Nyāya definition is invalid.[134]

CRITICISM OF PRESUMPTION (ARTHĀPATTI).—Presumption is defined as the knowledge of what removes inconsistency produced by the perception of two inconsistent facts.[135] Devadatta is known to be alive and absent from home. So it is assumed that he must exist outside his house. Otherwise, the inconsistency between his being alive and his absence from his house cannot be reconciled with each other. Some regard presumption as inference: "Devadatta lives outside his house, because though alive, he is absent from his house, like what has been proved." This argument is invalid, because his house is the locus of his absence, and because for this reason his absence is not an attribute of Devadatta, and because his existence outside his house cannot be inferred from his house. Citsukha refutes Kumārila's view thus. He asks whether Devadatta's absence from his house prior to the assumption of his existing outside is known by valid knowledge or not known by it. If it is known by valid knowledge, his existing outside his house can be inferred from it without any hindrance. If it is known by valid knowledge, presumption is not possible because of the absence of its cause.[136] According to the Nyāya-Vaiśeṣika absence is known by perception. Perception is stronger than testimony. So it disregards testimony, and infers the existence of Devadatta outside his house from his absence from his house as the probans known by perception. If Devadatta's absence from his house is known by nonapprehension, nonapprehension being weaker than testimony, presumption cannot prove Devadatta's existence outside his house, which is opposed to his absence from his house. Nonapprehension can function only when apprehension of existence does not exist. It is said, "When five pramāṇas cannot prove the existence of an object, nonapprehension proves its nonexistence."[137] Further, if there is a cause of persumption, it is either invariably concomitant with the presumed object, or it is variably concomitant with it. In the first alternative, the so-called presumption is nothing but inference, and is not an independent pramāṇa. In the second alternative, the object cannot be presumed, since the cause of presumption is variably concomitant with the presumed object. Furthermore, the demonstration without which the presumed object cannot be demonstrated is either known by valid knowledge, or it is not known by valid knowledge. In the first alternative, presumption cognizes what is already cognized, and therefore it is not valid knowledge.[138] In the second alternative, there can be no presumption of an object qualified by the qualification, since the qualification is not proved owing to the absence of the cause of presumption. In the absence of its cause presumption cannot arise.[139]

CRITICISM OF NONAPPREHENSION.—Nonapprehension is defined as noncognition of the absence of an object, which is capable of being cognized. A jar does not exist in the ground. The nonexistence of the jar is known by nonapprehension. The cognition is not perception, since it is not produced by sense-object-intercourse. The intercourse of nonexistence with a sense-organ is neither conjunction nor inherence, for they are the attributes of positive entities. Nor is the relation between them that of the qualified (viśeṣya) and the qualification (viśeṣaṇa), because it is included in an original relation, which being absent, it is absent. If the relation of the qualified to the qualification be admitted to exist even without an original relation, it is known by perception. The Nyāya holds that absence is known by perception produced by the intercourse between absence and a sense-organ called qualified-qualification (viśeṣaṇatā). But this relation is not cognizable. Nor is nonapprehension included in inference, because, if it were so included, it would be an instrument of nonapprehension also, which is not knowable, like the visual organ. Otherwise, nonapprehension also being cognized by nonapprehension, there would be infinite regress. So nonexistence is cognized by nonapprehension.

Citsukha refutes this view by adducing the following arguments against it. If mere nonapprehension has the capacity for cognizing nonexistence, inference also should be able to cognize nonexistence. If is contended that mere nonapprehension does not cognize nonexistence, but that appropriate nonapprehension or nonapprehension of an object, which is capable of being perceived, cognizes its nonexistence. The qualification 'appropriate' excludes mere nonapprehension. This contention is false, because if appropriate nonapprehension invariably produces the knowledge of nonexitence, as smoke invariably produces the knowledge of a fire, it is nothing but inference, and not an independent pramāṇa. Further, nonapprehension is entirely unknown, and so its being an instrument of valid knowledge cannot be known. So the knowledge of nonapprehension must be admitted. If nonapprehension is known by nonapprehension, this will lead to infinite regress. Furthermore, nonapprehension is either the absence of valid knowledge or the absence of knowledge in general. The first definition is too wide, because it applies to the absence of the knowledge of silver in a nacre to which silver is attributed. Otherwise, there would be no attribution of silver to a nacre. If the second definition were true, a person perceiving a white conch would not have an illusory perception of it as yellow, when his eyes are jaundiced. So nonapprehension is not the absence of knowledge in general. Hence nonapprehension is indefinable.[140]

Śrīharṣa and Citsukha are called by some scholars advocates of scepticism, because they prove all kinds of valid knowledge and categories as indefinable. They prove that they are false appearances. But they prove self-manifestness of Ātman and the other doctrines of the Advaitist. So they are not really sceptics.

CRITICISM OF HYPOTHETICAL REASONING (TARKA).—Hypothetical reasoning is defined as discovering contradiction in supposing that a probans is not always pervaded by a probandum. It is criticized in 'Prakṭārthavivaraṇa' in the following manner. That hypothetical reasoning is a part of inference is vitiated by interdependence. Inference is proved to be valid, when hypothetical reasoning is proved to be a part of inference. Hypothetical reasoning is proved to be a part of inference, when inference is proved to be valid.[141] Hypothetical reasoning removes a doubt that a suspected upādhi may vitiate the invariable concomitance between a probans and a probandum. It discovers an instance (e.g., a lake) from which a probandum (e.g., a fire) is absent. "If a lake were smoky, it would be fiery ; but a lake is not fiery ; therefore, a lake is not smoky." Tarka proves vyāpti. If vyāpti is not proved, an inference is not proved. Thus tarka is a part of inference. But that it is a part of inference is proved by inference. Thus there is vicious interdependence. Tarka is again defined as the attribution of a probandum because of the attribution of a probans. "If there were smoke in the lake, there would be a fire in it." This definition is too wide, because it applies to inference including tarka, a part of it. Further, a probans being proved, a probandum would be proved, and a probandum being proved, a probans would be proved. Thus it involves vicious interdependence. So there would be no valid inference anywhere ; all inferences would be hypothetical reasonings. An imaginary inference would prove an object. So the Nyāya would accept the view of the Advaita Vedāntin, who regards the world as a false appearance. So tarka is based on a weak foundation, supposes an undesired contingency to prove a desired contingency, ends in false knowledge, has no locus, and is vitiated by interdependence.[142] If another tarka unvitiated by these flaws proves an inference to be valid, the inference proves the tarka to be flawless, and the process goes on without proving any truth.

CRITICISM OF RECOLLECTON.—Citsukha refutes the definitions of recollection, illusion, and doubt, which are not regarded as pramāṇas. Recollection is either cognition produced by a residual impression (saṁskāra) without being produced by an instrument of valid knowledge, or such cognition marked by not being produced by a fault, or cognition produced by a residual impression of an object of a similar cognition, or cognition in which the genus of recognition exists. The first definition is too wide, for it applies to illusion, which is not produced by an instrument of valid knowledge, and which is produced by a residual impression. The second definition is not possible, since a residual impression also is a cause of valid knowledge inasmuch as from it the collocation of its causes is inferred. The third definition also is not possible, because the recollection "he is my father" cognizes more than the previous perception, the residual impression of which produces the recollection. The previous perception did not cognize 'he', the subject of the judgment of recognition. The element 'he' is not presented to consiciousness by some other cause through association for such a cause is not ascertained. In the recognition "this is that Devadatta" 'that'-part being not presented to consciousness by a residual impression through association, and 'this-part depending upon conjunction with a sense-organ alone, the nature of recognition qualified by 'this'-part and 'that'-part is unproven.[143] Further, a residual impression is not of the nature of consciousness. So it has not an object, and cannot have an object of a similar cognition. What is not of the nature of a cognition cannot cognize an object. If it had an object, a desire also would have an object, because the cognition which produces it has an object. Recollection is defined as cognition produced by a residual impression having for its object one similar to that of the cognition which produced it. This definition is invalid, since in the recollection 'he is my father' the part 'he' is not similar to the object of the apprehension. The fourth definition is invalid, since the manifester of the genus of recollection is not determined by a pramāṇa. The manifester of the genus of recollection must be qualified by a qualification which distinguishes it from doubt and illusion. But such a qualification is not ascertained. There is no manifester of the genus of mediate knowledge. If there is a manifester of the genus, it is either valid knowledge which is not produced by sense-object-intercourse, or it is produced by the instrument of valid knowledge, like a probans. The first alternative is inadmissible, because, if it were true, God's knowledge would be mediate. The second alternative also is untenable, since, if it were truce, recollection would not be mediate knowledge. For the same reason, mediateness of knowledge is not a common property other than a genus. A manifester of a genus being refuted, its being a common property other than a genus also is refuted.[144] So recollection is indefinable.

CRITICISM OF RECOGNITION.—Śriharṣa refutes recognition in the following manner. It is an experience in the form "this is that jar." It is either two cognitions : recollection and perception, or one cognition with one part as recollection and with another part as perception, or recollection, or perception. In the first alternative, the identity of the entity qualified by 'thisness' with the entity qualified by the past time, viz., 'thatness', which is manifested by the experience, is not recollection, because it was not perceived before, because there is no residual impression of it, and because there can be no recollection of it in the absence of the impression. So the first alternative is not justified. So the third alternative also is inadmissible. Recognition is not recollection. The second alternative also is not admissible, since perception cannot cognize the past condition of the object, viz., 'thatness', and since, if it is perceived, recognition is nothing but perception. This will amount to the acceptance of the last alternative. It is contended that the object 'this' 'identical with what is qualified by its past condition' has two parts : the part 'qualified by the past condition' cognized by recollection, and the part 'identical' cognized by perception. This contention is false, because, if it were true, recognition would not be the experience 'what is qualified by the past condition itself is this' because, 'that' qualified by the past condition and 'this' qualified by 'thisness' and 'identical' are brought to consciousness by recollection and perception respectively, but because identity abiding in the object qualified by the past condition is not manifested in consciousness by any experience.[145] Further, if recognition is one cognition with recollection of 'that' as one part and perception of 'this' as another part, then the cognition is a mixture of reccollection and perception. The cognition is the substantive (dharmin), and recollection and perception are its attributes (dharma). The residual impression produces the cognition of 'thatness' alone or the cognition of the substantive qualified by 'thatness.' In the first subalternative, recognition will not cognize 'that', since 'thatness' alone is brought to consciousness by the residual impression. In the second alternative, recognition will not cognize 'this', since 'thisness' alone is cognized by perception. When a residual impression and a sense-organ, the causes of the experience of the substantive cognition, act together, Śrīharṣa asks whether recollection and perception constitute a cognition of the qualified (viśeṣya) part, or whether a residual impression and a sense-organ in union produce a cognition of identity alone. In the first subalternative, recognition ceases to be a single cognition, and is vitiated by the flaws of different cognitions. In the second subalternative, in the substantive (dharmin) part of recognition there is a mixture of perception and recollection, and their natures are not determined by their objects. It is contended that the conflict between recollection and perception may not be avoided by considering their objects, but that it is avoided by considering their causes. A residual impression produces recollection, and sense-object-intercourse produces perception in recognition. This contention is false for the following reasons. Valid knowledge represents the real nature of its object ; invalid knowledge does not represent the real nature of its object ; the genus of valid knowledge is not admitted ; validity and invalidity depend on the object cognized by valid and invalid knowledge. Though recollection and perception are produced by different causes as shown above, they refer to the same object, which is the substantive endued with the nature of recollection and the nature of perception as attributes, although they are produced by different causes.[146] Thus valid knowledge and invalid knowledge will pertain to the same object. Further, because the nature of recollection and the nature of perception are manifested in recognition, and because their different objects are not admitted, the nature of recollection will be known in 'thisness' and the nature of perception will be known in 'thatness'.[147] Being produced by a residual impression is the condition of the nature of recollection, and of its conflict with perception, and of the condition of the removal of the conflict. This reasoning involves self-dependence. It is contended that the nature of recollection is its being produced invariably after a residual impression, and that invariability consists in being produced without cognizing the same form common to many individuals. The contention is false, because, if it were true, there would be interdependence : the nature of recollection is the condition (upādhi) of the nature of being produced by a residual impression ; the nature of being produced by a residual impression is the condition of the determination of the nature of recollection. So the intermixture of perception and recollection is unavoidable.[148] Furthermore, either the collocations of the causes of recollection and perception operate in producing recognition, or they do not operate in producing it. In the first subalternative, they will produce their separate effects, because each can produce its effect, and because different causes produce different effects. In the second subalternative, the nature of recollection and the nature of perception cannot appear as parts in recognition. If the nature of recollection is admitted to appear as a part in recognition without being produced by a residual impression, then it will lead to an unwarranted stretch of a general rule : the nature of recollection will exist in perception, and the nature of perception will exist in recollection, and there will be intermixture of recollection and perception.[149] It is contended that where the collocations of the causes of recollection and perception are separately produced without depending on each other, they produce their effects separately, but that in recognition they are produced simultaneously and depending on each other, and that, therefore, they produce their mixed effects. Śrīharṣa asks whether the collocations of the causes of perception and recollection aid each other in producing their mixed effect, or whether they do not aid each other in producing their mixed effect, where they operate together in producing their effects. In the second subalternative, the particular feature characterized by their union is unfit to produce its effect ; without aiding each other the causes will produce their separate effects, since there is no special function of their union. In the first alternative, the collocations of the causes of perception and recollection aid each other, and a residual impression will operate in perception-part, and a sense-organ will operate in recollection-part, and, consequently, there will be perception in recollection and recollection in perception, and thus there will be intermixture of the nature of perception and the nature of recollection in recognition. The fourth main alternative that recognition is perception also is inadmissible, because the cognition of the object qualified by 'thatness' or its past condition and its being the abode of identity, is not produced by a residual impression or by sense-object-intercourse. So recognition cannot contain such cognitions. So it is not perception.[150] Thus recognition is indeterminable.

CRITICISM OF ILLUSION.—Bhūṣaṇakāra defines illusion as false determinate knowledge. Citsukha refutes this definition. It is false, since falsity is indeterminable. False knowledge is either invalid knowledge, or knowledge disagreeing with its object, or knowledge which does not lead to the obtainment of the object shown by it, or knowledge incapable of producing an effective action. The first alternative is untenable, since, if it were true, recollection would be illusion in that it is invalid knowledge and yet determinate knowledge. The second alternative is inadmissible, because, if it were true, a valid knowledge of a past object or a future object would be illusion in that it disagrees with its object in time and place. The third alternative is unjustified, because valid knowledge of the moon and stars can never lead to the obtainment of them. The illusion "this is silver" in a nacre is partly valid, according to this definition, since it brings about obtainment of 'this'-part, which is therefore valid. The fourth alternative also is illegitimate, because the dream of a false snake-bite produces fear and trembling, but because dream is not illusion. The contention that knowledge in general produces an effective action, and that an object does not produce it, is invalid, because, if it were true, invalid knowledge also would produce an effective action.[151]

Uddyotakara defines illusion as knowledge of that which does not exist in an object (e.g., "this (nacre) is silver"). Citsukha refutes it thus. This definition is too wide, since it applies to doubt. On perceiving a tall anthill, a person has a doubt "Is it a post or a man ?" It is contradicted by the knowledge that it is neither a post nor a man. So doubt is the knowledge of that which does not exist in an object. But it is not an illusion.

Illusion is defined as knowledge which is contradicted by a sublating knowledge, or as knowledge produced by an instrument of knowledge vitiated by a fault. This definition is too wide, since it applies to doubt as shown above, and since sublation is not determined. Sublation is either opposite valid knowledge, or valid knowledge opposing illusion, or taking away its object. In the first alternative, sublation will apply to antecedent and succeeding valid cognitions, the former being destroyed by the latter, and so the definition will be too wide, because they are not illusions. The second alternative involves interdependence : illusion is sublated by valid knowledge opposed to it ; the latter is sublated by the former. The third alternative also is inadmissible, because the subalternatives involved in it are unjustified. Taking away the object of illusion is either producing knowledge of the nonexistence of the object manifested in the cognition, or valid knowledge of such an object, or producing the knowledge of the nonexistence of its object in the place and at the time qualified by which an object is manifested in consciousness. The first subalternative is inadmissible, because, if it were true, the cognition of Devadatta being contradicted by the illusion "this is not Devadatta, and does not live" would be invalid. The second subalternative also is untenable, since, if it were true, the cognitions of a jar and the like would be proved to be invalid by the valid knowledge of their nonexistence in another place and at another time. The third subalternative also is illegitimate, because the definition does not apply to the cognitions of objects in another place and at another time inasmuch as the place and the time do not exist in another place and at another time. Sublation is not taking away the fruit of knowledge, because a cognition also the fruit of which has not been produced is admitted to be contradicted. Illusion is not the substrate of the genus of illusion, because in the illusion "this is silver" there will be intermixture of genera. 'This'-part is valid knowledge, and 'silver'-part is invalid knowledge. So illusion is indefinable.[152]

CRITICISM OF DOUBT.—Citsukha refutes doubt thus. Doubt is either indefinite cognition, or cognition oscillating between two conflicting alternatives, or cognition specialized by the mark of indefiniteness, or false cognition producing a desire to know for certain, or false cognition other than illusion, or cognition in which the genus of doubt exists, or cognition which cannot be determined by any means. The first definition is invalid, for definite knowledge being undetermined, indefinite knowledge is undetermined. Definite knowledge is either knowledge in general, or knowledge with the form of one object, or knowledge opposed to doubt, or valid knowledge opposed to doubt. According to the first definition definite knowledge is knowledge in general. So indefinite knowledge is knowledge which is not the locus of the genus of knowledge, and so involves self-contradiction. According to the second definition of definite knowledge, the valid cognition of a variegated cloth, and valid cognitions of Chaitra and Maitra would be doubt, for they are not cognitions with the form of one object. The third and fourth definitions of definite knowledge are not valid, since knowledge and valid knowledge opposed to doubt are indeterminable in that doubt is indefinable. Further, if they were true, knowledge other than that opposed to doubt would be doubt, and so valid knowledge being produced in which doubt has not yet been produced would be doubt because of its not being opposed to doubt. The main second alternative is not admissible, because, if doubt were knowledge touching two conflicting alternatives, the valid cognitions of heat and cold, difference and identity etc., would be doubt. The third main alternative is not justified, since the nature of 'indefinite' is undetermined inasmuch as the nature of 'definite' is undetermined. If the word 'indefinite' means unsettledness between two alternatives, it is either the nature of the two alternatives or their attribute. It is not their nature, because, if it were so, the certain knowledge of the two alternatives would be doubt. It is not their attribute, because, if it were so, the valid knowledge cognizing the two alternatives endued with the attribute would be doubt. The fourth main alternative is not tenable, since the definition is too narrow, for it does not apply to doubt in a post or the like, which does not produce a desire to know for certain. The fifth main alternative is not justified, since the alternatives involved in it are inadmissible. Doubt is different from illusion in regard to its special object, or in regard to its cause, or in regard to its genus. The first subalternative is untenable, for the special nature of the object of doubt is not determined. The object of doubt is not the affirmation and denial of both alternatives, because, if it were so, the certain knowledge of the aggregate of two alternatives "these are a post and a man" would be doubt. Nor is the object of doubt the denial of two alternatives, because, if it were so, the knowledge "this is not a post; this is not a man" would be doubt. Nor is the object of doubt the denial of one of the alternatives, since that would presuppose the certain knowledge of the other alternative. Nor is the object of doubt the affirmation and denial of both alternatives, because, if it were so, the knowledge "this is a post, this is not a post, this is a man, this is not a man" would be doubt. So doubt would be certain knowledge of affirmation and denial of both alternatives. "Is this eternal or noneternal?" In this doubt the affirmation of one alternative is the denial of the other. So affirmation and denial of both alternatives are not possible. The second subalternative is untenable, because the special cause of doubt is not determined, because neither its collocation of causes nor its part is determined. Its collocation of causes is supersensible and so imperceptible. Nor can it be inferred, since there is no probans from which it can be inferred. Because its collocation of causes is not known, its part also is not known. The third subalternative also is inadmissible, for it involves intermixture of genera (jātisāmkarya). "This is either a post or a man". In this knowledge 'this'-part is certain, and two alternatives are subject to doubt. Thus the same doubt would be the substrate of the genus of certain knowledge, and of the genus of doubt. The sixth main alternative also is refuted by this argument, for the genus of doubt does not exist in doubt.[153]

CRITICISM OF WORD-FORM (SPHOṬA).—Ānandajñāna refutes the Śābdika doctrine of sphoṭa. According to Bhartṛhari a word is known through a word-form. But there is no evidence for the existence of a word-form (padasphoṭa). The experience of one word does not cognize a word-form, because it cognizes the constituent letters of the word, and because it does not cognize one form called a sphoṭa. Many letters cannot manifest a sphoṭa. They produce the experience of one word according to an object or condition (upādhi) of experience, as many trees are experienced as a forest, which is perceived. The assumption of a sphoṭa is unnecessary to account for the experience of one word.[154] A word-form cannot inhere in a word, because it will lead to unwarranted stretch of a general rule.

CRITICISM OF YOGIPRATYAKṢA.—Yogic perception is mystic intuition due to proficiency in meditation. It is defined as perception, the object of which is not fit to be perceived by us, and which is not perceived by God. Ānandajñāna refutes this definition. The second adjective (viśeṣaṇa) is not possible according to an atheist. According to a theist the first qualification is not possible. The Naiyāyika is a theist, and believes in the yogic perception of persons like us due to proficiency in meditation. We also can acquire yogic perception through the manas. If nondivine perception means nonyogic perception, it is contradicted, because it means yogic perception also. If it means yogic perception, the definition is circular and involves self-dependence (ātmāśrayatā) : yogic perception is perception of a yogin.

The Naiyāyika argues that yogic perception is valid, because it is an object of valid knowledge, like a jar. Ānandajñāna refutes his view. Yogic perception does not cognize dharma, because it is derived through the sense-organs, and because dharma is supersensible. The opponent contends that according to the Advaitavādin the locus of the reason (hetu) is unproven (āśrayāsiddha). The contention is false, because according to the Advaitavādin dharma is perceived by Hiraṇyagarbha, and because according to him it is perceived by the witness-self (sākṣin). The opponent argues that the buddhi of Vyāsa, who has achieved embodied release, does not cognize dharma, which is known from the Vedas alone, because it is buddhi, like our buddhi. This argument is false, because the buddhi of God cognizes dharma, which is not like our buddhi. The opponent argues that the buddhi of Vyāsa does not cognize dharma, because it is like the buddhi of non-God. According to the atheist the qualification is useless, because he does not believe in God. According to the theist also buddhi exists in Hiraṇyagarbha, who cognizes dharma. So the opponent's reason is unproven (asiddha). So yogic perception is not valid.[155]

CRITICISM OF DREAM.—A dream is defined as a cognition produced by the manas tainted by sleep. Ānandagiri refutes the definition. It is faulty, because the qualification is needless in that all produced cognitions, untainted or tainted, are produced by the manas. If the qualification is said to distinguish a dream from a percept produced by an external sense-organ, the argunent in defence is false, because a dream and a percept do not differ from each other as experiences. If a dream is defined as a cognition produced in sleep and uncontradicted at the time, and recognized on waking from sleep, the definition is faulty, because a sense-organ also is recognized on waking from sleep and uncontradicted in sleep. If a dream is defined as an illusion in sleep, then it is included in illusion, and the refutation of illusion applies to a dream, both being due to defects in their causes and being contradicted. A dream is not recollection because of its being produced by a residual impression, because recognition is not recollection because of its being produced by a residual impression. The Vaiśeṣika division of dreams into three kinds being caused by the strength of residual impressions, bodily humours (e.g., bile), and merits and demerits is false, because different causes do not always produce different effects. Further, individual dreams being endless, three kinds of dreams only are unreasonable.[156]

CRITICISM OF FAULTY REASONS.—Ānandajñāna refutes faulty reasons (hetvābhāsa). A reason (hetu) with distinctive characteristics is not determined. So a faulty reason devoid of them is not determinable. 1. A reason or probans (hetu) which is not known for certain to exist in the subject of inference (pakṣa) is defined to be unproven (asiddha).[157] This definition is too wide, because a valid reason also is not known for certain to exist in the subject of inference by some person or another. A valid reason cannot be known for certain by all persons to exist in the subject of inference, because it is not possible, and because person are not omniscient. Further, a subject of inference also cannot be defined. This reasoning refutes the definition of an unproven reason as a reason which is not proved to be pervaded by the probandum (sādhya) or predicate of inference, and as such to exist in the subject of inference. Invariable concomitance of a reason with the probandum (vyāpti) and the subject of inference have already been refuted. A reason cannot be proved to exist in the subject of inference by some person or by all persons for the reasons stated above.[158] Śrīharṣa refutes the second definition by observing that other faulty reasons also are included in an unproven reason, because they cannot arise without violating the conditions of pervasion (vyāpti) of a reason or probans by the probandum, and of a reason pervaded by the probandum existing in the subject of inference (pakṣadharmatā), and of both being proved.[159] So the second definition is too wide. 2. A reason, which exists in the subject of inference (pakṣa) and in dissimilar instances (vipakṣa) in which the probandum does not exist, is defined as contradictory (viruddha). "Sound is eternal, because it is produced". Ānandagiri refutes this definition. This definition is false, because a valid reason entirely existing in the subject of inference and in all dissimilar instances cannot be known in that its nonpervasion (avyāpti) of the subject of inference and all dissimilar instances cannot be prevented. If it exists partly in them, it is not present in them all. If its mere presence in them is sought to be affirmed, it cannot be proved, because its mere existence in both is not well-known.[160] A contradictory reason is also defined as a reason pervaded by the absence of the probandum. Ānandagiri refutes it. A contradictory reason cannot be known, because the probandum is unproven, because the pervasion of the reason by the probandum is unproven, and because from such a reason its contradictoriness to the probandum cannot be known.[161] Śrīharṣa urges that an inconclusive (anaikāntika) reason also is included in a contradictory reason, because it exists in dissimilar instances wherein the probandum does not exist. Ānandapūrṇa makes the point clear by observing that an inconclusive reason does not differ from a contradictory reason, because it coexists with the absence of the probandum inasmuch as it exists in the subject of inference, similar instances, and dissimilar instances.[162] 3. An inconclusive (anaikāntika) reason is defined as a reason existing in the subject of inference, similar instances, and dissimilar instances.[163] "All are eternal, because they are knowable". Ānandajñāna urges that the definition is false, because a contradictory reason also is covered by it as shown above.[164] A contradictory reason also is inconclusive, because it has variable concomitance (vyabhicāra) with the probandum. There is no cause for doubt about the existence of the probandum, until the probandum is determined.[165] Śrīharṣa also urges that a contradictory reason is included in an inconclusive reason according to the definition stated above. Ānandapūrṇa illustrates it. "A sound is noneternal, because it is unproduced". The reason 'unproduced' exists in a dissimilar instance, e.g., a soul, which is eternal. So it is an inconclusive reason. Thus the definition of a contradictory reason is too wide. "Sound is eternal, because it is a special quality of ether (ākāśa)". Here the reason is said to be an uncommon (asādhāraṇa) inconclusive reason, because it exists in the subject of inference alone. The definition of an inconclusive reason stated above does not apply to this inference, because the reason does not exist in dissimilar instances. "Sound is eternal, because it is knowable by a pramāṇa". The reason is said to be a common (sādhāraṇa) inconclusive reason, because it exists in the subject of inference, similar instances, and dissimilar instances. If a reason does not exist in similar instances or dissimilar instances, the definition stated above is too narrow, because it does not apply to such a reason.[166] 4. A contradictory (bādhita) reason is defined as a reason in an inference, which is contradicted by a means of valid knowledge. "A fire is cold, because it is a substance". It is contradicted by perception. Ānandajñāna refutes this definition. It is too narrow, if it means that a reason is contradicted by all pramāṇas, because in all cases a reason is not contradicted by all pramāṇas. The definition is too narrow, if it means that a reason is contradicted by any pramāṇa, because 'contradicted by any pramāṇa' means 'contradicted by all pramāṇas'.[167] Further, the nature of contradiction (bādha) is not determinable by the opponent. If it means that a reason appears to a person to be contradicted, then a valid reason also will sometimes be contradicted, because it appears to some person to be contradicted. If it means that a reason is really contradicted by all pramāṇas, it can never be known to be so contradicted, because all persons are nonomniscient.[168] 5. A proponent's reason is defined as counterbalanced, if it is countered by an equally strong reason of the opponent. A reason of one inference is countered by a reason of another inference. The second probandum is the contradictory of the first probandum. "Sound is eternal, because it is audible, like the genus of sound". "Sound is noneternal, because it is produced, like a jar". The second probandum 'noneternal' is the contradictory of the first probandum 'eternal'. So the first reason 'audible' is countered by the second reason 'produced'. Ānandagiri refutes the definition of a counterbalanced (satpratipakṣa) reason. It is too narrow, if it means a particular proponent and a particular opponent, because it does not apply to all proponents and opponents. It is not possible, if it means all proponents and all opponents. If the reasons of the proponent and the opponent are flawless, the object is of an alternative nature. So one reason cannot be flawless in both inferences. If either reason is flawless, both inferences cannot be equally strong. If they are said to be equally strong to experience, their reasons also may appear to be equally strong to experience, but are not really so. Therefore, the definition is too wide. If they are entirely equal in strength, they cannot be said to be of similar characteristics (tulyalakṣaṇa). Only reasons contradictory to each other can be countered by each other.[169] Śrīharṣa has elaborately criticized the faulty reasons, and his commentators have elucidated his criticisms.[170] Vācaspati Miśra (1500 A.D.), a Nyāya-Vaiśeṣika syncretist, refuted Śrīharṣa's criticisms of some Vaiśeṣika categories, valid knowledge and means of valid knowledge in 'Khaṇḍanoddhāra' later.

[1] SNS., iii, 83. [2] Bhām., i, 1, 1. [3] PPV., p. 102.
[4] Ibid. [5] Ibid. [6] Ibid. [7] Ibid, p. 103.
[8] VPS., p. 100. [9] Ibid, p. 101. [10] Ibid.
[11] Ibid, 101-02. [12] Ibid, p. 102. [13] Ibid.
[14] TPD., p. 122. [15] ACK., pp. 269-71.
[16] VP., pp. 332-33, 336 & 338.
[17] ACK., p. 270. IPC., Vol. I, pp. 199-210, IEP., pp. 184-86, HIP., Vol. I, pp. 833-35.
[18] ACK., p. 270. [19] Ibid, p. 137. [20] Ibid, p. 271.
[21] PKM., p. 38. [22] Ibid. TPD., pp. 122-28.
[23] SLS., p. 337.
[24] Ibid, pp. 334-40 ; pp. 353-55 ; VP., pp. 57-58.
[25] SLS., pp. 357 & 362. [26] Ibid, p. 362.
[27] Ibid, pp. 363-64. [28] Ibid, p. 369.
[29] Ibid, pp. 377, 382 & 386. [30] Ibid, pp. 387 & 395.
[31] Ibid, pp. 409-12, 414, 416-17. [32] ĀNM., p. 145.
[33] Ibid, p. 149. [34] Ibid, pp. 149-50.
[35] Ibid, p. 154. Ibid, pp. 153-54. [36] NMV., pp. 154-55.
[37] ĀNM., p 155. [38] Ibid, p. 302.
[39] SNS., iii, 96, p. 336. [40] Ibid.
[41] Ibid, iii, 83. Ibid, iii, 84. [42] Ibid, iii, 86. Ibid, iii, 85.
[43] VPS., pp. 230 & 232.
[44] TA., pp. 115-18, 122, 112-14 ; VP., pp. 403-04.
[45] ŚBS., iii, 1, 11 ; ŚB., Muṇḍ Up., i, 2, 12 ; ŚB., Br. Up., iii, 3, 1 ; VP., p. 38.
[46] IPC., Vol. I, pp. 128-39.
[47] VP., p. 105. IPC., Vol. I, pp. 374-75.
[48] VP., pp. 121-37 ; BRS., pp. 149-50 ; IPC., Vol. I, pp. 292-95 ; IEP., pp. 96-99. Cp. TS., p. 134.
[49] VPS., pp. 41-42 ; IPC., Vol. I, pp. 287-88 ; IEP., pp. 83-87.
[50] VPS., pp. 34-35. IPC., Vol. I, pp. 288-90 ; IEP., pp. 80-83.
[51] VPS., 26-28. [52] Ibid, pp. 28-29. IEP., pp. 93-94; 114-17. IPC., Vol. I, pp. 299-302.
[53] VPS., pp. 33-34. Cp. IS., pp. 39-48, 10-3-13, 113-23, 152-69, 288-323. ĀNM. IPC., Vol. I, pp. 285-306 ; IEP., pp. 80-120.
[54] VP., p. 186, 198 & 201. [55] Ibid, p. 203.
[56] Ibid, p. 205. [57] Ibid, Ch. II, MVV., Ch. I & Ch. II.
[58] VP., Ch. III. [59] 'Studies in Vedāntism' (K. C. Bhattacharya), pp. 62-63. (C. U.).
[60] ŚDP., p. 208 ; PP., p. 71. [61] NS., i, 1, 6. VP., ch. V.
[62] ŚDP., p. 214. [63] PP., pp. 113-15. [64] VP. ch. V.
[65] Ibid. [66] PP., p. 123. [67] STK., 5.
[68] ŚDP., pp. 235-36. [69] SM., p. 263.
[70] VP., p. 239 ; BRS., p. 40. IEP., pp 213-18.
[71] Ibid, pp. 241-60.
[72] Ibid, p. 269. [73] ŚBS., i, 3, 28.
[74] VP., p. 304 ; BRS., iv, 3, pp. 157 & 40 ; AUD., p. 16.
[75] BRS., p. 40. [76] Ibid, pp. 40 & 41.

[77] MP., p. 20 ; ŚMN., p. 20 & 152.
[78] BRS., pp. 40-41 ; Bhām., i, 1, 4 ;
VP., pp. 20, 37, 55-57, 75 & 171.
[79] TA., pp. 266-67. IEP., pp. 211-13.
[80] IS., pp. 82-83.
[81] VPS., p. 39. Ibid, pp. 38-39. Cp. TS., pp. 5-6.
[82] SP., p. 59 ; KKK., p. 145. Cp. TS., pp. 84-85.
[83] KKK., p. 146. [84] Ibid, p. 148. [85] Ibid, pp. 145-48.
[86] Ibid, p. 244. NKS., iv, 5. [87] Ibid.
[88] Ibid, pp. 245-46. [89] Ibid, pp. 246-47.
[90] Ibid, p. 249. [91] Ibid, p. 250.
[92] Ibid. [93] Ibid, p. 251. [94] NBT., p. 5.
[95] KKK., p. 255. [96] Ibid. [97] Ibid. [98] Ibid, p. 256.
[99] NBT., p. 5. [100] ŚMV., p. 257. [101] KKK., p. 256.
[102] Ibid, ŚMV., 256-57. [103] KKK., p. 256.
[104] Ibid, p. 257. [105] Ibid, p. 258.
[106] PĀV., ii, 2, 41, p. 562. [107] Ibid, pp. 562-63.
[108] NS., i, 1, 4 ; KKK., p. 293. [109] Ibid, p. 295.
[110] Ibid, p. 297. [111] Ibid, p. 302.
Ibid, pp. 293-95, 297-98, 300-01.
[112] TPD., p. 218. [113] Ibid, pp. 218-20.
[114] PĀV., ii, 2, 41, p. 565. [115] Ibid. [116] Ibid, pp. 565-66.
[117] Ibid, pp. 232-33. [118] TPD., p. 237.
HIP., Vol. I, pp. 717-34. [119] TPD., p. 237.
[120] Ibid, p. 238. [121] Ibid, pp. 241, 243-44.
[122] PĀV., ii, 2, 41, p. 566. [123] Ibid, p. 567.
Ibid, pp. 566-67.
[124] NS., i, 1, 6 ; TPD., pp. 255-56. [125] NV., i, 1, 6 ;
TPD., p. 256.
[126] TPD., pp. 253-56. [127] Ibid, p. 256.
[128] Ibid, pp. 257-58. [129] Ibid, pp. 261-62.
[130] Ibid, pp. 262-63. [131] Ibid, p. 263. [132] Ibid, p. 265.
[133] Ibid. [134] Ibid, pp. 265-66. [135] Ibid, p. 266.
[136] Ibid, p. 267. [137] Ibid, p. 268. [138] Ibid, p. 269.
[139] Ibid. [140] Ibid, 269-71 & 272.
[141] PĀV., ii, 2, 41, p. 571. [142] Ibid. [143] TPD., p. 227.
[144] TPD., pp. 228-29. [145] KKK., p. 158.
Ibid, pp. 156-57.
[146] Ibid, p. 160. ŚMV., p 160. [147] ŚMV., p. 161.
[148] KKK., p. 162. [149] Ibid, p. 162. ŚMV., p. 162.
[150] KKK., pp. 156-58, 159-63. [151] TPD., pp. 224-25.
[152] Ibid, pp. 224-26. [153] Ibid, pp. 222-24.
[154] TS., pp. 105-06, 119-20. [155] Ibid, pp. 88-89.
[156] Ibid, pp. 83-84. [157] TS., p. 97. [158] Ibid, pp. 96-97.
[159] KKK., (Ch.S.S.), p. 806. ĀVS., pp. 806-67.
[160] TS., p. 97. [161] Ibid. KKK., (Ch.S.S.), p. 841.
[162] ĀVS., p. 842. [163] TS., p. 97. [164] Ibid. [165] Ibid.
[166] KKK., (Ch.S.S.), ĀVS., pp. 850-52. [167] TS., p. 98.
[168] Ibid. [169] Ibid, pp. 98-99.
[170] KKK., (Ch.S.S.), ĀVS., pp. 875-958.

CHAPTER XI

CRITIQUE

BHĀSKARA.—The doctrine of difference and nondifference or identity (bhedābheda) was advocated by some Vedāntists before Śaṁkara, which is evident from Bādarāyaṇa's aphorisms (i, 4, 20-23), which refer to the views of Āśmarathya, Auḍulomi and Kāśakṛtsna. Śaṁkara explains their views in the following statement. "According to Kāśakṛtsna unmodified supreme Lord (Īśvara) Himself is the individual soul, and no other being. According to Āśmarathya, on the other hand, the soul's difference from Īśvara is desired, so that by knowing Him it may know all ; Īśvara is somehow the cause, and the soul is the effect. According to Auḍulomi the difference between the soul and Īśvara is clearly due to that of states ; the soul is a different state of Īśvara, so that there is difference as well as identity between them".[1] Śaṁkara himself accepts Kāśakṛtsna's view. Bādarāyaṇa refers to the doctrine of difference-cum-identity in the aphorism (iii, 2, 27) : Brahman and the individual soul are like a serpent and its coiled state, because both difference and identity between them are stated in the Upaniṣads. "The soul attains the Supreme luminous Person". "That thou art". The soul is like a ray of light of a luminous body (e.g., the sun) ; it is neither entirely different nor entirely nondifferent from the latter.[2] Sureśvara, Śaṁkara's disciple and contemporary, criticizes the doctrine of difference-cum-identity probably advocated by Bhartṛprapañca. Bhāskara interprets the 'Brahmasūtra' in the light of the doctrine of difference-cum-identity. Vijñānabhikṣu, Vallabha and Jīva Gosvāmī propound different types of difference-cum-identity. Some kind of difference-cum-identity appears to the author of this book nearer the truth than Śaṁkara's doctrine of absolute identity and Madhva's doctrine of absolute difference.

Bhāskara's identification of Brhaman with the Lord or Īśvara invested with excellent attributes, consideration of Him as both different and nondifferent from the souls and the world, concept of the soul as a knower, agent, enjoyer and sufferer, and atomic in magnitude, and concepts of the world as real, and of causation as transition from the unmanifest to the manifest accord with the views of the later theistic Vedāntists, and are on the right lines. His doctrine of Brahman's modification into the world is severely criticized by the later Śaṁkarites, Veṅkaṭanātha, Madhva and others. His doctrine of combination of works with knowledge is generally accepted with modifications by the Vaiṣṇava Vedāntists, some Śaivas (e.g., Śrīkaṇṭha and Śrīpati Paṇḍita) and Vijñānabhikṣu. Though knowledge due to meditation (yoga) is superior to works and devotion, because it yields mystic union with the Supreme Spirit with enlightenment, the majority of aspirants for self-realization and God-realization ought to perform their specific duties pertaining to their station in society in order to promote the good of mankind and transform their life into divine life. Bhāskara's rejection of embodied release is reiterated by the later theistic schools of Vedānta, and even by some Śaṁkarites (e.g., Prakāśānanda).

PRATYABHIJÑĀ ŚAIVISM.—Śaivism of the Pratyabhijñā school is better than Śaṁkara's absolute idealism from the monistic standpoint. Śiva as ever invested with Śakti (divine power), inseparable from each other, integral unity, absolutely free, pure consciousness, perfect 'I'-consciousness and manifestation, Absolute, unlimited Knower, with artistic delight is a better concept than Brahman as infinite existence-consciousness-bliss devoid of power, the substratum of nescience, which is regarded as an inexplicable cause of false appearances. The concept of 'all-Śiva' is more satisfactory than that of 'all-appearance'. All schools of Śaivism explain the thirty six principles in their own ways from the monistic and dualistic standpoints. The important facts of spiritual life, grace of God or descent of divine power (śaktipāta), mantra as a ray of the Divine Spirit, initiation, Master (guru) as a self-realized person through whom God imparts divine power to a disciple are explained. Worship as meditation is emphasized, without which self-realization and God-realization are not possible. Pratyabhijñā Śaivism describes how the Absolute becomes the soul, and how the soul becomes the Absolute. The philosophy of Pratyabhijñā Śaivism and Śākta monism are very similar to each other. Utpaladeva admits them to be allied doctrines, and does not criticize Śākta monism. Self-surrender, devotion, knowledge of identity, and Kuṇḍalinīyoga are common to them. Works are not discarded but given a subsidiary place as a propædeutic to knowledge. Śāktaism wants to harmonize works and devotion with knowledge, and transform a householder's life into divine life for service to humanity.[3] Meditation on Śiva-Śakti at the different centres of mystic consciousness is emphasized by both Pratyabhijñā Śaivism and Śāktaism. Meditation at the heart-centre on Śiva as 'Om' is emphasized by the 'Pāśupata Sūtra' and Śrīkaṇṭha. Śrīpati Paṇḍita commends Kuṇḍalinīyoga in addition to the esoteric Vīraśaiva doctrine of ṣaṭsthala. Śaṁkara naturally gives a subordinate place to devotion in spiritual discipline, because God is a phenomenal appearance, and because the worship of God is intended for persons of dull intellect. Self-surrender and devotion are much emphasized by Śaivism and Śāktaism. The way of knowledge is intended for the contemplative type of persons, who are but very few.

PĀŚUPATA ŚAIVISM.—Pāśupata Śaivism is followed by the Naiyāyikas and the later Vaiśeṣikas, though the former is principally a system of logic and epistemology, and though the latter is chiefly a philosophy of nature. Bhāsarvjña, a Naiyāyika, makes an important contribution to the Pāśupata philosophy. The author of the 'Pāśupatasūtra' recognizes the Sāṁkhya cosmology prevailing before the 'Sāṁkhyakārikā', mentions prakṛti, buddhi, ahaṁkāra, sense-organs, subtle elements, and gross elements, and does not trace the world to the atoms as the Nyāya-Vaiśeṣika does. He regards God (pati) as the ruler of prakṛti and the efficient cause of the world, and prakṛti as the material cause of the world. Madhva, like him, accepts the view, among the theistic Vedāntists. God, for the Pāśupata, is independent of the souls' merits and demerits in creating the world out of prakṛti. This view is not accepted by any other school of Śaivism. His concept of liberation as the soul's achievement of supernatural powers such as omniscience, omnipotence, and lordship retaining its integrity, and attaining complete union with God is entirely different from the Nyāya-Vaiśeṣika concept of liberation as the complete destruction of its specific qualities. His emphasis on self-surrender, devotion, offering of all actions and even the self to God (ātmadāna), muttering His name or mantra, constant recollection of Him is like that of a Vaiṣṇava theist. His stress on the eligibility of the Brāhmaṇa ascetics alone for absolution forestalls Śaṁkara's view. There are some repulsive elements in the Pāśupata practice, which do not accord with social norms of behaviour, and should be dispensed with. The Pāśupata ontology is dualistic, because it regards God as distinct from prakṛti and souls of which He is the ruler. He binds the individual souls and liberates them through His grace. They acquire merits and demerits by their voluntary actions. But they bear fruits if God favours them. He is absolutely free and independent of their merits and demerits in creating the world out of prakṛti. Liberated souls, who acquire lordship, do not lose their identity in Him.

ŚAIVA SIDDHĀNTA.—The Śaiva Siddhānta propounded by Bhojadeva and the 'Mṛgendra Tantra' is dualistic, because it regards God as distinct from souls and bonds. It considers God to be the efficient cause, His conscious power to be the instrumental cause, and His unconscious power of māyā to be the material cause, of the world. It tries to overcome dualism by conceiving of God, in His own nature, as its efficient cause, and through His unconscious power of māyā, as its material cause, and by conceiving of God Himself as becoming an atomic soul by veiling His qualities, and a taint, which is a trace of His power. Unlike the Pāśupata, it makes God dependent on the souls' merits and demerits in creating the world. Like Jīva Gosvāmi, it regards māyā as an unconscious power of God, a real positive principle. Śrīkumāra's arguments for the existence of God and criticism of the antitheistic objections closely resemble those of the Naiyāyikas. The Śaiva Siddhānta admits māyā to be the material cause of prakṛti and the world, and avyakta of the nature of sattva, rajas and tamas to be the cause of the bound souls' pleasures and pains. It considers God, souls and māyā to be eternal. But souls are essentially of the nature of God —omniscient, omnipotent and ubiquitous, but become atomic and endowed with limited knowledge and power because of taints. Souls are active, like God. They become omniscient, omnipotent, ubiquitous and infinitely blissful, when their taints are destroyed. They retain their integrity in emancipation, though their minds and egos are destroyed. So the Śaiva Siddhānta advocates dualistic ontology.

ŚRĪKAṆṬHA AND ŚRIPATI PAṆḌITA.—Both are profoundly influenced by Rāmānuja's Viśiṣṭādvaitavāda, and propound types of Śaiva qualified monism. The latter calls the former a follower of Rāmānuja, himself closely follows him, and sometimes reproduces 'Śrībhāṣya' verbatim in 'Śrīkarabhāṣya'. Both regard Brahman as invested with excellent qualities, as the material and efficient cause of the world, and as qualified by the powers of conscious souls and unconscious physical things, and consider Him to be their Soul. Śrīkaṇṭha admits inseparable relation (apṛthaksiddhi) between God and the souls and the world, like Rāmānuja. Both Śrīkaṇṭha and Śrīpati Paṇḍita recognize the importance of works, meditation and knowledge as means to emancipation. Both admit the reality of the world and satkāryavāda. Both consider individual souls to be atomic in magnitude, and knowers, agents, enjoyers and sufferers with limited freedom, and parts of God.

Śrīpati Paṇḍita severely criticizes Śaṁkara's concepts of attributeless Brahman, of

Īśvara as a phenomenal appearance, of an individual soul as a limitation of Brahman by avidyā, or as a reflection of It in avidyā, and as identical with Brahman, and of the world as a false appearance of Brahman due to avidyā. He also conceives of individual souls as atomic in magnitude and as knowers, agents, enjoyers and sufferers, both different and nondifferent from God, and becoming identical with God through His grace in release. But Rāmānuja does not recognize identity of a released soul with God. Śrīkaṇṭha rejects embodied release, like Rāmānuja and other Vaiṣṇavas. But Śrīpati Paṇḍita admits both embodied release and disembodied release. He regards the performance of duties, devotion and knowledge as means to emancipation. Both Śrīkaṇṭha and Śrīpati Paṇḍita are proponents of avikṛtapariṇāmavāda, difference and nondifference between souls and God, and jñānakarmasamuccayavāda.

The Pāśupata does not worship Umā, divine power, Consort of Śiva. Śrīkaṇṭha worships Śiva-Umā, God united with divine power inseparably, represented by 'Om', meditates on 'Om' in the heart-cavity, and is an adept in daharavidyā. Śrīpati Paṇḍita enjoins the practice of Kuṇḍalinīyoga. He believes in Śiva and Śakti as nondifferent from each other, and refers to the Vīra Śaiva esoteric doctrine of ṣaṭsthala. He criticizes Śrīkaṇṭha's doctrine on some points. Śrīkaṇṭha criticizes some views of Rāmānuja. Abhinava Gupta, a staunuch advocate of Pratyabhijñā Śaivism and commentator on the 'Parā Triṁśikā', a Śākta work, worships Śiva-Umā, and elaborately expounds Tantric yoga. All schools of Śaivism believe in devotion and the grace of God, like Śāktaism. The Pratyabhijñā school of Śaivism equates devotion with the intuitive knowledge of Brahman. But the Advaita Vedānta treats God as a phenomenal appearance, and the worship of Him with devotion as a purificatory process at best.

POST-ŚAṀKARA ADVAITA VEDĀNTA.—There are some texts in the earlier Upaniṣads, which can be harmonized into a system of unqualified idealistic monism (kevalādvaitavāda), like that of Śaṁkara. But there are other texts, which clearly assert the reality of the individual souls and Īśvara, the reality of the world, and difference among them. Bādarāyaṇa's aphorisms do not unequivocally teach absolute monism. The 'Śvetāśvatara Upaniṣad' and the 'Bhagavadgītā' do not teach absolute monism. So Śaṁkara and his followers misinterpret them in the light of their doctrine of unqualified monism, and make too much of their doctrine of inexplicable avidyā, and Śaṁkarites continually make compromises and modifications and adaptations to meet the challenges of the different schools of theistic Vedānta. But within its main framework absolute idealistic monism is incontrovertible, if all tenets of it are accepted to be true. So controversy between it and various types of theistic Vedānta will continue for ever. They will never accept the same fundamental tenets, and meet on the same ground. This truth holds good of the modern exponents of the different schools of Vedānta, who reinterpret the old doctrines in the light of their knowledge of Western philosophy in modern phraseology. The author of this book is not enamoured of absolute idealistic monism for reasons which will be expounded later in his subsequent works.

But there are some misconceptions about Advaita Vedānta, which must be removed. It does not deny the reality of the world, the reality of the individual souls, and the rôle of morality and religion. It recognizes them as empirically real for practical purposes.

For those of us, who have not yet achieved embodied release, they are real. Advaitavāda recognizes three degrees of reality from the practical standpoint,—the ontological reality of Brahman, the empirical reality of the souls and the world, and the illusory reality of illusions. There is not much difference between the realization of the soul as an eternal part of God and as identical with Brahman. Both can be realized when a soul transcends bodily, vital, and mental consciousness, conquers egoism and consequent emotions and passions. Complete community (sādharmya) with God and absolute identity with Brahman are not contradictory to each other. Unseemly controversy about the final state of emancipation is not of practical importance, because it is beyond the reach of most of the disputants. Again, cognition, emotion and action are interrelated to one another, and so the intuitive knowledge of Brahman presupposes good conduct and direction of emotions to the Supreme. Performance of duties, devotion to the Divine, and intuitive realization of Brahman are closely related to one another. Only active persons emphasize works, emotional persons stress devotion, and contemplative persons emphasize intuitive knowledge. There are different types of philosophy, which appeal to different types of persons, and which satisfy their deep aspirations. But true philosophy must facilitate our elevation from animality to divinity, egoism to altruism and humanism. It must not countenance escapism and monasticism, deny freedom and creativity and purposefulness of the individual souls, their social intercourse, and power of creating a new order, and negate the environment in interaction with which they can realize their goals. It must not deny, but help us solve the problems of life. True philosophy should recognize the reality of the world, the reality of the individual souls and their power of transcending their narrow individuality and transforming their life into divine life and contributing to a new order based on fellowohip of humanity. The experiences of the self-realized souls in the final state of release described by Śaṁkara, Rāmānuja, Vallabha and the like are almost the same despite the difference in the metaphysical subtleties of their doctrines. But certain souls' self-realization or God-realization is not of much avail at present. We must think of elevating human consciousness to a higher level by cultivating collective thinking, collective good-will, and collective meditation to save humanity from destruction. So negation of the world, unreality of the souls and their freedom, escape from life, and exaggeration of avidyā do not fit in with the present age.

The Advaita concept of Brahman as mere existence-consciousnessness-blish and infinitude, devoid of omniscience, omnipotence, lordship, and the power of creating, maintaining and dissolving the world, controlling the individual souls, and bestowing grace on them, and redeeming them, is not satisfactory. Consciousness, which is not self-consciousness or 'I'-consciousness, is almost insentient, as Abhinava Gupta shows. Knowledge without a knower and an object is inconceivable as Yāmuna and Rāmānuja point out. (Cp. Hegel). Bliss without a blissful being is inconceivable. Brahman devoid of power, freedom, activity, creation and direction, and yet perfect, is not satisfactory. The Absolute of Pratyabhijñā Śaivism, Śiva-Śakti, endowed with manifestation and perfect 'I'-consciousness, infinite freedom, and æsthetic delight is more satisfactory than Brahman of the Advaita Vedānta. Śaṁkara's concept of Īśvara associated with māyā as a false appearance imagined by a worshipper of dull intellect infected with nescience, incapable of meditating on Brahman, does not satisfy our religious aspirations. The theistic Vedāntists rightly identify Brahman with Īśvara invested with infinite excellent qualities (saguṇa), and consider Him to be the creator, maintainer, and destroyer of the world, Inner Controller of individual souls, bestower of His grace on them, and Lord of the moral law of karma. Śaṁkara treats indeterminate Brahman as superior to Īśvara while Kṛṣṇadāsa Kavirāja, a follower of Jīva Gosvāmī, treats attributeless Brahman as a ray of the light of the divine body of Īśvara (tanubhā) and inferior to Him.[4] The 'Bhagavadgītā' conceives of Īśvara as the foundation of Brahman.[5] Śaṁkara thinks the indeterminate experience of Brahman to be superior to the determinate knowledge of Īśvara invested with excellent attributes while Madhva thinks the determinate knowledge of Īśvara as superior to the indeterminate knowledge of Brahman. Madhva, Vallabha and others deny indeterminate knowledge. Śaṁkara's concept of avidyā or māyā as neither real nor unreal nor both but indefinable is extremely unsatisfactory. It is inexplicable in itself, and does not explain Īśvara, individual souls, the world, morality and religion adequately, but explain them away as false appearances. It does not really reside in Brahman or individual souls, because it is not real. Yet there is a hot controversy among the Śaṁkarites about this question. There is a similar controversy about the number of nesciences, and the annulment of nescience or nesciences. The doctrine of one individual soul (ekajīvavāda) is solipsism repugnant to common experience, and makes morality impossible. Dṛṣṭisṛṣṭivāda reduces external objects to momentary perceptions of an individual soul perceiving them. Prakāśānanda is an exponent of it. Sṛṣṭidṛṣṭivāda advocated by the Vivaraṇa school is more satisfactory than Dṛṣṭisṛṣṭivāda. The doctrine of many souls accords with common experience, and should not be lightly brushed aside. Śaṁkara's view of Ātman is better than those of the Cārvākas, the Yogācāras, the Mādhyamikas, the Nyāya, Kumārila, Prabhākara, and Śāṁkhya. But his concept of self or Ātman as mere knowledge or transcendent consciousness, and not as a self-conscious knower of objects, free agent, and enjoyer or a sufferer, is not rational. His concept of the relation of Ātman to ego (ahaṁkāra) is not adequate. His treatment of the individual soul as a false appearance makes a mockery of morality and religion. The reality and rôle of the finite selves and their interaction with one another are completely ignored by the Advaita Vedānta. To identify them with Brahman is not to glorify them, but to deny their real existence, freedom and creativity. They are self-conscious and self-determined agents, free unique centres of consciousness, with unique purposes in the world-order, holding communion with God, Who helps them in their free struggles in the physical and social environment to convert them into a rational universe. The problem of the finite self is ignored by the Advaita Vedānta, which denies its ontological reality and free agency. The theistic schools of Vedānta also do not unequivocally and emphatically recognize its freedom and creativity, and almost reduce it to a puppet of God. Morality is relative, but a social reality indispensable for social cohesion and realization of values. It should not be reduced to a false appearance. Religion, in the sense of spirituality as distinguished from blind dogmas, rituals and ceremonies, is necessary to man as a perpetually self-transcending being in eternal quest for God, the source of his intellectual, moral, æsthetic, and religious aspirations. It should not be cast aside as an irrational superstition despite great scientific and technological advance in the present age.

The Advaita concept of the world as a false appearance from the ontological standpoint does violence to our common experience. The theists consider it to be a manifestation of God, an expression of His power, which is real. They admit external objects to be real and transitory, though not momentary. Most Advaitins recognize relative stability, externality, and presentability of perceived objects, even of unperceived objects. They are treated as real for practical purposes. They are admitted to evoke responses in the form of practical actions. So there is no difference between the Advaitists and the Theists in the treatment of the world until Brahman is intuited and realized. The false world appearance is contradicted by the mystic intuition of Brahman. The theists also consider the world to be finally experienced as a manifestation of God bathed in His light and glory. They experience their souls as eternal parts of the Divine Spirit suffused with His knowledge and bliss, and participating in His experience, and the world of difference as expression of His glory and united in His integral unity.

Prakṛti or māyā is a real power of God. The world is real, and an expression of divine power. Causation is modification—transition from the undifferentiated to the differentiated, unfoldment of powers. Knower-known-relation is real. The world is known, but not false, because it is known. It is not false, because it is insentient. It is not false, because it is composed of parts. Space, time, and causality are real relations among the objects and events in the world. Categories invovle relations, but are not false for this reason. Power is real, and God is endowed with power or powers. God is not false, because He is known ; He is known incompletely as Rāmānuja and Madhva maintain.

It is true that a jīva is self-manifest, and of the nature of knowledge, which is self-manifest, and that it has avidyā and identifies itself erroneously with its mind-body-complex. Yet it is a knower and free agent. It can transcend its vital, mental, intellectual, and egoistic nature, and realize its spiritual nature akin to divine nature. It is a free spirit. It is not ubiquitous, since its ubiquity implies omniscience and omnipotence. Śaṁkara appears to advocate its empirical necessity and transcendental freedom. The Advaita discipline requires very stringent self-restraint and ascetic discipline, which presuppose freedom of the finite soul. Yet the Advaitist slurs over the problem of moral freedom.

The problem of evil does not arise in absolute monism. Evil is due to avidyā, which is inexplicable. Knowledge is higher than devotion. Devotion to Īśvara, a phenomenal appearance, is irrational. Devotion is higher than works. Knowledge also is higher than works. But renunciation of works, nonperformance of one's specific duties pertaining to one's station in society and order in life, and life of asceticism are not conducive to a full, all-round, harmonious life. Life of contemplation and life of works for self-realization and good of humanity are more satisfactory ideals. Selfless, disinterested performance of one's duties for the solidarity of humanity as enunciated and inculcated by the 'Bhagavadgītā' is a much better ideal.[6] Śaṁkara regards the disinterested performance of one's duties and duties performed and dedicated to God as conducive to purification of mind, and increase of sattva, and as a propaedeutic to the dawn of the saving knowledge.[7] He gives an inferior place to works. Asceticism emphasized by the Advaitins is not necessarily a higher life or more conducive to spiritual life. A householder's life is conducive to spiritual life for a sincere, vigilant and persevering aspirant. It is fuller and more balanced and harmonious life.[8]

Asceticism is escapism and life of negation and does not fit in with the modern outlook on life. It cannot be a universal ideal. It encourages monasticism, which will not be permitted by the future human society. The final state of release is indeed a positive state of experience of infinite knowledge and bliss of Brahman. But until it is reached, the world is real to us, and the finite self is a free centre of activity. Even in the final state a finite self does not possess the power of creation, maintenance and dissolution of the world, which are only empirically real. Somānanda's doctrine of "All are Siva" is better than Śaṁkara's doctrine of the finite self, Īśvara and the world as false appearances.[9] Considering bondage and liberation as phenomenal appearances is to explain away the problem of life. Still absolute idealism of Śaṁkara and his followers is an intellectual concept, which satisfies the uncompromising monistic impulse of some scholars and aspirants with an intellectual bent of mind. Within its framework Advaitavāda is incontrovertible, if its fundamental principles are accepted as unquestionable and indubitable truths. The controversy between a Śaṁkarite and a Mādhva is likely to continue for ever showing greater and greater dialectical skill.[10] It holds good of the contemporary exponents of the doctrines armed with the knowledge of Western philosophy as contemporary English works in Indian philosophy amply testify.[11]

[1] ŚBS., i, 4, 22. [2] BS., ŚBS., iii, 2, 28.
[3] ŚM., pp. 20-53. [4] CCA., i, 1, p. 1.
[5] BG., xiv, 27. [6] Ibid, iii, 20 & 25.
ŚBG., Introduction, p. 2.
(Ashterar & Co, Poona, 1916.)
[8] BG., V, 2, 6, 10, 12 ; vi, 39 ; xviii, 45-46 & 56.

[9] Supra, pp. 78-82. [10] AS., Nyāyāmṛta (Vyāsatīrtha).
[11] 'A Critique of Mādhva Refutation of the Śaṅkara School of Vedānta' (K. Narain) ; 'Philosophy of Śrī Madhvācarya' (B. N. K. Sharma) ; 'Advaita Concept of Falsity' (Nirod Baran Chakravarty), Calcutta, 1967.

INDEX OF AUTHORS

INDEX OF SUBJECTS

APPENDIX

REFERENCES

CHAPTER I

1. ब्रह्मपरिणतेरिति भास्करगोत्रे युज्यते । NKS., p. 332.
2. न च सिद्धरूपे ब्रह्मणि विधिः सम्भवति । साध्यार्थविषयो हि सः । BBS., i 1, 3.
10. परमात्मा स्वयमात्मानं कार्यत्वेन शक्तिविक्षेपं कृतवान् । अनन्ताश्च तस्य शक्तयोऽचिन्त्याश्च । Ibid, i, 4, 25.
11. भेदाभेदरूपं ब्रह्मेति समधिगतम् । Ibid, iii, 2, 11.
12. इतश्च प्रपंचाकार-विनिर्मुक्तं निदिध्यासितव्यम् । Ibid, iii, 2, 23.
13. भोक्तृभोग्यनियन्तृरूपस्य प्रपंचस्य ब्रह्मात्मता, न प्रपंचरूपता ब्रह्मणः । Ibid, iii, 2, 13.
    चैतन्यमात्रं रूपान्तररहितम् । Ibid, iii, 2, 17.
14. न चात्रापि विकारभावो विवक्षितः । किन्त्पाधिकृतभेदाभिप्रयासः । Ibid, ii, 3, 17.
    स्वाभाविकं चास्य ब्रह्मरूपमौपाधिकमितरत् । Ibid, ii, 3, 18.
15. तदिदम् औपाधिकमणुत्वं जीवस्यातो द्रष्टव्यम् । मनसोऽणुत्वाद् आत्मनोऽनियतमुच्यते । Ibid, ii, 3, 29.
16. न स्वाभाविकं कर्तृत्वमनिर्मोक्षप्रसंगात् । Ibid, ii, 3, 40.
18. भेदाभेदव्यपदेशात् । परमात्माऽहिस्थानीयः कुण्डलस्थानीयो जीव इति । Ibid, iii, 2, 27.
    यस्मादभेदः स्वाभाविकः ततो हेतो रनन्तेन परमात्मना विधूयाविद्याजलम् एकत्वं प्रतिपद्यते । Ibid, iii, 2, 26.
20. नेश्वरस्य संसारित्वमविद्यायोगात् निरतिशयानन्दस्वरूपत्वात् स्वभावसिद्धविद्यारूपत्वाच्च । Ibid, i, 2, 6.
    कस्येयमविद्या न तावज्-जीवस्य वस्तुभूतस्य तस्यानभ्युपगमात् । नापीश्वरस्य नित्यविज्ञानप्रकाशत्वाद् अज्ञानं विरुध्यते । तस्मादन्य ईश्वरस्तदंशो जीव. संसरतीति बलादभ्युपेयम् । Ibid, i, 4, 21.
21. स च भिन्नाभिन्नस्वरूपोऽभिन्नरूपं स्वाभाविकम् औपाधिकं तु भिन्नरुपम् । Ibid, ii, 3, 43.
    अवस्तुनः शशविषाणकल्पस्य चेतनस्य कुतो बन्धो मोक्षो वा कर्माधिकारो वा । Ibid, ii, 3, 50.
    बन्धः संस्टतिरज्ञानाद् विपर्ययो मोक्षः सम्यग्ज्ञानात् । Ibid, iii, 2, 5.
    तस्मादन्य ईश्वरस्तदशो जीवः संसरतीति बलादभ्युपेयम् । Ibid i, 4, 21.
22. अवस्थातद्वतोश्च नात्यन्तभेदः । कारणकार्ययोर्भेदाभेदावनुभूयेते । Ibid, ii, 1, 18.
25. अतो भिन्नाभिन्नरूपं ब्रह्मेति स्थितम् । कार्यरूपेण नानात्वमभेदः कारणात्मना न प्रपंचदर्शनम् (अविद्या) ब्रह्मकार्यत्वात् प्रपंचस्य वस्तुत्वम् । Ibid, i, 1, 4.
26. नित्यकर्मसमुच्चिताद् आत्मज्ञानाद् अविद्याकामकर्मलक्षण-बन्ध-निवृत्तिः । कर्मणा समुच्चितं ज्ञानं क्षेमप्राप्तिनिमित्तम् । Ibid, i, 1, 4. न च विरोधात् कर्मत्यागः अविरोध-दर्शितत्वात् । Ibid, iii, 4, 26.
    साधनभूतविद्याकर्मोत्कर्षापकर्षापेक्षया मुक्तिरेव फलम् ।
    परमात्मावस्था हि मुक्तिरवधारिता, सा चैकरूपा ॥ Ibid, iii, 4, 50.
27. विषयविषयो रागो बन्धहेतुः ब्रह्मविषयो मुक्तये । Ibid, iv, 4, 7. स्वप्ने सुषुप्तौ चाविद्या-कलुषितो जीव इह शुद्धेन परमात्मरूपेण सम्पद्यत इति विशेषः । Ibid, iv, 4, 2. परमकारणे सायुज्यं गतानां निरवधिकमैश्वर्यम् । इतरेषामैश्वर्यं सावच्छेदं परमेश्वरानुविधायीति स्थितम् । Ibid, iv, 4, 17.

CHAPTER II

1. भागव्यवस्था यन्निष्ठा तस्याहंभावभागिनः । व्यापित्वमनुसंधानं तज्जडस्य न युज्यते ।। APS., 26.

2. एष हि स्वानुभवप्रमाणकः । SpPR., p. 3. ŚSVM., i, 3. Cp. Śaṁkara. स्तानुभव एव अत्र साक्षी । PHV., 1.

4. अद्वयवादः स्थितः । स्वयूथ्यानद्वयवादिनः प्रतीदानीमारम्भः । तथा च तैरुक्तम् । यस्या निरूपाधिज्योतीरूपायाः शिवसंज्ञया । व्यपदेशः परां त्वामम्बां नित्यमुपास्महे ।। ŚDV., iii, 1.

5. न शिवः शक्तिरहितो न शक्तिर्व्यतिरेकिणी । शिवशक्तिमतोर्भेदः शैवे जातु न वर्ण्यते । ŚD., iii, 2-3. तदिच्छया सर्वं शिवात्मकम् । ŚD., iii, 20. शिवशक्तिमतामुक्ता सर्वत्रैव ह्यभेदिता । ŚD., iii, 64-65. SpPR., p. 11.

7. ज्ञानं बोधमयं तस्य शिवस्य सहजं सदा । ŚD., i, 27. भवत्युन्मुखिता चिता सेच्छायाः प्रथमा तुटिः । ŚD. i, 8.

8. इत्थं शिवो बोधमयः स एव परनिर्वृतिः । सैव चोन्मुखतां याति सेच्छाज्ञानक्रियात्मताम् ।। पदार्थत्वेन भगवान् सर्वत्रैव तदात्मता । ŚD., i, 39 & 41. एवं भेदात्मकं नित्यं शिवतत्त्वमनन्तकम् । तथा तस्य व्यवस्थानान्नानारूपेऽपि सत्यता । ŚD., i, 49.

9. यदयमनुत्तरमूर्ति-निजेच्छयाखिलमिदं जगत्स्रष्टुम । पस्पन्दे स स्पन्दः प्रथम. शिवतत्त्वमुच्यते तज्ज्ञैः । ṢṬTS., 1. शिवतत्त्वं नाम इच्छाज्ञानक्रियात्मककेवलपूर्णानन्दस्वभावरुपः परमशिवे एव । PPR., p. 6. अस्य जगत स्रष्टुमिच्छां परिगृहीतवतः परमेश्वरस्य प्रथमस्पन्दः एवेच्छाशक्तितत्वम् अप्रतिहतेच्छत्वात् । PPR., pp. 6-7.

11. सदाशिवतत्त्वे अहन्ताच्छादित-अस्फुटेदन्तामयं यादृशं परापररूपं विश्वं ग्राह्यम् । PHV., 3.

12. ईश्वरतत्त्वे स्फुटेदन्ताहन्तासामानाधिकरण्यात्म यादृक विश्वं ग्राह्यंम् । Ibid.

13. सा भवति शुद्धविद्या येदन्ताहन्तयोरभेदमतिः । ṢṬTS., 4. अहन्तेदन्तयोरैक्यप्रतिपत्तिः शुद्धविद्या । PPR., p. 7.

14. स्वस्वरुपेषु भावेषु भेदप्रथा माया । PPR., p. 7. माया विभेदबुद्धि-र्निजांशजातेषु निखिलजीवेषु । ṢṬTS., 5.

15. अत्र कला नाम अस्य पुरुषस्य किंचित्कर्तृताहेतुः, विद्या किंचिज्ज्ञत्वकारणम्, रागो विषयेष्वभिव्यंगः, कालो हि भावानां भासनाभासनात्मकानां क्रमः अवच्छेदको भूतादिः, नियतिः ममेदं कर्त्तव्यं नेदं कर्त्तव्यम् इति नियमनहेतुः, एतत् पंचकम् अस्य स्वरुपावरकत्वात् कंचुकमिति उच्यते । PPR., pp. 8-9.

16. यदा तु परमेश्वरः पारमेश्वर्या मायाशक्तया स्वरूपं गृहयित्वा संकुचित-ग्राहकतामश्नुते तदा पुरुषसंज्ञः । PPR., pp. 7-8.

17. इच्छादित्रिसमष्टिः शक्तिः शान्तास्य संकुचद्रूपा । संकलितेच्छाद्यात्मक-सत्त्वादिकसाम्यरुपिणी तु सती । ṢṬTS., 13.

18. निश्चयकारिणी बुद्धिः । PPR. p. 10 अहंकृतिः अहंप्रतीतिकरी । मनः विकल्पकरी । ṢṬTS., 14-15. शब्द-स्पर्श-रूप-रस-गन्धाः सामान्याकाराः पंच तन्मात्राणि । PPR., p. 10.

20. मायापरिग्रहवशाद् बोधो मलिनः पशुर्भवति । काल-कला-नियतिवशाद् रागाविद्यावशेन संबद्धः ।। PS , 16. आणव-मायीय-कार्ममलस्वभावानां पाशानां भाजनम् । PSV., 16.

22 चित्प्राधान्यपक्षे सहजे, प्रकाशमात्रप्रधानत्वे विज्ञानाकलता ; प्रकाश-परामर्शप्रधानत्वे तु विद्याप्रमातृता ।

समाधिप्रयत्नोपार्जिते तु चित्प्रधानत्वे शुद्धात्मप्रमातृता क्रमात्क्रमं प्रकर्षवती। संकोचप्राधान्ये तु शून्यादि-प्रमातृता। PHV., 5.

25. तुर्याभोगमयाभेदख्यातिरख्यातिहारिणी। VŚSV., i, 10, śl., 55. तुर्यातीतमयं योगी प्रोक्तचैतन्यमामृशन्। Ibid, i, 10, 56. शिवशक्तिपातविमले धीतत्त्वे भाति भारुपः। PS. 9.

26. स्वातन्त्र्यहानिर्बोधस्य स्वातन्त्र्यस्याप्यबोधता। द्विधाणवं मलमिदं स्वस्वरुपापहानितः। ĪPK., iii, 15. भिन्नवेद्यप्रथात्रैव मायाख्यं जन्मभोगदम्। कर्तर्यबोधे कार्मं तु मायाशक्त्यैव तत्त्रयम्। Ibid, iii, 16.

27. मध्यविकासाच्चिदानन्दलाभः। PH., 17. मध्यभूता संविद् भगवती विकसति। PHV., 17. विश्वोत्तीर्णनिजाहन्तासमावेशितचेतसः। VSSV., iii, 44, śl., 205.

29. चिदेव भगवती स्वच्छस्वतन्त्ररुपा तत्तदनन्तजगदात्मना स्फुरति। अस्यां च प्रसरन्त्यां जगत् उन्मिषति व्यवतिष्ठते च, निवृत्तप्रसारायां च निमिषति। PHV., 1. पदार्थत्वेन भगवान् सर्वत्रैव तदात्मता। ŚD., i, 41. एवं सर्वपदार्थानां समैव शिवता स्थिता। Ibid, i, 48. स्वशक्तिप्रचयोऽस्यविश्वम्। ŚS., iii, 30. HIP., Vol. II, 1952, pp. 738-39n.

30. आत्मैव सर्वभावेषु स्फुरन्निर्वृतचिद्विभु.। ŚD., i, 2.

31. भोक्तैव भोग्यभावेन सदा सर्वत्र संस्थितः। Spk., 29.
शिवो भोक्ता शिवो भोज्यं शिवावस्था भोक्तृरुपता। ŚD., vii, 99-100.
भोग्यं भोक्तरि लीनं चेद् भोक्ता तद्वस्तुतः स्फुटः। TA., iii, 191.
अनुत्तरानन्दमयो देवो भोक्तैव कथ्यते। Ibid, iii, 190.
इच्छादिकं भोग्यमेव तत एवास्य शक्तिता। Ibid, iii, 191.
तस्यापि परं वीर्यं पंचभूतकलात्मकम्। भोग्यत्वेनान्नरुपं च शब्दस्पर्शरसात्मकम्। Ibid, iii, 228.

32. ज्ञानज्ञेयस्वरुपिण्या शक्तया परमया युतः। पदद्वये विभुर्भाति तदन्यत्र तु चिन्मयः॥ Spk., 18.

33. किंतु निर्माणशक्ति. साप्येवंविदुष ईशितुः। तथा विज्ञातृविज्ञेयभेदो यदावभास्यते॥ ĪPK., ii, 8.

34. ज्ञेयस्य हि परं तत्त्वं यः प्रकाशात्मकः शिवः। न ह्यप्रकाशरुपस्य प्राकाश्यं वस्तुताऽपिवा। TA., i, 52. तस्य देवादिदेवस्य परापेक्षा न विद्यते। परस्य तदपेक्षत्वात् स्वतन्त्रोऽयमतः स्थितः। TA., i, 59-60. विभुत्वात् सर्वगो नित्यभावादाद्यन्तवर्जितः। विश्वाकृतित्वाच्चिदचित्तद्वैचित्र्यावभासकः। TA., i, 61-62. वेदकं वेद्यमेकं तत्त्वम्। चैतन्यं विश्वस्य स्वभावः। ŚSVM., i, 1. ज्ञाता ज्ञेयं ज्ञानमिति ज्ञानस्यैव त्रिधा स्थितिः। SpPD., p. 30 ज्ञानादृते स्वतोऽस्ति न ज्ञेयस्य सत्ता क्वचित्। Ibid, p. 30.

35. शिवः कर्त्ता शिवः कर्म शिवोऽस्मि करणात्मकः। शिवः एव फलावस्था व्यापार इति साधुषु। ŚD., vii, 100-01. कार्यता क्षयिणी तत्र कर्तृत्वं पुनरक्षयम् Spk., 14.

36. यदा त्वेकत्र संरुढस्तदा तस्य लयोदयौ। नियच्छन् भोक्तृतामेति ततश्चक्रेश्वरो भवेत्। Spk., 51.

37. ज्ञानाधिष्ठानं मातृका ŚS., i, 4. कवर्गादिषु माहेश्वर्याद्याः पशुमातरः। ŚS., iii, 19. शब्दराशिः स एवोक्तो मातृका सा च कीर्तिता। क्षोभ्यक्षोभकतावेशान्मालिनीता प्रचक्षते। TA., iii. 232.

38. विद्याशरीरसत्ता मन्त्ररहस्यम्। ŚS., ii, 3. शुद्धे चिन्मात्रतावेशादुन्मेषः सहसैव यः। स्वप्रकाशविकासाख्या सा विद्येति निरुपिता। शरीरसत्ता सा मान्त्री रहस्यं परमं च तत्। BŚSV., ii, 3, śl., 9-10.

39. गुरुरुपायः ŚS., ii, 6. यद्वा गुरुः परा शक्तिरीश्वरानुग्रहात्मिका। VSSV., ii, 6, śl. 26.

40. दीक्षाशब्द इह प्रोक्तो दानक्षपणलक्षणः। योविपस्यो ज्ञाहेतुश्च। ŚS., iii, 28-09.

42. द्विष्ठस्यानेकरुपत्वात् सिद्धस्यान्यानपेक्षणात्। पारतन्त्र्याद्ययोगाच्च तेन कर्तापि कल्पितः ĪPK., i, 16.

43. न चेदन्ताकृतानन्तः विश्वरूपो महेश्वरः । स्यादेकश्चिद्पुर्ज्ञानस्मृत्यपोहनशक्तिमान् । ĪPK. i, 23. प्रागिवार्थोऽप्रकाशः स्यात् प्रकाशात्मतया विना । न च प्रकाशो भिन्नः स्यादात्मार्थस्य प्रकाशता । Ibid, i, 33. प्रकाशात्मा प्रकाश्योऽर्थो नाप्रकाशश्च सिध्यति । Ibid, i, 34. चिदात्मैव हि देवोऽन्तःस्थितमिच्छावशाद्बहिः । योगीव निरुपादानमर्थजातं प्रकाशयेत् । Ibid, i, 38.

44. परेशशक्तिरात्मेव भासते नत्विदन्तया । Ibid, i, 51. अहंप्रत्यवमर्शो यः प्रकाशात्मापि वाग्वपुः । Ibid, i 53.

45. तदेवं व्यवहारेऽपि प्रभुर्देहादिमाविशन् । भान्तमेवान्तरर्थौघमिच्छया भासयेद्बहिः । ĪPK., i, 59. देशकालक्रमजुषामर्थानां स्वसमापिनाम् । सकृदाभाससाध्योऽसावन्यथा कः समन्वय. । Ibid, 66.

46. चिन्मयत्वेऽभासानामन्तरेव स्थितिः सदा । मायया भासमानानां बाह्यत्वाद्बहिरप्यसौ । Ibid, i, 84. तदैक्येन विना न स्यात् संविदां लोकपद्धतिः । प्रकाशैक्यात्तदेकत्वं मातैकः स इति स्थितम् । Ibid, i, 87.

47. अस्माकं सर्वसत्यता । ŚD., vi, 7.

53. अनादिनिधनं ब्रह्म शब्दतत्त्वं यदक्षरम् । विवर्ततेऽर्थभावेन प्रक्रिया जगतो यतः । ŚD., ii, 9. VPD., i, 1. HIP., Vol. I, pp. 863-64.

54. असत्या यदि पश्यन्ती पश्यन्ती ब्रह्म चित्रता । ŚD., ii, 24.

57. पश्यन्तं सा किमात्मानं पश्यन्ती जड़मेव वा । जड़े जडेत्वमेत्रास्याः, पश्यती ह्यनवस्थता । ŚD., ii, 56.

58. यो हि पश्यति पश्यन्तीं स देवः परमो मतः । ŚD., ii, 64.

59. यथा सर्वपदार्थानां भगवच्छिवरुप्ना । तद्वागिन्द्रियस्यापि न पुनः सा परा दशा ।। ŚD., ii, 88.

60. शिवस्य तादृगात्मत्वमुत्पद्येतात्र योगिवत् । इच्छया सर्वभावत्वमनेकात्मत्वमेवच । नात्र स्वात्मविकारेण जनयेद्भावमण्डलम् । ŚD., iii, 34-35.

62. नासत्ये सत्यबुद्धित्वखण्डनात्रास्ति काचन । ŚD., iii, 71. व्यवहारो न वस्तुगः । स्वरुपं वस्तुगं विद्धि व्यवहारो न जातुचित् । ŚD., iii, 77.

63. न हि शिवो घटादिरुपः, अपितु घटादिः शिवरुप । ततश्चिद्रपस्य देशकालस्वभावभेदाभावान्न भेदः । ŚDV., iii, 96.

64. ध्यानमनस्तमितं पुनरेष हि भगवान् विचित्ररुपाणि । सृजति तदेव ध्यानं संकल्पालिखितसत्यरुपत्वम् । PS., 77. भुवनावलीं समस्तां तत्त्वक्रमकल्पनामथाक्षगणम् । अन्तर्बोधे परिवर्तयति यत्सोऽस्य जप उदितः ।। PS., 78. सर्वभावाः शिवाकारा अन्तर्भूताः शिवानले । सोऽहं शिवः सुतृप्तोऽस्मि होम इत्युदितः परः । ŚD., vii, 90-91. शिवोऽस्मि साधनाविष्टः शिवोऽहं याजकोऽप्यहम् । शिव एवानया स्थित्या सत्यया याग उत्तमः । ŚD., vii, 96-97.

65. मत्स्वरूपानुभवरुपां परां काष्ठामधिरुढा भक्तिरेव विज्ञानम् । RKBG., ix, 24. भक्तिरद्वयचिन्मात्रस्वरूपब्रह्मतत्त्वभावनया आत्मन एवोपासनम् । Ibid, ix, 27.

66. यस्मिन्नर्थे सदात्यागः स योगः परयोगिनः । ŚD., vii, 81.
भाविते‌ऽभाविते वापि शिवत्वे शिवतैव मे । सर्वदा पितृमात्रादितौल्यदार्ढ्येन योगिता ।। Ibid, vii, 82.

67. ज्ञानमन्नम् । ŚS., ii, 9 , अनात्मन्यात्मताज्ञप्तिरन्नं ग्रस्यत इत्यतः । VŚSV., ii, 9, śl. 56.

68. शुद्धतत्त्वसंधानाद्वाऽपशुशक्तिः । ŚS., i, 16.
शुद्धं तत्त्वं परं वस्तु यत्तत्परशिवात्मकम् । तत्संधानं प्रपंचस्य तन्मयत्वेन भावनम् ।। VŚSV., i, 16, śl., 82-83.
वितर्क आत्मज्ञानम् । ŚS., i, 17.
वितर्कः प्रोक्तसंधानध्वस्तबन्धस्य योगिनः । विश्वात्मा शिव एवाहमस्मीत्यर्थविचिन्तनम् । VŚSV., i, 17, śl. 85.

69. शिवतुल्यो जायते । ŚS., iii, 25. तुर्यपरिशीलनप्रकर्षात् प्राप्ततुर्यातीतपदः, स्वच्छन्दचिदानन्दघनेन शिवेन भगवता तुल्यः जायते । KŚSV., iii, 25.

70. शुद्धविद्योदयाच्चक्रेशत्वसिद्धिः । ŚS., i, 21. जगत् सर्वमहमेवेति या मतिः । सा शुद्धा निर्मला विद्या । VŚSV., i, 21, śl., 99-100.

71. गर्भे चित्तविकासोऽविशिष्टविद्या स्वप्नः । ŚS., ii, 4.
सैवाविशिष्टा विद्येति किंचिज्ज्ञत्वस्वरूपिणी । अशुद्धविद्या सा स्वप्नो विकल्पप्रत्ययात्मकः ॥ VŚSV., ii, 4, śl., 18.

72. स्वशक्तिप्रचयोऽस्य विश्वम् । ŚS., iii, 30. तद्विमुक्तस्तु केवली । ŚS., iii, 34. सुखदुःखाभ्यां विशेषेण मुक्तः संस्कारमात्रेणापि अन्तरसंस्पृष्टः केवली केवलं चिन्मात्रप्रमातृरूपं यस्य । KŚSV., iii, 34.

73. हृदये चित्तसंघट्टाद् दृश्यस्वापदर्शनम् । शुद्धतत्त्वसंधानाद्वाऽपशुशक्तिः । ŚS., i, 15-16.
हृदयं तद्विजानीयाद्विश्वस्यायतनं महत् ॥ इत्युक्तनीत्या हृदयं विश्वविश्रान्तिभित्तिभूः ।
खसंवित् तत्र संघट्टश्चित्तस्य चलतः सतः ॥ तदैकात्म्यपरामर्शजागरूकस्वभावता ।
खाङ्गरूपेषु भावेषु प्रमाता कथ्यते पतिः ॥ खाङ्गकल्पतया तस्य यथावत् प्रथनं भवेत् ॥ VŚSV., i, 15, śl., 77-79, 80-81.

74. पौरुषज्ञानं ज्ञानमुदितं सत् अन्यनिरपेक्षमेव मोक्षकारणम् । तच्च ज्ञानमात्रस्वभावम्, अख्यात्यभाव एव हि पूर्णख्यातिः, सैव च प्रकाशानन्दघनस्यात्मनस्तात्विकं स्वरूपं, तत्प्रथनमेव मोक्षः । TAV., i, 24, p. 57.

75. चैतन्यमात्मा । ŚS., i, 1. ज्ञानं बन्धः । ŚS., i, 2. द्वैतप्रथा तदज्ञानं तुच्छत्वाद् बन्ध उच्यते । TA., i, 30. अपूर्णं ज्ञानमपर्णत्वाच्च तदेव अपूर्णमन्यता-शुभाशुभ-वासना-शरीर-भुवनाकार-स्वभाव-विविध संकुचित-ज्ञान-रूपतया मलत्रयात्मा बन्ध इति उच्यते । TAV., i, 30, p. 61.

76. तत्र दीक्षादिना पौंस्नमज्ञानं ध्वंसि यद्यपि । तथापि तच्छरीरान्ते तज्ज्ञानं व्यज्यते स्फुटम् । TA., i, 43.
दीक्षया गलितेऽप्यन्तरज्ञाने पौरुषात्मनि । धीगतस्यानिवृत्तत्वाद्विकल्पोऽपि हि संभवेत् ॥ TA., i, 48.
बौद्धाज्ञाननिवृत्तौ तु विकल्पोन्मूलनाद् ध्रुवम् । तदैव मोक्ष इत्युक्तं धात्रा श्रीमन्निशाटने ॥ TA., i, 50.

77. बन्धमोक्षौ न भिद्येते सर्वत्रैव शिवत्वतः ॥ विज्ञानमीदृक् सर्वस्य कस्मान्न स्याद्विमोहिता ॥ सैवैषा च संसारो बन्धमोक्षावतः स्थितौ ॥ प्रतीतिमात्रमेवात्र तावता बन्धमोक्षता । तथा तथा शिवावस्था स्वेच्छातः स तदात्मकः । तदात्मत्वे नास्ति बन्धस्तदभावान्न मोक्षणम् । ŚD., iii, 68-69 ; 70 & 72.

78. अज्ञानग्रन्थिभिदा स्वशक्त्यभिव्यक्तता मोक्षः । भिन्नाज्ञानग्रन्थिः पराकृतभ्रान्तिः । प्रक्षीणपुण्यपापो विग्रहयोगेऽप्यसौ मुक्तः ॥ PS., 60-61.

79. इह तावदात्मज्ञानं मोक्षः । अतो यदेवात्मनो लक्षणं तदेव मोक्षस्य । TAV., i, 31.
यत्तु ज्ञेयसतत्त्वस्य पूर्णपूर्णप्रथात्मकम् । तदुत्तरोत्तरं ज्ञानं तत्तत संसारशान्तिदम् । TA., i, 32.
बद्धोऽविद्यया जीवो मुक्तिस्तस्य हि तत्क्षये । SpPR., p. 5.

80. मोक्षो हि नाम नैवान्यः स्वरूपप्रथनं हि सः । स्वरूपं चात्मनः संविन्नान्यत्तत्र तु याः पुनः ॥ TA., i, 156-57.

81. आत्मा संवित्प्रकाशस्थितिरनवयवा संविदित्यात्तशक्तिव्रातं तस्य स्वरूपं स च निज-महसश्छादनाद्बद्धरूपः । TA., i, 330.

86. सर्वं शिवात्मकम् । ŚD., iii, 61 ; iii, 20. यथा सर्वपदार्थानां भगवच्छिवरूपता । Ibid, ii, 88. तस्मात्समग्राकारेषु सर्वासु प्रतिपत्तिषु । विज्ञेयं शिवरूपत्वं खशक्त्यावेशनात्मकम् । Ibid, iii, 17.

87· आत्मैव सर्वभावेषु स्फुरन्निर्वृतचिद्विभुः । अनिरूद्धेच्छाप्रसरः प्रसरद्-दृक्क्रिय. शिवः ।। ŚD. i, 2.
भावानां प्रतिबिम्बत्वे आत्मनोऽपि न युक्तता । प्रतिबिम्बेष्वसत्यत्वादर्भूतेष्वगोचरात् । Ibid, v, 33-34.
चिदात्मैव हि देवोऽन्तःस्थितमिच्छावशाद्बहिः । योगीव निरूपादानमर्थजातं प्रकाशयेत् ।। IPK., i, 38.
स्वामिनश्चात्मसंस्थस्य भावजातस्य भासनम् । अस्त्येव न विना तस्मादिच्छामर्शः प्रवर्तते ।। Ibid, i, 41.
चिन्मयत्वेऽवभासानामन्तरेव स्थितिः सदा । मायया भासमानानां बाह्यत्वाद्बहिरप्यसौ ।। Ibid, i, 84.
आभासरुप एव जडचेतनपदार्थः । ŚSVM., iii, 1, 1. तत्तद्रूपतया ज्ञानं बहिरन्तः प्रकाशते ।
ज्ञानादृते नार्थसत्ता ज्ञानरूपं ततो जगत् । TA., iii, 30. ज्ञानं न भवतो भिन्नं ज्ञेयं ज्ञानात् पृथङ् न हि ।
अतो न त्वितरत् किंचित् तस्माद् भेदो न वास्तवः । Ibid, iii, 2.

89. अतोऽसौ परमेशानः स्वात्मव्योमन्यनर्गलः । इयतः सृष्टिसंहाराडम्बरस्य प्रदर्शकः ।। TA., iii, 3.
निर्मले मुकुरे यद्वद् भान्ति भूमिजलादयः । अमिश्रास्तद्वदेकस्मिंश्चिन्नाथे विश्ववृत्तयः ।। Ibid, iii, 4.
भावानां यत् प्रतीघाति वपुर्मायात्मकं हि तत् । तेषामेवास्ति सद्विदयामयं त्वप्रतिघातकम ।।
तदेवमुभयाकारमवभासं प्रकाशयन् । विभाति वरदो बिम्बप्रतिबिम्बदृशाखिले । Ibid, iii, 10.
संविदात्मनि विश्वोऽयं भाववर्गः प्रपंचवान् । प्रतिबिम्बतया भाति यस्य विश्वेश्वरो हि सः । Ibid, iii, 268.
अतएवान्तरं किंचिद्धीसंज्ञं भवतु स्फुटम् । यत्रास्य विच्छिदा भानं संकल्पस्वप्नदर्शने ।
अतो निमित्तं देवस्य शक्तयः सन्तु तादृशे ।। Ibid, iii, 64.
इत्थं विश्वमिदं नाथे भैरवीय-चिदम्बरे । प्रतिबिम्बमलं स्वच्छे न खल्वन्यप्रसादतः ।। Ibid, iii, 65.
यः प्रकाशः स सर्वस्य प्रकाशत्वं प्रयच्छति । न च तद्व्यतिरेक्यस्ति विश्वं सद्वावभासते । Ibid, , iii 2.
प्रतिघात्यप्रतीघात्यात्मकम् आभासमात्रसारमेव एतत्, न तु तात्विकम् । Ibid, iii, 11.

93. चिदिच्छाशक्तिसम्बुद्धः स्पन्द आत्मबलेरितः । SpPD., p. 37. विमर्शः स्पन्दः । PPR., p. 2.
शिव एकः स्पन्दवान् स्वप्रतिष्ठितः । SpS., 1. इह परमेश्वरस्य एकैव परामर्शशक्तिः किंचिच्चलत्ताभास-रूपतया स्पन्द इति, स्फुरत्ता इति, ऊर्मिः इति, बलम् इति, उद्योगः इति, परा-इत्याद्यनन्तसंज्ञाभिः आगमेषु उद्घोष्यते । SpS., p. 5.

CHAPTER III

1. आक्षपादा नैयायिकास्तेषां मते देवो दर्शनाधिष्ठायकः शिवो महेश्वरः । LV., 13, p. 11. वैशेषिकाणां नैयायिकैः सार्द्धं शिवदेवताऽभ्युपगमे भेदो नास्ति. तत्त्वेषु भेदो विद्यते । Ibid, p, 6C. कणादस्य पुरः शिवेनोलूकरूपेण मतमेतत् प्रकाशितम् । पशुपतिभक्तत्वेन पाशुपतं प्रोच्यते । देवविषयो भेदो वैशेषिकाणां नैयायिकैः समं नास्ति । TRD., p. 266. SDSm., ch. vi. HIP., Vol. II, 1952, pp. 731-33. Criticism, SBS., ii, 2, 37-40.

3. प्रमितिः संवित् संचिन्तनं संबोधो विद्याभिव्यक्तिः । प्रमाता पुरुषः । प्रमेयाः कार्यकारणादयः पंच पदार्थाः । प्रमापयिता भगवान् । PAB., i, p. 7.

4. क्रीड़ावानेव स भगवान् विद्याकलापशुसंज्ञकं कार्यमुत्पादयन् अनुगृह्णाति तिरोभावयति चेत्यतो देवः। Ibid, ii,2. कार्ये स एव कारणं परम् । Ibid, ii, 21.

5. स्वेच्छयैवाशेषकार्योत्पत्यादिकारणस्वभावः क्रीड़ा, तद्धर्मित्वं देवत्वम् । RT., p. 11. परिपूर्णपरितृप्त-त्वाच्छिवः । PAB., V, 47.

6. कर्मकामिनश्च महेश्वरमपेक्षते, न तु भगवानीश्वरः कर्म पुरुषं वापेक्षते। अतो न कर्मापेक्ष ईश्वरः। Ibid, ii, 6.

7. पुरुषश्चेतनो भोक्ता क्षेत्रज्ञः पुद्गलो जनः। अणुर्वेदोऽमृत. साक्षी जीवात्मा परिभूः परः॥ Ibid, v, 3.

9. सति विभुत्वे स्ववृत्या कार्यकारणयोः सर्वगतत्वेऽपि स्ववृत्त्यसंकरः। नित्यं कार्यम्। कारणेश्वरनित्यत्वात् पतिनित्यत्वम्। Ibid, ii, 5. भव इति विद्याकलापशूनां ग्रहणम्। अत्रोत्पादकानुग्राहकतिरोभावकधर्मि कारणम्, उत्पाद्यानुग्राह्यतिरोभाव्यधर्मि कार्यमित्येत् कार्यकारणयोर्लक्षणम्। Ibid, ii, 42 & 44.

10. तत्र पाशा नाम कार्यकारणाख्याः कलाः। अस्वातण्त्र्यमनैश्वर्यं बन्ध। पश्यनाच्च पाशनाच्च पशवः। Ibid, i, 1. विद्यानां धर्मार्थकामकैवल्यतत्साधनपराणाम् ईशानः। Ibid, v, 42.

11. कार्यकारणाञ्जना निरञ्जनाश्च पशवः। अनैश्वर्यं बन्धः। कारणशक्तिसन्निरोधलक्षणमस्वातन्त्र्यमनैश्वर्यं बन्धोऽनादिः। Ibid, i, 1.

12. आत्मेश्वरयोगो योगोः प्रत्येतव्यः। Ibid, i, 20.

20. सदा रुद्रमनुस्मरेत। PSS., v, 34. सिद्धयोगी न लिप्यते कर्मणा पातकेन वा। Ibid, v, 20. एवमोङ्कारमिति ध्येयमुक्तम्। PAB., v, 28. छित्वा दोषाणां हेतुजालस्य मूलम्। PSS., v, 35. कृत्स्नस्य तपसो लक्षणमात्म-प्रत्यक्षं वेदितव्यम्। PAB., iii, 19.

22. लभते रुद्रसायुज्यम्। PSS., v, 33. अप्रमादी गच्छेद् दुःखानामन्तम् ईशप्रसादात्। Ibid, v, 40. अन्यत्र कैवल्यादिफलको योगः इह तु पारमैश्वर्यदुःखान्तफलकः। SDS., vi, 14. दूरदर्शनश्रवणमननविज्ञानानि चास्य प्रवर्तन्ते। सर्वज्ञता। मनोजवित्वम्। कामरुपित्वम्। विकरणः। धर्मित्वम्। PSS., i, 21-26. तत्त्वव्याप्तसदोदितसिद्धिज्ञानं सर्वज्ञत्वम्। SDS., vi, 6. सर्वेषामेव रूपाणां युगपदेवाधिष्ठाता भवति। PAB, i, 24. विकरण इति कैवल्यम्। Ibid, i, 25. अत्र गुणधर्मणायं धर्मो भवति। अस्य सिद्धस्य प्रभुत्वं बिभुत्वं गुणधर्मित्वं च व्याख्यातम्। Ibid, i, 26. निरतिशयमपराधीनत्वमवश्यत्वम्। सत्त्वान्तरानभिभाव्यज्ञान-सम्बन्धित्वमनावेश्त्वम्। समस्तभयातिक्रान्तत्वमभयत्वम्। कायेन्द्रियवैकल्यफलेनात्यन्तासम्बन्धित्वमजरत्म्। प्राणादियोगजदुःखासंस्पर्शित्वमरत्वम्। GKV., p. 10.

24. उपायफलं लाभः ज्ञानतपोदेवनित्यत्वस्थितिशुद्धिभेदात् पंचविधः। SDS., vi, 2. गुरूभक्तिः प्रसादश्च मतेर्द्वन्द्वजयस्तथा। धर्मश्चैवाप्रमादश्च बलं पंचविधं स्मृतम्। Ibid, vi, 4. अज्ञानमधर्मश्च विषयाभ्यासः स्थितेरलाभश्च। अनैश्वर्यं च मला विज्ञेयाः पंच पंचार्थे॥ प्रथमो विद्यालाभस्तपसो लाभोऽथ देवनित्यत्वम्। योगो गुणप्रवृत्तिर्लाभा. पंचेह विज्ञेयाः। वासो ध्यानमखिलकरणनिरोधस्तथा स्मृतिश्चैव। प्रसाद इति चोपाया विज्ञेयाः पंच पंचार्थे॥ PAB., v, 30.

CHAPTER IV

2. शैवागमेषु मुख्यं पतिपशुपाशा इति क्रमात् त्रितयम्। तत्र पतिः शिव उक्तः पशवो ह्यणवोऽर्थपंचकं पाशः। TP., i, 5.

3. चिद्घन एको व्यापी नित्य. सततोदितः प्रभुः शान्तः। जयति जगदेकबीजं सर्वानुग्राहकः शम्भुः॥
ज्ञानक्रियास्वभावं तत् तेजः शाम्भवं जयति॥ तामेकां चिद्रूपामाद्यां सर्वात्मनास्मि नतः।
सोऽनादिमुक्त एको विज्ञेयः पंचमन्त्रतनुः॥ पंचविधं तत् कृत्यं सृष्टिः स्थितिसंहृती तिरोभावः।
तद्वदनुग्रहकरणं प्रोक्तं सततोदितस्य॥ Ibid, i, 3, 1-3, 6-7.

4. शक्तिशिवौ वस्वैक्यं मणिप्रभावद् यतो युक्तम् । ŚR., TD., i, 3, p. 18.
यानुभूतिरजामेयानन्तात्मानन्दविग्रहा । महदादिजगन्मायाचित्रभित्ति नमामि ताम् ।। TD., i, 3, p. 15.

5. सर्वज्ञ: सर्वकर्तृत्वात् साधनांगफलै: सह । MT., i, 5, 13. तच्चास्यावृत्तिशून्यत्वान्न व्यञ्जकमपेक्षते । Ibid, i, 5, 14. नाध्यक्षं नापि तल्लैङ्गं न शाब्दमपि शांकरम् । ज्ञानमाभाति विमलं सर्वदा सर्ववस्तुषु । Ibid, i, 5, 16.

6. तेन विभुस्तद्युक्तयै कुरुते तनुकरणभुवननिष्पत्तिम् । कर्त्रा विना न कार्यं न तथोपादानकरणाभ्याम् ।। TP., ii, 17.

8. शुद्धानि पंचतत्त्वान्याद्यन्तेषु स्मरन्ति शिवतत्वम् । शक्तिसदाशिवतत्त्वे ईश्वरविद्याख्यतत्त्वे च ।।
पुंसो ज्ञकर्तृतार्थं मायातस्तत्वपंचकं भवति । कालो नियतिश्च तथा कला च विद्या च रागश्च।। Ibid, ii, 1-2.

9. व्यापकमेकं नित्यं कारणमखिलस्य तत्त्वजातस्य । ज्ञानक्रियास्वभावं शिवतत्त्वं जगदाहुराचार्या: ।। Ibid ii, 5.

10. चिदचिदनुग्रहहेतोरस्य सिसृक्षो यं आद्य उन्मेष: । तच्छक्तितत्त्वमभिहितमविभागान्नमस्यौव ।। Ibid, ii, 7.
पत्यु: शक्ति: परा सूक्ष्मा जाग्रतो द्योतनक्षमा ।। तया प्रभु: प्रबुद्धात्मा स्वतन्त्र: स सदाशिव: ।। मातंगे । TD., ii, 7, p. 79.

11. ज्ञानक्रियाख्यशक्तयोरुत्कर्षनिकर्षयोरभावेन । य: प्रसरस्तं प्राहु: सदाशिवाख्यं बुधास्तत्वम् ।। TP., ii, 8.
ज्ञानक्रियाख्ये न्यक्तुल्ये शक्तीछोद्रेकमश्नुते । यदा सदाशिवाख्यस्तु तदासौ शिव उच्यते ।। TD., ii, 8, SH.

12. न्यग्भवति यत्र शक्तिर्ज्ञानाख्योद्रिक्ततां क्रियां भजते । ईश्वरतत्त्वं तदिह प्रोक्तं सर्वार्थंकतृ सदा ।। TP., ii, 9.
ज्ञानेच्छे न्यक्समे शक्ती क्रियाधिक्यं यदाश्नुते । तदासावीश्वराख्यां तु लभते परमेश्वर: ।। TD., ii, SH.

13. न्यग्भवति कर्तृशक्तिर्ज्ञानाख्योद्रेकमश्नुते यत्र । तत् तत्त्वं विद्याख्यं प्रकाशकं ज्ञानरूपत्वात् ।। TP. ii, 10.
उद्रिच्यते ज्ञानशक्ति: क्रियेच्छे न्यक्समे यदा । तदासौ शुद्धविद्याख्य: सर्वविद्यानिधि: शिव: ।। TD., ii, 10.

14. तत्त्वं वस्तुत एकं शिवसंज्ञं चित्रशक्तिशतखचितम् । शक्तिव्यापृतिभेदात् तस्यैते कल्पिता भेदा: ।। TP., ii, 13.

15. ईश: कर्ता कारकञ्च शुद्धविद्या प्रकाशिका । एभिरीशोऽनुगृह्णाति क्लृप्तैर्भेदैश्चराचरम् ।। TD., ii, 14.

17. चिदनुग्रहस्त्वयं किल यन्मोक्ष: शिवसमानतारुप: । सोऽनादित्वात्कर्मण इह भोगमृते न याति संसिद्धिम् । TP., ii, 16.

18. शक्तय इहास्य करणं मायोपादानमिष्यते सूक्ष्मा । एका नित्या व्यापिन्यनादिनिधना शिवा सोक्ता ।। TP., iii, 1.

19. साधारणी च पुंसां कारणमपि चेयमखिलभुवनानाम् । निखिलजनकर्मखचिता स्वभावतो मोहसञ्जननी ।। TP., iii, 2.
माया विमोहनी प्रोक्ता विषयास्वादभोगत: । यत्र तत्र स्थितस्यास्य स्वकर्ममलहेतुत: ।। किरण, TD., iii, 2.

20. नानाविधशक्तिमयी सा सृजति कालतत्त्वमेवादौ । TP., iii, 4.

21. नियतिर्नियमनरूपा मायात: साप्यनन्तरं भवति । नियमयति येन निखिलं तेनेयं नियतिरुद्दिष्टा ।। Ibid, iii, 5.

22. मायातस्तदनु कलामलं नृणामेकस्तु कलयित्वा । व्यञ्जयति कर्तृशक्तिं कलेति तेनेह कथिता सा ।। TP., iii, 6.

23. बुद्धिर्यदास्य भोग्या सुखादिरुपा तदा भवेत् करणम् । विद्यायं करणं स्याद् विषयग्रहणे पुनर्बुद्धि: ।। Ibid, iii, 10.

25. तत्वैरेभि: कलितो भोक्तृत्वदशां यदा पशुर्नीत: । पुरूषाख्यतां तदायं लभते तत्वेषु गणनां च । Ibid, iii, 12.

26. पुरुषस्य हि भोगार्थं किलैत्र तस्मात् प्रसूयतेऽव्यक्तम् । अनभिव्यक्तगुणत्वादव्यपदेशं तदव्यक्तम् ।। Ibid, iv, 1.

27. अव्यक्ताद् गुणतत्त्वं प्रख्याव्यापारनियमरुपमिह । सत्त्वं रजस्तमोऽपि च सुखदुखं मोह इति च । भवति गुणत्रयतो धीर्विषयाध्यवसायरुपिणी चेति । Ibid, iv, 2-3.

28. मायायाः परतोऽत्रा शुद्धः शक्तौ निलीयते सकलः। सर्वात्मनि सापि शिवे तिष्ठत्यविभागमापन्ना ॥
माया पुरूषः शिव इत्येतत् त्रितयं महार्थसंहारे। अवशिष्यते पुनस्तत् प्रनर्तते पूर्ववत् सृष्टौ ॥ Ibid, v, 6-7.

29. तदनुग्राहकं तत्वं कलाख्यं तैजसं हरः। मायां विक्षोभ्य कुरूते प्रवृत्त्यंङ्गं परं हि तत्। तेन प्रदीपकल्पेन तदा स्वच्छचितेरणोः। प्रकाशयत्येकदेशं विदार्य तिमिरं घनम् ॥ MT., i, 10, 4-5.
पशवस्त्रिविधा ज्ञेया विज्ञानप्रलयाकलाः सकलाः। मलयुक्तस्तत्राद्यो मलकर्मयुतो द्वितीयश्च ॥ TP., v, 8.

34. चैतन्यं दृक्क्रियारूपं तदस्त्यात्मनि सर्वदा। सर्वतश्च यतो मुक्तौ श्रूयते सर्वतोमुखम्। सदप्याभासमानत्वात्तन्निरुद्धं प्रतीयते। वश्योऽनावृतवीर्यस्य सोऽत एवाविमोक्षणात्। MT., i, 2, 5-6.

35. तत् पारतन्त्र्यं बद्धत्वं तस्मिन्नित्ये चिदादिवत्। मुक्तिसाधनसन्दोहो व्यर्थीऽलमनयाधिया ॥ Ibid, i, 7, 4.

35. गताधिकारनीहारवीर्यस्य सत एधते। पशोरनुग्रहोऽन्यस्य तादर्थ्यादस्ति कर्मणः॥ बोद्धृत्वपरिणामित्वधर्मयोरनुवर्तनम्। मलस्य साधिकारस्य निवृत्तेस्तत्परिच्युतौ ॥ MT., i, 21-22.

37. तदाधाराणि कार्याणि शक्तिरूपाणि संहृतौ। विवृतौ व्यक्तिरुपाणि व्याप्रियन्तेऽर्थसिद्धये ॥ MT., i, 9, 13

38. तस्मान्नियामिका जन्यशक्तिः कारकस्वतुनः। सान्वयव्यतिरेकाभ्यां रूढितो वावसीयते ॥ MT., i, 9, 19.

39. तद्व्यक्तिर्जननं नाम तत्कारकसमाश्रयात्। तेन तन्तुगताकारं पटाकारावरोधकम्। MT., i, 9, 20.
नासतः क्रियते व्यक्तिः कलादेर्ग्रथितस्तथा ॥ MT., i, 9, 21.

40. सा माया वस्तुरूपा परमार्थभूता विश्वमूलत्वादीश्वरुवत्। TD., i, 8 ; p. 62.

41. माया वस्तुरुपा शिवरुपा तत्कार्यं च जगच्छिवरुपम्। शिवाद् भिन्नस्य कस्यचिदसम्भवाद्। TD., i, 18 ; pp. 71-72.

42. परिपक्वमला ये तानुत्सादनहेतुशक्तिपातेन। योजयति परे तत्त्वे स दीक्षयाचार्यमूर्तिस्थः ॥ TP., i, 15,
बद्धाञ्छेदान् विनियुङ्क्ते भोगमुक्तये पुंसः। तत्कर्मणामनुगमादित्येवं कीर्तिताः पशवः ॥ TP., i, 16.
द्विविधा हि परमेश्वरस्य शक्तिः, बन्धकरा मोचिका चेति। TD., i, 15, p. 54.

43. एको ह्यनेकशक्तिर्दृक्क्रिययोश्छादकोमलः पुंसाम्। TP., i, 17.

44. पाशानुग्राहित्वात् पुरूषतिरोधायिका विभोः शक्तिः। पाशत्वेनाभिहिता पाशाश्च चतुर्विधास्त्वेवम् ॥ TP., i, 19.

CHAPTER V

1. न वयमत्यन्ताभेदवादिनः। ŚKBS., ii, 1, 22. ब्रह्मणः कदाचिदपि न निर्विशेषत्वम्। Ibid, i, 1, 2.
2. वयं न च भेदाभेदवादिनः। Ibid, ii, 1, 22.
3. शक्तिः शक्तिमद्रूपाद् व्यतिरेकं न वाञ्छति। तादात्म्यमनयोर्नित्यं वह्निदाहिक्ययोरपि। Ibid, i, 2, 1; BPD., 3.
4. चिदात्मैव हि देवोऽन्तःस्थितमिच्छावशाद्बहिः। योगीव निरुपादानम् अर्थजातं प्रकाशयेत्। ĪPK., i, 38 ; ŚKBS., ii, 2, 38 ; i, 2, 9.
5. भेदाभेदकल्पं विशिष्टाद्वैतं साधयामः। ŚKBS., ii, 1, 22.
6. चिदचित्प्रपंचरूपशक्तिविशिष्टत्वं स्वाभाविकमेव ब्रह्मणः। Ibid, i, 1, 2. चिदचिद्वस्तुशरीरकः परमेश्वरः। Ibid, 4, 27.
7. किन्तु शरीर-शरीरिणोरिव गुणगुणिनोरिव च विशिष्टाद्वैतवादिनः। Ibid, ii, 1, 22.
8 जीवशरीरतया जीवविशिष्टस्य ब्रह्मणोंऽशो जीवः। Ibid, ii, 3, 45.

9. सूक्ष्म-चिदचिद्विशिष्टं ब्रह्म कारणं स्थूलचिदचिद्विशिष्टं तत् कार्यम् । Ibid, i, 1, 2.
10. न वयं भेदवादिनः । Ibid, ii, 1, 22.
सृष्टिकाले भगवतः शरीरं चिदचित् स्मृतम् । अन्तर्यामिण एतेन विशिष्टाद्वैतमेव यत् ॥
तदेकदेशि विज्ञेयमित्युक्तं तै विचक्षणैः । शैवोऽप्येतेन विध्वस्तो यतश्चोर एव हि ॥ ŚAM., 63.
शैवस्तावद्विशिष्टाद्वैतमङ्गीकृत्य रामनुजमतचोरः । ŚAMP., 63, p. 38.
15. ज्ञानस्थितिलयतिरोभावानुग्रहरूपं कृत्यम् । Ibid, i, 1, 2, p. 9.
16. चिदचित्-प्रपंचशक्तिविशिष्टत्वं ब्रह्मणः, न कदाचित् निर्विशेषत्वम् । Ibid.
17. अपरिच्छिन्नशक्तिविशिष्टत्वमनन्तशक्तित्वम् । Ibid.
18. स्थूलसूक्ष्म-चिदचित्प्रपंच-विशिष्टः परमेश्वरः एव कार्यकारणरुपः । Ibid, i, 1, 5, p, 27.
19. सूक्ष्मचिदचिद्-विशिष्टं ब्रह्म कारणम्, स्थूलचिदचिद्-विशिष्टं ब्रह्म कार्यं भवति । Ibid, p. 14.
20. अतएव वेदानाम् अपौरुषेयत्वम् ईश्वरकार्यत्वं च । Ibid, i, 1, 3, p. 16.
21. सर्ववेदकर्तृत्वम् ईश्वरस्य सिद्धम् । Ibid, p. 18.
22. अतः सर्वातीतः परमेश्वर इति सर्वोत्कृष्टत्वं ब्रह्मण एव । Ibid, iii, 2, 31.
23. अतः परब्रह्म सर्वोत्कृष्टतयैव सर्वनमस्कारविषयोऽवगम्यते । Ibid, iv, 1, 5.
24. हेयगुणराहित्येन कल्याणगुणसाहित्येन चोभयलिंगं ब्रह्म । Ibid, iii, 2, 17.
26. आकाशशरीरं ब्रह्म आकाशः प्रकाशश्चिदम्बरमुच्यते । Ibid, i, 1, 2, p. 11.
27. ब्रह्मणः प्रपंचरुपत्वं न निषिध्यते, किन्तु एतावन्मात्रं न भवति । Ibid, iii, 2, 21.
28. चिदचिदात्मकत्वेऽपि ब्रह्मणस्तद्धर्मप्रतिषेधात् चिदचिद्-विशिष्टमपि ब्रह्म निर्दोषं निखिल-मंगल-गुणास्पदं च । Ibid, iii, 2, 29.
30. सकल-चिदचिदाकार-परमशक्ति-विलास-समरसात्मनः सर्वदोष-वासना-कलंक-रहितात् परमात्मनः किंचिदपि वस्त्वन्तरं नास्ति । Ibid, 2, 30.
34. नामरुपयोरन्तराले तत्कार्यस्पर्शरहित एव वर्तते । Ibid, iii, 2, 14.
35. निरवद्यं कल्याणगुणास्पदं च ब्रह्म इत्युभयलिंगमिति । Ibid, iii, 2, 15.
38. सुखदुःखभोगहेतुभ्यो जीवशरीरभ्यो ब्रह्मरूपस्यास्ति हि वैशेष्यम्, इच्छागृहीतत्वादस्य तेषां कर्ममूलत्वाच्च । Ibid, i, 2, 8.
42. तुरीयं च तुरीयातीतं च शिवस्थानम् । उत्तरगीता । Ibid.
45. परप्रकृतिरुपा परमशक्तिर्हि चिदम्बरमुच्यते । परप्रकृतित्वं चिदाकाशस्य । Ibid i, 1, 2. शक्ति-शक्तिमतोरभेदः । Ibid, i, 2, 7. सकल-चिदचित्-प्रपंच-महाविभूतिरूपा महासच्चिदानन्दसत्ता देशकालादि-परिच्छेदशून्या परमशक्तिः परब्रह्मणः शिवस्य स्वरुपं च गुणश्च भवति । Ibid, i, 2, 1.
46. अचिदवस्तुरूपा माया । अतो न निमित्तमात्रमीश्वरः । Ibid, ii, 3, 37. अतो निमित्तादनन्यमुपादानम । Ibid, 1, 4, 24. न केवलं मायायाः जगदुत्पत्तिः, महेश्वराच्च, किन्तु मायिनः परमेश्वरात् । Ibid, i, 4, 27.
47. प्रणवपर्यायेणोमाशब्देन परप्रकृतिरुपा पराशक्तिरुच्यते । Ibid, iv, 4, 22.
49. तस्मादीश्वर एव दहराकाशोऽपहतपाप्मत्वादिगुणक इति । Ibid, i 3, 13.
53. जगदुपादान-निमित्तभूतस्यापि परमेश्वरस्य निर्विकारत्वम् । मायादि-प्रपंच-शक्तिमतः शिवस्यैवोपादानत्वमव-गम्यते । Ibid, ii, 2, 38.
54 यथा निमित्तस्य प्रकृतित्वेऽपि न विकारादिस्पर्शः तथा परिणामिण सम्भवात् । Ibid, i, 4, 27.

55. नामरुपविभागरहित-सूक्ष्मचिदचिद्वस्तुशरीरकः कारणावस्थः परमेश्वरः संविभक्तनामरूप-चिदचिद्वस्तु-शरीरको भवेयमिति संकल्पमकरोत् । Ibid, i, 4, 27.

56. सच्चिद्रूपेण शिवेन यदि न व्याप्तं जगत्, तदा सत्ता-स्फूर्तिभ्यां विनाकृतं कथमस्ति स्फुरति । Ibid, ii, 1, 17.

57. संकोचावस्था प्रलयः विकाशावस्था सृष्टिः । Ibid, ii, 1, 18.

58. परमकारणात् परब्रह्मणः शिवात् अभिन्नमेव जगत् कार्यम् । Ibid.

59. न वयं ब्रह्मप्रपंचयोरत्यन्तमेव भेदवादिनः, न वात्यन्ताभेदवादिनः न वा भेदाभेदवादिनः वस्तुविरोधात् । Ibid, ii, 1, 20.

60. किन्तु शरीर-शरीरिणोरिव गुणगुणिनोरिव च विशिष्टाद्वैतवादिनः । Ibid, ii, 1, 22.

62. अतः परिपूर्णस्य तस्यैव कार्यत्वं कारणत्वं च सम्भवति । Ibid, ii, 1, 27.

63. विचित्रनामशक्तिशवलमाया-परमशक्ति-विशिष्टः परमेश्वरः स्वशक्तिशकलेन प्रपंचाकारः स्वतः प्रपंचातीतश्च भवति । Ibid, ii, 1, 31.

64. कर्मप्रवाहसिद्धोऽयं संसारः । Ibid, ii, 1, 35.

68. अतः संसारे किंचिज्ज्ञत्वं मुक्तौ सर्वज्ञत्वमिति ज्ञातैवात्मा । Ibid, ii, 3, 19.

70. जीवः स्वेच्छया प्रवृत्ति-निवृत्ति-हेतुं करोति स्वकर्मपाकवशेन, जीवकृतप्रयत्नं प्रवृत्तिनिवृत्तिहेतुमवेक्ष्य तदनुमति-दानेन परः प्रवर्तयति । Ibid, ii, 3, 41.

71. जीवात्मा परमेश्वरांशो मूर्त्येकदेश एव । Ibid, ii, 3, 42.

72. तस्माज् जीवो ब्रह्मणोंऽशभूत एव तत्स्वरूपं प्रतिपद्यते । Ibid.

73. जीवशरीरतया जीवविशिष्टस्य ब्रह्मणोंऽशो जीवः । Ibid, ii, 3, 45.

74. तद्विशिष्टतया स्वरुपभेदश्च सिद्धः । Ibid, ii, 3, 46.

77. जीवस्यानाद्यपचारप्रवाहेन पराभिध्यानात् परमेश्वर-संकल्पात् तस्य सत्यसंकल्पत्वादिकं तिरोहितम् । Ibid, iii, 2, 4.

78. परमेश्वर-संकल्पादस्य बन्धमोक्षौ भवतः । Ibid, iii, 2, 5.

79. अनाद्यज्ञानवासनावष्टम्भ-विजृम्भित-विचित्रकर्मफल-भोगानुगुण-वहुशरीर-प्रवेश-निःसीमतापसहिष्णुत्वं हि जीव-त्वम् । Ibid, i, 1, 1, p. 7.

80. अस्य सर्वोत्कृष्टस्य व्याप्तिदृष्टया सर्वेषां प्रतीकानामुपास्यत्वम् । Ibid, iv, 1, 5.

82. स्वात्मतया नैरन्तर्येण ब्रह्मणि भाविते हि तद्रूपमुपासकेषु प्रकाशते । Ibid, iv, 1, 12.

84. उमासहितं परं ब्रह्म सर्वात्मकं मुक्तिसाधकम् । अतः परब्रह्मणः स्वरूपधर्माणामलोप एव । Ibid, iii, 3, 39.

85. ब्रह्मप्राप्तस्य जीवस्य मलतिरोहितं ब्रह्मसदृशगुणं स्वरुपं पूर्वं सदेव मलावरणापगमाद् आविर्भवति । Ibid, iv, 4, 1.

87. मुक्त आत्मा सादृश्यात ब्रह्मस्वरुपाविभागेन स्वरुपमनुभवति । Ibid, iv, 4, 4.

88. भोगमात्रसाम्यं मुक्तस्य ब्रह्मणश्चेति समीचीनमिति । Ibid, iv, 4, 21.

89. अतो ज्ञानस्वरूपं स्वयंप्रकाशमपहतपाप्मत्वादियोगात् कल्याणगुणविशिष्टं च ब्रह्मसदृशं मुक्तस्वरुपं युक्तम् । Ibid, iv, 4, 7.

90. मुक्तेन ब्रह्माकारं हि दृश्यते विश्वमेतत् । Ibid, iv, 4, 14.

92. स एक एव निरंकुशप्रकाशः सर्वसाक्षी, पशुपाशयोर्न स्वरुपसत्ता निषिध्यते, किंतु नामरूपविभागार्हस्थूलत्वम् । Ibid, i, 2, 9.

94. ततः स्वरुपपृथगवस्थान-सूक्ष्ममायापुरूषः पर एव स्वयमुपादानमपीत्युच्यते । Ibid,

95. मृद्द्रव्यमेव व्यवहारसिद्धयर्थं जायमानावस्थान्तरं तु मृदो द्रव्यान्तरम् । Ibid, ii, 1, 16. कार्यस्य कारणे सत्वाच्च कारणाद् अनन्यदेव कार्यम् । Ibid, ii, 1, 17.

CHAPTER VI

5. तस्मात् स्वरुप-व्यवर्तक-तटस्थ-लक्षणत्रयेण सर्ववेदान्तानां ब्रह्मप्रतिपादकत्वं युक्तम् । ŚRBS., i, 1, 4, p. 45.

6. सृष्टि-स्थिति-संहाराविर्भाव-तिरोधानानि पंचकृत्यान्यर्थवादः । Ibid.

7. परशिवस्य ब्रह्मण एव सर्वदेवतामयत्वेन च तदुपासनस्यैव मोक्षोपदेशत्वदर्शनात् । Ibid.

8. निर्विषया निराश्रया च संविद् अनुभवसिद्धेति तुच्छम् । Ibid, p. 51.

9. तत्-त्वं-पदयोः सविशेषजीवपरत्व-ब्रह्म-व्यपदेशात् । Ibid. p. 52.

11. माया परशिवशक्तिः । Ibid, i, 1, 2, p. 33.

13. भक्तानुग्रहार्थं दिव्यमंगलविग्रहधरस्य महेश्वरस्य मूर्तामूर्तप्रपंचकल्पनेऽदोषः । Ibid, p. 30.

14. जगदुपादान-परमेश्वरशक्तेस्तु तदेकदेशवृत्तित्वम् । तस्मादभिन्ननिमित्तोपादानकारणत्वम् न त्वेककारणत्वम् । Ibid.

15. आत्मप्रत्ययविषयतया अपरोक्षत्वेन प्रत्यगात्म- प्रसिद्धे रित्युक्तिविरोधात् । Ibid, p. 31.

16. नाहंप्रत्ययविषयो ब्रह्मेति चेत्, जीवब्रह्मभेदानंगीकारात् ब्रह्मणः व्यवहारिकदृश्यत्वानंगीकारे निरधिष्ठान-ब्रह्मप्रसंगः । Ibid, i, 1, 4.

17. शक्तिसंकोचतया सृष्टेः प्राक् परमेश्वरस्य निर्गुणत्वात् । सगुणश्रुतीनां सृष्टयुन्मुख-परमेश्वर-शक्ति-विकास-कालपरत्वम् । Ibid, i, 1, 2, p. 31.

18. सेश्वरद्वैतभाने तु सर्वं शिवमयं जगत् । Ibid.

22. न स्वप्नवत् प्रपंचस्य मिथ्यात्वम् अर्थसिद्धिक्रियासिद्धि-दर्शनात् । Ibid, i, 1, 1, p. 5.

23. नाभाव उपलब्धेः । वैधर्म्याच्च न स्वप्नादिवत् । BS., ii, 2, 27-28.

27. शक्तिशक्तिमतोरभेदः । मृद्घटादिवत् कार्यकारणयोरभिन्नत्वमंगीकर्तव्यम् । ŚRBS., ii, 1, 14.

28. ब्रह्मसत्त्वे प्रत्यक्षानुमानागमप्रमाणदर्शनात् । Ibid, i, 1, 1, p. 4.

30. पृथिव्यादिभूतचतुष्टयसंयोगेनैव चेतनाचेतनसृष्टिः स्वतो भविष्यतीति यदुक्तं तदयुक्तम् । Ibid.

32. जीवब्रह्मणोर्भेदाभेद एवांगीकर्तव्यः । जीवो ब्रह्मणः अंश एव, न त्वितरे । Ibid, ii, 3, 40.

33. न च भेदाभेदयो विरोध इति वाच्यम् । वयं श्रुतिप्रमाणवादिनः । Ibid.

34. प्रकाशादिवज् जीवः परमात्मनोंऽशः । Ibid, ii, 3, 43.

35. विशेषणविशेष्ययो रंशांशित्वेऽपि स्वभाववैलक्षण्यं दृश्यते । एवं जीवपरयोः विशेषण-विशेष्यकृतं स्वभाव-वैलक्षण्यम् आश्रित्य भेदनिर्देशाः प्रवर्तन्ते । अभेदनिर्देशस्तु पृथक्सिद्धयनर्हे-विशेषणानां विशेष्यपर्यन्तत्वमाश्रित्य मुख्यत्वेनोपपदयते । Ibid.

37. जीवानामन्योन्यभेदाणुत्वेन प्रतिशरीरं भिन्नत्वाच्च भोगव्यतिकरो न भवति । Ibid, ii, 3, 46.

40. नानात्वव्यपदेशस्तावत् स्रष्टृत्व-सृज्यत्व-नियन्तृत्वनियाम्यत्व सर्वज्ञत्वाज्ञत्व-स्वाधीनत्व-पराधीनत्व-शुद्धत्वा-शुद्धत्व-कल्याणगुणाकरत्व-तद्विपरीतत्व-पतित्व-शेषत्वादिभिर्दृश्यते । Ibid, ii, 3, 40.

41. उभयव्यपदेशोपपत्तये जीवोऽयं ब्रह्मणोंऽश इत्यभ्युपगन्तव्यम् । Ibid.

42. तस्माद् द्वैताद्वैतमतमेवांगीकर्तव्यम् । Ibid.
43. तस्मात् जीवब्रह्मणो: स्वाभाविकभेदो निर्दिष्टः । Ibid, ii, 1, 22.
44. चेतनजीवस्यापि परमेश्वरोपासनया तदनुग्रहवशात् अबाधितशिवत्वं सिध्यति । Ibid.
45. भेदाभेदमतमेव सूत्रकारमतमिति बालानामपि विज्ञायते । Ibid.
46. अंगांगित्वस्वीकारे जीववत् परिच्छिन्नत्व-प्रसक्तिर्दुर्वारा । Ibid.
47. तयोरभेदत्वे पूर्वोक्तदोषाः प्रसज्येरन् । जीवब्रह्मणो: स्वभावभिन्नत्वे तन्निवृत्यसम्भवाच्च । Ibid.
48. जीवालोकत्व-जीवैकत्व-जीवब्रह्मत्ववादो ह्ययुक्तः । Ibid, ii, 3, 42.
51. ईश्वर-नियामकत्वेऽपि चेतनत्वेन किंचित्कर्तृत्वमविरोधम् । Ibid, ii, 3, 48.
52. तस्माज्-जीवेश्वरयोरुभयकर्तृत्वविधायकश्रुतीनामविरोधः । जीवानां ब्रह्मांशत्वेन परिच्छिन्नत्वात् । अंशांशिनोरभेदात् । Ibid, ii, 3, 49.
54. ब्रह्मविद्यामहिम्ना जीवस्य स्वाभाविकाविद्यानिवृत्तिपूर्वक-शिवत्वप्राप्तिवादो युक्तः । Ibid, iv, 4, 1,
56. बद्धाबद्धवन् मुक्तावस्थायां जीवब्रह्मणो र्भेदः नांगीकर्तव्यः । Ibid, iv, 4, 4.
62 ज्ञ एव जीवः ज्ञातृस्वरुपः । Ibid, ii, 3 ,17.
63. ज्ञ एव । अयमात्मा ज्ञानस्वरुप एव न ज्ञानमात्रं नापि जडस्वरुपः । Ibid.
70. तद्वज्-जीवस्य परशिव-पाशशक्तया स्वशक्तिसंकोचेन स्वपरज्ञान-तिरोहितत्वमुपपद्यते । Ibid, ii, 3, 35.
72. शिवाकारकारित-बुद्धिसत्त्वावस्था समाधिरूपदिश्यते । Ibid, ii, 3, 36.
73. बुद्धे र्मोक्षकाले जडत्वेन नष्टत्वादात्महनन-प्रसंगः । Ibid.
83. निर्मुक्तानामिहैव जीवन्मुक्तिदशायामेकत्वं परशिवे सम्भवति । Ibid, iii, 4, 52.
87. परमेश्वरार्पितं कर्मानुष्ठानं तु परम्परा मोक्षहेतुरिति विधीयते । Ibid, iii, 4, 12.
92. आश्रमकर्माणि विदुषामविदुषां च कर्तवयानि इति निर्णीयते । Ibid, iii, 4, 32.
93. धर्मब्रह्मोभयसहकारित्वेन च मोक्षावगमात् । ज्ञानकर्मसमुच्चयानुष्ठानं सर्वेषामाश्रमानां विधेयम् । Ibid, iii, 4, 33.
95. आश्रमानाश्रम-साधारण्येन सर्वेषां मुमुक्षूणां ब्रह्मविद्याधिकारः Ibid, iii, 4, 39.

CHAPTER VII

2. यथा च सद्भेद औपाधिकः, एवं सज्ज्ञानानन्दभेदोऽपि, सत्त्वरहितज्ञानानन्दयोः शून्यत्वप्रसंगाद्, बोधात्मत्व-रहितसतश्च भानाभावप्रसंगाद्, दृश्यत्वे कल्पितत्वेन सत्त्वायोगात् सद्बोधात्मकसाक्षिणश्च परमप्रेमास्पदत्वेना-नन्दस्वाभाव्यावगमादिति । तथा च कल्पितभेदसामान्यतदपेक्षव्यक्तयाकारबाधेन सत्यज्ञानानन्दात्मकं ब्रह्म निश्चीयते । सत्यादिवाक्यं विशिष्टार्थपरत्वरहितम् । VKT., i, 1, 2, p. 95.
3. यत्र तु ब्रह्म निरस्तसमस्तोपाधिभेदं ज्ञेयत्वेनोपक्षिप्यते, तत्र शास्त्रम्—'अशब्दमस्पर्शमरूपमव्ययम्' इति प्रवर्तते । Bhām., i, 1, 20, p. 195.
4. स्वतोऽसंगस्य ब्रह्मणः कालत्रयेऽपि स्वाभाविकं यन्निष्प्रपञ्चस्वरूपं तदेवास्थूलादिशब्दैः प्रतिपाद्यते VPS., p. 97.
5. तत्र ज्ञानशब्दोऽनेकविकारयुक्तान्तःकरणवृत्तिप्रतिबिम्बितचैतन्ये व्युत्पन्नः । आनन्दशब्दश्च शुद्धसात्त्विकान्तः-करणवृत्त्यभिव्यक्तायामत्यनुकूलतया स्फुरुन्तयां कस्यां चिद्व्यक्तौ लोके प्रसिद्धः । तथा च वृत्तित्यागांशे लक्षणा इतरांशे तु मुख्यवृत्तिः । Ibid, p. 229.

6. एकसत्यानन्तशब्दाः स्वगतभेदाभावमिथ्यात्वाभावसजातीयविजातीयद्वितीयाभावाभिधानद्वारेण तत्र लक्षणया वर्तन्ते । Ibid.
7. गुणस्य गुणिना भेदाभेदयोरनिरूपणादुपपन्नं निर्गुणत्वम् । Ibid, p. 217.
8. लक्षणरुपेण ब्रह्मस्वरुपप्रतिपादनपरं सत्यादिवाक्यम् । Ibid, p. 215.
9. अस्ति तावद् ब्रह्म नित्यशुद्धबुद्धमुक्तस्वभावं सर्वज्ञं सर्वशक्तिसमन्वितं । ŚBS., i, 1, 1, pp. 79-80.
10. बुद्धेत्यपराधीनप्रकाशमानन्दात्मानं दर्शयति, आनन्दप्रकाशयोरभेदात् । Bhām., i, 1, 1. p. 80.
11. तदेवमनौपाधिकं ब्रह्मणो रूपं दर्शयित्वाऽविद्योपाधिकं रूपमाह— सर्वज्ञं सर्वशक्तिसमन्वितम् । तदनेन जगत्कारणत्वमस्य दर्शितं, शक्तिज्ञानभावाभावानुविधानात् कारणत्वभावाभावयोः । Ibid.
मायाप्रतिबिम्बितं हि चैतन्यं सर्वज्ञं सर्वशक्तिसमन्वितं जगत्कारणम् । PĀV., i, 1, 2. p. 39.
12. स्वरूपलक्षणं तु तस्य सत्यं ज्ञानमनन्तं ब्रह्मेत्यादिश्रुतिषु प्रसिद्धम् । VPS, p. 195. श्रुत्यन्तरं च यो वै भूमा तत्सुखमिति सुखस्यैव ब्रह्मधर्मत्वमाह । Ibid, p. 216.
13. तत्र तावज्जन्मादिकारणत्वं मायाविशिष्टब्रह्मणः स्वरुपलक्षणत्वेऽप्यविरुद्धम् । शुद्धब्रह्मणस्तु तत्तटस्थलक्षणम् । Ibid, pp. 194-95.
14. तस्य चोपादानत्वे सति कर्तृत्वं तटस्थलक्षणम् । ACM., p. 40.
15. उपादानत्वं च कार्यतादात्म्यवत्कारणत्वम् । Ibid, p. 41.
16. उपादानगोचरकृतिमत्त्वमेव कर्तृत्वम् । Ibid, p. 42.
17. अनानन्दात्मके हि जगत्कारणे ब्रह्मशब्दप्रयोगो न युज्यते । जन्मादिधर्मजातस्योपलक्षणत्वाद् ब्रह्मसंस्पर्शाभावात्सर्वज्ञं सर्वशक्तिसमन्वितं ब्रह्मेति जन्मादिसूत्रेण ब्रह्मस्वरुपं लक्षितमिति सिद्धम् । PPD., p. 81.
18. तस्मान् जगज्जन्मादिकारणत्वमेवोपलक्षणमिति । PPV., p. 205.
19. न हि नानाविधकार्यक्रियावेशात्मकत्वं तत्प्रसवशक्त्यात्मकत्वं वा विशुद्धब्रह्मान्तर्गतं भवितुमर्हति । Ibid.
20. शुद्धब्रह्मसम्बन्धाभावेऽपि मायाविशिष्टकारणब्रह्मसम्बन्धित्वात् । VPS., p. 195.
21. अविद्यासहितब्रह्मोपादानं जगत् ब्रह्मण्येवास्ति तत्रैव च लीयते । Bhām., i, 1, 2, p. 95.
22. एवं ब्रह्मापि मायाकार्यकुम्भादिकल्पितव्यक्त्यनुगतं सत्तया लक्ष्यमाणं सत्त्वं न हास्यति । तथा ज्ञानत्वानन्दत्वाभ्यामप्यन्तःकरणवृत्युपधानलब्धभेदचिदानन्दविशेषानुगताभ्यां लक्ष्यमाणचिदानन्दव्यक्तयोरपि योज्यम् । VKT., i, 1, 2, p. 94.
24. न तावद्ब्रह्मधर्मः क्रिया, तस्याः स्वाश्रयविकारहेतुत्वेन ब्रह्मणो नित्यत्वव्याघातात् । Bhām., i, 1, 4, pp. 126-27.
25. त्रिविधोऽपि धर्मलक्षणावस्थापरिणामलक्षणो विकारो नास्ति । Ibid, p. 135.
26. न देशकालादिविशेषयोगः परमात्मनि कल्पयितुं शक्यते । ŚBS., iv, 3, 14, p. 998.
27. तदेवं निरवयवं ब्रह्म न परिणमते, किं तु विवर्तते इति पक्षो अङ्गीकार्यः । VPS., p. 206.
28. 'अज आत्मा महान् ध्रुवः' इति ध्रुवशब्देन परिणामविरुद्धकौटस्थ्याभिधानात् । कूटस्थत्वं च ब्रह्मणो निरवयवत्वादुपपन्नम् । Ibid, p. 204.
29. सर्वस्य हि प्रपंचजातस्य ब्रह्मैव तत्त्वमात्मा । प्रपंचस्त्वनाद्यविद्योपदर्शितोऽपरमार्थसन् । Bhām., i, 3, 4, pp. 134-35.
30. प्रपञ्चोपाधिकतया तेषामनिर्वचनीयत्वात् । VPS., p. 217.
31. न च सर्वं खल्विदं ब्रह्मेत्याद्युपासनाप्रकरणपठितवाक्यानि सप्रपञ्चं ब्रह्म प्रमापयन्ति । आरोपितरुपेणाप्युपासनोपपत्तेः । तस्मान्निष्प्रपञ्चब्रह्मप्रमितौ न कश्चिद्विरोधः । Ibid, p. 97.

32. न च ब्रह्मणो निष्प्रपञ्चप्रतिपादनेन सप्रपञ्चग्राहकप्रमाणविरोधः। तादृशप्रमाणस्यैवाभावात्। Ibid.
33. सर्वज्ञः सर्वशक्तिरित्यादिशब्दाश्चानिर्वचनीयप्रपञ्चोपाधितया तत्र वर्तन्ते। Ibid, p. 229.
34. निर्गुणमपि सद्ब्रह्म नामरूपगतैर्गुणैः सगुणमुपासनार्थं तत्र तत्रोपदिश्यते। ŚBS., i, 2, 14, p. 248.
35. अन्यदेव तद्विदितादथो अविदितादधीति श्रुत्या वेद्यत्वस्यापि निषेधात्। अवेद्यत्वेऽप्यखण्डैकरसब्रह्माकारान्तःकरणवृत्त्या चैतन्याभिव्यक्तियुक्तया शास्त्रजन्यया विद्ययाऽविद्यातत्कार्यनिवृत्तेर्ब्रह्मणः शास्त्रवेद्यत्वमुपचर्यते। VPS., p. 244. ब्रह्मणः स्वप्रकाशत्वात् प्रमातृव्यापाराधेयप्रकाशातिशयवत्त्वं कर्मत्वं नास्ति। PĀV., i, 1, 4, p. 66.
36. अत्र संक्षेपशारीरकानुसारिणः केचिदाहुः। शुद्धमेवोपादानं जन्मादिसूत्रतद्भाष्ययोः उपादानत्वस्य ज्ञेयब्रह्मलक्षणत्वोक्तेः। SLS., pp. 71-72.
37. विवरणानुसारिणस्तु (आहुः)। सर्वज्ञत्वादिविशिष्टमायाशबलमीश्वररूपमेव ब्रह्मोपादानम्। Ibid, p. 72. न च जगदुत्पादनाय मायाख्यायाः शक्तेरङ्गीकार्यत्वादन्यसद्भावः शङ्कनीयः। आत्मशक्तित्वेनावस्तुत्वेन च मायायाः पृथग्गणनानर्हत्वात्। AUD., p. 3. उपादानाधिष्ठानत्वयोरेकस्मिन्नेवात्मनि सम्भाव्यते। अधिष्ठानाभिन्न उपादानकारण आत्मन्यखण्डैकरसत्वम्। AUT., p. 27.
38. कृत्स्नस्य व्यावहारिकप्रपञ्चस्य ब्रह्मैव उपादानं, जीवस्तु प्रातिभासिकस्य स्वप्नप्रपञ्चस्य च। SLS., p. 87.
39. अत्राहुः पदार्थतत्त्वनिर्णयकाराः। तत्र ब्रह्म विवर्तमानतया उपादानमविद्या परिणममानतया। Ibid, p. 90.
40. संक्षेपशारीरककृतस्तु ब्रह्मैव उपादानं कूटस्थस्य स्वतः कारणत्वानुपपत्तेर्मायाद्वारा कारणम्। Ibid, p. 95.
41. वाचस्पतिमिश्रास्तु जीवाश्रितमायाविषयीकृतं ब्रह्म स्वत एव जाड्याश्रय-प्रपञ्चाकारेण विवर्तमानतया उपादानमिति माया सहकारिमात्रं, न कार्यानुगतं द्वारकारणमित्याहुः। Ibid, pp. 96-97. अनिर्वाच्याविद्याद्वितयसचिवस्य प्रभवतो विवर्ता यस्यैते वियदनिलतेजोऽबवनयः। Bhām., Introduction, p. 1. आत्मनः परिणममानाविद्याधिष्ठानत्वेन विवर्तोपादानत्वं तस्याश्च परिणामित्वं च सूचितं भविष्यति। AUT., p. 26.
42. ब्रह्मसिद्धिकारास्त्वेवमाहुः। जीवा एव स्वाविद्यया प्रत्येकं प्रपञ्चाकारेण ब्रह्मणि विभ्राम्यन्ति, ब्रह्म तु मायाविशिष्टं बिम्बरूपं प्रतिबिम्बरूपं वा न जगत्कारणम्। यत्त्वया दृष्टं तन्मया दृष्टमिति संवादस्तु बहुपुरुषावगतद्वितीयचन्द्रवत्सादृश्यादुपपद्यते। VPS., p. 224, BRS., pp. 9-13.
43. स्वरूपेणाधिष्ठानत्वमपेक्ष्य ब्रह्मणो जगत्कारणत्वव्यपदेश इतीष्टसिद्धिकाराः प्रकारान्तरेण वर्णयन्ति। ब्रह्मैकमेव स्वाविद्यया जगदाकारेण विवर्तते स्वप्नादिवत्। Ibid, p. 225. आत्मवादिनस्त्वात्मनोऽव्यवहार्यत्वेऽपि स्वमायावशेनैव तस्य सर्वव्यवहारास्पदत्वोपपत्तेर्न व्यवहारलोपः। IS., i, 120, p. 192,
45. Cp. IS., i, 107-19, pp. 187-91 ; i, 36, pp. 145-47.
48. विवर्तवादस्य हि पूर्वभूमिः वेदान्तवादे परिणामवादः। व्यवस्थितेऽस्मिन् परिणामवादे स्वयं समायाति विवर्तवादः॥ SŚR., ii, 61.
50. 'अत्रायं पुरुषः स्वयंज्योति' रिति श्रुतेश्चात्मा स्वयंप्रकाशः। TPD., p. 26. आत्मा स्वप्रकाशः। स्वप्रकाशत्वञ्च स्वसंविन्नैरपेक्ष्येण न स्फुरणम्। PĀV., i, 1, 1, p. 14.
51. आत्मैव चित्प्रकाश इति बलादङ्गीकार्यत्वात्। आत्मानुभवयोरभेदात्। VPS., p. 57.
52. तस्मात्परिशेषात्स्वप्रकाशत्वेनैवात्मनोऽपरोक्षत्वम्। Ibid, p. 85.
54. अस्मत्प्रत्ययत्वाभिमतोऽहंकारः। स चेदमनिदंरूपवस्तुगर्भः सर्वलोकसाक्षिकः। PPD., p. 17.
55. तस्मात्प्रत्यगात्मा स्वयंप्रसिद्धः स्वमहिम्नैवापरोक्षत्वादध्यासयोग्यः। Ibid, p. 29.
56. तेनान्तःकरणोपरागनिमित्तं मिथ्यैवाहंकर्तृत्वमात्मनः स्फटिकमणेरिवोपधाननिमित्तो लोहितिमा। Ibid, p. 20.

57. तदेवं स्वप्रकाशानुभवस्य नित्यत्वादात्मस्वरूपत्वमविरुद्धम् । तथा चात्मैव विषयोपाधिकोऽनुभव इति व्यपदिश्यते अविवक्षितोपाधिश्चात्मेति । VPS., p. 58. अहंप्रत्ययगम्यत्वाकारेण यदा विवक्ष्यते तदा जीव उच्यते । AUD., p. 27.

58. अहंकारस्यानाद्यनिर्वचनीयाऽविद्या उपादानम् । अविद्यायाः परमेश्वराधिष्ठितत्वं निमित्तम् । कर्तृत्व-भोक्तृत्वादिकं च कार्यम् । सुषुप्तेरन्तःकरणप्रलयरूपत्वान्न तत्र सद्भावः । VPS., p. 62.

59. अध्यासमन्तरेणासंगस्यात्मनो निर्व्यापारस्य प्रमाऽजनकत्वेन कारकप्रयोक्तृत्वलक्षणप्रमातृत्वानुपपत्तेः । Ibid, p. 88. Cp. आत्मनोऽहंकारादिसाक्षित्वेनाहंधीविषयत्वस्य निरस्तत्वान्न लोकसिद्धता । RP., i, 1, 4, p. 78.

61. कर्मफलभोक्तुर्जीवात् उदासीनप्रकाशरुपसाक्षिणः पृथगाम्नानात् । SLS., p. 240. चिदाभासविशिष्टाहं-काररूपजीवभ्रमाधिष्ठान-कूटस्थचैतन्यात्मा साक्षी । Ibid, p. 242.

62. सर्वप्रत्यग्भूतं विशुद्धं ब्रह्म जीवाभेदेन साक्षीति प्रतिपाद्यते । Ibid, p. 243. TPD., 374. Cp. सर्वकरणतद्वृत्तिव्यतिरिक्तः स्वप्रकाशात्मकः सर्वसाक्षी सर्ववृत्त्यनुगत एक आत्मा शोधितः। AUT., p. 86.

63. परमेश्वर एव जीवप्रवृत्तिनिवृत्त्योरनुमन्ता स्वयम् उदासीनः साक्षी नाम । SLS., p. 245. Cp. PĀV., i, 1, 4, p. 69.

64. ब्रह्मकोटिरेव साक्षी प्रतिभासती जीवकोटिः । SLS., p. 249.

65. केचित्तु अविद्योपाधिको जीव एव साक्षात् द्रष्टृत्वात् साक्षी लोकेऽपि हि अकर्तृत्वे सति द्रष्टृत्वं साक्षित्वं प्रसिद्धम् । तच्च असंगोदासीनप्रकाशरुपे जीव एव साक्षात् सम्भवति । Ibid, pp. 249-50.

66. तस्मात् अन्तःकरणोपधानेन जीवः साक्षी । Ibid, p. 253. जीवो नामान्तःकरणावच्छिन्नचैतन्यं, तत्साक्षि तु अन्तःकरणोपहितचैतन्यम् । VP., p. 102.

67. बोधरूप आत्मा । आत्मनः सुषुप्तिसाक्षित्वान्न तत्र तदभावः, मातृमानमितिमेयानां व्यभिचारित्वेऽपि तद्भावाभावसाक्षिणः कालत्रयेऽप्यव्यभिचारात् । SB., p. 12. SBBS., p. 13.
देहद्वयाधिष्ठानभूतं कूटस्थचैतन्यं साक्षीत्युच्यते । SLS., p. 234.
Cp. सर्वकरणतद्वृत्तिव्यतिरिक्तः स्वप्रकाशात्मकः सर्वसाक्षी सर्ववृत्त्यनुगत एक आत्मा शोधितः । AUT., p. 86.

68. तमेतमविद्याख्यमात्मानात्मनोरितरेतराध्यासं पुरस्कृत्य सर्वप्रमाणव्यवहाराः प्रवृत्ताः । ŚBS., i, 1, 1, p. 40. आत्मनः प्रमातृत्वादि न पारमार्थिकं, किंत्वविद्यामूलैव प्रमाणादिप्रवृत्तिः । PĀV., i, 1, 1, p. 16.

69. सत्यं प्रत्यगात्मा स्वयंप्रकाशत्वादविषयोऽनंशश्च तथाप्यनिर्वचनीयानाद्यविद्यापरिकल्पितबुद्धिमनःसूक्ष्मस्थूल-शरीरेन्द्रियावच्छेदेनानवच्छिन्नोऽपि वस्तुतोऽवच्छिन्न इव, अभिन्नोऽपि भिन्न इव, अकर्तापि कर्तेव, अभोक्तापि भोक्तेव, अविषयोऽप्यस्मत्प्रत्ययविषय इव, जीवभावमापन्नोऽवभासते । बुद्ध्यादीनामनिर्वाच्यत्वेन तद्भेदस्याप्यनिर्वचनीयत्वात् । Bhām., i, 1, 1, p. 38.

70. प्रमायां खलु फले स्वतन्त्रः प्रमाता भवति । अन्तःकरणपरिणामभेदश्च प्रमेयप्रवणः कर्तृस्थश्चित्स्वभावः प्रमा । कथं च जड़स्यान्तःकरणस्य परिणामश्चिद्रूपो भवेत्, यदि चिदात्मा तत्र नाध्यस्येत् । कथं चैष चिदात्मकर्तृको भवेत्, यद्यन्तःकरणं व्यापारवच्चिदात्मनि नाध्यस्येत् । तस्मादितरेतराध्यासाच्चिदात्मकर्तृस्थं प्रमाफलं सिध्यति । Ibid, p. 42.

71. प्रमातृत्वं हि प्रमां प्रति कर्तृत्वं, तच्च स्वातन्त्र्यम् । स्वातन्त्र्यं च प्रमातुरितरकारकाप्रयोज्यस्य समस्त-कारकप्रयोक्तृत्वम् । न च कूटस्थनित्यश्चिदात्माऽपरिणामी स्वतो व्यापारवान् । तस्मादव्यापारवद् बुद्ध्यादितादात्म्याध्यासात् व्यापारवत्त्वया प्रमाणमधिष्ठातुमर्हतीति । Ibid, p. 41.

72. चिदचिद्रूपसंवलितप्रमाया: आश्रय: प्रमातापि तत्स्वभावो भवितुमर्हति, न च चिदचित्संवलनमध्यासमन्तरेण संभवति। VKT., i, 1, 1, p. 42.

76. वेदान्तेभ्य: यद्यपि च चैतन्यानन्दधन: कर्तृत्वभोक्तृत्वरहितो निष्प्रपञ्च एक: प्रत्यगात्मावगम्यते, तथापि कर्तृत्वभोक्तृत्वदु:खशोकमोहमयमात्मानमवगाहमानेनाऽहंप्रत्ययेन। Bhām., i, 1, 1, p. 46.

77. तदनेनान्त:करणाद्यवच्छिन्न: प्रत्यगात्मा इदमनिदंरूपश्चेतन: कर्ता भोक्ता कार्यकारणाविद्याद्वयाधारोऽहंकारास्पदं संसारी जीवात्मा इतरेतराध्यासोपादान:; तदुपादानश्चाध्यास इत्यनादित्वाद्बीजाङ्कुरवन्नेतरेतराश्रयत्वमित्युक्तं भवति। Ibid, p. 45.

78. सर्वानर्थसंसारभाजनं जीवात्मा। Ibid, p. 45.

79. न चैवं कर्तृत्वादे: प्रत्यायकाभाव: शङ्कनीय:। साक्षिण: प्रत्यायकत्वात्। VPS., p. 98.

80. ब्रम्ह कतृत्वादिप्रपञ्चोपेतस्य जीवस्य कथमात्मा स्यात्। उच्यते। साक्षिवेद्या एव कर्तृत्वादय। Ibid, pp. 97-98.

83. चिदात्मन: स्वयंप्रकाशस्यैव अनवच्छिन्नस्य अवच्छिन्नेभ्यो बुद्धयादिभ्यो भेदाग्रहात्, तदध्यासेन जीवभाव:। Bhām., p. 38.

84. जीवो हि चिदात्मतया स्वयंप्रकाशतयाऽविषयोऽप्यौपाधिकेन रूपेण विषय इति भाव:। Ibid, p. 39.

85. जीव एव तु तत्तदुपाधिरहित: शुद्धबुद्धादिस्वभावो ब्रह्मेति गीयते। Ibid, p. 58.
जीवात्मानश्चाविद्यादर्पणा ब्रह्मप्रतिबिम्बका:। Ibid, iv, 1, 4, p. 939.

86. जाग्रद्दशा नाम इन्द्रियजन्यज्ञानावस्था। इन्द्रियजन्यविषयगोचरापरोक्षान्त:करणवृत्यवस्था स्वप्नावस्था। सुषप्तिर्नामाविद्यागोचराऽविद्यावृत्त्यवस्था। VP., pp. 387 & 394.
सुषुप्तौ जीव: स्वोपाधिविलये सति परमानन्दरूपं ब्रह्म प्राप्नोति। AUD., p. 1.

88. न चायं क्रियाकारकफलात्मक आभास ईषदपि परमार्थवस्तु स्पृशति। तस्य मोहमात्रोपादानत्वात्। SNS, ii, 51. बुद्धयुपहितस्य तत्तादात्म्यापन्न: स्वचिदाभासाविवेकाज्जीव: कर्ता भोक्ता प्रमातेति च कथ्यते इति वार्तिककारपादा:। SB., p. 27.

89. अज्ञानविषयीभूतं चैतन्यमीश्वर:, अज्ञानाश्रयीभूतं च जीव इति वाचस्पतिमिश्रा:। अस्मिंश्च पक्षे अज्ञाननानात्वाज्जीवनानात्वम्। प्रतिजीवं च प्रपञ्चभेद:, जीवस्यैव स्वाज्ञानोपहिततया जगदुपादानत्वात्। प्रत्यभिज्ञा च अतिसादृश्यात्। ईश्वरस्य च सप्रपञ्चजीवाविद्याधिष्ठानत्वेन कारणत्वोपचारादिति। अयमेव चावच्छेदवाद:। SB., p. 29. न वयमविद्यां सर्वजीवेष्वेकामाचक्ष्महे, किंत्वियं प्रतिजीवं भिद्यते। Bhām., i, 4, 3, p. 377.

90. नाविद्या ब्रह्माश्रया, किन्तु जीवे, सात्वनिर्वचनीयेत्युक्तं, तेन नित्यशुद्धमेव ब्रह्म। Bhām., i, 1, 4, p. 126.

91. जीवो नामान्त:करणावच्छिन्नचैतन्यम्। VP., p. 102.

92. अनाद्यविद्याप्रतिबिम्बकृतविभागस्यैव जीवस्य तदुत्पन्नाहंकारादिविशेषेषु स्थूलप्रतिबिम्बापेक्षया सर्वेषामुपाधित्वं न विरूध्यते। PPV., p. 67.. अविद्याप्रतिबिम्बिताच्चिद्धातोर्जीवाख्यादन्य: परमेश्वरो न निषिध्यते। तत्रापि विशिष्टयोरभेद: कल्पित:। PĀV., i, 1, 17, p. 113. अज्ञानोपहितं बिम्बचैतन्यमीश्वर:, अन्त:करणतत्संस्कारावच्छिन्नाज्ञानप्रतिविम्बितं चैतन्यं जीव, इति विवरणकारा:। SB., p. 28 स ईश्वर: एवाज्ञानप्रतिबिम्बिततया- द्रष्टा जीव:। PĀV., i, 1, 4, p. 69. उक्तञ्चैतदभेदेऽपि विम्बप्रतिबिम्बयोर्धर्मव्यवस्थेतिभाव:। RP., ii, 3, 46, p. 688. अव्यतिरेकेऽपि च ब्रह्मणो जीवानां बिम्बप्रतिबिम्ववद्विद्याव्यवस्था। BRS., p. 12.

93. एकमेव चैतन्यं विम्बत्वाक्रान्तमीश्वरचैतन्यं प्रतिबिम्बत्वाक्रान्तं जीवचैतन्यम्। बिम्बप्रतिबिम्बकल्पनोपाधिश्चैकजीववादे अविद्या, अनेकजीववादे अन्त:करणान्येव। VP., p. 381.

94. जीवपरमेश्वरसाधारणचैतन्यमात्रं बिम्बं तस्यैव बिम्बस्याविद्यात्मिकायायां मायायां प्रतिबिम्बमीश्वरचैतन्य-मन्तःकरणेषु प्रतिबिम्बं जीवचैतन्यम्। Ibid, p. 380.

95. तत्रापि प्रतिबिम्बो जीवः बिम्बस्थानीय ईश्वरः। तथा सत्येव लौकिकबिम्बप्रतिबिम्बदृष्टान्तेन स्वातन्त्र्य-मीश्वरस्य तत्पारतन्त्र्यं जीवस्य च युज्यते। SLS., p. 152.

96. स चान्तःकरणसाक्षी जीवात्मा परमेश्वरस्य प्रतिबिम्बः। तस्मात् सत्यज्ञानानन्दात्मको जीव ईश्वरस्य प्रतिबिम्बः। अन्तःकरणमेव जीवोपाधिः। ACM., pp. 30 & 38.

97. तत्र सत्त्वरजस्तमोगुणात्मकमज्ञानं प्रतिबिम्बोपाधिः। भावरुपाज्ञानमेव प्रतिबिम्बोपाधिरिति सिद्धम्। सत्यज्ञानानन्दात्मकौ जीव ईश्वरस्य प्रतिबिम्बः। Ibid, pp. 32, 35 & 38.

98. अज्ञानप्रतिबिम्बितं चैतन्यमीश्वरः, बुद्धिप्रतिम्बितं चैतन्यं जीवः, अज्ञानोपहितं तु बिम्बचैतन्यं शुद्धमिति संक्षेपशारीरककाराः। SB., p. 28.

99. संक्षेपशारीरके अविद्यायां चित्प्रतिबिम्ब ईश्वरः, अन्तःकरणे चित्प्रतिबिम्बो जीवः। SLS., p. 103.

100. अत्र उक्तं प्रकटार्थविवरणे 'एका अनादिरनिर्वाच्या भुतप्रकृतिः चिन्मात्रसम्बन्धिनी माया। तस्यां चित्प्रतिबिम्ब ईश्वरः। तस्या एव परिच्छिन्नाऽनन्तप्रदेशेषु आवरणविक्षेपशक्तिमदविद्याभिधानेषु चित्प्रतिबिम्बो जीव' इति। Ibid, p. 99 ; PĀV., i, 1, 1, p. 8.

101. शुद्धसत्त्वप्रधाना माया तदभिभूतमलिनसत्त्वा अविद्येति मायाऽविद्याभेदं परिकल्प्य मायाप्रतिबिम्ब ईश्वरः, अविद्याप्रतिबिम्बो जीव इति उक्तम्। SLS., p. 102.

103. एको जीवस्तेन च एकमेव शरीरं सजीवम्, अन्यानि स्वप्नदृष्टशरीराणीव निर्जीवानि, तदज्ञानकल्पितं सर्वं जगत्। Ibid, p. 160.

104. जीवेश्वरोपाधिरज्ञानमेव। तदप्येकमेव तत्प्रतिबिम्बो जीवः, उपाधेरेकत्वात्। ACK., p. 40.

105. तस्याज्ञानस्यैकत्वात् तत्र प्रतिबिम्बोऽप्येक इत्येकजीववादिनः। ACM., p. 36.

106. मुख्यो वेदान्तसिद्धान्त एकजीववादाख्यः। इममेव च दृष्टिसृष्टिवादमाचक्षते। अस्मिन् पक्षे जीव एव स्वाज्ञानवशाज्जगदुपादानं निमित्तं च, दृश्यं च सर्वं प्रातीतिकम्। SB, p. 29.

107. हिरण्यगर्भ एको ब्रह्मप्रतिबिम्बो मुख्यो जीवः। अन्ये तु तत्प्रतिबिम्बभूता जीवाभासाः संसारादिभाज इति अनेकशरीरैकजीववादमातिष्ठन्ते। SLS., p. 162.

108. एक एव जीवोऽविशेषेण सर्वं शरीरमधितिष्ठति। Ibid, p. 164.

109. इतरे तु अन्तःकणादीनां जीवोपाधित्वाभ्युपगमेन अनेकजीववादमाश्रित्य बद्धमुक्तव्यवस्थां प्रतिपद्यन्ते। Ibid, pp. 165-66.

110. मलिनसत्त्वप्रधाना अविद्या मालिन्यवैचित्र्यादनेकधा तदुपहितो जीवोऽपि तथैव। अस्मिन् पक्षे नाना जीवः। ACK., p. 38.

111. बिम्बप्रतिबिम्बकल्पनोपाधिश्चैकजीववादे अविद्या, अनेकजीववादे अन्तःकरणान्येव। VP., p. 381.

113. अत्र केचिदाहु। पूर्वपूर्वकल्पिताविद्योपहित उत्तरोत्तराविद्याकल्पकः। SLS., p. 478.

114. आत्मा तथा मूढबुद्ध्या जगद्रूपः प्रकाशते ॥ २१ ॥ आत्मन्येव जगत्सर्वं दृष्टिमात्रं सतत्त्वकम् ॥ २२ ॥ योगवाशिष्ट, VSM, p. 104.

115. अन्यस्तु दृष्टिरेव विश्वसृष्टिः, दृश्यस्य दृष्टिभेदे प्रमाणाभावात्। SLS., p. 484.

116. तानि चान्तःकरणानि प्रतिपुरुषं व्यवस्थितानि। तत्कथं सर्वपुरुषभोगसांकरः। VPS., p. 72.

117. तथा चान्तःकरणोपाधिश्चैतन्यस्य विषयोपरागसिद्ध्यर्थो भविष्यति। Ibid, p. 73.

118. नन्वेवमसंगिनः साक्षिचैतन्यस्याविद्यानावृतस्य जीवत्वेऽपि स्यादेवान्तःकरणवशाद्व्यवस्था। Ibid, p. 74.

120. अन्तःकरणावच्छिन्नः प्रत्यगात्मा चेतनः कर्ता भोक्ता जीवात्मा । Bhām., i, 1, 1, p. 45.

121. जीव एव तु तत्तदुपाधिरहितः शुद्धबुद्धादिस्वभावो ब्रह्मेति गीयते । Ibid, p. 58.

122. सर्वोपाधिरहितं हि स्वयंज्योतिरितिगीयते, न तूपहितमपि । Ibid.
तस्योपहित रूपं जीवः, शुद्धन्तु रूपं तस्य साक्षि । Ibid, i, 1, 4.

124. अनाद्यविद्योपाधानलब्धसर्वशक्तिज्ञानस्यापि परमात्मनः वेदानां योनेः । Bhām , i, 1, 3.

125. सर्वगन्धत्वादिरौपाधिको ब्रह्मण्यध्यस्तः । Ibid, iii, 2, 11.

126. निर्विशेषमेकरूपं चैतन्यैकरसं सद् ब्रह्म । परमार्थतोऽविशेषाश्च सर्वगन्धत्वादय उपाधिवशादध्यस्ता इति सिद्धम् । Ibid.

127. उपाधिगत एव रूपभेदो ब्रह्मण्युपचर्यते ध्यानार्थम् । Bhām., iii, 2, 12.

128. वस्तुतोऽनवच्छिन्नचैतन्यं तत्त्वान्यत्वानिर्वचनीयनामरूपविषयावच्छिन्नं कार्यम्, तस्य कर्ता ईश्वरो ज्ञाता सर्वज्ञः सर्वशक्तिरिति सिद्धम् । Bhām., i, 1, 5.

129. संसारिणां वस्तुतो नित्यज्ञानत्वेऽप्यविद्यादयः प्रतिबन्धकारणानि सन्ति, न त्वीश्वरस्याविद्यारहितस्य ज्ञान-प्रतिबन्धककारणसम्भव इति भावः । Ibid, pp. 171-72.

131. उक्तैश्वर्यतिरोभावे देहाभिमानो हेतुः । RP., iii, 2, 6.

133. अविद्याप्रतिबिम्बितं चैतन्यं जीवः ; अविद्योपहितं चैतन्यमीश्वरः । TA., p. 38.

134. इयं समष्टिरुत्कृष्टोपाधितया विशुद्धसत्त्वप्रधाना । एतदुपहितं चैतन्यं जगत्कारणमीश्वरः । VS., p. 9.

135. एवं च स्वाविद्यया जीवभावमापन्नस्यैव ब्रह्मणः प्रपञ्चकल्पकत्वादीश्वरोऽपि जीवकल्पितः । SLS., p. 159.

136. जीवोपाधिना अन्तःकरणादिना अवच्छिन्नं चैतन्यं बिम्बभूत ईश्वर एव । Ibid, p. 139.

137. परमार्थदर्शिनस्तु य ईश्वर स एव प्रत्यगात्मेति मन्यन्ते । VPS., p. 191.

142. न हि भिन्नोऽयम् इत्यभेदबुद्धिमनिराकृत्य भेदबुद्धिः पदार्थमालिङ्गते । भिन्नाभिन्नं विशेषैश्चेद् दुःखि स्याद् ब्रह्म ते ध्रुवम् । अशेषदुःखिता च स्यादहो प्रज्ञात्मवेदिनाम् ।
SNS., i, 78, p. 102. Ibid, i, 68-78. Introduction, p. 15.

144. एवमयं प्रमातृप्रमाणप्रमेयव्यवहारः सर्व एव पराचीनविषय एव, न प्रतीचीनमात्मानम् अवगाहयितुमलम् । SNS., iii, 52.

145. पराञ्च्येव तु सर्वाणि प्रत्यक्षादीनि नात्मनि । प्रतीच्येव प्रवृत्तं तत् सदसीति वचोऽञ्जसा । Ibid, iii, 45.

146. आत्मनश्च अशेषप्रमेयवैलक्षण्यात्, सर्वानर्थैकत्वज्ञानापनोदि ज्ञानदिवाकरोदयहेतुत्वं वस्तुमात्रयाथात्म्यप्रकाशन-पटीयस्त्वत्त्वमस्यादिवचस एव । Ibid, ii, 1.

147. आत्मज्ञानं हि स्वतःसिद्धपरमार्थात्मवस्तुस्वरूपमात्राश्रयादेवाविद्यातदुत्पन्नकारकग्रामप्रध्वंसि स्वात्मोत्पत्तावेव शास्त्राद्यपेक्षते नोत्पन्नमविद्यानिवृत्तौ । Ibid, i, 36.

148. नाप्रमेये स्वतःसिद्धेऽविश्वासः कथमात्मनि । Ibid, i, 89.

149. तत्त्वमस्यादिवाक्यानां स्वतःसिद्धार्थबोधनात् । अर्थान्तरं न संद्रष्टुं शक्यते त्रिदशैरपि ॥ Ibid, i, 98.

150. सर्वत्राव्यभिचारात् कूटस्थनित्यत्वं सिद्धं स्वत एव, न प्रमाणापेक्षम् । US., ii, 93, p. 80.

153. नीलाद्यनुपलम्भेऽपि स्वाभाविकस्वरूपोपलम्भस्य दुर्निवारत्वात् । ĀNM., p. 144.

154. तत्राजानतो भेदानुपलम्भात् । Ibid.

156. तस्मात् संवित्स्वरूपतायामात्मनो न दूषणं पश्यामः, सा च स्वयंप्रकाशेति सिद्धा तद्रूपस्यात्मनः स्वप्रकाशता । Ibid, i, 145.

157. उपाध्युपहितस्यानुपलम्भेऽपि स्वरूपस्योपलम्भान्न क्षणिकत्वसिद्धिः । NMV. pp. 143-44.

159. आत्मनो निरतिशयसुखहिताव्यतिरेकसिद्धेः अहितस्य स्वत एवानभिसम्बन्धात् । SNS., i, 30.

160. 'हितं मे स्यादहितं मे मा भूत्' इति मिथ्याज्ञानं प्रवृत्तिनिमित्तम् । Ibid.

161. परमानन्दरूपता तु परप्रेमास्पदया प्रकाशत एव । ĀNM., p. 173.

162. तदेवं परमप्रेमास्पदभावः परमानन्दभावमन्तरेणात्मनि नावकल्पत इति सिद्धम् । Ibid, p. 175.

163. आत्मनि प्रेमा निरुपाधिकः, तथा चायं परिशेषतः परमानन्द. प्रकाशत इत्युक्तम् । Ibid, p. 176.

164. प्रकाशमानोऽप्ययमानन्दोऽनाद्यनिर्वाच्याविद्योपदर्शितविविधविचित्रनामरूपप्रपञ्चतया विवेकतः स्फुटतरमनवभासमानो न भासत इव सांसारिकदशायाम् । Ibid, pp. 176-77.

165. ब्रह्मसाक्षात्कारोन्मीलितनिखिलाविद्योपप्लवस्तु परितः प्रद्योतमानपरिशुद्धभावो मुक्ताविति भेदसिद्धिः । Ibid, pp. 177-78.

166. परमप्रेमास्पदत्वेन तस्यानन्दरूपत्वात् निर्धर्मकनित्यस्वप्रकाशसुखात्मक एवात्मा । SB., p. 19.

167. नित्योऽक्रमदृगात्मैको व्याप्नोतीव धियोऽनिशम् । SNS., ii, 69.

168. निर्यत्नोऽविक्रियोऽनिच्छन्निच्छन्तीं चाप्यलुप्तदृक् । Ibid, ii, 71.

169. निस्त्रिकालस्थां कूटस्थः क्षणभंगुराम् । Ibid, ii, 74.

170. निरपेक्षश्च सापेक्षां पराचीं प्रत्यगद्वयः पश्यति । Ibid, ii, 75.

171. दुःखिनः साक्षिताऽयुक्ता साक्षिणो दुःखिता तथा ॥ Ibid, ii, 76.

172. नर्ते स्याद् विक्रियां दुःखी साक्षिता का विकारिणः । धीविक्रियासहस्राणां साक्ष्यतोऽहमविक्रियः । Ibid, ii, 77.

173. एवं सर्वस्मिन् व्यभिचारिणि, आत्मवस्त्वेवाव्यभिचारि । Ibid, ii, 78.

174. अस्याश्च क्षणभंगुरत्वे स्वयमेवात्मा साक्षी । न हि कूटस्थावबोधमन्तरेण बुद्धेराविर्भावतिरोभावादिसिद्धिरस्ति । Ibid, p. 191.

175. परिणामिधियां वृत्तं नित्याक्रमदृगात्मना । षड्भावविक्रियामेति व्याप्तं खेनाङ्कुरो यथा ॥ Ibid, ii, 82.

176. अतो नित्यमविकारो स्वयंदृशिः । Ibid, ii, 83.

177. प्रत्यर्थं तु विभिद्यन्ते बुद्धयो विषयोन्मुखाः । न भिदावगतेस्तद्वत् सर्वास्ताश्चिन्निभायतः ॥ Ibid, ii, 86.

178. तस्माज्जगद्धियां वृत्तं ज्योतिरेकं सदाक्षते । Ibid, ii, 89.

179. दृष्टेर्द्रष्टारमात्मानं न पश्येद् दृश्यमानया । विज्ञातारमरे केन विजानीयद्धियां पतिम् ॥ Ibid, ii, 92.

180. आत्माऽनात्मा च लोकेऽस्मिन् प्रत्यक्षादिप्रमाणतः । सिद्धस्तयोरनात्मा तु सर्वेषामात्मपूर्वकः ॥ Ibid, iv, p. 3.

181. इदमित्येव बाह्योऽर्थेह्यहमित्येव बोद्धरि । द्वयं दृष्टं यतो देहे तेनायं मुह्यते जनः ॥ Ibid, iv, 6.
विद्यात् अनन्तरमबाह्यार्थं प्रत्यक्स्थं मुनिरञ्जसा । Ibid, iv, 8.

182. ऋते ज्ञानं न सन्त्यर्था अस्ति ज्ञानमृतेऽपि तान् । Ibid, ii, 97.

183. यस्मात् प्रमाणप्रमेयव्यवहार आत्माऽनवबोधाश्रय एव, तस्मात् सिद्धमात्मनोऽप्रमेयत्वम् । Ibid, ii, 98.

184. ग्राहकग्राह्यविभागे योऽविभागवान् । हानोपादानयोः साक्षी हानोपादानवर्जितः ॥ Ibid, 108.

185. नित्यावगतिरूपत्वात् कारकादिर्नचात्मनः । Ibid, ii, 113.

186. नित्यं संविदमाश्रित्य स्वतःसिद्धामविक्रियाम् । सिद्धायन्ते धियो बोधास्तांश्चाश्रित्य घटादयः ॥ Ibid, ii, 115.

187. धीवन्नापेक्षते सिद्धिमात्माऽन्यस्मादविक्रियः । निरपेक्षमपेक्ष्यैव सिद्धन्त्यन्ये न तु स्वयम् । Ibid, ii, 110.

72. चिदचिद्रूपसंवलितप्रमाया: आश्रय: प्रमातापि तत्स्वभावो भवितुमर्हति, न च चिदचित्संवलनमध्यासमन्तरेण संभवति। VKT., i, 1, 1, p. 42.

76. वेदान्तेभ्य: यद्यपि च चैतन्यानन्दघन: कर्तृत्वभोक्तृत्वरहितो निष्प्रपञ्च एक: प्रत्यगात्मावगम्यते, तथापि कर्तृत्वभोक्तृत्वदु:खशोकमोहमयमात्मानमवगाहमानेनाऽहंप्रत्ययेन। Bhām., i, 1, 1, p. 46.

77. तदनेनान्त:करणाद्यवच्छिन्न: प्रत्यगात्मा इदमनिदंरूपश्चेतन: कर्ता भोक्ता कार्यकारणाविद्याद्वयाधारोऽहंकारास्पदं संसारी जीवात्मा इतरेतराध्यासोपादान: ; तदुपादानश्चाध्यास इत्यनादित्वाद्बीजाङ्कुरवन्नेतरेतराश्रयत्वमित्युक्तं भवति। Ibid, p. 45.

78. सर्वानर्थसंसारभाजनं जीवात्मा। Ibid, p. 45.

79. न चैवं कर्तृत्वादे: प्रत्यायकाभाव: शङ्कनीय:। साक्षिण: प्रत्यायकत्वात्। VPS., p. 98.

80. व्रम्ह कतृत्वादिप्रपञ्चोपेतस्य जीवस्य कथमात्मा स्यात्। उच्यते। साक्षिवेद्या एव कर्तृत्वादय:। Ibid, pp. 97-98.

83. चिदात्मन: स्वयंप्रकाशस्यैव अनवच्छिन्नस्य अवच्छिन्नेभ्यो बुद्ध्यादिभ्यो भेदाग्रहात्, तदध्यासेन जीवभाव:। Bhām., p. 38.

84. जीवो हि चिदात्मतया स्वयंप्रकाशतयाऽविषयोऽप्यौपाधिकेन रूपेण विषय इति भाव:। Ibid, p. 39.

85. जीव एव तु तत्तदुपाधिरहित: शुद्धबुद्धादिस्वभावो व्रह्मेति गीयते। Ibid, p. 58.
जीवात्मानश्चाविद्यादर्पणा व्रह्मप्रतिबिम्वका:। Ibid, iv, 1, 4, p. 939.

86. जाग्रद्दशा नाम इन्द्रियजन्यज्ञानावस्था। इन्द्रियजन्यविषयगोचरापरोक्षान्त:करणवृत्यवस्था स्वप्नावस्था। सुषप्तिर्नामाविद्यागोचराऽविद्यावृत्त्यवस्था। VP., pp. 387 & 394.
सुषुप्तौ जीव: स्वोपाधिविलये सति परमानन्दरूपं व्रह्म प्राप्नोति। AUD., p. 1.

88. न चायं क्रियाकारकफलात्मक आभास ईषदपि परमार्थवस्तु स्पृशति। तस्य मोहमात्रोपादानत्वात्। SNS., ii, 51. बुद्ध्युपहितस्य तत्तादात्म्यापन्न: स्वचिदाभासाविवेकाज्जीव: कर्ता भोक्ता प्रमातेति च कथ्यते इति वार्तिककारपादा:। SB., p 27.

89. अज्ञानविषयीभूतं चैतन्यमीश्वर:, अज्ञानाश्रयीभूतं च जीव इति वाचस्पतिमिश्रा:। अस्मिंश्च पक्षे अज्ञाननानात्वाज्जीवनानात्वम्। प्रतिजीवं च प्रपञ्चभेद:, जीवस्यैव स्वाज्ञानोपहिततया जगदुपादानत्वात्। प्रत्यभिज्ञा च अतिसादृश्यात्। ईश्वरस्य च सप्रपञ्चजीवाविद्याधिष्ठानत्वेन कारणत्वोपचारादिति। अयमेव चावच्छेदवाद:। SB., p. 29. न वयमविद्यां सर्वजीवेष्वेकामाचक्ष्महे, किंत्वियं प्रतिजीवं भिद्यते। Bhām., i, 4, 3, p. 377.

90. नाविद्या व्रह्माश्रया, किन्तु जीवे, सात्वनिर्वचनीयेत्युक्तं, तेन नित्यशुद्धमेव व्रह्म। Bhām., i, 1, 4, p. 126.

91. जीवो नामान्त:करणावच्छिन्नचैतन्यम्। VP., p. 102.

92. अनाद्यविद्याप्रतिविम्बकृतविभागस्यैव जीवस्य तदुत्पन्नाहंकारादिविशेषेषु स्थलप्रतिबिम्बापेक्षया सर्वेषामुपाधित्वं न विरूध्यते। PPV., p. 67. अविद्याप्रतिबिम्बिताच्चिद्धातोर्जीवाख्यादन्य: परमेश्वरो न निषिध्यते। तत्रापि विशिष्टयोरभेद: कल्पित:। PĀV., i, 1, 17, p. 113. अज्ञानोपहितं बिम्बचैतन्यमीश्वर:, अन्त:करणतत्संस्कारावच्छिन्नाज्ञानप्रतिविम्वितं चैतन्यं जीव, इति विवरणकारा:। SB., p. 28 स ईश्वर: एवाज्ञानप्रतिबिम्बिततया-द्रष्टा जीव:। PĀV., i, 1, 4, p. 69. उक्तञ्चैतदभेदेऽपि विम्बप्रतिबिम्बयोर्धर्मव्यवस्थेतिभाव:। RP., ii, 3, 46, p. 688. अव्यतिरेकेऽपि च व्रह्मणो जीवानां बिम्बप्रतिबिम्ववद्विद्याव्यवस्था। BRS., p. 12.

93. एकमेव चैतन्यं विम्बत्वाक्रान्तमीश्वरचैतन्यं प्रतिबिम्बत्वाक्रान्तं जीवचैतन्यम्। बिम्बप्रतिबिम्बकल्पनोपाधिश्चैकजीववादे अविद्या, अनेकजीववादे अन्त:करणान्येव। VP., p. 381.

94. जीवपरमेश्वरसाधारणचैतन्यमात्रं बिम्बं तस्यैव बिम्बस्याविद्यात्मिकायायां मायायां प्रतिबिम्बमीश्वरचैतन्य-मन्त:करणेषु प्रतिबिम्बं जीवचैतन्यम् । Ibid, p. 380.

95. तत्रापि प्रतिबिम्बो जीव: बिम्बस्थानीय ईश्वर: । तथा सत्येव लौकिकबिम्बप्रतिबिम्बदृष्टान्तेन स्वातन्त्र्य-मीश्वरस्य तत्पारतन्त्र्यं जीवस्थ च युज्यते । SLS., p. 152.

96. स चान्त:करणसाक्षी जीवात्मा परमेश्वरस्य प्रतिबिम्ब: । तस्मात् सत्यज्ञानानन्दात्मको जीव ईश्वरस्य प्रतिबिम्ब: । अन्त:करणमेव जीवोपाधि: । ACM., pp. 30 & 38.

97. तत्र सत्त्वरजस्तमोगुणात्मकमज्ञानं प्रतिबिम्बोपाधि: । भावरुपाज्ञानमेव प्रतिबिम्बोपाधिरिति सिद्धम् । सत्यज्ञानानन्दात्मकौ जीव ईश्वरस्य प्रतिबिम्ब: । Ibid, pp. 32, 35 & 38.

98. अज्ञानप्रतिबिम्बितं चैतन्यमीश्वर:, बुद्धिप्रतिम्बितं चैतन्यं जीव:, अज्ञानोपहितं तु बिम्बचैतन्यं शुद्धमिति संक्षेपशारीरककारा: । SB., p. 28.

99. संक्षेपशारीरके अविद्यायां चित्प्रतिबिम्ब ईश्वर:, अन्त:करणे चित्प्रतिबिम्बो जीव: । SLS., p. 103.

100. अत्र उक्तं प्रकटार्थविवरणे 'एका अनादिरनिर्वाच्या भुतप्रकृति: चिन्मात्रसम्बन्धिनी माया । तस्यां चित्प्रतिबिम्ब ईश्वर: । तस्या एव परिच्छिन्नाऽनन्तप्रदेशेषु आवरणविक्षेपशक्तिमदविद्याभिधानेषु चित्प्रतिबिम्बो जीव' इति । Ibid, p. 99 ; PĀV., i, 1, 1, p. 8.

101. शुद्धसत्त्वप्रधाना माया तदभिभूतमलिनसत्त्वा अविद्येति मायाऽविद्याभेदं परिकल्प्य मायाप्रतिबिम्ब ईश्वर:, अविद्याप्रतिबिम्बो जीव इति उक्तम् । SLS., p. 102.

103. एको जीवस्तेन च एकमेव शरीरं सजीवम्, अन्यानि स्वप्नदृष्टशरीराणीव निर्जीवानि, तदज्ञानकल्पितं सर्वं जगत् । Ibid, p. 160.

104. जीवेश्वरोपाधिरज्ञानमेव । तदप्येकमेव तत्प्रतिबिम्बो जीव:, उपाधेरेकत्वात् । ACK., p. 40.

105. तस्याज्ञानस्यैकत्वात् तत्र प्रतिबिम्बोऽप्येक इत्येकजीववादिन: । ACM., p. 36.

106. मुख्यो वेदान्तसिद्धान्त एकजीववादाख्य: । इममेव च दृष्टिसृष्टिवादमाचक्षते । अस्मिन् पक्षे जीव एव स्वाज्ञानवशाज्जगदुपादानं निमित्तं च, दृश्यं च सर्वं प्रातीतिकम् । SB , p. 29.

107. हिरण्यगर्भ एको ब्रह्मप्रतिबिम्बो मुख्यो जीव: । अन्ये तु तत्प्रतिबिम्बभूता जीवाभासा: संसारादिभाज इति अनेकशरीरैकजीववादमातिष्ठन्ते । SLS., p. 162.

108. एक एव जीवोऽविशेषेण सर्वं शरीरमधितिष्ठति । Ibid, p. 164.

109. इतरे तु अन्त:कणादीनां जीवोपाधित्वाभ्युपगमेन अनेकजीववादमाश्रित्य बद्धमुक्तव्यवस्थां प्रतिपद्यन्ते । Ibid, pp. 165-66.

110. मलिनसत्त्वप्रधाना अविद्या मालिन्यवैचित्र्यादनेकधा तदुपहितो जीवोऽपि तथैव । अस्मिन् पक्षे नाना जीव: । ACK., p. 38.

111. बिम्बप्रतिबिम्बकल्पनोपाधिश्चैकजीववादे अविद्या, अनेकजीववादे अन्त:करणान्येव । VP., p. 381.

113. अत्र केचिदाहु: । पूर्वपूर्वकल्पिताविद्योपहित उत्तरोत्तराविद्याकल्पक: । SLS., p. 478.

114. आत्मा तथा मूढबुद्धया जगद्रूप: प्रकाशते ।। २१ ।। आत्मन्येव जगत्सर्वं दृष्टिमात्रं सतत्त्वकम् ।। २२ ।। योगवाशिष्ट, VSM., p. 104.

115. अन्यस्तु दृष्टिरेव विश्वसृष्टि:, दृश्यस्य दृष्टिभेदे प्रमाणाभावात् । SLS., p. 484.

116. तानि चान्त:करणानि प्रतिपुरुषं व्यवस्थितानि । तत्कथं सर्वपुरुषभोगसंकर: । VPS., p. 72.

117. तथा चान्त:करणोपाधिश्चैतन्यस्य विषयोपरागसिद्धयर्थो भविष्यति । Ibid, p. 73.

118. तदेवमसंगिन: साक्षिचैतन्यस्याविद्यानावृतस्य जीवत्वेऽपि स्यादेवान्त:करणवशाद्व्यवस्था । Ibid, p. 74.

120. अन्तःकरणावच्छिन्नः प्रत्यगात्मा चेतनः कर्त्ता भोक्ता जीवात्मा। Bhām., i, 1, 1, p. 45.

121. जीव एव तु तत्तदुपाधिरहितः शुद्धबुद्धादिस्वभावो ब्रह्मेति गीयते। Ibid, p. 58.

122. सर्वोपाधिरहितं हि स्वयंज्योतिरितिगीयते, न तूपहितमपि। Ibid.
तस्योपहित रूपं जीवः, शुद्धन्तु रूपं तस्य साक्षि। Ibid, i, 1, 4.

124. अनाद्यविद्योपाधानलब्धसर्वशक्तिज्ञानस्यापि परमात्मनः वेदानां योनेः। Bhām , i, 1, 3.

125. सर्वगन्धत्वादिरौपाधिको ब्रह्मण्यध्यस्तः। Ibid, iii, 2, 11.

126. निर्विशेषमेकरूपं चैतन्यैकरसं सद् ब्रह्म। परमार्थतोऽविशेषाश्च सर्वगन्धत्वादय उपाधिवशादध्यस्ता इति सिद्धम्। Ibid.

127. उपाधिगत एव रूपभेदो ब्रह्मण्युपचर्यते ध्यानार्थम्। Bhām., iii, 2, 12.

128. वस्तुतोऽनवच्छिन्नचैतन्यं तत्त्वान्यत्वानिर्वचनीयनामरूपविषयावच्छिन्नं कार्यम्, तस्य कर्ता ईश्वरो ज्ञाता सर्वज्ञः सर्वशक्तिरिति सिद्धम्। Bhām., i, 1, 5.

129. संसारिणां वस्तुतो नित्यज्ञानत्वेऽप्यविद्यादयः प्रतिबन्धकारणानि सन्ति, न त्वीश्वरस्याविद्यारहितस्य ज्ञान-प्रतिबन्धककारणसम्भव इति भावः। Ibid, pp. 171-72.

131. उक्तैश्वर्यतिरोभावे देहाभिमानो हेतुः। RP., iii, 2, 6.

133. अविद्याप्रतिबिम्बितं चैतन्यं जीवः ; अविद्योपहितं चैतन्यमीश्वरः। TA., p. 38.

134. इयं समष्टिरुत्कृष्टोपाधितया विशुद्धसत्त्वप्रधाना। एतदुपहितं चैतन्यं जगत्कारणमीश्वरः। VS., p. 9.

135. एवं च स्वाविद्यया जीवभावमापन्नस्यैव ब्रह्मणः प्रपञ्चकल्पकत्वादीश्वरोऽपि जीवकल्पितः। SLS., p. 159.

136. जीवोपाधिना अन्तःकरणादिना अवच्छिन्नं चैतन्यं बिम्बभूत ईश्वर एव। Ibid, p. 139.

137. परमार्थदर्शिनस्तु य ईश्वर स एव प्रत्यगात्मेति मन्यन्ते। VPS., p. 191.

142. न हि भिन्नोऽयम् इत्यभेदबुद्धिमनिराकृत्य भेदबुद्धिः पदार्थमालिङ्गते। भिन्नाभिन्नं विशेषैश्चेद् दुःखि स्याद् ब्रह्म ते ध्रुवम्। अशेषदुःखिता च स्यादहो प्रज्ञात्मवेदिनाम्।
SNS., i, 78, p. 102. Ibid, i, 68-78. Introduction, p. 15.

144. एवमयं प्रमातृप्रमाणप्रमेयव्यवहारः सर्व एव पराचीनविषय एव, न प्रतीचीनमात्मानम् अवगाहयितुमलम्। SNS., iii, 52.

145. पराञ्च्येव तु सर्वाणि प्रत्यक्षादीनि नात्मनि। प्रतीच्येव प्रवृत्तं तत् सदसीति वचोऽञ्जसा। Ibid, iii, 45.

146. आत्मनश्च अशेषप्रमेयवैलक्षण्यात्, सर्वानर्थैकत्वज्ञानापनोदि ज्ञानदिवाकरोदयहेतुत्वं वस्तुमात्रयाथात्म्यप्रकाशन-पटीयसस्तत्त्वमस्यादिवचस एव। Ibid, ii, 1.

147. आत्मज्ञानं हि स्वतःसिद्धपरमार्थात्मवस्तुस्वरूपमात्राश्रयादेवाविद्यातदुत्पन्नकारकग्रामप्रध्वंसि स्वात्मोत्पत्तावेव शास्त्राद्यपेक्षते नोत्पन्नमविद्यानिवृत्तौ। Ibid, i, 36.

148. नाप्रमेये स्वतःसिद्धेऽविश्वासः कथमात्मनि। Ibid, i, 89.

149. तत्त्वमस्यादिवाक्यानां स्वतःसिद्धार्थबोधनात्। अर्थान्तरं न संद्रष्टुं शक्यते त्रिदशैरपि॥ Ibid, i, 98.

150. सर्वत्राव्यभिचारात् कूटस्थनित्यत्वं सिद्धं स्वत एव, न प्रमाणापेक्षम्। US., ii, 93, p. 80.

153. नीलाद्यनुपलम्भेऽपि स्वाभाविकस्वरूपोपलम्भस्य दुर्निवारत्वात्। ĀNM., p. 144.

154. तत्राजानतो भेदानुपलम्भात्। Ibid.

156. तस्मात् संवित्स्वरूपतायामात्मनो न दूषणं पश्यामः, सा च स्वयंप्रकाशेति सिद्धा तद्रूपस्यात्मनः स्वप्रकाशता। Ibid, i, 145.

157. उपाध्युपहितस्यानुपलम्भेऽपि स्वरूपस्योपलम्भान्न क्षणिकत्वसिद्धिः। NMV. pp. 143-44.

159. आत्मनो निरतिशयसुखहिताव्यतिरेकसिद्धेः अहितस्य स्वत एवानभिसम्बन्धात्। SNS., i, 30.

160. 'हितं मे स्यादहितं मे मा भूत्' इति मिथ्याज्ञानं प्रवृत्तिनिमित्तम्। Ibid.

161. परमानन्दरूपता तु परप्रेमास्पदया प्रकाशत एव। ANM. p. 173.

162. तदेवं परमप्रेमास्पदभावः परमानन्दभावमन्तरेणात्मनि नावकल्पत इति सिद्धम्। Ibid, p. 175.

163. आत्मनि प्रेमा निरुपाधिकः, तथा चायं परिशेषतः परमानन्दः प्रकाशत इत्युक्तम्। Ibid, p. 176.

164. प्रकाशमानोऽप्ययमानन्दोऽनाद्यनिर्वाच्याविद्योपदर्शितविविधविचित्रनामरूपप्रपञ्चतया विवेकतः स्फुटतरमनवभासमानो न भासत इव सांसारिकदशायाम्। Ibid, pp. 176-77.

165. ब्रह्मसाक्षात्कारोन्मीलितनिखिलाविद्योपप्लवस्तु परितः प्रद्योतमानपरिशुद्धभावो मुक्ताविति भेदसिद्धिः। Ibid, pp. 177-78.

166. परमप्रेमास्पदत्वेन तस्यानन्दरूपत्वात् निर्धर्मकनित्यस्वप्रकाशसुखात्मक एवात्मा। SB., p. 19.

167. नित्योऽक्रमदृगात्मैको व्याप्नोतीव धियोऽनिशम्। SNS., ii, 69.

168. निर्यत्नोऽविक्रियोऽनिच्छन्निच्छन्तीं चाप्यलुप्तदृक्। Ibid, ii, 71.

169. निस्त्रिकालस्थां कूटस्थः क्षणभंगुराम्। Ibid, ii, 74.

170. निरपेक्षश्च सापेक्षां पराचीं प्रत्यगद्वयः पश्यति। Ibid, ii, 75.

171. दुःखिनः साक्षिताऽयुक्ता साक्षिणो दुःखिता तथा॥ Ibid, ii, 76.

172. नर्ते स्याद् विक्रियां दुःखी साक्षिता का विकारिणः। धीविक्रियासहस्राणां साक्ष्यतोऽहमविक्रियः। Ibid, ii, 77.

173. एवं सर्वस्मिन् व्यभिचारिणि, आत्मवस्त्वेवाव्यभिचारि। Ibid, ii, 78.

174. अस्याश्च क्षणभंगुरत्वे स्वयमेवात्मा साक्षी। न हि कूटस्थावबोधमन्तरेण बुद्धेराविर्भावतिरोभावादिसिद्धिरस्ति। Ibid, p. 191.

175. परिणामिधियां वृत्तं नित्याक्रमदृगात्मना। षड्भावविक्रियामेति व्याप्तं खेनाङ्कुरो यथा॥ Ibid, ii, 82.

176. अतो नित्यमविकारो स्वयंदृशिः। Ibid, ii, 83.

177. प्रत्यर्थं तु विभिद्यन्ते बुद्धयो विषयोन्मुखाः। न भिदावगतेस्तद्वत् सर्वास्ताश्चिन्निभायतः॥ Ibid, ii, 86.

178. तस्माज्जगद्धियां वृत्तं ज्योतिरेकं सदाक्षते। Ibid, ii, 89.

179. दृष्टेर्द्रष्टारमात्मानं न पश्ये दृश्यमानया। विज्ञातारमरे केन विजानीयद्धियां पतिम्॥ Ibid, ii, 92.

180. आत्माऽनात्मा च लोकेऽस्मिन् प्रत्यक्षादिप्रमाणतः। सिद्धस्तयोरनात्मा तु सर्वेषामात्मपूर्वकः॥ Ibid, iv, p. 3.

181. इदमित्येव वाह्योऽर्थोह्यहमित्येव बोद्धरि। द्वयं दृष्टं यतो देहे तेनायं मुह्यते जनः॥ Ibid, iv, 6.
विद्यात् अनन्तरमवाह्यार्थं प्रत्यक्स्थं मुनिरञ्जसा। Ibid, iv, 8.

182. ऋते ज्ञानं न सन्त्यर्था अस्ति ज्ञानमृतेऽपि तान्। Ibid, ii, 97.

183. यस्मात् प्रमाणप्रमेयव्यवहार आत्माऽनवबोधाश्रय एव, तस्मात् सिद्धमात्मनोऽप्रमेयत्वम्। Ibid, ii, 98.

184. ग्राहकग्राह्यविभागे योऽविभागवान्। हानोपादानयोः साक्षी हानोपादानवर्जितः॥ Ibid, 108.

185. नित्यागमगतिरूपत्वात् कारकादिर्नचात्मनः। Ibid, ii, 113.

186. नित्यं संविदमाश्रित्य स्वतःसिद्धामविक्रियाम्। सिद्धायन्ते धियो बोधास्तांश्चाश्रित्य घटादयः॥ Ibid, ii, 115.

187. धीवन्नापेक्षते सिद्धिमात्माऽन्यस्मादविक्रियः। निरपेक्षमपेक्ष्यैव सिद्धन्त्यन्ये न तु स्वयम्। Ibid, ii, 110.

188. दृश्यानुरक्तं तद्द्रष्टृ दृश्यं द्रष्ट्रनुरञ्जितम् । अहंवृत्त्योभयं रक्तं तन्नाशेऽद्वैततात्मनः ॥ Ibid, ii, 53.
189. अविक्रियस्य भोक्तृत्वं स्यादहंबुद्धिविभ्रमात् । Ibid, ii, 63.
191. यथा विशुद्ध आकाशे सहसैवाभ्रमण्डलम् । भूत्वा विलीयते तद्वदात्मानीहाखिलं जगत् ॥ Ibid, ii, 86.
192. तत् सिद्धमेतद्-'विज्ञानमर्थप्रकाशनसमये प्रकाशते तदुपाधावनन्तरं सन्देहायोग्यत्वादर्थवत्' इति । ĀNM., p. 138.
194. परिशेषतः स्वप्रकाशतैवास्याश्रयणीया । Ibid, p. 141.
196. न तावदर्थस्वभावो द्रवकठिनयोरिवजड़प्रकाशयो रैकात्म्यविरोधात् । क्षणभंगिनश्च प्रकाशस्य प्रकाश्यैक्यानुपपत्तेः । pp. 141-42.
197. नाप्यर्थान्तिरमर्थधर्मो विज्ञानाधेयमर्थप्रकाशनमिति युक्तम् । Ibid, p. 142.
198. यद्यान्तरमेवार्थप्रकाशनमाश्रीयेत विज्ञानमेव तत् संज्ञान्तरेणापन्नम् । Ibid.
199. तस्माद् विज्ञानमेव स्वपरप्रकाशस्वभावं प्रकाशत इत्याश्रयणीयम् । Ibid.
201. अतोऽनुभूयमानं विषयापरोक्ष्यं नापलपनीयम् । VPS. p. 54.
202. तदसत् । अविज्ञानरूपस्य बहिष्ठस्याप्यापरोक्ष्यदर्शनात् । Ibid.
203 अतो घटादि प्रमेयं विषयत्वेन प्रत्यक्षम् । प्रमितिस्तु स्वप्रकाशत्वेन न प्रत्यक्षा । Ibid, p. 55.
205. अध्यासपरिनिष्पन्नान्तःकरणसम्पिण्डितस्यात्मनो ज्ञानाकारपरिणामात् । PPV., p. 175.
206. अतोऽन्तःकरणपरिणामविशेषश्चैतन्यस्य विषयावच्छेदोपाधि. करणव्यत्पत्त्या ज्ञानं भावव्युत्पत्त्या तु संवेदनमेवार्थप्रकाशो ज्ञाप्तिर्ज्ञानमुच्यते । Ibid,
207. प्रमातृव्यापारः संविज्जनको ज्ञानम् Ibid, p. 174.
209. एकस्याः संविदो विषयविशेषैः सम्बन्धानामुत्पत्तिविनाशाभ्यामेव तत्सिद्धौ संविदोऽप्युत्पत्तिविनाशयोर्गौरवात् । VPS., p. 58.
211. एवमपि प्रमितेः (प्राकट्यस्य) स्वसत्तायां प्रकाशव्यतिरेकादर्शनात् न घटादिवदन्यवेद्यता युज्यते । VPS. p. 55.
212 अतः प्रमातृव्यापारस्य प्रमाणस्य फलभूतायाः प्रमितेः (प्राकट्यस्य) स्वप्रकाशत्वमादर्तव्यम् । Ibid.
215. प्रत्यभिज्ञा तु ज्वालायमिव सन्ततविज्ञानोदयसादृश्यादुपपद्यते । VPS., p. 182. सादृश्याद्दीपवद्धीः US., xvi, 23, p. 253.
218. अहमुल्लेखस्य तत्राध्यासिकत्वात् । VPS., p. 183.
219. न च ज्वालाप्रत्यभिज्ञावद् भ्रान्तत्वम् । तत्र सूक्ष्मदर्शने प्रत्यक्षत एव ज्वालानां भेददर्शनात् । अत्र तदभावात् । तदेवमेकः स्वप्रकाशः आत्मेति सिद्धान्तः । Ibid, p. 189.
220. आधारस्याप्यसत्त्वाच्च तुल्यता निर्निमित्ततः । US., xvi, p. 26.
222. न च शून्येऽहंप्रत्यय उपपद्यते । VPS., p. 182.
224. सर्वप्रकारज्ञानोपसंहारे बुद्धेः कारणात्मनाऽवस्थानम् PK., p. 2.
225. मिरवयवस्य च परमार्थत उपाधिसंसर्गायोगाद् युक्तं तस्मिन् सर्वस्य कल्पितत्वं चेतिभावः । USPY., xvi, 22, p. 252.
226. सदा निर्विशेषचिद्रूपः कूटस्थ एवात्माऽभ्युपेतव्यः । Ibid, xvi, 57, p. 270.
229. तदुत्पत्तिविनाशप्रतीत्योश्चावश्यकल्प्यविषयसम्बन्धविषयतयाप्युपपत्तेः । SB., p. 19.
234. तस्मादिमनिदमात्मकोऽहंप्रत्ययः । VPS., p. 53.
237. अथात्मप्रकाशेऽपि हेतुः, तदसत् । चिद्रूपस्य जडाधीनप्रकाशानुपपत्तेः । VPS., p. 57.
238. तत आत्मा स्वयमेव प्रकाशते चिद्रूपत्वे सत्यव्यवहितत्वादनुभववदिति प्राप्नोति । Ibid.

239. आत्मैव चित्प्रकाश इति बलादंगीकार्यत्वाद् । आत्मानुभवयोरभेदात् । Ibid.

240. अतो नाहंकार आत्मा सषुप्तावनवभासात् । Ibid, p. 58.

241. नापि बुद्धेः कर्तृत्वमात्मन्यारोपयितुं शक्यम् । अख्यातिवादे भ्रान्त्यभावात् । Ibid, p. 189.

242. किं तु चिद्रूपत्वेन दृश्यसाक्षित्वं भोक्तृत्वम् । तस्माद् भोक्तैवात्मेति सांख्यानां पक्षः । Ibid, p. 190.

243. तेषामात्मनो नित्यानुमेयत्वमहमित्यपरोक्षावभासविरुद्धम् । Ibid, p. 54.

244. विषयसंसृष्टान्तःकरणावच्छिन्नं चैतन्यं तदाकारमवभासत इति भावः । PPV., p. 70.

245. सर्वत्राविद्यावृततया अनभिव्यक्तस्वभावमपि चैतन्यमन्तःकरणं येन येनावस्थाविशेषेण विवर्तते, तेन तेनाकारेण व्यज्यते । Ibid.

246. स्वव्यापाराविष्टमिति परिणामसंसर्गादापन्नजाड्याभिभवलक्षणयोग्यत्वमुच्यते । अन्तःकरणं हि स्वस्मिन्निव स्वसंगिरण्यपि चैतन्याभिव्यक्तियोग्यतामापादयतीति भाव । Ibid.

347. अन्तःकरणावच्छिन्नतया प्रमाता विषयावच्छिन्नतया फलमिति भावः । विषयस्यापरोक्ष्यैकरसः फलम् । Ibid.

249. सर्वगतस्याप्यात्मनोऽविद्यावृतप्रकाशस्य परिच्छिन्नान्तःकरणपरिणामोपाध्यभिव्यक्त्यपेक्षया विषयविशेषं प्रति प्रमातृत्वम् । Ibid, p. 71.

250. परिणामसंसृष्टकर्मोपाधिनियमान्नासंसृष्टेषु चैतन्याभिव्यक्तिरिति नैकस्य प्रमातुः सर्वविषयावभास इति भावः । Ibid. असंगस्याप्यन्तःकरणप्रतिबिम्बद्वारा तद्वृत्तिसम्बन्धः । AUT., p. 84.

251. एतत् प्रमातृचैतन्याभिन्नतयैवाभिव्यक्तं तद्विषयचैतन्यं न प्रमात्रन्तरचैतन्याभेदेनाभिव्यक्तमतो न सर्वेषामवभास्यत्वमित्यर्थः । PPV., p. 71.

252. ननु केयमभिव्यक्तिः । आवरणाभिभव एव न स्वरूपातिशयः । Ibid. मनःपरिणामः संविद्व्यञ्जको ज्ञानम् । PĀV., i, 1, 1, p. 33. मनःसंसृष्टे विषये चैतन्यं प्रतिबिम्बते तद् विषयसंवेदनम् । Ibid, pp. 83-84.

254. प्रयत्नोपलम्भानुपलम्भयोरुपपत्तौ वास्तवपुरुषभेदपरिकल्पनस्याप्रामाणिकत्वात् । ĀNM., p. 28.

255. तत् सिद्धमेतन्न प्रतिक्षेत्रं क्षेत्रज्ञभेदः प्रमाणपदवीमध्यास्त इति । Ibid, p. 29.

256. यद्वा आत्मा द्रव्यत्वव्यतिरिक्तापरजात्याधारभेदन नाना न भवति नित्यत्वाद्विभुत्वान्निरवयवद्रव्यत्वाद्वा गगनवत् । Ibid, p. 30.

257. न खल्वात्मैकत्ववादिनो विशेषगुणाधिकरणतामात्मनोऽङ्गीकुर्वते येनायं हेतुः सिध्येत् । Ibid, p. 19.

258. न च वेद्यानां वेदनादीनां वेदितृगुणभावो युक्तः, न चानित्यगुणं नित्यं पश्यामो येनानित्या एव वेदनादयो नित्यस्य वेदितुर्गुणा भवेयुः । Ibid, pp. 19-20.

260. व्यवस्थातो नाना । *Vaiśeṣika Sūtra*, iii, 2, 20. ĀNM., p. 4.

CHAPTER VIII

1. चैतन्याभासखचितं शरीरद्वयकारणम् ॥ आत्माऽज्ञानं तदव्यक्तमव्याकृतमितीर्यते ।
न सन्नासन्न सदसद्भिन्नाभिन्नं न चात्मनः । PKV., 39-40.

2. न सभागं न निर्भागं न चाप्युभयरूपकम् । ब्रह्मात्मैकत्वविज्ञानहेयं मिथ्यात्वकारणात् । Ibid, 41.

4. एकाह्यविद्या अनादिर्भावरूपा अन्या पूर्वपूर्वविभ्रमसंस्कारः, तदविद्याद्वितयं, सत्त्वासत्त्वाभ्यामनिर्वाच्यम् । VKT., i, 1, 1, p. 3.

5. यद्यपि महाप्रलयसमये चान्तःकरणादयः समुदाचरद्वृत्तयः सन्ति, तथापि स्वकारणेऽनिर्वाच्यायामविद्यायां लीनाः सूक्ष्मेण शक्तिरूपेण कर्मविक्षेपकाविद्यावासनाभिः सहावतिष्ठन्ते। Bhām., i, 3, 30, p. 333.

6. ब्रह्मैवेक्षित्रनाद्यनिर्वाच्याविद्यासचिवं जगदुपादानम्। Ibid, i, 1, 5, p. 167.

7. अविद्याऽनर्थहेतुः। ततः सैव कर्तृत्वाद्यनर्थबीजमुपदर्शनीया। PPD., p. 30.

8. यच्चानादि स्वयं मिथ्या मिथ्योपादानमात्मसम्बन्धि च तदज्ञानमिति मिथ्याध्यास एव तथाविधाज्ञानोपादानं कारणमन्तरेणानुपपद्यमानस्तत् कल्पयतीत्युक्तम्। PPV., p. 13.

10. अत्र च साक्षिवेद्यस्याज्ञानस्य प्रमाणैरभावव्यावृत्तिः प्रदर्श्यत इति न तस्य प्रमाणवेद्यत्वप्रसङ्ग इति। Ibid, p. 43.

12. स्वाश्रयावरणमज्ञानं स्वाश्रयैकत्वेन न विरूध्यते। साक्षिचैतन्यस्य चाज्ञानावभासकत्वादतो न चिदाश्रयत्व-विरोधः। Ibid.

13. स्वरूपमात्रसम्बन्ध्यज्ञानं तत्र जीवब्रह्मव्यवहारभेदं प्रवर्तयति। Ibid, 45.

14. मायाऽविद्ययोश्चैकत्वमवोचाम। VPS., p. 49.

18. न चासंभवित्वं, भावाभावविलक्षणस्याज्ञानस्याभावविलक्षणत्वमात्रेण भावत्वोपचारादात्मवदनादिभावत्वेना-निवर्त्यत्वानुमानानुपपत्तेः। TPD., p. 57.

19. अस्मन्मतेऽज्ञानस्य साक्षिसिद्धतया प्रमाणावोध्यत्वात् प्रमाणज्ञानोदयात् प्राक्कालेऽज्ञानं तद्विशेषितोऽर्थः साक्षिसिद्धोऽज्ञात इत्यनुवादगोचरो भवति। Ibid, p. 60.

22. तत्र अनात्मनस्तावत् नाज्ञानेन अभिसम्बन्धः। तस्य हि स्वरूपमेवाज्ञानम्; न हि स्वतोऽज्ञानस्य अज्ञानं घटते। SNS., Ch. III, p. 226.

23. नानात्मविषयम् अज्ञानं सम्भवति इति ग्राह्यम्। एवं तावत् नानात्मनोऽज्ञानित्वम्, नापि तद्विषयम् अज्ञानम्। Ibid.

24. पारिशेष्यात् आत्मन एवास्त्वज्ञानम्। Ibid, p. 227.

25. अज्ञानानपेक्षस्य च आत्मनः स्वत एव स्वरूपसिद्धेः युक्तम् आत्मन एवाज्ञत्वम्। आत्मविषयम्। Ibid.

26. अज्ञानमात्रनिमित्तत्वात् तद्विभागस्य, सर्पात्मतेव रज्ज्वाः। Ibid.

27. तस्मादनादिनिधनं ब्रह्मतत्त्वमेवाविद्याश्रय इति वाच्यम्। ĀNM., p. 313.

34. जडस्याज्ञानाश्रयत्वे भ्रान्तिसम्यग्ज्ञानयोरपि तदाश्रयत्वप्रसंगात्। Ibid.

35. अनुपपन्नद्वयाश्रयत्वकल्पनाद्वरं संप्रतिपन्नस्वरूपाश्रयत्वोपादानम् मोक्षावस्थासंबन्धिन एव संबन्धाश्रयत्वात्। PPV., 45. आत्मन एवाविद्या आत्मन्येव च। IS., i, 140, p. 211.

36. अस्माकं त्वविद्यैवावच्छेदोपादानम्। द्वैधीभावोऽप्यविद्यानिष्ठ एव सन् आत्मनि अध्यस्यते। VPS., p. 47.

37. न चान्तःकरणमन्तरेणाविद्यासम्बन्धो न दृष्टचरः सुषुप्ते संमतत्वात्। Ibid, p. 48.

38. तदाऽप्यन्तःकरणचैतन्यतत्सम्बन्धानामेव विशिष्टत्वे चैतन्यस्ययाश्रयत्वं दुर्वारम्। Ibid.

39. अतश्चिन्मात्राश्रितमज्ञानं जीवपक्षपातित्वाज् जीवाश्रितमुच्यते। Ibid.

40. न हि साक्षिचैतन्यमज्ञाननिवर्तकं प्रत्युत तत्साधकमेव। अन्यथैतदज्ञानं सर्वैः प्रमाणैर्न्यायैश्च विरूध्यमानं कथं सिध्येत्। Ibid, p. 50.

41. न चाविचारितरमणीयाया आत्मानमाच्छादयितुमसामर्थ्यं शङ्कनीयम्। Ibid.

42. अनुभयते हि स्वयंज्योतिषोऽपि भोक्तुर्देहादिसंघाताद् व्यावृतत्वमज्ञानतिरोहितमेव। Ibid.

44. अविद्या स्वाश्रयाभिन्नविषया स्यात् तमो यतः। VSM., 6, p. 23.

45. तस्मात् जीवब्रह्मविभागशून्यमात्मानमाश्रित्य तमेव विषयीकरोति इति अज्ञानविषयत्वमात्मनः सिद्धम्। Ibid, pp. 29-30.

46. प्राप्तज्ञानानामग्रहणवतां चेतनानामेवावृतत्वाभिधानान्नान्तःकरणाश्रयमज्ञानं किन्तु चैतन्याश्रयम्। PPV., p. 46.

51. जाड्यदृश्यहेतुभ्यां मिथ्यात्वं वा प्रसाध्यताम्। PM., p. 11.

56. मिथ्येति अनिर्वचनीयता उच्यते। PPD., p. 4. पञ्चपादिकावचनात् सदसदनधिकरणत्वरूपमनिर्वाच्यत्वम्। AS., p. 48.

57. प्रपञ्चनिषेधाधिकरणीभूतब्रह्माभिन्नत्वान्निषेधस्य तात्विकत्वेऽपि नाद्वैतहानिकरत्वम्। AS., pp. 96-97.

59. ज्ञाननिवर्त्यत्वं वा मिथ्यात्वम्। ज्ञानप्रयुक्तावस्थितिसामान्यविरहप्रतियोगित्वं हि ज्ञाननिवर्त्यत्वम्। Ibid, p. 160.

60. स्वाश्रयनिष्ठात्यन्ताभावप्रतियोगित्वं वा मिथ्यात्वम्। Ibid, p. 182.

61. विषमसत्ताकभावाभावयोरविरोधः पूर्वमुपपादितः। Ibid, p. 189.

62. सदसद्विविक्तत्वं वा मिथ्यात्वम्। प्रमाणसिद्धभिन्नत्वेन मिथ्यात्वं सिध्यति। Ibid, pp. 195 & 197.

63. मिथ्यात्वमिथ्यात्वेऽपि प्रपञ्चसत्यत्वानुपपत्तेः। परस्परविरहरूपत्वेऽपि विषमसत्ताकयोरविरोधात्, व्यावहारिकमिथ्यात्वेन व्यावहारिकसत्यत्वापहारेऽपि काल्पनिकसत्यताऽनपहारात्। Ibid, pp. 210, 216-17.

67. तस्मात् मिथ्यात्वेऽपि अर्थक्रियाकारित्वसम्भवात् मिथ्यैव प्रपञ्चो, न सत्य इति। SLS., p. 497.

68. न हि भेदप्रपञ्चस्य तत्त्वश्चिदात्माऽभेदं वर्णयामः, किन्तु न भिन्नो नाप्यभिन्नो नापि भिन्नाभिन्नः, किं तर्ह्यनाद्यविद्याविलसित इति। ĀNM., p. 302.

71. सत्यानृतरूपेणात्यन्तविविक्तयोर्वास्तवैक्यस्यायोगात्। तस्मादध्यस्तमेवैकत्वम्। VPS., p. 14.

73. अध्यासो नाम अतद्रूपे तद्रूपावभास स मिथ्येति भवितुं युक्तम्। PPD., p. 4.

74. आत्माऽनात्मानौ विरुद्धस्वभावौ विषयिविषयत्वात्तेत्ररूपवदिति। VPS., p. 10.

77. परमप्रेमास्पदत्वेन च तस्यानन्दरूपत्वात्, निर्धर्मकनित्यस्वप्रकाशसुखात्मक एवात्मा इत्यादयः। SB., p. 19.

78. अध्यासो भेदाग्रहेण व्याप्तः, तद्विरुद्धश्चेहास्ति भेदाग्रहः, स भेदाग्रहं निवर्तयंस्तद्व्याप्तमध्यासमपि निवर्तयति। Bhām., 1, 1, 1, p. 8.

93. न खल्वभावो बाह्यस्यार्थस्यार्थस्याध्यवसातुं शक्यते। उपलब्धेः। न चोपलभ्यमानस्यैवाभावो भवितुमर्हति। ŚBS., ii, 2, 28, pp. 547-48.

94. उपलब्धिव्यतिरेकोऽपि बलादर्थस्याभ्युपगन्तव्य उपलब्धेरेव। न हि कश्चिदुपलब्धिमेव स्तम्भः कुड्यं चेत्युपलभ्यते। Ibid, p. 548.

95. बाध्यते हि स्वप्नोपलब्धं वस्तु प्रतिबुद्धस्य। नैवं जागरितोपलब्धं वस्तु स्तम्भादिकं कस्यांचिदप्यवस्थायां बाध्यते। Ibid, ii, 2, 29, p. 555.

96. यथा च स्वप्नमाये दृष्टे असद्रूपे तथा विश्वमिदं द्वैतं समस्तमसद्दृष्टम्। MKSB., ii, 31.

97. ज्ञानज्ञेयज्ञातृभेदरहितं परमार्थतत्त्वदर्शनम्। Ibid, iv, 1,

99. अत्र विज्ञानवादिनस्तु विज्ञानाभेदनिमित्त एव विषयस्यापरोक्षावभास इत्याहुः। तन्निराकरोति प्रमेयं कर्मत्वेनापरोक्षमिति। PPV., p. 50.

100. अतोऽनुभूयमानं विषयापरोक्ष्यं नापलपनीयम्। VPS., p. 54.

101. अविज्ञानरूपस्य बहिष्ठस्याप्यपरोक्ष्यदर्शनात्। Ibid.

102. प्रत्येतव्यप्रतीत्योश्च भेदः प्रामाणिकः कुतः। प्रतीतिमात्रमेवैतद्भाति विश्वं चराचरम्। VSM., 18, p. 103.

103. आत्मन्येव जगत्सर्वं दृष्टिमात्रं सतत्त्वकम् । Ibid, p. 104.

104. यस्य चित्तमयी लीला जगदेतच्चराचरम् । Ibid, p. 105.

114. गुणाश्रयो द्रव्यमित्यसङ्गतम् । संख्यारूपगुणवत्तया रूपादेरपि प्रतीतेः । KKK., p. 579.

115. 'अव्याप्तेरप्यतिव्याप्तेर्द्रव्यं नैव गुणाश्रयः । आद्ये क्षणे गुणाभावाद्गुणादावपि वीक्षणात्' । TPD., p. 175.

116. 'द्रव्यजातियोगित्वमपि नो द्रव्यलक्षणम् । तज्जातिव्यञ्जकाभावात्तन्मानस्यानिरूपणात् ।' Ibid, p. 178.

118. गुणाश्रयत्वं द्रव्यत्वमिति मन्दप्रतारणा । ACM., p. 5.

120. 'सामान्यवानगुण इत्याद्यस्य न लक्षणम् । अन्योन्याश्रयतापत्तेर्गुणस्याद्याप्यसिद्धितः ।' TPD., p. 181.

121. सिद्धे गुणे अगुण इति लक्षणसिद्धिस्तत्सिद्धौ च गुणसिद्धिरितीतरेतराश्रयत्वदूषणग्रस्तत्वात् । Ibid.

123. समवायिकारणेश्वरेच्छादेशकालादृष्टापेक्षणात् । Ibid, p. 184.

124. तस्मात्संयोगवत्कर्माऽप्यव्याप्यवृत्त्यैवेति । ACM., p. 13.

125. 'प्रत्यक्षादनुमानाद्वा न जातिः सेद्धुमर्हति । व्यञ्जकैरन्यथासिद्धेस्तद्वृत्तेश्चानिरूपणात् ।' TPD., p. 303.

126. 'अद्रव्यत्वान्न संयोगः साङ्कर्यान्नेतरावपि । पदार्थान्तरतापत्तेर्नान्यसम्बन्धसंभवः ।' Ibid, p. 305.

128. 'अतिव्याप्तया निराकुर्याद्यं पक्षचतुष्टयम् अनेकत्वानिरुक्तेश्च पक्षमन्त्यं प्रतिक्षिपेत् ।' Ibid, p. 190.

131. परमाणुष्वेव तादृशस्वरूपाभ्युपगमेन व्यावृत्तिसिद्धेः किमेतैः । ACM., p. 14.

143. एवं च शून्यतैव तात्विकी विश्वस्यापद्येतेति । ĀNM., p. 46.

144. न खलु स्वहेतुसमासादितस्वभावभावात्मतो भेदस्यान्यापेक्षा निरूप्येत । Ibid, p. 47.

145. तदपेक्षायां निरपेक्षभावस्वभावताविघातात् तद्विरुद्धधर्माध्यासस्यैकत्रानुपपत्तेः । Ibid.

146. तस्माद् भावस्वभावताभावाद् भेदस्य न विधायकमेवाध्यक्षं व्यावृत्तिगोचरमिति सिद्धम् । Ibid, p. 49.

147. 'मूलक्षयकरीं प्राहुरनवस्था हि दूषणम् ।' Ibid, pp. 49-50.

149. तत् सिद्धमेतन्न प्रामाणिको भेदनिर्भासः इति । Ibid, p. 55.

150. भेदसंवेदनं न प्रमाणनिबन्धनम् अनिरूपितप्रमाणकत्वाद् भेदसंवेदनत्वाद्वा स्वप्नभेदावभासनवद् इति । Ibid.

151. निखिलो भेदः अनाद्यविद्यातद्वासनाविरचितभ्रममात्रसिद्धः । Ibid, p. 56.

152. भेदो मिथ्या भेदत्वात् । दर्पणादिगतमुखादिभेदवदिति । PM., p. 7.

154. अभेदं नोल्लिखन्ती धीर्न भेदोल्लेखनक्षमा । तथाचाद्ये प्रमा सा स्यान्नान्त्ये स्वापेक्ष्यवैशसात् ।
KKK., i, 18, p. 113.

155. तस्मात्स्वरूपभेदे प्रमाणं भवत्प्रत्यक्षमद्वैते एव प्रमाणं भवति । Ibid, p. 117.

156. तस्माद् घटस्य न स्वरूपनिरूपणे पटप्रतीत्यपेक्षा । Ibid, p. 118.

158. अन्योन्याभावोऽपि यस्माद् भेद एष्टव्यस्तमात्मन्येवान्तर्भावयेदुक्तयुक्तिभिः । Ibid. p. 119.

164. न वयं भेदस्य सर्वथैवासत्त्वमभ्युपगच्छामः, किं नाम, पारमार्थिकं सत्त्वम् । अविद्याविद्यमानत्वं तु तदीयमिष्यते एव, तदेव कार्यकारणभावोपयोगि । Ibid, p. 129.

190. तथा च तेनैवानुगतव्यवहारोपपत्तौ कृतं विलक्षणलक्षणपरीक्षाप्रयासेन । TPD., p. 310.

191. यादृगाश्रयेऽणुमहदादिपरिमाणसमवायः परेणाङ्गीक्रियते तादृगाश्रयविशेषादेव तद्व्यवहारोपपत्तौ तदतिरिक्त परिमाणकल्पनायां कल्पनागौरवाच्च । Ibid.

199. महत्त्वापकर्षतारतम्यस्य क्वचिद्विश्रान्तिसाधने त्रसरेणुष्वेव तद्विश्रान्तिसिद्धेः सिद्धसाधनत्वात् ।
TPD., p. 283.

218. सर्वानिर्वाच्यत्ववादिनो दुर्निरूप्यत्वस्यालंकारत्वात् । VPS., p. 211.

219. प्रतीतिमात्रशरणत्वे चानिर्वचनीयवादापातः । सर्वज्ञः सर्वशक्तिरीश्वर एव कारणम् । Ibid.

220. असत्यप्रतिष्ठं ते जगदाहुरनीश्वरम् । अपरस्परसम्भूतं किमन्यत्कामहेतुकम् ।। BG., xvi, 8.

221. स्वाभाविकमेव जगद्वैचित्र्यम् । MSBG., ŚRBG., Ibid.

222. सर्वे भावाः क्षणिका अर्थक्रियाकारित्वाद् व्यतिरेके शशविषाणवत् । VPS., p. 78.

223. अतो भावानामेकस्मिन्नेव क्षणेऽर्थक्रियाकारित्वलक्षणत्वम् । Ibid.

CHAPTER IX

19. दुःखराशेर्विचित्रस्य सेयं भ्रान्तिश्चिरन्तनी । मूलं संसारवृक्षस्य तद्बाधस्तत्त्वदर्शनात् । SNS., ii, 103. साऽविद्या संसृतेर्बीजं तन्नाशो मुक्तिरात्मनः । Ibid, i, 7.

20. एकात्म्यप्रतिपत्तिर्या स्वात्मानुभवसंश्रया । Ibid.

21. नित्यनिरतिशयसुखाभिव्यक्तिर्निःशेषदुःखोच्छेदलक्षणमाचार्याः, स पुनरविद्यास्तमय एवेति । Ibid, p. 271.

23. तथा चाऽद्वैतात्मविद्यावशादेवाशेषाविद्याविनिवृत्तिर्निःश्रेयसमिति चतुरस्रम् । Ibid, p. 289.

25. वेदनब्रह्मभवनयोरेककालत्वनिर्देशात् । PPD., p. 89.

26. ब्रह्मदर्शन-सर्वात्मभावयोरेककालत्वनिर्देशान्मध्ये क्रियान्तरं वारयति । Ibid, pp. 89-90.

27. इह पुनर्न सर्वात्मभावस्य ब्रह्मदर्शनातिरेकेण प्रयत्नान्तरापेक्षा विद्यते । Ibid, p. 90.

28. मिथ्याज्ञानापायश्च ब्रह्मात्मैकत्वविज्ञानाद्भवति, न क्रियातः । मिथ्यैव भेदावभास स्तस्य प्रतिपक्षाद् अभेदावभासादपनय इति गम्यते । Ibid.

29. तस्मान्न संपदादिवत् पुरुषव्यापारपरतन्त्रा ब्रह्मविद्या, किन्तु प्रत्यक्षादिजनितज्ञानवदपरामृष्टहानोपादानवस्तु-स्वरूपमात्रनिष्ठेत्यभ्युपगन्तव्यम् । Ibid, p. 91.

30. तस्मान्मिथ्याज्ञाननिवृत्तिमात्रं मोक्ष इति श्रुतिन्यायाभ्यां सिद्धम् । Ibid.

31. एवं च नित्यमुक्तात्मस्वरूपसमर्पणान्न मोक्षस्यानित्यत्वदोषः । Ibid, p. 91.

32. ततो वास्तवसम्बन्धाभावे सत्यशरीरत्वं स्वाभाविकं, सशरीरकत्वं तु मिथ्याज्ञानकृतमित्यभ्युपेयम् । VPS., p. 239.

33. न च मिथ्याज्ञानं कर्मभिर्निवर्तते । नाप्यशरीर एव मोक्षः कर्मभिरन्यथा परिणम्यत इति वक्तुं शक्यम् । कूटस्थस्य परिणामायोगात् । Ibid.

63. अनारब्धकार्ये एव तु पूर्वे तदवधेः । भोगेन त्वितरे क्षपयित्वा सम्पद्यते । BS., iv, 1, 15 & 19.

64. तद्धि समुदाचरद्वृत्तितया इतरेभ्यः पशुवृत्तिभ्यो बलवत् । Bhām., iv, 1, 15, p. 958.

65. अनिर्वाच्याच्चानिर्वाच्योत्पत्तौ नानुपपत्तिः । Ibid, p. 959.

66. निरतिशयस्तु स्थितप्रज्ञः । स च सिद्ध एव । Ibid.

67. न वयं साहित्यं ब्रूमः, कदाचिदसम्प्रज्ञातात्मैकत्वदर्शनं कदाचिदारब्धकर्मोपस्थापितदोषनिमित्तद्वैतदर्शनं चेति । PPV., p. 284.

68. प्रारब्धकर्मवशतश्च तत्त्वदर्शनं सशरीरस्यैव सम्भवति, व्यासादीनां च सशरीराणामेवापरोक्षदर्शनं श्रूयते । Ibid.

69. तत्त्वदर्शिनोऽपि द्वैतदर्शनाभास उपपद्यते । Ibid.

72. यद्यपि तत्त्वज्ञानमशेषकर्मोपादानभूतामविद्यां निवर्तयति, तथापि प्रारब्धकर्मणो न निवर्तकम् । स्वयं तत्फलत्वात् । Ibid, p. 263.

73. लेशानुवृत्तौ तज्जन्यकर्मादेरनुवृत्तितः । उत्पन्नात्मावबोधस्य जीवन्मुक्तिः प्रसिध्यति । TPD., p. 385.

75. "भूयश्चान्ते विश्वमायानिवृत्तिः ।" Ibid, p. 386. स्थितप्रज्ञस्तावन्न विगलितनिखिलाविद्यः सिद्धः किन्तु साधकः । BRS., iii, 107½, p. 130.

78. अनिर्वचनीयेऽज्ञानांशाभ्युपगमे बाधकाभावात् । Ibid, ACM., p. 75.

80. जीवन्मुक्तिस्तत्त्वज्ञानवासनाक्षयमनोनाशाऽभ्यासात् । TA., p. 358.

81. ब्रह्मवित् जीवन्मुक्तो भोगेन प्रारब्धभोगे क्षीणे वर्तमानशरीरपातेऽखण्डरसब्रह्मानन्दात्मनाऽवतिष्ठते । Ibid, pp. 413-14.

82. अन्ये तु भाविशरीराऽनारम्भो विदेहमुक्तिः । Ibid, p. 349.

88. शास्त्रस्य जीवन्मुक्तिप्रतिपादने प्रयोजनाभावात् । VSM., p. 274.

92. कुर्वन्नेवेह कर्माणि जिजीविषेच्छतंसमाः Īśa Up., 1 ; SNS., i, 18.

93. प्रवृत्तिनिवृत्ती प्रति कर्तुः स्वातन्त्र्यम् । SNS., i, 81, p. 106.

95. अज्ञानहानिमात्रत्वान्मुक्तेः कर्म न साधनम् । कर्मापमार्ष्टि नाज्ञानं तमसीवोत्थितं तमः ।। Ibid, i, 24.

96. नित्यस्याफलवत्त्वाच्च न मोक्षः कर्मसाधनः । Ibid, i, 28.

98. तन्मूला संसृतिर्यस्मात्तन्नाशोऽज्ञानहानतः । Ibid, i, 43.

99. उत्पाद्यमाप्यं संस्कार्यं विकार्यं च क्रियाफलम् । नैव मुक्तिर्यतस्तस्मात् कर्म तस्या न साधनम् ।। Ibid, i, 53.

100. असक्तो हि ईश्वरार्थं कर्म कुर्वन् परं मोक्षमाप्नोति पुरुषः सत्त्वशुद्धिद्वारेणेत्यर्थः । ŚBG., iii, 19.

101. अयथावस्त्वविद्या स्याद् विद्या तस्याविरोधिनी । समुच्चयस्तयोरेवं रविशर्वर्योरिव । SNS., i, 56.

102. स्वरूपलाभमात्रेण यस्त्वविद्यां निहन्ति नः । न तदङ्गं प्रधानं वा ज्ञानं स्यात् कर्मणः क्वचित् ।। Ibid, i, 64.

103. अज्ञानमनिराकुर्वन् ज्ञानमेव न सिध्यति । विपन्नकारकग्रामं ज्ञानं कर्म न ढौकते । Ibid, i, 65.

104. हेतुस्वरूपकार्याणि प्रकाशतमसोरिव । विरोधीनि ततो नास्ति सांगत्यं ज्ञानकर्मणोः । Ibid, i, 66.

108. ननु ज्ञानमपि ध्यानवन्मानसक्रियेति चेत्, न । फलतः कारणतश्च ज्ञानक्रिययोर्वैलक्षण्यात् । ज्ञानं न पुरुषेच्छातन्त्रमिति क्रियातो विलक्षणमेव । VPS., p. 249.

109. तत्र तत्सम्पादनलक्षणक्रियायामेव पुरुषस्य स्वातन्त्र्यं, न ज्ञानाज्ञानयोः । Ibid, p. 251.

111. एवं स्मृतिज्ञानमपि संस्कारोद्बोधाधीनं, न पुरुषप्रयत्नाधीनम् । Ibid.

112. न चासौ साध्यसाधनभावो मिथ्या । ततो भावनस्यायथावस्तुत्वेऽपि न शास्त्रस्य काचिद्धानिः । भावनस्य च पुरुषतन्त्रत्वमस्माभिरभ्युपेयत एव । तस्य ध्यानक्रियारूपत्वात् । Ibid, pp. 251-52.

113. ननु ध्यानमप्यनुभवतन्त्रमेव धारावाहिकस्मृतिज्ञानरूपत्वादिति चेत् न । अननुभूते स्मृत्ययोगात् । Ibid, p. 252.

114. क्रियाभाजो मनस आकारविशेषसमर्पकत्वात् । Ibid.

115. ततश्च श्रुतिसमर्पिताकारविशिष्टाया मानसक्रियायाः प्रवाहो ध्यानं, न तु स्मृतिप्रवाहः । Ibid.

116. अपरोक्षतयाऽनुभूतेष्वपि वस्तुषु स्मृतिर्ध्यानाद्विशिष्यते । Ibid, p. 253.

117. अतः कर्तुमकर्तुमन्यथा वा कर्तुमशक्या यथानुभूतं वस्त्वविलङ्घयन्ती तत्संस्कारोद्बोधमात्राधीना स्मृतिरित्युच्यते । Ibid.

119. न हि ज्ञानं प्रयत्नान्तरमेव जायते, किन्तु तेन प्रयत्नेन प्रमाणादिसामग्र्यां सम्पादितायां पश्चादुत्पद्यते । Ibid, p. 256.

120. न च ध्यानमपि प्रयत्नसम्पादितसामग्रीतन्त्रं न प्रयत्नतन्त्रमिति वक्तुं शक्यम् । प्रयत्नातिरिक्तसामग्र्यभावात् । Ibid.

123. न च पराभिमतकार्यानङ्गीकारे प्रवर्तकाभावः । कृतियोग्येष्टसाधनस्य प्रवर्तकत्वात् । Ibid, p. 237.

124. इष्टसाधनस्यैव कृतियोग्यस्य कार्यताभ्युपगभात् । Ibid, p. 238.

125. एकमेव वस्तु कृतिनिरूप्यतया कार्यमुच्यते, इष्टनिरुप्यतया चेष्टसाधनमिति । Ibid, p. 238.

126. तस्मात् कृतियोग्येष्टसाधनमेव विध्यर्थो न तु नियोगः । तत्राविद्यानिवृत्तिलक्षणो मोक्ष इष्टस्तस्य च साधनं ब्रह्मात्मैक्यतत्त्वज्ञानम् । Ibid.

127. तस्मात् ब्रह्मण्येव वेदान्तप्रामाण्यम् । Ibid, p. 238. न तावन्नियोगब्रह्मणी उभे अपि वेदान्तैः प्रमातुं शक्येते । विरूद्धत्रिकद्वयापत्तिप्रसङ्गात् । Ibid, p. 236.

129. न च स्मृतिसन्तान एव ध्यानम् । स्मृतिसन्तानस्य वस्तुगोचरत्वाद् ध्यानस्यारोपितविषयतयाऽपि सम्भवात् । Ibid.

130. नैतत् सारम् । स्वतःप्रामाण्यहानिप्रसङ्गात् । Ibid, p. 237.

132. नैवम् । अपुरुषतन्त्रत्वाद् वस्तुयाथात्म्यज्ञानस्य । SNS., i, 88 p. 113.

133. अनात्मादर्शनेनैव परमात्मानमुपास्महे । Ibid.

135. नियोग एव प्रवर्त्तकः, स च कालत्रयविविक्तः शब्दैकसमधिगम्यः कार्यरूपो ऽर्थविशेष इति । ĀNM., p. 230.

136. उपपादितं च तादृश्याः श्रेयःसाधनतायाः प्रवृत्तिहेतुत्वम् । Ibid, p. 231.

137. न चासौ नियोगः, तस्य कालत्रयविविक्तिस्य खपुष्पकल्पस्य प्रेरणाश्रयत्वासम्भवात् । Ibid, 242.

138. ततो वेदेऽपि लिङ्‌आदिभ्यः प्रवृत्तिहेतुः कश्चिद्धर्म एवावगम्यते । Ibid.

139. कालातिरेकिणो हि सत्ता कालसम्बन्धव्याप्ता, सचाकालात्मनो नियोगाद्व्यापको व्यावर्तमानः स्वव्याप्यामपि सत्तां व्यावर्तयेद् दहन इव धूमम् । Ibid, p. 255.

140. तदेवं प्रयोगमधिरोहति—वेदः सिद्ध एवार्थे प्रमाणं प्रमाणत्वात् प्रत्यक्षवत्, पराभिगतकार्यवैपरीत्यं च सिद्धशब्दार्थः । Ibid, pp. 256-57.

187. इड़ापिङ्गले दक्षिणोत्तरे नाड्यौ हृदयान्निःसृते निरुध्य तस्मादेव हृदयादूर्द्ध्वगमनशीलया सुषुम्नया नाड्या हार्दं प्राणमानीय कण्ठावलम्बितं स्तनसदृशं मांसखण्डं प्रापय्य तेनाध्वना भ्रुवोर्मध्ये तमावेश्य अप्रमादवान् ब्रह्मरन्ध्राद्विनिष्क्राम्य परमपुरुषमुपगच्छति । AGBG., viii, 11.

189. यदा योगी पद्मासने उपविश्य गुल्फाभ्यां गुदमूलं निष्पीड्य प्राणधारणया सुषुम्नामार्गेण मूलाधारात् कुण्डलिनीमुत्थाप्य स्वाधिष्ठानमणिपूरानाहतविशुद्धाज्ञानिर्वाणाख्यषटचक्रभेदक्रमेण सहस्रदलकमलकर्णिकायां विद्यमानपरमात्मना सह संयोज्य तत्रैव चित्तमचलं कृत्वा स्वात्मानन्दरसं पिबति । SBD., on VS., p. 47.

206. भावस्यैव चाभावो निवृत्तिरभावस्यैव च भावः । न चा ज्ञानं भावोऽभावो वा । तस्यानिर्वाच्यताऽभ्युपगमात् । ĀNM., p. 354.

207. न चैवं सदद्वैतव्याहतिरनिर्मोक्षो वा । तस्याः सद्रूपताऽनङ्गीकाराद् अनिर्वाच्यताभावाच्चानविद्योपादापादानत्वात् । Ibid, p. 356.

208. अतोऽनिर्वाच्या वाऽविद्याव्यावृतिः । Ibid.

209. आत्मैवाज्ञानहानिर्वेति । Ibid, p. 357.

210. नैवम् । निवृत्तिमदुपाधित्वेनापि तदुपपत्तेरनिर्वाच्यतायाः स्वाभाविकप्रतिबन्धानिरूपणान्निवृत्तेरस्तु निवृत्यन्तरानङ्गीकारात् । Ibid, p. 358.

211. तदेवं सदसद्वैलक्षण्येऽप्यनिर्वाच्यलक्षणे न काचनानुपपत्तिः । Ibid, p. 359.

212, सदसत्सदसदनिर्वचनीयप्रकारेभ्योह्यन्यप्रकारैर्वाऽज्ञानस्य निवृत्तिर्युक्ता । IS., p. 85.
आत्मातिरिक्तस्य अवस्त्वावगमात् पञ्चमप्रकारा निवृत्तिर्मिथ्येत्येव रहस्यम् । ISV., p. 452.

213. भावस्याभावो निवृत्तिरभावस्य च भावः भावाभावविलक्षणस्याज्ञानस्य कथमभावो निवृत्तिः स्यात्। TPD., p. 380.

214. नापि पञ्चमप्रकारा सदसद्विलक्षणतया तस्या अप्यनिर्वचनीयत्वप्रसङ्गात्। सदसद्विलक्षणमनिर्वचनीयमिति-लक्षणाङ्गीकारात्। Ibid, p. 381.

215. नाप्यात्मैवाज्ञाननिवृत्तिः, आत्मनः सदातनत्वेनाज्ञाननिवृत्तेरपि तथात्वे संसाराभावप्रसङ्गात्। आत्मन-स्तत्त्वज्ञानसाध्यत्वप्रसङ्गाच्च। Ibid, p. 382.

216. अनृतजडदुःखानात्मद्वैतविरोधिसत्यज्ञानानन्ताद्वयलक्षणं ब्रह्मैव वेदान्तवाक्यजनितब्रह्मैकाकारान्तःकरणपरिणाम-दर्पणप्रतिबिम्बितं सविलासाज्ञाननिवृरिति युक्तमभ्युपगन्तुम्। Ibid.

217. तस्मादुत्पन्नात्मविज्ञानस्य ज्ञात आत्मैव सविलासाज्ञाननिवृत्तिरिति स्थितम्। Ibid, p. 383.

233. तस्मादात्मैवानन्दः, अन्यथा मोक्षोऽपुरुषार्थः स्यात्, सुखाभावात्। सर्वस्यात्मार्थत्वेन प्रियत्वाच्चात्मेवे प्रियः। अत आत्मैव मुख्यं सुखम्, इतरत्तादर्थत्वात् सुखम् अतोऽमुख्यम्। IS., pp. 29 & 30.

234. आत्मनः सुखरूपत्वं श्रुतियुक्त्यनुभवसिद्धं नापलपनीयम्। तस्मादात्मैवानन्द इति स्थितम्। आत्मत्वादानन्द-विग्रहा अनुभूतिः। Ibid, p. 31.

236. कश्चिद् ब्रह्मानन्दस्याभावः काल्पनिको यावदविद्यमनुवर्तते। SLS., p. 702, SL., p. 110.

237. न हि स्वव्यवहारानुकूलचैतन्याभेदमात्रमापरोक्ष्यम् किं त्वनावृतार्थस्य तदभेदः। Ibid, 704.

238. तथा च अनावृतत्वांशस्तत्त्वसाक्षात्कारे सतय एवेति निरतिशयसुखापरोक्षस्य पुरुषार्थस्य विद्याप्राप्यत्वं युक्तमित्याहुः। Ibid, SL., pp. 110-11.

239. अज्ञाननिवृत्तौ तु चिदानन्दभेदप्रविलयात्तादाऽपरोक्ष्यमिति तस्य विद्यासाध्यत्वमित्याहुः। Ibid, p. 705.

240. ज्ञेयभिन्नमिदं यस्माज् ज्ञेयवस्त्वनुसार्यतः। न प्रवृत्तिं निवृत्तिं वा कटाक्षेणापि वीक्षते॥ SNS. iv, 54.

241. सम्यग् ज्ञानशिखिप्लुष्टमोहतत्कार्यरूपिणः। सकृन्निवृत्तेर्बाध्यस्य किं कार्यमवशिष्यते॥ Ibid, iv, 59.

255. तथा ब्रह्मणः स्वात्मप्रकाशस्यानन्दस्वभावो न संवेद्यः, कर्मत्वाभावात्। न चासंवेद्यः, स्वप्रकाशत्वात्। BRS., p. 4.

256. तस्मादात्मप्रकाशप्रकृष्टानन्दस्वभावमेव ब्रह्मेति युक्तम्। आनन्दस्वभाव आत्मा, परमप्रेमास्पदत्वात्। Ibid, p. 5.

257. ब्रह्मापि स्वयंप्रकाशं सच्च नास्ति न प्रकाशते चाज्ञानाम्। IS., i, 9. p. 71.

258. अतः प्रमाणं तत्रार्थवत्, यथा संवित्तेः सत्त्वात्मकप्रकाशकत्व-प्रतिपादनमर्थवत्। Ibid.

259. तस्मात् स्वयंप्रकाशमपि प्रमाणप्रकाश्यमेव। तस्य चाप्रकाशनमज्ञानमेवेति तन्निवर्तनमेव तत्प्रकाशत्वं प्रमाणस्य। स्वयंप्रकाशस्यापि, अप्रकाशत्वादप्रकाशकल्पत्वात्। Ibid, p. 72.

260. तस्मात्प्रकाशकमेव प्रमाणमित्यस्मिन्नपि पक्षे अज्ञाननिवर्तकत्वं सिद्धं तस्य प्रकाशकत्वायैव। यदा तु निवर्तकमेव, अर्थात् प्रकाशनमिति स्थितिः—तदा सुतरां निवर्तकत्वं सिध्येत्। Ibid.

261. अविद्याया निवर्त्यत्वान्मानं चार्थवदात्मनि। अनात्मत्वादविद्यायास्तद्ध्वंसे नात्मनः क्षतिः॥ Ibid, i, 156, p. 216.

263. नापि प्रपंचाभावावगमाय (अलम्), प्रत्यक्षादिषु सत्सु तदसम्भवात्। आगमोऽपि न तावताप्रप्रणेतृकोऽत्र क्रमते, प्रमाणान्तराधिगतगोचरत्वात्। BRS., pp. 22-23.

264. आम्नायतः प्रसिद्धिं च कवयोऽस्य प्रचक्षते। भेदप्रपंचविलयद्वारेण च निरूपणम्। Ibid, i, 2, p. 23.

265. सार्वात्म्यविद एव तेन ध्यानोपदेशः। अधिगतसार्वात्म्यस्य सतो ध्यानोपदेशः। Ibid, p. 17.

266. वाग्रूपान्वितं च जगत्; अतो वाचः विपरिणामो विवर्तो वावसीयते। Ibid, p. 18.

267. वाक्शक्तिरेव वा चितिः ; तत्प्रतिसंहारेऽपि सूक्ष्मा वाक्शक्तिरित्येके ; सर्वथा वाग्रूपाधीनो ज्ञेयबोध इति सर्वं ज्ञेयं वाग्रूपान्वितं गम्यत इति तद्विकारस्तद्विवर्तो वा । Ibid, p. 19.

268. न चात्मा शब्दः, अप्रसिद्धेः शब्दज्ञत्वाच्च । न च ज्ञेयो ज्ञाता स्यात् घटवत् । अज्ञेयस्याशब्दत्वात् ज्ञेयस्य च घटादिवदब्रह्मत्वाद् न ब्रह्मणः शब्दत्वम् । IS., i, 75, pp. 172-73.

269. अज्ञेयत्वं चात्मनः प्रसिद्धम्, ज्ञातृत्वप्रसिद्धेः । न ह्येकस्यैव अनंशस्य ज्ञातृत्वं तज्ज्ञेयत्वं च युगपत् क्रमेण वा सम्भवति । ...अतोऽज्ञेय आत्मा, ज्ञत्वादात्मत्वाच्च । Ibid, p. 175.

270. अतः शब्दस्य ज्ञेयत्वात् ब्रह्मत्वं प्रत्यक्षादिविरुद्धं, न त्वात्मनः, अतद्विषयत्वात् । Ibid.

271. शब्दस्य पराक्त्वेनैव प्रतीतेः प्रत्यक्ता ब्रह्मणो नोक्ता स्यात् । न ह्यज्ञः शब्दः शब्दात् परागर्थात् ब्रह्मणः प्रत्यक्त्वं प्रतिपत्तुं क्षमते । Ibid, pp. 175-76.

272. तस्मादात्माद्वैतमेव सिध्यति, न शब्दाद्वैतं घटाद्वैतं वेति सिद्धम् । Ibid, p. 176.

273. विद्यैव चाद्वया शान्ता तदस्तमय उच्यते । BRS., iii, 106, p 119.

274. विद्यैव चाविद्यानिवृत्तिः यद्यग्रहणमेविद्या, यतो भाव एव अभावव्यावृत्तिः ; अथ विपर्यासः, तथापि विरोधितत्त्वज्ञानोदय एव तन्निवृत्तिः । Ibid, pp. 121-22.

275. नन्वेकत्वे तुल्यकालताप्यनुपन्ना ; न, एकस्यापि वस्तुनो भावाभावरूपेण व्यपदेशात् । Ibid, p. 122.

276. प्रपंचप्रविलयः शब्देन प्रतिपद्यते । Ibid, iv, 3, p. 157. किं तर्हि शब्देन प्रतिपाद्यते ? प्रपंचाभावः । तत्र प्रपंचपदार्थोऽपि सिद्धः, निषेधोऽपि सिद्धः । Ibid.

CHAPTER X

1. अपूर्वाधिगमं कुर्वत् प्रमाणं स्यान्न चेन्न तत् । SNS , iii, 83.

2. अबाधितानधिगतासन्दिग्घबोधजनकत्वं हि प्रमाणत्वं प्रमाणानाम् । तच्च स्वतः । Bhām., i, 1, 1.

3. अर्थतस्तु व्यक्तिभेदेन व्यवस्थीयते । PPV., p. 102.

4. अर्थक्रियासंवादज्ञानात्प्रामाण्यनिश्चयेऽपि तुल्योऽनवस्थादिदोषः । Ibid.

5. तद्वदेव साधनज्ञानानामपि तत् स्वत एव स्यात् । Ibid.

6. तस्माज् ज्ञानोत्पत्तिमात्रप्रयुक्तार्थव्यवहारदर्शनात् प्रतीतितोऽर्थतश्च स्वत एवार्थनिश्चयः प्रामाण्यम् । अप्रामाण्य-जन्म दोषसहितात् कारणात् तत्प्रतीतिर्बाधादिति परत एवाप्रामाण्यं युक्तम् । Ibid.

9. अतो नोत्पत्तौ परतस्त्वम् । VPS., p, 101. प्रामाण्यनिश्चयस्तु स्वत एव । TA., p. 269.

10. प्रामाण्यं नाम ज्ञानस्यार्थपरिच्छेदसामर्थ्यं, तत् किं गुणजन्यत्वज्ञानादवगम्यते अर्थक्रियासंवादज्ञानाद्वा । VPS., p. 101.

11. विमतं साधनज्ञानं स्वत एव प्रमाणं ज्ञानत्वात् फलज्ञानवत् । Ibid.

12. तस्मात् प्रामाण्यस्योत्पत्तौ ज्ञप्तौ च ज्ञानोत्पादकज्ञापकातिरिक्तानपेक्षत्वलक्षणं स्वतस्त्वमभ्युपेयम् । अप्रामाण्यस्य तु ज्ञानकारणगतदोषादुत्पत्तिर्बाधाच्च ज्ञप्तिरिति परतस्त्वम् । Ibid, p. 102.

13. स्वतःप्रामाण्यस्यापि दोषबलादप्रामाण्यमविरुद्धम् । Ibid. Cp. TA., p. 276.

14. विज्ञानसामग्रीजन्यत्वे सति तदतिरिक्तहेत्वजन्यत्वं प्रमायाः स्वतस्त्वं नाम । TPD., p. 122.

32. 'मायामयत्वसिद्धौ तु प्रपञ्चस्य प्रमाणतः । प्रत्यक्षादिप्रमाणानां प्रामाण्यं व्यावहारिकम् ॥
अद्वैतागमवाक्यन्तु तत्त्वावेदकलक्षणम् । प्रमाणभावं भजते बाधवैधुर्यहेतुतः ॥" ĀNM., p. 145.

33. सांव्यवहारिकप्रामाण्यभावस्यैव प्रत्यक्षादेः स्वरूपसिद्धाम्नायेनापेक्ष्यमाणत्वात्, तात्त्विकांशबाधनेऽपि विरोधाभावात् । Ibid, p. 149.

34. आम्नायस्यापि स्वतःसिद्धप्रमाणभावस्य प्रमितावनपेक्षतासाम्याद् युक्तं तस्य परस्यैव बलीयस्त्वम् । Ibid, pp. 149-50.

35. परमात्मतत्त्वसाक्षात्कारोऽप्यविद्यात्मकोऽविद्यावभासान्तराणि संहरन् स्वयमपि संहि्रयमाणः परिशुद्धमात्मतत्त्वं व्यवस्थापयति । Ibid, p. 154.

36. प्रमाणस्यालीकत्वादद्वैताविधातः । NMV., pp. 154-55.

37. "तस्मान्मायामयत्वेऽपि युक्ता ब्रह्मणि मानता, अद्वैतागमवाक्यानामिति तावत् व्यवस्थितम् ।" ĀNM. p. 155.

39. न तु प्रमाणं सत् प्रमाणान्तरेण विरुध्यत इत्यसकृदवोचाम । SNS., iii, 96, p. 336.

40. यत्रापि वाक्यप्रत्यक्षयोर्विरोधाशङ्का तत्रापि पुरुषमोहवशादेव सा जायते, न तु परमार्थत इति । Ibid.

41. न विरोधस्ततो युक्तो विभिन्नार्थावबोधिनोः । Ibid, iii, 83.

42. स्वमहिम्ना प्रमाणानि कुर्वन्त्यर्थावबोधनम् । इतरेतरसाचिव्ये प्रामाव्यं नेष्यते स्वतः ।। Ibid, iii, 86.

43. तत्त्वमस्यादिवाक्यम् अखण्डार्थनिष्ठं कार्यकारणव्यतिरिक्तद्रव्यनिष्ठत्वे सति समानाधिकरणत्वात् सोऽयं देवदत्त इति वाक्यवदिति । VPS., p. 230. एवं सत्यज्ञानादिवाक्येऽप्यखण्डार्थता योजनीया ।। Ibid p. 232.

44. सामानाधिकरण्यञ्च विशेषणविशेष्यता लक्ष्यलक्षणभावश्च । अखण्डत्वं नाम विजातीय-सजातीय-स्वगत-भेदशून्यत्वम् । TA., pp., 116 & 117.

55. तच्चानुमानमन्वयिरूपमेव न तु केवलान्वयि सर्वस्यापि धर्मस्यास्मन्मते ब्रह्मनिष्ठात्यन्ताभावप्रतियोगित्वेन अत्यन्ताभावाप्रतियोगिसाध्यकत्वरूपकेवलान्वयित्वस्यासिद्धेः । VP., p. 203.

56. नाप्यनुमानस्य व्यतिरेकिरूपत्वं साध्याभावे साधनाभावनिरूपितव्याप्तिज्ञानस्य साधनेन साध्यानुमितावनुपयोगात् । Ibid, p. 205.

69. यस्य वाक्यस्य तात्पर्यविषयीभूतसंसर्गो मानान्तरेण न बाध्यते तद्वाक्यं प्रमाणम् । Ibid, p. 239.

72. तच्च जातेरेव न व्यक्तेः व्यक्तीनामानन्त्येन गुरूत्वात् । कथं तर्हि गवादिपदाद्व्यक्तिभानमितिचेत् जातेर्व्यक्तिसमानसंवित्संवेद्यतयेति ब्रूमः । p. 269.

74. सर्गाद्यकाले परमेश्वरः पूर्वसर्गसिद्धवेदानुपूर्वीसमानानुपूर्वीकं वेदं विरचितवान्, न तु तद्विजातीयं वेदमिति न सजातीयोच्चारणानपक्षोच्चारणविषयत्वं पौरुषेयत्वम् । Ibid, p. 304.

75. तत्त्वानुभूतिः प्रमा । KKK., p. 145 तत्त्वानुभवः प्रमा । SP., p. 59. यथार्थानुभवो मानम् । NKS., iv, 1. यथार्थानुभूतिः प्रमा । TA., p. 266.

76. धर्म्यंशे विशिष्टे च प्रमाया अप्रमात्वापातात् । Ibid, p. 146.

77. देशकालसम्बन्धांशे प्रमाया अप्रमात्वापातात् । Ibid, p. 148.

79. मितिः सम्यक्परिच्छित्तिस्तद्वत्ता च प्रमातृता । NKS., iv, 5. KKK., p., 244.

80. न खलु सम्यक्त्वं तत्त्वविषयता याथार्थ्यं वा सम्भवति, उक्तदोषात् । Ibid.

81. विशेषमात्राभिधाने रजतत्वादिना विशेषेण सहैव शुक्तिव्यक्त्यादेर्भ्रमेणावगाहनात्तस्यापि प्रमात्वं स्यात् । Ibid, pp. 245-46.

82. न तावदेवंविधो विशेषोऽभिधातुं शक्यः यदवगमस्य न भ्रान्तित्वादिसम्भवः, स्वप्नदृशः सर्वविशेषोपलम्भात् । Ibid, pp. 246-47.

83. बाधस्य च तद्विपरीतार्थप्रमात्वेन तदर्थाननुगमात्, प्रमायाश्चाद्याप्यव्यवस्थानात् । Ibid, p. 249.

84. परिच्छेदशब्दश्चानुभूतिपर्यायोऽनुभूतिदूषणं नातिक्रामति । Ibid, p. 250.

85. अव्यभिचार्यनुभव. प्रमा । Ibid. यद् अतस्मिंस्तदिति, तद् व्यभिचारि । यत्तु तस्मिंस्तदिति, तदव्यभिचारि । NBh., i, 1, 4.

86. नापि तृतीय:, ज्ञानार्थभेदवादे सर्वाकारेण तत्साम्याननुपत्ते:, अभेदवादे भ्रमस्यापि तथाऽभ्युपगन्तव्यत्वप्रसङ्गेन विशेषणवैयर्थ्यापातात् । Ibid, p. 251.

87. अविसंवाद्यनुभव: प्रमा । Ibid, 251. अविसंवादकं ज्ञानं सम्यग्ज्ञानम् । NBT., p. 5.

88. वास्तवतदर्थक्रियात्वस्य च दुर्निरूपत्वेन व्यवहारानर्हत्वात् तथा प्रतीतिमात्रस्याप्रमासाधारण्यात् । KKK., p. 255.

89. न, सामान्यतो विवक्षायां भ्रान्तावपि प्रसङ्गात् । प्रतीयमानरूपेणार्थक्रियाकारित्वमर्थस्य विवक्षितम्, इति चेन्न, दुरवधारणत्वात् । Ibid.

90. तदर्थक्रियादर्शनात्तदवधारणमितिचेन्न, विनाप्यर्थक्रियां तद्दर्शनसम्भवात् । Ibid.

91. कालान्तराविसंवादस्य च दुरवधारणत्वात् । Ibid, p. 256.

92. एतेन 'प्राप्त्यादियोग्यता संवादार्थ:' इत्यपि निरस्तम् । Ibid. ज्ञानमपि स्वयं प्रदर्शितमर्थं प्रापयत् संवादकमुच्यते । NBT., p. 5.

94. अबाधितानुभूति: प्रमा । KKK., p. 256.

96. तर्कसंशयविपर्ययस्मृतिव्यतिरिक्ता प्रतीति: प्रमा । Ibid.

97. प्रमात्वलक्षणजात्यभिसम्बन्धात् प्रमा । Ibid, p. 257.

98. एतेन 'शक्तिविशेष: प्रमात्वं, तद्योग: प्रमालक्षणम्' इत्यपास्तम्, दुरवधारणत्वात् । Ibid, p. 258.

99. इन्द्रियार्थसन्निकर्षोत्पन्नं ज्ञानमव्यभिचारि प्रत्यक्षम् । NS., i, 1, 4. KKK., p. 293.

100. न तावदिन्द्रियार्थसन्निकर्षोत्पत्ति: प्रत्यक्षा, अप्रत्यक्षविशेषणत्वात् । KKK., 295.

101. साक्षात्कारित्वावगममन्तरेण तदवगमानुपपत्ते:, तदवगमाच्चास्य प्रतीतावन्योन्याश्रयप्रसङ्ग: । Ibid, p. 297.

102. अस्ति ह्ययात्मनो भासमानत्वं कदाचित्कैनचित्, अन्यथाऽप्रमेयत्वप्रसङ्गात् । Ibid, p. 302.

103. 'विवादाध्यासितं ज्ञानमर्थाव्यभिचारि । समर्थप्रवृत्तिजनकत्वात् । मैवं, हेतोर्विरुद्धत्वात् । TPD., p. 218.

105. केयं व्याप्ति:, किमविनाभाव:, किं वा स्वाभाविक: सम्बन्ध:, निरुपाधिक: सम्बन्धो वा । Ibid, pp. 232-33.

106. उपाधिर्हि साधनाव्यापकत्वे सति साध्यव्यापक: । Ibid, p. 237. HIP., Vol. I, pp. 717-24.

107. एवं व्याप्तिसिद्धौ उपाधिसिद्धि:, तत्सिद्धौ च तद्रहितसम्बन्धस्य व्याप्तित्वसिद्धि:, इति कथं नान्योन्याश्रयत्वम् । TPD., p. 237.

108. भवतु नाम या काचन व्याप्तिस्तस्याव्याप्तेरनुमितेश्च व्याप्तिरेष्टव्येत्यात्माश्रय: । सत्यामेव व्याप्तौ अनुमितिभावात् असत्यामभावात् । Ibid, p. 238.

110. 'प्रसिद्धसाधर्म्यात् साध्यसाधनम् उपमानम् ।' NS., i, 1, 6. TPD., pp. 255-56.

111. 'आगमाहितसंस्कारस्मृत्यपेक्षं सादृश्यज्ञानमुपमानम् ।' NV., i, 1, 6. TPD., p. 256.

113. शास्त्रं 'शब्दविज्ञानादसन्निकृष्टेऽर्थे विज्ञानम्' इति मीमांसका: । TPD., p. 256.

117. अन्तरेण च सम्बन्धं शब्दस्यार्थविशेषप्रतीतिजनकत्वेऽध्यक्षानुमानयोरपि सम्बन्धसमर्थनवैयर्थ्यापात: । Ibid, p. 263.

118. संकेतस्यापि जातौ व्यक्तौ विशिष्टे वाभिहितन्यायेन दुर्ग्रहत्वात् । Ibid, p. 265.

119. तस्माच्छास्त्रं शब्दविज्ञानादसन्निकृष्टेऽर्थे बुद्धिरिति लक्षणमलक्षणम् । Ibid.

121. अन्यथानुपपन्नदर्शनादुपपादके बुद्धिरर्थापत्ति: । Ibid, p. 266.

122. 'आदयेऽनुमानं तेनैव तिष्प्रत्यूहं प्रवर्तताम् । द्वितीये कल्पकाभावादर्थापत्त्युदय: कुत: ।।' Ibid, p. 267.

123. 'प्रमाणपञ्चकं यत्र वस्तुरूपे न जायते वस्तुसत्तावबोधार्थं तत्राभावप्रमाणता ।' Ibid, p. 268.

124. किं चोपपादकेन येन विनानुपपद्यमानत्वं तत्प्रमितं न वा । प्रथमे गृहीतग्राहिकार्थापत्तिर्न प्रमा स्यात् । Ibid, p. 269.

125. द्वितीये तु विशेषणासिद्धेः तद्विशेषितानुपपद्यमानार्थप्रतीतौ कल्पकाभावान्नार्थापत्तिरुदयमासादयेत् । Ibid.

127. सोऽयं देवदत्त इति प्रत्यभिज्ञाप्रत्यये तदित्यंशस्य संस्कारानुपनीतत्वे सत्ययमित्याकारस्य च संयोगमात्राधीनतया विशिष्टप्रत्यभिज्ञास्वरूपासिद्धिप्रसङ्गात् । Ibid, p. 227.

129. प्रागवस्थाविशिष्टाश्रयतया त्वभेदः केनापि न प्रकाशित इति 'य एव प्रागवस्थाविशिष्टः, स एवायम्' इति प्रत्यभिज्ञायाः शरीरं न स्यात् । KKK., p. 160.

130. न । प्रमात्वसामान्यानङ्गीकारे प्रमारूपताया विषयव्यवस्थित्यैवोपगमनेनोपाध्यन्तरोपन्यासेऽपि स्मृतित्वानुभूतित्वयोरेकस्मिन्नेव धर्मिण्यर्थे निवेशात् प्रमात्वाप्रमात्वयोरेकविषयतयैव । Ibid, p. 160.

132. तस्मात् स्मृत्यनुभवसङ्करो दुर्वार एव । Ibid, p. 162.

154. नापि स्फोटात्मके शब्दे प्रमाणम् । एकशब्दप्रतीतिस्तु वर्णविषयत्वात् न स्फोटं गोचरयति । TS., p. 105-06. न च स्फोटस्य शब्द-समवायः, अतिप्रसङ्गात् । TS., p. 120.

157. अनिश्चितपक्षवृत्तिः हेतुः असिद्धः । Ibid, p. 99.

158. एतेन व्याप्यत्वपक्षधर्मत्वाभ्याभप्रमितो हेतुः असिद्धः इति निरस्तं, व्याप्तिपक्षयोः निरस्तत्वात्, अप्रमितस्यापि केनचिद्वा सर्वे र्वा इति निर्वक्तुमयुक्तत्वात् । Ibid.

159. व्याप्तिं पक्षधर्मतां तत्प्रमितिं वा न विरून्धतां हेतुदोषत्वासम्मवात् । ĀVS., pp. 806-07.

160. तत्र कार्त्स्न्येन तद्वृत्तावव्याप्तेरनिवारणात् । एकदेशेन तद्वृत्तावपि सा न निवर्तते ।। TS., p. 97.

161. साध्यासिद्धेरसिद्धेश्च व्याप्ते रूक्तेन हेतुना । विरोधस्याप्रसिद्धेश्च न प्रसिद्धा विरुद्धता ।। Ibid. तथा चानैकान्तिक एवायम् । KKK., Ch. S.S., p. 841.

162. पक्षत्रयवृत्तेरनैकान्तिकस्यापि साध्यव्यतिरेकसामानाधिकरण्यमस्तीति ततो भेदो न स्यादित्यर्थः । ĀVS., p. 842.

163. विरुद्धनीतेरत्रापि निवेशात्तदनुत्थितेः । व्यभिचारविचारस्य विरुद्धेऽपि प्रसङ्गतः ।। TS., p. 97.

164. साध्यसन्देहहेतुत्वं साध्यासिद्धेर्न सिध्यति । Ibid.

167. मानव्यक्तेस्तथाभावे कथं नाव्याप्तिरापतेत् । तन्मात्रस्य तु तद्भावे सर्वत्राव्याप्तिरेव ते ।। Ibid. p. 98.

168. आपातिकस्य चेदिष्टः सद्धेतावपि सज्यते । सर्वथा चेन्न तज्ज्ञानमसर्वज्ञस्य लभ्यते ।। Ibid. सर्वथा न हि तुल्यत्वं विकल्पानवकल्पनात् । यथाकथञ्चित्तद्भावे नात्यापत्तिः कथं भवेत् ।। Ibid.

169. मिथो विरुद्धसाध्यत्वं न चैवमुपपद्यते । साध्ये विरुद्धे तुल्यत्वं न हि सिद्धिमुपाश्नुते ।। Ibid, pp. 98-99.